Film Production Technique

Creating the Accomplished Image

From the Wadsworth Series in Television and Film

Production for Broadcast, Video, and Film

Video Basics   Herbert Zettl

Television Production Handbook, 5th Ed   Herbert Zettl

Crafting News for the Electronic Media: Writing, Reporting, and Production
Carl Hausman

Lighting for Film and Electronic Cinematography   Dave Viera

Institutional Video: Planning, Budgeting, Production, and Evaluation   Carl Hausman

Video Communication: Structuring Content for Maximum Program Effectiveness
David L. Smith

Sight-Sound-Motion: Applied Media Aesthetics, 2nd Ed   Herbert Zettl

Electronic Cinematography: Achieving Photographic Control Over the Video Image
Harry Mathias/Richard Patterson

Electronic Moviemaking, 2nd Ed   Lynne Gross/Larry Ward

Audio in Media, 4th Ed   Stanley R. Alten

Modern Radio Production, 4th Ed   Carl Hausman/Philip Benoit/Lewis B. O'Donnell

Writing for Broadcast and Film

Scriptwriting for High-Impact Videos   John Morley

Copywriting for the Electronic Media, 2nd Ed   Milan D. Meeske/R. C. Norris

Writing for Television and Radio, 5th Ed   Robert L. Hilliard

Writing the Screenplay: TV and Film, 2nd Ed   Alan A. Armer

Broadcast Selling, Advertising, and Programming

Broadcast and Cable Selling, Updated 2nd Ed   Charles Warner/Joseph Buchman

Broadcast/Cable Programming: Strategies and Practices, 4th Ed   Susan T. Eastman

Other Broadcast Titles

Announcing: Broadcast Communicating Today, 3rd Ed
Lewis B. O'Donnell/Carl Hausman/ Philip Benoit

Radio Station Operations: Management and Employee Perspectives
Lewis B. O'Donnell/Carl Hausman/Philip Benoit

Stay Tuned: A Concise History of American Broadcasting, 2nd Ed
Christopher H. Sterling/John M. Kitross

Directing TV and Film, 2nd Ed   Alan A. Armer

World Broadcasting Systems: A Comparative Analysis   Sydney W. Head

Film History and Analysis

Movie History: A Survey   Douglas Gomery

Working Cinema: Learning from the Masters   Roy Paul Madsen

Immediate Seating: A Look at Movie Audiences   Bruce A. Austin

Film Production Technique

Creating the Accomplished Image

NEW ENGLAND INSTITUTE
OF TECHNOLOGY
LEARNING RESOURCES CENTER

Bruce Mamer

Minneapolis Community College

 Wadsworth Publishing Company

I(T)P™ An International Thomson Publishing Company

Belmont ■ Albany ■ Bonn ■ Boston ■ Cincinnati ■ Detroit
London ■ Madrid ■ Melbourne ■ Mexico City ■ New York ■ Paris
San Francisco ■ Singapore ■ Tokyo ■ Toronto ■ Washington

4/96

#32541900

Editor: Katherine Hartlove
Editorial Assistant: Jessica Monday
Production Services Coordinator: Debby Kramer
Production: Robaire Ream, Ideas to Images
Designer and Art Director: Gary Palmatier
Print Buyer: Barbara Britton
Permissions Editor: Robert Kauser
Copy Editor: Elizabeth von Radics
Technical Illustrator: Ideas to Images
Cover Designer: Gary Palmatier, Ideas to Images
Cover Photographer: Ken Sax
Compositor: Ideas to Images
Printer: Courier Companies, Inc./Kendallville
Cover Printer: Color Dot Litho, Inc.

Printed in the United States of America

1 2 3 4 5 6 7 8 9 10 — 01 00 99 98 97 96

For more information, contact Wadsworth Publishing Company.

Wadsworth Publishing Company
10 Davis Drive
Belmont, California 94002, USA

International Thomson Publishing Europe
Berkshire House 168-173
High Holborn
London, WC1V7AA, England

Thomas Nelson Australia
102 Dodds Street
South Melbourne 3205
Victoria, Australia

Nelson Canada
1120 Birchmount Road
Scarborough, Ontario
Canada M1K 5G4

International Thomson Editores
Campos Eliseos 385, Piso 7
Col. Polanco
11560 México D.F. México

International Thomson Publishing GmbH
Königswinterer Strasse 418
53227 Bonn, Germany

International Thomson Publishing Asia
221 Henderson Road
#05-10 Henderson Building
Singapore 0315

International Thomson Publishing Japan
Hirakawacho Kyowa Building, 3F
2-2-1 Hirakawacho
Chiyoda-ku, Tokyo 102, Japan

Library of Congress Cataloguing-in-Publication Data

Mamer, Bruce.
    Film production technique : creating the accomplished image /
Bruce Mamer.
        p.   cm.
    Includes index.
    ISBN 0-534-20568-2
    1. Motion pictures—Production and direction—Handbooks, manuals,
etc.   2. Cinematography—Handbooks, manuals, etc.   I. Title.
PN1995.9.P7M278   1995
791.43 ' 0232—dc20   95-14856

To Ellen, Rebecka, and David

Brief Contents

Contents

Preface

THIS book is about creating images. People embark on their first filmmaking projects for a variety of reasons. Some want to express a vision that is unique and challenging. Others have a story to tell or something they feel needs saying. Some want to master techniques that they have admired on the screen, whereas others are busy dreaming up ways to subvert mainstream commercial product. Whatever brings a person to the medium, the starting place in film is the moving image.

Whatever shape a beginning filmmaker's desire takes, his or her aims will be best served by a broad-based understanding of film technique. Anyone who has learned to play a musical instrument knows that before a musician is ready to play before an audience, a huge commitment of hours learning time signatures and practicing scales is required. Any aspiring painter discovers the same requirement of apprenticeship: One cannot master any art form overnight.

Film is no different. But perhaps because Hollywood's images look so easy and effortless, novice filmmakers are often shocked to discover how much attention each individual shot is given. Commercial film producers generally consider that a film crew has done a good day's work if it has produced a little more than a minute of what will wind up being finished film. The budgets for commercial films today are astronomical: $20 million is an average figure, which puts the cost of a ninety-minute film at around $200,000 a minute. Although a film's budget would never be expressed like this, the figure reflects at least some of the extensive resources devoted to each individual image.

Clearly, beginning independent filmmakers need not, and in most cases could not, emulate this scale and approach. But even on the smallest scale, filmmaking is an extremely costly and complicated endeavor. For this reason, a mastery of the technical elements of filmmaking—the ability to control the variables of focus, exposure, lighting, and composition, for example—is essential to creating images of worth, value, and weight—images that function within a film as parts of an integrated whole.

A common but unnecessary stumbling block for many beginning film students is "technophobia." Despite the computer revolution, the problem continues to be widespread among people regardless of age, gender, and background. Although this book takes a comprehensive approach to covering the technical aspects of filmmaking, the intent is to present the information in a straightforward and practical way. There may nevertheless be portions that require study and rereading because of the complexity of the processes described, but it is my hope that the text will make the process of mastering basic film technique an empowering rather than intimidating experience.

Another underlying assumption is the importance of understanding and mastering traditional technique. To that end, this book focuses on conventional (Hollywood) film style: breaking down scenes for dramatic emphasis, lighting for atmosphere, editing for pace and efficiency, and so forth. While more adventurous and experimental techniques should be encouraged, it is clear that this topic could not be effectively addressed within the scope of a book like this without shortchanging and trivializing vital and complex issues. I would encourage anyone interested in experimenting with film form and technique to follow that impulse, but I would also advise that there are many reasons for understanding the workings of conventional narrative films. The most radical techniques often, though not always, evolve from conventional approaches and are effective precisely because the artist knows his or her way around the "norm."

In film as in other fields, there is a tendency to divide people into "creative" and "technical" roles, in some cases subordinating the latter (the technical mastery of the craft) as less important, perhaps less "artistic." Certainly there are technical people who are not creative, but there are also creative people who are not productive because they do not understand the technical fundamentals. In filmmaking, which could reasonably be called the most "technical" of the arts, those who truly excel (whether as directors, cinematographers, editors, or other skill positions) are both technically expert and creatively engaged. It makes no sense and is indeed counterproductive to separate these qualities in any discussion of the filmmaking process. Another assumption underlying this text, therefore, is that the creative ideas that work in film are grounded in technical understanding.

To that end, this text approaches the process of making films from the perspective of projects that involve at least a small crew. It recognizes the contributions of individual crew members and the general common sense with which crews are organized. The desire to be an excellent gaffer (lighting electrician) or grip (the crew's jack-of-all-trades) is a worthy pursuit. Moreover, for those who aspire to direct, working from the bottom up and serving in a number of capacities provides both a fuller knowledge of the craft and a better understanding of the interpersonal dynamics on a set. Many aspiring filmmakers wish to create films on their own. If this is the case, this text still applies: you just have to be responsible for all the elements detailed herein (no easy task!).

This book distinguishes between working on productions with a big budget and working on smaller, low-budget projects. This represents an inescapable fact. As an independent or student, you are probably working without access to the resources and support equipment that filmmakers working on large productions take for granted. You are making films on the edge and have to scrape and struggle for everything you can get. This book's practical emphasis is on technologies most independent filmmakers can realistically gain access to; it also encourages as much ambition as possible in obtaining advanced equipment. Despite the tribulations of working outside the commercial mainstream, this book is being written on the crest of a new wave of vital independent films, and it is my fervent hope that the independent ethic will both prosper and flourish.

A final note about the rapidly developing technologies associated with video: Film and video have emerged as interdisciplinary fields, each useful for specific approaches and purposes, and a significant interface is developing between the two technologies. Until recently, many film-trained editors were reluctant to abandon film editing for video editing, because of the inflexible nature of most of the early systems. With the emergence of new digital video-editing systems, this reluctance is rapidly disappearing. The last great barrier is the development of digital video-editing systems that educational programs and independent filmmakers can afford. At this writing, these systems are just around the corner. Because of the importance of these developments, some basic comments on video are incorporated into the text, and relevant parts also have a "Video Applications" segment at the end.

Despite new video technology, interest in film remains high. University film programs are turning applicants away. A substantial amount of film is still being shot, though much ends up being edited on video. For a great many professionals and artists, film will continue to be the medium of choice for the foreseeable future.

One of the major purposes of this book is to give the reader an appreciation of just what it takes to produce the images we see on-screen. It may take quite some time to achieve the level of control being recommended in this text. You may start out working with small lights or a cheap light meter. You may be working on your own or with insufficient help. But at all times, you want to be moving toward the basic goal presented: controlling the elements in and in front of the camera. My hope is that this book will help you develop the confidence that comes with an understanding of both the craft and the art of filmmaking.

Acknowledgments

This book owes its existence and overall quality to many people, but credit must go first and foremost to my friend and developmental agent par excellence, Paul Nockleby. Without Paul's crucial and timely assistance, this project may never have come into being, and his help since contract signing has been invaluable.

Readers of early versions of this text included Peter Bundy, Gwynneth Gibby, and Bill Caulfield. At various stages of the manuscript, Beth Berg, Tania Kamal-Eldin, and Martha Boehm were also invaluable in this regard. M. Walker Pearce and Charles Harpole were extremely helpful in both reading and supporting this project in its early stages. Martha Davis Beck, in particular, has been a friend and valued reader throughout the entire project.

There have also been numerous people who have contributed to specific sections of the book. Craig McKay, A.C.E., the editor of *Something Wild,* was most gracious in giving pertinent details about the editing of the scene reproduced in chapter 6. Those who have read and commented about specific sections include Del Olson of Delden Film Labs on general lab work; Greg Meyers of Lighthouse, Inc., on lighting equipment; and John Fillwalk and Stephen Solum of Minneapolis Community College on video and sound, respectively. Fred Ginsberg of Equipment Emporium, Dennis O'Rourke of Cinesound II, and Gerard Bonnette, freelance sound mixer, gave welcome input on location and studio recording issues. Brian McGraw of Cinequipt, Inc., was exceptionally helpful in providing details about equipment and logistical help in finding photographs. Colleagues Stephen Andrews and Gary Reynolds both had useful comments on the composition section. In addition, colleagues Abdel Hafidh Bouassida and Mary Ahmann were generous with their time and comments on content and overall structure.

Institutional support has been greatly appreciated as well. Minneapolis Community College was most gracious in giving me both release and sabbatical time to complete this project. Thanks go to Joe Anderson, Chuck Berg, and Ed Small of the Department of Theater and Film at the University of Kansas, who made a place for me during my sabbatical and then so generously gave me both room and their valued insights when this project came along. Dave Barnhill of the University of Kansas Computer Center helped immensely in deciphering the many competing video grab technologies.

Brian Jennings has been invaluable in helping me keep my finger on the pulse of day-to-day production. Steve Pecchia-Bekkum has also been most helpful in this regard. Gregory Winters, Gregory M. Cummins, and Jay Horan have contributed to many of the insights and stories that are part of this text. Most significant in this regard, many thanks to Miroslav Janek and Roger Schmitz, with whom I shared many hours lugging and using cameras, lights, and sound gear—necessary experience to obtain the unique perspective required to truly understand the filmmaking process.

From Wadsworth, I would like to thank my editor, Katherine Hartlove; production supervisor Debby Kramer; and Robert Kauser, who assisted with obtaining permissions to use some of the more complex reproductions. I would particularly like to thank Gary Palmatier and Robaire Ream of Ideas to Images for their fine work in illustration and design, and copy editor/proofreader Elizabeth von Radics, who was both thoughtful and diligent in helping to manage and refine this at times overwhelming amount of information.

Thanks must also be given to the many reviewers who patiently toiled over the numerous versions of this text: Robert B. Musburger, Ph.D., University of Houston; Rob Sabal, University of Arizona; William D. Schmidt, Central Washington University; Paul Younghouse, Indiana State University; Ken Portnoy, California State University, Northridge; Robert L. Synder (retired), University of Wisconsin, Oshkosh; Jack Ofield, San Diego State University; Robert Miller, Northern Illinois University; and Brian Patrick, University of Utah.

In the final analysis, the biggest share for the inspiration for this text must go to all the students over the years who have challenged me in ways I still find extraordinary. Those moments when the passion for filmmaking starts to crystalize and move forward are what has made teaching most rewarding. My parents, Donna and Stuart Mamer, have provided highly valued support in so many ways as has the rest of my extended family. And most of all, to my wife, Ellen, whose support and editorial skills over the years have always inspired me to take everything I do to a higher level, and to my children, Rebecka and David, who make all the other parts of life so much fun.

PART 1

Creating the Shots

1

1

The Camera

The Language of the Camera

Motion picture film is made up of a series of still photographic images. **SEE 1-1** When projected in succession, these provide the illusion of movement. Each individual photographic image is called a *frame*—a discrete entity that, just as in painting, has shapes and forms arranged in a *composition.* A sequence of frames is called a *shot,* which is commonly defined as the footage created from the moment the camera is turned on until it is turned off. Despite several styles of film that have specialized approaches, the shot is generally considered to be the basic building block of a film.

If the shot is the basic building block of a film, the *setup* is the basic component of a film's production. A setup, also referred to as a camera position, placement, or, simply, *angle,* is just what the name suggests: it is when you *set up* the camera to execute a shot. If you need a simple shot of a character saying "Yes," you have to set up the camera, do some basic set decoration, work out the lighting, record the sound, and so on. If you then want another character to respond "No," you have to go through the same process to execute the shot. A setup may involve something as simple as a single line of dialogue or cover extensive material that is going to be used throughout a *scene*—the basic unit of a script, with action occurring in a single setting and in real time—or even throughout the entire film.

Beyond these basic definitions, it is important to start thinking of the shots as *accomplishing goals,* dramatic or otherwise. A shot may show us a necessary piece of information or help to create an atmosphere. It may serve as a simple delivery device for a line of dialogue; it may produce associations that were not implicit without its presence. A shot does not necessarily have to be discussed in a purely *narrative* (story) context. Like a detail in a pointillist painting, it may be one piece in a grander abstract plan. It may add to the kinetic energy (movement) of a piece, such as in music videos. But all shots have a purpose and must be thought out in terms of their relationship to the greater whole of the film. A shot has to do something because, whatever its content, its presence will have an impact.

When discussing shots, the idea of *choice* is key when considering the filming of any action—simple or complex, conventional or unconventional. Filmmakers repeatedly face a deceptively simple question: Where do I put the camera to "cover" this action (this line of dialogue, this facial expression) in a way that is involving and dramatically effective? Although covering the action implies a purely functional approach, there must be an internal logic to the way the camera is being used—a

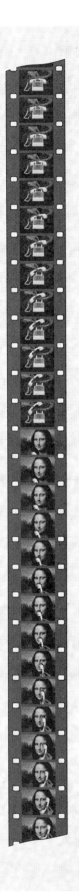

1-1

A motion picture shot comprises individual frames
that when projected in succession provide the illusion
of movement

logic that fits the dramatic context and the formal approach of the material being shot. There must be a reason why a closer shot is used at a specific point. There must be a reason why you withdraw from the action with a wider shot at another point. A scene in which the presentation has not achieved some internal logic will appear shapeless and "undirected." The choices made will structure the viewer's perception of the scene and contribute to defining the shape and meaning of the film. The determining factors in choosing specific shots are the context of the material and the greater structure of shots in which the single shot participates.

Overshadowing this idea of choice should be an awareness that all the decisions made on a set (camera, lighting, sound, and so on) are driven by the demands of the editing room. Experienced filmmakers will attest to the importance of approaching each shot with a sense of the whole film in mind—a process called *shooting for the edit*. A film crew is made up of many skilled professionals, all of whom must understand how the scene being filmed is going to cut together. The sound people must know what the editors need in order to cut the audio tracks. The cameraperson must think about what compositions will cut together, and whether the scenes are being appropriately covered. The lighting crew needs to understand that the quality of light must be continuous from one shot to the next.

With the exception of a few specialized approaches, virtually every film, whether narrative, experimental, documentary, or animated, has to confront this question of the relationship of the camera to the subject and surroundings. Some common strategies for shooting scenes—and having a strategy is crucial—will be developed throughout this text, but any plan must come from the filmmaker's understanding of the materials at hand and the dramatic needs of the subject matter. Whatever the approach to shooting, keep in mind that someone (possibly you) will have to fit all the pieces together. The beginning of the process must be informed by the end.

Movement and Perception

In the late 1880s, Thomas Edison and W. L. K. Dickson produced what now constitutes the basic mechanism of the motion picture camera. The phenomenon that allows us to perceive this series of still images as being a continuous representation of motion has been called *persistence of vision*, although there is increasing evidence that the physiological response is much more complex than has generally been recognized. Persistence of vision is based on the idea that the human eye will hold an image for a split second. For an example, just look at a light bulb for a few seconds and then look away. The eye will hold the imprint of that light for a short period. When presented with a succession of images, each one making a momentary imprint, the eye blurs them into movement. The key to this process is that a person's view must be disrupted between each drawing or photograph. If not, all one will see is a complete blur.

Prior to the advent of motion pictures, inventors and tinkerers had perfected many contraptions that allowed people to perceive motion created from individual drawings of sequences of movement. Invented in the 1830s, the zoetrope is probably the most famous of these. **SEE 1-2** It was a simple drum set up on a turntable. The drum had vertical slits, spaced equally all the way around the drum.

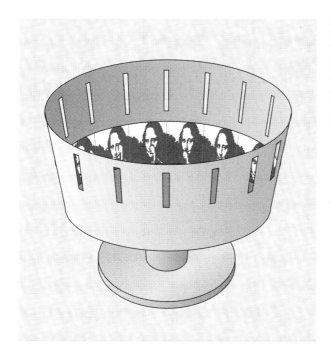

1-2

The zoetrope, circa 1830, was an early example of simulating motion by viewing a series of individual drawings

A set of individual drawings, each representing sequential points in a simple movement, were placed around the edges of the inside of the drum. When the drum was rotated, viewers would look through the slots at the pictures on the far side of the drum. They would see one picture, and then their view would be disrupted by the exterior of the drum. The next slot would allow them to see the next picture, and so on. When the drum was rotated at the correct rate, viewers would see the pictures as a continuous movement.

These experiments quite naturally began to incorporate the relatively new technology of still photography. The most famous early experiments were by Eadweard Muybridge. The story goes that Leland Stanford, the namesake of the university and then governor of California, bet a friend that there were times in a horse's gallop when none of the animal's four feet was touching the ground. Stanford hired Muybridge to test this hypothesis. In 1878, Muybridge set up an ingenious testing ground in which he used still cameras with strings attached to their shutter releases. At brief intervals along a racetrack, he rigged a sequence of several dozen such cameras. As the horse ran by, the camera would take a picture of a discrete point of the horse's progress. When finished, Muybridge had a series of pictures, representing sequential points in the motion of a running horse. It was a simple matter to adapt these pictures to a zoetrope, and the result was a smooth representation of the horse's gallop. This is precisely what film is—a series of still photographs that when presented in sequence re-create movement. The only thing needed at that point was a more efficient way of capturing the image and a more sophisticated presentation device.

The technology to produce still photographs had existed since 1839, when Louis-Jacques-Mandé Daguerre introduced a device that could capture and transform light into a permanent image. The big step for motion pictures was to design both the equipment that could photograph a sequence of images and a medium on which those images could be recorded. Edison and Dickson were poised to provide a solution to the first requirement, and when George Eastman provided them with strip celluloid film, their problems were solved. Despite many design variations, what they invented more than a hundred years ago remains *the* basic film mechanism. It is a relatively simple device, not unlike a sewing machine, but all filmmakers need a sophisticated understanding of how it works to get the desired images on film. In the age of home video, many beginners come with the expectation that the camera is just going to magically work. In film, you find that it takes a measured and thoughtful approach to make the process work.

The Basic Mechanism

The fundamental mechanism that transports and exposes the film is made up of a small number of essential elements which are present in some form in virtually every camera you use. Their relatively simple interrelationship, what is called the camera's *action*, is the "how" of recording the images.

The following photo shows a typical camera interior. **SEE 1-3** This particular design includes the *film chamber*—the space in the camera where the unexposed film is stored. Many cameras employ a separate *magazine (mag)* as the film chamber. The design pictured here will have a *cover plate*, or *lid*, that closes over the film chamber. An illustrated view is shown on the facing page. **SEE 1-4** Each of the elements plays its own individual role.

1-3

A typical camera interior, showing the film chamber where the unexposed stock is stored

Interior of a Bell & Howell DR-70 (16mm) camera

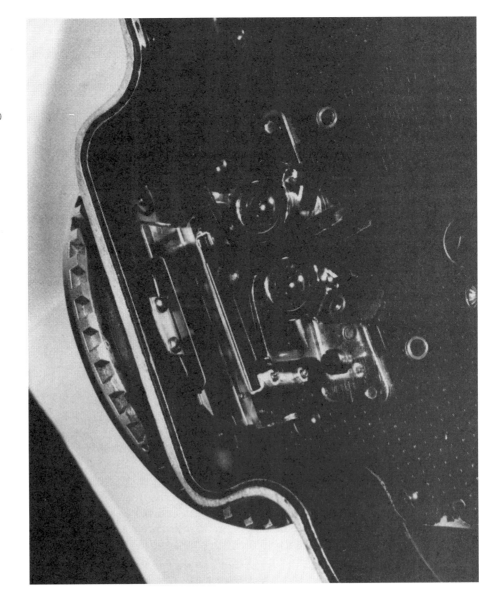

1-4

All the parts shown here are important, but the real action occurs with the pull-down claw and shutter

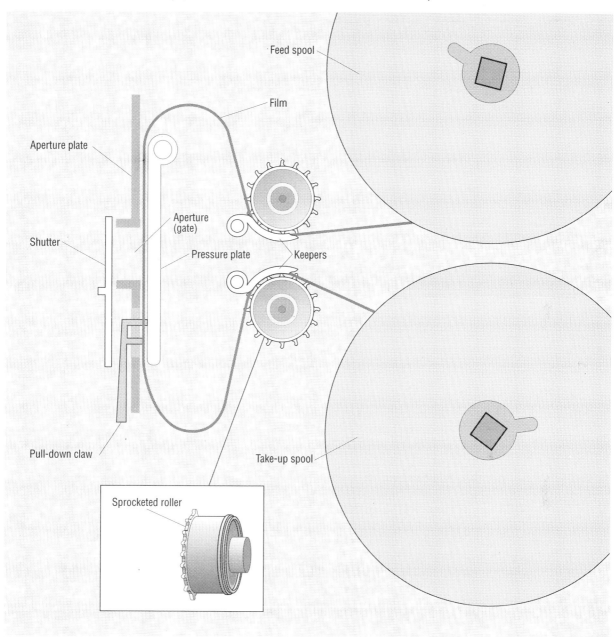

The ***feed spool*** and ***take-up spool*** do what one would expect. The feed spool holds the unexposed film, referred to as ***raw stock***, that you have bought from the manufacturer. The take-up spool winds the film after it has been exposed. Both spools are mounted on ***spindles***, the take-up being driven by the camera's motor. The feed spool turns as the film feeds off it. Some feed spools have a slight backward resistance—referred to as torque—that ensures even feeding into the mechanism.

The ***sprocketed rollers*** feed the film into and out of the area where each image is exposed. Each roller has sprocket teeth that correspond to the ***pitch*** (distance between sprocket holes) of the film. These rollers drive the film continuously forward. The two rollers are geared together so that they run at precisely the same speed. As the top roller is feeding the film in, the bottom roller

1-5

In a single–sprocketed roller design, one side of the roller feeds the film in as the other side feeds it out

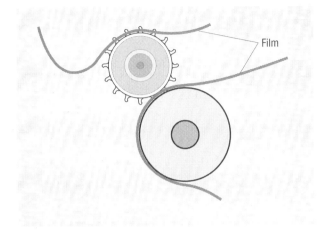

Film

is feeding it out at precisely the same rate. This is key because the rollers keep a consistent amount of film in the gate area. When viewed from the front, the actual sprocket teeth are on the edge of the roller toward the body of the camera—away from the side you would be looking at.

This two–sprocketed roller configuration is quite common, but there are some camera designs that employ a single sprocketed roller, in which one side of the roller is feeding the film in as the other is feeding it out. **SEE 1-5** The CP-16 (*CP* stands for Cinema Products) is a good example of a 16mm camera with this approach.

Keepers do exactly what their name suggests; they simply keep the film tight against the sprocketed roller. Their sole function is to make sure the film does not slip away from the sprocketed roller, which would throw the whole system out. They usually can and need to be pivoted out of the way for loading and cleaning. A spring-loaded pin (one that has a spring that pulls it back into position after it has been disengaged) locks them back in place. Forgetting to close the keepers can lead to camera jams and ruined film, although most cameras have safety features guarding against this mistake.

The *aperture*, usually referred to as the *gate*, is the place where each individual frame is exposed. Although the gate is a rather unassuming rectangular hole, it is a finely machined opening, and its care and maintenance are essential to producing a quality image. The film plane is the place toward which all efforts, hopes, and fears are directed. All issues of focus, focal length, exposure, and a host of others get resolved (or not) right here.

The *aperture plate* is the polished metal plate that guides the film to the gate, where it is exposed. It is also referred to as the *film guide*.

The *pressure plate* is usually mounted on spring-loaded pins and holds the film flat against the aperture plate. The film has to be held flat so the pull-down claw will engage properly. The pressure from the spring-loaded pins is also the main force that holds the film stable as it is being exposed, as well as flat against the gate for uniform focus. Film has a natural curl that would leave its edges closer to the lens than its center if not held flat. The pressure plate is removable to make cleaning the camera easier.

These parts of the mechanism are important, but the real action occurs with the pull-down claw and shutter.

The *pull-down claw* is the mechanism that advances each individual frame for exposure. **SEE 1-6** It is usually recessed in the body of the camera and, when rolling film, comes out and grabs each individual frame and pulls it down to be exposed. It then retracts, goes up and grabs the next frame, and pulls it down. This sequence occurs continually and, in this manner, every frame is pulled in front of

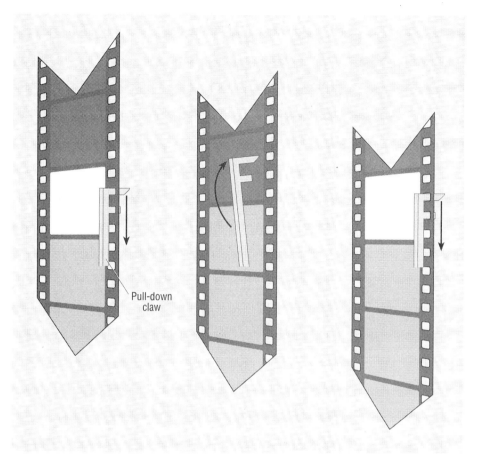

The pull-down claw advances each frame of film for exposure

Pull-down
claw

the gate and exposed. This is called ***intermittent movement***, because the frames are alternately moving and stationary as they rush past the gate.

The ***shutter*** is the other key element. As stated, both the production and projection of the film image is based on disrupted vision. If there were nothing to block the light from the film as the pull-down claw advances each frame, the image would blur because it was being exposed while the film was moving. The shutter is the necessary response to the action of the pull-down claw. It continuously rotates in front of the film, blocking the light while the film is moving, and allowing the light to reach the film for the brief moment that it is stationary in front of the gate. Many cameras employ a half-disc–shaped shutter called a ***half-moon shutter***. **SEE 1-7** In most designs, they are actually slightly smaller than 180 degrees of a circle. Other shutter designs are discussed later in this chapter in the section on viewing systems.

This is how each frame is brought to the gate for exposure. The pull-down claw brings each frame to the gate. The shutter blocks the light as the frame is being moved into place. As the claw is going up to get the next frame, each frame is exposed while it is stationary in front of the gate. All the other elements in the basic mechanism support this simple action.

The ***Latham's loops***, named after their discoverer, are not really part of the basic mechanism of the motion picture camera. Rather, they are an idiosyncrasy of the film. But they are so essential to the way the image is formed that they warrant equal consideration. It is apparent that the basic mechanism employs two different types of motion. There is both the continuous motion of the sprocketed rollers and the intermittent movement of the pull-down claw. There clearly has to be someplace for these two movements to be reconciled. That place is in the loops. When loading

1-7

Many cameras employ a half-moon shutter, which is actually slightly less than 180 degrees of a circle

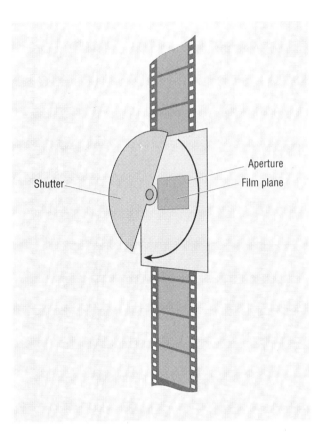

Shutter
Aperture
Film plane

film, you form a small loop with the film both above and below the gate. These flexible loops are where the give-and-take of the two movements occurs. If you run a "dummy load" with the lid open, you will see the film "chattering" (vibrating slightly) on the top and bottom.

With most cameras, these loops are set at the start and, unless there is a malfunction or the camera gets rough treatment, there should be little concern about losing the loop. High-end professional cameras have ways of checking the loops between shots, and you will see them being checked with relative frequency. These loops are crucial to achieving a usable image. Most everyone has seen a projector lose the film loop, whether during a classroom film presentation or at a commercial theater. When this happens, the image starts to blur vertically. Most projectors have a loop restorer, a lever that pushes the film back into the correct position. If not, someone has to stop the projector and reset the loops.

When the loop is lost, the film becomes taut between one of the rollers and the pressure plate. **SEE 1-8** As the illustration suggests, the camera usually loses the loop on the bottom, with the excess film collecting at the top. When this happens, the pull-down claw is no longer engaging with the sprocket holes—striking the film between sprockets. Rather than being driven by the intermittent movement of the claw, the film is being driven by the continuous movement of the sprocketed rollers. It is thus moving while it is being exposed. This is what creates the blurring effect, which is most noticeable in the bright areas of the image. Fluorescent lights, for example, will look like hanging bedsheets.

Whereas losing the loop in the projector can be easily corrected, its loss while shooting is disastrous. The image is exposed while the film is moving, and the resulting blur is not correctable. Reshooting or abandoning the material are the only options. Experimental filmmakers have occasionally used footage with a lost loop to good effect, most notably Bruce Baillie's *Castro Street* (1966). In most situations, though, it is undesirable.

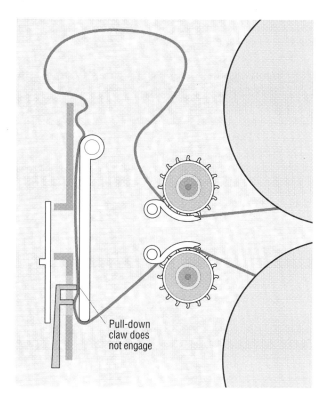

1-8

"Losing the loop" means that the film becomes taut between one of the rollers and the pressure plate

Pull-down claw does not engage

Cameras do not lose the loop often, but when they do, the camera will usually sound different. Although it happens infrequently, you should nevertheless be constantly checking and guarding against it. The biggest culprit of lost loops is improper loading—one of the many reasons why learning proper loading technique is critical. Not closing the keepers is a common loading mistake that causes lost loops. Another cause can be the film's *plastic memory*. If the camera sits loaded and unused for an extended period (as little as half an hour), the film will conform to the shape in which it was left. When the camera is started again, that semirigid shape can cause the film to run through the mechanism poorly, thus losing the loop. A jar to the camera (which should always be avoided for obvious reasons) or flaws in the raw stock (which are extremely rare) can also create the problem. Camera malfunction, such as with the pull-down claw or the sprocketed rollers, can also be the cause. These would result from serious mechanical breakdowns and thus would occasion major repair costs.

There are two other design options that are part of the basic mechanism on many cameras. A registration pin and an inching knob are not absolutely necessary, but they are generally desirable.

The purpose of a *registration pin* is to hold the film absolutely steady as it is being exposed. It is usually below the film gate and, like the pull-down claw, extends out and engages a sprocket hole.

In the explanation of the basic mechanism, it is apparent that nothing is holding the film in place except the force of the pressure plate and the friction of the movement. The pull-down claw has retracted and is going up to grab the next frame. Oddly enough, this is just when the film is exposing, and the stability of the image is critical. All cameras hold the image reasonably stable, but the registration pin guarantees that the frame will not move at all. The pin extends from the body of the camera and engages the sprocket hole as each individual frame is being exposed. It retracts as the next frame is being pulled down.

Most high-end 16mm cameras have a registration pin, and almost all modern 35mm cameras have one. When perfect registration is a must, a *pin-registered camera* is necessary. Perfect registration is essential in many applications, including animation, when the film has to be projected a long distance, when the film is being transferred to video, and when it is going to be blown up to a larger frame size.

An *inching knob* is used to manually move the basic mechanism backward or forward. It is usually found on the exterior of the camera, though occasionally it is inside the film chamber (a design that can be irritating). The knob is helpful in loading because the mechanism can be advanced to ensure that the film is properly threaded—the pull-down claw and sprocket teeth properly engaged and the loops correct. It is particularly helpful in moving the shutter to enable you to see through the viewing system or check the gate for dirt and hair (see page 48). The inching knob is also used to roll film with the plastic memory effect out of the sprocketed rollers, thus avoiding problems with the loop. Inching knobs are essential parts of projectors as well.

Although both these features are desirable, many fine cameras have neither. The Bolex camera, for example, can produce an exceptional image but has neither a registration pin nor an inching knob.

Most basic technical mistakes with the camera occur because of a lack of knowledge about the camera's inner workings. In the age of video, when many people just pop in a cartridge and expect things to work, producing a film image takes careful attention to detail. It begins to strike the aspiring filmmaker that the aspects of film that ought to be simple (such as getting a useable image) are difficult, and those that ought to be hard (such as being an artist) are near impossible. An understanding of the basic mechanism will serve both your ability to create images trouble-free and your awareness of film's possibilities.

As the mechanical age yields to the electronic age, there is nevertheless something irresistibly beautiful about the action of a well-designed camera. This appreciation not only enables you to know if a camera is malfunctioning, it allows you to understand any camera with which you might have to work. Comprehending what is going on in a camera is also critical to understanding what can and cannot be accomplished visually. The deceptively straightforward task of making sure the camera operates correctly will always require your careful attention.

Frames per Second

Frames per second (fps), or the more general *frame rate*, refers to the number of individual frames being photographed each second. The professional frame rate is *24 fps*, that is, 24 individual photographs are recorded per second. Many cameras come with a choice of several different frame rates, with rates lower and higher than 24 used for fast- and slow-motion effects (see page 41). The standard rate for projection equipment is 24 fps as well.

Prior to the introduction of sound in the 1920s, films were shot at 16 fps—the minimum number of frames that could reproduce normal motion without the flicker created by a slow-moving shutter. The change to 24 occurred with the advent of sound and was made necessary by the faster speed required to produce adequate sound fidelity. Many cameras, particularly Super 8 cameras, still include the option of running at 16 fps or, more frequently, 18 fps, as this has remained the amateur standard.

Motors

Camera motors can be divided into two useful categories: *synchronous* and *wild*. A synchronous motor, referred to as a *crystal* or a D.C. Servo-controlled motor, is a speed-controlled motor that produces a virtually perfect 24 fps. This allows sync-sound filming—shooting in which the actual location sound is recorded *in sync* with the image. Sound for film is recorded separately on conventional audio equipment, and precision speeds are necessary for the two to run in sync. (See chapter 13 for a further discussion of the synchronization of sound and picture.) Wild motors, on the other hand, will deviate slightly from the set frame rate. If set to run at 24 fps, the speed of a wild camera could vary a percentage point or two from a true 24 fps. Although this deviation would never be visible to the eye, the lack of precision makes later synchronization virtually impossible. Wild cameras are used in situations where sound is not needed or, more commonly, when sound effects will be edited in later. They receive much more use than one might at first suspect.

Beyond this key distinction, there are two types of motors in common use: **spring-wound** and **electric**. Electric motors are the standard, but spring-wound types see substantial use in the 16mm format. There are still a few older spring-wound models floating around in 35mm, but they are rare in Super 8. Cameras with spring-wound motors are by definition wild cameras. Sync filming requires an electric motor, although not all battery-operated cameras have crystal motors. Electric motors generally run on rechargeable nickel-cadmium batteries, referred to as **nicads**. Super 8 cameras can usually be run off disposable batteries or nicads. Most battery-operated motors can be run off wall power (AC power, as opposed to the DC power of batteries) but require step-down transformers to convert the voltage of conventional outlets—always 110 volts—to the voltage of the individual camera. Individual cameras have different voltage requirements, usually somewhere between 8 and 20 volts.

Spring-wound motors are generally found on older camera designs. The motor is driven by a spring similar to that found in a mechanical clock. There is a hand crank on the side of the camera to manually wind the spring tight. The camera is driven by the spring releasing its bound-up energy. Winds generally last about thirty seconds when filming normal motion, although this varies from camera to camera. The camera has a governed motor that allows it to run at a constant speed —it does not slow down as the spring gets to the end of its wind.

The major advantages of spring-wound motors are their low cost and their ability to be used in situations in which electricity, either for camera operation or battery recharging, is either unavailable or impractical. Prior to the days of portable battery-operated cameras, spring-wound cameras were used to shoot most location documentaries, particularly combat footage and exploration footage. Unless preventive measures are taken, batteries perform poorly in the cold, making the spring designs particularly helpful in frigid climates. The drawbacks to the spring-wound motor are limitations on shot length, the constant rewinding, and the inability to run at a perfectly controlled speed.

Once you step into sync shooting, you enter a world where costs limit access, and personnel demands call for a larger crew (sound mixer, boom operator, and others). A bare-bones 16mm sync **camera package** (camera, lenses, magazines, batteries, battery chargers, tripod, and any other camera needs specific to the shoot) rents for roughly $300 to $400 a day. Access to this high-end equipment can be limited, particularly in university film programs. For this reason and many others, initial projects are usually shot with wild cameras, often spring-wound types. In this age of electronic everything, spring-wound cameras may appear old-fashioned, but they are still precision instruments that can produce stunning images. The filmmaker, not the motor, is the variable on whether the camera produces beautiful images or not. While most everyone thinks in terms of dialogue scenes, it is surprising the relatively high number of shots that do not require sync—having sound effects added later. This said, battery-operated cameras are the standard for professional use.

Formats

The term *format* refers to the size of the film stock and the size of the image. There are three standard formats in general use: 35mm, 16mm, and Super 8. A fourth format, Super 16, is an adaptation of the 16mm format. **SEE 1-9** The biggest of the three formats is 35mm. It demands a substantial budget both in terms of the stock itself and the equipment used to shoot and edit it. Super 8 is the smallest and is relatively inexpensive. There are a number of other formats (65mm, Imax, Omnivision, and so on), but these have highly specialized applications and are prohibitively expensive. A 16mm frame is roughly one-quarter the size of a 35mm frame. A Super 8 frame is roughly one-quarter the size of a 16mm frame. The frame's width-to-height relationship is called the *aspect ratio*.

The 35mm film stocks have perforations on both sides of the film, referred to as *double perf* or two row. The 16mm stocks are available in double perf as well as *single perf* or one row—sprocket holes on one side only. Most 16mm shooting is done with double perf because it is easier to manipulate in the editing process. Super 8 is all single perf.

Beyond cost, the biggest difference among the formats is in image quality. The larger formats are able to contain more information, thus creating a more defined image. More definition aids in projectability and, of more importance recently, a higher-quality transfer to video. In a commercial theater, the projected image is as much as 300,000 times larger than the 35mm frame from which it originated. A 16mm image will not stand that kind of expansion without significant image deterioration because there is less information. A Super 8 image would produce a dim blur. The harsh reality is that 35mm is the format for people interested in theatrical exhibition.

35mm

If you see a film at a commercial theater, odds are that it was shot on *35mm* film. Music videos and commercials are also frequently shot on 35mm, then transferred to video for editing and finishing.

The 35mm stocks have four individual sprocket holes per frame. The high number allows for more gentle handling of the film in cameras and projectors, sparing a single perforation from supporting the entire bulk and weight of the larger frame size. It is difficult to think in terms of the weight of an individual frame, but the film is so flexible and is being transported at such a high speed that it needs all the stability possible.

Aspect ratio for 35mm film is expressed as 1.33:1, meaning that the frame is four fields wide to three fields high. This is referred to as the Academy Aperture. The name derives from the standardized frame size and sound track configuration accepted by the Academy of Motion Picture Arts and Sciences shortly after the introduction of sound. The area to the left of the frame is for the optical track in final prints. This area also remains unused by the gate in the camera, though there are some applications in which the full frame is used.

In effect, the Academy Aperture is frequently shot but rarely projected. It is usually masked in the projector to create *widescreen*. The masked image in widescreen has an aspect ratio of 1.85:1, almost two fields wide to one field high. This is the way most feature films are presented in commercial theaters. Clearly, much of the frame is lost when a film is shown on television.

Ratios larger than 1.85:1 are generally achieved with an anamorphic process. The film frame itself is the standard 35mm size (actually, the image area is slightly larger than the Academy Aperture), but the anamorphic process uses a camera lens that "squeezes" the image so it appears to be stretched vertically. It is then

1-9

Film formats are distinctions based on the size of the film stock and the size of the image

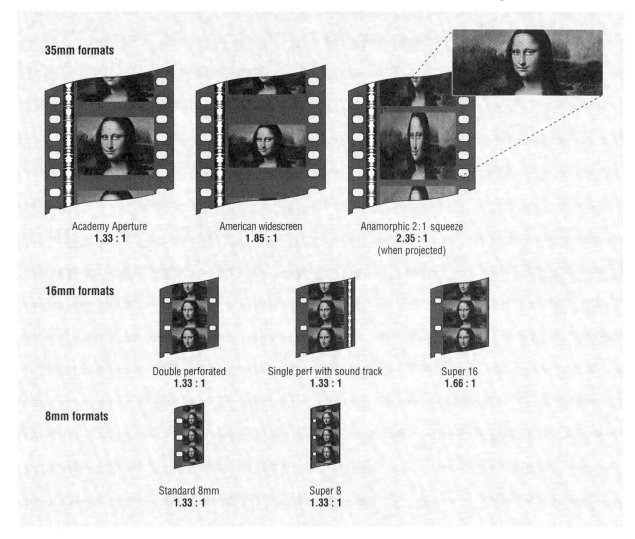

35mm formats

Academy Aperture
1.33 : 1

American widescreen
1.85 : 1

Anamorphic 2:1 squeeze
2.35 : 1
(when projected)

16mm formats

Double perforated
1.33 : 1

Single perf with sound track
1.33 : 1

Super 16
1.66 : 1

8mm formats

Standard 8mm
1.33 : 1

Super 8
1.33 : 1

"unsqueezed" in projection. The best-known anamorphic process, CinemaScope, has a projection aspect ratio of 2.35:1. When shown on television, title sequences are often left squeezed so the sides of credits are not cut off, thus allowing the viewer to see this strange squeezed image.

Cameras for 35mm are large, expensive to rent, and require substantial technical support (both in terms of crew and equipment). The use of 35mm is virtually impossible for students and very difficult for low-budget independents. The reality, unfortunately, is that it is difficult to get anything shown if it is not in 35mm. Few theaters of any size are equipped with 16mm projectors, and almost none with Super 8.

16mm

The *16mm* format is used in many independent film projects and most intermediate and advanced film production classes. This is the format that can support, in terms of equipment and technical resources, a level of production that students both need to learn and can afford. The term *afford* is used advisably, because it is still quite expensive.

The 16mm format was introduced in the 1920s and quickly became the amateur stock of choice. It took on greater significance with the rise of instructional filmmaking in the 1930s and 1940s, and came to wide acceptance during World War II—the majority of combat footage being shot with 16mm cameras. It has developed into a full-blown professional format in the years since, though video has made a dent in its popularity.

The 16mm film stock has one sprocket hole per frame. The sprocket hole is right at the *frame line*, the hairline dividing one frame from another. The pitch for most production cameras is .2996mm. Film stocks with different pitches are either print stocks or designed for other specialized purposes. The aspect ratio of 16mm is also 1.33:1, four fields wide to three fields high.

Super 16 is an adaptation of the 16mm format. Many independent projects used to be shot in standard 16mm with the intention that there would be a blowup to 35mm for theatrical presentation. One drawback is that the dimensions of a 35mm widescreen frame are wider and shorter (1.85:1) than the 16mm frame. To transfer to 35mm, the top and bottom of the 16mm composition had to be eliminated to conform to the 35mm frame. Not only did this have to be considered by the person shooting the film when framing shots, it reduced the already small amount of information available to create the 35mm image.

Super 16 was introduced to counter this problem. Super 16 uses standard, single perf 16mm stock and a modified 16mm camera. The area of the film that would be taken up by the second row of sprockets is used for additional image area. This produces a composition with the same dimensions as widescreen 35mm, as well as substantially increases the information available for blowing up.

Super 16 requires a wider-than-normal gate as well as a modified lens and viewing system. Most of the newer production cameras, such as the Arri SR and the Aaton, are designed to be easily converted to Super 16. Older cameras would require extensive retooling, an approach that generally is not cost-effective unless you foresee doing a substantial amount of work in Super 16. Even then, the adaptation may be questionable.

When the destination is a final film print, Super 16 is shot only when a blowup to 35mm is a certainty. Finishing in 16mm would be counterproductive. The area of the second set of sprocket holes will eventually be devoted to the sound track. Finishing in 16mm would mean eliminating that entire portion of the frame. Those beautifully balanced compositions might suddenly look as though something were missing.

Super 16 is now receiving additional attention as a source of visuals for the new high-definition television (HDTV), which is widescreen in format.

Super 8

Super 8 is the smallest of the three formats and was the amateur standard for many years. It replaced the Regular 8 format, which is still available but increasingly difficult to find. Desiring a way for students to shoot a lot of film inexpensively, Super 8 was, and to a lesser extent still is, the format of choice for many university film programs. Recent years have seen enormous inroads into the popularity of Super 8 by home video. The low cost, immediate results, and ease of incorporating home video into existing television systems made the cost, delays in processing, and cumbersome, finicky projectors of Super 8 an easy target for the burgeoning market.

For a period there was a large Super 8 movement in the United States consisting mostly of independents wanting to produce out of the Hollywood mainstream. This impetus still remains but was radically altered by the realities of the video age. The low- and midrange Super 8 cameras and much of the support equipment have largely disappeared. What remains are the high-end Super 8 cameras with high-quality lenses and sound capabilities. These cameras have held on as a relatively inexpensive and less cumbersome way of generating a film image that can be transferred to video. Super 8 has been particularly popular in remote location work, where video's electrical requirements and climatic limitations can pose difficulties. As Super 8 grows increasingly rare, more university programs are switching to 16mm or video for beginning production classes.

In its heyday, sophisticated postproduction strategies were devised for editing in Super 8. These included handling audio separately to facilitate the kind of complex sound layering that one associates with 16mm and 35mm. This led to a number of highly sophisticated films being shot on Super 8, particularly Derek Jarman's *The Last of England* (1987). Although this trend is encouraging, the support for high-end Super 8 is not widespread enough to recommend it to the beginner. Without a clear understanding of how the equipment is supposed to perform, Super 8 can be very frustrating. Even Jarman himself recommended learning in a larger format first, so one understands what the Super 8 equipment can and is supposed to do. Once 16mm has been mastered, a move to Super 8 can be quite productive.

Frame configurations for Super 8 are different from those for other formats, a fact that can be disconcerting for editors new to the format. The frame line of most formats is aligned with the sprocket hole. In Super 8 the frame line is between the sprocket holes. The splicers still cut at the frame line, but this is the only format that so configures the frame.

Camera Loads

Raw stocks in 16mm can be purchased loaded in two different ways: on *daylight spools* and on *cores*. In 35mm, film is available only on core loads. Super 8 film is available in cartridges. Daylight spools and core loads each have advantages, although daylight spools are used more frequently on small projects, and core loads are the industry standard. *Core loads* are more complicated to use because they must be loaded in absolute darkness, usually in a *photographic darkroom bag*, often referred to as a *changing bag*.

Daylight Spools

Daylight spools are so named because they allow the camera to be loaded in the light. They have two black metal flanges on a core with a hollow center. **SEE 1-10** The square holes on each side of the flange are for mounting the spool on the spindles in the camera. The side flanges protect the film from accidental exposure.

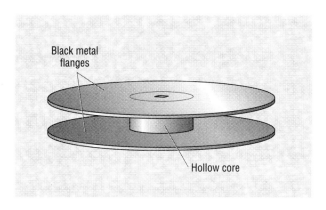

1-10

Daylight spools allow a camera to be loaded in lighted conditions

Black metal flanges

Hollow core

1-11

Reciprocally fed film on a daylight spool

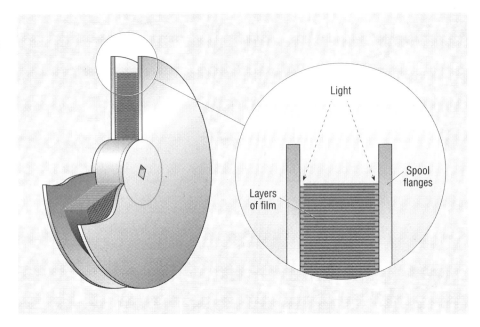

The flanges of a daylight spool are slightly farther apart than the actual width of the film to prevent the film from binding as it feeds off. **SEE 1-11** In order that light does not seep down into the center of the roll, the film is fed onto the spool with a reciprocal action. One layer of film is fed against one flange of the daylight spool. Then the film is shifted slightly to one side, and the next layer is fed against the other flange. The next layer is fed against the first flange, and so on. The outer layers of film block light from getting to the center of the roll in the loading process.

The 100-foot daylight spool, which runs for 2 minutes 40 seconds in normal filming for 16mm, is the most commonly used size on beginning projects. Daylight spools are generally used in smaller 16mm cameras, ones with the film chamber designed specifically for them. They are also handy when working in remote locations and when just a shot or two is needed. Also available are 400-foot daylight spools, which run just under 11 minutes in 16mm, but their use has diminished since video replaced film for shooting TV news. Television news photographers often had to change rolls on the fly, and daylight spools were more convenient. Their major drawback is that they are noisier in a magazine. Several cameras have felt-lined interiors to deaden the noise, an approach that might appear to deserve wider acceptance barring the difficulty of keeping the cloth clean.

Core Loads

Core-loaded raw stock is the norm in professional film applications. A core is a circular plastic piece on which the film is wound. Unlike the daylight spool, there are no flanges to protect the film, meaning that all core loads have to be loaded in changing bags. The most common size is the 400-foot load; 1,200-foot loads are available but are practical only in highly controlled situations due to the bulk and extra weight of the attendant equipment. The 1,200-foot loads were popular in 16mm for formal interviewing situations, but so much of that type of application has gone to video that their use has diminished.

The cores themselves come in a variety of sizes and are also used extensively in the editing process. **SEE 1-12** Camera loads use 2-inch cores, whereas most editing applications use 3-inch cores or larger. The 3-inch cores limit the stress on the inner layers of film, which is particularly important for sound stock. Labs frequently wind processed film on 4-inch cores to eliminate as much stress as possible on the fragile emulsion.

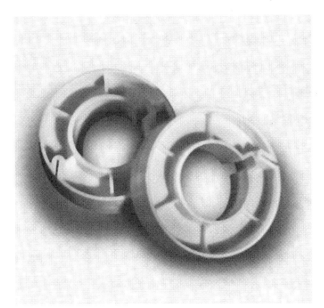

1-12

Camera loads use 2-inch cores, which have no flanges, necessitating the use of a darkroom bag

Cartridges

There have been many experiments with cartridge-loading films. The only one that remains is the Super 8 cartridge, although there are a number of loading approaches that share its design. **SEE 1-13** Super 8 has a plastic cartridge that simply slips into the camera's body and is discarded in the processing stage.

The Super 8 cartridge uses the *coaxial* feed and take-up compartments, based on the design strategy of modern coaxial film magazines (see "Magazines" later in this chapter). The coaxial design has the supply roll in a chamber on one side of

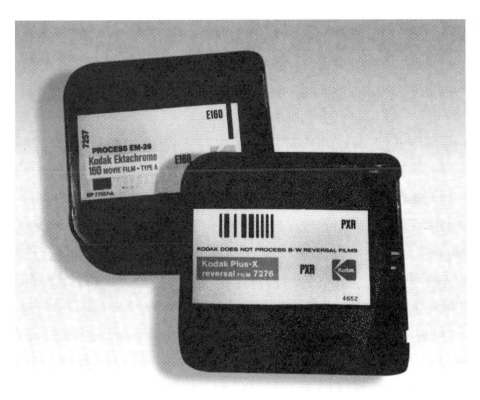

1-13

The Super 8 cartridge is the only remaining cartridge-loading film the cartridge and the take-up in a second chamber on the other side. The film has two slight twists so it can curve from one side to the other. In terms of the camera's basic mechanism, a Super 8 camera consists of just the gate, aperture plate, pull-down claw, and shutter. All the other elements must, by necessity, be in the cartridge. Each Super 8 cartridge comes with a built-in pressure plate as well as a form of roller-and-keeper system, the cartridge employing a slightly different strategy here. The cartridge also has to dedicate space in its interior for the loops.

Cameras

In terms of what is available, the range of camera types has consolidated considerably since the advent of video. Only a small number of companies have been able to weather the reduced demand. Many oddball cameras have rotated out of the bottom of the loop due to age and peculiarity of design, but a number of 16mm cameras have held on through the lean years: the Bolex, the Scoopic, the Aaton, the Eclair, Arriflex cameras, and the Bell & Howell series. Some of these are no longer produced, but their durability and quality have kept them around and working, particularly in education programs. Production cameras in 35mm generally come from two companies: Arriflex and Panavision. A small number of Super 8 cameras are still produced, Nizo being one company that is still making quality cameras. In the prime of their popularity, Super 8 cameras were produced by many companies, and many good deals can be found on used models. This discussion focuses on 16mm cameras and the choices that are out there.

The first four cameras discussed are all wild—that is, nonsync—cameras. All four have film chambers designed for daylight spools, although there are models available that can be adapted for magazine use. **SEE 1-14**

1-14

Nonsync cameras generally use daylight spools, although some can be adapted to mag use

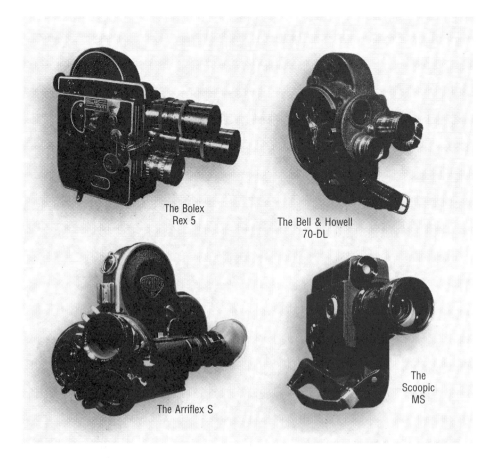

The Bolex
Rex 5

The Bell & Howell
70-DL

The Arriflex S

The
Scoopic
MS

The Bolex and the Bell & Howell are both spring-wound cameras. The Bolex is a finely engineered piece of equipment and has been the camera of choice for independent and nonsync professional work for many years. It is still being produced, and a wide variety of accessories are available, including electric motors that can be mounted on the side.

The Bell & Howell is lovingly referred to as the "nail pounder," so named because it is so rugged people said it could be used to drive in tent stakes (do not try it). It was designed to withstand situations where tender treatment was difficult, such as being thrown off landing barges during World War II. The Bell & Howell is no longer produced, although many of them are still available and providing excellent results.

Both the Arriflex S (Arri S) and the Scoopic are battery operated. Some models of the Scoopic and all Arri S cameras can accept magazines. The Arri S is the only one of these cameras that has a registration pin and is thus the most expensive of the four. The Scoopic is specifically designed for easy handheld work and is still extensively used in sports filming. Some models of Scoopics have motors that allow the camera to do sync sound, though it is generally too noisy and inflexible for critical applications. Neither the Arri S nor the Scoopic are still produced.

The five cameras in the group below are all designed for sync-sound filming. **SEE 1-15** All of them are magazine-loading cameras with no room in the camera body for daylight spools (see following section). The first three are no longer being produced, though they are still common in rental and educational situations. The last two are state-of-the-art and are the two major production cameras currently in use.

1-15

Sync cameras are magazine loading and are used for sync-sound filming

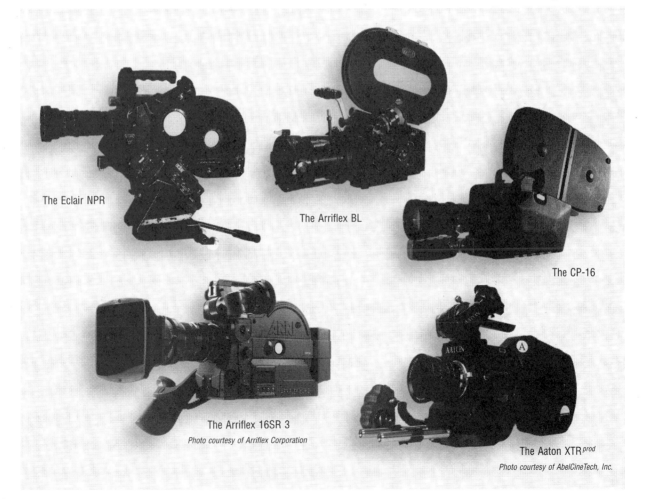

The Eclair NPR

The Arriflex BL

The CP-16

The Arriflex 16SR 3

Photo courtesy of Arriflex Corporation

The Aaton XTR^{prod}

Photo courtesy of AbelCineTech, Inc.

The Eclair revolutionized the industry in the early 1960s. The camera's light weight and the coaxial design of its magazine made it both portable and flexible enough to use in almost any situation, allowing it to go places a camera had never gone before. It, along with the Arriflex BL, became the production cameras of the '60s and '70s. Both cameras have registration pins. Although the Eclair was a revolutionary handheld camera, it is a shoulder wrecker compared with the modern Aaton and the Arri SR. The Arri BL is considered a studio camera, with an extensive and bulky housing to make it noiseless. The CP-16, the most portable and lightweight of the older cameras, was designed to be used in television newsfilming. It does not have a registration pin, though it is an excellent and frequently used piece of equipment.

The Arri SR and the Aaton are both pin registered and adaptable to the Super 16mm format. They also are designed to interface with many video systems, adaptable to record a number of time-code formats. Arriflex cameras have been widely used since the 1930s, and the Arri SR is a commonly available and frequently used system. The Aaton is less common in the United States but is considered the equal of the Arri SR.

Basic Threading Procedures

Although the basic theory is consistent, threading procedures vary slightly from one camera to the next. Some cameras are relatively easy to thread, whereas others require a modicum of understanding and skill. A number of wild cameras have automatic threading—mechanisms designed to feed the film unassisted. Most cameras, however, must be manually threaded. Wild cameras that employ daylight spools are covered here; tips for the more complicated magazines are discussed in chapter 15.

Finding a manual and following the instructions is the first step. In addition, cameras often have either a printed diagram somewhere on their bodies, or lines in the film chamber that indicate the threading path. These guides are indispensable, but the best way to learn about a camera is to be walked through it by someone with extensive experience. An hour or two with a person who really understands a camera can be an eye-opening experience on many counts. The following overview provides some basic tips.

All cameras are designed with as little excess space as possible in the film chambers. Space means bulk and bulk means weight. There is precious little finger room, so keep the film chamber as free as possible, particularly by removing the take-up daylight spool.

On automatic-threading cameras, a small cutter in the film chamber is used to create an edge on the film. The film is fed into the top sprocketed roller as the camera is being run, the film thus feeding all the way through the mechanism. Automatic-threading cameras employ *loop setters*—small guards above and below the gate that create loops of the appropriate size and shape. The loop setters are closed to thread the film and open for shooting. Most cameras with this design have a release that automatically opens the loop setters when the cover plate is put in place. Some older models have loop setters that must be opened manually, a step that if forgotten will result in ruined film. The Bolex and Scoopic are examples of cameras with automatic-threading mechanisms. **SEE 1-16**

All other cameras must be manually threaded. This simply means opening the keepers and inserting the film, creating the loops, and threading the film in front of the pressure plate. Two major considerations are making sure that the loops are the correct size and that the sprocket holes of the film are engaged in the teeth of the rollers.

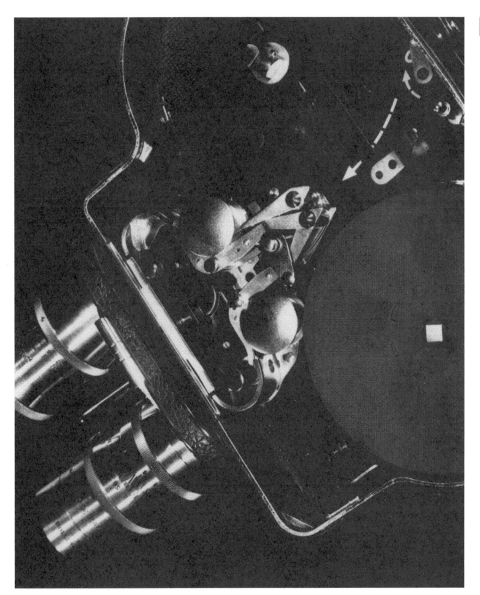

1-16

Interior of a Bolex with loop setters closed

Making the loops just the right size is a requirement that may leave some people scratching their heads, but it should be clear on each individual camera. The loops must not be so big that the film strikes the interior of the film chamber. Any contact brings with it the possibility of scratches on the film. Oversized loops may also cause poor registration, because the film is bouncing off the camera body as it is being exposed. In addition, the loops must not be so small that they prevent the give-and-take between the continuous and intermittent movements.

In the latter case, check to make sure that the sprocket holes of the film are engaged in the teeth. This usually requires visually checking, or gently pulling the film back and forth over the roller to ensure that it is engaged. Failure to check this will result in the film feeding through the rollers at an incorrect rate, leading to a jam or lost loop. Again, make sure the keepers are closed before proceeding.

Before putting on the cover plate, run the camera for two or three seconds to make sure all systems are go. Check the loops to ensure that they are both the correct size and holding their shape. Make sure the daylight spools are taking up correctly. In school and rental situations, the take-up spool is the previous user's empty feed spool. Make sure it has not been pinched or otherwise damaged. If it has been pinched, the film will collect around the edges of the spool. Even if the film then seems to be falling onto the reel after passing the pinched section, you will have problems later—the film will be loose on the take-up reel, and the full 100 feet will not fit onto it; the camera will jam toward the end of the reel. When you take off the cover plate, it will be like opening a jack-in-the-box—the "accordioned" film popping out of the camera because it had no place to go.

Beyond being threaded correctly in the mechanism, the other major consideration in loading a camera is that as little film be exposed to light as possible. As in 35mm still photography, manufacturers make the rolls a little longer than their stated length to allow for some spoilage during loading. Footage that is exposed to light in the loading process is referred to as *light struck,* and all efforts are made to minimize the amount of film subjected to this effect. As stated, the daylight spool can be loaded in lighted conditions, though manufacturers recommend loading in subdued light to conserve as much unexposed film as possible. Daylight spools can be loaded in bright daylight without difficulty, though it should be done only if absolutely necessary; you just lose more film at the beginning.

Once you close the camera, use *camera tape* to cover all places where the camera body meets the cover plate. Camera tape protects against *light leaks*—unwanted light striking the film caused by any irregularities in the camera's tight-fitting junctions. An opaque, 1-inch-wide adhesive tape, it can be found at any film-supply company or rental house.

Light leaks can be a problem on any camera but particularly on older cameras, where constant use has weakened latches or metal seams. Light leaks can be responsible for minor occasional flaws to completely destroyed film, clearly a problem to be avoided regardless of severity. Leaks are not common, but compulsory taping follows the old maxim: An ounce of prevention is worth a pound of cure. It is far better to expend a few cents worth of tape than risk having an undetected problem ruin the film. Most rental houses test for light leaks, and newer, constantly maintained cameras often do not need to be taped.

Gaffer's tape is the same material as camera tape only it is 2 inches wide. These tapes look similar to common silver duct tape, but *no substitutes should be used.* Any other tape, particularly duct tape, will leave a gummy residue or tear off the camera's exterior covering. The residue is particularly destructive in that it attracts dirt that can eventually work its way into the camera. Gaffer's tape is a handy problem solver used by almost every member of a film crew.

Once the camera is closed and taped, it should be run for several seconds to get past the film that was light struck in the loading process. This can be done with the assistance of the *footage counter,* also called the gas gauge, an indicator that keeps track of how much film has been shot. Some cameras have rolling numbers similar to the odometer on a car; others have a simple tension bar that rests on the film inside the film chamber, driving a gauge on the body of the magazine or camera. On cameras using daylight spools, the counter will have some room beneath the zero point (negative footage numbers) so the film can be run past the light-struck footage. This is called "running the camera to zero." The following summary list may prove helpful:

1. Make sure the camera is wound or the battery attached.

2. If the camera has automatic threading, close the loop setters before threading the film.

3. On automatic-threading cameras, a small film cutter can usually be found just below the bottom loop setter in the film chamber. Trim the front edge of the film with it. Insert the film in the top sprocketed

roller with the trigger depressed—the camera running. When it feeds through to the bottom, stop the camera.

4. On manual-threading cameras, open the keepers and pressure plate and insert the film.

5. Set up the bottom daylight spool for take-up.

6. Make sure that the loops are set as they should be—not too big and not too small. This will require opening the loop setter on automatic-threading cameras.

7. Check that the take-up reel is taking up correctly. If a daylight spool is pinched, the camera will jam later.

8. Close and tape the camera. Run the camera to the zero point so you get past all the light-struck film.

When *downloading* (unloading) the film, greater care must be taken to avoid light-struck film. The reciprocal feeding process described does not occur during take-up in the camera, and light can find its way deep into the spool, ruining many shots. Find a dark place or cover the camera with a heavy shirt. Do whatever you can to minimize contact with light. The last several shots on the roll will usually be ruined in downloading; if these are important to you, they can be saved by downloading in absolute darkness. Because you only have to take the reel out and get it into its packaging, this is not difficult to accomplish, since there is no unthreading involved. Finding a dark place may be the only obstacle. A friend tells the story of one shoot where he wanted to save every possible frame of the last shot on a roll. The only dark place he could find was the trunk of his car. His crew locked him in and he emerged in a few moments with the carefully preserved roll. He was quite pleased with his inventiveness until the police arrived with guns drawn, demanding that the assembled crew "let the guy out of the trunk." Seeing only the first part of the action, an onlooker had assumed some Jimmy Cagney–style mayhem was about to occur.

Develop good camera habits from the start. Beginners often get rushed and forget important procedures, then cross their fingers and just hope the film turns out. Work toward eliminating luck as part of the equation. Shooting takes a measured and logical approach that takes all potential problems into consideration. Misthreading a camera is the most basic and destructive mistake that can be made.

Magazines

In the magazine (mag) design, the film chamber is separate from the camera. The magazine is loaded with film and then mounted on the camera. Core loads are used almost exclusively in magazines, although magazines can be adapted to use daylight spools. Most 16mm magazines are designed for 400-foot loads, although both 200- and 1,200-foot ones are occasionally found. Again, core loads require the use of a photographic darkroom bag. There are two styles of magazines in general use: front-to-back and coaxial.

Front-to-Back

The front-to-back style of magazine is probably the most familiar. Some versions of these, particularly older designs, resemble and are thus called "Mickey Mouse ears." The front-to-back approach employs a front chamber that holds the feed

1-17

The front-to-back magazine design employs a front chamber that holds the feed roll, and a rear chamber that holds the take-up

CP-16 magazine

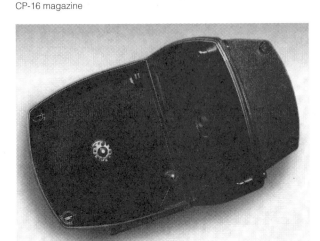

1-18

This modification of the front-to-back design employs sprocketed rollers in the lighttrap

Arri BL magazine

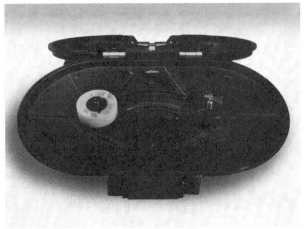

roll and a rear chamber that holds the take-up. The film is fed out of the feed side and into the take-up chamber by means of a *lighttrap*, which guarantees that light will not seep into the chamber. The front-to-back magazine design has become less common in 16mm, although it is still used in a number of 35mm cameras.

In the front-to-back design, a loop of film is held out of the magazine to be threaded through the sprocketed rollers and gate area. The inside of the camera itself is a standard basic mechanism, only there is no room for daylight spools. The sprocketed rollers of the camera drag the film through rollers in the magazine's lighttrap. The drawback to this method is that it can take some time to thread the camera. The CP-16 employs this design. **SEE 1-17**

A modification of the front-to-back design employs sprocketed rollers in the lighttrap. Rather than having simple rollers in the lighttrap, sprocketed rollers transport the film out of and back into the magazine. The magazine takes more time in the changing bag because the film must be threaded through both rollers. However, the film only has to be inserted in front of the pressure plate in actual threading. The magazine requires more attention because the correct number of frames must be between the rollers to make the loops the right size. The Arriflex BL 16mm camera is the best-known camera employing this configuration. **SEE 1-18**

There are two basic styles of magazine lids in the front-to-back design. One design hinges the front chamber and the rear chamber separately. In this style, all that has to be done in the darkroom bag is get the film in the front chamber and fed out through the lighttrap. Lock the front compartment and you are done. The back can be set when you get out of the bag or when you are threading the camera. The CP-16 magazine employs this approach.

The other type of mag has a single-hinged lid for the entire film chamber, with the feed and the take-up being side by side. This of course means that both feed and take-up have to be threaded in the changing bag. If the film is not properly attached to the take-up core, the camera will jam quickly because there will soon be no place for the film to go. Tape is never used to attach the film because it attracts dirt and causes problems in the processing machines. You should put about an $\frac{1}{8}$-inch fold in the film that is slid into the core's slot. Having to thread this style of magazine can be somewhat intimidating at first, but it is easily mastered. The Arri BL magazine is a typical example of this design.

Coaxial

Most of the newer generation of cameras, particularly in 16mm, use the coaxial design. Like the Super 8 cartridge, all the elements that transport the film to the gate (sprocketed rollers, keepers, pressure plate, room for loops) are in the magazine itself. The actual cameras themselves look quite odd because all they are is a lens mount, pull-down claw, gate, registration pin, and viewing system attached to a motor. The main bulk of the camera comes when the magazine (and the lens) is attached. The Arriflex SR, the Aaton, and the older Eclair NPR are examples of 16mm cameras that use this design.

With the coaxial design, the feed side has to be set up in the bag, and the rest can be done in the light of day. It is somewhat similar to the Arriflex BL design, because the film has to be threaded through the magazine's first set of sprocketed rollers. When you emerge from the bag, the film will be threaded out the front of the magazine on top of the pressure plate. It is then fed in at the bottom of the pressure plate. You will have to leave out enough film to form the loops. Every camera will have a specific number of frames that have to be left out, usually twelve. These frames are then pushed back into the magazine both above and below the pressure plate. The only nerve-racking aspect of this magazine is that the loops on some designs are hidden behind a facing plate, where you cannot see or test them.

The beauty of the coaxial design is that once loaded, it is as easy to change a magazine as it is to change a Super 8 cartridge. When a roll runs out, you pop off the magazine and pop on the next one. The change should take a second or two, whereas conventional magazines can take several minutes. Camera assistants are responsible for making sure there is always a fresh magazine available.

Magazines and magazine loading with core loads are the standard industry approach. Daylight spools are handy for quick-and-dirty shooting or when you have just a few shots to get, but their drawbacks—noise and short length—generally exclude them from most professional situations.

Viewing Systems

The viewing system allows the cameraperson to view the image being filmed. Different makes of camera employ different strategies to facilitate this. There are two different types generally available: the rangefinder system and the reflex viewing system. With the rangefinder, the operator looks through a facsimile lens that is mounted on the side of the camera. In the reflex system, you are actually looking through the camera's lens while filming. Cameras with some kind of reflex viewing system are the industry standard.

Rangefinders

Rangefinder viewing systems are found on older cameras, but there are enough of them still around to warrant inclusion here. The biggest drawback to the rangefinder system is that the operator is not looking at the exact framing of what is being filmed. This can result in minor framing errors, although there is an adjustment that should take care of most cases. This problem is called *parallax*, and most rangefinder cameras have some method of *parallax adjustment*.

The parallax adjustment is usually found around the eyepiece and controls a hinge with which the viewing system can be either swivelled away from or toward the body of the camera. The control knob is usually calibrated with the same numbers as would be found on a focus ring. The reason for this is that parallax becomes more exaggerated the closer the subject is to the camera. A subject a long

1-19

Parallax is exaggerated at close range

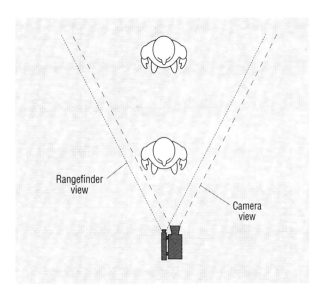

1-20

The parallax adjustment control swivels the viewing system to make the center of the viewer image the same as that of the film image

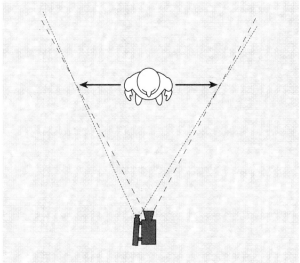

distance from the camera has enough room on either side that minor parallax differences are going to be relatively unnoticeable. When the subject is closer to the camera, these difficulties are increased. **SEE 1-19**

The parallax control swivels the viewing system to make the center of the viewer image the same as the center of the film image. **SEE 1-20** If filming a subject 8 feet away, a parallax adjustment set to 8 feet will give the same center point for both images. This strategy is clearly useful for simple images, but it breaks down with complex images incorporating camera/subject movement and multiple focus points.

Reflex Viewing

Reflex, or *through-the-lens (TTL)*, viewing systems employ several different strategies for diverting light to the camera operator's eye. All reflex viewing systems must be engineered with the camera shutter in mind. Either there is something in front of the shutter that is diverting the light, or the shutter itself is part of the viewing system. The Bolex employs a split-prism viewing system. A prism in front of the gate diverts a percentage of the light up through the viewing system. The rest of the light continues unhindered to the film plane. Split prisms are an excellent viewing strategy with one minor drawback: the light diverted to the viewfinder reduces the amount of light that is exposing the film. The amount of light is not large, but is enough that it must be compensated for in exposure. In low-light situations where you need all the light you can get, the lost light can be a significant complication. It also means that the light available to the viewfinder is sometimes insufficient. Viewfinders can be dim, occasionally making the framing difficult, particularly with darker shots. Dark viewfinders can be a problem with almost any camera.

A second viewing system has achieved wider acceptance. It was introduced by Arriflex in the 1930s, and to this day the simplicity and logic of the design remains a thing of beauty. The design employs a *mirrored butterfly shutter*. **SEE 1-21** The shutter has the shape of a butterfly, with *front-surfaced mirrors* for "wings." As opposed to the vertical design of conventional shutters, this shutter is set at a

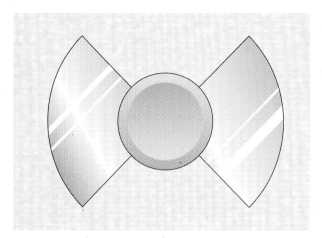

1-21

A mirrored butterfly
shutter is equipped with
front-surfaced mirrors
for "wings"

45-degree angle to the film plane. As it rotates, the shutter alternately sends light
to the film plane, or the mirrors send the light to the viewing system. **SEE 1-22** As
all shutters do, the mirrored wings block the light from reaching the film as it is
being transported. In so doing, the mirror also diverts the light up to the operator's
eye. There is no reduction of light in this system. The shutter allows 100 percent of
the light to reach the film plane in exposure, and then 100 percent of the light is
diverted to the viewing system.

Caution: Front-surfaced mirrors should be cleaned professionally. If you
attempt to clean the mirror with a cloth or tissue, you may wipe off the mirror silver
itself! Household mirrors are rear-surfaced mirrors; you look through glass to see

1-22

Viewing system with a rotating mirrored butterfly shutter, which alternately sends light to the film plane
and whose mirrors send light to the viewing system

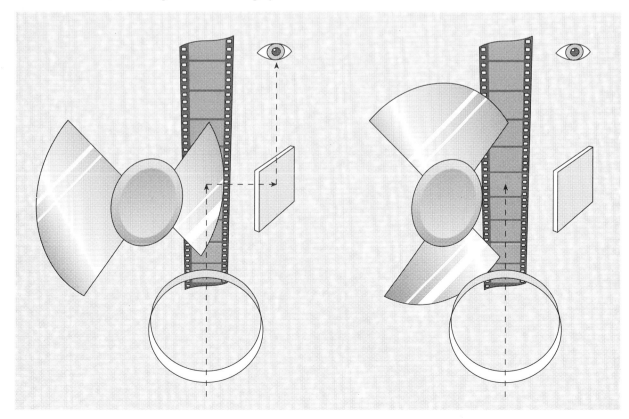

your image. Minor distortion is not a problem in a household mirror, but in critical optics any distortion is unacceptable. With the mirror on the surface of the shutter, care must be taken that the surface is not damaged.

Viewing Screens

As you look through the viewing system, you will see the viewing screen. **SEE 1-23** The screen is usually a piece of ground glass mounted just above where the light is diverted into the viewing system—adjacent to the butterfly shutter in that common design. The viewing screen, referred to as a *target*, has a series of markings that usually consist of *crosshairs*, the *TV safe frame*, and the film frame itself. The crosshairs are right in the center and can be quite helpful in planning and executing movements. The TV safe frame shows the boundaries that ensure appropriate framing when film is transferred to video, some of the edge areas of the film frame being lost in the transfer. Most professional cameras have some extra viewing room around the film frame so you can see elements that are approaching the frame.

1-23

The viewing screen usually displays crosshairs, the TV safe frame, and the film frame

Diopters

All reflex viewing systems must be set to the operator's eye. This is achieved by setting the *diopter*—an adjustable glass element in the eyepiece. Every human eye is slightly different, and the diopter allows you to adjust the viewing system for the peculiarities of your eye to ensure as sharp an image as possible while shooting. Even two people with 20/20 vision need to set the diopter to the slight differences in their vision. The diopter also plays an essential role in focusing with the viewing system, an approach that is more rare than one might first imagine. Failing to properly adjust the diopter usually has serious consequences on focus quality.

Although manuals for individual cameras should be followed to the letter, most 16mm and 35mm cameras employ similar methods for adjusting the diopter. The control for the diopter is found on or near the eyepiece. Diopters are set with the lens removed from the camera. The lens is a confusing factor because you are not setting the lens to your eye, you are setting the viewing system to your eye. The lens is set to the film. The diopter will have a setscrew or locking ring for making adjustments. Most camera manufacturers recommend that you rotate the diopter until all the framing aids are crisp and sharp. This includes crosshairs and any boundaries for the frame. Once they are perfectly focused, lock the setscrew or ring.

Once the diopter is set, you do not need to touch it again. The viewing system is set to your eye and the process is complete. The focus ring on the lens will be used to focus each individual shot. Occasionally, people get confused about this and will fiddle with the diopter during filming. This can be a recipe for disaster. Remember, you are setting the viewing system to your eye, not trying to use it to focus on any one object. The only caution on all this is that the human eye can change during the course of a long day of shooting. Your eye can get fatigued, and as it tires it actually changes shape. It is a good idea to check the diopter when you start to sense the strain of a long day.

Super 8 cameras with factory-attached lenses usually have complicated and often inadequate ways to set the diopter. Unfortunately, the kinds of situations in which Super 8 cameras are frequently used are precisely where one needs a good focusing system the most. You may be working in a hurry with few or no people helping you. In this kind of situation, spending an inordinate amount of time on focusing can distract you from other important issues. Despite this, you must still spend the time to get the focus right.

The Shots

Although mastering the technical aspects of the camera is an immediate and necessary pursuit, developing a thoughtful and intelligent approach to using the camera is the long-term goal. These first chapters include the development of a menu of what many consider to be the resources, or the "language," of cinema (see page 124 for a summary). As suggested, there are limitless choices in determining a strategy for filming any action, whether simple or complex. The following are commonly used shots, employed to achieve specific dramatic goals within individual scenes.

Proxemics

Proxemics, from the word *proximity*, refers to the distance between subject and camera. Essentially, there are three basic positions: long shot, medium shot, and close-up. There are many points in between and outside these three, such as medium close-ups and extreme long shots. But these alternative positions can be seen, and will be treated, as variations of the basic three. In studio television production, shot descriptions are very clearly defined and, especially when given as part of instructions to a camera operator, have very specific meanings. In film, interpretation of specific positions is not so rigid, because the basic structure of scenes is generally a process of moving closer to the subject.

Long Shot

A *long shot (LS)* is any shot that includes the full human body or more. **SEE 1-24** A shot that includes just the person from head to toe is alternately called a *full-body shot* or full shot. A shot in which the subject is exceptionally far away from the camera is called an extreme long shot.

1-24

A long shot includes the full human body or more
Kate Maberly in Agnieszka Holland's *The Secret Garden* (1993)

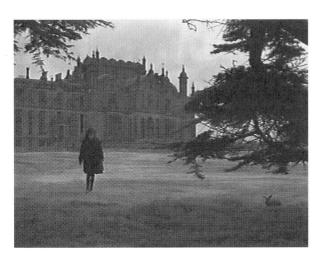

1-25

A full-body shot, or full shot, includes just the person from head to toe
Charlie Chaplin's *One A.M.* (1916)

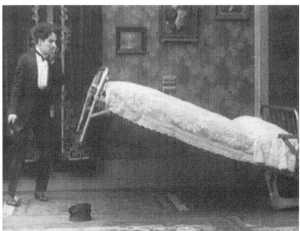

The LS tends to be random in the information it presents. If there is a general shot of people in a space, it would be difficult for viewers to distinguish which character or characters are supposed to be the focus of the shot. Momentarily discounting the notion that many elements, such as lighting, costume, and composition, can direct our attention to specific parts of the frame, we cannot logically value one character over another in a long shot. Closer shots are then used to identify characters or objects that, for narrative or atmosphere reasons, are important.

The full-body shot was much used by filmmakers in the early years of filmmaking but has fallen into some disfavor in recent years. Director Charlie Chaplin shot almost exclusively in full-body shots. **SEE 1-25** He wanted the viewer to see both his body language and his facial expressions, without the involvement of closer shots.

The long shot, and even more so the *extreme long shot (ELS)*, can also be used to diminish the subject. Presented with a lone figure in a vast landscape, the figure will appear to be overwhelmed by the surroundings. Westerns are well known for using both the LS and the ELS to achieve this effect, giving us rugged individuals within vast panoramas of untamed space. Sam Peckinpah's *Ride the High Country* (1962) dwarfs its participants against vistas of California's Sierra Nevada Mountains. **SEE 1-26** These vistas serve not only as a reminder of the puniness of human activity, but also as a metaphor for a struggle to answer larger human questions. The riders' destination is not simply a mining camp high in the mountains but a higher moral ground.

Medium Shot

The shot of a person from the waist up gives more detail than the full-body shot but is generally neutral in its presentation of the subject. **SEE 1-27** The *medium shot (MS)* represents how we interact with people in life, at least in American culture. When two people speak, they generally address each other in something roughly approximating the medium shot. The medium shot literally puts the viewer on equal footing with the subject being filmed. We rarely get right up into other people's faces to speak. In current parlance, that would be "invading their space." On the other hand, we rarely address people in long shot except as a part of a stiff, formal

1-26

In an extreme long shot, the subject is exceptionally far away from the camera
Sam Peckinpah's *Ride the High Country*

1-27

A medium shot shows a person from the waist up
Bruno Ganz in Wim Wenders's *The American Friend* (1977)

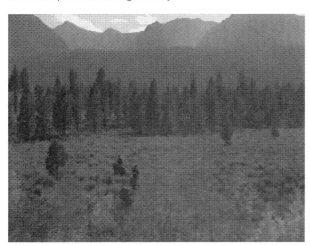

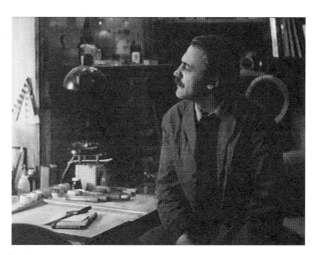

address or in the initial stages of being introduced to someone. In a medium shot, the subject is neither diminished nor unduly emphasized.

The key word in describing the MS is *neutral*. This is an arguable distinction because many see the full-body shot as being equally neutral if not more so, because it does not necessarily emphasize any particular element. There is merit to this argument, but the medium shot seems to have taken over this role, due in part to the general disfavor into which the long shot has fallen.

Close-up

The *close-up (CU)* is essentially a head shot, usually from the top shirt button up. **SEE 1-28** Anything closer than that is an *extreme close-up (ECU)*. The *medium close-up (MCU)*, which is from midchest up, is also frequently employed.

The CU is the shot that provides the greatest psychological identification with a character as well as amplifies details of actions. It is the point in which the viewer is forced to confront the subject and create some kind of internal psychological self. This identification in a CU can occasionally be so intense that the shot becomes claustrophobic. The close-up creates a tight and confined space. It has very strict

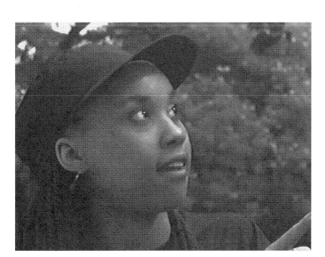

1-28

A close-up is essentially a head shot
Ariyān Johnson in Leslie Harris's *Just Another Girl on the IRT* (1993))

A push-in to a tight close-up
Ingrid Bergman in *Notorious*

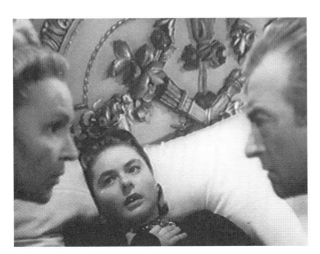 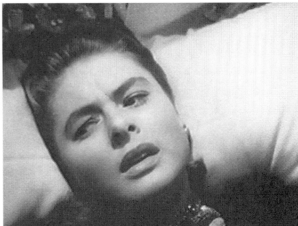

boundaries both for an actor's performance and a viewer's sense of a character's freedom of movement. The viewer can get the sense of an oppressive and menacing closeness—an "in your face" effect. Although the example of Alfred Hitchcock's *Notorious* (1946) also gets into issues of camera movement, the sequence pictured above is famous for this effect: When the main character (Ingrid Bergman) realizes that she is being poisoned, the camera moves in for a tight close-up to accentuate her discomfort. **SEE 1-29** A close-up can be equally as disorienting for the invader as it is for the invaded. The viewer can eventually become uncomfortable with being either too close or too familiar with a subject.

Close-ups are also used to amplify details. The interrelationship of these shots can be particularly successful in creating suspense. A classic example of this is in Alfred Hitchcock's *Sabotage* (1936), in which a woman (Sylvia Sidney) realizes that her husband (Oscar Homolka) has been involved in the death of her younger brother. As she serves him dinner, she starts glancing at a large carving knife. The film cuts from close-ups of the carving knife to the woman looking at it. It then cuts to the man looking at the woman. She looks at the carving knife. He looks at the carving knife and then at her. This goes on for a brief period as the tension mounts. She finally takes the knife and stabs him. This type of editing is a very common and effective device for creating suspense. (Basic principles of scene structure are discussed in chapter 5.)

It is clear that the sequence of these three shots represents a natural and logical progression of moving closer to a subject. It also represents a general movement from information that is random and undifferentiated toward more-specific information. This simple progression is one of the mainstays of the conventional approach to scene construction.

Angles

Although the term *angle* is often used on the set to designate simple camera position (setup), it also has a more limited meaning in terms of camera resources, that is, the height and orientation, or level, of the camera in relationship to the subject.

1-30

In a low-angle shot, the camera is below the subject, angled upward

1-31

The effect of this typical low-angle shot is to make the character seem powerful and intimidating
Bill Nunn in *Do the Right Thing*

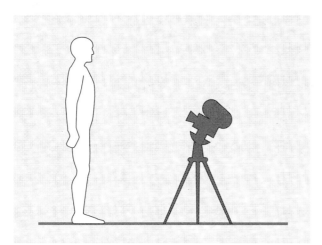

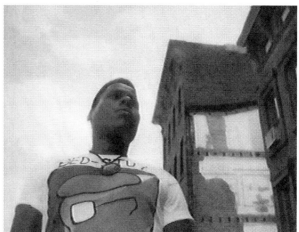

Low-Angle Shot

A *low-angle shot* is one in which the camera is below the subject, angled upward. **SEE 1-30** It has a tendency to make characters or environments look threatening, powerful, or intimidating. A classic example of the extended use of this shot is the presentation of Radio Raheem (Bill Nunn) in Spike Lee's *Do the Right Thing* (1989). **SEE 1-31** The effect of a low-angle presentation is equally applicable to objects. A scene involving a country kid's first day in the big city is a good, albeit cliché, example. The viewer is presented with low-angle shots of skyscrapers looming over the awed onlooker.

The low-angle shot can also give a distorted perspective, showing a world out of balance. This can produce a sense of both disorientation and foreboding. Ceilings and other high background elements become part of the scene. Orson Welles's *Citizen Kane* (1941) has many examples of this. The constant presence of ceilings in *Citizen Kane* gives the film a closed in, claustrophobic tone. **SEE 1-32**

Another good example comes from Alfred Hitchcock's *Vertigo* (1958). In an eerie cemetery scene, James Stewart is consistently filmed from below, making the framing of foreground and background elements disorienting. The

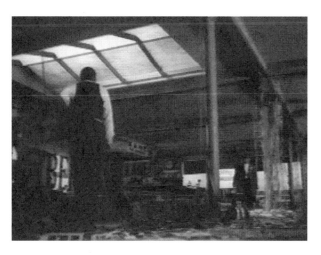

1-32

The inclusion of ceilings creates a closed-in feel in this typical low-angle shot
Orson Welles's *Citizen Kane*

1-33

This low-angle shot features distortion between the foreground and background, which can be intentionally disorienting

James Stewart in *Vertigo*

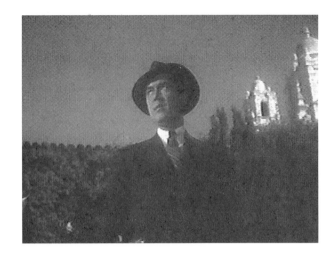

arrangement of the steeple and trees in the background gives the shot a very ominous tone. **SEE 1-33**

Foreground elements can also become distorted. Experimental video artist Bill Viola uses this to good effect in one of the movements of *Ancient of Days* (1978–81). The section has a lengthy shot of what is apparently a huge boulder in the foreground with a group of tourists milling around in the background. As the tourists move, we slowly start to realize that the perspective may be fooling us as to the size of the boulder. By the end of the shot, we realize that the rock is no more than a foot or so tall.

High-Angle Shot

The *high-angle shot* is obviously the opposite of low-angle, and its effects are the opposite as well. The camera is placed above the subject, pointing down. It tends to diminish a subject, making it look intimidated or threatened. This is the traditional way of making characters look insignificant.

Fritz Lang's masterpiece *M* (1931) has a classic exchange that incorporates both high- and low-angle shots. The film has a scene involving two men arguing, one of whom suspects the other of being the child murderer who is the focus of the film's story. One man is short (the accused) and the other tall (the accuser). The scene starts out with a shot that establishes where the characters are in relationship to each other. The scene is then an interplay—a shot/reverse shot sequence—between high-angle and low-angle shots in which the viewer sees each man's perception of the other. **SEE 1-34**

1-34

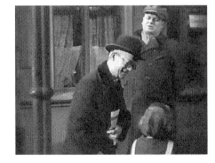

A. Establishing shot

Fritz Lang's *M*

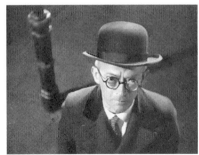

B. High-angle shot

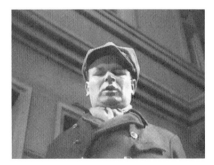

C. Low-angle shot

Eye-Level Shot

Eye-level shots are those taken with the camera on or near the eye level of the character being filmed. This also includes objects or landscapes that are seen from roughly eye level.

Eye-level shots tend to be neutral. Much like the medium shot, they represent the perspective of someone meeting people in daily life. An eye-level shot puts the viewer on equal footing with the subject being filmed. It has none of the diminishing or exaggerating qualities of the high- and low-angle shots.

A significant majority of shots in theatrical films are shot at eye level, as well as a high percentage of shots in episodic television. Unless one wishes to make specific comments on a character, high- and low-angle shots are often misused. For all the stylistic bravura of the Radio Raheem shots in *Do the Right Thing*, some critics have wondered if the character should have appeared so threatening.

All this said, most directors will tell you that they will not put the camera directly at eye level—they will position it just slightly above or below, but not enough to convey any kind of judgment or implication. The true eye level is considered too confrontational, too direct to the audience. Much as with medium shots, the neutral approach is preferred unless specific effects are desired.

Bird's-eye View

The *bird's-eye shot*, also called an overhead shot, is actually a variation of the high-angle but is so extreme that it has an effect all its own. This shot is from directly above and tends to have a godlike, omniscient point of view; people look antlike and insignificant. Its use is quite extreme and generally has such ominous associations that it appears only infrequently.

The classic example of the bird's-eye shot is, of course, Alfred Hitchcock's *The Birds* (1963). In one of the film's early bird attacks, the townspeople are gathered in a diner. A gas station attendant is struck by a bird, and gas spills out around the pumps. It is ignited and the birds start to attack as the firefighters and townspeople try to cope with the blaze. Suddenly, Hitchcock cuts to a perspective several hundred feet above the action. **SEE 1-35** As birds float serenely in the foreground, the futility and chaos of the human response to nature's revenge looks small and pitiful.

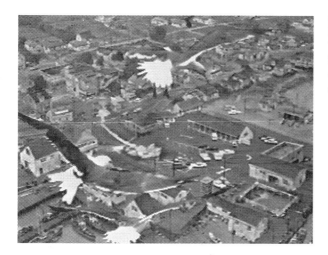

1-35

The bird's-eye view takes the high-angle shot to an extreme

Alfred Hitchcock's *The Birds*

Oblique Shot (Dutch Angle)

In an *oblique shot*, also called the *Dutch angle*, the camera is tilted laterally on a tripod so it is no longer straight with the world. The oblique shot takes the straight lines of the world and presents them as diagonals. Although it can exaggerate uphill or downhill motion, it is generally used to give the world an overwhelming sense of being unbalanced or out of kilter. One of the classic employments of the oblique angle is in Carol Reed's *The Third Man* (1949), a mystery set in post–World War II Vienna. The tilted shot is largely responsible for the film's overall sense of a world where human values and actions are distorted. **SEE 1-36**

The 1960's "Batman" television show also used the oblique angle extensively. In this case the effect is campy, the action highly stylized and overplayed to exaggerated the effect. To a certain extent, the oblique angle is problematic for just this reason. It is so transparent in its effect that it virtually announces its own cliché. Many critics have found fault with *The Third Man*, claiming the use of the oblique angle eventually becomes predictable and finally banal. Spike Lee's *Do the Right Thing* also makes liberal use of the oblique angle, a stylization that some argue does not survive repeated viewings well.

Although these may be valid critiques, the oblique angle does have subtle uses to good effect. Neil Jordan's *The Crying Game* (1992) has a number of thoughtful uses of the oblique angle. In the scenes between Jody (Forest Whitacker) and Fergus (Stephen Rea), the camera often starts out level and then, as it moves toward the characters, lists to the side a little. **SEE 1-37** The technique invests the scenes with a foreboding atmosphere, helping to develop tension.

When a technique like the oblique angle is used, we must also recognize that employing a camera that is level with the world has its own aesthetic assumptions. With the camera level in such a high percentage of what we see in films, it begins to appear so natural that we rarely even question it. As with some of the other approaches, such as medium shots and eye-level shots, a level camera is used when subjective judgments are not desired. The level camera approximates our general perception of the world, since we rarely walk around with our heads cocked to one side or the other.

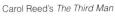

The oblique shot (Dutch angle) is generally used to convey a world that is off balance or out of kilter
Carol Reed's *The Third Man*

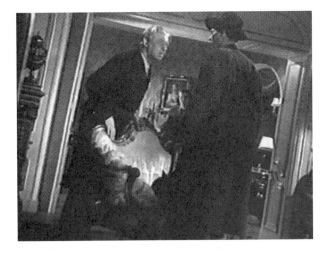

1-37

The camera is level in the establishing shot, but shifts to a Dutch angle in the close-up

Neil Jordan's *The Crying Game*

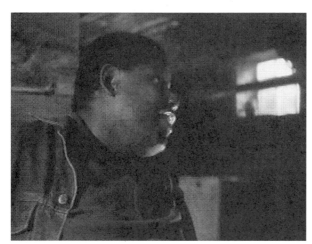 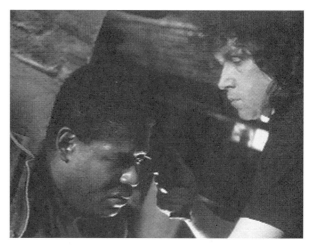

Point-of-View Shot

A *point-of-view shot* represents the perception or viewpoint of a specific character. It is not used as frequently as one might at first presume, primarily because camera vision and human vision are decidedly not the same. The constantly shifting gaze of the human eye is somewhat random and chaotic in its choice of attention. The eye has unselective focus. If you watch a dance, your eye might randomly go from the dancer's feet, to her hands, to her face, then back to her feet. The human gaze shifts with only minimal structure to the view it creates. Film vision is considerably more focused and selective. In addition, sight is only one aspect, albeit an important one, of how we interpret the world. All our other senses combine to form an impression of our surroundings.

Despite these differences, many films use the point-of-view shot effectively. Horror films have come to use it quite extensively—replicating the point of view of the killer as he relentlessly stalks his prey. The selective focus actually seems to aid the effect, representing a maniacally focused perception. Robert Montgomery's *Lady in the Lake* (1946) may be the classic exploration of the point-of-view shot. The entire film is played from a detective's perspective. The viewer sees what he sees. It is an interesting experiment, but eventually becomes so artificial that the approach is seldom duplicated except as snippets within a larger whole. Hitchcock's *Vertigo* has a much more common and successful approach to the point-of-view shot. The film constantly shifts from the looker (James Stewart) to what he is looking at. The film is very voyeuristic, as are many Hitchcock films, in its constant positioning of the viewer and the viewed.

There are certainly other angle variations. With the advent of the sewer-dwelling mutants, we could suggest some subterranean variation. Direct address to the camera is not employed frequently in film, although it is widely used in television. There are others, but one need not be rigid or schematic about this. A preponderance of what you shoot could well be done from roughly eye level, but employing other possibilities will give variety and texture to your film.

2

Camera Options and Supports

Variable Frame Rates

Many cameras come with the capability to vary the frame rate. **SEE 2-1** Continuous running at frame rates other than 24 frames per second yields either *slow-motion* or *fast-motion* effects. Some cameras, including the Bolex and most Super 8 models, have a switch that gives a number of relatively common options. Other cameras, particularly certain Arriflex models, have a rheostat that lets you dial to the rate you want.

This may at first appear contradictory: faster frame rates (36, 48, 64, et cetera) produce slow-motion shots, and slower frame rates (9, 12, 16, et cetera) produce fast motion. The key to understanding this is remembering that all projectors run at 24 fps. If you record 48 frames in one second and project that same piece at 24 fps, what took one second to shoot is going to take two seconds to project. Time is expanded, so 48 frames per second makes the action twice as long. Conversely, if you shoot at 12 fps, the material that is filmed in two seconds is presented in one second. In this case, the time is collapsed. **SEE 2-2**

There are two considerations you should be aware of when creating motion effects. The first is that you should *never run a camera empty at speeds greater than 24 fps.* The claw is designed to go out and engage a sprocket hole, and it overreaches if there is no film in the camera. At high speeds, the life of the mechanism can be significantly reduced. The second issue is that the basic mechanism, and thus the shutter, is running at a different speed when creating motion effects, and the film is receiving a different amount of light than at the 24 fps standard. Cameras with built-in exposure meters automatically compensate for this, but in most situations you need to know how to make the adjustments. Specific calculations are covered in chapter 11, but this should be kept in mind.

To create really dramatic slow-motion effects, a specialized camera is often necessary. General-use cameras that have variable frame rates usually go up to only 48 frames per second or at most 64. At 48 fps, action is expanded to twice its natural length. For actions that take some time to unfold, such as human movements, 48 to 64 fps can create nicely stylized effects. For actions that take a brief time, this slowdown may be almost imperceptible. Students often ask how to achieve that lovely slow-motion ripple effect when a drop falls into water. It is useful to ask yourself how long this event takes in real time. A drop falling in water may take less than a second. If you then double that time, it is still under two seconds. The attempted slow-motion effect is almost imperceptible.

2-1

Frame rate determines the number of frames photographed per second

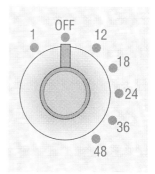

2-2

Shooting time versus projection time

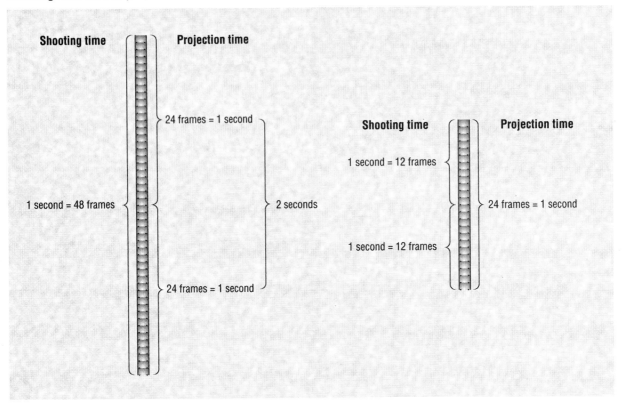

To get the kind of effect that will make a speeding bullet visible takes a substantial number of frames per second. Both PhotoSonics and Arriflex make cameras capable of running up to 150 fps. Specialized cameras can shoot up to 10,000 fps. Some basic math indicates that what took one second to shoot at this rate takes almost seven minutes of projection time. High-speed cameras are used extensively in motion analysis, and this is one of the few areas where video has not made inroads on film territory. NASA uses high-speed cameras to shoot a tremendous amount of footage of every takeoff. Construction and manufacturing companies also use them to analyze how products and structures will resist stress. A zoologist might use high-speed photography to study the movement of animals. High-speed cameras can create many dramatic effects, though their use necessitates many technical considerations that are not immediately evident.

All filmmakers will quickly become conversant with all the multiples and divisors of twenty-four. This is particularly true when editing; but whenever you need to determine how long a shot needs to be or how much screen time it is going to take, it can always be determined in frames. Time becomes a physical length of film. A shot that is 72 frames long is going to take three seconds of screen time, and so on.

Single Framing

Many cameras also come with a single-framing function, enabling you to shoot one frame at a time. One of the primary uses of this is, of course, *animation*. The most familiar animation is the cartoon style of Walt Disney films and others of that ilk. This approach is called *cel* animation. There are many other types of animation, including clay animation, pixillation, cameraless animation, and computer animation.

The majority of animations, cel and otherwise, attempt to re-create the natural movements of characters and objects. In this approach, one creates artwork that represents sequential points in movement. The movement of someone waving a hand would mean creating many points within that motion, from the hand at the character's side to points along the movement upward.

Animation is an immensely painstaking activity. Some basic math gives you a sense of this. If fluid movement is the goal, the maximum number of frames you can shoot of any single piece of artwork is two. If you shoot more, the movement will look staggered—it will not flow from one drawing to the next. If you are shooting two frames per drawing, one second of screen time takes 12 separate drawings. At 12 drawings for one second, a minute's worth of animation requires 720 drawings. A 90-minute film would need 64,800 drawings. The classic animations of the major studios were all done shooting one frame of film for each drawing. Just multiply all the previous figures by two if this approach is chosen. If all this does not give you a moment's pause, you might have a future as an animator.

Camera Features

There are a number of other options common on many cameras. The basics include the following:

Frame counter   These can be found on many wild cameras but only infrequently on sync cameras. Usually located close to the footage counter, the *frame counter* counts individual frames and is particularly helpful in such applications as animation. Usually there is one dial that counts individual frames and another that keeps track of the frames in increments of 50 or 100. At normal running speeds, the frames fly by so fast that counting is useful only in specialized situations like backwinding.

Backwinding   With *backwinding*, the basic mechanism of the camera can be driven backward with a hand crank. One can do a shot, back up, and make another *pass* over the same piece of film. This is useful for doing superimpositions, matte shots, and a variety of other effects. Exposure is a consideration when doing multiple-exposure techniques. Multiple passes are possible, though modern multiple-exposure shots are usually done on separate pieces of film and later printed together on a single piece of film. Be aware that when you are backwinding, you wind the film through the entire mechanism, including the shutter. The lens must be blocked or the film will be exposed while being backwound. The Arri S can be run in reverse, but is no longer being manufactured. At present the only commercially available 16mm camera with a backwinding feature is the Bolex.

Battery tester   Most cameras with electric motors have rudimentary battery-testing functions. Usually, a small scale with a pointer indicates whether there is adequate power. These scales are functional, but a handheld *battery tester* is a much more useful tool. Many of the new multitesters on the market are good for testing batteries, and some of their other functions can be helpful as well. Generally, one tests the voltage of the battery to see if it is at the level necessary for the camera to perform properly. There is further discussion on the care of batteries in the next section.

Lens turret   A *lens turret* is an option on a small number of cameras. It is a moveable plate in front of the film gate with which you can rotate different lenses in front of the film, allowing you to switch lenses between shots. These are more common on wild cameras than on high-end production cameras. The Bolex and Arri S are examples of cameras with turret systems.

Filter slots and holders   Many cameras have small *filter slots* either in the film chamber or on the exterior of the camera. The desired filter is mounted in a holder (a slide) which is then slid into a slot that positions it between the rear element of the lens and the film gate. **SEE 2-3** The use of these slides is somewhat controversial. Many cinematographers prefer filters that mount on the front of the lens, because rear filters effect the rear-element-to-film-plane relationship. Dirt or markings on rear filters are disastrous, as well as being more difficult to control because they are unseen. Filter slots can also be used for opaque slides with patterns cut in them, such as a binocular-shaped cutout.

There are two cautions with the use of filter slots. First, if the filter slot is on the exterior of the camera, be sure that there is an empty slide in the slot. An empty slot allows a direct route to the film gate, and light will fog the film. Even if no filtering is being done, make sure a dummy slide is inserted. Both the Bolex and Scoopic have this design. Second, make sure that whoever used the camera before you did not leave an unwanted filter in the slide. An unwanted filter will add undesired color and change exposure. This should be checked, although the presence of an unwanted filter should be apparent when you are cleaning the camera anyway.

Variable shutters   A small number of cameras come with a *variable shutter*—a means of changing the size of the shutter. Variable-shutter controls most often make the shutter bigger, with smaller shutters not allowing time for the pull-down claw to advance each frame of film. The 180-degree shutter configuration is the size that gives optimum recording of natural movement. Shutters that are larger record such a small percentage of the action that movements do not blur from frame to frame. This causes a strobelike effect that can be interesting but is generally undesirable. The variable shutter is useful in a small number of situations (to limit the rolling bars when shooting off a television screen is one

2-3

Filter slots are located either in the film chamber or on the camera exterior

Filter slot on a CP-16

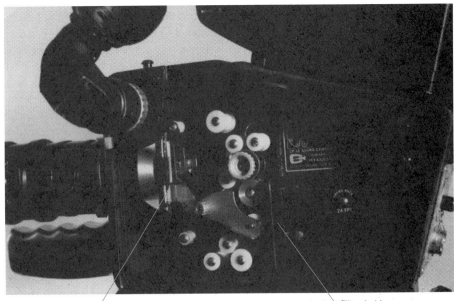

Filter slot   Filter holder

example) but is not a frequently used option. It can be used to create fades, though they usually show the imperfections of moving the control by hand. Closing the variable shutter entirely is a good way of blocking light when back-winding the camera.

Tripod threading holes   On the bottom of the camera body are one or more *tripod threading holes* that are used to attach the camera to the head. Smaller, lighter cameras have a small hole matching the screws found on lightweight tripods. Larger, heavier cameras have a bigger hole matching the threading on heavyweight tripods. Smaller cameras sometimes have both sizes, allowing them to be used on any tripod. Larger cameras often have a choice of two similar-sized holes, one toward the front of the camera, the other toward the back. This is to compensate for the weight of the lens you are using. To keep the weight of the camera evenly distributed on the tripod, if you are using a heavy lens, you would use the front hole. The back hole is used with a light lens.

Cleaning and Care

Whoever coined the phrase "cleanliness is next to Godliness" must have been a filmmaker. It is absolutely crucial that the camera be clean. If it is not, the resulting footage may be jeopardized. Bright hopes are often dashed, and pocketbooks emptied, when film comes back from the lab scratched or otherwise ruined. It is clear that a few front-end preparations can deter a substantial percentage of disappointments. When film is ruined, the only cure is reshooting.

The cleanliness and care of the camera is but one among the numerous responsibilities of the *1st assistant cameraperson (1st AC)*—a key player in the daily operation of a film shoot and one who usually has several assistants as well. In multiple-camera shoots, such as concert films, the loading and cleaning of the cameras can keep quite a few crew members employed, with people being hired to clean, other people to load, and some just to run the mags back and forth to the camera. However many people are working on the camera crew, monitoring the quality of the technical work is the 1st AC's responsibility.

Cleaning Kit

The AC always carries a cleaning kit. Experienced ACs often have very sophisticated kits, but for people shooting their first films, it is easy to put together a simple one. The following items are inexpensive and available at either a camera shop or discount store:

Swabs   Many ACs use cotton *swabs*, although they have some very apparent drawbacks. The main one is that fibers on the tip can come off and work their way into the camera. In the past few years, swabs with sponge tips have been introduced and are in general use. Unfortunately they are substantially more expensive and, particularly if you live in a small community, you may have to order them from a video-supply catalog.

Alcohol   Denatured *alcohol* is preferable, although isopropyl will do in a pinch. Isopropyl alcohol has a lubricant that many ACs will warn you against, although I have never had a problem with it.

Orange stick   You can buy an *orange stick* for about a dollar at a camera store or pay seventy-nine cents for a half-dozen at a discount store. They are so named because they're made of the wood of an orange tree. They are used by manicurists to push back cuticles. For our purposes, they are used to clean the gate; nothing else, unless designed by a camera's manufacturer, should be substituted.

Blower brush or camel-hair brush   Inexpensive *blower brushes* are available at camera stores and are simple rubber squeeze bulbs with a gentle bristle brush attached to where the air is blown out. Rather than this, many ACs use *camel-hair brushes*, which have a very gentle bristle, but these can be somewhat expensive. Most come in lipstick-style tubes in which the bristles can be extended or withdrawn. This is important because it is essential that you never allow the bristles to get dirty. Touching them leaves skin oils that attract dust. Eventually you will be brushing dirt into your camera. Brushes that get dirty are usually thrown away. If you have a simple blower brush, use the same care.

Lens-cleaning tissue and lens-cleaning fluid   Both *lens-cleaning tissue* and *lens-cleaning fluid* are available at any camera store and are necessary parts of any cleaning kit. They are produced by a number of different companies, but are very specific items and no substitutes (such as facial tissue or a shirt sleeve) should be used. (Lens care is covered in chapter 3.)

Canned air   This is an optional item used to blow dust out of the camera body and magazines. *Canned air* used to contain CFCs, which are listed as one of the major contaminants of the world's ozone layer, but many of the newer canned-air products do not. You may want to check the contents of specific canned-air products to determine if they are environmentally friendly. This is the most expensive element in the cleaning kit.

Cleaning Method

Cleaning techniques are specific to individual ACs, and there are probably those who would disagree with some of the following recommendations. But I have used these procedures enough, and have seen other ACs use them, to feel comfortable with their applications. You are free to work out your own methods, although there are some very important "don'ts" that are discussed as part of the process.

All pieces of the camera must be cleaned—from the lens, to the body, to the magazine. It would be silly to spend a half hour making sure the body of the camera is immaculate, then not clean the magazine. The film stock will just carry all the dirt from the magazine right into the body when you start filming.

The first step is take the brush and dust out the camera completely. The canned air can also be used here. You will be able to see many dust particles. Clean out what is visible and make every effort to get out anything else that may be in there. This applies to the magazines as well. Also clean the film chamber's cover plate or door in this manner, but do not open or remove the pressure plate.

The next step is to use the alcohol and swabs. Moisten the swab and clean all metal pieces that the film is liable to come in contact with. This does *not* include the pressure plate and the gate. Clean the rollers and keepers and anything else that the camera's specific design includes. Do not reinsert a dirty swab into the alcohol, as it will contaminate what remains in the bottle.

You will always encounter the two roller designs illustrated. **SEE 2-4** The sprocketed rollers are specifically designed to drive the film forward; all other rollers guide the film either from the feed or to the take-up. All cameras are designed so that the film's emulsion touches as few surfaces as possible. Any contact carries with it the possibility of scratching or abrading the film. All rollers, both sprocketed and ordinary, have a recessed center so that the film touches them only at its edges—in the area of the sprocket holes. Whenever you see either of these designs,

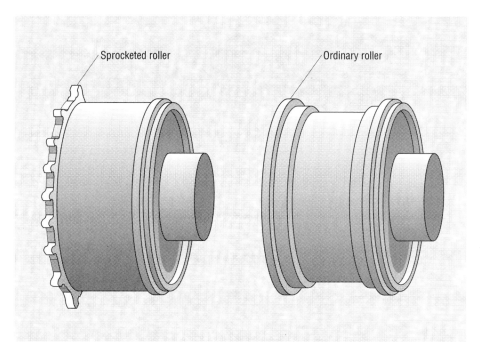

Sprocketed roller   Ordinary roller

Both types of film transport rollers have a recessed center so that the film touches them only at its edges

the emulsion almost invariably goes toward it. Much of the rationale for camera and magazine design is made with protecting the film in mind.

As you are cleaning the camera, parts of the roller may be toward the keepers and thus inaccessible. In this case, use the camera's inching knob to move the entire mechanism so you can access these areas. If the camera does not have an inching knob, it may have a single-framing capability that will allow you to move the mechanism in the increments necessary to get the whole assembly clean. In many cases, not much more than the rollers and keepers need cleaning in this step.

Now for the pressure plate and gate area. The first step is to remove the pressure plate. With a clean, dry finger, just wipe the pressure plate. Then wipe the film guide. If the pull-down claw is extended (not retracted), be careful not to unduly jostle it, as that can cause damage. Many ACs use a small chamois to wipe this area, but I have found wiping it with a finger to be perfectly adequate. Although skin oils attract dirt, this should be a relatively dirt-free environment.

The cleanliness of the gate is the chief goal of this step. Everyone knows how distracting it can be when hair gets in the projector gate at a theater. If this happens while shooting, the offending strand is going to be recorded for posterity. In addition, dirt can collect around the edges of the gate or, more significant, cause scratches. As with hair, once it is on the film there is no way to get rid of it.

▶ **RULE:** *Regarding cleaning the gate itself, do not clean it if you cannot see any dirt.*

Excessive cleaning will start to wear down the finely engineered edges of this critical area. Any dirt or hair that can cause a problem should be visible to the naked eye, although many ACs carry some type of magnification device for careful inspection. If there is dirt or hair in the gate, clean it immediately. The orange stick is used to clean the gate area. Do not use anything else, such as a paper clip or toothpick. The orange stick is used because it is a very soft wood. Anything hard can cause immediate damage to the aperture. If there is dirt or hair in the gate, take the stick and gently flick it off.

After this, give the camera another quick brushing to get rid of any dirt that may have been dislodged in previous steps. It is impossible to get anything absolutely, guaranteeably clean, but the idea is to get the interior of the camera as clean as humanly possible. This should take twenty to thirty minutes at the beginning of the day, and the camera should be checked frequently during shooting. Magazines are thoroughly cleaned every time they are reloaded. The film chamber is also cleaned as the camera is being reloaded.

The cleanliness of the gate is the most important consideration. All production cameras have a means of checking the gate in between takes. Usually the lens is removed and the inching knob is used to rotate the shutter out of the way. The AC can then see if there is anything in the gate, often with the aid of a flashlight and magnifying device. Many ACs check the gate with the lens still on the camera—using the lens as a magnifying glass—but this takes some experience to know what to look for.

Checking the gate is usually done immediately after the shooting from an individual setup has been concluded. No lights are struck and no actors excused. Nothing is changed until the 1st AC gives the go-ahead. If a substantial amount of material is being done from a single setup, the gate will be checked after each individual segment. If there is hair or dirt in the gate, all the preceding material will have to be reshot.

Canned air, blower brushes, and alcohol should not be used on anything to do with the gate or pressure plate. The air and blower brushes will just knock dirt into the shutter mechanism. Alcohol should not be used because the interior of the gate is covered with an antireflectant coating that will eventually break down. Pressure plates are generally covered with this material as well.

In many beginning courses, it is just you and your camera. Crew work and specific job responsibilities are yet to come. In this case, remember that the cleanliness of the camera is *your* responsibility. Do not expect rental house or equipment room personnel to do your job for you, even though they should be giving you a clean and well-maintained camera. Rental houses are generally reliable in this regard, although this is sometimes understandably not the case in schools. No matter whose hands you take the camera from, you should look it over and clean it before you shoot. The gate should be checked constantly and the entire camera recleaned between every roll of film. Nothing is more disheartening than looking at your lab report and seeing those words that strike terror into the heart: "hair in gate" or "scratches."

The notion of an ounce of prevention being worth a pound of cure applies here. Check the loop to ensure that it is the correct shape. Use camera tape to ward off potential light leaks. Clean the camera and check the gate on the off chance that there might be a hair. Start developing good habits. With most camera problems, the only cure is to reshoot—always a costly and dispiriting proposition.

Batteries

If you were to speak to every person who had ever shot with a motion picture or video camera, you would probably hear a battery-related horror story from each of them. Battery care and maintenance are essential to proper operation of the camera. There is no feeling quite like having to scrap an expensive and preparation-heavy shoot right in the middle because of battery problems. **SEE 2-5**

Most batteries designed for film (or video) are the slow-charging type. They are usually plugged in in the evening and ready for use the next morning, although they need a long night's charge (twelve or more hours). Quick-charging batteries are made for some cameras, but the slow-charging models are generally more reliable and less expensive. The lengthy charging time does take preplanning so you do not get caught without power. The 1st AC, who is in charge of the batteries, will have at least one to three backups. The number of magazines a battery will drive varies from camera to camera, but a fully charged battery should run at least four or five 400-foot magazines.

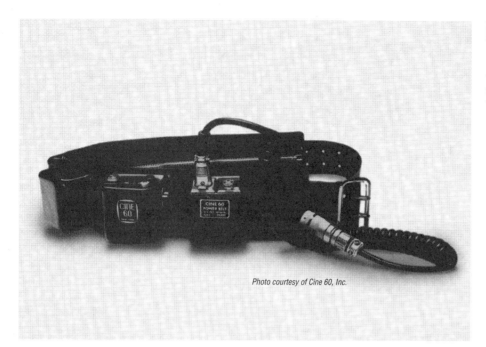

2-5
Battery care and
maintenance is essential
to proper operation of
the camera
The Cine 60 battery

Photo courtesy of Cine 60, Inc.

The key to long battery life is frequent, complete discharging. If not, they can develop *memory*. If a battery is not totally discharged over a period of time, it will memorize the small amount of charge it needs to be topped off. When the battery is completely discharged after it has developed a memory, it will recharge only the amount it has memorized, thus not giving its full potential. This problem is correctable, but the whole process significantly cuts down on the life of the battery. The way to avoid this problem is to make sure that the battery is fully discharged relatively frequently—once every week or so when in constant use.

Beyond the battery itself, most cameras employ a cable to hook the camera to the battery. This also requires care and attention. A general rule is to unplug the battery whenever the camera is not in use—even on relatively short delays between takes. The battery will discharge even if the camera is not running. Although this is standard procedure, it can cause quite a bit of wear and tear on the cable. When picking up the camera package, first make sure the cables are present—you will not shoot if you get out on location and they are not there; second, make sure they are in working order. As many shoots close down over bad cables as over bad battery power.

Be sure that you have determined the voltage requirements of the camera before you use an adapter to plug it into the wall. Improper electrical connection can cause a meltdown, and I'm sure there's no feeling quite like melting down a $20,000 camera. Batteries often come with a switchable choice of voltages. Again, make sure you know the requirements of the camera.

Movement

Creating steady moving shots has been a goal since the experiments of the pioneer filmmakers. A handheld camera, while having a viable aesthetic of its own, does not offer adequate shot stability thus necessitating sophisticated camera supports for movement. The Germans in the 1920s are credited with exploring and perfecting many of the effects that can be achieved with the moving camera. They are responsible for what is generally referred to as *fluid camera technique*—an approach to shooting that smooths out or eliminates entirely any bumpy camerawork, moving from composition to composition in an efficient and timely manner. This was the approach adopted by classic Hollywood cinema and, although challenged by more informal camera techniques, remains an important philosophical approach to shooting.

Equipment that supports camera movement is referred to under the general category of *camera mounts* or *camera support systems*, both umbrella terms that include tripods, dollies, cranes, the Steadicam, and many other specialized mounts. Camera movement can be used to achieve many different ends. It can go from different proxemic positions; it can go from high-angle shots to low-angle shots and vice versa, and it can reveal previously unseen elements in the frame.

In discussing camera movement as an aesthetic tool, however, one must first state the self-evident: a significant amount of camera movement is used solely to follow or, more accurate, anticipate character movement in the frame. Often, this movement is designed to help create a visual dynamic and is rarely noticed by the average viewer. Having the camera in a static position all the time becomes visually uninteresting. Working in movement can help provide a flowing, moving texture to the film. A great deal of this type of movement is to create space for other action to occur—action as simple as another character entering the frame or as complex as incorporating whole new fields of information. Movement to recompose and anticipate action is described in chapter 7.

What follows is a summary of common camera moves, the equipment used to achieve them, and some attendant aesthetic effects.

Tripods

A *tripod* is a three-legged camera support that is familiar to most readers. What is referred to as a tripod is actually two separate pieces: the *legs*—the actual tripod—and the head. The *head* is the mechanism on which you mount the camera and which has pan and tilt controls. The head-to-legs mount is usually a bowl design in which sits the rounded bottom of the head. A bolt and knob (usually a wingnut or a similar design) extend from the bottom of the head for locking it in place. This knob-and-bolt arrangement plays a key role in leveling the tripod.

A tripod, of course, is used as much for camera stability as it is to facilitate movement. Tripods are a key part of the camera package for most smaller projects, even though their use on larger projects is not quite as common as it used to be. This is simply because the more versatile support systems, such as the new generation of relatively lightweight crab dollies, have become more the standard. The camera can simply be rolled to the next setup with a dolly, rather than taking down and resetting the tripod. On films with a decent budget and a large camera/grip crew, the high rental cost, weight, and size of a dolly are easy obstacles to overcome. For smaller, inexperienced crews, the tripod is still the camera mount of choice.

Legs

There are two common types of legs available: wooden legs and the newer metal legs. Wooden legs were the industry standard for many years and, while they still have many followers, their use has become less prevalent. The metal legs have become popular because of their versatility and lightweight, sturdy design.

Wooden legs are designed so that one set of legs moves inside the other. A twist lock allows the user to set them at the desired height, as it does on some of the metal leg designs. **SEE 2-6** This lock must be used to tighten the legs together. If the lock pushes the legs away from each other, damage can eventually result.

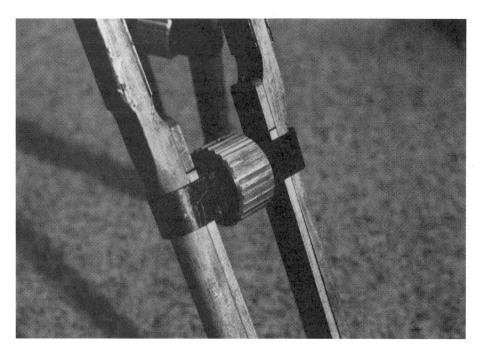

2-6

A twist lock on a wooden leg enables you to set the leg to the desired height

Wooden legs come in two different forms: standard legs and baby legs. **SEE 2-7** *Standard legs* are about 4 feet tall and extend from roughly that height to around 7 feet. As their name implies, standard legs are used for shots that are done at a standard height (eye level or thereabouts). *Baby legs* are used for low shots. They are about 2 feet tall and can be extended to the lower end of the standard legs'

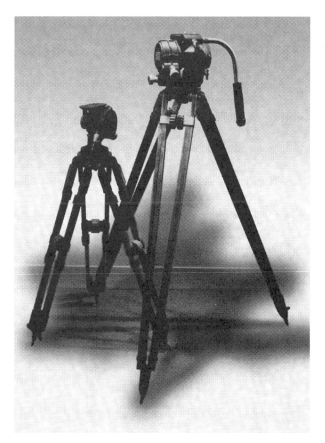

2-7

Standard legs are used for eye-level shots; baby legs are used for low shots

range. To get lower than this, one needs to put the head on a high hat. A ***high hat*** is basically a head mount with three feet. It stands about 6 inches tall and is also useful for mounting on tabletops and other surfaces. The head of the tripod is removable and is switched among these three, depending on the shot.

The wooden tripods do not have stops on the legs like many amateur and newer professional tripods. That is, the tripod will collapse spread-eagle on the floor if something is not used to hold the legs in place. For stability, they require ***spreaders***, also called ***spiders*** or ***tri-downs***. The spreader is put on the floor and has three arms that extend to hold the tripod legs in position. The tripod legs have ***spurs*** (small pins at the base of the legs) that are put in the cups of the spreader. A large spring-loaded pin holds the legs in place. The spreader is an absolute necessity on smooth surfaces. If you are working on a rough surface, such as the ground or a carpet, the spurs dig in to hold the tripod steady. Most camera crews will use a spreader anyway, because it eliminates the possibility of someone carelessly knocking out the legs.

The new metal legs are becoming more and more popular because they generally incorporate all three heights in their design. With wooden legs, you have to bring three-leg systems (standard, baby, high hat) and switch the head among them as the shot demands. This is not as big a hassle as some people make it out to be, but it does complicate the task. But with the metal leg extensions sliding into each other, much greater height range can be achieved in a single leg. Metal legs stand about the height of baby legs, but can be extended to the highest range of standard legs. They usually have stops that allow the leg to be locked in the normal upright position, eliminating the need for a spreader. Many makes of tripods have stops that allow the legs to be spread out so they get the camera down to almost high hat level.

Heads

There are three basic types of heads: mechanical/friction heads, fluid heads, and gear heads. Fluid heads are generally preferred for initial efforts, although mechanical and friction heads also see substantial use. Gear heads are the industry standard for 35mm shooting. New fluid-effect heads are also making an impact on the amateur market and are discussed under fluid heads.

The head is solely involved in pans and tilts. A ***pan*** is a shot in which the camera is simply pivoted horizontally on the tripod. A ***tilt*** is similar to a pan except its movement is vertical. **SEE 2-8**

All heads have independent pan and tilt locks. With the exception of gear heads, the fineness of these controls plays a big part in the quality of the moves you are attempting to make. Many heads also have knobs to control the amount of resistance in the pan and tilt movements. ***Resistance*** is the force against ones move-ment—a tightness that makes it more difficult to move the tripod head. At first this seems to be a contradiction. Why would anyone want something to be harder than it needs to be? Without this resistance, however, the operator tends to start over- or underpushing. If one is overpushing, the tendency is to respond by slowing down, and the move becomes uneven. Underpushing produces the opposite result. When there is resistance to the movement, one can push more uniformly.

Mechanical and friction heads Many people do not distinguish between mechanical heads and friction heads, but there are slight design differences that warrant separate treatment. ***Mechanical heads*** are both the most rudimentary and most common type of tripod head. They are designed for still photography, and people use them in film solely because of their availability. They are functional but are inadequate for finely defined movements. The movements of the pan and the tilt are simply metal on metal. The tilt and pan are either locked

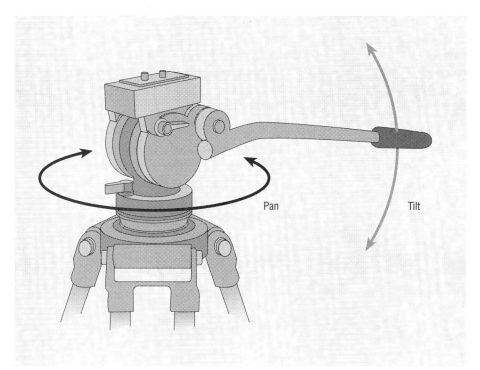

2-8

Pan and tilt controls
enable you to swivel and
tilt the camera

or unlocked. There is no attempt made to cushion the move or create any resistance, because they are designed to simply get the camera from one position to another for still photographs.

Friction heads are close cousins to the mechanical heads. They also have metal-on-metal interiors, although there is an effort to cushion movement usually in the form of an internal swelling ring. Thus the pan and the tilt controls will give some gradations of resistance between completely loosened and locked. Friction heads are a small step up from straight mechanical heads, although you have to fight for the smoothness of movement easily achieved on professional heads. They are an older design expressly produced to be an inexpensive alternative to fluid and gear heads, a role largely taken over by the new fluid-effect heads.

Fluid heads   The fluid head will probably be the tripod of preference for the work you will be doing. *Fluid heads* actually employ a hydraulic fluid that is forced from chamber to chamber in the head. The pan and tilt knobs are labeled *pan fluid* and *tilt fluid*, respectively, and allow the user to regulate the firmness of resistance to movement.

Many tripods are being billed as *fluid-effect heads*, and some of them are surprisingly good. They seem to be quite useful with smaller cameras, though larger cameras still require a true fluid head (or a gear head). The only indefinite at this point is durability. They appear to be a development worth following for people interested in an inexpensive, quality system, but their performance over time remains to be seen.

Gear heads   These are the standard in 35mm shooting. The pan and the tilt of *gear heads* are controlled by separate gears that are in turn controlled by hand cranks. The operator turns the pan crank and the tilt crank to the desired positions. Resistance is not an issue, because the head is responding to the gears being cranked. With a gear head, moves can be preplanned—an assistant can put erasable marks on the head so they can crank to a specific position.

Gear heads yield exceptionally smooth movements, but one has to learn how to hand-crank both the tilt and the pan gears simultaneously. This can be tricky though easily mastered by people with some coordination. Gear heads are heavy and bulky as well as expensive to rent. They are largely intended to make smooth moves with big cameras. They can certainly be used with smaller cameras, but fluid heads can often yield moves of equal quality.

Good movements can be made with inexpensive or poorly designed heads, but they certainly make the task much harder. On small projects, you often have to use whatever tripod you can get your hands on. Such is the reality of the way you may have to work, but it is difficult to get the performance you want from tools that are inadequate or not designed for the purpose. You should get in the habit of doing everything possible to obtain the tools designed for the job, regardless of the dent it puts in your budget. Using equipment that makes the task harder can lead to hidden costs (lost time with location, talent, light, and so on) that can be greater than anything expended on the front end.

Leveling the Head

Almost all heads being sold specifically for film or video work come with some means of leveling to ensure that the head is straight with the world. Most employ a leveling bubble—a small bubble centered inside a circle—similar to that found on a carpenter's level. The knob and bolt on the underside of the head are part of one leveling design called *ball joint leveling*. Turning the knob slightly clockwise loosens the head in the bowl. You can then position the head so the leveling bubble is in the center of the circle. This is done with the camera on the head, because the weight of the camera may change the level slightly. This method is popular on 16mm tripods, whereas tripods for 35mm employ a variety of means. With some tripods you have to adjust the legs to achieve level, an approach that is irritating until one gets used to it.

Leveling the head should become automatic. It is the first thing the AC does when moving to a new setup, even if there is a possibility that the camera position may still be changed. No effective evaluation of shot and composition can be done without a level tripod head. Shots can be set up that appear straight with the world, and a simple movement turns the world askew.

Attaching the Camera

There are two types of threading on the screws used to attach the camera to the head. The first is found on small and amateur cameras and the second is the professional standard. The first screw type is a ¼-20 (quarter-twenty). Most Super 8, consumer video, and small 16mm cameras have the ¼-20 threading. The ¼ refers to the diameter of the screw in inches; the 20 refers to the pitch of the screw threading. This is a common screw size available in any hardware store. With a few carpentry skills, you can use this knowledge to build many nifty camera supports. Be cautioned, however, that the screw thread is not deeper than the hole in the camera. The camera body often has circuitry above the hole. A thread that is too long can cause extensive—and expensive—damage.

The second type of camera screw is a ⅜-16. Again, this refers to the diameter of the screw and the thread pitch. This is the attaching screw for most larger 16mm and all 35mm cameras, used simply because the professional cameras are heavier. The ¼-20 screw is not strong enough to support the weight of the larger cameras.

Tripods and heads are rated for the maximum-weight camera that they can support. Never put a camera on a tripod and head not rated for its weight. If you do, with some effort you may still be able to create decent movements, but the arrangement will be an accident waiting to happen. The camera will be top-heavy and fall over with the least encouragement. The ⅜-inch hole in larger cameras will generally stop you from putting the camera on an inappropriate tripod. Occasionally, there is cause to adapt between the smaller threading and the larger hole. There are bushings available that will adapt a ⅜-inch camera-mounting hole to ¼-20 tripod threading. On smaller cameras that have only the ⅜-inch threading, such as older Bolexes, these can be quite useful. Cameras bigger than the Bolex should not be adapted to the ¼-20 threading.

Older heads come with the attaching screw permanently mounted in the *camera plate*—the plate on which the camera rests. Access to the screw is from underneath the camera plate. It is impossible to get the screw absolutely tight by hand, so most heads incorporate a *critical tightener*. This is a bar between the screw head and the plate that can be turned to expand the relationship between the screw and the camera. **SEE 2-9** With this you will be able to fully tighten the camera on the head—a requirement for both creating decent moves and ensuring the safety of the camera.

Newer head designs employ a *quick-release plate* which is detachable and screwed independently into the bottom of the camera. Plate and camera are then simply secured to the head without all the time-consuming tightening. The plate does not have a critical tightener, the now-independent screw being easily reached with a screwdriver. Particularly in documentary shooting, the quick release is quite handy for breaking the camera off the tripod quickly if a new shot suddenly presents itself.

The quick-release plate is also helpful in moving the tripod between setups in narrative and commercial situations. The camera can easily be taken off and set in a safe place. The tripod can then be set up and the camera reattached. With the older design, the AC would carry the whole camera-and-tripod system to the new setup rather than go to the bother of taking the camera off the head. An experienced AC can transport the whole system safely, but this method's potential for accidents can leave an inexperienced camera crew holding its collective breath.

When attaching the camera to the quick-release plate, be sure the camera is straight on the plate. If it is cockeyed, it will affect how straight the camera is with the world. Even if the head is level, the shots will not look level, particularly when panning and, to a lesser extent, tilting.

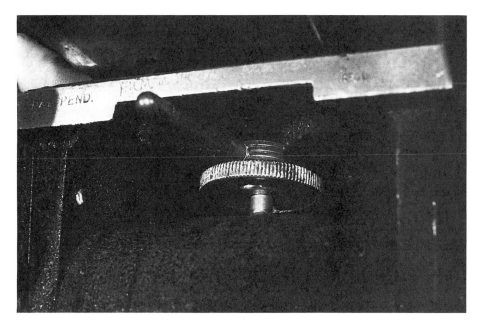

2-9

Critical tighteners help ensure a securely mounted camera

Caution: When attaching a camera to a head, whether with a quick release or the traditional design, make certain the camera is properly attached before leaving it. Both the threads and the plates can appear to be attached without actually making a connection. If you step away, you may find the camera on the floor when you come back. Test the connection by lifting the camera slightly. If the screw is properly threaded, the tripod will come with it.

Pans and Tilts

Both pans and tilts can be used to reveal new elements within the frame, elements of which the viewer may have been unaware. A typical example might be a shot of a couple walking down a street hand-in-hand. The camera then pans over to show a crestfallen suitor, seeing them together for the first time.

With that revelation, we can create association and in some cases a sense of causality. An example of the use of the pan to create an association comes from D. W. Griffith's *Birth of a Nation* (1914). There is one shot that starts with a wide view of a Civil War battle and then pans to a woman huddled with small children on a wagon. To further emphasize the point, Griffith includes a pan back to the battle. The conclusion is inescapable. The misery is a by-product of the battle. Some might argue that the same effect could be accomplished with a cut between the two subjects. There is some truth to this, but the pan creates a bonding of subjects to which the cut can only come close. By panning, these two subjects are spatially, and thus philosophically, connected.

Although the pan can be employed as described, its overall use can be problematic because it does not really duplicate the movement of the human eye. When following a lateral movement, your eyes move by themselves or in conjunction with head and body movement. The pan is somewhat like pivoting your head without moving your eyes. We occasionally view movement in this manner—such as at a tennis match—but it is often in specialized circumstances and it feels and looks unnatural.

Pans have to be carefully planned, in terms of both their execution and eventual use. The word *pan* will quickly become part of your everyday vocabulary, but it is generally used in conjunction with subject movement or as part of larger camera movements rather than as an expressive technique. You can prove this to yourself with a few simple tests. Pan from one person sitting in a chair to another, or go to a theater rehearsal and pan from subject to subject on the stage. Unless you are following movement, the pans will probably look mannered and stagy. Upon further contemplation, even the shot from *Birth of a Nation* recounted above looks arguably unnatural.

The general application of the tilt is similar to that of the pan—revealment and so on—except that it can also go from one angle to another, say, from eye level to low angle. A common example would be a child running down a street and then straight into someone's knees. We then see the tilt from the knees to an intimidating low angle of a disapproving adult.

Camera Safety Checklist

☑ There is one essential rule of tripod safety: Never leave a camera on a tripod without being 100 percent sure that the tilt is locked. If the tilt is not locked, the weight of the lens can start the camera tilting forward. As it moves it will gain momentum, and the lens can smash into a tripod leg, damaging or even ruining the lens. If the tripod itself is not secure, the whole system can fall over or the threading screw can shear off. In both cases, the camera smashes to the floor. Some ACs never leave the camera for any reason. It is under their protection. If they absolutely must leave, they will get the 2nd AC to mind the camera until their return.

☑ Along the same lines, the balance mechanisms on tripods are wonderful, but they can give camera personnel a false sense of security. With ball joint leveling, the head can be made level while the legs are uneven, leaving the whole system in a precarious position. Often the legs will have a leveling bubble as well and, although it is not necessary that it shows absolute level, the closer to level it is, the better.

☑ It is a good idea to set up the tripod so one of the legs is pointing in the same direction as the lens. As suggested, the greatest weight of a camera is usually toward the lens. If a camera falls over, it tends to fall lens first. With one leg pointed forward, the majority of the camera weight is supported.

☑ If a particular setup is the least bit insecure, use ***sandbags*** or other weights on the legs. The use of sandbags to secure light stands is fairly common, and several should be brought along for the camera. Sandbags can be used for "lockdowns," situations in which the framing must be absolutely consistent from shot to shot, superimpositions, and matte shots, for example. They are also frequently hung from the knob used for leveling, to ensure even greater stability.

☑ The camera must be secure at all times. One thing you can count on is that if you set up the camera so some fool can knock it over, some fool will knock it over. There can be dozens of people wandering around a film set, and the odds are that at least one of them has no common sense around equipment. A top-of-the-line 16mm production camera with a good lens can easily cost $35,000. An improperly set tripod can be responsible for damage that either makes a rental company very unhappy or destroys your own investment. Cameras can be repaired, but they often cannot be brought back to their original condition. After a careless crew dropped it lens-first from a tripod, one camera was never again as quiet.

☑ Never leave a camera in an exposed position. As much as many of us enjoy building odd camera mounts and encourage students to experiment with same, the camera should never be put in jeopardy. The camera extending from a car on a 2 by 4 is precarious. It makes no sense to risk damage to the one tool that is indispensable in making films.

☑ Get set up and comfortable. Be sure that the tripod legs are not going to get in the way of any of your movements while executing the shots. Pans often require moving around the tripod, and anything blocking your way can affect the shot. Having to strain or stand on your tiptoes to look through the eyepiece is going to affect your ability to execute the shot smoothly. Find something secure to stand on or reposition the camera so you feel completely comfortable. Do not change the shot unnecessarily for your comfort—just find a way to make yourself comfortable.

Dollies, Cranes, and Arms

The past several decades have seen a profusion of specialized devices to assist camera moves, some involving computer technology but more incorporating electronically assisted movement. As technology evolves, distinctions between these types of movements are blurring significantly. For example, many dollies have modest crane capabilities. Cranes can be adapted to do other tasks. Dollies, cranes, and their technological brethren are presented together here because, as a viewer, it is difficult on occasion to determine on what kind of camera support a shot has been executed. It is, of course, unproductive to sit there and try to guess. What the equipment allows you to do is the concern. Although students rarely get their hands on the newest technologies, you should be familiar with what is available. This prepares you for professional experience and sets you to thinking about inexpensive ways of duplicating complex effects.

Dollies

A *dolly* is a wheeled vehicle with a camera-mounting device on it. **SEE 2-10** The earliest dollies were large, heavy vehicles that were used almost solely in the studio. Many new lightweight dollies have been introduced that make dolly work on location so easy that their use has almost become the norm. These are not exactly lightweight, but can be moved easily by four people. Dollies can also be as simple as a go-cart–style platform with wheels on which you mount a tripod. The more sophisticated designs have seats for the camera operator and assistant, with movement controlled by a variety of complex controls.

Dolly movements are frequently done on specially built *dolly track*. **SEE 2-11** This eliminates the shock of any floor unevenness and allows the dolly to be guided accurately to the end of its movement. Making sure that the track is not in camera view can affect what kind of shot you plan. Track is often too expensive or too cumbersome for smaller projects. You can even out rough surfaces by putting down plywood or wooden planks on which to run the dolly.

Dolly shots can be quite effective because they can go from one proxemic position to another. They can go from the random information of a long shot to

2-10

Dollies can be as simple as a go-cart–style platform on wheels or as sophisticated as a computerized vehicle complete with seating

The Chapman Super PEEWEE II dolly   The Matthews Doorway dolly

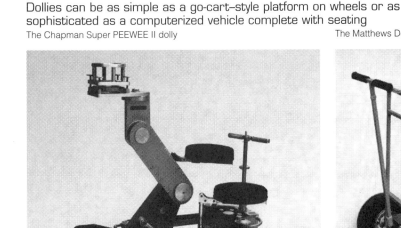
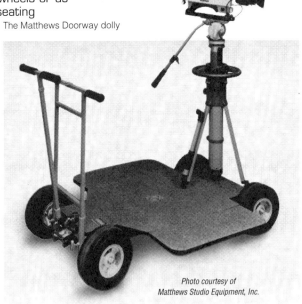

Photo courtesy of
Chapman/Leonard Studio Equipment, Inc.

Photo courtesy of
Matthews Studio Equipment, Inc.

2-11

A dolly track eliminates unevenness and allows the dolly to be guided accurately

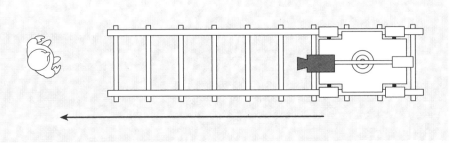

2-12

Dolly shots can be effective for going from the random information of an establishing shot to the specific information of a close-up

Milos Forman's *Amadeus*

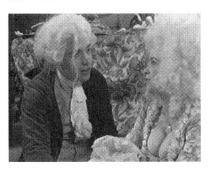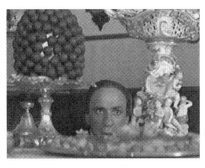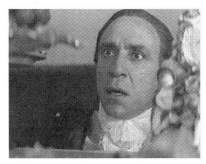

the very specific information of a close-up or vice versa. The camera moving in, called a push-in, can be used to clarify detail, identify objects of importance, or amplify emotion. Moving out, called a pull-out, can loose people in bigger spaces or, as with a pan, reveal elements heretofore unseen.

Milos Forman's *Amadeus* (1984) contains many examples of effective dolly shots. Although the elderly Salieri (F. Murray Abraham) narrates the film, his dialogue in the film's flashback story is quite limited. Much of the film is composed of reaction shots, often incorporating movement, of Salieri responding to the impetuousness of the young Mozart. One sequence shows Salieri seeing Mozart for the first time. **SEE 2-12** Salieri is hiding in the room as Mozart (Tom Hulce) flirts lewdly with his future wife (Elizabeth Berridge); the scene is composed of a traditional shot/reverse shot sequence. Salieri is stunned by the sudden realization that this "dirty child," as he calls him, is the great composer. Here, Foreman uses the dolly to emphasize Salieri's reaction, the movement amplifying the shocked look on his face.

With the camera mounted on a dolly, it can be moved toward or away from the action. It can also move alongside or around a stationary action. Although it may be an arbitrary distinction, a dolly shot is distinguished from a *tracking shot* solely in that a tracking shot follows alongside, in front of, or behind a *moving* subject; that is, the character position remains roughly the same and what changes is the background. **SEE 2-13** While this may not appear to be a significant

2-13

A tracking shot follows alongside, in front of, or behind a moving subject

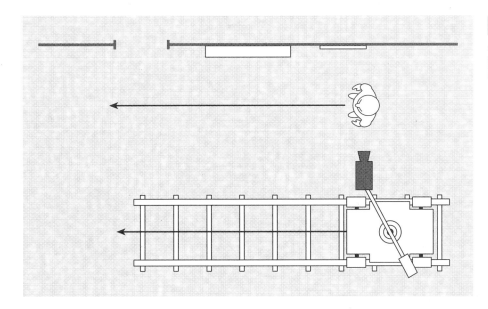

2-14

The background shifts in a typical tracking shot whereas character position remains roughly the same
Buster Keaton's *The General*

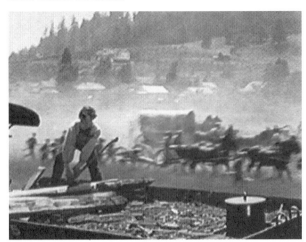 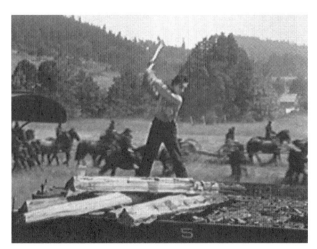

difference, it can be played for some clever effects. Buster Keaton's *The General* (1925) has several shots of a moving train that are good examples of this. **SEE 2-14** With the camera on a train running on parallel tracks, Keaton is on top of another moving train, furiously chopping wood and oblivious to his surroundings. Keaton's position within the frame remains relatively consistent, but in the background we see the entire Confederate Army pass behind him. Moments later the entire Union Army passes behind him as well, again entirely unnoticed. Thus in one sequence, Keaton's character has unknowingly passed from behind friendly lines to behind enemy lines.

The tracking shot can also be used to observe a continuous action covering a wide space. The concluding scene of Andrei Tarkovsky's *The Sacrifice* (1986) consists of a spectacular six-plus-minute tracking shot that explores how action can gain momentum if allowed to unfold naturally. It chronicles the final mental disintegration of the main character, a man who has just set fire to his own home. Following the action, the camera tracks back and forth over his home and the long driveway leading to it. **SEE 2-15** He races toward the burning house, and his family

2-15

The duration of tracking shots often aids dramatic effect
Andrei Tarkovsky's *The Sacrifice*

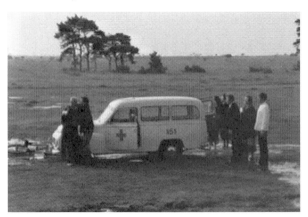 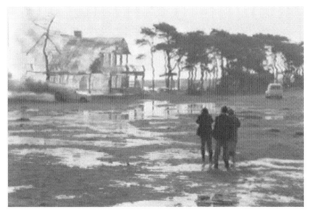

catches him. An ambulance arrives and he runs away from it. The duration of the shot—the fact that it is not broken into separate pieces—has a cumulative effect on the viewer as the character's desperation mounts. By the end of the shot, the main character has been restrained and loaded into the ambulance, presumably to be incarcerated for his mental breakdown. His family forlornly watches the burning house collapse as the ambulance drives away.

Cranes

A camera *crane* has a single elevating arm on a rolling vehicle. Cranes vary from the small ones incorporated into dollies, to large vehicles that can get the camera high in the air. Cranes generally have seats for the camera operator and at least one assistant. The crane can accomplish many of the same things as the dolly but whereas the dolly, in its strict definition, only has horizontal possibilities, the crane has full freedom of movement both horizontally and vertically. The ability to get above or below a subject allows one to vary height in relationship to the subject. Frequently, the camera goes up to give the viewer an omniscient view. **SEE 2-16 & 2-17**

2-16

Camera cranes enable you to get above or below a subject, thus varying height in relationship to the subject

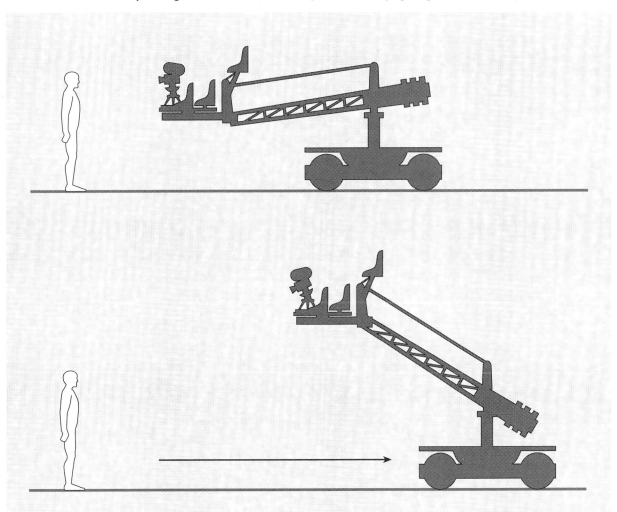

2-17

A camera crane has full freedom of movement both horizontally and vertically
The Chapman Mobile Titan crane
The Crane by Matthews

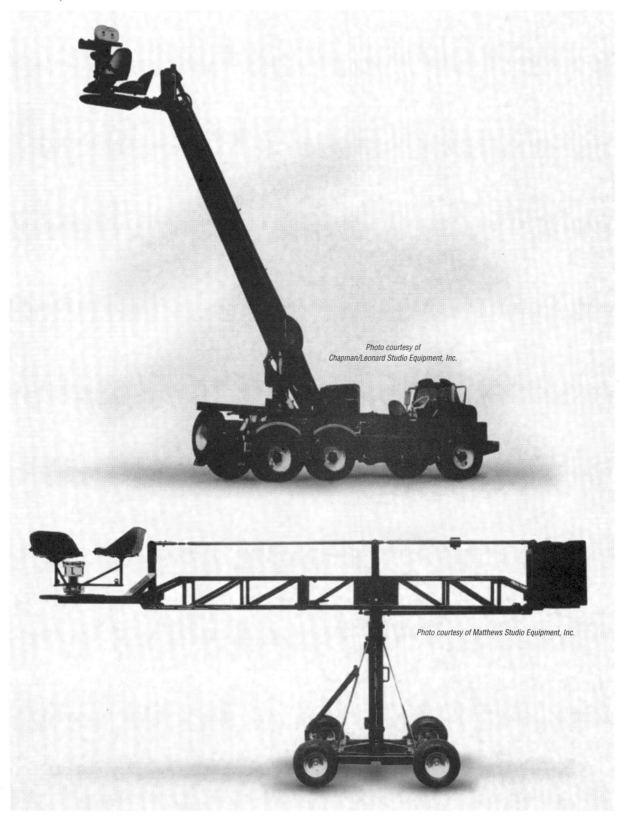

Photo courtesy of
Chapman/Leonard Studio Equipment, Inc.

Photo courtesy of Matthews Studio Equipment, Inc.

2-18

This classic crane shot goes from a very general establishing shot to a very specific close-up
Alfred Hitchcock's *Notorious*

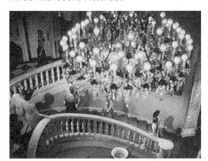 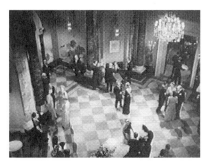 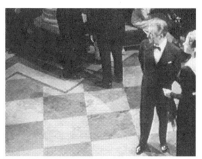

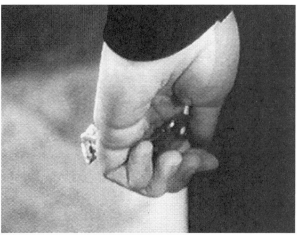

A good example of a crane shot is an oft-cited one from Alfred Hitchcock's *Notorious*. **SEE 2-18** The shot starts with a dollylike movement, showing a wide shot of people at a party. Filmed from a balcony, the information is random and undifferentiated. It simply establishes "formal party." It appears to be just a routine shot designed to create a simple transition between one scene and the next. Due to the conventional nature of this opening, what comes next catches the viewer off-guard. The camera cranes all the way down to a tight shot of Ingrid Bergman's hand. We see that she is tightly grasping a key—a key stolen from her husband. The shot thus goes from a random view to a very specific piece of information that is crucial to the plot. The complexity of the technical execution of a shot like this is breathtaking, given that the position of the key has to be coordinated to be in just the right place in the final composition. It is similar to shooting an arrow through the hole of a moving donut at fifty paces.

Arms

There are many other types of movement devices, particularly modifications to the basic crane design. *Arms* suspend the camera on the end of a crane-style device. **SEE 2-19** Lacking a place for the operator, the camera is moved by a remote operator with electronic control of the movement. A joysticklike control allows the operator to execute pans and tilts while watching a video picture of what the camera is seeing.

Spike Lee's *Do the Right Thing* has a spectacular shot that was filmed with an arm or similar device. **SEE 2-20** The shot starts with Mother Sister (Ruby Dee) and the Mayor (Ossie Davis) sitting on a bed. They get up and start walking toward the

2-19

Arms suspend the
camera on the end of
a crane-style device
The Chapman Lenny Arm II

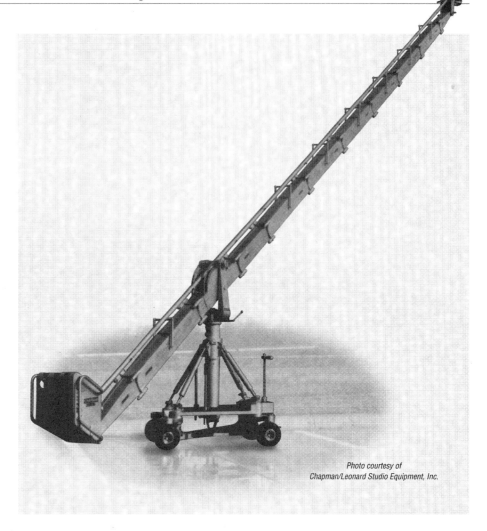

*Photo courtesy of
Chapman/Leonard Studio Equipment, Inc.*

2-20

This spectacular shot was executed with a jib or an arm
Spike Lee's *Do the Right Thing*

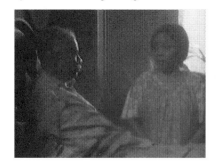 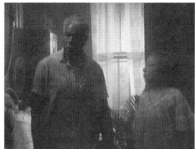 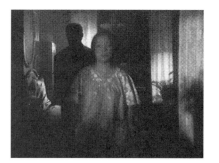

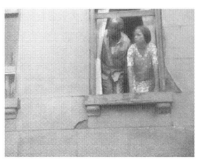 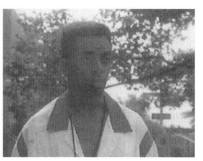

camera. The camera pulls all the way back and out of a window. As they look out of the window, the camera cranes around to Mookie (Spike Lee) on the street. It is a spectacular shot, tying many of the film's elements together.

The arm is only one example of new developments in camera support equipment, all designed to make life easier for the filmmaker as well as to create shots previously considered impossible. Most of these are out of reach of most small projects, in terms of both the cost and the technical expertise to execute them. One can, however, always dream and plan….

Although students may not be able to get their hands on many of these technologies, they should always be prepared to improvise creative substitutes. Wheelchairs are particularly popular for creating dolly-style shots; I have seen people use grocery carts, skateboards, and a wide variety of other vehicles. Lumber can be used to build an infinite variety of mounts, including seesaw-style cranes and mounts for moving vehicles, mostly cars. Be inventive in figuring out ways to move the camera. Again, the safety of the camera should always be a primary consideration.

Handheld Camera

With the *handheld camera*, shots lack the smoothness to which so many technical resources are devoted. The handheld camera can give a "you are there" feel to the shots, a sense of the viewer being a participant in the action. If desired, the "camera as a participant" approach can lend a sense of urgency or chaos to action. The handheld camera can also give scenes an informal and spontaneous tone, though its use to achieve this end has a number of pitfalls.

The handheld camera has been very popular in documentary and experimental films and has made inroads in feature films as well. It has had a role in documentary films for many years but has been a central feature since the late 1950s, when the development of lightweight portable cameras and sound recorders allowed documentary filmmakers to go on location and shoot under almost any conditions. While recognizing many exceptions, there are a significant number of experimental films that use the handheld camera as an alternative to the often rigid formal approach of commercial cinema. In Jonas Mekas's *Reminiscences of a Journey to Lithuania* (1971), the filmmaker took a trip to his homeland, photographing short snippets of subjects that interested him. The resulting film, which Mekas narrates in a fragmented, poetic style, is a free-form collection of home movie–like shots, very few of which are more than a second or two long. This produces an effect far different from the stately, some might say rigid, use of the camera in classic American film.

Although there are infrequent earlier examples, handheld camera use became more frequent in commercial feature films in the 1960s. Stanley Kubrick's *Dr. Strangelove* (1964) has some beautiful examples of thoughtful use of the handheld camera. It is used most effectively in the scenes of the attack on Jack D. Ripper's compound and in those of the crippled bomber as it wings for Russia. **SEE 2-21** The assault on Ripper's compound emulates the chaos of combat footage. It is particularly effective when intercut with the highly formal images of the war room, where the fate of the world is being decided.

The scenes in the bomber are even more effective. Just after the plane is hit, sparks and smoke are everywhere. The handheld camera charges in and gives the appearance of capturing the action as it happens. The images, when looked at individually, take on an almost abstract quality. Many of *Dr. Strangelove*'s scenes are played for comedy, and the handheld scenes seem to be saying that there is

2-21

The free-form use of a handheld camera in this scene emulates the chaos of the
action on-screen

Stanley Kubrick's *Dr. Strangelove*

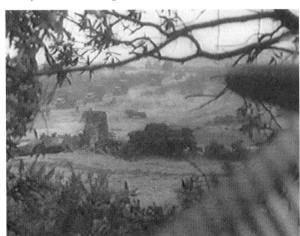 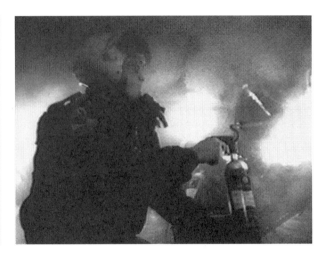

also something very real and very dangerous occurring. The sense of impending
doom in both scenes plays as a stark and effective contrast to the tone of outrageous
parody in the rest of the film.

Special Rigs

Steadicam The Steadicam™ was designed in recognition of the freedom of
movement offered by the handheld camera, while also recognizing the desire to
eliminate its attendant shakiness. It is a device that mounts on the camera operator's
chest. It incorporates balanced weight and reciprocating movement to give fluid
movement to what are essentially handheld shots. It is an expensive piece of
equipment that requires a trained operator in top physical condition. Its use has
become widespread, particularly in commercial production.

One of the first uses of the Steadicam in a theatrical feature was in John
Schlesinger's *Marathon Man* (1976). In one scene, Dustin Hoffman is chased on
foot through New York's Central Park. He runs up and down stairs. He runs through
a tunnel. He runs across cobblestone streets. The camera either follows or precedes
him everywhere he goes. These shots would have been almost inconceivable
without the Steadicam, requiring either a handheld camera or extensive track. In
the first case, the shot would have reflected each and every one of the camera
operator's footsteps. In the second case, laying track probably would have been
unfeasible because specialized track that could accommodate the shape of the steps
would have been necessary. Even had it been technically feasible, it probably would
not have been economically practical.

Car rigs Shots from moving vehicles are commonly called for. Often these are
just standard close-ups or medium shots of the vehicle's occupants. They would
be routine, except engine vibration and road bumps are major complications when
planning these kinds of shots. Special mounts, called car rigs, are used to securely
attach the camera to the vehicle and, with a design almost like a shock absorber,
minimize pavement bumpiness.

Shooting out of the window of a moving vehicle can also be used as a point-of-view shot. This approach can be employed to establish a sense of place or create an impression of great expanse. Terrence Malick's *Badlands* (1973) has many exceptional vehicle shots, utilizing moving shots of the arid northern plains as representations of the emptiness of the film's rootless and unconnected characters. Toward the end of the film, distant mountains serve as both an actual and metaphorical destination that are continuously moved toward but never reached.

Aerial Aerial shots (from planes and helicopters) have their own particular aesthetic and again need specialized mounts to reduce vibration. *Aerial shots* can be used as variations of crane shots, but the movement and the elevation makes their general feel different. Ken Burns's television series "The Civil War" (1989) employed long aerial shots with the camera literally floating down some of the back-country rivers of the battle areas. These shots served as transitional devices, background for oral material, and a means to give the viewer a strong sense of place. One lengthy shot traveling down a beautiful, hazy river at sunset is juxtaposed against a speech by Frederick Douglas about the openness and promise of America versus the reality of slave life.

These rigs thus give smoothness and fluidity to shots that were previously impractical or impossible. Any avid viewer of early David Letterman TV shows may well also suggest the "Thrillcam" or the "Monkeycam," both of which are actually based on complex and viable technologies. New developments in technology will undoubtedly allow filmmakers many new opportunities. The use of these may not be feasible on smaller projects for many years. Some take on the character of parlor tricks.

Camera supports are a key ingredient in the shots you attempt to execute. Many students, with teacher encouragement, do their shooting handheld under the conviction that the tripod inhibits movement, encouraging the creation of static shots. This is fine, though the goal is to eventually be as free on a camera mount as you are handheld. It is no easy trick, but certainly a worthy pursuit. Very little that you see in commercial films is shot handheld. As suggested, the handheld camera has its own aesthetic, but if it is not appropriate to what you are doing, it should not be used. Some people think it gives film a more informal style, but informal style generally relies on other methods. Director Robert Altman is known for using an informal camera style, but very little in his films is shot handheld. The equipment necessary to shoot feature films is just too heavy and bulky to be handheld effectively. Get used to tripods, and camera support systems in general, because a high percentage of what you see is shot with some kind of support.

3

Lenses

THE camera *lens* **is the vehicle** that transfers light to the film. It can be as simple as a single piece of glass, called an *element*, or as complicated as multiple elements that can be moved in relation to one another.

The lens always includes three basic features that will be part of the decision-making process whenever you are shooting. On most lenses, two of these features are in the form of moveable rings that have to be set for every shot: the focus ring and the *f*-stop ring. The third refers to the length—wide-angle, normal, telephoto—of the lens, what is referred to as focal length. In a zoom lens, focal length is a variable as well and will also have a ring devoted to it.

The camera itself is based on the idea of the *camera obscura*, a phenomenon that has been observed for centuries. When rays of light pass through a pinhole on a surface, they create an upside-down representation of the world on the other side. A lens simply transmits the light more efficiently, since the pinhole does not allow light through in sufficient quantity to create a workable exposure. The lens does the same thing as the pinhole: it takes an image and presents it to the film upside down. When the film is later projected on a screen, the projector reverses the process. **SEE 3-1**

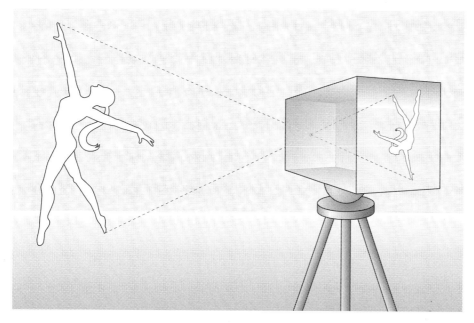

3-1

The camera obscura phenomenon projects an inverted image of the light entering through a tiny aperture

Focus

Light rays emanate from a point on a subject. They strike the surface of the lens and, as they travel through the lens and exit the rear element, are bent toward the film plane.[1] After they pass out of the rear element, they converge and are represented as a point on the film plane. The illustration below shows a single-element lens, though virtually all lenses used for film or video are composed of multiple elements. **SEE 3-2** If this light comes from a subject at the distance for which you have set focus (point B), the light comes to a point right at the film plane. If the subject is at a different distance (A or C), the light comes to a point either in front of or behind the film plane.

Every shot you execute must be focused, and many shots (more than one would anticipate) may require shifts of focus to accommodate all of a scene's action. In a given composition, you have to choose a subject that you want to be in focus. You can focus on only one distance at a time. Everything in front of and behind that point is going to be out of focus to some degree. How much out of focus is dependent upon depth of field, an issue that complicates any discussion of focus and which is explained fully later in this chapter.

In a simple lens, the *focus ring* controls the position of the front element of the lens in relation to the film plane. The front element is moved forward or backward as you turn the ring. As the front element is moved, the points where the light rays converge change. **SEE 3-3** The focus ring gives a series of distances, from the closest focus point that the lens is able to achieve to infinity. **SEE 3-4** The universal symbol for infinity is ∞. A hatch mark against the focus ring is used to set the desired distance. If the subject is 8 feet away, you set the ring to 8 feet. **SEE 3-5** Focus rings are often marked in both feet and meters. Be sure you know which one you are using. Reading the meters indicator when you're thinking feet will obviously ruin many shots.

---

1. The path the light rays travel can be substantially more complicated in some lenses.

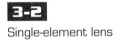

Single-element lens

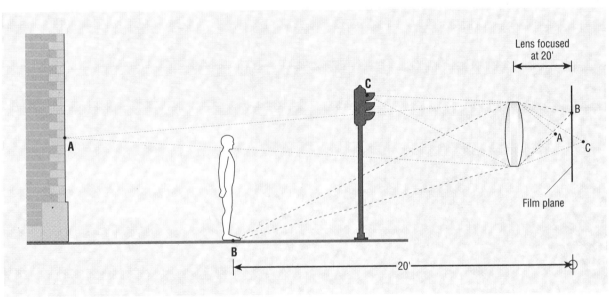

3-3

The streetlight resolves at the film plane when focused at 12 feet

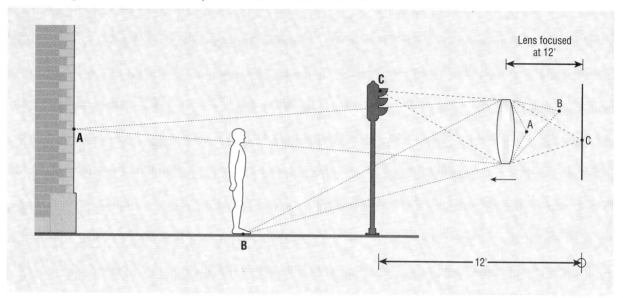

3-4

Subjects resolve at different points when the focus ring is shifted

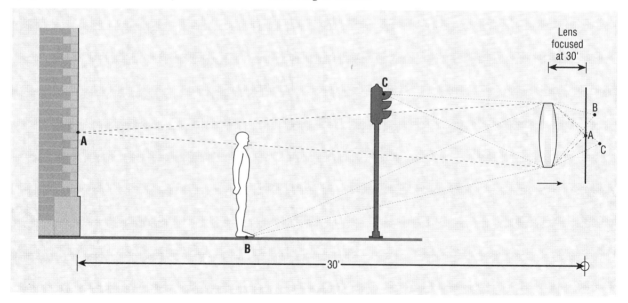

3-5

The focus ring controls the position of the front element of the lens in relation to the film plane

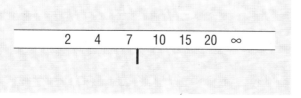

3-6

A ground-glass
focusing configuration
splits the image; you
then rotate the focus
ring until the bottom of
the ground glass lines
up with the top

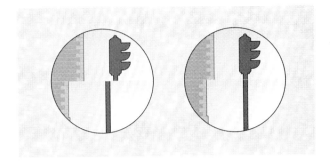

There are two methods of focusing. The first method works effectively only with cameras equipped with a reflex viewing system and a zoom lens. In this method the lens is *focused to the eye* as you look through it. To focus to your eye, you must have the diopter set properly. The first step is to zoom in all the way to the subject, gradations of focus being much more distinct with a telephoto lens. With most cameras, you then rotate the focus ring until the subject is as sharp as possible. If you try to focus with a short lens or even a normal lens, you can rotate the focus ring a fairly substantial distance without seeing a significant difference in the sharpness of the image.

In a variation on this first method, many cameras, particularly Super 8 models, employ a split *ground-glass* configuration for critical focusing. **SEE 3-6** When you zoom in to an object, the ground glass will split the image; you then rotate the focus ring until the bottom of the ground glass lines up with the top—rather than until you see a sharp image. Although some makes of camera have excellent ground-glass approaches, this method of focusing is generally rather poor and is further complicated by the inexactness of the diopter-setting systems on many Super 8 cameras. If the diopter is set incorrectly in either the ground-glass method or the "to the eye" method, you will not get the results you want. It's like a computer: if you put junk in, you'll get junk out. No matter how simple and friendly the focusing system on a Super 8 camera appears, it may be better to use the following method.

This can come as a shock to many newcomers to the process, but the second method of setting focus is by using a tape measure. This might appear time-consuming and disruptive, but it is by far the preferred method. You simply measure from the camera to the subject, and set the ring accordingly. It is virtually foolproof. You measure to the universal symbol for the film plane not, as some might expect, to the front of the lens. This symbol can be found on the body of virtually every camera. **SEE 3-7**

3-7

The universal symbol
of the film plane is
found on the body of
virtually every camera

Although some viewing systems can be difficult to use, the biggest culprit in focus problems is inattention to detail by the user. Not setting the diopter properly causes a substantial percentage of the problems, but the primary reason is simply inexactness of approach. When working by yourself or with small, inexperienced crews, it is easy to overlook many details. So many things demand attention, and there is constant pressure to keep the whole process moving forward. It will quickly become apparent that focus is one detail that can be overlooked only at the cost of your entire film. When even one piece of the puzzle is bad, it can be difficult to fit the whole thing together.

Focus is one of the two major areas in which beginning filmmakers consistently make technical mistakes; exposure is the other. The key to remember is that *focus must be set for every shot that you are going to execute*. Failure to do this will result in blurred and unusable images.

Focus Effects

Occasionally, beginners expect that, as a rule, everything should be in focus. However, focus can be used to create many effects—ones both so subtle that they are rarely noticed by the viewer and others so big that they demand to be interpreted on a thematic level. The play between soft and sharp focus can be used to achieve a number of different effects:

- Suggesting other planes of action without allowing them to dominate viewer attention.

- Isolating a subject in a space.

- Suggesting that a subject lacks clarity.

- Shifting focus for a form of dramatic emphasis or to draw viewer attention to a specific part of the frame.

- Acting as a transition from one scene to the next.

There is substantial overlap among these categories, and several of the following examples demonstrate one or more of the concepts. The last two effects listed are discussed in the next section.

Allowing the background to go out of focus to suggest peripheral action is a common effect. A scene in a diner from Jonathan Demme's *Something Wild* (1986) provides an excellent example of this. **SEE 3-8** When working in a public place such as this, it is generally desirable to suggest the presence of other customers but not allow them to distract viewer attention. Placing the background out of focus can achieve this suggestion. If there was no one in the background at all, the scene might appear empty and set up; if the people were in sharp focus, they might attract attention and diminish viewer involvement with foreground action.

Planes of focus can also direct viewer attention to specific parts of the frame. Just as you can choose different shots—LS, MS, CU—you can choose different areas of the frame to be in focus. Gordon Willis's cinematography for Herbert Ross's *Pennies from Heaven* (1982) has a number of examples of this. When Arthur Parker (Steve Martin) meets a young blind woman in a tunnel, he is stunned by her purity and grace but has no context to articulate his feelings. As they emerge from the tunnel, Arthur is out of focus in the background, an effect that forces the viewer to focus on her. **SEE 3-9** This shot also amplifies the unfocused longings of Arthur, a character who is virtually made mute by the grimness of his surroundings.

3-8

Leaving the background action out of focus prevents the viewer from being distracted by it

Ray Liotta in *Something Wild*

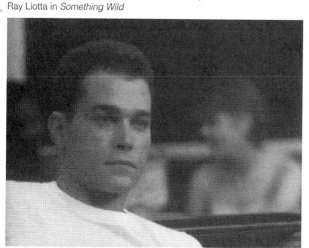

3-9

Focus isolates the background subject, forcing the viewer to concentrate on the subject in the close-up

Herbert Ross's *Pennies from Heaven*

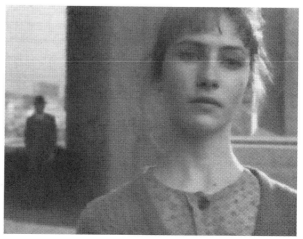

Shifting Focus

The discussion so far has left out an obvious complicating factor: movement. Not only does the subject move, but camera movement is often incorporated into a shot as well. As either the subject or camera moves, focus is necessarily going to have to change. You therefore have to *rack focus*, which is physically shifting the focus ring as the shot is being executed. Racks are usually done by the 1st AC. There is actually a separate credit for "focus puller" on British films, a recognition that suggests how frequently their talents are employed. Planning and executing a rack focus usually requires setting up marks on the floor as well as on a piece of tape on the focus ring. Be prepared to devote some time to the process on the set. Practical aspects of a rack focus are covered in chapter 15.

3-10

A rack focus can be used metaphorically, such as to symbolize a character's confusion and then sudden comprehension

Mike Nichols's *The Graduate*

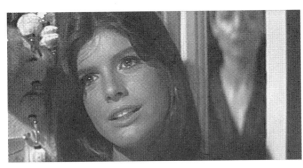
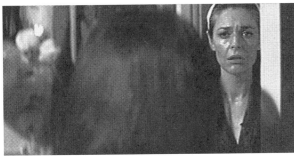
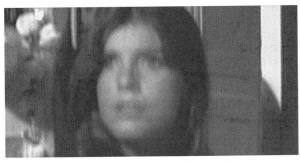
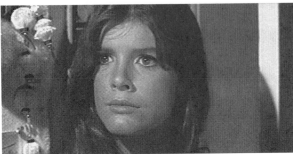

Rack focuses are employed frequently, although they are most often used to keep a moving subject in focus. As such, they go largely unnoticed. Occasionally they are used as transitional devices to get us from one scene to the next: a shot will be slowly racked out of focus, and then the first shot of the new scene will start out of focus and be racked into focus. Another technique is to start with some foreground element in focus and then rack to a background element. Focusing on some tree branches in the foreground and then racking to some action in the background is a typical example. Occasionally a director may try to milk a technique like this for some metaphorical content, but it is often effective as a simple transitional moment before launching into a new direction. It can be almost like a pause in music.

Focus can also be used effectively to delineate different elements of a shot—to change the emphasis, and hence the viewer's attention, from one area of the frame to another. The dramatic emphasis is created by shifting focus from one subject to another, not by editing or camera proximity to subject.

A shot from Mike Nichols's *The Graduate* (1967) illustrates this effect well. **SEE 3-10** It occurs in a scene in which Elaine (Katherine Ross) learns that Benjamin (Dustin Hoffman) has been having an affair with her mother (Ann Bancroft). The revelation is handled visually. Benjamin looks at Mrs. Robinson, who is standing behind Elaine. Mrs. Robinson is out of focus. As Elaine turns, there is a rack focus to Mrs. Robinson that makes Elaine's sudden comprehension of the situation inescapable. As Elaine turns back to Ben, she remains out of focus for several seconds, then she is racked back into focus. Keeping Elaine out of focus serves to amplify her emotional confusion at that point. Focus racks are often timed to specific movements so they are less noticeable.

Racking focus between characters in conversation to achieve an effect similar to editing is occasionally tried. One character says her line and then it racks to another character who says his line. Then it racks back again. This was a popular approach in a number of films in the 1960s and 1970s. Occasionally it is still employed, though if overused, the effect can appear mannered and artificial.

f-stop

The *f-stop ring* controls a small *diaphragm*, also referred to as an *aperture* (though not to be confused with the film gate), in the lens that regulates the amount of light reaching the film plane. **SEE 3-11** The *f*-stop is determined by using a *light meter*. Discussion of the role of the *f*-stop in exposure dominates part III of this text, but many people already know that it is something on the lens that is set to get proper exposure.[2] You will eventually come to see the *f*-stop as the starting point for any understanding of the creation of the motion picture image. How it interrelates with what is created in front of the camera in terms of light is one of the dominant controls of the dramatic and expressive power of an image. Its complex integration with what is in front of the camera plays *the* key role in photographic quality, and thus dramatic quality, of the film image.

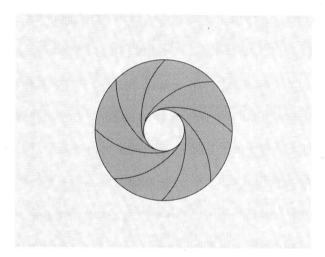

3-11

The aperture in the lens regulates the amount of light reaching the film plane

Everyone has seen underexposed or overexposed film and, in its most simplistic sense, the *f*-stop is used to obtain a usable exposure. If the *f*-stop is improperly set, the film will be over- or underexposed. The *f*-stop ring has a series of numbers. **SEE 3-12** Most lenses do not have numbers either as high or low as are shown here, but these are the general parameters. Theoretically, the *f*-stops could go on to infinity.

---

2. Shutter speed, which is a familiar concept to still photographers, is not a significant factor in motion picture production (see page 209).

1	1.4	2	2.8	4	5.6	8	11	16	22	32	45	64

3-12

The *f*-stop ring is used to set the *f*-stop for the correct exposure

3-13

Relative sizes of *f*-stops correspond to the size of the aperture

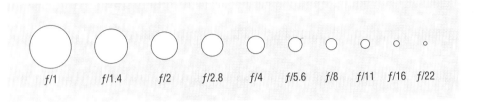

f/1   *f*/1.4   *f*/2   *f*/2.8   *f*/4   *f*/5.6   *f*/8   *f*/11   *f*/16   *f*/22

The numbers can be somewhat confusing because the smallest number represents the widest opening, or *maximum aperture*, and the highest number represents the smallest opening, or *minimum aperture*.

▶ **RULE:** *The lower the number (e.g., f/1), the larger the opening; the higher the number (e.g., f/22), the smaller the opening.*

Thus the smaller *f*-stops let in more light, and the larger *f*-stops let in less light. Most lenses do not have anything numerically larger than *f*/22. There are also lenses with *f*-stops less than *f*/1—Stanley Kubrick used one to shoot in candlelight in *Barry Lyndon* (1975)—but they are so rare that *f*/1 serves as a sensible starting point.

Circles are used to represent approximate size relationships between the stops. **SEE 3-13** The actual size of any stop will depend on the focal length of the lens.

This more-light/less-light approach is invariably the way *f*-stops are presented, but it is somewhat of a backdoor tack. The goal in choosing an *f*-stop is often, though certainly not always, a clear and true-to-life picture. This is referred to as *normal exposure*. It takes a certain and reasonably consistent amount of light to produce a normal exposure, and the *f*-stop is used to transmit this light. In bright light, the stop must be small so too much light does not reach the film. In low light, the stop must be large.

The term *lens speed* refers to the maximum aperture, as wide as the lens diaphragm will go. A lens with a maximum aperture of *f*/3.5 would be considered a slow lens; a lens with a maximum aperture of *f*/1.8 is a fast lens. Due to the length of the lens and the construction of the lens barrel, telephoto lenses are almost always slower than wide-angle lenses. It makes sense that a short, squat lens would have a wider aperture than a long, narrow one. If you want to use a telephoto lens in a low-light situation, you can almost surely anticipate some problems due to its slow speed. But properly prepared, any situation of this nature can be handled.

It is recommended here that you bite the bullet and memorize the *f*-stops. They will be your constant companions if you have anything to do with *technical camera*—everything concerning camera except calling different shots. If an aid to memorization is helpful, here is a useful mnemonic:

▶ **RULE:** *Every stop is a numerical double of the second previous stop, that is, 2.8 is twice 1.4, 8 is half of 16, and so on.* **SEE 3-14**

They cheat and round it off between 5.6 and 11. A second way is even more fun: All of these numbers, starting with 1, are multiples of the square root of two (1.4). Maybe if you are an autistic savant, this will be an acceptable method, but the point is made. Perhaps rote memorization is your preferred modus operandi.

As with the focus ring, there is a hatch mark with which you set the number. There is usually a *detent*, or a click stop, at each number. You can, and frequently will, use in-between settings called half stops, quarter stops, and so on. Some cameras have internal light meters, and the *f*-stop is controlled by a scale near the viewing screen. This is particularly true of Super 8 cameras.

3-14

Every stop is a numerical double of the second previous stop

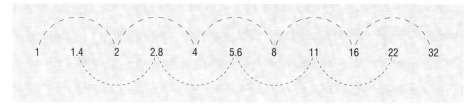

The numbers shown here are the true f-stops, referred to as ***full stops***, and they represent specific points in the transmission of light. They are derived from a mathematical formula which divides the focal length of the lens by the diameter of the diaphragm opening. Expressed as a formula, that is:

$$\frac{focal\ length}{diameter}$$

In terms of what you need to know to light a scene, this is not particularly earth-shattering information. It is important, though, to understand that f-stops have a mathematical derivation. Everything becomes very mathematical once you start to light. You will occasionally see different numbers, but these are midpositions and are specific to the lens you are using.

This is a simplification but in general, the higher-numbered f-stops are used in bright-light situations, such as outdoors, and the lower-numbered f-stops in low-light situations, such as interiors. In essence, you must determine the correct f-stop to get the exposure you want. It is worthwhile to think of the process of learning exposure technique as determining how to avoid major mistakes. At some basic level, mistakes result in under- or overexposure. The term *mistake* is used carefully, because one might ask if there are not times when we actually *want* over- or underexposure. If we have a shot of a person walking down a dark alley at night, the image would certainly incorporate many elements of underexposure. As we will come to see, virtually all film images have a wide range of volumes of light; an image without a range results in a shot that is flat and uninteresting. Eventually you will come to see the task as controlling all the levels of exposure in what will often be a very complex image.

Thus the key to exposure is understanding the f-stop and how it relates, in terms of light, to what exists in front of the camera and what is happening at the film plane. Once lighting is added, what exists in front of the camera will eventually be something over which you have complete control. Once you fully understand f-stops, their use will appear to be somewhat easier. That said, though, the use of the f-stop will never be simple.

Focal Length

The third feature of the lens is ***focal length***. It is usually measured in millimeters (mm) and is the measurement from the optical center of a lens, which is usually in the front element, to the film plane. **SEE 3-15** Lenses are referred to as, for example, a 25mm lens or a 75mm lens, although the numbers should not be confused with the millimeters of the common formats. The focal length of a lens can be generally found on the barrel next to the front element of the lens. It is expressed as $f = n$; thus, $f = 25$ is a 25mm lens. Older American lenses often have focal lengths

3-15

Focal length is the distance from the optical center of a lens to the film plane

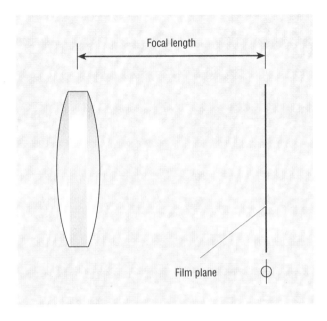

Focal length

Film plane

expressed in inches. Every inch is equal to 25mm, so a 2-inch lens is a 50mm lens, a 3-inch lens is a 75mm lens, and so on.

There are two major categories of lenses: prime and zoom. A *prime lens* is any *fixed focal length lens*, that is, it gives a fixed angle of view. Essentially a prime lens is any nonzoom lens. Zoom lenses have many different focal lengths and are spoken of in terms of their range. For example, a lens having a range from 12mm to 120mm is referred to as a 12–120 lens. The zoom ring on the lens will have a sequence of numbers that indicate at what focal length the lens is set. **SEE 3-16**

3-16

The zoom ring on a lens has a sequence of numbers that indicate focal length
Zoom ring on an Angienieux 12-120 lens

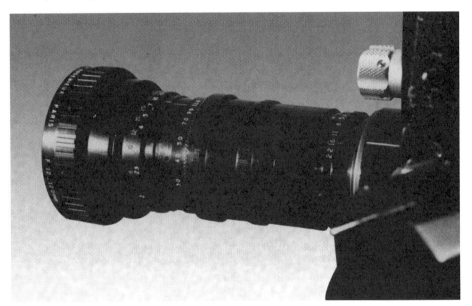

3-17

Focal lengths in different formats

	Wide-angle (short)	Normal	Telephoto (long)
Super 8	<12	12	>12
16mm	<16	16–25	>25
35mm	<50	50	>50

Lenses can be grouped into three different categories: wide-angle (short lens), normal, and telephoto (long lens). Wide-angle lenses make us appear farther from the object we are filming. Normal lenses do just what their name suggests: give a normal view of the scene. Telephoto lenses, like binoculars, make objects appear closer than they actually are. The zoom lens allows us to go uninterrupted from a wide shot to a close shot, or vice versa. The zoom lens incorporates all three categories.

The lens size required to achieve a specific distance effect varies with the size of the format being used. A smaller format requires a shorter lens to fill the smaller area of the frame. Many readers who have done 35mm still photography, one of the most common formats in still photography, know that a 50mm lens is generally considered a normal lens. This is true in motion picture cinematography as well, though you will hear much discussion about what constitutes "normal." In 16mm, a normal lens is roughly a 25mm lens. In Super 8, a normal lens is roughly 12mm. The pattern here is clear: as you halve the format size, you need roughly half the length to create the same effect. **SEE 3-17** The cutoff points here are rather arbitrary. Many people consider the 50mm lens the normal lens in the 35mm format, and some people consider it to be somewhat less than 50.

Lens Perspective and Characteristics

Lens perspective refers to the way lenses represent space. Different kinds of lenses have different effects on the way we perceive depth and dimensionality within an image. Lens perspective is less well known than the simple characteristics described above, but this aspect of lenses will eventually have a greater impact on the process of choosing a lens. Directors and cinematographers generally do *not* choose lenses for how close they bring the viewer to the subject. That can be controlled by simple camera placement. Lenses are usually chosen for how they represent space. As a developing pattern might suggest, the normal lens is probably the most commonly employed lens.

Wide-angle

The defining characteristic of *wide-angle lenses,* also called short lenses, is that they elongate space, that is, objects appear more distant from each other than they

3-18

The wide angle of this shot maximizes the sense of tiny figures against a vast landscape

Bernardo Bertolucci's *The Sheltering Sky*

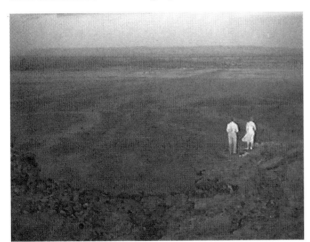

3-19

This extreme wide-angle shot gives the interaction between the characters an unsettling subtext

Orson Welles's *Touch of Evil*

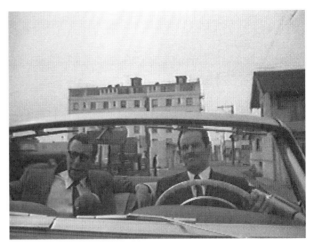

actually are. A number of objectives can be accomplished with this. Like the long shot, which can diminish a character, the wide-angle lens can be a critical element in this effect. It can take a big space and make it even bigger. Using a wide-angle lens on a lone figure within a vast landscape can increase the effect of isolation and diminishment. Orson Welles's *Citizen Kane* was one of the first films to extensively explore the use of the wide-angle lens for effect. In *Kane*'s examples of low-angle shots (see page 35), the short lens adds to the sense of a cavernous and oppressive space. One impressive shot from Bernardo Bertolucci's *The Sheltering Sky* (1990) has a vista with characters looking off a cliff, the desert stretching out in front of them. **SEE 3-18** It is clearly shot with a wide-angle lens to maximize the sense of tiny figures against a vast indifferent landscape.

There are a number of by-products of wide-angle lenses that are not really perspective issues but that figure into the decision-making process. Wide-angle lenses make things appear farther away from the camera. You may have to be right on top of a subject to achieve a close-up. Wide-angle lenses also bend lines in the composition outward. Orson Welles used an extreme wide-angle lens for several car shots in *Touch of Evil* (1958), giving the conversation between the two men an unsettling subtext. **SEE 3-19** Extreme wide-angle lenses bend corners and give almost funhouse-mirror distortion to objects or people being filmed. They are rarely used for portraiture because they balloon people's faces and make them look heavy or freakish. The closer to the subject, the more pronounced the effect. The most familiar distorting lens is called a *fish-eye*, which sees almost a full 180 degrees in front of the camera. Its effects are so extreme that it is not actually used that frequently.

The most inappropriate use of a wide-angle lens that I can remember came from a film about a family farm being foreclosed. There was a shot of the farm woman looking on sadly as all the household goods are being sold. The cinematographer shot her with a wide-angle lens, which made her look grotesque and freakish. To this day I have not been able to discern why the cinematographer chose that lens for that shot. Possibly he thought it would make the woman look miserable and downtrodden. It was clearly a carefully considered decision on his part, because he had to get right up into her face to get the shot—something that, being a nonprofessional, made her quite uncomfortable. Wide-angle lenses are used extensively, but care must be taken with some of their more extreme characteristics.

Normal

A *normal lens* basically gives a normal representation of perspective. Subjects look roughly the same size as they did from the camera, and the distances between the subjects look unaltered. One must remember, however, that the film image is a two-dimensional image. Just because you use a normal lens does not mean that you will have an image that accurately represents three-dimensional space. You have to think of many more issues, such as composition, focus, and lighting, if you want to create an image that appears to have some depth.

Telephoto

Telephoto lenses do the opposite of wide-angle lenses. Rather than elongating perspective, telephoto squashes perspective, that is, things look closer together down the camera's field of view than they do in real life. This is a very common effect, and, once pointed out, many examples come to mind. In films set in big cities, directors and cinematographers like to use telephoto lenses to shoot crowd shots on streets. It makes people look jammed together and cramped. It exaggerates the effect of people crowded like rats in a too-small space.

The long lens can also make movement toward the camera look distorted, giving a subject an almost dreamlike inability to reach its destination. Another shot from Mike Nichols's *The Graduate* provides an excellent example of this effect. Near the end, Benjamin is running toward a church where Elaine is getting married. To amplify his desperation, one of the key shots is clearly executed with a long lens. Hoffman is running as fast as he can, but he does not appear to cover any appreciable space. **SEE 3-20**

As the shot starts, you can see how compressed the space appears. You can tell that the car and the telephone pole are at different distances from the camera, but you would be hard pressed to tell how far apart they actually are. It is also very difficult to tell if Hoffman has passed the car or is still behind it. The second frame represents a point four seconds into the shot, four seconds being a much more substantial amount of screen time than at first would appear. While you can tell that he is closer to the camera, it is impossible to judge how much distance he has covered. The third frame represented is eight seconds into the shot. Again, it is difficult to determine how much space he has covered. The effect is not quite like he is running in place, but it does seem as though he is spending a great deal of time and exerting a tremendous amount of energy to cover what appears to be a very short distance. The entire action of this segment of the shot takes eighteen seconds, and the squashing effect makes it seem like an eternity. In the words of the Red Queen in *Alice in Wonderland,* "The faster I go, the behinder I get."

The effect can even jam things together to the extent that it almost makes the image appear abstract. Landscapes can take on an exaggerated and heightened form. With the compressed space, things can emerge suddenly from behind objects blocking the view. Telephoto lenses also flatten surfaces in a way that can be considered the opposite of the ballooning effect of wide-angle lenses. The human face can appear narrow and compacted, with the nose flattened and the eyes closer together. This is not as unflattering an effect as the wide-angle effect, but you should be aware of it.

3-20

This telephoto shot gives a dreamlike aspect to the character's desperate yet seemingly futile pursuit

Mike Nichols's *The Graduate*

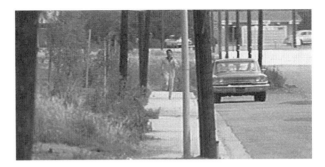

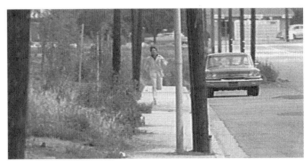

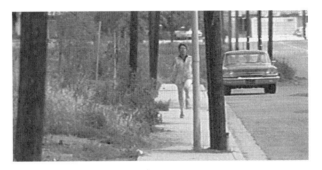

Zoom

The term *zoom* has worked itself far enough into the language that most people understand what it means. The ***zoom lens*** includes all of the focal lengths discussed previously. It may strike some people as odd that the zoom lens was left out of the section on camera movement. It has been left out so far because it is not truly a camera movement. The zoom effect is created by movable elements in the lens that either bring the subject closer to or push it farther away from a stationary camera.[3] This allows shots, like some camera movements, to go from very random information to very specific information and vice versa. It has side effects, though, that are clearly specific to the zoom and for that reason is always distinguishable from traditional camera movement.

The major difference between camera movement and the zoom is that the zoom includes a transition from the spatial characteristics of one focal length to the spatial characteristics of another. If we zoom in to a subject, we go from the elongation of the wide-angle lens to the squashed perspective of the telephoto lens. The dolly shot looks decidedly different because it is usually done with a fixed lens, thus the perspective characteristics remain the same throughout the movement. The dolly has the feel of independently moving through a space, whereas the zoom feels like one is being mechanically moved through space. In effect, the dolly brings the viewer to the subject, and the zoom brings the subject to the viewer.

---

3. Moving the camera and zooming at the same time is a tricky but relatively common practice.

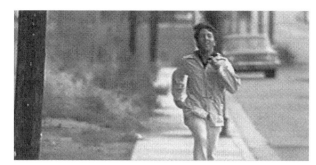

3-21

The perspective shifts in
the zoom shots

Dustin Hoffman in *The Graduate*

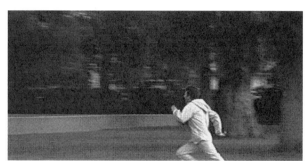

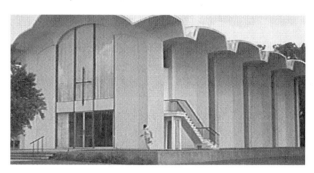

Despite this difference, many directors still tend to use the zoom like the dolly. It takes much less set-up time and equipment, thus accomplishing roughly the same effect at a much cheaper price. In the faster working climate of television, it is particularly popular. As such it has gotten a reputation as the poor man's dolly or the hack director's dolly. It is rarely used thoughtfully as a means of representing different spatial approaches.

The previously mentioned shot from *The Graduate* of Dustin Hoffman running toward the church is one of the few good examples of how the spatial characteristics of both extremes of the zoom lens can be used to good effect. **SEE 3-21** Hoffman's run toward the camera is only one segment of a longer shot. When Hoffman reaches the camera, the camera pans and zooms out at the same time. **SEE 3-22** The result is the transition from a lens that squashes space to a lens that elongates space. Suddenly Hoffman is a tiny figure dwarfed by a huge church. It is difficult for some people to see the zoom, but just watch for the point where his figure starts getting smaller in the frame.

Despite the negatives associated with the zoom, it can be quite effective and has seen increased use in recent years. John Singleton's *Boyz N the Hood* (1991) has several effective uses of the zoom to amplify emotion. In one sequence, the young Tre (Desi Arnez Hines II) arrives home from a trip with his father (Larry Fishburne) just as several of his neighborhood friends are being taken away by the police. **SEE 3-23** As the police drive away, the shot zooms in to a close shot of Tre. As is the case with telephoto lenses (the final position of this zoom), the background drifts out of focus. This effect isolates viewer attention on the young

3-22.

The simultaneous pan and zoom changes the perspective from a squashed space to an elongated space

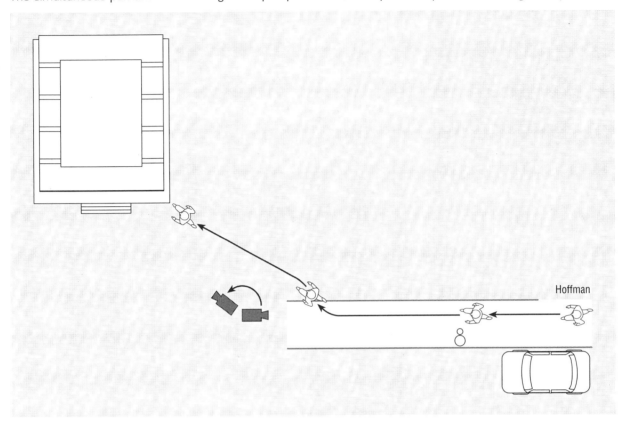

Hoffman

man's visible sense of disappointment and helplessness. Dolly shots also have the potential to change the background focus because of the attendant rack focus, but the effect is more exaggerated with a zoom.

The zoom lens can also be used for what has become known as a vertigo shot, popularized in the Alfred Hitchcock film of the same name. In a vertigo shot, the lens is zoomed in as the camera is dollied out, or vice versa. If this is done carefully, the framing of the composition remains exactly the same while only the perspective characteristics change. The perspective of the shot is thus smashed or elongated like an accordion, which can give a very distorted or subjective sense of screen space. In the film *Vertigo,* it is used to re-create the point of view of a man terrified of heights. In Martin Scorsese's *Goodfellas* (1990), the technique is employed to represent the subjective perspective of the Ray Liotta character in his most drug-addicted and paranoid state.

Lenses are key parts of the camera package. The employment of a specific lens brings with it both the lens's representation of space and any characteristics inherent in the lens. Occasionally someone comes up with the mistaken notion that telephoto lenses are used for close-ups and wide-angle lenses for long shots. You can use a telephoto lens for a full-body shot, only the field of view will be narrow and you will have to be some distance from the subject. Wide-angle lenses are often used for close-ups, though one must be aware of their distorting qualities. It is all dependent on what you are trying to achieve visually. Lenses are chosen for how they represent space—for their perspective characteristics. If a director wants a scene to have a sense of open space, he or she will opt for a wide-angle lens. Scenes that require a very constrained sense of space often call for telephoto lenses. Start understanding the properties of individual lenses, because their choice has a big impact on the image and thus occasions many preshooting discussions.

3-23

The zoom shot effectively amplifies emotion by focusing on the boy's face, the background drifting out of focus
John Singleton's *Boyz N the Hood*

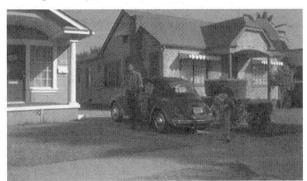
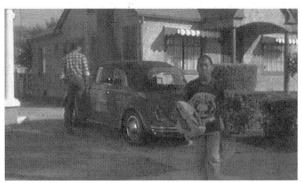
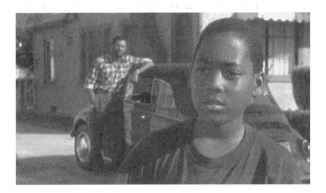

Depth of Field

Depth of field refers to the distances down the field of the camera's view that remain in sharp focus. As stated, focus must be set one distance at a time. When you have chosen the focus point, everything in front of and behind that point is going to be out of focus to some extent. The focus at different distances is a matter of what is referred to as *acceptable sharpness*—a way of speaking of the crispness or clarity of the detail of subjects or areas in an image. The range of distances before subjects become unacceptably soft—the depth of field—is dependent on several technical variables.

The overriding variable on depth of field is format size. The lenses used with larger formats have shallower depth-of-field characteristics than their counterparts in smaller formats. That is, if you use a lens that produces a normal perspective in the 35mm format (a 50mm lens) and a lens that produces normal perspective with a 16mm camera (25mm), the latter lens will produce more depth of field. Clearly, you would never choose a format based on depth-of-field concerns; usually, format is selected for reasons such as presentation, economics, and so on.

Beyond the choice of format size, the three variables on depth of field that are used while shooting are the same three found on lenses: *f*-stop, focal length, and focus point. There are two ways of determining the depth of field in a given situation: markings on the lens or printed depth-of-field tables. There are complex technical reasons for depth-of-field effects, but some general rules are presented here.

***f*-stop**   Higher *f*-stops yield greater depth-of-field characteristics—more will be in focus. Lower *f*-stops yield shallower depth-of-field characteristics—less will be in focus. If you are shooting at $f/16$, you will have greater depth of field than if you shoot at $f/2.8$. Do not take this to mean that you can arbitrarily set the f-stop to achieve greater or lesser depth of field. The f-stop is dependent on the lighting conditions under which you are shooting. If you were to get a reading of $f/5.6$ and decide to set the f-stop ring to $f/22$ to get more depth of field, the image would be completely underexposed. This may appear to make the f-stop an inflexible variable on depth of field, though in part III we suggest how there can be room for changes.

Focal length   Wide-angle (short) lenses yield greater depth of field. Telephoto (long) lenses yield shallower depth of field. This is why we said earlier that gradations of focus are more distinct with a long lens. If you are shooting with a 20mm lens, you will achieve greater depth-of-field characteristics than if you shoot with a 70mm lens. Again, filmmakers tend to choose lenses for the way they render space. If you are attempting to achieve specific focus effects, the depth-of-field characteristics of the lens clearly become part of the decision-making process. You would not choose a 10mm lens if it defeated the way you envision the space; but filmmakers desiring a deep focus effect generally shoot with a wide-angle lens. The film noir style of the 1940s and early 1950s incorporated tremendous depth within the image, and short lenses were clearly a central factor in the production of these films. A film such as *Citizen Kane* employs the depth of field inherent in a wide-angle lens in conjunction with the lens's elongation effect to create its extraordinary wide fields of focus.

Focus   Far focus settings yield greater depth of field. Close focus settings yield shallower depth of field. There is greater depth of field focused at 20 feet than if focused at 10 feet. Thus, focus becomes more critical the closer the subject is to the camera. Focus is generally less of a variable than the previous two elements. If something needs to be in focus, you will frequently set focus to it. Focus, however, is often manipulated to create effect.

The depth of field, that is, how much of the image is in focus, is thus dependent on these three variables. Clearly, there are ways to minimize or maximize focus for effect. Factors that maximize focus are short lenses, high f-stops, and far focus points. Factors that minimize depth of field are long lenses, low f-stops, and close focus points.

Determining Depth of Field

There are the two possible methods of determining depth of field for a given shot. The first is an option found on many prime lenses. These lenses have hatch marks that give the parameters of depth of field. **SEE 3-24** There is a sequence of f-stop numbers on either side of the focus hatch mark. In this example, if you were shooting at $f/4$ and focused at 8 feet, you could tell that you would have everything from roughly 6 to 12 feet in focus; *roughly* is the key word here because this method gives only general parameters. Many lenses use these markings, although there are different methods of marking the boundaries. Bolex lenses, which usually have the

3-24

The markings on the lens barrel give the depth-of-field parameters

name Switar or Paillard on them, have a clever strategy that employs gold dots that appear as you close the aperture. Zoom lenses do not have these markings because the focal length varies as you zoom, and thus no single chart would be correct.

The second method is far more common, mostly because of the inexact nature of the first method. ***Depth-of-field tables*** have a chart of the near and far parameters of focus for the common focal lengths. These tables generally list the depth of field down to inches. The *American Cinematographer Manual*, which is published by the ***American Society of Cinematographers (ASC)***, is generally used as a source for these tables, though they can be found elsewhere. The pocket-sized ASC manual is used constantly on the set.

Because lens length is a constant, there will be tables devoted to specific lens lengths. You need a table for the format being used—the ASC manual has tables for 35mm and 16mm, but not Super 8. You might have to do some searching for a Super 8 table. If you are shooting 16mm and using a 35mm table, your results will be skewed. In 16mm, the ASC manual has individual tables for 8, 9.5, 12, 16, 25, 35, 50, 85, 100, and 135mm lenses.

If you are shooting 16mm film with a 25mm lens, you first would look up the 25mm table. The tables have axes for both the focus and the *f*-stop. Tables are set up somewhat like mileage tables in an atlas, where you can look down a column and across a row to see how far it is from Minneapolis to Indianapolis. The following sample table includes only a few numbers but is representative of depth-of-field tables in general. **SEE 3-25**

If you are using a zoom lens, you can read the focal length off the zoom ring. If the ring is between numbers, you should probably round up to the nearest focal length for which you find a table.

In looking at these numbers, notice that there is always more depth of field behind the focus point than there is in front of it. This has given rise to the *⅓-⅔ rule*, which states that one-third of the depth of field is in front of the focus point and two-thirds is behind. It does not always work quite this perfectly, but as a rule of thumb it is relatively close. Just remember that there is always more depth of field behind the focus point than there is in front.

3-25

Sample depth-of-field table

Lens focus	f/1	f/1.4	f/2	f/2.8	f/4	f/5.6	f/8	f/11	f/16	
50'	36' 80'			25' Infinity					7' Infinity	Near Far
25'	21' 1" 30' 8"									
15'						9' 3" 40'				
10'					7' 9" 14' 3"	7' 1" 17' 2"			4' 7" Infinity	
8'					6' 6" 10' 6"	6' 12'				
6'										
5'										
4'										
3'	2' 11" 3' ¾"									
2'	1' 11¾" 2' ½"			1' 11" 2' 1"					1' 7½" 2' 7½"	

3-26

Depth of field and
focusing at infinity

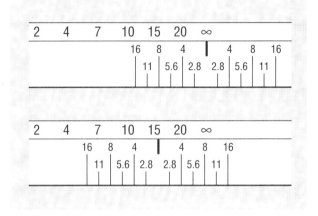

The shallowest depth of field is always in the lower-left corner of the table. Factors that maximize depth of field are in the upper-right corner. Note, however, that the maximum depth of field is not actually in the farthest upper-right box; it is actually down the column where we are focused at 10 feet. Here everything from 4 feet 7 inches to infinity is in focus. This is because as we draw the focus point closer to the camera, we continue to include infinity in the depth of field. You can easily see this on the barrel depth-of-field markings. If you are shooting at $f/11$ with focus set at infinity, the far end of depth of field will extend well past infinity. **SEE 3-26** You do not need to consult a philosopher to realize that the concept of "well past infinity" is absurd.

The point at which you are focused as close as you can be to the camera and still include infinity in the depth of field is called the *hyperfocal distance*. Each f-stop on each length lens has its own hyperfocal distance, because the depth of field expands and contracts with different f-stops. Hyperfocal distances are listed on most depth-of-field tables, and a knowledge of them can be handy, particularly in documentary work where many things may be happening spontaneously at different distances from the camera. Setting an arbitrary focus point for a specific depth of field, one that either includes or excludes objects in the frame, is a common practice.

Depth of Field and Setting Focus

In pragmatic terms, you should determine the depth of field in virtually every shooting situation. Let us say that you are shooting a scene in which one person is in the foreground at 8 feet and another person is in the background at 15 feet. **SEE 3-27A** You have determined—and this, of course, is not always the case—that you want both people in focus. A light meter reading determines that you will be shooting at $f/5.6$. You consult the depth-of-field table and find that if you focus on the person in front, everything from 6 to 12 feet will be in focus. In this situation, the second person would be out of focus. Conversely, when focused at 15 feet, the depth of field will be from 9 feet 3 inches to 40 feet, and focus will exclude the person in the foreground.

What would the options be if the goal was having both figures in focus? As any clever person would be quick to point out, you can simply move the characters closer together. This is obviously a very reasonable approach, and many minor difficulties can be solved in this manner. That said, do not get in the habit of allowing technical limitations to determine the content of your compositions. If for some narrative or aesthetic reason you wanted the character positioning to remain as designed, what would be some other options? The first would be to shoot at a higher

3-27

Depth of field and setting focus

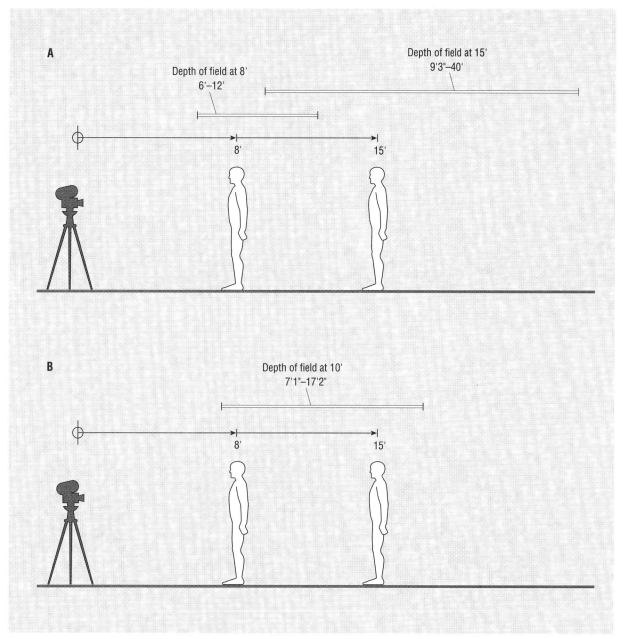

A

Depth of field at 8'
6'–12'

Depth of field at 15'
9'3"–40'

8'   15'

B

Depth of field at 10'
7'1"–17'2"

8'   15'

f-stop; however this would require more lights. This is a relatively common solution, though we will skip over it for now.

The easiest solution here would be to pick a focus point that included both of the figures. Another look at the table determines that if focus is set at 10 feet, you will achieve the desired depth of field. **SEE 3-27B**

In this case, you would set focus at 10 feet, and both subjects would be in focus. There may be no object in the image that is actually 10 feet away, but the focus setting is arbitrary to achieve a specific depth of field.

Conversely, there may be situations in which you do not want both subjects to be in focus. If a situation has subjects at 10 feet and 14 feet, and you focus on the

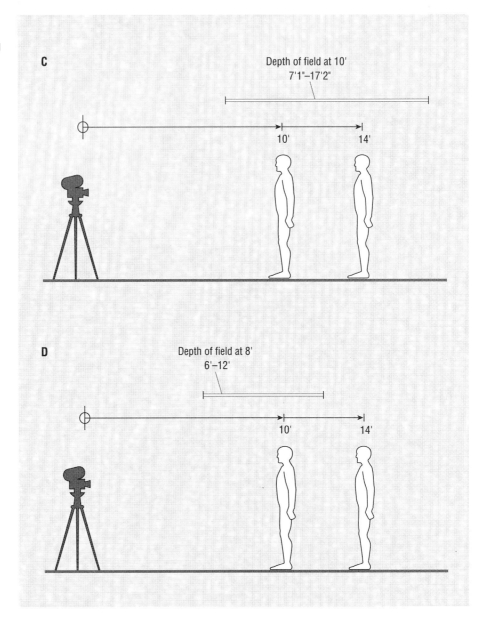

C

Depth of field at 10'
7'1"–17'2"

10'   14'

D

Depth of field at 8'
6'–12'

10'   14'

first figure, the depth of field includes the second figure as well. **SEE 3-27C** If you want the second figure out of focus, you would consult the table and find that focusing at 8 feet would reduce the depth of field to everything from 6 feet to 12 feet, thus achieving the desired effect. **SEE 3-27D**

So the focus point can be set arbitrarily to achieve specific effects. If you wanted the foreground figure out of focus, you could find a focus point that would achieve that effect. All of this must be done in consultation with a depth-of-field table or the hatch marks on the lens. Never arbitrarily shift a focus point without being very sure of the attendant result.

As with everything, subject movement complicates these issues. In the first example, if the person in front moves toward the camera, a rack would be necessary to keep him or her in focus. That rack focus would certainly cause us to lose focus on the background person. If our goal was to keep both figures in focus, the only solution might be to bring in more light to achieve a higher f-stop. Consulting the table would tell us what f-stop we would need to create the effect.

The key is that focus points can be set arbitrarily to achieve specific depth-of-field effects. Just because a subject is at 8 feet does not mean you have to focus at 8 feet. As you set up your shots, you must always be concerned with what will and won't be in focus. As suggested, you do not automatically want everything to be in focus all the time, but you do want to be in control of what is and is not. Achieving the effects you want takes extensive reference to depth-of-field tables and complex manipulation of focus point.

Deep Focus

The approach that keeps all elements in the frame sharp is called *deep focus*. It has been written about extensively and has many champions in the critical and theoretical world. Theorists interested in deep focus are usually champions of a realist approach to cinema. Orson Welles, Jean Renoir, and Alain Resnais, among others, have been generally recognized as creators of some of the great experiments in deep focus. Renoir's *The Rules of the Game* (1939) is often cited as an early example of the use of many different planes of focus to facilitate complex, multilevel action. Working with the technical elements that maximize depth of field is critical to deep focus.

Shallow Focus

Shallow focus is an approach in which, as described in the examples from *Pennies from Heaven* and *The Graduate,* several different planes of focus are incorporated within a single image. This can create a purposefully less realistic image—one that manipulates viewer attention and suggests different planes of action, both literally and figuratively. Shallow focus is less of a theoretical construct than deep focus is. It does not have as strong a critical following, probably because realist critics have so firmly hitched their wagons to deep focus. However, it can be every bit as much of an aesthetic approach.

Bernardo Bertolucci's *The Last Emperor* (1987) has many examples of a shallow-focus approach. The young emperor (John Lone) is frequently portrayed as being alone and isolated. To emphasize this, both foreground and background elements are often purposefully placed out of focus. In this approach, there is usually frequent rack focusing. **SEE 3-28** This shot includes a carefully calculated rack from the man in the foreground to the emperor in the midground.

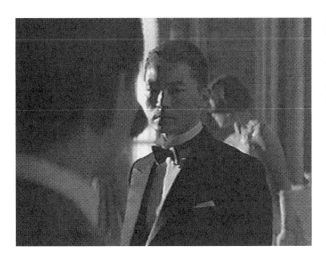

3-28

In a shallow-focus approach, several planes of focus are incorporated within a single image
Bernardo Bertolucci's *The Last Emperor*

As suggested, shallow focus is generally considered to be less realistic than deep focus, even though it may more closely approximate our actual perceptual processes. When we look at an object, our eyes focus on it. Although we may not be conscious of it, everything else is slightly out of focus. This lack of awareness of objects being out of focus is probably why we respond to deep focus as if it were somehow realistic. Out-of-focus elements in a frame generally call attention to the "plastic" qualities of film, reinforcing the notion that we are watching the creation of a photographic process. As such, they tend to break realistic identification and, though relatively common, have not found the same kind of acceptance as deep-focus shots.

Some of the great deep-focus films use all the technical elements possible to maximize depth of field. *Citizen Kane*'s cinematographer, Gregg Toland, has recounted how he employed these elements, and many of the film's shots are oft-cited examples of the unmanipulated spaces of deep focus.[4] It is particularly instructive to read how newer, faster film stocks facilitated his shooting much of *Kane* at higher f-stops ($f/8$ and above) than previously possible in similar situations. He also recounts how short lenses played an important role. Films that employ shallow focus as an aesthetic tool, such as the opening sequences of *The Last Emperor*, are equally instructive in how to creatively use elements that minimize depth of field.

For beginners, depth of field may seem to be more an effect that happens to you—one of those characteristics of the nature of lenses that buffets and batters you. But the more control you exert over the medium, the more you will be able to manipulate the variables to achieve the kinds of effects you desire. Often, as a beginner, you are forced to settle for the effect you can get; you do not have the resources to control the image that a larger project would have. If the background comes back out of focus, it may be because you did not have the lights or the lenses to achieve a different effect. This is largely unavoidable, though the long-term goal is to attain complete control.

Notes on Depth and Movement

An issue that requires clarification is the difference between depth of field and the concept of depth. Students often confuse them because both the terms and the issues are clearly interrelated. *Depth of field* is a technical consideration with highly defined parameters. It may be manipulated for aesthetic effect, but its determinants are technical. *Depth* is an aesthetic consideration in which you have to make a decision as to how you want your two-dimensional image to suggest space. If you want a decidedly three-dimensional feel to an image, you have to consciously manipulate elements in front of the camera to suggest depth. Lighting is a factor. Placement of objects in the foreground and background is a factor as well. Depth of field is simply one more factor.

Movement is also affected by lens length. Wide-angle lenses are better for obtaining smooth handheld shots as well as complicated moves done on camera supports. The telephoto lens magnifies both the subject and any movement on the part of the cameraperson. Handheld shots done with very long lenses can be almost unwatchable when projected, even though no significant movement was detected while shooting. On the screen, the image jumps all over—an effect that can cause symptoms similar to seasickness in the viewer. If you have to shoot some distance from the subject, such as when filming animals in a zoo, it can be difficult to use a wide-angle lens. This means that a tripod is indispensable for this kind of

---

4. Toland's article has been reprinted frequently, most recently in the August 1991 issue of *American Cinematographer.*

filming. Normal lenses are simply in between the extremes of telephoto and wide-angle, in both focus and the ability to be handheld. If both normal perspective and deep focus are desired, a lens on the low end of normal may be required.

Prime Versus Zoom

Although less true now than ten or fifteen years ago, prime lenses are generally used more than zoom lenses because they have better optical qualities. Zoom lenses are very complex, being composed of a number of elements. The more surfaces the light has to pass through, the more the light deteriorates. Prime lenses, because of their relative simplicity, generally give sharper images. This said, it should be noted that zoom lenses have been steadily improving, and some of the new generation of zooms have been billed as being the optical equals of their prime brethren. Cinematographers seem to be split pretty evenly on this issue. When you are going to be zooming, only a zoom lens will do. When the shot is static or it is the camera doing the movement, the prime lens is still the most common choice.

Cinematographers sometimes prefer a zoom lens because it gives them more compositional flexibility. If they want a slightly closer shot, they can just zoom in and not have to go through the time-consuming process of moving and releveling the entire camera. This also can be handy in moving from medium shots to close-ups without having to change the setup, although there are some pitfalls when you do this. The biggest concern is how the two lens lengths represent space. In the medium shot, a wall may appear to be several feet behind a subject whereas in the close-up, when zoomed in to a longer focal length, it can appear to be just off the subject's shoulder. It can be disconcerting to have shots with differently represented backgrounds included in the same scene. Some cinematographers, usually with director input, will go ahead and change the setup to maintain consistent spatial relationships. How this is handled will be your decision, as you will no doubt see scenes that approach it both ways.

A further deterrent to the use of zooms is that rack focuses executed on zoom lenses have a slight zooming effect. The moving front element of the rack focus does the same thing as the moving element of the zoom, only to a lesser extent. This is called *breathing*, and is difficult to see as the shot is being executed. The effect can be quite disconcerting if it is not desired. Some of the newer generation of zoom lenses have corrected this problem, but these are very expensive and may be out of reach of novice filmmakers.

Zoom lenses, however, can be a very attractive feature for many beginners. Nowhere can you push or turn anything and get such immediate results. But because of this, they tend to be overused. Infatuated with this minor but gratifying feature, students will zoom in and out. And in and out. I discourage beginners from doing more than a couple of zooms in their first films, and those only to get it out of their systems. When you start looking for them in films, you will be surprised by how few you see. Very few directors use them intelligently, Robert Altman and Sergio Leone being notable exceptions.

Lens Mounts

Lens mount refers to the method with which the lens is attached to the camera. As with many situations in which manufacturers are competing for markets, lens mounts are not standardized. Arriflex has one mount. Bolex uses C-mount lenses, and the CP-16 has a different mount altogether. Both the Arri and the CP mounts are called *bayonet mounts*. The part of the lens that is inserted into the camera is called the *flange*. C-mount lenses have threaded flanges, and attaching them is a simple matter of screwing the lens in. Bayonet mounts have an extended pin that interlocks with the lens. Some lenses can be adapted to other makes of cameras whereas others cannot be. For example, there is an adapter available that allows some Arriflex lenses to be used on the CP-16, but not vice versa. The relationship of the rear element of the lens to the body of the camera is just too different to be matched.

This area where the flange meets the camera is crucial. There is virtually no room for error in the flange-to-camera relationship because it will affect the highly critical distance between the rear element and the film plane. If a lens is improperly mounted even slightly, whatever film is shot will most likely be out of focus. This leads to one of the fundamental rules of camera care:

▶ **RULE:** *Never pick up a camera by its lens.*

This puts undue stress on the flange area and will eventually cause the lens to be loose in its mount, leading to rear-element-to-film-plane difficulties.

Many lenses, particularly zooms, are so heavy that they could put undue stress on the camera's lens mount. These lenses generally have a *lens support system*, consisting of rods that extend from the body of the camera, to support the weight of the lens. This is a very common strategy in 35mm shooting. A lens that is too heavy may damage the lens mount if not properly supported.

When deciding on lenses, make sure you have an appropriate match of lens and camera. When you are going to a rental house, they will know the appropriate lenses, even though it is still *your* responsibility to make sure everything works together. Low-budget filmmakers often get a special lens from a friend of a friend, and the camera from some other source altogether. This is where you can run into trouble. Be sure the pieces match. Shoot a test roll if you can.

The lens should *not* be mounted on the camera when it is being transported. Again, the flange area is critical, and any shocks to the camera while the lens is mounted can jar the position of the lens. A bumpy ride in a car might cause significant focus problems. The lens should be packed in a material that will absorb as many shocks as possible.

Front-Filters and Matte Boxes

Virtually all lenses have some method of front-mounting filters. Most *front-filters* for 16mm lenses are round, thin glass pieces that can be mounted in rings that screw into the front of the lens. **SEE 3-29** Several lenses use rectangular filters that are mounted in a holder that attaches to the front of the lens, an approach more common in 35mm. *Series 9* filters (series refers to a size) and their attendant ring adapters are the most common in 16mm, particularly for zoom lenses. These rings are designed to screw into each other so a director of photography (DP) can sandwich as many filters together as desired. The more surfaces the light passes through, however, the more its quality degrades. When multiple filter effects are needed, DPs generally prefer single filters that combine effects or will sandwich no more than two at a time.

A *matte box* is an accordion-like *bellows* attachment that is mounted on the front of the lens. **SEE 3-30** It can be used to mount filters or to shade the lens from direct light. A *sunshade* is also used for this purpose.

3-29

Most front-filters for 16mm are round, thin glass discs mounted in rings that screw into the front of the lens
Series 9 filters and adapter rings

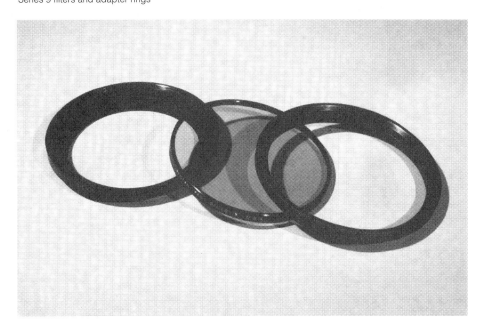

3-30

A matte box is an accordion-like bellows attachment mounted on the front of the lens
Aaton XTR^{prod} with matte box

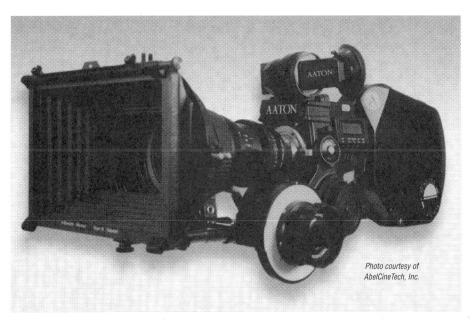

Photo courtesy of AbelCineTech, Inc.

It was originally designed to create shots that matte out (block light from) certain areas of the frame. The mattes are generally made out of heavy cardboard or metal and are inserted in the front of the matte box. They can be used to create a variety of patterns (keyholes, binoculars, question marks, and such) or, in conjunction with a camera's backwinding functions, to make multiple passes on the film, blocking out areas intended for other information in later passes. The most common example of this is the split-screen effect, in which you see two separate images side by side on the screen. You block off one side of the lens on one pass and then block off the other side on the next pass. With this approach, you can create many-layered effects.

As attractive as this feature might appear, this type of matting is done infrequently. Most matte shots are now done with blue screen mattes, and effects like the split screen are usually editorial decisions that involve optical printer work. Blue screen mattes are dark blue curtains behind the subjects being filmed. Registration, the positioning of the individual elements next to each other, and the quality of black necessary for multiple printing are much easier to achieve with this type of matte. Although the matte box can be used to create many interesting effects, its professional use is mostly for filtering and lens shading.

Care and Maintenance

All modern lenses have a purplish antireflectant coating. This coating reduces stray light bouncing around in the lens, a phenomenon that reduces *contrast*, the play between lights and darks. If a lens is cleaned unnecessarily, that coating will eventually wear down. Only clean a lens if there is some noticeable mark, such as a smudge or fingerprint, and then clean the lens immediately. The oil from your finger can etch a permanent pattern in the antireflectant coating if it is left for any significant amount of time.

▶ **RULE:** *If a lens is not dirty, don't clean it. If it is dirty, clean it immediately.*

When you do have to clean a lens, use only the materials specifically designed for the purpose—commercially produced lens-cleaning tissue and lens-cleaning fluid. The tissue should be used first, and the drops only as a last resort. If there is substantial dust or grit on the lens, clean it off with a camel-hair brush before using tissue; otherwise the dirt can get into the paper and scratch the coating and possibly the lens itself. I roll up the tissue like a cigarette and then swirl the end around the mark until it's gone. If this doesn't get rid of the mark, then, and only then, use the fluid in conjunction with the tissue.

When you have to use the fluid, put a drop on the center of the lens, and use the tissue as just described. This should get rid of most anything. Be careful that the fluid does not run down into where the glass meets the barrel of the lens. All lenses are cemented into position, and the fluid, if not used carefully, will eventually start to break down that cement. If the cement gets broken down, any shock to the lens may cause the elements to shift. The distance between the elements and the film plane are precisely engineered, and the movement of even a fraction of a millimeter will seriously degrade the image. All shocks to the lens should be minimized, but transportation is the biggest culprit; excessive heat can also weaken these cements and cause problems.

All these recommendations also apply to filters, and their care is a significant issue. It would be foolish to spend half an hour cleaning a lens and then put a dirty filter in front of it. If anything, you will see the AC spending more time with filters than with the lens itself.

There is substantial disagreement about the role of dust on the lens and filters. Some people claim it reduces contrast; others say that a modest amount has no significant effect because it could not conceivably be in the range of focus. It is virtually impossible to eliminate all dust, but cleaning is called for if there is a substantial amount of it. The camel-hair brush is the tool of choice for this job.

As important as the front element of a lens is, always check the rear element as well. Given that the lens is removed frequently to either check the gate for hair or to mount a new lens, dust and marks can be a factor here as well. In fact, something on the rear element degrades the image more dramatically than front-element marks. The distance between this rear element and the film plane is absolutely crucial to the quality of the image. Anything that may degrade the quality of the light must be avoided at all costs, so be sure to check both ends of the lens.

The flanges of both the lens and the mount on the camera should be cleaned as well. If a piece of dirt or grit gets lodged between the lens and the camera, it can actually change the distance between the rear element of the lens and the film plane. Again, even the slightest shift can jeopardize the sharpness of the image. Alcohol and a swab are the accepted materials for cleaning these critical areas.

Don't make the mistake of cleaning a lens with alcohol and swabs, even though they're part of a standard cleaning kit. This would make the antireflectant coating look like the swirls on a poorly cleaned window. It is extremely important to use the appropriate materials on the appropriate parts. Do not use facial tissue. Do not use a corner of your shirt sleeve. Do not attempt to blow the dust off with your breath; no matter how hard you try, you will just get spit on the lens. Watch how ACs take care of their lenses, and develop your own good habits from the start.

Any discussion of lenses can get quite complicated. Optics is a highly developed science, and lenses are extensively researched and tested. You will eventually hear such terms as *astigmatic aberrations, coma,* and *longitudinal chromatic aberrations,* as well as an endless list of technical reasons why what's in front of the camera never arrives at the film plane in perfect shape. To avoid these problems, remember that any lens is an amalgamation of compromises. The manufacturer had to give up one thing to get something else. Older zoom lenses in particular can sacrifice quite a bit of sharpness to get longer zoom ranges. The molded-plastic lenses in cheap cameras give up just about everything. These kinds of optics will just not do for motion pictures. If you start with an impoverished image, there may not be much left by the time it has been projected 90 feet.

Still, there are lenses that yield beautiful results and, with proper use and care, will serve your needs for many years. Cinematographers tend to latch on to specific lenses and go to great lengths to hold on to them and care for them. Start thinking about how you want a lens to perform and what lenses live up to your standards.

4

Film Stocks and Printing Processes

FILM **stocks are distinguished by a number of key factors.** These include the stock's general construction; the exposure index, which rates the film's responsiveness to light; the color balance, which is the way the stock responds to different colors of light; and the latitude, the range of lighting values within which a film stock will produce a usable exposure. Although latitude is important in choosing a film stock, it is intrinsic to discussions of lighting and is covered in part III. All other elements are primary factors in choosing a film stock.

Construction of the Film Stock

Motion picture film is a strip of celluloid covered with a light-sensitive emulsion. It has **sprocket holes**, also called **perforations**, which facilitate the transportation and thus the exposure of the film. The construction of color film can be quite complex, but black-and-white film is relatively simple. There are several layers of coatings and adhesives, but black-and-white film is essentially made up of three basic elements: emulsion, base, and antihalation backing. **SEE 4-1** Film that has not yet been exposed is referred to as raw stock.

The **emulsion** is a solution of **silver halide crystals** suspended in a gelatin bath. When these silver halides are struck by light—that is, exposed—they change their properties. They further change their properties when subjected to chemical developers. In the case of negative film, the exposed halides harden and become opaque. In reversal film, the film is bleached and reexposed to reverse the areas that would be opaque in a negative. Either way, the film is barely touched by the light as it leaves an imprint. The analogy of a fingerprint can be invoked here. The chemical processing brings out the latent qualities of this "fingerprint." The emulsion side is a neutral color, usually tan or light green.

4-1

Black-and-white film stock is composed of emulsion, base, and antihalation backing

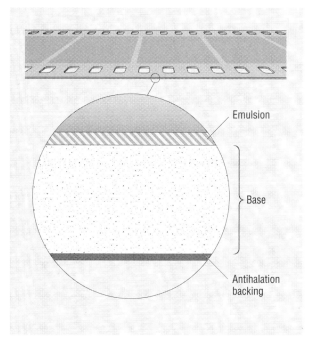

Emulsion

Base

Antihalation backing

If the silver halide crystals are large, they can be discernible to the viewer as shimmering building blocks of the image, called *grain*. Grain is similar to pixels, which is short for picture elements, on a computer. The smaller the grain and the smaller the pixel, the less likely a viewer is to notice that the image is made up of small dots. In the majority of commercial films, substantial effort is devoted to making grain as unnoticeable as possible. Grain is used to good effect in many films with a highly expressive image, calling attention to the construction of the photographic image and enhancing its abstract qualities.

The *base* is just the celluloid vehicle on which the emulsion is laid. The opposite side of the film, the *antihalation backing*, is dark and shiny. This coating minimizes reflections that can cause bright areas to bleed into adjacent parts of the frame. In the early days of motion picture and still photography, there was no antihalation backing, and the camera operators, under a light-tight hood, actually looked through the base of the film as they were filming. Before the development of modern viewing systems, this was the way cinematographers checked composition. This antihalation backing is completely removed in the developing process.

Color film stocks have a much more complicated construction. Although there are a number of different processes, the industry-standard color negative stocks are probably the best example. They work on the principle of separating the colors into three different layers of emulsion, with dye couplers and interlayer filters incorporated in the design. Each layer is sensitive to one segment of the color spectrum, although it does not break down as simply as just the three primary colors of light: red, green, and blue—referred to as *RGB*.[1] The top layer records the blue record, the next layer the blue and green record, and the final layer the blue and red. The base and antihalation backing are the same. There are other designs, but this one is fairly typical.

Negative and Reversal

Raw stock comes in two forms: negative and reversal. Most readers are familiar with negative film. *Negative film* has all the lights and darks reversed from how they are normally perceived. *Reversal film* is the opposite: all colors and shades are rendered normally, photographic slides being a common example.

Negative stock cannot be used as a primary projection medium but must be printed onto a second piece of film that is a frame-for-frame replication of the *original*, the film that actually ran through the camera when shooting. These duplicate prints are called *workprints* and are made by a motion picture processing laboratory—the *lab*. As the term *workprint* suggests, one does all the work of editing with these prints. Due to fears of damaging the fragile emulsion, the original is touched only when absolutely necessary. Except in a few limited applications, the original is never projected. A film's original exists as a medium used to produce either the workprint or the final product, a *projection print*.

Negative stock is the professional standard. It generally yields an image with tighter grain structure and is responsive to a wider range of light values. With reversal film, the reversing process is another level of manipulation of the film. The reversed original in a sense becomes the second *generation* of the innate negative. The term *generation* refers to making copies from an original. A workprint is one generation from the original, and thus a second-generation print. A print of a print would be a third generation. The farther one gets away from the original, the more the quality degrades, a reason why so many versions of early films have lost much of their original visual grandeur. In this process, grain increases and contrast

1. Whereas the primary colors on a color wheel are red, yellow, and blue, light differs in that its primary colors are red, green, and blue. The subtractive colors of light—cyan, magenta, and yellow—can also be important.

decreases. Negative film stock also provides a higher-quality transfer to video, further cementing its dominant position. Virtually all commercial features are shot on negative film.

Negative stock becoming the standard has led to some confusion in terminology. In the press and trade journals, the **camera original** produced on location is often referred to as the negative, leading one to think that *negative* and *original* are synonymous terms. But if one shoots reversal film, the piece of film that ran through the camera is an original as well. The term *original* simply refers to the film run through the camera during shooting. Even when the original is on reversal, which can be projected without a print, workprints are made when protecting the original is an issue.

Exposure Index

Exposure index (EI) rates how sensitive a film stock is to light, what is referred to as film *speed*. Different sources may refer to this as ASA (American Standards Association) or ISO (International Standards Organization), but they are just different names for the same thing. Under whatever name, EI is a somewhat arbitrary number that is found on the film's packaging. This number will be set on the light meter and it is the sole variable in the conversion of an amount of light in front of the camera to the corresponding *f*-stop. How the film stock will respond to different volumes of light depends solely on how the manufacturer—Kodak and Fuji are the primary ones—has designed and produced the stock.

▶ **RULE:** *The lower the EI number, the less sensitive the film is to light; the higher the EI, the more sensitive the film is to light.*

All manufacturers produce a number of different film stocks. The most significant difference in the construction of these stocks is the size of the silver halides and how closely they are packed together, which controls how sensitive the film is to light. Film stocks with large, loosely packed silver halide crystals respond better to low volumes of light. Film stocks with smaller crystals and tighter construction require more light to expose them. A film stock with a low EI, such as Kodak Plus-X black-and-white reversal film (EI 40), is less sensitive to light, thus you need a greater amount of light to expose it. Plus-X would therefore be easier to use in a high-light situation, such as outdoors in sunlight. A film stock with a higher EI, such as Kodak Ektachrome Color Negative 7298 (EI 500), is more sensitive to light. Less light is required to expose it, thus making it easier to use in low-light situations, such as indoors.

At least in the early stages, you will probably want to determine your film stock by the lighting conditions in which you are going to shoot. Most beginners will make this simple distinction: when shooting outdoors, use a stock with a lower EI; when shooting indoors, use a stock with a higher EI. This is not a bad way to start out, but be aware that most film professionals do not choose their film stocks on this basis. If someone is shooting indoors but wants the *look* of Plus-X, he will just light the set so he can shoot with Plus-X. This idea of the look of a film stock is quite complicated, but it mostly has to do with issues of grain, color separation, and how stocks respond to under- and overexposure.

For now, you should probably use the manufacturer's recommendation on the film's packaging. It will say that the stock has an EI of 80 or 320 or whatever. There will be a place to set the number on your light meter, and this should be done immediately. In Super 8, there are notches on the film cartridge that automatically set the EI on the camera's light meter, so you do not have to do anything. Once you have decided on a film stock and have set its EI on the light meter, the EI becomes a constant.

Color Balance

All types of light sources have their own color qualities. Daylight is generally somewhere close to white. Tungsten light, which includes the majority of indoor illumination and most motion picture lighting instruments, is reddish-orange (we will refer to it as red). Fluorescent light is, unfortunately, green.

Film stocks are balanced for these different light sources; and the way the stock responds to different colors of light is called the *color balance*. Although the human eye can take a wide variety of color sources and average them roughly as white, the film stock can respond to only one color at a time. When we are under tungsten light, do we perceive it as red? When we are under fluorescent light, do we perceive it as green? If you look carefully, you actually will perceive these colors. In reality, though, you probably don't pay much attention and average everything as a relatively even color. The film, of course, does see the difference. If a light source is red, it is red, and that is the light reaching the film plane. Color film stocks, then, are balanced for different types of light sources. If you are shooting red light (tungsten), the film stock must be appropriately balanced or the result will be just what you see: red.

The distinct color of a given source is rated by its *color temperature*, and it is important to note that color temperature is an issue only when shooting with color film. If you are shooting black-and-white, it is not a concern. Color temperature is measured in *degrees Kelvin (K)*, which refers to the temperature at which a black-bodied object—a surface that does not reflect light—changes color as it is heated. Most people have seen films on making steel and know that as metal is heated it changes color; first yellow, then red, then white, and finally blue. The temperature at which the black object turns a specific color is arbitrarily assigned to the color of a light source. *Tungsten (T)* lamps rated for motion picture photography are 3,200° Kelvin. They produce the same color as a black-bodied surface when heated to 3,200°. *Daylight (D)*, or photographic white, is 5,500° K. Other light sources will fall in the scale at different points. Standard household tungsten bulbs (40-watt, 60-watt, et cetera) will be less, say 2,800° K or 2,900° K. Fluorescent light, though not truly having a color temperature, will fall in at about 4,600° K. An overcast day will actually be blue and can fall in anywhere from just above 8,000° K to 20,000° K.

Tungsten and daylight color temperature are the two that are most important to photography (T = 3,200° K, D = 5,500° K). All film stocks will be balanced to one of these two, that is, all film stocks are designed to be shot under one light source or the other. Shooting under the wrong light with the wrong film will yield strange results. Many have probably seen this in personal still photographs. If you shoot with daylight film under tungsten light, the film will come back with an orange cast. If tungsten-balanced film is shot in daylight, the film will come back with a blue cast.

The solution seems simple: just shoot with the right stock in the right situation. Of course, nothing is ever that simple. The first problem arises when you have to move from a tungsten situation to a daylight situation. Switching rolls constantly is time-consuming and involves too much handling of the film, so a method had to be devised to use a stock balanced for one source under the other source. That is, there had to be a way to use either a film stock balanced for daylight under tungsten light or a film stock balanced for tungsten light in daylight. For a variety of reasons, mostly having to do with versatility, the latter approach is prevalent, although recent years have seen a rebound for daylight-balanced stocks.

That being the case, what is going on when you shoot under tungsten light with a film stock balanced for tungsten light? The color of the light is red, but you want the film to read it as white or normal. The manufacturer has simply made the red layer of the film less sensitive than the other green and blue layers. There

4-2

The red layer of tungsten-balanced film is less sensitive than the green and blue layers, hence it is less responsive to the red spectrum

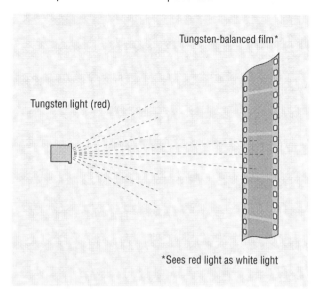

Tungsten-balanced film*

Tungsten light (red)

*Sees red light as white light

4-3

Using an 85 filter when shooting tungsten-balanced film in daylight turns the white light red, which the film then reads as white

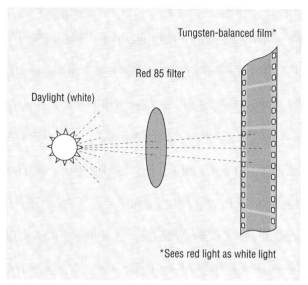

Tungsten-balanced film*

Red 85 filter

Daylight (white)

*Sees red light as white light

is physically less emulsion that responds to the red spectrum. Being less responsive to the red spectrum, the film stock will take red light and read it as white light. **SEE 4-2**

To use this film stock in a daylight situation, the adjustment is quite simple. Simply use an 85 filter, which is reddish (orange/amber) colored. **SEE 4-3** The logic of this step is straightforward. The 85 filter takes the white light of daylight and adds a red component to it. The tungsten-balanced film, which reads red light as white light, then renders that light as white. To state it another way, the 85 filter turns the white daylight red, and the tungsten-balanced film stock then reads it as white light.

"Why bother going through all this?" one might reasonably ask. It is because the opposite transition has tremendous drawbacks. Shooting daylight-balanced film stock under tungsten light requires the use of a deep-blue 80a filter. All filters will reduce the amount of light reaching the film plane. The 80a filter cuts out two and two-thirds stops of light, whereas the 85 cuts out just two-thirds of a stop.

The problem becomes apparent in a hypothetical situation in which we take a daylight-balanced film stock into a tungsten situation. In these circumstances, you are usually going from a bright area (outside) to a darker area (inside), and if you lose two and two-thirds stops on top of that, you may not have enough light to get an exposure. Losing so much before you even start can really deter you. Add to this the probability that you started with a pretty low EI stock, needed for exteriors, and you can see how untenable the situation is.

The 85 filter makes much more sense because of its versatility. For that reason, a majority of color film stocks, particularly those designed primarily for professional use, are balanced for tungsten light. For several years, there were not even any daylight-balanced color negative film stocks available from the most prominent manufacturers. This has been rectified, but tungsten-balanced film still dominates the field.

Most manufacturers recommend a different EI that automatically adjusts for the two-thirds of a stop lost when you use the 85. On the film's packaging, you will find one EI for tungsten light (T) and one EI for daylight (D). After the daylight EI number it will always say "with 85 filter." The daylight number is always lower than the tungsten EI, and the "with 85 filter" is the reason why. The manufacturer is simply compensating for the lost light in the EI.

To make the correction from tungsten to daylight, there are glass front-filters that can be mounted on the front of your lens. Virtually all lenses will have ring adapters that screw into the lens. Rather than use the front-filter method, some cameras have a filter slot directly in front of the film plane in which you can insert a small piece of gel. Many people who have worked in Super 8 will remember that this was handled quite simply with the tungsten/daylight switch on the camera. When the switch was in the daylight position, the reddish 85 was inserted (Super 8 stocks are balanced for tungsten). In 16mm and 35mm, you are on your own, as you are anyway with virtually everything else.

This is all relatively uncomplicated. If you are outdoors shooting with a tungsten-balanced stock, you use the 85 filter. If you are indoors shooting in tungsten light, you do not. Where this really gets complicated is when you have to shoot a scene that has a mix of several sources with different color temperatures. Clearly, you have to consider the color of the light source and how it is going to be rendered on film. Even more important, you have to match the light sources to each other if you want realistic rendition. If you are mixing all types (and thus colors) of light sources, you will get a shot back that is all colors. Lighting crews spend a substantial amount of time on this, and it is an issue that eventually will have you jumping through hoops, too.

Raw Stocks

As stated, film that has not been exposed to light is called *raw stock.* For beginning cinematographers, the primary factor in the choice of a raw stock is usually the film's speed—the EI—the number that rates how sensitive a film stock is to light. Lower-speed stocks are generally more suitable for high-light conditions, and higher-speed stocks are used in low-light situations. Lower-speed stocks have tighter grain structure and better reproduction of blacks than higher-speed stocks, although the latter have shown dramatic improvement in recent years. Filmmakers with limited resources and smaller lights often choose the stocks with higher EIs, because of their versatility when working with low volumes of light and the greater depth of field achieved with the resulting higher *f*-stops.

Color Stocks

The bulk of commercial work is done in color and is shot predominantly on negative. Most black-and-white shooting is done on reversal, although negative should be seriously considered for advanced projects.

Color reversal film stocks were very popular prior to the video revolution, because they did not require printing to be viewed. Applications where scratches and permanency were not major issues, such as television news and amateur sporting events, used miles of reversal film, because the film could be slapped onto a projector or telecine—the machine that converts film into a video broadcast signal—and shown as frequently as needed. Then it could be put on a shelf, or in a garbage can, never to be seen again. Once this "shoot and show" function was taken over by video, the higher quality of negative stocks ensured that they would become the standard for professional work, at least in color. There are a few color reversal stocks, but both lower image quality and inadequate lab support make them less desirable. The world has become a negative place, at least for color film.

4-4

Available tungsten-balanced stocks

	Kodak		Fuji	
	Film stock	E I	Film stock	E I
Low Speed	7248	100 (T) 64 (D)		
Midrange Speed	7293	200 (T) 125 (D)	F-125	125 (T) 80 (D)
			F-250	250 (T) 160 (D)
High Speed	7298	500 (T) 320 (D)	F-500	500 (T) 320 (D)

There are presently two major producers of film stock: Kodak and Fuji. Kodak remains the dominant producer, although Fuji has initiated aggressive marketing strategies. Check with the manufacturers about student discounts. Each manufacturer's film stocks have a slightly different look, both boasting excellent color rendition, tight grain structure, and good reproduction of dark areas in the frame. The best way to learn about the characteristics of individual stocks is to shoot the film and talk to labs and DPs who have dealt with the specific stocks.

The film stocks that these manufacturers produce change according to technological developments driven by the demands of the industry. Any listing of stocks will eventually become out-of-date, although there are some considerations that remain consistent. Film stocks are usually referred to by their numbers, for example, Kodak 7248 or Fuji F-500. Although 35mm has a more significant share of the market, the following discussion will be couched in terms of the 16mm stocks frequently used by students and independents. Most 16mm stocks have a 35mm equivalent.

The chart above lists the stocks designed for tungsten (T) that are available at this writing. All stocks come with two EIs, the lower rating for daylight (D) reflecting the compensation for the light lost when using the 85 filter. **SEE 4-4**

The most surprising recent trend in film stocks has been the resurgence of daylight-balanced negative film stocks. Selection was very limited for many years, but demand has evidently convinced manufacturers that there is a market for it. In fact, Fuji even discontinued its low-rated tungsten stock, F-64, the stock that was commonly used by filmmakers outdoors with the 85 filter. Higher-EI stocks had tight enough grain structure, and the daylight stocks were eliminating that use. Both Kodak and Fuji offer daylight-balanced stocks, both having one low-speed and one high-speed version. The manufacturers generally do not list tungsten ratings on daylight film stocks, the 80a filter reducing the EIs to the extent ($2\frac{2}{3}$ stops) that the stocks become difficult to use. The higher-speed stocks are actually very difficult to use in bright exteriors, since the high EIs yield higher *f*-stops than many lenses have. They are primarily designed for arena and stadium shooting, many of which use lights producing 5,500° Kelvin light or thereabouts. **SEE 4-5**

Only Kodak and Fuji offer color reversal stocks. Fuji offers one high-speed stock. Kodak offers a total of four: a low-speed and high-speed stock for both tungsten and daylight.

4-5

Available daylight-balanced stocks

	Kodak		Fuji	
	Film stock	E I	Film stock	E I
Low Speed	7245	50 (D)	F-64D	64 (D)
High Speed	7297	250 (D)	F-250D	250 (D)

Black-and-white Stocks

The preference for raw stock is the opposite in black-and-white, with reversal being the prevalent choice. Although a few notable exceptions come to mind, such as Spike Lee's *She's Gotta Have It* (1986), Steven Spielberg's *Schindler's List* (1993), and Martin Scorsese's *Raging Bull* (1980), the majority of black-and-white shot is on nonprofessional projects. This includes early student exercises and producers who have not switched over to video, such as high schools that do not have adequate stadium lighting to support video. Thus, reversal is dominant and more plentiful than negative, and filmmakers will have an easier time finding competent processing. However, negative should be carefully considered if the final product is going to be a film print or high-end transfer to video. You may have to do some modest searching for both the stock and quality laboratory services, but if image clarity is a goal, negative is the better choice.

Kodak is the only manufacturer that still produces black-and-white film. There are two negative and two reversal film stocks. Black-and-white film stocks list an EI for both tungsten and daylight, the tungsten rating being lower. This, of course, has nothing to do with color temperature. Black-and-white film is less sensitive to the red spectrum, and thus with the lower EI, Kodak is recommending slightly more exposure under tungsten light. Black-and-white generally costs about two-thirds to three-quarters what color costs. **SEE 4-6**

Product catalogs list several other choices you need to make. One is whether to buy the film on core loads or daylight spools. This largely depends on the camera you are using and, to a lesser extent, the size of the shoot. Smaller cameras generally require 100-foot daylight spools. Although magazines can run daylight spools, 400-foot core loads are the professional standard used in magazine-loading cameras.

4-6

Available black-and-white film stocks

	Kodak B&W			
	Reversal		Negative	
	Film stock	E I	Film stock	E I
Low Speed	Plus-X	40 (T) 50 (D)	Plus-X	64 (T) 80 (D)
High Speed	Tri-X	160 (T) 200 (D)	Double-X	200 (T) 250 (D)

35mm is available in 1,000-foot loads. Another choice in 16mm is whether to choose single- or double-perf film. Again, most producers shoot double-perf film because it is more versatile in editing.

Product brochures list catalog numbers and all ordering information. The film business being what it is, manufacturers are wary of sending stock without 100 percent guarantee of payment. Establish credit if possible or be ready to pay up front. Personal checks generally must clear before shipments will be made. Credit cards open most doors.

Processing

Motion picture film has to be taken to a professional processing lab. Although the services required of a lab can become quite complex, initial services on a film usually consist of processing the original and making a workprint. Unlike still photography, where a short piece of film is loaded onto a small reel to be developed, motion picture film processing requires large tanks to accommodate the longer camera loads. The film is moved on rollers and literally dragged through the processing chemicals. This ensures that layers of film do not become sandwiched together, which would impede the chemical process.

Today, finding the processing services you need may mean dealing with a number of far-flung labs. As with any other business, labs specialize, and students and independents outside of major urban centers may have to do some searching. Lab services are generally expressed in cents per foot. Processing might cost ten cents per foot, for example. Although the figures look small on the paper, they add up quickly enough. A number of labs have special student pricing, a boon to any on-the-edge producer. You might find one lab that charges forty-five cents a foot for processing and workprinting and another that charges twenty-five. The difference between these two prices may not amount to much for a commercial project, but for a student it can be a significant sum.

Printing

The processed film is put on a *printer*, where it is sandwiched with a piece of raw stock. **SEE 4-7** The workprint is thus a frame-for-frame *contact print* of the original film. Printers have one high-wattage bulb that shoots a single piece of bright light toward the film gate. In the path to the gate, there are two levels of filters and front-surfaced mirrors positioned at 45-degree angles. These filters and mirrors separate the light into its three primary colors—red, green, and blue—for individual control. The three colors of light are individually controlled by *light valves*, shutterlike devices that can be opened and closed to control the volume of a color in the print. These valves are generically referred to as the *printer lights,* and their role throughout the entire photographic process is essential. Although there are slight differences among individual printers, the path of the light generally resembles the illustration. **SEE 4-8**

The first filter on the top row diverts all red light down through the light valve. It allows all the blue and green light to pass through to a second filter, which diverts the green light down to its own light valve. The remaining blue light is diverted by a front-surfaced mirror to a third valve that controls the volume of blue. The bottom row recombines the three lights to expose the film at the printer gate. The intensity of the three primary colors of light in the printer can thus be adjusted to make corrections to compensate for any mistakes in exposure. The manipulation of these printer lights is a key element in the life of a film and is covered in detail in chapter 18.

4-7

Making a contact print involves sandwiching the processed film with a piece of raw stock

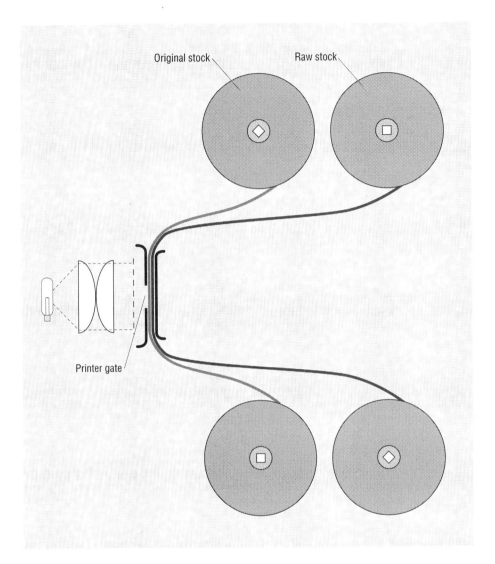

4-8

Path of light in film printing

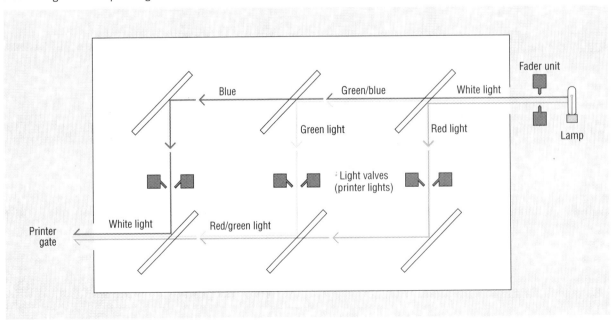

As stated, most labs price their services in cents per foot. Processing may cost ten cents a foot; workprint may cost twenty-five. It sounds inexpensive, but the total mounts extremely quickly. Labs usually list prices for three different types of workprints:

- **One light**—the lab uses the standard light in the printer, which is often not useful for beginners who may have exposure difficulties.

- **Best light**—more expensive and indicates that the lab will look through the negative and choose the best light for the entire roll. Generally the best approach for newcomers who are learning the complexities of exposing and processing film.

- **Timed**—indicates that the lab checks the original and determines the best printer light for each individual shot, which is very expensive and used only infrequently, even for projects that have the budget to support it.

Communication about such issues should be as clear and unambiguous as possible. Mistakes are costly and could jeopardize the integrity of the exposed film itself. Other information that needs to be communicated to the lab is covered in chapter 15.

Motion picture laboratories are becoming increasingly rare, and finding the right one will take some research. The video revolution has put a dent in the demand for processing and, particularly, workprinting. This loss of business eliminated most of the labs that processed limited amounts of film, particularly in small urban areas. Only labs in the largest and most film-active American cities have been able to remain open. Start collecting lab brochures and price lists to determine which ones provide the services needed at a price that is acceptable. As labs become more dependent on big jobs from commercials and feature films, finding quality processing and reliable service is becoming increasingly difficult for students and independents, a reality sadly complicated by irresponsible independents who fail to pay bills. Despite this, there are still many labs that wisely see these newcomers as the future of the business. Try to talk to film teachers or independent filmmakers in your area to find out what labs have provided quality service in the past.

Working with labs is one of the realities of the field. However, jury-rigged processing can be done to create extraordinary effects. It is said that the North Vietnamese processed their propaganda films in garbage cans during the Vietnam War. The product was rough, but, if anything, the undiluted roughness added to the persuasiveness of the footage. One of the most beautiful student films I have ever seen was self-processed, with the sandwiching causing the sprocket patterns on the unprocessed layers to swirl in abstract patterns. The approach is not useful, however, unless you are willing to accept the attendant effects.

Viewing Dailies

There is nothing quite so exhilarating as watching *dailies*, also called *rushes*, which is the footage from the previous day's work. All the painstaking effort that went into execution has a concrete representation in the final product. Viewing dailies can be a tension-inducing experience as well. This is where you see any unpleasant surprises that were not anticipated during the shoot. With experience, you should be able to avert any outright disasters, but there are almost always things that you wish were better.

Dailies should be watched with a critical eye from several different perspectives. The first time through, thoroughly check the condition of the workprint and, by extension, the original. If there are flaws or damage, they should be identified and addressed at this stage. If you do not find the problem on the workprint, have the lab check the original. Damaged or dirty film is generally discarded and the material reshot, so be completely conversant with any flaws and identify their source immediately. If the problem is caused by the camera, early identification may avert further damage. In addition, the more the film is handled in editing, the more it will show stress. If you notice damage later in editing, you may wonder at what stage it occurred if the film is not checked at the start.

Properties of Film Editing

Editing is time-consuming and technically challenging and can either perfect or ruin a film. The mechanics of editing are discussed in the final sections of this book. What is described here is the traditional way of editing and finishing a film. For most beginners with limited resources, this may be the way your film is finished, if indeed a print on film is your final destination.

In the editing stages, a film exists as a number of pieces. You do not really get to see the whole thing together until the film is virtually finished. As such, it is useful to start with the final product, called the final print. Indeed, editing is a process of moving toward this final print, the first version of which is called an ***answer print***. The version of the film that is created during the editing process is called the ***edited workprint***. All the truly creative work of editing is done at this stage.

Sound complicates editing immensely. Although sound and picture are edited at the same time, all sound is handled on separate pieces similar to the film. Sound is generally recorded on a traditional magnetic medium, such as cassette tape or conventional quarter-inch reel-to-reel tape, although the newer ***DAT*** (digital audio-tape) format is seeing increased use. Sound is then transferred to a magnetic medium called ***mag stock*** or fullcoat (a name that actually implies a specific type of mag stock) which is the same size and dimension as the film itself. It has sprocket holes of the same size and pitch as film and is covered with the same magnetized oxide coating that standard cassette and quarter-inch audiotapes have. In the traditional approach to finishing a film (before video and digital audio, that is), mag stock is *the* primary medium for editing sound. Mag stock runs at the same rate (24 fps) as the film itself and is available in all the formats in general use—35mm, 16mm, and even Super 8, though its use is less prevalent in this smallest format. For people who have done basic video editing, mag stock is a requirement that may appear prehistoric until one understands the freedom it allows, a freedom now matched by digital editing technologies.

Most film editing is done on either ***flatbed*** or ***upright*** editing machines. **SEE 4-9** The uprights are an older design than the flatbeds, although many old Hollywood hands still swear by them. Although there are bigger versions, the most common flatbeds have three film ***transports***, one picture and two sound. **SEE 4-10** The ***picture gate*** is where each individual frame is projected and the film can be run at normal speed and at fast and slow motion, or can stop on individual frames. The sound transports have magnetic playback heads that correspond precisely with the picture gate in terms of frames. These can be controlled in the same manner as the picture, all three being able to be run in either forward or reverse. There are sprocketed rollers on the left and right of each transport, each left-to-right pair, which is what the term *transport* refers to, controlling one roll of picture or sound. This allows the editor to work with one picture roll and two rolls of mag stock, referred to as ***mixtracks***, at a time. The transports can be run individually or can be interlocked to feed all the tracks past the heads at precisely the same rate. With all the tracks locked together and the rollers feeding the film past the heads at an even rate, you can position specific sounds against specific images. If you have a sound that is precisely 24 frames long and a shot that can be made the same, they can be cut against each other.

4-9

Most film editing is done on either flatbed or the older upright editing machines
Moviola M—77AH flatbed editing table

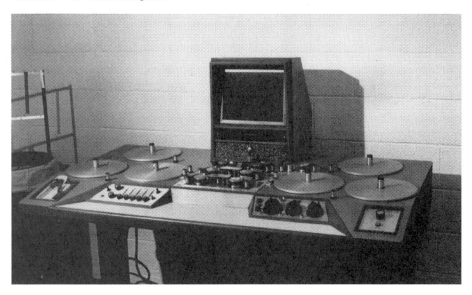

4-10

The most common flatbeds have three film transports—one picture and two sound

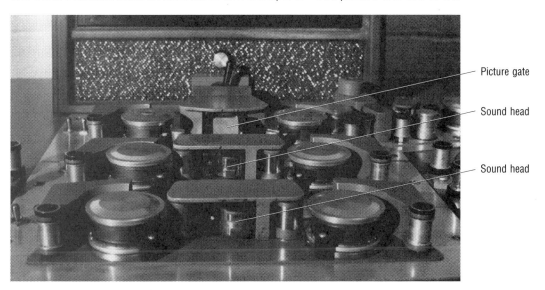

Picture gate

Sound head

Sound head

Each sound is transferred to an individual piece of mag stock, and specific sounds can by analyzed for the number of frames they occupy. A car horn may occupy five frames and its echo another dozen. In the 16mm format, a popular song may occupy 100 feet of film. The Gettysburg Address might occupy 90 feet of film, depending on the pace of delivery. Even at these lengths, songs, speeches, and a host of other sounds can be broken down to frames in order to find specific events (for example, measures, beats, individual notes, words, or sentences) within them. Once sound events are located on the mag stock, specific shots can then be edited against specific sounds. Multiple sound tracks can be built out of these individual pieces, and specific relationships between sound and image can be created. Synchronizing sound and image is controlled by the frames.

Thus sound can be manipulated against picture and, just as significant, picture can be manipulated against sound. A famous story of Charles Laughton and director Leo McCarey during the making of a classic studio-age comedy, *Ruggles of Red Gap* (1935), illustrates this latter capability. A scene called for Laughton to recite the Gettysburg Address to a saloon filled with grizzled frontier patrons. The problem was that Laughton was incapable of getting through the address without breaking into hysterics. He was able to get the first few lines out but, because of whatever demons had hold of him that day, was unable to continue. The longer the attempts went on, the worse the situation became. Wanting to avoid the expense of holding the set and the extras another day, McCarey shot several dozen cutaways of the crowd of saloon patrons in awed silence. When Laughton regained his composure several days later, McCarey had him record the address on an audio recorder, and the scene was made up of this recording overlaid with the shots of the barroom patrons. We see Laughton only for a few lines at the beginning, briefly in the middle, and pleased with the effect he has created at the end. Virtually the entire speech is composed of the ***reaction shots*** of the saloon patrons.

This example can clarify many basic principles. The reading of the Gettysburg Address would be transferred to magnetic film stock; in 1935 it would have actually been transferred to a photographic medium. It is then represented as a specific length of film, which can have image of the same length built against it. **SEE 4-11A** If we wish to have specific images positioned against specific events in the speech, we simply find the sound we want and cut the image we want on the picture roll across from it. If we wish to have the sound of a honkytonk piano in the background, for example, it is transferred to a separate piece of stock and positioned on another mixtrack against the image and existing sound. **SEE 4-11B** If the sound effect of a clock chiming in the background is desired, another track is required. **SEE 4-11C** This sound can also be very precisely positioned wherever it is wanted. If you want the sound of horses galloping by outside, that, too, is handled separately. **SEE 4-11D** Any sound that you want layered in will require separate handling.

The final product is one picture roll—the edited workprint—and a number of mixtracks all the same length as the picture. The number of sound tracks will

4-11

Compiling mixtracks enables sound to be manipulated against picture and vice versa

Picture						
Laughton	Cowboys	Bartenders	Ruggles	Over the shoulder (Laughton)	Old men	Laughton

Sound

A Fourscore and 7 years ago, our fathers... the last full measure of devotion... and for the people, shall not perish from the earth.

B Honkytonk piano...

C Clock chiming

D Horse galloping   Horse galloping

depend on how complex and layered your sound is. A music video may have only one track, the music track. More complex sound requires more complex track building. All narrative films require multiple tracks. Francis Ford Coppola's *Apocalypse Now* (1979) was said to have had more than seventy sound tracks. Jean-Luc Godard once made a feature film with only three sound tracks. When queried on why so few, he replied that it was because he had only three hands.

Once you have every element where you want it, you start the final steps of finishing a film: *negative cutting, final audio mixdown* (the creation of the final sound track), and the actual *printing* of the film. Although the filmmaker has substantial input, these three processes are either laboratory procedures or handled by experienced professionals. All are expensive. When you start these processes, all the creative decisions of editing have been made. There is almost no turning back. These processes are a matter of locking all the elements into place and combining them on one piece of film—the answer print. If the answer print meets your approval, it is used as a guide for all subsequent prints, which are called *release prints*.

When all the mixtracks are built, the mixtracks and picture are taken to a professional mixing facility for the final mix. All the tracks of sound are mixed down to a single sound track. The *rerecording mixer*, an employee of the mixing facility, will orchestrate the mix at your instructions, operating the mixing board as well as any sideboard signal processors. It is here that you finalize all the volume levels, any manipulations of sound quality, the sound fades planned by the editor, and so on. Although it will soon be in a different form, the *master mix* represents *the* sound for the film.

This master mix is turned into an *optical master*, a piece of film that is blank except for a narrow strip of diamond-shaped patterns opposite the side with the sprocket holes. **SEE 4-12** These patterns are the sound for the film, all sound in film being handled photographically. The optical master is used to print the sound track on the final film, where it is called an *optical track*.

When the film is edited exactly the way you want it, you then return to your original film and have it "conformed" to what you did in the edited workprint. The film is usually given to a professional, listed in credits as the *negative cutter* (also called the conformist), who makes an entirely new film out of the original, using the edited workprint as a guide. The film has latent *edge numbers* (see page 403), which serve as a guide to the negative cutter. This is generally the only time the original is handled and cut. This conformed original is still only a printing medium. Everything projected on a screen will be a print struck from this edited original.

In the negative matching process, the original film is actually cut into two separate rolls called *A & B rolls* (there can be more than these two). In the A & B rolls the picture is *checkerboarded*, with all the odd-numbered shots (1, 3, 5, 7 . . .) on one roll and the even-numbered shots (2, 4, 6, 8 . . .) on the other. This is done for a number of reasons, but mostly to achieve color and exposure control in the printing process and to facilitate dissolves, superimpositions, and other effects.

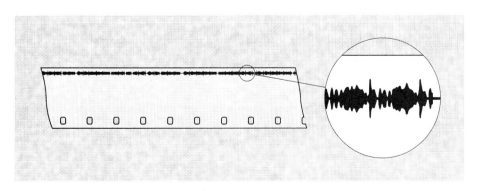

4-12

The optical master is a piece of film that is blank except for a strip of patterns opposite the sprocket holes

4-13

Flowchart representing the process of finishing a film

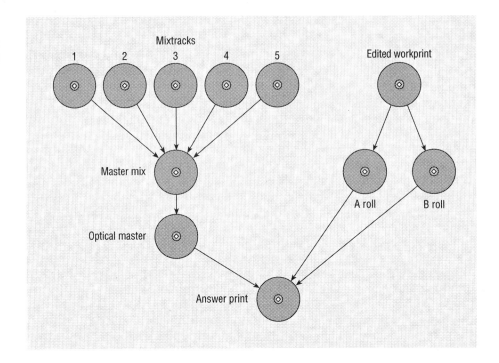

The process of finishing a film can be represented as a flowchart. **SEE 4-13** The sound and the image have two separate paths. Sound and image are cut at the same time, but they are not represented on the same piece of film until at the very end in the answer print. A final print is also descriptively called a *married print*, where the two entities are finally joined together.

To summarize, the mixtracks and the edited workprint are created in editing. The mixtracks are mixed down into a master mix, which is then converted into an optical master. The edited workprint is used as a guide to re-create the film out of the original, making the A & B rolls. The A & B rolls and the optical master are then used to create a final print. Unless there are complications, the answer print is the guide for all subsequent release prints. Hollywood commercial films generally do not cut the precious original. The original is used as the head of a family tree of printing and projection versions of the film. Often what you see at the theater is many generations away from that original piece of film, particularly when films are released in numerous theaters.

The final processes of completing a film, including conforming, mixing, and printing, are costly. The following estimates assume that you are finding vendors that will provide services at reasonable rates. If you want to mix the sound where George Lucas mixes his films (which is probably not an option even if you could afford it), multiply your costs by about five. The mix on a five-minute 16mm film might cost $150 to $200, assuming reasonably uncomplicated sound. If your film has an average number of cuts and you can find a negative cutter who will negotiate, you might get conforming done for $200. A final print of a color film would be around $200 to $250, including the creation of the optical master. Black-and-white is cheaper. This does not include titles and a host of other hidden costs.

Few students take their first films all the way to a final print. It is far more expensive than most tentative first efforts warrant. The complex process of creating sound tracks and carefully executed visuals should not be attempted until you have done some basic image manipulations. On the other hand, I have known aspiring filmmakers to take three or four years to make their first married film, apparently fearing the commitment of finalizing all their decisions. Do not tarry too long with your formative efforts.

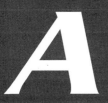

A VIDEO APPLICATIONS

The Camera

For those interested in the interface between film and video, the production video camera may be the most irrelevant part of the system. The predominant trend, at least when film is part of the scenario, is to *shoot on film and edit on video*. Frequently, projects that are commenced like this are designed to never return to film, with all exhibition planned on video. There are many different options, however, and going back to a finished film print is an increasingly viable one. Even if a project is started, edited, and finished on film, it is most probably going to be transferred to video for expanded exhibition opportunities, as submission material for grant proposals, or as demo reels for job applications. In addition, some notion of how a video camera works is necessary for an understanding of film-to-video transfer options. Thus, one must be intimately involved with video technology even if one is still shooting and finishing film.

The Video Camera

A video camera is comparable to a film camera in both dimension and weight. It is a body with a lens. The major difference is that the film camera captures light photographically whereas the video camera turns the light into an electrical signal—the *video signal*—that is recorded on magnetic tape in a manner analogous to sound recording. Although the internal workings of the film camera are impressive, they are essentially a nineteenth-century technology. A video camera is a product of the electronic age and, as with all things electronic, it is beginning to interface with digital technologies. **SEE A-1**

The video signal itself has been around since the advent of television. In fact, the earliest broadcasts existed only as signals with no method of recording. The first studio recorders were developed in the 1950s, and portable video started to become a dimly envisioned possibility in the mid-1960s with the first half-inch reel-to-reel recorders. Video began

A-1

Whereas a film camera captures light photographically, a video camera turns light into an electrical signal that is recorded on magnetic tape
Panasonic AG-DP800 "SUPERCAM" S-VHS camcorder

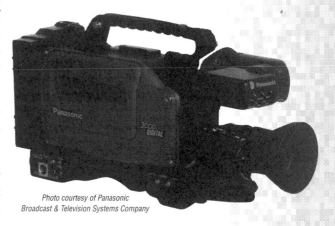

*Photo courtesy of Panasonic
Broadcast & Television Systems Company*

115

transforming the industry in the late 1970s. Television news stations, which shot millions of feet of film a year and had sophisticated in-house processing setups, quickly converted to the newer, cheaper, more immediate medium, and the primacy of film was over in short order.

The biggest difference between a film and video camera is in what happens to the light. Rather than striking the film plane, light passes through the lens of a video camera and strikes a *CCD* (charge-coupled device), generally referred to as a *chip*, which converts the light to a complex electrical signal. The chip is a flat board covered with thousands of light-sensitive pixels. Cameras are designed with three chip sizes: 1/3 inch, 1/2 inch, and 2/3 inch. Chip size can be found in a camera's manual and is somewhat similar to format size in film in that it is one of the variables on depth of field and the perspective characteristics of a lens.

When light strikes the chip, it makes an impression that is converted into the video signal. Most high-end cameras are *three-chip cameras*, devoting a chip to each of the primary colors of light—red, green, and blue. Many studio cameras, as well as older field cameras, employ a tube technology that similarly converts light into an electrical signal.

The technology to convert light into an electrical signal has been around for years and, in fact, is the basis of the most common approach to film sound. One of the most exciting aspects of the encoded electrical video signal is that it can be almost endlessly manipulated. The film image is in many ways written in stone. Although there are complicated and potentially costly reprinting options, a film image is photographically imprinted and must essentially be changed manually from one print to the next. With the potential for electronic manipulation, the recorded video signal can be modified in many different ways both before it gets to the tape in initial recording and, particularly, as it is being edited in postproduction phases. As such, it can be seen as a starting place for a complex and highly manipulated image. The ease of implementing optical effects and the increased creative possibilities have brought a new dimension to the process of creating a finished work.

Equipment and Formats

There are two basic approaches to video shooting and recording: the video camera with a separate *VTR* (videotape recorder), and the *camcorder*. In its infancy, the video camera and the recorder came as separate units with the camera generating the video signal and the VTR recording it. As the technology evolved, these units could be combined in the smaller camcorder package.

Just as film is shot in frames per second, video is broken down into *video fields* per second. Whereas film frames are arranged consecutively down the celluloid, the video frame does not have such discrete boundaries. The video frame is recorded diagonally on the tape, referred to as helical recording, with each frame composed of two diagonal lines of information. Although the video frame is not a distinct viewable entity like the film frame, the editor can stop and look at a frame just as with film. Video runs at 29.97 fields per second, usually just called 30. And though the recording method is very similar to that of audio, video recording requires much higher speeds to record a stable, usable image. Therefore, the helical scan record head rotates in the direction of the tape to *multiply* the speed of the tape.

The configuration of tracks on the videotape can be different from format to format. Many formats mix some signals, whereas other tracks have optional uses. All formats have at least two audio tracks, with some of the professional ones having room for one or two more. Employing four separate tracks, a typical half-inch VHS videotape is representative of most track configurations. The image track is in the

A-2

A typical half-inch videotape employs four separate tracks

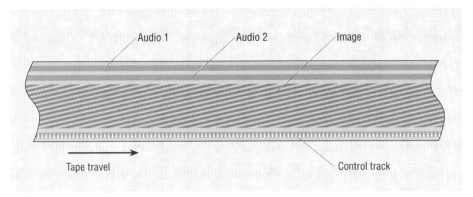

center and takes up the largest portion of the tape. The audio is on two narrow tracks at the top of the tape. **SEE A-2**

The bottom of the tape is reserved for the fourth track, the *control track*, which is recorded during shooting. Composed of a series of pulses, the control track, and its emulators, is central to the way video works. Much like a crystal camera, the pulses are referenced in playback to reproduce perfect speed. Any imperfection in the control track will cause image breakup. There is 1 pulse per video frame—30 pulses per second (PPS). The control track also allows the easy identification of frames in the editing process.

One of the major distinctions between video cameras, and by extension the entire recording chain, is whether they produce a *broadcast-quality* signal. Broadcast quality refers to the creation of a video image that meets certain emission standards. In a manual, equipment fulfilling this requirement is listed as meeting RS-170A standards. Although these standards are based on specific objective technical specifications, including signal-to-noise ratio, resolution, and color accuracy among others, just what constitutes a broadcast-quality signal can be a matter of some disagreement. The problem is that most professional equipment exceeds the established standards to the extent that many people in the field subjectively establish higher standards. While a hard-and-fast definition of broadcast quality is elusive, amateur video is not generally considered of sufficient quality to gain wide use. There are, of course, the home-video clip shows, and the lower image quality of the submitted clips clearly demonstrates the differences.

There are a number of formats available, many with competing claims to being the format with the best image quality. There are three camera standards: consumer, industrial, and broadcast quality. Although most industrial cameras actually conform to broadcast standards, subjective standards exclude them from most commercial television applications.

VHS is the most common video format, with the majority of consumer *VCRs* (video cassette recorders) and camcorders using this standard half-inch format. VHS produces an acceptable image, particularly when playing back prerecorded movies and producing images for the home market.

Super VHS was introduced in the late 1980s and is a step up in image quality and stability from its predecessor. It is an industrial-quality medium, being used extensively in schools and in-house business training.

Betamax was the main competitor with VHS for the half-inch consumer market for many years. VHS won the battle, but little pockets of Beta users still remain.

Betacam SP is presently one of the most significant broadcast-quality professional standards. Beta SP camcorders are common, the format used by a

A-3

Beta SP camcorders are used by most television news departments
Sony Betacam SP BVW-600 digital camcorder

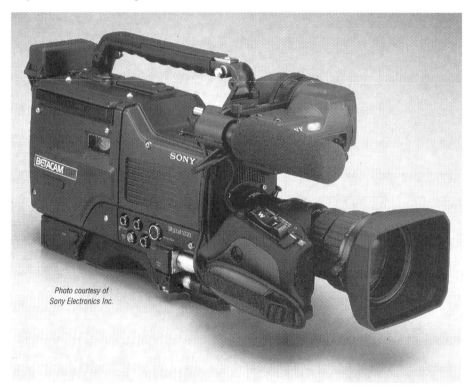

Photo courtesy of
Sony Electronics Inc.

majority of television news departments. Separate camera and VTR setups are
common for a more film-style shoot, an approach that also allows someone to be
at the deck, monitoring and mixing the audio signal. The *SP* stands for superior
performance. **SEE A-3**

Hi 8 is a Sony product and, like Betacam, receives substantial use as an
industrial-quality medium. Employing a conveniently small camera, Hi 8 tapes are
similar in size and dimension to standard audiocassettes. One drawback of Hi 8 is
that editing can be problematic, due to problems with dust and dirt on such a small
format. Shooting on Hi 8 and then transferring to another format to edit is a
common approach.

Video 8 uses the same cartridge style as Hi 8, but the format is not to the
same standard. Both tape formulation and general technical standards are
consumer-grade.

MII was designed by Panasonic to be a competitor in the broadcast-quality
professional market. It has been very popular among independents as a low-cost
alternative to the Betacam systems.

Three-quarter-inch, or *U-matic*, was the most significant professional standard for the first years of the video revolution. Employing a separate camera and
VTR, most TV news was shot on three-quarter, although the equipment was eventually deemed too bulky and heavy for flexible location use. A significant amount
of three-quarter-inch equipment is still in use, although the format does not have
quite the same share of the market as it did before Betacam was introduced.

Digital videotape recording is making inroads in the high end of the field and
will play a greater role in the future. Sony was a leader with its introduction of the
D-1 system. This was followed by D-2, D-3, and D-5, all coming from several

manufacturers including Sony, Panasonic, Hitachi, and Ampex. At this point, digital equipment is prohibitively expensive for the typical independent, although it most assuredly will come down in price and, presumably, go up in popularity. Cameras and recorders that digitize the image are in development, and this technology will undoubtedly play a significant role as well.

Technical Features

In many of its functions, the video camera is, of course, similar to the film camera. It has a lens with a focus ring, some form of exposure control, and a lens with something akin to a focal length—usually a zoom lens. Although video equipment must address the same technical issues, filmmakers are often frustrated by the lack of clearly defined technical parameters in video. Issues that are reasonably concrete in film, particularly EI, depth of field, and exposure, become somewhat more slippery in video. All three of these issues are in some way dependent on the construction of the chip for individual cameras, not on the technical quantification of light as they are in film.

Videotape does not have an EI as such, with sensitivity to light based on the number and design of pixels, not the formulation of the tape in a way similar to the construction of the film emulsion. Theoretically, each model of video camera creates its own EI, with most newer cameras responding well in extremely low light situations. One needs to become familiar with how specific cameras perform under different lighting conditions.

Beyond this consideration, video camera lenses have a focal length and f-stop that are based on mathematical formulations just as in film. Despite this, depth of field and exposure are not generally taken into account in a similar fashion. In video as in film, depth of field is dependent on the size of the "format" being used, in video's case, the chip size. Wide-angle, normal, and telephoto focal lengths can be identified for each chip size. Despite this, video manuals rarely list depth-of-field charts because videographers tend to chart depth-of-field and focus effects by eye as the shots are being set up. This is a perfectly acceptable method except that it does hamper the ability to plan for focus effects in advance. For those who have a hard time abandoning the film approach, the three chip sizes roughly translate to the three basic film formats; a Super 8 chart is close to a ⅓-inch chip, a 16mm chart can be used for a ½-inch chip, and 35mm converts to ⅔ inch. That these are only rough equivalents should be emphasized. Depending on a film depth-of-field chart for precise focus parameters would be a mistake.

In terms of exposure, there is still a diaphragm calibrated in f-stops on all video cameras. The volume of light the lens transmits is the same, but the camera's response to that light varies on a camera-to-camera basis, again based on the design of the chip. As stated, converting a volume of light to an f-stop depends on the EI of the film stock. With no fixed EI, light does not translate into an f-stop so easily. Videomakers tend to use their eyes or depend on a *waveform monitor*, an oscilloscope-style machine that represents the character of the video signal.

Although these issues can be frustrating, the method of handling color temperature is substantially easier in video. Unlike photographic mediums, the video signal can be trimmed electronically to conform to virtually any color source—to see almost any color source as white. This is referred to as *white balance*. White balancing is done by holding a white card in front of the camera. Under tungsten light, for example, the white card will reflect the light's red color. The camera will see this and adjust the levels of individual colors (RGB) until it sees the card as white. Thus everything shot under the tungsten light will read the light as white. This eliminates the need for color balance filters, particularly film's omnipresent 85 filter. Although the 85 is not really a significant burden, more-difficult lighting situations—fluorescent, mercury vapor, and so on—can be easily addressed in video. While this may appear to simplify the entire issue of color temperature, it actually eliminates only a modest number of basic changes. One must still consider the more significant issue of matching color sources in front of the camera to each other (see page 273).

Film-to-Video Transfer

There are a number of ways to transfer film to video, from the relatively inexpensive means to methods that can make film costs look reasonable. The most common approach in professional situations is to shoot color negative, with the image being reversed in the transferring process. Shooting a video camera straight into a projector with a five-bladed shutter is a common approach for consumer transfers. Filming the image off a rotating prism or a series of mirrors is another. The *flying spot scanner* is employed on many professional transfer machines. Many new professional transfer machines use a three-chip configuration in a way similar to a high-end video camera, only with a slightly different optical and recording strategy.

One key consideration is the difference between frame rates in film and video. The twenty-four frames of film must be converted to the thirty frames of video. The *three-to-two pull-down method* prints three film frames normally on the video with the fourth frame printed twice, thus reconciling the difference between the two frame rates. This method is the professional norm.

When you transfer film to video, you need to consider how a project is going to be both edited and finished. There are two considerations that will be further explored in the video-editing section (see page 472), but be sure you understand them before proceeding. The first issue is what form of control track you will use for the edit and at what stage in the process it should be introduced. The control track used in standard VHS is the most basic approach. When greater control is needed, *time code, window burns,* and, because they are the guide for producing a film print, interfacing film edge numbers with the video control track will become important factors.

The second issue is the quality of transfer needed. It is common to edit with a slightly lower quality video copy, with the intention of returning to the original to finish. In this case, returning to the original may indicate either a high-quality video transfer made at the same time as the workprint, or going all the way back to the film negative itself. In this situation, one is working with something akin to a video workprint, what some refer to as *video dailies.* In both cases, you need to know the endgame before you blindly choose a transfer method.

PART II

Blocking for the Camera

5

Scene Construction

ONE of the most important steps in planning the filming of a scene is to develop a strategy for shooting. Although this involves developing a specific approach in the form of a storyboard or shot list or the like, some basic principles of scene construction must be considered before trying to sketch anything out.

In theater production, *blocking* refers to planning where the actors will be and how action occurs in relationship to the set and stage space. In film, this is complicated by the presence of the camera. The term **blocking for the camera** refers to staging action for the camera. As much or more than any other element, blocking for the camera must be done with a clear conception of how the scene is going to be edited. It might be useful to think of a film as a jigsaw puzzle, each piece of which must be created individually and have a specific place in the finished pattern. Unlike a puzzle, though, there is not one right way to put a film together. The design of each film bears the mark of the filmmaker's personal style, with the result being a unique piece of work.

The choices you make in terms of setups are entirely up to you, but seeing all choices as being equal is a mistake. Shooting a scene should be done with the knowledge not only of a wide set of rules intrinsic to film, but also of accepted folk wisdom that has evolved over the years and of many aesthetic principles developed by filmmakers and artists in other media. There are approaches that many talented people have determined work; there are others that simply do not. If the goal is to create a scene that is clear and coherent to the viewer, understanding basic scene construction is crucial.

The Director

Directors are usually involved from around the beginning of a project all the way to, in some cases, the creation of the final print. A film is organized into three critical phases: preproduction, production, and postproduction. *Preproduction* constitutes the planning and preparation—the process of identifying and securing all the elements, both human and material, that will be needed for the film. This includes fine-tuning the script, casting, location scouting, set design, finding props, organizing the shooting into a series of manageable tasks, and whatever else it takes to get into a position to shoot. *Production* includes all the actual shooting. The *director* is usually the key decision-making force in both these stages of a film. Although some directors are also involved in *postproduction*, the editing and all the detailed finishing processes, that aspect is covered in part V.

It is the director's choices, including many of the visual resources presented so far, that drive the rest of the crew. On fictional films, the director is responsible for determining the look of the film, rehearsing and organizing the actors' performances, selecting the setups and all attendant details, and marshaling all forces toward the completion of the material. The director interprets the script in terms of both a theatrical, dramatic interpretation and the story's visual presentation. Actors develop an approach to their characters, and the director must assist them in shaping the performance and creating a consistent characterization. The director is the overriding organizational force within the production of the film, in both the practical day-to-day aspects and the overall conceptual vision of the film.

The Menu

Before discussing scene construction itself, a summary of the visual resources presented so far is in order. **SEE 5-1** Lists such as this risk constant editorializing. On close scrutiny, some of the categories begin to break down, and there are always exceptions to any suggested effect, such as situations in which a technique is successfully played against its common use. However, knowledge of these basics can serve as a starting point for anyone wanting to learn conventional film technique. Their application will eventually appear to be much more wide ranging than many people recognize. Although the content of the shots may be different, certain techniques, such as close-ups, are often consistent from the most adventurous independent production to conventional television product.

Certain patterns start to suggest themselves with these shots. If you want an essentially neutral portrayal, for example, you might choose specific approaches, such as a medium shot, at eye level, with a level camera. Many of the shots of Radio Raheem in Spike Lee's *Do the Right Thing* are from a low angle, but there are several that have even more extreme characteristics. One shot of the character is from a low angle, photographed with a wide-angle lens, and with the camera at an oblique angle. **SEE 5-2**

The wide-angle exaggerates the character's features, and the oblique angle gives the sense of a world out of balance. Whether or not one agrees with the intimidating nature of the combination of these effects, one can appreciate how a shot like this figures into the grand plan of the film. One of the major elements of *Do the Right Thing* is the increasing tension caused by the hot and stifling day on which the action occurs. The shot of Radio Raheem, as well as many other elements of the film, create an atmosphere where everything is distorted and on the edge.

5-1

The menu of the camera resources presented so far

Proxemics	**Camera Movement**	**Lens Perspective and Characteristics**
Long shot	Pan	
Medium shot	Tilt	
Close-up	Dolly	Wide-angle
Camera Angles	Tracking	Normal
Low	Crane, arm, and so on	Telephoto
High	Handheld	Zoom
Eye level	Steadicam	
Bird's-eye view	Aerial	**Focus**
Oblique/level		Shifting focus
Point-of-view		Deep focus
		Shallow focus

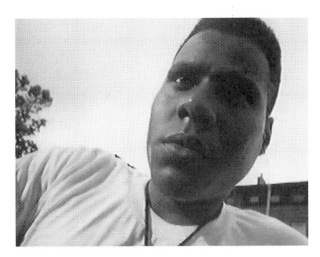

5-2

Oblique, low-angle shot with wide-angle lens exaggerates the character's features and conveys a world out of balance

Bill Nunn in *Do the Right Thing*

Although lists like figure 5-1 can give valuable ideas, these effects should not be treated as a mix-and-match recipe. It is not a matter of, if you want diminishment, you mix two-thirds long shot with one-third high angle.... That approach would most likely be stereotypical and cliché. Rather, the camera should be approached as a meaning-producing instrument. A list like this should never be seen as an end, as something mastered and then ignored. The myriad subtleties continue to be explored more than a century after the first frame of film saw a glimpse of light.

Basic Scene Structure

It is clear from the discussion of shots and other resources that where the camera is placed in relation to the scene plays a central role in guiding how the viewer interprets character and action. A long shot of a character responding to something, for example, does not draw us in as persuasively as the same response in a closer shot. As suggested, the sequence of long shot–medium shot–close-up also represents a process of moving closer to the action, of moving from a random view to much more specific information.

Dramatic Emphasis

The concept of **dramatic emphasis** lies at the heart of narrative filmmaking and can be a critical component of experimental and documentary film as well. Simply stated, this means that the director uses the camera to show us the action in the order and with the amplification that he or she wants. The director *breaks down the scene* into an interrelationship of dramatic perspectives (shots) that focus viewer attention on specific information, characters, dialogue, action, and so on.

Alfred Hitchcock's *Notorious* has many remarkable sequences, but one of its more subtle scenes provides a clear example of this concept. **SEE 5-3** The scene takes place about one-quarter of the way into the film and involves Alicia (Ingrid Bergman) trying to have a discussion with an unresponsive suitor, Dev (Cary Grant). Struggling with a shady past, Alicia is trying to start over—making an insult Dev delivers in the middle of this scene all the more humiliating. The entire beginning of the scene is played in a *two-shot*, so named because it shows two people from roughly the waist up. The timing of the cut to the close-up is key to the scene's effect. The exact positioning of the cut is indicated by the horizontal line, right at the end of Dev's line of dialogue, and the camera subtly emphasizes the emotional deflation visible in Bergman's face.

5-3

Dramatic emphasis—when the camera shows the action in the order and with the emphasis that the director wants—lies at the heart of narrative filmmaking

Ingrid Bergman and Cary Grant in *Notorious*

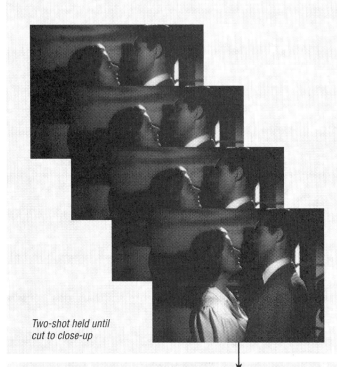

Two-shot held until cut to close-up

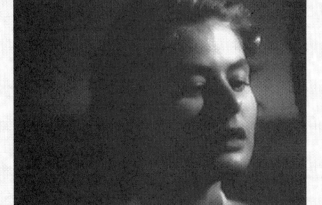

ALICIA

I wonder if it is too cold out here. Maybe we should eat inside.

She kisses him.

Hasn't something like this happened before? What's the matter? Don't look so tense. Troubles? Well, handsome, I think you'd better tell mama what's going on. All this secrecy is going to ruin my little dinner.

Pause.

Come on, Mr. D, what is darkening your brow?

DEV

After dinner.

ALICIA

No, now. Look, I'll make it easy for you. The time has come when you must tell me that you have a wife and two adorable children and this madness between us can't go on any longer.

DEV

I bet you've heard that line often enough.

ALICIA

Right below the belt every time. That isn't fair, Dev.

The two-shot is played out for an unusually long period of time—almost forty-five seconds. Some argument could be made that the director could have broken the scene down into other shots to emphasize Grant's taciturn response or Bergman's attempt to draw him out. And yet, the choice of playing this part of the scene in a two-shot has an unquestionable logic to it. There is nothing occurring that cries out for emphasis. It is just a simple exchange of dialogue, and a cut is not necessary until the intensity of the interchange increases. When the cut finally does come, its logic is inescapable. If anything, cutting the lengthy two-shot would dilute the impact of the cut when it finally does come.

You need not look far to see examples of scenes that use shot selection for dramatic emphasis. Simply turn on the television and watch any episodic television program, news program, talk show, or commercial. The technique is pervasive. In the hands of a competent craftsperson, the approach is so natural to the logic of the scene that we barely notice it. Indeed, most commercial films are purposely designed so that the editing—how the scenes are constructed—is virtually invisible.

Master Scene Technique

As suggested, the sequence of LS-MS-CU represents a common movement from random, general information to very specific information. Scenes often begin with a relatively random long shot, and then the focus becomes tighter and more specific. In most cases, a wide view of the whole scene is shot first, and then the shooting is broken down into medium shots and close-ups. This process has a variety of permutations and goes under several different names, but it is generally referred to as *master scene technique*. This is the process of breaking down scenes into their constituent elements. Elements are simply those things—people, objects, places—that are key aspects of the scene being shot. If a scene has two characters talking, there are two elements. If they are arguing over the restaurant check in front of them, the check might become a third element. The elements are then presented in the groupings and the order that the director desires to create dramatic and engaging scenes. Though there were others experimenting at the same time, the early filmmaker D. W. Griffith is generally credited with pioneering this concept.

Master scene technique is an approach in which the director stages the scene essentially as it would be staged in a theater. All or part of the scene is shot in a *master shot*—a shot in which all, or most, of the elements are presented together. This shot is also called, more descriptively, an *establishing shot*, because it establishes the space in which the scene is occurring, where the characters are in relationship to each other, any important objects that may be present, and so on. The director then stages the scene many more times, only shooting it in a variety of MS and CU shots. Medium shots convey more-specific information but not with the emphasis or intensity that can be achieved with the close-up. Directors will tell you that they generally save close-ups for the most intense part of an individual scene—the climax. The material is then given to an editor who cuts it into an effective sequence.

This method has an almost factorylike approach and, in the heyday of the Hollywood studio system—the 1920s through the 1950s—films were literally ground out on an assembly line. One production unit at Warner Brothers even referred to itself as the "Sausage Factory." Directors who had some clout, or who worked on such low-budget films that no one paid much attention to them, were able to make films with some individual character, but the assembly-line approach influenced virtually all films. There is, after all, a certain logic to this progression of moving closer to a subject. As with so many other techniques in the Hollywood approach, this is a natural replication of human perceptual experience. When we are curious about something, we move closer to it.

This method has been recognized under a variety of different names, such as invisible editing, continuity style, classical Hollywood style, and master shot discipline, among others. By whatever name, the approach was, and still is, standard operating procedure in American film. Different and more adventurous styles have been experimented with, particularly in the 1960s and 1970s, but the approach still holds profound influence.

5-4

Shot/reverse shot involves shooting all of person A's dialogue from setup #1, then moving the camera to setup #2 and shooting all of person B's dialogue

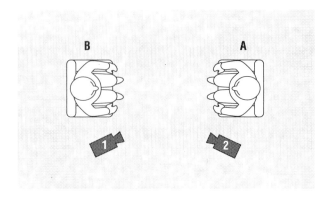

Shot/Reverse Shot

In its simplest and most common manifestation, called *shot/reverse shot*, master scene technique provides an easy way to handle a conversation between two or more characters. Once pointed out, it is an approach familiar to everyone, particularly to those who watch television interview programs such as "60 Minutes." It is the bread-and-butter of thousands of movies and countless television shows. The concept of shot/reverse shot is not so much a theoretical approach as it is an expansion on the previous two topics.

Quite simply, shot/reverse shot involves shooting all of person A's dialogue from setup #1 and then picking up the camera and moving it to setup #2—called the *reverse shot*—and shooting all of person B's dialogue. **SEE 5-4** The results are then intercut as a simple back-and-forth exchange of dialogue. We have a shot of person A saying a line of dialogue and then a shot of person B responding. To keep things visually interesting, other types of shots are worked in, such as an *over-the-shoulder (OTS)* shot (done over a character's shoulder), or a two-shot.

The usefulness of this basic approach in shooting interviews is obvious. Several hours of an interview with person A are shot. When the interview is over, the subject is excused and the camera is moved to the reverse shot (setup #2). Several minutes of the interviewer (person B) nodding in assent (or maybe staring blankly in disbelief) are then shot. The inevitable dull interludes in the actual conversation can simply be cut out in the editing, the resulting jump in the footage covered with a shot of the interviewer responding to what is being said. This method of shooting allows the footage to be manipulated into the desired order and length. This flexibility can also extend to manipulating the context and content of what is said. Although many films, from Orson Welles's *Citizen Kane* to the work of Robert Altman, try to find more adventurous approaches, shot/reverse shot remains a common method of delivering dialogue.

Although they are relatively straightforward to describe, these techniques—master scene technique, dramatic emphasis, and shot/reverse shot—require practical experience to truly understand and control. Moreover, it is important to recognize the function they serve. These techniques are essentially tools that enable you to communicate narrative information clearly and effectively. Certainly, one wants to find a method of presentation that is more daring than the standard way of doing things, but this remains the basis—the starting point—for much visual storytelling. On occasion, a more adventurous shot selection may overcomplicate material that demands a straightforward presentation. These techniques also serve a purpose common to most narrative art forms: they start with a general view of things and move to a closer, more specific perspective of the subject.

A Typical Scene

In the majority of films, scenes are included because they accomplish a narrative goal, there usually being at least one central idea that a scene is trying to convey. Sometimes a scene serves to introduce a character; sometimes it delivers a subtle piece of information that gives a clue to character and motivation. Sometimes the scene is a key piece of action or information; sometimes it just gets us from here to there in the story or establishes some kind of mood or atmosphere. The scene is always there to drive the story forward in some fashion. As a director, you must try to discern what the purpose of each scene is and focus on conveying that purpose. Once the goal is determined, many of the resources listed in the menu are employed to achieve that end. Remember that this is still a partial list, one limited to camera resources at that. There are other elements that aid a scene in accomplishing its purpose—lighting, sound, and design being major ones.

Although it is difficult to call it typical, Alfred Hitchcock's *Vertigo* has a brief, almost wordless scene in a museum that typifies some of these concepts. Scottie (James Stewart), a detective, has followed Madeleine (Kim Novak) to a museum, where he finds her sitting on a bench, staring at a painting. Scottie had been asked to follow Madeleine by her husband, who is concerned that she believes she is possessed by a long-dead relative named Carlotta Valdes. As Madeleine sits in the museum oblivious to Scottie's presence, he quietly moves behind her to observe her actions. He notices that she has brought a bouquet of flowers just like the one in the painting. He also notices that her hair is put up in a bun just like the woman in the painting. Scottie moves out of the gallery and finds a museum guard, who tells him that the painting is titled "Portrait of Carlotta."

In analyzing the scene, it is easy to delineate some of the things that it is attempting to accomplish on a narrative level. Although there are many other areas that could be discussed on both a formal and content level, we can determine a minimum of four goals that the scene is attempting to convey to the audience:

1. Madeleine is transfixed, if not unhealthily obsessed, by the person in the painting.

2. There is a correlation between the flowers that she has brought and the flowers in the painting.

3. There is a correlation between the bun in her hair and the bun in the painting.

4. The portrait is of the woman who is supposed to have taken possession of Madeleine.

What are the elements?

- Scottie
- Madeleine
- The painting
- The flowers on the bench
- The flowers in the painting
- The bun in Madeleine's hair
- The bun in the painting
- The museum guard

5-5

The purpose of a typical scene is to accomplish a narrative goal—to convey an idea
or in some fashion drive the story forward

Alfred Hitchcock's *Vertigo*

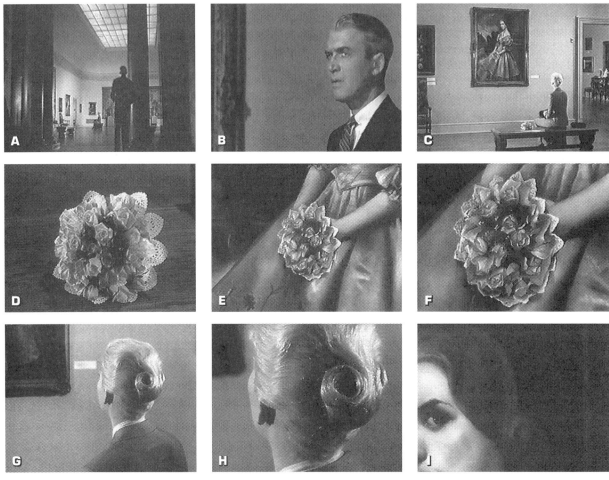

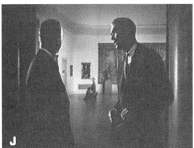

How does Hitchcock emphasize these elements so that the simple associations in the scene are communicated to the viewer? Think strategies. The following discussion leaves out some shots, reproducing just those that aid in accomplishing the scene's central purpose.

The scene starts with a master shot that establishes the spatial relationships. **SEE 5-5A** Scottie is in the foreground observing Madeleine in the background. She is sitting alone, staring at a single painting. Although the museum gallery itself has relatively even lighting, Scottie stands outside the gallery in the darkness. The lighting has an eerie, atmospheric feel, and the shot is from a low angle that makes the space appear cavernous and overwhelming.

Scottie moves behind Madeleine. The film then cuts between elements associated with Madeleine and shots of Scottie studying all the details of the setting. These shots have Scottie in a medium shot, but the MCU represented here is used when he starts to grasp the association between Madeleine and the painting. **SEE 5-5B**

From Scottie's position, we see what amounts to a second master shot—Madeleine, the painting, and all the pertinent elements. **SEE 5-5C** It is also a point-of-view shot from Scottie's perspective. It establishes all the important details more specifically than the original master shot, although they still remain undifferentiated. It is going to be the job of the closer shots to emphasize what is important. The film cuts back to Scottie as he notices the flowers on the bench (figure 5-5B). It then cuts to a close-up of Scottie's view of the flowers on the bench. **SEE 5-5D** The camera cranes up to a close-up of the flowers in the picture. **SEE 5-5E & 5-5F**

After an MS of Scottie (figure 5-5B), we see Scottie's point of view of the back of Madeleine's head. **SEE 5-5G** The camera then dollies in to a close-up of a bun in her hair, the viewer being given a general view of Madeleine with the camera being pushed into the detail that the director wants us to see as significant. **SEE 5-5H** The camera then moves up to the same detail, a bun in the hair, in the painting. **SEE 5-5I** This is essentially the same presentation that occurred with the flowers, and the associations between the two hairstyles are thus strongly emphasized. Scottie exits to a shot similar to the first master and speaks to the museum guard. **SEE 5-5J**

The relationship between Madeleine and the painting is very carefully emphasized, so the viewer's awareness of the connection is unavoidable. As a director, you have to ascertain the key things that the scene is attempting to accomplish and then determine a strategy for emphasizing them. Like the crane shot in *Notorious,* both of these big crane shots from *Vertigo* are technically complicated. The entire scene is a little less than two minutes long. It is reported that it, along with another even briefer scene that takes place in the same space, took four days to shoot.

The idea of the presentation of shots and scenes requiring some internal logic bears repeating. There is a certain rightness to a close shot of Ingrid Bergman at a specific point in *Notorious.* There is a rightness to using a low-angle shot of Radio Raheem in *Do the Right Thing.* The determining factors in choosing a specific shot are the context within which it is presented and the greater structure of shots in which the single shot participates. The rightness of the individual part must serve the coherence of the whole.

Continuity

The director of the film is responsible for the film's style and the way the camera narrates the story line. There are also a number of general organizing principles that influence shot selection and general scene construction. Style in American film has largely been subservient to the goal of presenting seamless and involving stories that, at least in their parts, are portrayed as unfolding in real time. Scenes are put together in such a way that their construction—the shot selection, the editing—goes largely unnoticed by the viewer. In film criticism, this has most aptly been referred to as invisible editing.

A substantial part of this approach is based on *continuity shooting*—the creation of shots that when cut together represent continuous action. The style employs both story structures and formal elements that do not deviate substantially from realistic portrayals of events. Although this style has indeed been pervasive, other traditions have evolved that either present alternatives or, in many cases, are conscious assaults on the ideological assumptions of this dominant approach. The remainder of this chapter explores some of the underlying principles of continuity shooting.

The general application of the concept of continuity in film is familiar to most viewers. It is most noticeable in scenes where it is lacking—sequences where the action does not match from shot to shot. For example, in one shot a character has on a tie; in the next shot, the tie is missing and the character's shirt is casually unbuttoned. In one shot, a character reaches for a drink with her right hand; in the next, she picks up the drink with her left hand. In a master shot, there is a full glass of beer on a table; in the medium shot, it is empty. The mistake reaches comical proportions when the master shows the glass full again. Some of the mistakes are so obvious that it seems unthinkable that someone could have missed the problem. But, during the lengthy delays between setups and the press of never-ending competing demands, elements are easily shifted, lost track of, and mislaid.

These examples are common things that most observant viewers have noticed at some time or another. However, *shooting in continuity* has a broader definition that has wide-ranging implications for the way elements have to be monitored while shooting a scene: When you are shooting in continuity, you are creating a real-time relationship between the shots. Films are not even shot in order, much less in real time. A scene that takes several minutes of screen time could easily have taken a day or more to shoot. Shooting in continuity means you are creating pieces of film that will later be cut together in such a way as to suggest that what the viewer is seeing is occurring in real time.

Continuity editing is dependent on a very common type of cut, the match cut. A *match cut* is simply a cut in which the action matches from one camera angle to the next. If a person is going out of a door, he or she starts to open the door in one shot, and the next shot picks up the action at the exact point, from the opposite side of the door. In a cut from a long shot of someone sitting down in a chair to a closer shot, the action in the two pieces should match. This is, of course, both a shooting and an editing decision. You must have the plan in mind when you are shooting, but the actual matching of the action occurs when cutting the shots together.

The opposite of a match cut is a jump cut, something that was virtually heretical in the golden age of the Hollywood studio system. The *jump cut* is a cut between shots in which there is a jump in time—an *ellipsis*—between the shots. In his landmark film *Breathless* (1959), French director Jean-Luc Godard incorporated the jump cut into a structure that both made narrative sense and subverted dominant stylistic approaches. In this formally radical approach, when Godard wanted to get a character from one side of town to another, he simply cut him from one place to the other. When he wanted to get from one part of a conversation to another, he simply cut out all the intermediate material. The result is that characters jump from one place to another, creating a jumbled, chaotic sense of reality. These are cuts that draw attention to themselves and, by extension, to the process of making a film. Godard's film openly subverted the conventional approach, giving the viewer a highly subjective representation of space and action. American films still attempt to create a relatively seamless sense of real time and real space, but Godard's influence has had a profound impact on everything from conventional product to commercials to music videos.

Continuity Shooting

Shooting out of sequence requires careful attention to detail in order to ensure that all the elements of a scene remain consistent from shot to shot. Something shot early in the morning may have to be matched with something you are going to shoot late in the afternoon. Even if you are doing shots relatively close together, you can run into problems. A student film from several years ago had an example of this. The film had a simple sequence of a woman entering a house. The student put the camera outside to shoot the first part of the movement. When that shot was completed, he moved the camera indoors to do the match shot of the completion of the entrance. The actor sat down to wait and, as it was a bright, sunny day, put on her sunglasses. When the next shot was done, she had forgotten to take off the sunglasses. One can appreciate the sinking feeling the student had on getting the film back and seeing the mistake which, as glaring as it was, would be noticed by most viewers.

In the old days, continuity was monitored by the "scriptgirl"—a hopelessly outdated credit. Now, the continuity person is called a *script supervisor*. Prop people, makeup artists, and set dressers are usually enlisted to help ensure that the appropriate elements are in the frame. Continuity used to be monitored by making rough sketches and detailed notes describing the action, the elements within the frame, and the position of performers. Although sketches and notes are still essential, Polaroid cameras had a big impact on how continuity was accomplished. The script supervisor could produce an instant representation of how all the elements within a frame were arranged. The use of Polaroids quickly became commonplace, and they are still used extensively, particularly in the costume and makeup departments. Their sole drawback is that they can represent only individual moments within larger movements, and their sound and frequently needed flash make them unusable during takes.

In recent years, Polaroids have been replaced with a virtually foolproof method—the video assist. The *video assist* is a tiny video pickup device mounted in the viewing system of the film camera. It gives a video record of the shot, albeit not a particularly high-quality representation. With it, the script supervisor can go back to check where specific movements occurred in relationship to dialogue and action or to find the specific positioning within a frame. This can be time-consuming, however, if the script supervisor and video assist person have to roll through a substantial amount of tape to find what they need. If other people feel the need to get involved, the whole set can come to a standstill, and pretty soon everyone is standing around drinking coffee and watching the monitor. Nevertheless, the use of video assist on sets is becoming prevalent, although the equipment and the people to operate it can be beyond the financial means of most low-budget films. On small crews, often there is no specific person responsible for continuity, in which case the task usually falls to other key personnel, such as the director or cinematographer.

Types of Continuity

The script supervisor is actually involved in only a few types of continuity. Some elements, such as lighting, are so specialized that they are left to their respective departments. The following categories of continuity are just general areas, rather than rigid classifications that have been defined and elaborated on over the years.

Action   The position of performers and other moving elements within the frame is called action continuity. This refers to where a subject is in movement, as opposed to what he is wearing or how props are arranged in a scene. When the goal is to match actions between closer and longer shots, the position of the actor on the set and how he is moving must be relatively consistent.

If an actor says his line *before* sitting down in the master shot but says it *after* he sits down in the medium, the two shots will be uncuttable. If he is scratching his chin in the medium but has his hands at his side in the master, the pieces again will be uncuttable. This is always a difficult issue because, although you have to communicate to the actors the need for continuity so their actions match between setups, you also do not want to inhibit them. Experienced professionals are generally very knowledgeable about the requirements of the medium. For nonprofessionals, it can be quite disconcerting.

Props, costume, and makeup   Shooting a short scene can easily take a day or more. Invariably elements are moved around as you light, and objects are moved to balance compositions. Costumes and makeup also require constant attention. Responsibility for the consistency of these elements is shared by the script supervisor and the crew members in the respective departments.

Apparently simple things such as candlelight can drive the script supervisor to distraction. Over the course of a shoot, candles will have to be carefully controlled so they remain consistent. If the candles are allowed to burn down, they may not match from the beginning of the scene to the end. A script supervisor would probably ask the prop person to bring a substantial number of extra candles. They may even burn some candles to certain lengths the night before, so they can substitute specific lengths. Assuming the standard delays between takes and setups, the candles might have to be blown out between shots. This is no problem, except it necessitates lighting them again. Since many smaller projects do not have a continuity person, or have one who has other responsibilities, something like this can easily be overlooked.

Historical   Particularly important in period pieces, historical continuity refers to checking that all elements are historically accurate to the context of the film. People reading printed books in a version of Chaucer's *The Canterbury Tales* would be inappropriate; similarly television antennas in a film set in the Civil War would be out of place. Many films play fast and loose with this. You will often hear of films including a song or some other element that was created after their action occurs. This is often a matter of research, the responsibility for which can fall on a number of different shoulders. For a song, it may fall to the screenwriter or, if the song's inclusion is an editorial decision, the film's postproduction team. For elements in the frame, the research may often fall to people in the ***art department***, an umbrella term for everyone involved in the design elements of the image. Extensive researching abilities may be part of the job description for many crew positions, again particularly for period pieces.

As with everything, purposefully breaking the conventions can create interesting results. Alex Cox's *Walker* (1988) is set in 1850 Nicaragua, with the title character installing himself as the imperialist president of the war-torn country. To emphasize parallels to modern events, the film includes such historical impossibilities as Walker and his men being saved by army helicopters, images that are eerily reminiscent of the fall of Saigon in 1975. There are many other improbable elements, including a computer-outfitted command center and Walker's pride in making the cover of *Time* magazine. The purpose is clearly to create parallels with modern events and break with realistic modes of historical interpretation. However, this type of experiment is so artificial and specific that it is used very infrequently.

As you watch films more carefully, you will notice unintentional historical continuity errors with some frequency. One of director Anthony Mann's great westerns, *The Far Country* (1955), has jet trails in the sky above scenes supposedly occurring in the 1880s. The more actual film production experience you get, the more you realize that things like this are usually not mistakes but rather the unavoidable compromises one must make when under time and budgetary constraints. Perhaps they were losing the light and were forced to shoot despite the conditions. The more you know, the more you may be amazed that films get made at all! The production of a film is such a complex tangle of marshaling elements to occur at just the right time that you are often forced to work, even when you do not have everything you want in place.

Lighting   Matching will be a problem if shots that are to be cut together look different in terms of the color and quality of the light. This issue is often referred to as ***photographic consistency***, and it will drive many of the technical considerations you need to be concerned with while shooting. The script supervisor is generally not involved in lighting continuity issues, other than occasionally taking notes for the director of photography (DP).

Continuity is one concern that delineates motion picture photography from still photography. Still photography is usually not sequential in its presentation. Even if a still photographer is attempting to create some kind of photo montage, the images are nevertheless presented as discrete entities, and anything but major differences in lighting is not going to be noticed. In film, however, if you want the illusion of shots occurring in real time, the quality and intensity of light must match from shot to shot.

Still photographers who visit film sets are often amazed at the complexity of the lighting approach. They invariably suggest that a simpler approach might work, until they are made aware of the kinds of matching that are being attempted. Even then, some cannot grasp the difference. Still photographers usually have extensive control in the printing process, including dodging specific elements or areas of the image and manipulating exposure and processing times. When they are shooting, if they just get a decent negative, they can create the kind of product they want. Although there is some room for image manipulation in film, these discriminations can generally be applied only to the whole shot and the entire frame. *It is imperative that you work out all matching issues when you are shooting.*

One story may give some sense of the kind of hoops you have to jump through in this regard: I was once working on an exterior shoot in a midwestern state on one of those days that people who forecast the weather like to call "partly sunny"— an ambiguous term that leaves up to question whether there are going to be more clouds or more sun. This was definitely a "more clouds" day, weather that reminds one why filmmakers prefer the largely cloudless skies of southern California. It was a relatively simple scene that the ***production manager (PM),*** the person responsible for all scheduling, had budgeted the morning for shooting with the intent of shooting another scene in the afternoon. The problem in such a situation is that the quality and intensity of light between the sunny and the cloudy periods do not match. The scene would have proved uncuttable had we attempted to shoot under both conditions. The three- or four-hour shoot became a daylong ordeal in which a succession of hapless souls tried to estimate, with limited success, how much sunshine we were going to be blessed with at any given time. The production manager was tearing her hair out because the afternoon shoot, which was logistically complicated, had to be canceled and rescheduled while a large number of costly elements (talent, extras, props, and the like) cooled their heels.

If it had been a bigger shoot, we probably would have had the resources to overcome our difficulties. There are lights that, as the manufacturers love to boast, "outshine the sun at twenty paces." But our options were limited and we spent substantial time just waiting. Natural light has a nasty habit of changing quite frequently. Artificial light requires a level of control that can come only with experience.

Sound   This refers to creating a sound track that is consistent, with no big shifts in either the volume or the quality of the recorded sounds. Although the location recordings must be as consistent and high quality as possible, sound continuity is largely an editorial issue. Many imperfections can be covered or fixed, either during the editing process or when mixing the final sound track in the studio.

Sound can also have implications for historical continuity. When doing period pieces, modern sounds can present problems. The sound mixer on a film set in the 1840s, for example, shot about forty yards from a major highway and a half mile from a private airport, had to jump through many hoops to get usable sound.

Performance   With action being shot from so many setups, performance must be standardized so that it matches between camera angles. This is generally not a problem on larger productions, where most actors, as well as the director, are experienced professionals. But on films where you may be working with nonprofessionals, it can be a big issue, both in terms of what a performer can produce and how an inexperienced director evaluates that performance. Before shooting, details of a performance—the level and tone—should be completely worked out between the talent and the director. A director who asks for anything different between takes can cause enormous editing problems. Although this is not the script supervisor's domain, a good one will recognize glaring errors.

I had one job working with an inexperienced director who was directing a very emotional performance from an untrained actor, a bad mix if there ever was one. He was not getting from her what he wanted, but time constraints forced us to start shooting anyway. We did several takes of the master shot of one of the actor's long speeches, then moved in for medium shots and close-ups. Between setups, the director decided that her performance was too unrestrained in the master, so he asked the actor for less. The next time he got too little, so he asked for more. He got too much. He was trying to shape the performance as we were shooting, and the resulting footage proved uncuttable. The editor was eventually forced to play the whole thing in master, an option that suited neither the scene nor the shape of the film. If this kind of mistake were made on a larger project, the eventual outcome would probably be a reshoot (and people would be fired). On smaller budgets, this option does not always exist.

Spatial continuity   This refers to creating an understandable sense of space, and is the focus of the following section.

The Line

A director friend likes to call the line "the central organizing principle" of narrative cinema. The *line*, also called the *180-degree rule* or the *axis of action*, refers to a principle used to create an understandable sense of the space in which the action is occurring.

The line is relatively easy to understand on a superficial level, but its role in production is something that takes on-set experience to truly understand. Simply stated, the rule says that if shooting is begun on one side of an action, it must stay on that side. If the camera jumps to the other side of the action, that is, crosses the line, the sense of an understandable and continuous space can be disrupted. Before doing storyboards or blocking the action for the camera, this line is drawn in the shooting space. This rule has broken down somewhat in recent years, but if the goal is to create a logical and continuous sense of space, application of the concept of the line is a must. As with anything painted with such a broad stroke, there are exceptions, but they are fewer than might be expected. Even if a distorted sense of space is desired, a knowledge of the line's effect is still necessary.

The line is generally based on one of two factors: sightlines or direction of action.

Sightlines

With *sightlines*, the line is created by drawing a straight line that represents a character's direction of vision. The line is based on the sightlines of the character who is on camera and can change as his or her direction of view changes. Often the line is drawn between two people in conversation, though it applies to an individual character watching an action as well as to multiple-character situations.

If you start on one side of the sightlines between two characters, you must stay on that side. If you use a setup from the other side of the line, the characters will not appear to be looking at each other.

If you start shooting from setup #1, the rest of the setups should be on that side of the sightlines. **SEE 5-6** If you cut to anything on the setup #2 side, you will have problems with matching sightlines, and the characters will appear to be looking at some unseen third space. It does not make any difference on which side of the sightlines you start. That should be an aesthetic determination based on what you want to see in the background, which profile of the performers you want to film, and anticipated character movement. But once you have started on one side, you have to stay on that side.

This can be difficult to conceptualize, so taking the most extreme example should make it easier to understand. In this example, setup #1 is at a right angle to person A, and setup #2 is at a right angle to person B on the opposite side of the line. **SEE 5-7**

5-6

The "line" refers to a principle used to create an understandable space in which the action is occurring

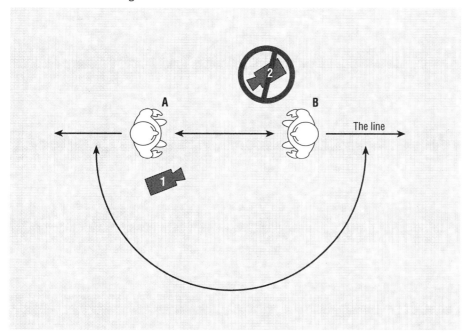

5-7

Mismatched camera positions help illustrate the concept of the line

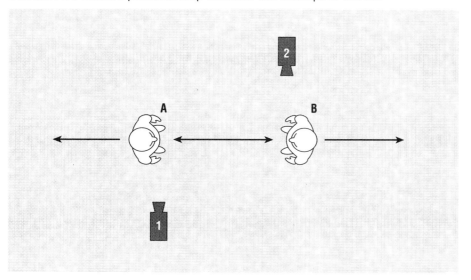

The key to understanding this is to consider the direction that the character will be looking in the resulting film. If we can transpose the shot from setup #1 to see how it would look on the screen, the character would be looking screen-right. **SEE 5-8**

If the same thing is done with setup #2, which way would the character be looking? This may be more difficult to visualize, but if we pull the camera around while moving the character with it, the direction can be determined. **SEE 5-9** Again, the character would be looking screen-right.

The problem comes when we attempt to cut the two pieces together. **SEE 5-10** It appears as though person A is talking to the back of person B's head. If the angles chosen are less extreme than in this example, the problem still remains. This is more difficult to visualize, but characters will appear to be looking at some abstracted third space. Though audiences will not point to the screen and say, "Look, they crossed the line," on an unconscious level it will be difficult to discern a logical space, that is, understand where the characters are in relationship to each other and the space. This confusion, this sense that something is wrong with the scene, will disrupt viewer involvement with the drama.

5-8

The subject from setup #1 is looking frame-right

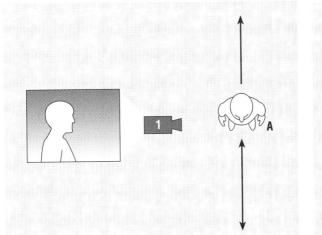

5-9

The subject from setup #2 is also looking frame-right

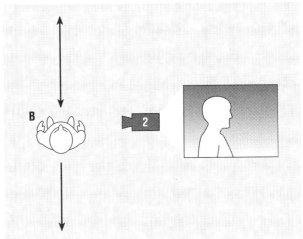

5-10

The characters do not appear to be looking at each other

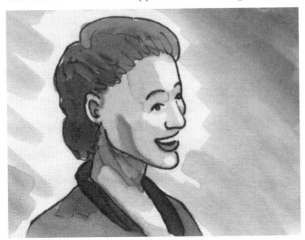
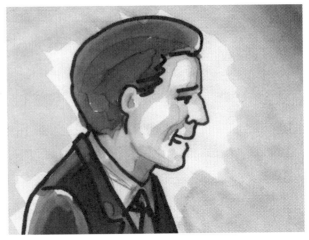

Clearly, there are many filmmakers who *want* to disrupt this seamless, unimpeded involvement. Or they wish to intentionally create a confused sense of space and action. If you want to deliberately create a disrupted sense of space, you must understand the application of the line just as clearly as when you want a conventional representation of the space. In many situations, a confused sense of space does not serve the narrative context, even if what you are doing is unconventional. The director who calls the line "the central organizing principle" of narrative cinema is no dull conventionalist. He has won international awards for some odd and unconventional stories. But he does not want confusion over spatial relationships to distract the viewer's attention from the action of his films. Planning out the entire scene in terms of setup, character position, and the line is a necessary component of scene construction.

Character movement complicates the line in regard to sightlines, although the line simply changes as a character's sightlines change. Sightlines also become more complicated when there are more than two characters. Usually, when filming a conversation involving multiple characters, one should try to simply stay to one side of the action or the other.

Action

In terms of action, the concept of the line is even more clear. If you film a car driving down the street from its right side, it will be moving from left to right in the resulting shot. If you then cross the street and film the same car continuing in the same direction, it will be moving from right to left in the resulting shot. When you try to cut the two pieces together, the car will appear to have changed directions. **SEE 5-11**

D. W. Griffith certainly understood this idea by the time of *Birth of a Nation.* The Civil War battle scenes would have been virtually incomprehensible without following this rule. In one sequence, the Confederate troops charge the Union lines. Because all setups are to the right of the charge, the Confederate troops are always

5-11

Crossing the line in an action shot causes the car to appear to have changed direction

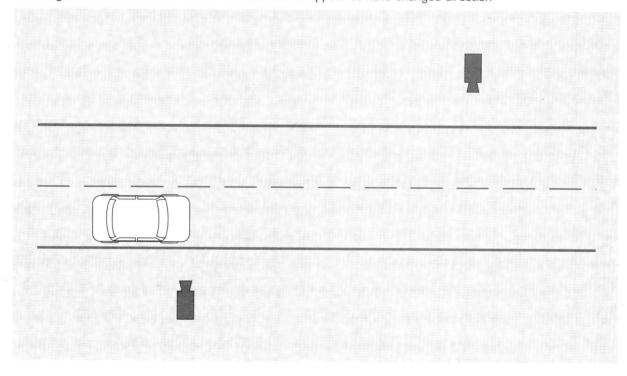

moving from left to right. **SEE 5-12** However, what would happen if Griffith had tried to mix in some setups from the left side of the Confederate charge? The Confederate troops would move from right to left. **SEE 5-13** Clearly, they would look like they were retreating when intercut with shots from the other side. When shooting any action that depends on a continuous sense of direction, from battle scenes to football games, the line must be a chief consideration.

5-12

Setup showing action moving left to right

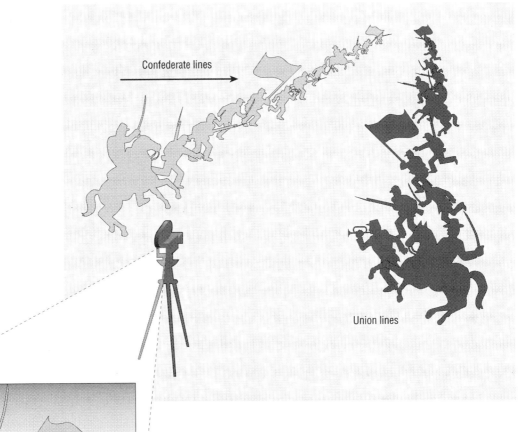

Confederate lines

Union lines

5-13

Crossing the line reverses the action

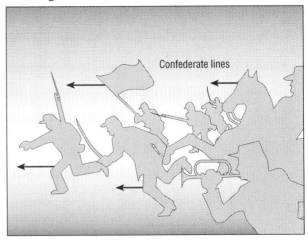

Confederate lines

Conceptual Errors

Other than disregarding the line altogether, the biggest mistake beginning filmmakers make is thinking that the line is from the camera to a character, when it is actually between one character and another. As a character's sightlines change, the line changes. If you are shooting person A from setup #1, and she looks from person B to person C, the line shifts across the camera with her sightlines. **SEE 5-14** Whereas setup #2 would have been unacceptable previously, it is now perfectly within bounds. If person A returns her view to person B, you have effectively made a shift to the left side of the conversation.

Music videos have had a tremendous impact on many of these "rules" of film construction. Many music videos do not have a clearly thought-out strategy toward many issues such as the line, nor should they. Despite this, there are still examples of the 180-degree rule being broken that clearly do not work. An editor friend recently showed me a video that eventually got some play on MTV which, were it not for video's inherent ability to manipulate the image, would have included a very disruptive *line jump*. **SEE 5-15**

The video had a sequence of shots of a grave digger wielding a pickax. The director had made one of the most basic conceptual errors possible. He shot the full shot of the grave digger from one side of the action (setup #1), then, inexplicably, he shot a close-up of the pickax gliding through the frame in slow motion from the other side of the action (setup #2). With an action of this nature, it is very easy to figure out what the line is. The direction of the motion matches the sightlines, and the line is the plane of the motion of the pickax. Imagine these two pieces cut together, and you can get a sense of how incongruous some simple line jumps look. The motion of the pickax is in an arc from left to right in the first shot and is an arc from right to left in the second shot. **SEE 5-16** The scene was salvaged only because it is possible, with the appropriate high-end video gear, to flip the video image

5-14

As a character's sightlines change, the line changes

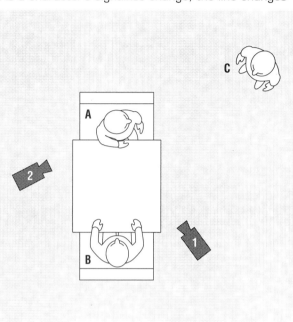

5-15

Music video setup

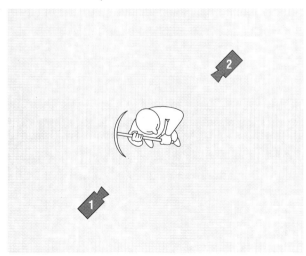

5-16

Line jump results in the ax swinging from the other side of the action

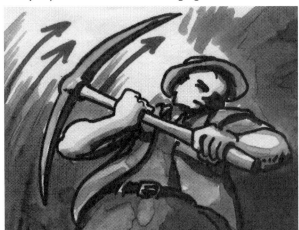 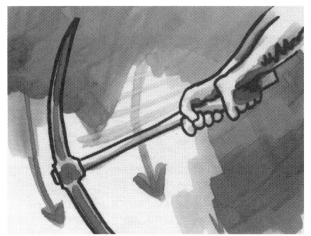

side-to-side, much in the same way as with many computer graphics software programs. Unaltered, though, these two pieces do not fit together except as a disjointed representation of a simple movement.

After several sessions of having the line drilled into him, one student was gloating about finding a line jump in Nicholas Ray's *Rebel Without a Cause* (1955). Occasional line jumps are found in classical-era Hollywood films. Sometimes they appear to be mistakes that could not be fixed. Other times they simply represent the director avoiding complicated steps to reposition the camera, assuming the audience will be able to follow the action. Indeed, when the space is straightforward or innately understood—a baseball field is a good example—certain "leaps of faith" can be taken with the camera. Some line jumps are simply not a big problem. It may be just as well to brazen your way across, being more efficient than going through some fancy, schematic footwork to cross over. There are other line jumps, however, that cause noticeable breaks in continuity.

Sometimes line jumps can be part of a greater plan; other times they are just irreversible mistakes in conception with which one must live. There are films that owe their informal effect to a complete or partial disregard for the line. A line jump is essentially a jump cut, and, just as Godard employed jumps in time in *Breathless*, disruptions of conventional space can create specific effects, most notably confusion or chaos. If jumps are part of an organized approach, they can be effective. If they are not, they look like mistakes. At the other extreme is a film like Milos Foreman's *Amadeus*, which is so dependent on emphasizing Salieri's response to Mozart's actions—on Salieri watching Mozart—that it is virtually immaculate in terms of the line. Whatever the approach, the line must be clearly understood to achieve desired spatial effects.

Crossing the Line

There will be situations in which you need to start a scene on one side of the line and at some point shoot action from the other side. Reasons for this can range from requiring different elements in the background to needing to completely change the area in which the action is occurring. Once you have established the position on one side of the line, there are a number of accepted ways of getting to other parts of the shooting space. All such transitions should be preplanned. A director should not capriciously or arbitrarily decide while filming that he wants to get to the other side of the line or, worse yet, find that he suddenly needs to be on the other side because of poor planning. If the director, cinematographer, and script supervisor are standing around scratching their heads with one hand and drawing imaginary lines on the floor with the other, you know someone has made a mistake. As with everything, there should be a reason why particular decisions are being made.

Many of these line-crossing solutions are not particularly good ones, which is another reason for careful planning. The solutions come with their own baggage: they all demand some kind of narrative justification. To a certain extent, they are included here to reinforce the importance of thinking out the line as well as to explore further complications.

Cutaway   One way to get to the other side of the line is to employ a cutaway. A *cutaway* is just what its name implies—a shot that the editor can cut away to. If you are in the middle of a scene, you can cut away to some unrelated element— a dog under the table, a child smiling, clouds passing in front of the moon, or a clock tower chiming midnight. Because the space has been disrupted, you then can return to whatever side of the line you wish. Creating and employing cutaways can be both a shooting and an editorial decision. Directors shoot cutaways to protect themselves and ensure that the editors will have enough material to make the scene work. Editors employ them when they encounter difficulties, such as continuity, the line, poor camera work, and so on, while cutting the scene. When a scene is just not working and there is no material to fix the problem, it may be necessary to go back and shoot some cutaways if complete reshooting is not possible.

The examples of cutaways are purposefully cliché. "The dog under the table" shot is a standing joke among directors and editors. When animals or children are around, insecure directors will often shoot some footage of them attentively watching the action. If there are any problems in the cutting, the editor can simply cut away to the dog to get out of it. It is so obviously a scene-repair shot, or an attempt at cuteness, that it is used only at risk of peer ridicule.

This approach clearly has more drawbacks than its potential for cliché employment. Unwarranted interruptions may ruin the pace of a scene, deflect viewer attention from important elements, or unnecessarily mislead the viewer as to the direction of the scene. They tend to sidetrack the internal logic of how a scene builds to its climax.

Dolly   Another way to cross the line is simply to dolly around to the other side. When the camera is on one side of two characters' sightlines, you dolly the camera behind one of the characters. It is generally unwise to dolly *through* the sightlines, as a character will have to look at or near the camera. It is also somewhat like walking between two people who are talking, an awkward action in most circumstances. The major drawback to using the dolly in this manner is that it must fit into the overall visual approach of a scene. If you are doing a conventional shot/ reverse shot, the sudden employment of a dolly may feel as if it is thrown in. If you simply dolly to the other side of a conversation and then return to a standard shot/ reverse shot, the dolly can stick out like the proverbial sore thumb.

Point-of-view   Cutting to a point-of-view shot puts you right on the line, and from there you can go anywhere you want. The problem is the same as with the dolly, however: the shot must be dramatically justified. You cannot just throw in a point-of-view shot to get to the other side of the line. When the line is a consideration, you are by definition working with an omniscient camera—the camera is an uninvolved observer of the scene. To suddenly change the narrative context of the storytelling brings with it associations that may not be appropriate.

Changing sightlines or the position of characters   These are probably the best ways to change the line, though again they demand narrative justification. The first solution, described in the discussion of sightlines, is to have one of the characters look in a different direction, that is, move sightlines while keeping the camera stationary. If there is narrative justification (some reason for the character to look away), this can be an effective way to change positions. In the second method, you can simply have one of the characters move to another part of the space. Most directors like to keep characters moving anyway, so the scene does not become static. As characters move, the sightlines, and thus the line, move with them. When characters move, dollying the camera to new positions also can be better integrated. Both of these solutions are a matter of blocking. Examples of changing sightlines and moving characters are discussed further in chapter 6 in the breakdown of a scene from Jonathan Demme's *Something Wild*.

Screen Direction

The concept of screen direction comes into play when a character leaves a shot and then has to reenter in another shot. This is essentially a function of the line, although the difference is that screen direction ties separate spaces together by direction of movement. Simply stated, the way to achieve consistent screen direction is by having characters enter the frame from the opposite side they exited. If they exit frame-left, they must enter the next shot frame-right. If this simple rule is not followed, it will look as though the characters have turned around and gone in the other direction. Of course, the idea can also be applied to create a discontinuous or confused sense of space.

When the spaces in which consecutive scenes are taking place are not closely related, failure to think out screen direction can create at most some modest disorientation. If a character's next scene is across town, the direction he exits and enters the frame may not make much difference. When spaces for scenes *are* closely related, however, failure to think out screen direction can be disastrous. A good example of the latter would be a sequence of shots of someone getting up and going from one room to another. **SEE 5-17**

5-17

Screen direction comes into play when a character exits a shot and then reenters in a subsequent shot

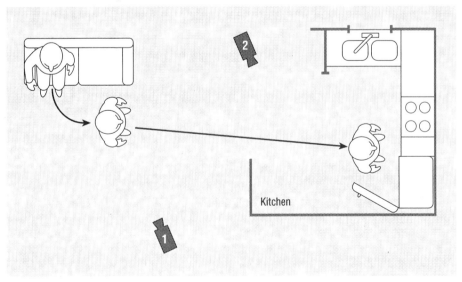

Kitchen

If you start the movement from setup #1, the character will exit the frame screen-right. If you make the mistake of shooting the next part of the movement from setup #2, the character will enter from the right and move to the left. It will appear as though she changed directions rather than walked in a straight line. It may even appear that she walked around behind the camera.

As suggested, the problems of improper screen direction are less crucial when spaces are more widely separated—where the setting has changed to the extent that the viewer will immediately accept it as new space and not be concerned about direction. If communicating the idea that a character is moving in a consistent direction is important, however, you will want to keep screen direction in mind. Sometimes you can give a sense of a character wandering or being lost by manipulating screen direction.

Although this is only tangentially related, there are generally accepted expectations that certain types of movement go in specific directions. This is particularly true of points on the map. When characters travel east, we expect them to move from left to right; if they are traveling west, right to left. When Woody Allen flies to California in his 1977 film *Annie Hall,* viewers would probably not accept the plane moving from left to right. Westerns also incorporate substantial right-to-left movement indicating a westward direction.

A number of film critics and theorists have suggested that the line is a by-product of the theatrical heritage of film, that cutting to the far side of action would be tantamount to making the audience jump to the opposite side of the stage, or suddenly viewing the play from backstage. Early filmmakers, realizing that the audience's closest frame of reference was watching stage productions, were loathe to disrupt conventional audience positioning to the action.

There is a certain amount of truth to this, but the 180-degree rule mainly serves to create matching sightlines and continuous direction of action. If the line is not followed, people will just not appear as though they are looking at each other, and action will appear discontinuous. Again, very few audience members will recognize this on a conscious level. As some of the rigid rules of narrative filmmaking break down, the line may be becoming less important, or maybe filmmakers are just paying less attention to it. Nevertheless, it is crucial that its application be understood no matter what one is attempting to accomplish.

6

Previsualization

ARMED **with some basic principles,** the next step is to formulate a strategy for shooting each individual scene. This strategy is largely the director's responsibility, although other craft positions will become involved, and the process overlaps with many of those described in chapter 12. This strategy can take a variety of forms: shooting scripts, shot lists, storyboards, and so on. Whatever form the strategy takes, the key is to be prepared. Although this will be amplified throughout this chapter, nothing sows the seeds for failure more effectively than not being mentally and organizationally ready to shoot a scene.

Preparation

A prepared director has planned the visual and dramatic approach to the day's work, including thinking out the blocking of the scene, the setups, the personality and motivation of all the characters, and the importance of the action within the larger context of the script. There are a number of ways to prepare a scene. You can plan each shot meticulously, including the exact framing and incorporation of all movement, or determine the rough parameters of the shots, intending to work out the finer points on the set. You can also come in armed with only a clear mental picture of the scene, so long as that picture has been communicated to the key creative people. This last approach should not be attempted by beginners. Whatever the method of preparation, a director should walk "on the floor" knowing the movements of all the characters, where they should be when they deliver their lines, and how the camera is going to cover the script.

Maximum efficiency on the set is an important goal. In all but the most specialized situations, there is material from a script that must be accomplished, that is, a certain number of setups to be shot, and action to be covered. No matter how high the budget, you are always working with limited resources on a limited time schedule. On a practical level, a lack of organization causes lengthy delays, poorly communicated needs for props and technical setups, and frequent duplication of effort. This produces anxiety and tension on the set, inhibiting productivity in a way that usually shows in the final product. On a conceptual level, it can indicate fundamental flaws in the way a director is shaping the visual approach to the material. An unprepared director tends to create scenes that are shapeless and paceless, with the internal logic—the logic of dramatic emphasis—clearly missing.

A certain case can be made for a spontaneous approach to filming, although that case tends to be both overstated and overromanticized. In most instances, it is a surefire way to create an uncuttable mess. Even films that appear informal are more planned than people realize. The simple fact is that unpreparedness can be disastrous, particularly for inexperienced and independent directors. Independents often depend on the donation of time and materials from many people. Film schools abound with stories of talent or crew who took a walk because they did not understand the commitment required of them or, worse yet, felt their time was being wasted. There are few things more destructive to the morale on a set than crew members being forced to cool their collective heels while decisions that should have been made earlier are being pondered. These are particularly sticky issues for inexperienced directors, because they are still learning the organizational skills needed to avoid such problems in the first place.

Methods of Previsualization

Being able to visualize a film in advance, to dream it out, is a difficult skill to develop. While it may be easy to come up with great ideas for individual shots, planning an entire scene is a formidable challenge. Previsualization requires experience and a knowledge of all the things that do and do not work in specific situations. There are a number of important tools to aid in previsualizing scenes, including overheads, storyboards, shot lists, and, to a lesser extent, shooting scripts. These tools also play an essential role in giving crew members the information they need to do their jobs effectively.

These tools are invaluable in forming a strategy for covering the action. Presented with an action, what *choices* do you make to film it? If a character crosses a room, do you dolly or pan? Would planning a cut to a wider shot be a better strategy? If a character looks off-screen, an expectation is created of seeing what the character sees. Do you plan a cut to what is seen? Do you pan to it? This action can be uncomplicated—simply getting the character from one place to another; or it can be invested with all manner of figurative overtones, whether symbolic, metaphoric, or allegoric.

As the rationales for the following previsualization tools are being discussed, keep in mind that most scenes are shot with a single camera. This is done for a variety of reasons, most notably to avoid complications in lighting design and expenses of extra cameras and crew. With the cost of producing a film becoming so exorbitant, however, the preference for single-camera shooting has been changing. When it costs what it does to get a full crew onto a location and create the required look for a film, needing to go back for reshoots or missed shots may simply not be possible. Pressure to produce something cuttable increases, and a second or even third camera may ensure that enough material is generated. Despite this, these discussions will stay with the still-prevalent single-camera model.

Overheads

Overheads, views of the scene from directly above, are the best starting place, being a good prelude to storyboarding. Draw an overhead of the location or set and start thinking out the movements of the characters as they go through actions or deliver dialogue, blocking the scene as if it were on a theatrical stage. In a best-of-all-worlds situation, this blocking is developed with the actors in rehearsal. Once you have determined where the characters are going to be during the scene, you can devise a few potential setups. Then you can start deciding what material from the script you want to be covering from each individual setup. Drawing a vertical line on a copy of the script to denote the material covered is a good method for cross-referencing setups against the dialogue and action. For some directors, this is all that is needed for an organized approach to a scene, although moving on to storyboarding is highly recommended.

Once some basic setups are worked out, other things start to fall into place. You can work in some complicated shots, some atmosphere shots, or a variety of other effective options. You might eventually wind up discarding the original setups altogether, but at least there is a starting point from which to develop engaging ideas.

Overheads will also help you with the line. When looking at a scene from above, the line can be drawn, based on sightlines or direction of action, and a determination can be made about where to start shooting. Having all this determined in advance can prevent getting worked into a corner. One beginning filmmaker was shooting a scene in which he made a central mistake that could have easily been avoided with some forethought. The scene involved a conversation between a person in a kitchen and another seated on a couch across the room. **SEE 6-1** Without carefully considering the ramifications, he began shooting the person on the couch from an apparently logical place—setup #1. When he went to shoot the second character, he had a problem. Setup #2 would have been the logical place for shooting the second character, but this would create a sightline mismatch. To preserve the line, he wound up shooting this part from setup #3. This left the actor's back to the camera as he turned to talk to the character on the couch, a solution that neither pleased the actor nor made much sense in the final product. To incorporate setup #2 and preserve the continuity of sightlines, the appropriate place to shoot the first character would have been from roughly setup #4.

When a specific setup is logical or desired for a scene, such as setup #2 in the previous example, it can be drawn on the overhead, then the other setups can be determined in relation to it. A basic, conventional approach to shooting a scene

6-1

Overheads of scene are helpful for blocking and determining camera setups

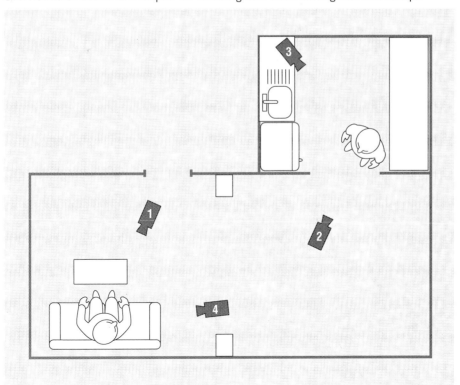

should be easy to work out. Overheads are extremely useful, both in understanding line issues and in preplanning the shooting of a scene. Many commercial storyboard forms come with two rectangles—one for drawing the image and the other for sketching an overhead view of the individual setup. Experienced directors may forgo this process because they have a clear understanding of all the spatial issues. Inexperienced directors need to be as prepared as conceivably possible.

Storyboards

A *storyboard,* or simply *board,* has each shot drawn on one side of the page, with the script material it covers—dialogue, action, objects—on the other side. In a certain sense, it is the comic book version of the film. A standard storyboard form will have room for three storyboard frames vertically down one side of the page, with room for the dialogue and action on the other. Some commercial forms are quite elaborate, with space for camera directions, continuity notes, overheads, and whatever else is necessary. Computer software has been developed that can generate the forms, many programs having clip art based on commonly used framings. Creating a simple storyboard form by hand or on a computer is not complicated. All that is needed are three rectangles arranged down the side of a page.

A simple starting place is to determine a limited number of camera setups on the overhead and apportion the action and dialogue to those setups on the storyboard. Though this sounds similar to drawing vertical lines through the script, the storyboard gives the framing of the shots and all the movement of the camera and subjects. If six setups are envisioned, you can start assigning lines and action to those specific cameras. If a line of dialogue is to be done in a medium shot from a particular camera angle, the storyboard would include a drawing of the character in medium, including rough positioning against the background, with the dialogue to the side. If the shot includes camera movement, the storyboard would have representations of key framings in the movement, with arrows indicating direction of movement. The storyboard draws out every shot, not just general positions or a few representative shots. The storyboard can represent action as simple as the shot described above or as complicated as the opening 8-minute shot from Robert Altman's *The Player* (1992), a shot that, if indeed it was storyboarded, would have had many drawn frames representing all the specific points in the movement.

Storyboards can be formal, consisting of elaborate drawings indicating precise framing and movement. These are created according to the director's instructions and are usually the handiwork of *storyboard artists* hired specifically for the purpose. Storyboards can also be exceedingly simple, with stick figures and crude line drawings to show rough positioning. Whatever the form, the purpose of the storyboard is the same: to communicate the shooting strategy to the appropriate individuals.

Certain films demand scrupulous storyboarding, particularly those that employ extensive special effects. Robert Zemeckis's *Who Framed Roger Rabbit* (1988), with its carefully executed animation combined with live action, was storyboarded down to precise camera framing, character position, and even lens length. There are directors (Alfred Hitchcock was famous for this) who have the entire film completely storyboarded before shooting a frame of film. Hitchcock used the storyboard like a blueprint for a building, seeing the actual shooting as a messy afterthought to the truly creative part of the process.

Shooting Scripts and Shot Lists

Initial scripts are relatively bare-bones affairs. Camera directions and the specifics of character movement are largely left to the discretion of the director. Once everything is determined in terms of camera and movement, the director puts together a detailed version of the script, called the ***shooting script***. Essentially an annotated version of the script, the shooting script numbers the scenes for preparation and logging during shooting. This is not so much a previsualization tool as it is the *result* of previsualization, a formal version of the director's initial intentions.

The ***shot list*** is a less formal alternative to the storyboard. It lists brief written descriptions of the intended shots. Experienced directors frequently use the shot list because it is the minimum that will serve their purposes when, given their abilities to shape a scene, making a storyboard is unnecessary. For people who can visualize from it, the shot list can be as instructive as a storyboard.

A Typical Scene

Taking a simple script involving two characters as an example, these processes become clearer. **SEE 6-2** The numbers on the side of the heading denote the scene number from the shooting script.

The first step is to draw an overhead of the chosen location with rough positioning of talent. **SEE 6-3** A typical approach is to plan a master shot for the first several lines—setup #1. Medium shots of both characters are also conventional options for the ensuing dialogue, shooting John from setup #2 and Andrea from setup #3.

When the scene is storyboarded, the dialogue can be apportioned to the setups that have been devised. A potential storyboard, in this case, is a simple approach to shooting a few lines of dialogue. **SEE 6-4** The circled numbers in the upper right refer to the setup, although most storyboards do not cross-reference setups like this. The numbers on the left are scene numbers used to identify position in the script. How they are generated is explained in chapter 15.

6-2

Sample script of a typical scene

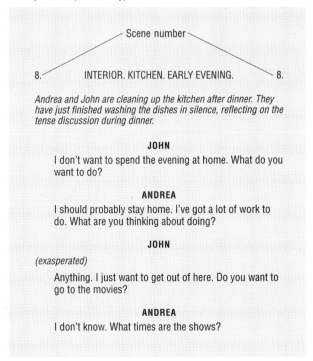

Scene number

8.   INTERIOR. KITCHEN. EARLY EVENING.   8.

Andrea and John are cleaning up the kitchen after dinner. They have just finished washing the dishes in silence, reflecting on the tense discussion during dinner.

JOHN

I don't want to spend the evening at home. What do you want to do?

ANDREA

I should probably stay home. I've got a lot of work to do. What are you thinking about doing?

JOHN

(exasperated)

Anything. I just want to get out of here. Do you want to go to the movies?

ANDREA

I don't know. What times are the shows?

6-3

Overhead of a typical
scene

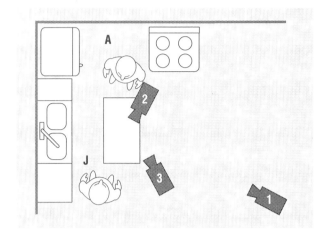

6-4

Storyboard of a typical scene

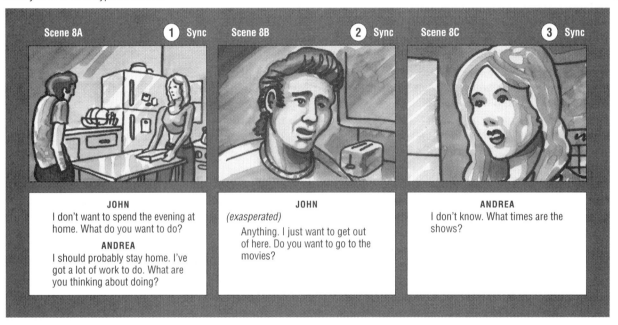

Although this is a bare-bones example, with the shot being used as a vehicle for the dialogue, the same process that breaks this scene down in such a straightforward manner could be applied to more elaborate ends as well. If the goal were in a more expressive realm, the shots would differ but the same basic reasoning applies.

This method, of course, represents the basic style of scene breakdown that D. W. Griffith pioneered: the interrelationship of shots for dramatic emphasis. While this approach can be highly effective, it can leave out subtle shadings and the active participation of the camera. It is a functional approach that values covering a scene, though some would argue that it has the potential to be dull. Many of the shots outlined in this approach can be a useful jumping-off point, even when a director intends some adventurous shooting. Although this approach may sound easy, it is difficult to make even the simplest of scenes work. Even the most conventional television product requires facility and experience to pull off.

Coverage

Coverage—shooting the action and dialogue of a scene from more than one setup—should always be built into your shooting plan. The initial storyboard examples may appear to suggest that lines in the script are shot from only one angle. This is not the case. Yes, directors must direct the setups so that their vision shapes the material, but they generally shoot individual dialogue and action from at least a few different angles, as well as covering longer portions of the script from the setups. This provides options in the editing room if there are any conceptual errors in the way the scene was shot.

In the most excessive variation of this approach, the director (and only a very insecure director would do this) shoots the material from almost every conceivable angle. The footage is then handed over to the editor with a simple "good luck" as the only guide. Editors hate this. It forces them into the position of redirecting the film. The idea of coverage should not deny the logic of using specific camera setups. One first-time director, overcompensating for the coverage mistakes he had seen in his experience as an assistant editor, felt the necessity to shoot his scenes from just about every conceivable angle. Every time the principal shooting appeared to be over, he would think of one more angle that he absolutely had to have to edit the piece. The crew was looking for a noose and a sturdy tree. The director should shape the scene while still providing options.

You may have heard of the opposite extreme in which directors shoot specific parts of the script from one and only one angle, imposing ultimate control by not providing any options for the editors. Both Alfred Hitchcock and John Ford were famous for maintaining this kind of tight control. Before you fall into what many call "the Hitchcock Syndrome," however, be aware that both Hitchcock and Ford achieved this control of the expressive powers of cinema only after directing many films. Ford made dozens of shorts and routine action films, many now lost, before making any of the films that contributed so much to his reputation. In Hitchcock's case, with a few notable exceptions, his first fifteen or so films are largely unremarkable.

Independents and students often attempt to conserve stock to stay within miniscule budgets, forgoing some angles to stay within an arbitrary amount of footage allotted for a scene. This can sometimes lead to false savings. Missing key shots can diminish a scene's total effect. Although shooting must be economical, do not skimp on the necessary pieces.

A Caveat

Preparing a script can be very methodical, and there are an increasing number of films that appear overplanned and devoid of life, bland executions of meticulously thought-out storyboards. In such films the shots are machine engineered and factory assembled to the extent that they lose any semblance of being a part of an organic whole. One episodic television program was so meticulously planned that it required only about one month's work from its star player. The star was in the studio for a week or two to shoot all the close-ups and mediums for the entire season. The rest of the cast was called in, and all the star's two-shots and masters were filmed. The star was then released, and the next several months were spent shooting the material for the rest of the cast. Thus, a shot of the star giving sage advice to a character may have had its reverse done weeks or even months later. Although the skills of the makers largely hid the approach, the result felt overly calculated.

Cautioning against overplanned films is important, but there is some danger of encouraging the opposite—completely spontaneous shooting. This approach rarely yields fruitful results. There is a tendency among some beginners to regard previsualization as overdetermined, somehow destroying the spontaneity of artistic creation. This perception can be a strong one. Marlene Dietrich was once reminiscing for a university audience about Orson Welles and his exceptional creative ability and vital imagination. Undoubtedly swept up in the moment, one questioner asked if Welles ever worked from storyboards and scripts. After a stunned pause, Dietrich's response was a contemptuous "of course," which spoke volumes about the naïveté of the question. The notion that ideas just jump out of the brain straight onto the screen has occasioned more bad beginning films than any other single misconception. Clearly, some middle ground is required.

The storyboard is certainly a key previsualization tool, but it is not set in stone and should not intimidate thoughtful improvisation on the set. However, any deviation from a well-thought-out game plan should be carefully considered in terms of how it will be integrated into everything else. After a long day, crews can get slaphappy and make decisions that at the time appear brilliant but later look ridiculous. Do not let yourself be put in a position in which wholesale changes occur, because the shape of a scene as a whole can get lost. All changes must be weighed and carefully incorporated into the shooting plan.

Production Design and Costume

Although they are not by definition storyboard issues, the planning for production design and costume is often done at the same time or included in the storyboarding process itself. The ***production designer***, the person responsible for designing all the film's settings, will often use the storyboards as a guide to create sketches of the settings. These elements often come under the general heading of ***decor***, which also includes props, makeup, and any other element that is part of the physical content of the frame. German filmmakers of the 1920s are generally credited with the first significant explorations in the use of decor to create effect. In films such as F. W. Murnau's *Nosferatu* (1922) and Fritz Lang's *Metropolis* (1926), the directors investigated how external settings suggested or reflected internal states of mind. Both theater and painting have precedents for this kind of approach, and film's incorporation of many common devices from these traditions was inevitable.

Design for realistic films has a great deal to do with visual stereotypes—the way the viewer expects certain things to look. If a script calls for the establishment of an upscale home, certain elements can be used to create that effect. If the goal is to establish an isolated, dilapidated mountain cabin, other components can be incorporated to suggest that. The designs for a fantasy film may be more the creation of an imaginative designer, but even they are done within the context of what viewers expect, though some play against visual stereotype, including the seedy, run-down futures of Ridley Scott's *Alien* (1979) and Terry Gilliam's *Brazil* (1985).

Production design can range from the relatively simple to the complex and costly. The war room scenes in Stanley Kubrick's *Dr. Strangelove* (Ken Adam, production designer) are dominated by strong design elements. **SEE 6-5** The peculiar credibility of the space makes the outrageous actions of the characters all the more absurd. The same designer's work on the early James Bond films was both influenced by, and influential to, modern design. Looking back at these films, one realizes that the novelty of their look was a substantial part of their appeal.

Visual environment helps to define character. A messy, cluttered environment tends to establish similar traits in the character. The opposite is a very cold, empty environment as featured in films like Paul Schrader's *American Gigolo* (1980) and Woody Allen's *Interiors* (1978), both films about cold, emotionally empty people. **SEE 6-6** Clearly there are many other elements that contribute

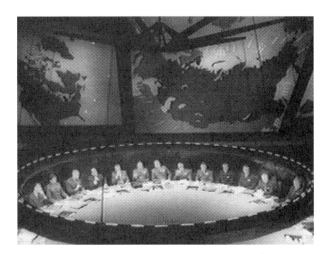

6-5

Strong production design elements can add underlying meaning to a scene
Stanley Kubrick's *Dr. Strangelove*

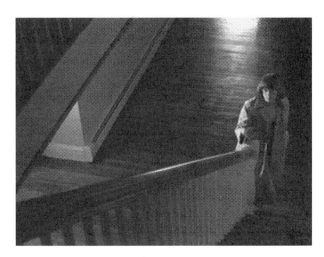

6-6

Visual environment can define character and context
Mary Beth Hurt in *Interiors*

to the tone and atmosphere of a scene. Color plays an important role, with scenes being conceived in a variety of emotional tones, from warm tones, to cool tones, to earth tones, and so on.

Another factor used to define character is costume. Emil Jannings's doorman in F. W. Murnau's *The Last Laugh* (1924) is an oft-cited example. When the doorman has his uniform, he is a proud and overbearing character; when he loses the uniform, he becomes small and pitiful. A major contrast in Julie Dash's *Daughters of the Dust* (1991) is between the stiff and repressed country women and the independent city women. The country women are all costumed in reserved darks and lights, with straight and harsh lines. **SEE 6-7A** The city women are dressed in cream colors, with decorative frills and fashionable hats. **SEE 6-7B**

Makeup is somewhat different because its use is often purely functional, although there are many films that employ makeup as either a major design element or for purposes of character definition. In either case, the employment of makeup is never simple. Beginners do not usually have experience with makeup, a fact that leads to a variety of pitfalls when they attempt basic effects. Many makeup people come to film with a theatrical background, and it is important to realize that the kind of makeup the performers need for an audience 20 to 100 feet away is vastly different from the kind needed for a camera that may be as close as several feet. Good makeup people understand how the materials they use will photograph and how the proximity of the camera will represent their work.

6-7

The conservative costuming of the country women is juxtaposed with the stylish garb of the city women

Julie Dash's *Daughters of the Dust*

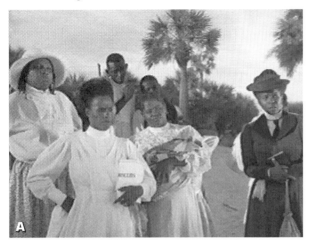
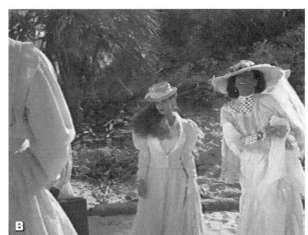

These are just a few possibilities of what design can produce. Clearly a film can go many different directions in terms of decor. The key is that it has to go somewhere. If low-budget films have a common failing, it is that they frequently lack a consistent approach to visual style. Often this is both a decor and camera matter, and is also largely an economic reality. The personnel and material for set design and decoration are frequently beyond the available resources. Low-budget films often get stuck in the locations that are available to them, shooting without the resources or the time to change things. Although viewers may not notice many design factors, a film with wildly different design elements can look very inconsistent.

The Shape of a Scene

It can be useful for beginners to take the backdoor approach to visualizing a scene: start with a scene in a finished film and work back to a storyboard. This gives a sense of what choices have been made in camera positions. It can also clarify issues of the 180-degree rule, allow speculation on some practical organizational principles, and suggest some approaches to technical issues as well.

Breaking down a scene like this produces a clear idea of what is occurring visually in relationship to the dialogue and action in the script. As always, the key words are *choice* and *strategy*. Creating overheads and storyboards facilitates planning the blocking of the scene, determining suitable setups, and apportioning the dialogue and actions to those setups. Reviewing the idea of elements is helpful. A scene consists of elements that the director must decide how to photograph, thus determining what should be emphasized at what point.

The straightforward and exceptionally effective diner scene from Jonathan Demme's *Something Wild* is a good example of this. The scene has the three main characters, Charles (Jeff Daniels), Lulu (Melanie Griffith), and Ray (Ray Liotta). Charles is attempting to get Lulu away from Ray, an ex-con on a crime spree. Charles uses the presence of several police officers sitting nearby to intimidate Ray. The film is from a script by E. Max Frye.

As you read the transcription of the dialogue, think about breaking down the scene into elements. **SEE 6-8** Who are the key characters, and what objects and actions are important to the scene? What are the potential setups?

6-8

Dialog from diner scene in *Something Wild*

90.   INTERIOR. DINER. NIGHT.   90.

RAY

Uh, let me have the "Rustler's Rhapsody."

DARLENE

"Rustler's Rhapsody."

Charles enters from behind Ray.

CHARLES

Just coffee for me . . . Darlene. You don't mind, do you, Ray?

LULU

Charlie, you gotta be outta your mind. You don't know what you're doing.

RAY

Charlie, you are one dumb son of a bitch. I'm almost starting to like you, Charlie.

DARLENE

(entering with coffee)

Here ya go.

CHARLES

Thanks, Darlene.

(to Ray)

I want Lulu.

RAY

Is that your name this week? Lulu?

LULU]

Yes.

RAY

You know, Charlie, she's not going to be too happy driving around in a station wagon the rest of her life. You better think about that. You better ask yourself if you really want her.

CHARLES

I really want her.

RAY

Ahhhh.

LULU

Great.

RAY

Charlie, you gotta fight for a woman like this.

CHARLES

I don't have to fight you, Ray. I'm gonna take Lulu and we're gonna waltz right outta here and there's not a damn thing you can do to stop me.

RAY

Ooh. Rrrrrr. Ha, ha. Oh, Charlie, you are somethin'. You are somethin'.

CHARLES

Take a look over there. Go ahead. Evening, officer.

OFFICER

How's it goin'?

CHARLES

Ray, you're a convicted felon. You're in the possession of one, if not several, concealed weapons. You robbed a grocery store. You assaulted that poor kid with a gun. You left the state of Pennsylvania, which is gonna come as a surprise to your parole officer. And I'd be willing to wager that that Cadillac of yours sitting out in the parking lot, I bet it's hot.

LULU

Charlie!

CHARLES

Now it's you with something to lose.

RAY

Fuck you.

LULU

He's got you, Ray.

RAY

Fuck you too, Lulu.

The police officer is joined by two others.

CHARLES

Evening, officers.

OFFICER

How ya doin'?

CHARLES

Oh, good, pretty good. Thank you.

(to Ray)

Hand over the car keys. Come on, hand over the car keys.

LULU

Let's go.

RAY

You're going to regret this.

CHARLES

Well, life's full of regrets.

RAY

No. You are really going to regret this.

CHARLES

Now your wallet.

LULU

Charlie, come on.

RAY

You think you're pretty smart, don't you, Charlie.

CHARLES

Pretty smart. Well look, Ray, just to show you there are no hard feelings, this one's on me.

Charles waves the check at Ray. Charles and Lulu exit.

CHARLES

(to police)

Good night.

OFFICERS

Good night.

DARLENE

(giving Ray the check)

The gentleman said you'd take care of this.

RAY

That son of a bitch.

What would be considered the elements of this scene? There are clearly five: Lulu, Charles, Ray, Darlene, and the police officers. The scene is thus an interrelationship of these five elements. What are some potential setups? The entire action is presented from eight setups, at least until everything very significantly changes when Charles and Lulu exit. The first setup is the master shot, the starting point of all conventional scene breakdown. There are two OTS shots, one of Ray

6-9

Overhead of the diner
scene

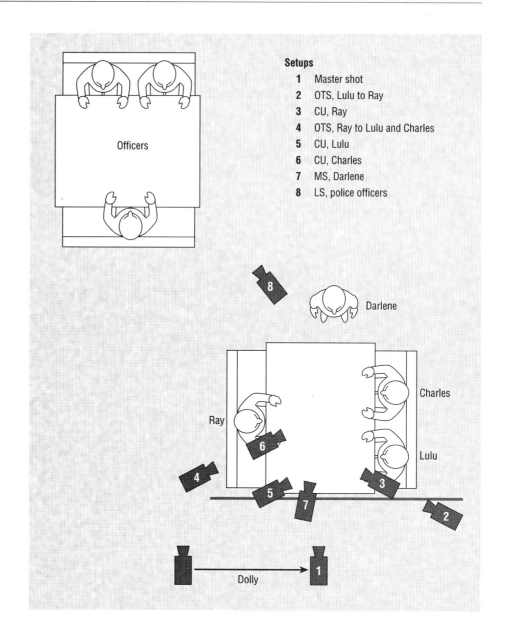

Officers

Darlene

Charles

Ray

Lulu

Dolly

Setups
1 Master shot
2 OTS, Lulu to Ray
3 CU, Ray
4 OTS, Ray to Lulu and Charles
5 CU, Lulu
6 CU, Charles
7 MS, Darlene
8 LS, police officers

over Lulu's shoulder and one of Lulu and Charles over Ray's shoulder. There are three close-ups of the key people: Lulu, Ray, and Charles. There is one setup for Darlene and one setup for the police officers. The two setups covering the exit are described later.

Note the overhead. **SEE 6-9** The positioning of the cameras for the close-ups (setups #3, #5, and #6) is slightly misleading, because the squashing of perspective and the out-of-focus background make it obvious that they were done using a longer lens, a telephoto, from roughly the positions of the OTS shots (setups #2 and #4). Even if they were done from precisely the same place as the OTS shots, the change of lens length marks them as different setups. All numbering is internal to this illustration and does not reflect any actual onset organization.

The scene is broken down in the following figure. **SEE 6-10** The ellipses (...) denote when a character's dialogue continues into the following shot. Pay attention to the way the shots break down in relation to the dialogue. How often are the reaction shots done without any dialogue? Is the 180-degree rule observed? How are the setups used to play the climax of the scene? Are the setups used in a logical way that reflect the shape of the scene?

6-10

Breakdown of the diner scene

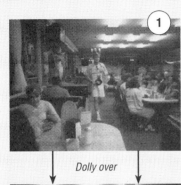

Dolly over

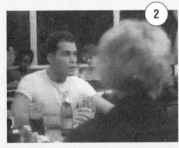

RAY

Uh, let me have the
"Rustler's Rhapsody."

DARLENE

"Rustler's Rhapsody."

CHARLES

Just coffee for me,
Darlene.

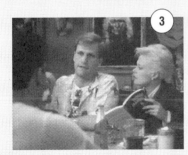

You don't mind, do
you, Ray?

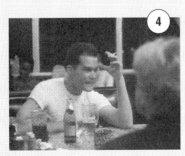

LULU

Charlie, you gotta
be outta your mind.
You don't know what
you're doing.

RAY

Charlie, ...

... you are one dumb
son of a bitch.

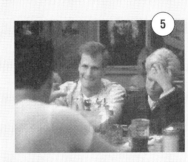

... I'm almost starting
to like ...

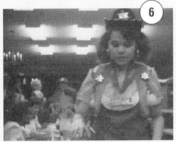

...you, Charlie.

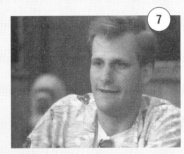

DARLENE

Here ya go.

CHARLES

Thanks, Darlene.
I want Lulu.

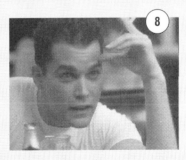

RAY

Is that your name this
week? Lulu?

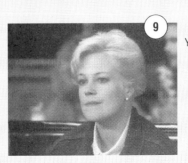

LULU

Yes.

6-10

Breakdown of the diner scene *(continued)*

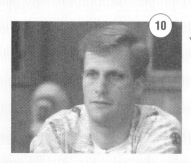

10 RAY
You know, Charlie, ...

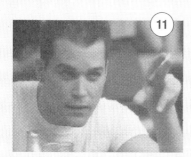

11
... she's not going to be too happy driving around in a station wagon the rest of her life. You better think about that. You better ask yourself if you really want her.

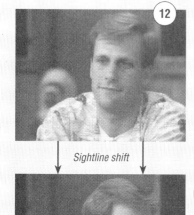

12

Sightline shift

CHARLES
I really want her.

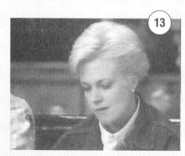

13 RAY
Ahhhh.

LULU
Great.

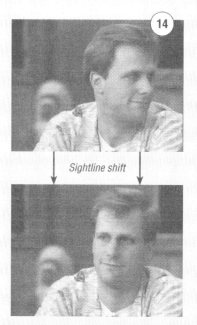

14

Sightline shift

15 RAY
Charlie, you gotta fight for a woman like this.

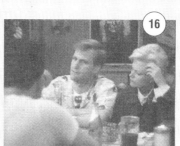

16 CHARLES
I don't have to fight you, Ray. I'm gonna take Lulu and we're gonna waltz right outta here and there's not a damn thing you can do to stop me.

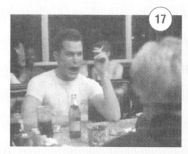

17 RAY
Ooh. Rrrrrr. Ha ha. Oh, Charlie, you are somethin'. You are somethin'.

6-10

Breakdown of the diner scene *(continued)*

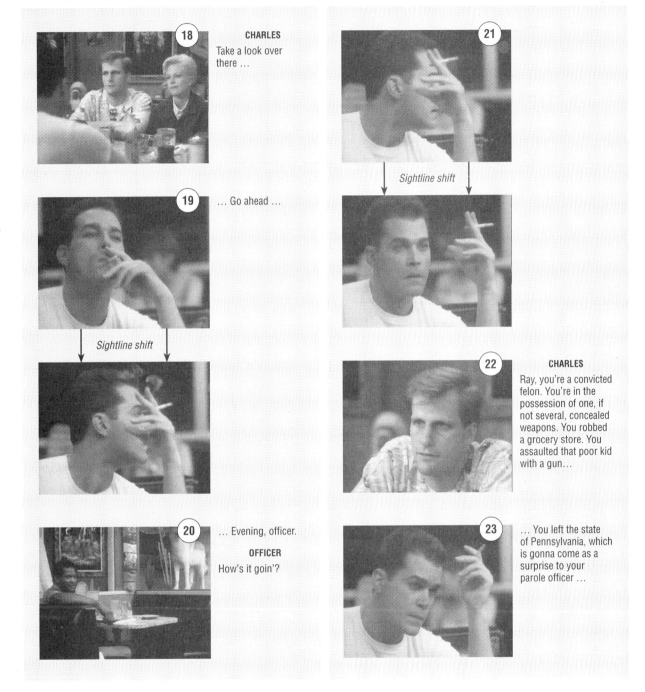

18 CHARLES
Take a look over there …

19 … Go ahead …

Sightline shift

20 … Evening, officer.
OFFICER
How's it goin'?

21

Sightline shift

22 CHARLES
Ray, you're a convicted felon. You're in the possession of one, if not several, concealed weapons. You robbed a grocery store. You assaulted that poor kid with a gun…

23 … You left the state of Pennsylvania, which is gonna come as a surprise to your parole officer …

As suggested, the master is used sparingly, three times to be exact (shots 1, 32, and 43). The first (1) does exactly what a classic master is supposed to do: present all the elements together. The police officer is shown seated as Charles enters behind him. Then the camera dollies over to show Darlene taking dessert orders from Ray and Lulu.

After the initial master, the scene quickly moves in for the medium shots and close-ups. The first cuts are between the two OTS shots (setups #2 and #4). Close-ups are then used to present the basic elements at issue. Since the most intense part of the scene is yet to come, the cutting retreats back to mediums. Parameters

6-10

Breakdown of the diner scene *(continued)*

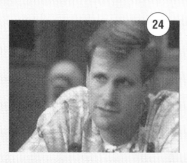

24   ... and I'd be willing to wager that that Cadillac of yours sitting out in the parking lot, I bet it's hot.

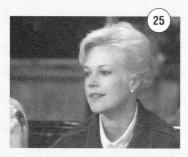

25   **LULU**

Charlie!

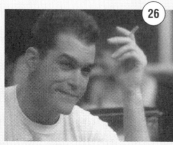

26

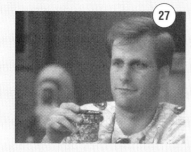

27   **CHARLES**

Now it's you with something to lose.

28   **RAY**

Fuck you.

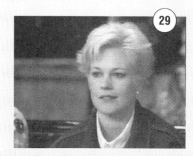

29   **LULU**

He's got you, Ray.

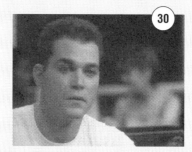

30   **RAY**

Fuck you too, Lulu.

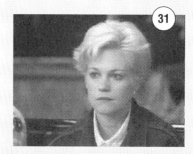

31

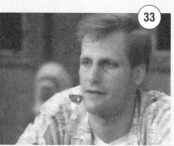

32   **CHARLES**

Evening, officers.

OFFICER

How ya doin'?

CHARLES

Oh, good, pretty good. Thank you ...

33   ... Hand over the car keys ...

6-10

Breakdown of the diner scene *(continued)*

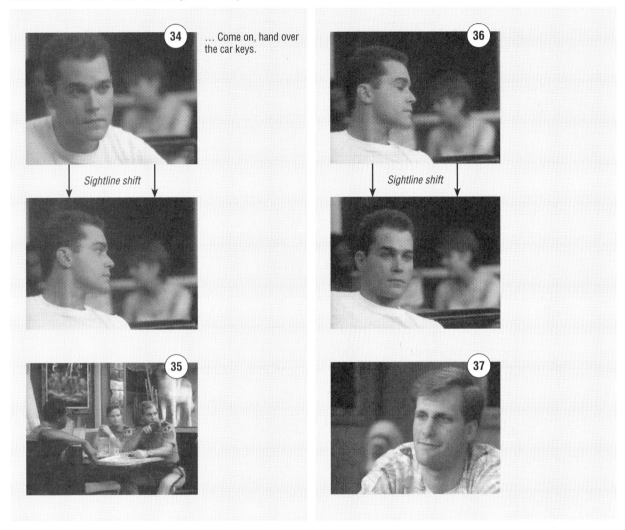

of performance, such as the body language, are always key issues. One shot where Ray mocks Charles with his entire body (17) clearly requires the medium shot. Although the logic of the scene may require an MS here anyway, it is clear that the MS is used facilitate Ray Liotta's exceptional performance.

The most intense part of this scene, the climax, is when Ray swears at Charles and Lulu. As expected, it is played entirely in close-ups (21–31). Immediately after this, the scene cuts to the master shot (32), in which Charles makes verbal contact with the police officers. Used in the middle of a scene like this, the master shot can act as a release valve for tensions that have built up in a scene. Both the intensity of a scene and the closeness to the subjects can be such that we literally need to back off. Because the content of this shot is slightly comical, one can almost feel oneself breathe a sigh of relief.

Despite this brief respite, the scene maintains its intensity. It returns to a sequence of close-ups for the exchange of the keys and wallet (33–42). As is so often the case, the master is also used to "bookend" the scene, although its final use (43) is somewhat before the end of the scene. As suggested, everything changes once Lulu and Charles get up to leave (46). This requires two more camera positions. **SEE 6-11** Setup #9 is used just once (49) and is essentially a variation on the master shot. Presumably it was shot at the same time. Setup #10

Breakdown of the diner scene *(continued)*

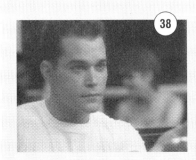

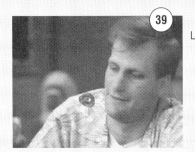

LULU
Let's go.

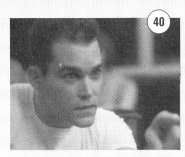

RAY
You're going to regret this.

CHARLES
Well, life's full of regrets.

RAY
No. You are really going to regret this.

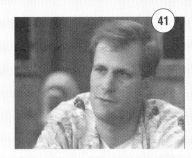

CHARLES
Now your wallet.

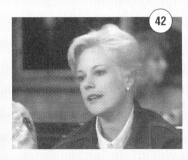

LULU
Charlie, come on.

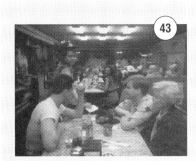

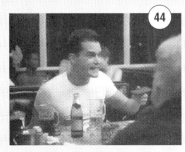

RAY
You think you're pretty smart, don't you, Charlie.

CHARLES
Pretty smart …

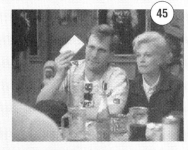

… Well look, Ray, just to show you there are no hard feelings, this one's on me.

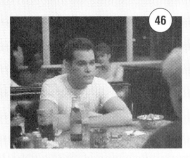

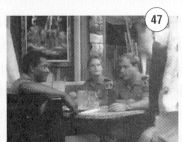

CHARLES
Good night.

OFFICERS
Good night.

6-10

Breakdown of the diner scene *(concluded)*

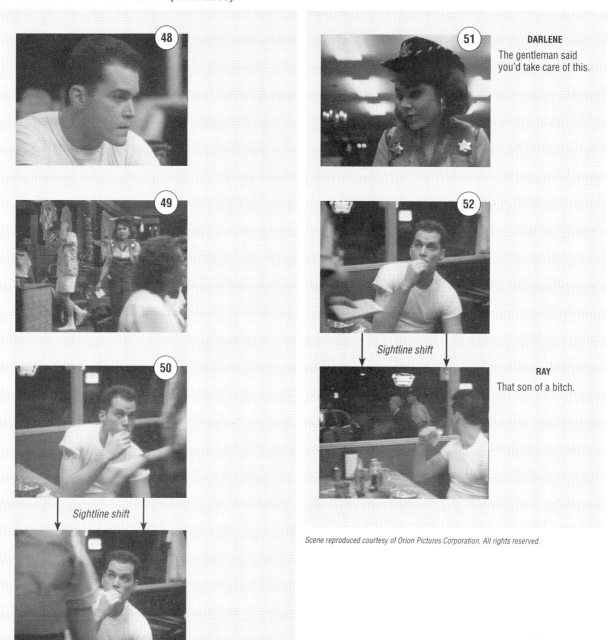

DARLENE
The gentleman said you'd take care of this.

Sightline shift

RAY
That son of a bitch.

Sightline shift

is used twice and has some significance in terms of the 180-degree rule (see below). The final two setups are:

- Setup #9: Alternative master

- Setup #10: Medium of Ray, with Lulu and Charlie running to the car in the background.

The logic of a specific shooting plan is always open to argument, but the sequence in this case has clearly been considered carefully in terms of the way the

6-11

Shooting the characters' exit requires two more setups

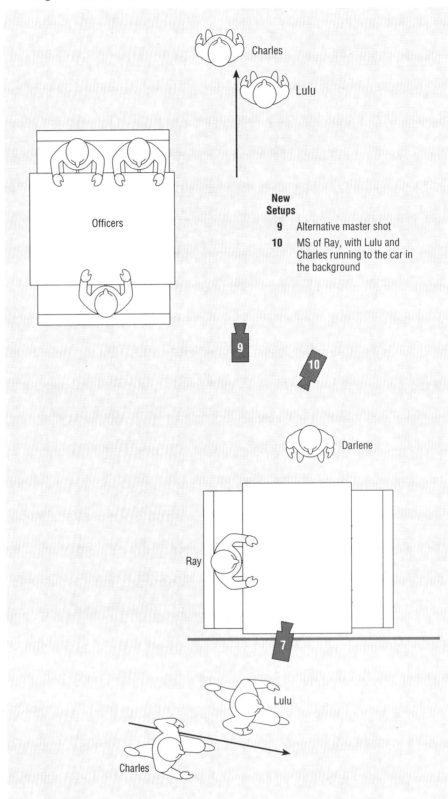

Charles

Lulu

Officers

New Setups

9 Alternative master shot

10 MS of Ray, with Lulu and Charles running to the car in the background

9

10

Darlene

Ray

7

Lulu

Charles

setups are used to cover the action. The "rightness" of the camera positions is virtually inescapable.

The Line

What occurs in terms of the line is interesting as well. The line clearly runs right through the table, and the camera is on the window side of the action, at least until Charles and Lulu leave. The line then switches from the window side to the restaurant side in the alternative master (49). Before this transition, the only camera position on the far side of the action is the one for the police officers (setup #8), which is used twice before Charles and Lulu's exit (20 and 35). On both occasions, the employment of this setup is justified by Ray's sightline shift prior to its inclusion. Some editors might argue that the shot could be used without the sightline shift. The setup maintains the direction of the action and is lined up pointing in the same general direction as the other setups. The setup is used a third time (47) as Charles and Lulu leave.

Shot 49, from setup #9, is the transition shot from one side of the line to the other. Then we can come back to shot 50 for the final interchange between Ray and Darlene. The original setup #7 of Darlene is used for this, although allowing her to pass in front of the camera in shots 50 and 52 constitutes a line cross. This could have been avoided by cutting before she passes in front of the camera, but the look of bewilderment on Ray's face would have been sacrificed. In this case, editor Craig McKay and director Demme determined that the emotional content of the scene required keeping Ray's response, thus overshadowing any slight dislocation caused by the change of direction. Such are the compromises that are often made.

Organizational Considerations

Although many considerations went into shooting this scene, the primary focus in the discussion here is on the sequence of shooting. Masters are usually shot first for a variety of reasons, the most significant being the director's desire to essentially rehearse the scene "in master" before shooting. Issues of performance, continuity, and movement are ironed out at this stage, which assists all departments in anticipating the needs of the closer shots. In particular, the script supervisor can watch the entire scene and make mental and written notes about the details that will require matching.

Another consideration is that the master shot usually requires the most bodies, an obvious concern in this instance. Keeping and feeding extras is expensive, and the *production manager (PM)* wants them to be cut loose as quickly as possible. For this reason, all the shots requiring extras are generally shot at the beginning. Being able to dismiss the extras in a timely manner reinforces the importance of organizing the sequence of shooting. The PM and *assistant director* (the *AD* is also responsible for day-to-day scheduling) need to know the direction of all the shots in the scene, thus allowing them to identify what elements—characters, extras, and so on—are going to be necessary and for how long. There is nothing like coming to a setup late in a shooting day and realizing that the appropriate elements are no longer available.

Matching the lighting from setup to setup is another consideration. It is relatively easy for an experienced crew to match lighting when moving from the master to close-ups. Going the other way, matching lighting from close-ups back to the master, is tricky. In the master, the position of the camera and the wide field of view can present obstacles to placing instruments. A crack crew can easily overcome these problems, but master shots commonly require compromises in the lighting. It is essential to know what compromises are going to have to be made before lighting the closer material. Re-creating the lighting from a close-up with an instrument repositioned to shoot the master can consume important time on the set as well as produce uneven results.

There are numerous other considerations. The tables had to be moved away from the wall to create space for the camera. Much changed in the final setups (#9 and #10), and time devoted to relighting is a key consideration. The inside of the restaurant needed to be lighted for the initial eight setups. When the whole thing turns in the other direction, the exterior of the restaurant becomes an issue, both in terms of lighting and the control of elements in the parking lot. Suffice it to say that the last setup required an entire relight—a demanding albeit common occurrence. This is something the production manager would have foreseen as the shooting script developed. Allowances for time, materials, and extra personnel would be anticipated.

Technical Considerations

One key technical consideration in this scene is how depth of field is employed for effect. The extras in the background of the close-ups, atmosphere as they are called, are purposefully out of focus. Demme and DP Tak Fujimoto undoubtedly wanted to suggest that there were other customers present but did not want them detracting from the foreground action. From the squashing of perspective, it is clear that Fujimoto used a long lens to minimize depth of field for the close-ups. When confronted with the choice of how to move from a medium shot to a close-up, the conventional approach is to do the opposite: reposition the camera closer to the subject. The main consideration is perspective characteristics, the conventional approach avoiding intercutting scenes with what some would consider disconcertingly different backgrounds. Minimizing depth of field with a long lens represents a conscious decision on the cinematographer's part, because other choices would have easily yielded a more deep-focus effect.

Another key technical consideration is the incorporation of the fluorescent lights in the background of the masters and the shots of Darlene. There are two approaches to this. One is to gel all the instruments with a filter that matches the color temperature of the fluorescents. This requires using a filter on the camera to reconvert the light to tungsten-balanced film. The second option is to completely replace the fluorescents with specialized bulbs that produce 3,200° K. As the shooting undoubtedly took several nights, this latter approach was presumably taken.

This scene represents the classical approach to scene breakdown at its best. Camera setups are devised, and the dialogue to be covered from each setup is determined. The scene is thus composed of an interrelationship of the different shots to emphasize the action and responses—the dramatic emphasis. While other approaches can be considered, the clarity achieved here is undeniable. This straightforward example may lead some to believe that the conventional approach is somehow easy. Nothing could be farther from the truth. The difficulties of creating a seamless scene can be understood only by trying to create one yourself. It takes the skill of many different people to make a scene work.

7

Composition

Composition in film, as in painting and graphic design, refers to the arrangement of shapes, volumes, and forms within an artistic frame. It is a key, possibly *the* key, element in a film's overall visual design. There are many films in which the composition is formulaic and uninspired. More often than not, though, the composition is thoughtful and workmanlike. On a few celebrated occasions, the composition is inspired—taking the film into that rare arena of visual poetry. Whether or not it reaches this lofty status, effective composition is rarely noticed. There are, however, poorly composed films that leave the viewer unsatisfied, with the uncomfortable feeling that something is amiss—that the film is creating a world that is not only out of balance but which lacks any internal cohesion.

Whereas a painter has the ability to thoughtfully predetermine the positioning of elements in a composition, the filmmaker has a more complicated task. This, of course, is because of the added dimension of movement. The key to composition for the film frame is the awareness that composition is dynamic, always in flux, ever changing. Whether you are dealing with camera movement, subject movement, or both, the elements in the frame will almost always be moving, and you have to think out each composition in terms of what is occurring at all times. You can start out with a perfectly balanced frame, and one small movement by a character—something as simple as shifting body weight—can make the composition fall apart, the frame becoming completely unbalanced. Thus the person shooting has to plan a response to the movement of both the subject being filmed and the camera itself.

The Director of Photography

Effective filming can be done by a single person with a camera or by a full-scale feature crew. Whether working on your own or with a crew, the creativity and care needed for effective shooting remains consistent. The *director of photography (DP)*, also referred to as *cinematographer*, has two primary responsibilities: composition and lighting. There are also many unstated expectations. Primary among these is the ability to evaluate whether the individual shots work within the greater context of the film. This can range from simply making sure the shots look good, to making sure that they have the appropriate pace and dynamic visual energy, to—most important—evaluating on a shot-by-shot basis whether the shots will cut together in the editing room. As with so many other skill positions, a DP with experience in the editing room brings a valuable perspective to the process.

When you view a film, you are looking at someone's (the DP's) conscious approach to composition. He or she has had to *line up the shots*—that is, look at what is in front of the camera and decide how to arrange it in relation to the boundaries of the film frame. Beginners quickly learn that there is a big difference between looking through a camera and shooting. Anyone can look through a camera, but it takes a creative eye to produce framings that are both consistently dynamic and part of a cohesive vision of the whole.

The DP's role is obviously central. Many beginners venture into filmmaking with an innocently formed intent to become a DP. Indeed, there is a certain romance to the camera. It sits at the center of attention on a set, almost like a throne, with its minions scurrying about, ministering to its needs. However, once you learn a little about the camera, you realize that DPs have to be part mathematician, part magician, and part personnel manager. It soon becomes clear that people have very high expectations of you. Beyond serviceable composition, the unwritten expectation is that you will bring life and animation to the subject—even if that subject is somewhat less than spellbinding on its own. I know DPs who cannot sleep the night before big shoots, with butterflies created by the tension associated with high expectations. There is no substitute for getting it right, and there are hundreds of things that will conspire against the easy execution of even the simplest of shots.

The Frame

Beyond content issues that can be analyzed on an interpretative level, the formal elements of a frame demand equal consideration. The term *formal* refers to the choices one makes beyond the narrative structure of a film—the lighting, the camera angles, employment of movement, and all the other resources discussed in the menu in chapter 5. In a sense, structure is the straight line of the narrative, and form is the variation in the presentation of details from that line. When Jim Jarmusch uses single takes to cover scenes in *Stranger Than Paradise* (1984), the scenes themselves and their order are the structural elements, and the single take is the formal approach. When cinematographer Haskell Wexler pre-exposes film to create a milky, old-feeling image in Hal Ashby's film biography of Woody Guthrie, *Bound for Glory* (1976), that is a formal approach. Mira Nair's *Mississippi Masala* (1992) is suffused with red, creating a visual analogy for the ease and warmth with which the people live. Color, shape, the play between light and dark, the texture of the image, the dynamics of movement, and a host of other formal elements all add immeasurably to the impact of an image. More than simply establishing atmosphere or mood, formal elements shape the way we perceive characters and events.

Composition should never be looked at schematically or as being dominated by any unbreakable rules. However, there are a number of commonly accepted principles that need to be considered. Examples that illustrate these principles could go on forever, as could examples of exceptions—compositions that play against accepted conventions. The goal here is to put forth a few straightforward ideas that can serve as an impetus for further exploration on your own.

Balance and the Frame, and the Rule of Thirds

The dominant compositional principle, the ***rule of thirds***, is not so much a rule as it is a guideline for creating a balanced frame. The rule of thirds draws four lines that divide the frame into thirds horizontally and vertically. **SEE 7-1** Areas and objects of visual interest are then put on these lines to balance the composition. A balanced frame simply means that elements in a composition are balanced by other elements. If a human face is by itself on one side of the frame, the composition looks off balance. When a second element is added on the empty side, it is possible to create some sense of balance.

Balance is a key to and a natural component of composition. Both human perception and movement are dependent on a sense of equilibrium. Observation has shown that human beings want to literally have both feet on the ground when either confronting visual phenomena or moving through it.[1] The human eye—actually the processes of the mind—relentlessly attempts to impose balance on natural phenomena. The mind can find balance in triangles, abstracting a center point or finding an axis that balances the weight of the form. Rectangles and squares immediately suggest their own internal balance. Trapezoids and a number of other shapes lend themselves to similar treatment.

Other shapes announce balance less openly but still lend themselves to the balancing desire of the eye. Circles have no immediate balance, and yet the eye will be drawn to the center, create an axis, and thus suggest balance. Even completely free-form shapes will often have some center of balance. Forms that do not suggest balance are said to have stress, which is discussed in the next section.

Just as the eye looks for order in abstract shapes, it desires to impose order on an artistic frame—a composition. The rule of thirds simply takes this natural human ability to create balance and gives it artistic form. Whereas balance in painting and still photography is at least superficially straightforward, balance in film is complicated by movement. Many framings that look unstable by themselves are balanced by movement. Still, some relatively straightforward examples can be shown. Terrence Malick's *Badlands* is an engagingly visual film. One scene,

---

1. Much of the experimentation regarding the psychological ordering of perceptual experience has been done from the perspective of Gestalt psychology. Donis A. Dondis's *A Primer for Visual Literacy* (Cambridge, Mass.: MIT Press, 1974) and the work of Rudolph Arnheim are excellent sources for those interested in studies of perceptual experience.

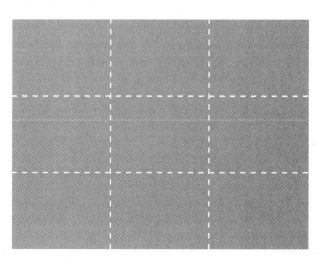

The rule of thirds is a guideline for creating a balanced frame

7-2

A typical rule-of-thirds framing

Terrence Malick's *Badlands*

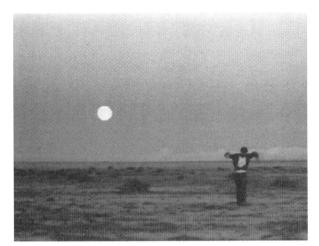

7-3

This classic balanced composition is a common strategy for handling shots with three characters

Fritz Lang's *Scarlet Street*

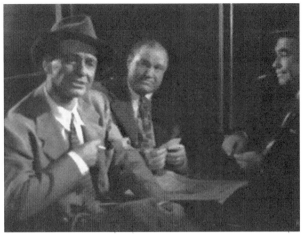

roughly halfway into the film, has Kit (Martin Sheen) aimlessly walking across the plains. **SEE 7-2** The horizon is on the bottom thirds line, with the moon in the upper left, balancing Kit on the right.

Fritz Lang's *Scarlet Street* (1945, Milton Krasner, DP) has a wealth of examples of classic balanced compositions. One scene has a group of reporters questioning the main character during a train ride. **SEE 7-3** The balancing of the three faces, the two characters on the vertical thirds lines, and the hands with the cards is a classic balanced composition—also a common strategy for handling a shot with three people.

It may be difficult for the experimental part of our nature to admit, but the basis for much film composition is the rule of thirds. Its application can be so conventional and lead to so much predictable composition that one almost wishes there might be another starting point. The rule of thirds is a natural reflection of human perceptual experience, however, and must be given careful consideration. If you were to take four strips of film tape and put them on your television set according to the thirds lines, the results would be stunning. You could marvel at the power of a simple straightforward composition or agonize over the depressing sameness of it all. Whether you are looking at a routine television show, a studio-age Hollywood film, or the most on-the-edge narrative piece, the lines would almost invariably intersect obvious areas of interest within the compositions. Although one may want to venture past this fundamental principle, the rule of thirds remains a starting place and constant point of reference as the dominant approach of the majority of international cinematography.

An acquaintance of mine sniffed when I mentioned that I teach students the rule of thirds. "A recipe for boring composition," he intoned. Despite the snootiness of the comment, it smacks of a certain amount of truth. Composition should be arresting and dynamic rather than formulaic and conventional. The past one hundred plus years of modern painting have been a direct reaction against conventions dating to the ancient Greeks and which were further rooted during the Renaissance. And yet, one has to learn how to draw a straight line before one can draw anything else. There is a big difference between composition that is new and challenging and composition that comes out of nowhere and is bad. Like it or not, a high percentage of the composition you see derives from the rule of thirds.

General Design Characteristics

Working DPs frequently invoke the names of great artists when discussing their approach to specific films. With the goal of creating rich, complex, and subtle images, a study of the historical development of the graphic arts—painting, graphic design, and photography—provides valuable schooling for the inexperienced cinematographer. A knowledge of the breadth of approaches to the arrangement of elements in a composition, the handling of line and shape, the shaping and direction of light, and the incorporation of content elements to produce meaning informs the framing and arrangement of any image. Student images are frequently criticized for concentrating on foreground elements (the subject) to the exclusion of a shot's *background*—an idea that is more complex than simply what is behind the subject. It is that extra information, that detail, that gives an image its context and character. This does not mean that cinematographers need to be imitative of specific works, nor should their work become static and arty. Just as there are books of painting and still photography designed for the coffee table, there can be coffee table movies. But the sense that a composition can have a "painterly" quality is a key first step in moving toward a necessarily complex approach to the image.

A laundry list of conventional design characteristics must by definition leave many things out. Images dominated by horizontals tend to be restful and stable. Verticals suggest strength and power. As might be suspected, diagonals tend to suggest imbalance, although when employed in highly structured arrangements, diagonals can create powerful images as well. The German expressionists, with their fascination with heroic myth, created paintings and films with dominant vertical elements. Leni Riefenstahl's famous and notorious *Triumph of the Will* (1935), an ode to Adolf Hitler and the Nazi Party, is an excellent example of a film that uses vertical and diagonal compositional elements to suggest strength and power.

Color is a key element in creating associations and tone. Blue is considered a cool color, both emotionally and physically. Red is hotter, suggesting warmer emotional content. Browns and greens are earth tones, suggesting naturalness and security. Lushness and brightness play a significant role in the texture of an image, as do muted and desaturated tones.

Compositions can also be arranged to direct viewer attention to specific parts of the frame. This can be done with lighting, arrangement of shapes, and design elements such as costume and makeup. Pools of light can be used to direct attention to specific areas. An example of two of these elements can be found in Milos Forman's *Amadeus* (Miroslav Ondricek, DP). **SEE 7-4** As Salieri hears Mozart conduct a recital for the first time, he advances through the audience in awe. The

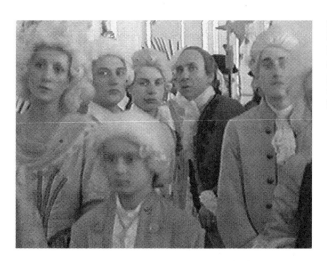

7-4

Costume and arrangement of peripheral characters direct viewer attention
Milos Forman's *Amadeus*

composition is designed to direct our eye to Salieri. The dark costume makes him stand out from the other concert goers, and the arrangement of peripheral characters creates lines that, when followed, lead the eye straight to Salieri.

Composition and Content

The foremost consideration in composing for film is that the image be a meaning-producing instrument. This is both difficult to accomplish and difficult to discuss. The concept of images producing meaning has long been analyzed in painting, graphic design, and photography, but no single discussion could ever be definitive. This is as it should be—the potential for any artistic expression being unlimited. It is not simply what is in the frame that creates meaning; it is also the way the subject is framed, arranged, and lighted, using all the resources discussed in previous chapters.

On a purely content level, a few typical examples will be helpful. Terrence Malick's *Days of Heaven* (1978, Nestor Almendros, DP) recounts a romance between a poor migrant worker (Brooke Adams) and a wealthy young farmer (Sam Shepard). Many of the film's images are dominated by the farmer's house, an impressive but isolated structure designed to suggest some of the same emotional qualities in its owner. Frequently the house is framed in the background of the migrants' activities, serving as a constant reminder of both the workers' reduced circumstances and the vast gap between them and the owner. One particularly telling sequence has the Brooke Adams character surprising the farmer as he sits in the tall grass, watching the sunset (see page 270 for a discussion of the lighting of this scene). As the two characters speak, the farmer's opulent home in the background dominates the space between them. **SEE 7-5** The visual arrangement of the shot itself suggests the relationship—the chasm—between the two characters. The house, and all it represents, will always separate them, no matter what events occur later in their relationship. What might appear to be an innocent encounter is literally over-shadowed by this dominating symbol of class distinction.

Ivan Passer's *Cutter's Way* (1981, Jordan Cronenweth, DP) provides a similar example. The story involves several friends living on the fringes of society, who suspect a rich man of committing a murder. At one point, two characters go sailing to escape the mounting tension. **SEE 7-6** As their boat plies the waves, an

7-5

Visual arrangement of elements symbolize the relationship of the characters

Terrence Malick's *Days of Heaven*

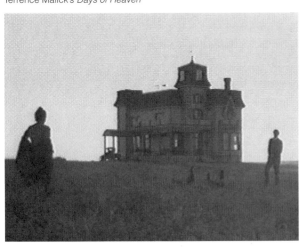

7-6

Visual subtext is meaningful information not present in the narrative but implicit in the visual presentation

Ivan Passer's *Cutter's Way*

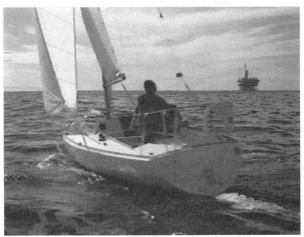

oil rig dominates the background of virtually every shot. As a symbol, the open sea generally suggests freedom and openness—a place where people can escape the ever-present demands of a complicated social existence. But here, the placement of the oil rig continually reminds us otherwise. It is omnipresent. The employment of *visual subtext*—information that is not present in the content and structure of the narrative but implicit in the visual presentation—is crucial in creating a complex image.

Composition and Stress

Whereas many shapes suggest internal balance, there are other shapes that cannot resolve their imbalance. These shapes and arrangements are said to have compositional *stress*, also referred to as tension. Both balance and stress have useful applications in any sophisticated concept of composition. Sometimes stress can be resolved by either implied or actual elements moving in the frame. Other times that stress is purposefully unresolved, creating an artwork that challenges conventional formal interpretation.

While most American films of the studio age relied on balanced compositions, film noir was the first style in commercial features to significantly exploit compositional stress to give a sense of a world in which something was catastrophically wrong. Joseph H. Lewis's *Gun Crazy* (1949, Russell Harlan, DP)—a classic independent, low-budget film noir—has many images that lack conventional balance. The film chronicles a couple's fascination with guns. Their eventual descent into criminality ends with the couple (Peggy Cummins and John Dahl) fleeing the police by car. In this final scene, the strain on the woman's face has a reciprocal representation in the imbalance of her composition. **SEE 7-7**

Although the impetus for the film noir sensibility faltered in the 1950s, the importance of compositional stress was rediscovered by cinematographers of the '60s and '70s, a sensibility continued in the films of David Lynch and others. Bernardo Bertolucci's *The Conformist* (1971, Vittorio Storaro, DP), a film that extensively influenced visual style of the period, has many intriguing examples of unbalanced compositions. An early scene in a radio station sets the visual tone with a stark composition of the film's protagonist (Jean-Louis Trintignant) having a conversation that is as ambiguous as the composition. **SEE 7-8**

7-7

Compositional stress gives a sense of a world in which something is very wrong

Joseph H. Lewis's *Gun Crazy*

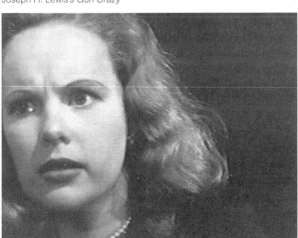

7-8

Stark, unbalanced compositions can reflect ambiguous content

Bernardo Bertolucci's *The Conformist*

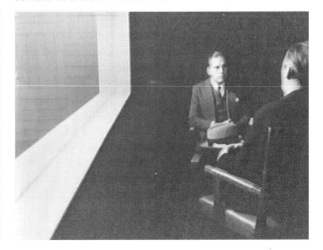

7-9

Compositional stress caused by elements with disproportional weight
Jean-Louis Trintignant in The Conformist

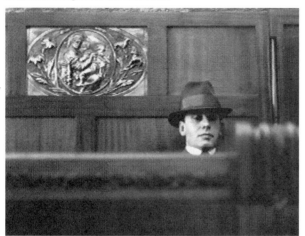

Another famous composition from *The Conformist* demonstrates a different kind of imbalance. **SEE 7-9** The lines of the image are very symmetrical, yet the face has too much weight to balance the other elements in the frame. In this case, there is an almost rule of thirds–like division, and yet the weight given individual elements creates a very unbalanced image.

Compositional stress often creates the expectation of resolution. When a space is left open, the expectation is created that it will be filled. An example of this is a shot of an individual sitting at a bar. If the empty bar stool next to the person is included in the shot, the expectation is created that the seat will be filled. If the shot is more conventionally balanced, someone *forcing* his way into the composition might be perceived as intrusive.

Horror films take particular advantage of this tension. Space is used to create the expectation on the part of the audience that something, usually bad, is going to happen. The open door behind the unsuspecting character is going to be filled by whatever representation of our inner fears the film is exploiting. Our expectations can be either fulfilled or frustrated. John Carpenter's *Halloween* (1978) has several situations in which the viewer is aware that the killer is near. Characters oblivious to the danger are shown in shots that have space left for the killer to enter. But the film purposefully increases tension—keeps us on the edge of our seats—by not delivering. When we get the relief of a more conventionally balanced composition, apparently signaling the passing of danger, Carpenter increases the shock by having the killer appear—violating the equilibrium.

Stress and Photographic Factors

Simple imbalance is a key factor in compositional stress; images, on the other hand, can achieve stress through different means. For example, elements specific to photography can be employed to create tension. Leaving elements out of focus can create confusion and frustration, particularly when the image is designed to make us want to see the subject. Distorting lenses can be a contributing factor as well, showing objects that are out of proportion in relation to the size of other elements in the frame.

Wide-angle lenses are frequently employed to create this type of stress. The bending of foreground elements mixed with the elongation—making background images appear smaller—can create exaggerated effects. The couple from *Gun Crazy* is often presented in shots that fragment their presence between the foreground and the background. **SEE 7-10** This is an issue of *scale*, the size of objects in relation to each other. Although it might be argued that these shots have some internal balance, the distortion of relationships definitely adds an element of stress.

Also from *Gun Crazy*, the companion shot to figure 7-10 is a good example of distortions of scale. **SEE 7-11** The steering wheel is so distorted in relationship to the face that, despite some internal balance, compositional stress is clearly an issue. Long lenses can create a confining and distorting perspective also. The prelude to one of the key musical sequences in Bob Fosse's *Cabaret* (1972) has an excellent example of this. **SEE 7-12** The song "Tomorrow Belongs to Me" is set in a beautiful

7-10
Use of wide-angle lens to create stress
Peggy Cummins and John Dahl in *Gun Crazy*

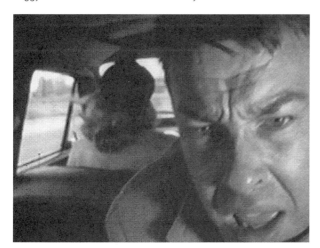

7-11
Use of distortions of scale to create stress
John Dahl in *Gun Crazy*

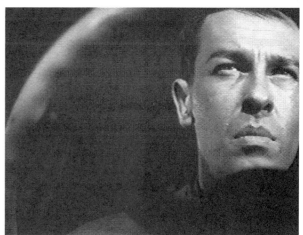

alpine beer garden. The establishment of this setting, however, which conventionally might be shot with a wide-angle or normal lens to give a complete view, is shot entirely with a long lens. The subtle claustrophobia—the lack of expected openness—creates apprehension that is born out when the deceptively bucolic atmosphere turns menacing as it evolves into a pro-Nazi songfest. In Jane Campion's *The Piano* (1993), the long lens is a factor in the scene where Ada's note to Baines (played by Holly Hunter and Harvy Keitel) falls into the wrong hands—a prelude to the film's violent action. **SEE 7-13** Filmed along a fence line in the hills, the squashed and angular compositions are so distorted that the scene is invested with an undertone foreshadowing the impending conflict.

7-12
The long lens can create a mood of claustrophobia and apprehension
Bob Fosse's *Cabaret*

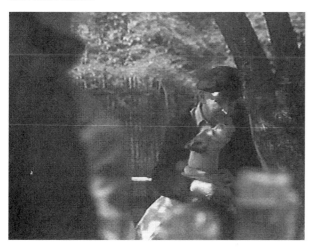

7-13
The squashed and angular composition foreshadows impending conflict
Jane Campion's *The Piano*

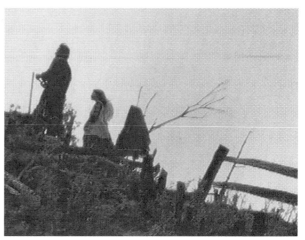

Lining Up the Shots

As stated, lining up the shots consists of looking at what is in front of the camera and deciding how to arrange it in relation to the boundaries of the film frame. This conscious approach to composition is generally the responsibility of the director of photography.

Headroom and Eyeroom

The predominant content element in most shots in narrative films is most frequently one or more people. When a person is the focus of compositional interest, where is the viewer's eye drawn? Usually to the eyes. When people are composed on film, the eyes are almost always on the top thirds line. **SEE 7-14** If you put the eyes any lower, you will frequently get into problems with *headroom*—the amount of space above the head. Cinematographers generally put the eyes on the top thirds line because too much headroom tends to diminish the subject. **SEE 7-15** This example obviously overstates the effect; less exaggerated effects diminish to a lesser degree.

Individual cinematographers handle headroom differently, but generally keep the top of the head close to the top of the frame. Headroom is more critical in close shots—close-ups with an inordinate amount of headroom definitely diminishing the subject. A little more headroom can be allowed in longer shots, although putting the eyes below the top thirds line can produce disagreeable results. Some cinematographers maintain that you can err on the side of too little headroom as well. Cropping that is too tight can make a character look constrained—as if in a room with a low ceiling.

Eyeroom, or *looking room*, refers to the practice of giving characters space in the direction they are looking. A character looking frame-right would be composed around the left thirds line and vice versa. If a character is not given eyeroom, the shot will feel confined, as if sight is somehow limited or the character's face is pressed up against something. Of course, there are times when a diminished or cramped effect can be useful, but if you do *not* want them, you must take care to compose accordingly.

Many cameras have viewing systems with crosshairs or ground-glass centers. Beginners occasionally mistake these for compositional aids, thinking that they

7-14

People are almost always composed with the eyes on the top thirds line

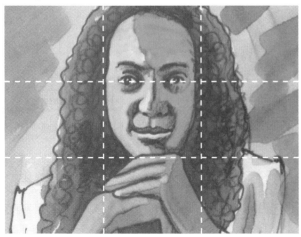

7-15

Too much headroom diminishes the subject

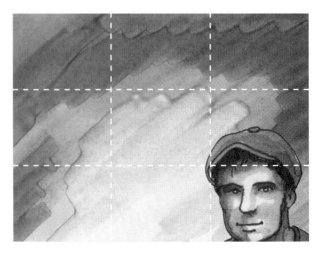

are supposed to put the crosshairs right between the subject's eyes. I like to call this the assassination theory of composition. I once saw this theory applied in a videotape of a man giving a very powerful speech. It was shot by an obviously inexperienced camera operator, who consistently kept the speaker's eyes right in the center of the frame. Given the limited options of taping a speech from a fixed camera position, the operator did about the only thing one can do—zoom in and zoom out. When the lens was zoomed in, the effect was bad though not entirely unacceptable. But when the lens was zoomed out, the cavernous space above the speaker's head made him appear tiny and unimpressive, completely subverting his powerful oration.

Cleaning the Image

It is usually necessary to "clean" the image of any elements that draw the viewer's attention to undesired parts of the frame or make for an odd visual presentation. In the first case, this refers to objects that either are an unwarranted distraction or are hovering around the edges of the frame. If an object, say, a chair leg, is barely protruding into the frame, it will draw attention to itself. The viewer's eye will unconsciously search it to see what it is. The more difficult it is to read, the more it will disrupt the frame. This is usually a matter of sloppy composition. The solution is to position the object entirely outside the frame or enough in the frame that the viewer can unconsciously read it without effort. The longer an image is held, the more the viewer will search the frame. If the viewer's attention is taken by an element in the frame that is confusing, it can detract from simple involvement.

Josef von Sternberg, one of the greatest of all visual directors, once stated that when presented with a shot of a character seated in a chair, he would be sure that all four chair legs were in the shot. His assumption was that the chair would appear to be on the verge of collapse if proper support were not evident. While this may show a lack of faith in the viewer's ability to understand images, the point is nevertheless made. That which an image needs, it must have. That which an image does not need should be eliminated.

The latter case refers to background, and to a lesser extent foreground, elements that are peculiarly positioned, such as telephone poles coming out of people's heads, and light switches, household plugs, and similar objects that because of their positioning appear to be attached to the body. Mel Stuart's *Willie Wonka and the Chocolate Factory* (1971) has an effective parody of the problem. **SEE 7-16** A television reporter is framed in such a way that the antlers of a trophy in the background appear to be coming out of his head. Although this example is a good gag, it can create peculiar effects when not desired.

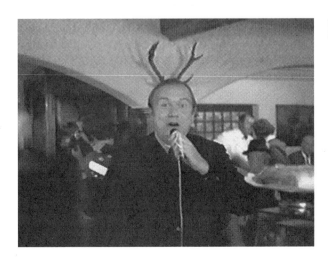

7-16

Distracting background image creates peculiar effect

Mel Stuart's *Willie Wonka and the Chocolate Factory*

7-17

This example of cheating in positioning the characters defies logic but represents an adventurous solution

Alfred Hitchcock's *The Man Who Knew Too Much*

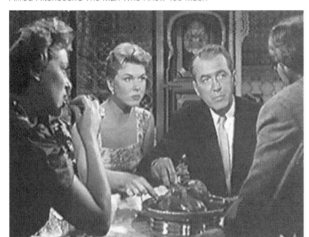
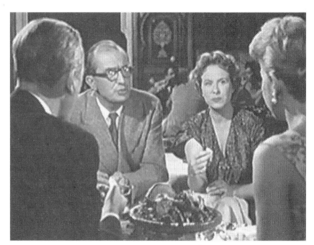

Cheating

Shifting elements in the composition to balance the frame, thus improving an otherwise problematic shot, is called *cheating*. Most cheats are relatively simple: moving items on a table, shifting furniture, or relocating artwork on a wall is frequently enough to fix an untenable frame. Continuity is a key concern when cheating, although experience helps to understand what you can get away with.

Cheating applies to the positioning of characters as well. If a character is blocked in a specific way for one angle, there may be a difficult background element that creates a problem—say a door frame or light switch—in another angle. To eliminate the problem, simply move the actor in the appropriate direction to either cover up the offending object or allow recomposition to exclude it.

Alfred Hitchcock, who seemed to delight in these simple manipulations, did a cheat in *The Man Who Knew Too Much* (1956, Robert Burks, DP) that defies logic, but which still goes largely unnoticed by the audience. The scene involves two couples sitting across each other at a table. **SEE 7-17** While both couples are shoulder-to-shoulder when facing the camera, they are several feet apart in their respective reverses. Shooting a conversation like this is always a challenge due to questions of the line and shifting perspective. This example represents an adventurous solution—one which may have left a less prestigious director making explanations to studio chiefs.

Directors of photography are always adjusting things, fussing with the set, and rearranging props to get the perfect composition. With eye to the camera, a camera operator asking a props person or set dresser to slide things a little bit one way or the other is quite common. Sloppiness is acceptable only in a few specific applications, and DPs will generally work hard to achieve an image that is clean and not confusing.

Movement and Anticipatory Camera

As suggested in chapter 2, much of the camera movement in film is not noticed by the viewer. It is movement that responds to or, more accurate, anticipates subject movement. *Anticipatory camera* is an approach to cinematography that is particularly associated with classic Hollywood cinema. It is structured, highly choreographed camerawork that leads rather than follows movement, making adjustments for the movement of characters in the frame or the entrances of others. Not all camerawork need be formal, but the approach so dominates all cinematography that it influences the way one thinks about shooting.

The DP must respond intelligently to shifting elements within the frame. A common example is a two-shot in which one of the characters exits. The initial frame can be balanced for two people, but that balance falls apart once the person leaves. The solution is to pan slightly in the appropriate direction to rebalance the frame. Whenever there is movement in the frame, the DP is confronted with a choice: What to do to compensate for the movement. Generally, failure to adjust results in poor framing.

Just as performance is rehearsed, camera is rehearsed as well. During the final blocking of the scene in rehearsals, the actor's movements should become consistent, and a plan for shooting can be devised and rehearsed. If the actor shifts her weight or turns to face a new direction, the responding movement of the camera can be perfectly timed to anticipate the action. If the actor is going through a bigger movement, the camera can accommodate it by drifting or moving boldly in the appropriate direction. The key is rehearsal so that the camera operator knows the movement and has a planned response.

The concluding scenes of Fritz Lang's *Scarlet Street* have many excellent examples of camera movement used to create a balanced composition and anticipate movement. In one scene, where the guilt-racked main character, Christopher Cross (Edward G. Robinson), is overwhelmed with guilt, he begins hearing the voices of the people whose deaths he has caused. In one shot, he tears away the canopy on his bed to find the source of the voices. The camera starts with a balanced composition of the bed sheets shielded by a canopy. **SEE 7-18A** In an exceedingly subtle move that is a perfect demonstration of this concept, a quick tilt is done to create room for Chris as he enters the frame. **SEE 7-18B** The camera does not react *after* Chris enters the shot; it starts the movement just before he enters the frame and is finished by the time he reaches his final position. On the surface a move like this appears to be almost inconsequential, but it is with responses such as this that camerawork achieves much of its subtlety and fluidity. Without this type of movement, camerawork can appear static and stagey.

Broader movements benefit from thoughtful planning as well. A shot following the one just described leads Chris through a complex movement. The shot starts with Chris seated on the bed. **SEE 7-18C** The camera starts to dolly out

7-18

Using camera movement to create balance and anticipate subject movement
Edward G. Robinson in *Scarlet Street*

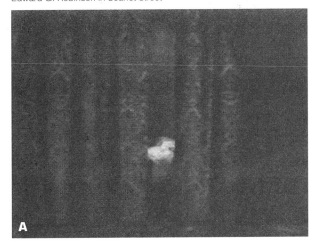

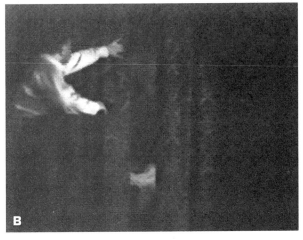

7-18

Using camera movement to create balance and anticipate subject movement *(continued)*

Edward G. Robinson in *Scarlet Street*

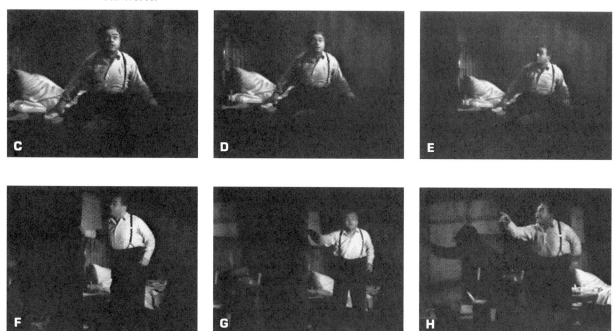

to give Chris room to stand. **SEE 7-18D** Before he stands, Chris looks frame-left. **SEE 7-18E** The camera anticipates this by drifting left to create eyeroom, also anticipating the direction Chris will go when he rises from the bed. The camera does not give full headroom for Chris's final position when standing, as that would create too much headroom while he is still on the bed. The top of the frame is completed in a tilt timed to his rising. **SEE 7-18F** The camera then continues to drift frame-left as Chris advances through the room. **SEE 7-18G** Both camera movement and character movement are then perfectly timed for an ending composition, allowing room for a striking shadow of Chris as he points to something. **SEE 7-18H**

Anticipatory camera movements are the result of choices that must be made constantly while preparing each shot—working out strategies for covering the action in front of the camera. A camera operator must respond to all subject movement. Failure to do so results in compositions that may begin well but wind up out of balance.

On a set there is constant dialogue among the director, the camera operator, and the talent as to the inclusion and arrangement of elements within the frame. Although most movements of this nature are planned out in advance, the camera operator should be ready for minor adjustments. The biggest mistake novice camera operators make is to find a good beginning composition and then lock down the tilt and pan, as if this is the framing the world should have forever. The camera operator generally wants to have the tilt and pan unlocked (usually both on tight fluid) in order to respond to subject movement.

Planning and executing movements that are assured and decisive is an important goal for a beginning cinematographer. You can always tell when a cinematographer has not quite decided what to do in a specific situation. There is a tentative quality to the movements that betrays the operator's lack of confidence. Part of maturing as a camera operator is building confidence in your judgment and showing conviction in the effects you are trying to accomplish.

Movement and Compositional Balance

Frequently, camera movement is necessary to create balance in a composition that has been disrupted by or simply needs to follow the action. DPs will often use elements in the foreground or background to balance off compositions. As characters move, however, these balancing elements can become liabilities unless appropriately managed. The opening of the previously discussed scene from *Scarlet Street* has Chris entering his rented room. Elements on a table in the foreground are used to create balance as he walks through the room. As he comes in, he is balanced by a bottle frame-right and a wall light fixture frame-left. **SEE 7-19A** As he moves across the room toward a window, the camera dollies left while panning right. **SEE 7-19B** In the resulting composition, Chris is balanced by a coffeepot and cup at frame-left and the window frame-right. **SEE 7-19C** Balance is a key goal here, but these elements are also used to create a sense of depth in the image.

7-19

Using camera movement and foreground and background elements for compositional balance
Fritz Lang's *Scarlet Street*

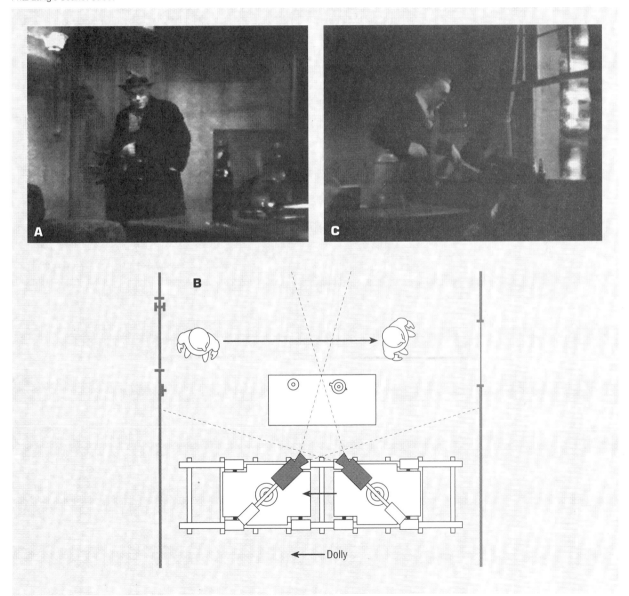

A question might be, why the dolly? Could a pan have been done instead? Although this movement may have been a feature of a grand plan on Lang's part—as befits the main character's name, there is much crossing imagery in the film—it also could have been just one of those things that was worked out on the set. Within the confines of the set, a pan may not have created the final composition that Lang and DP Milton Krasner felt was appropriate.

Subject Movement Toward or Away from the Camera

A subject moving toward or away from the camera almost always requires some adjustment. If the composition is correct at the beginning of the shot, a character would move out of the top of the composition as he approaches the camera if no correction is made. **SEE 7-20** A tilt is usually in order, often with a pan incorporated for any horizontal changes. The key to executing a good move is to find some aspect of the composition that is going to remain relatively stable; in this case, keeping the appropriate headroom would be a key issue.

The previously mentioned shot from *Amadeus* concludes with a stunned Salieri approaching the camera. **SEE 7-21A** As Salieri comes closer, the camera is subtly and fluidly tilted to give the appropriate headroom for the new composition. The timing is immaculate with the headroom kept perfectly even throughout the move. By the end, the camera is at a low angle that exaggerates Salieri's features and diminishes the peripheral characters in the background. **SEE 7-21B** Movement like this requires rack focusing as well.

7-20

A character approaching the camera moves out of the top of the composition, necessitating a tilt

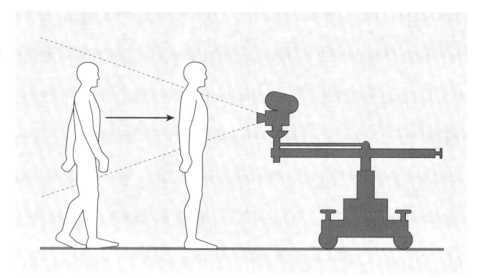

7-21

Tilting to give appropriate headroom as subject approaches the camera

F. Murray Abraham in *Amadeus*

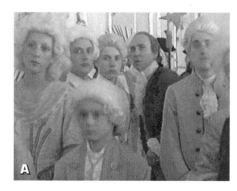
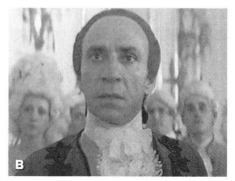

Camera Movement Toward or Away from a Subject

The same principles apply to dollies and zooms toward and away from a subject as with subject movement. There is almost always a tilt necessary, and often a pan as well. **SEE 7-22** Despite the aesthetic differences between a dolly and a zoom, when considering compositional adjustments made necessary by their use, they become virtually synonymous.

7-22

A dolly or zoom toward a subject usually requires a tilt

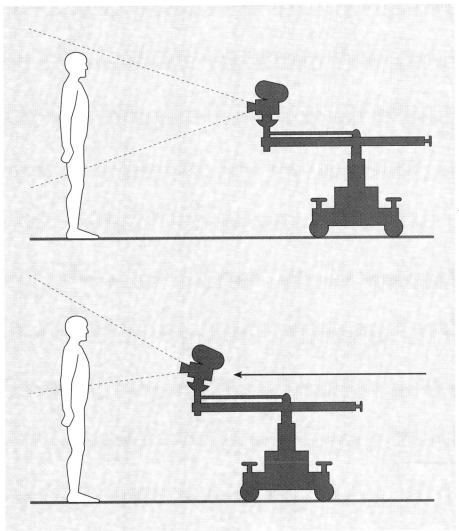

Movement to Create Space

Moving the camera to create room for a character entering the frame is a common approach. Director Nicholas Ray has garnered recognition for the fluid and thoughtful use of the camera in his films. Ray's *In a Lonely Place* (1950, Burnett Guffey, DP) has many examples of the camera being used to accommodate character entrances and exits. A typical shot features a literary agent (Art Smith) being joined by the main female lead, Laurel (Virginia Graham). Again, timing is

7-23

Gradually moving the camera to accommodate a subject entering the frame

Nicholas Ray's *In a Lonely Place*

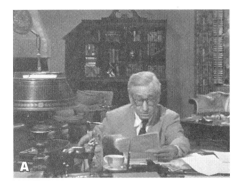 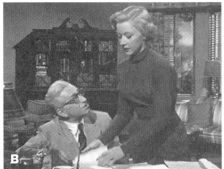

everything. The camera starts with a composition of the agent. **SEE 7-23A** The composition starts to drift right and slightly up to anticipate Laurel's entrance. When she enters the frame, the composition is completing as she reaches her final position. **SEE 7-23B**

Character Movement to Balance Composition

Having a character move to fill a compositional void is also a very common approach. Rather than planning some extensive and time-consuming camera move, simply have the talent move to positions that fill out the composition. *Scarlet Street* has an excellent, though almost comically transparent, example of this. The scene immediately following the previous example involves two police officers rousting the now derelict main character from a park bench. **SEE 7-24A** The entire scene is done in a single take and, though many viewers might not notice it, incorporates significant camera movement. This sequence of three frames illustrates how characters can be regrouped after they are set in motion.

The shorter officer in the foreground does all the talking, while the taller officer is essentially a shill to be played off of. As Chris starts to get off the bench, the first officer steps toward him to be assertive, disrupting the balance of the frame. **SEE 7-24B** The second officer steps frame-left—into the empty space— to reestablish balance. **SEE 7-24C** It is clear from its stiffness that this movement is done at someone's direction and is solely intended to rebalance composition.

Such movements are the subject of much discussion on the set. The DP often has to ask the talent to move to specific positions to be in proper composition. Again, this is what marks are for. If beginning film actors share a common short-coming, it is in neither understanding nor accommodating the requirements of composition. Occasionally directors have to take young performers (particularly stage-trained ones) aside and explain "the rules of the road." Shots are effective only if certain principles are considered while shooting.

7-24

Using character movement to fill compositional voids

Fritz Lang's *Scarlet Street*

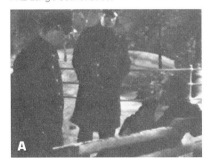 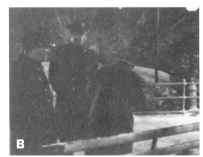 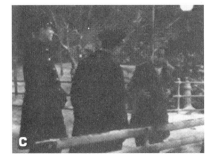

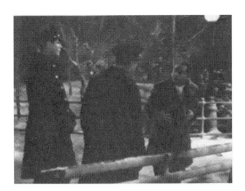 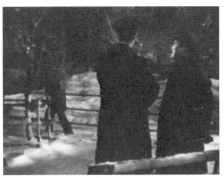

7-25

Creating emotional space with a pragmatic use of movement

Fritz Lang's *Scarlet Street*

Movement and Meaning

We have mainly been detailing the practical considerations of movement, but many thematic issues are dependent on movement as well, incorporating the creation of space for meaning. The end of the park bench shot from *Scarlet Street* provides an example of both: the creation of emotional space intermingled with a pragmatic use of movement. After the police have rousted Chris, he shuffles off behind them. **SEE 7-25** The camera drifts left to allow him space to leave. Not only is this a practical necessity, it also allows Chris to disappear miserably into the distance.

One final note: Although camera operators are given rehearsals for complicated moves, they are usually expected to handle simple ones on their own. It may be considerate to allow beginning DPs several practices, but this may not be the case in much standard production.

Practical Considerations

As always, practical considerations shape many of the decisions made for shooting. Whatever is planned will have complications, and being able to effectively readjust is essential.

Composition and Compromise

Composition often requires compromise. That is, either to avoid some bothersome element or to integrate a difficult camera move, a framing that is less than perfect has to be made. The camera might have to be tilted down to avoid a hanging light in a tight location. The camera might have to be panned one direction or the other to avoid an undesired background element. How do you respond when there is a substantial difference in the heights of the characters, or if one character is seated and the other is standing? Do you tilt up to make room for a character entering the frame, or start with too much headroom and let the character fill it?

The previously discussed shot from Nicholas Ray's *In a Lonely Place* is a good example of a typical compromise (figure 7-23). The initial framing of this shot is easy to criticize as being too loose, having unnecessary headroom in particular. However, the logic of the composition is made apparent when the second character enters. The move to the final composition would have been too extreme—the tilt would have covered too much distance too quickly—if the first framing had been tighter. The movement would not have been fluid, particularly when matching movement from other shots. As in this example, framings occasionally have to be left loose to incorporate some other element entering or exiting the frame. In this case, the first composition is left loose to facilitate a subtle move to the second, tighter composition.

Often, such compromises have to do with avoiding undesired elements in the foreground or background. If there are television antennas on the homes in a period piece, framing will have to be adjusted so the antennas are not in the shots. If a room has a low ceiling, high camera angles may have to be used to avoid hanging lights or microphones on booms. There are myriad obstacles that make slight changes in shots necessary.

Compromises are a necessity in situations in which achieving complete control of all the elements is impossible. (This notion is explored further in a variety of contexts.) A great deal of time and money goes into securing shooting spaces that can be manipulated to the needs of filmmakers. If something on the location is posing a problem, it will simply be eliminated. This can include a wide range of obstacles, many of them beyond the question of compositional challenges—from television antennas in period pieces to unattractive paint jobs to bothersome people. Without the money or time to change things, independents and students wind up shooting, in some cases literally, around obstacles. It is often a matter of what you are willing to give up compositionally to create something that is workable.

Camera and Performance

The dialogue between the DP and the talent is critical. The talent often has specific expectations of the DP, and the DP always needs the performers to respond to compositional requirements. Communication is constant and is essential to the visual shape of the film.

One expectation is that the DP must make the talent look good. There are legendary stories of actors who insisted that they be filmed and lighted in very specific ways. Although one might prefer not to be a slave to some cultural beauty stereotype, one needs to recognize that there are indeed angles on performers that do not do them justice. A certain amount of cinematography is still based on the old glamour approach of the studio age. Making sure that all the elements display the talent at their best can affect a wide range of decisions. Determining which side of the line to film from based on the actor's better side is a typical example.

Beyond this concern for appearance, talent is a critical component in composition. Performers' movements must be integrated into the needs of a balanced frame. Usually this is a matter of setting up marks for the talent to hit as they move through a scene, the approach representing a tightly choreographed interplay between camera and subject. A good example of this is when the director wants a moving subject in a close-up, in which case the DP has to make the performer move within tightly controlled parameters. The DP will draw a frame in the air that will give the boundaries of a performer's possible movements: "If you move too far this way, you will be out of composition. If you go too far that way…"

One concern is that if the space is too defined, actors can become so absorbed in the mechanical aspects of their movement that the performance gets lost. However, being able to work within the technical demands of the medium depends on the ability and professionalism of the actor. Alfred Hitchcock's *Notorious* (Ted Tetzlaff, DP), has many shots of characters in movement that are so tight that it clearly took much communication among talent, DP, and director to achieve the desired stability of composition. Shots of Alicia nervously pacing in the midst of a party as Dev searches for clues in the wine cellar are particularly good examples of moving shots that are very tightly controlled. One can clearly visualize the DP drawing the boundaries of her movement. This tight control is very purposeful in emphasizing the tension Alicia feels while trying to aid Dev's clandestine activities. To allow a wider frame for greater freedom of movement would have diluted the claustrophobic effect. Despite the constraints, Bergman's performance is one of the most luminescent in film. Every emotional shading shines within the tightly controlled technique that displays it. Considering all the technical adjustments that must have been transpiring, Bergman maintained focus on the smallest elements of her performance.

Still, inexperienced performers may have difficulties keeping compositional considerations from affecting their performance. Some actors may rebel at the tightly controlled parameters. One possibility is to have actors move in such a way as to remain framed appropriately, that is, they could reposition themselves or shift their body weight to conform to the needs of the composition. However, this usually occasions stiff, unnatural movement on the actors' part. Being sensitive to the performers' concerns is a necessity, but being firm about the demands of the medium is also important. Talent who cannot hit marks or understand abstract parameters are going to be the source of sloppy compositions.

Informal Camera Styles

The classical approach to camerawork is one more convention to be questioned and tested. The 1960s and 1970s saw a movement toward a more informal image in films—a movement that had its genesis in post–World War II Italian film and the French New Wave of the '50s and '60s. In films ranging from the work of Robert Altman and John Cassavetes to those of a new generation of experimental and documentary filmmakers, there was an attempt to create an image that was more spontaneous than the highly choreographed Hollywood prototype.

In such films as *Faces* (1968) and *Husbands* (1970), John Cassavetes was an innovator, particularly in the use of the handheld camera in fictional films. The most striking feature of these films is their improvisational tone. The majority of the scenes were shot handheld, and one gets a sense that the camera operator was given the camera and told to do the best he could, not knowing what was going to happen next. The films have an almost documentary shooting approach, the camera being used to film a narrative with improvised elements.

The handheld camera can create less structured and less static imagery, but informal imagery and the handheld camera are not synonymous. Robert Altman's early masterworks *McCabe and Mrs. Miller* (1971) and *The Long Goodbye* (1973) have images and sequences of shots that were largely undreamed of prior to these films. Altman and his cinematographer, Vilmos Zsigmond, specifically planned for the camera to be always moving in *The Long Goodbye*. The actors were also allowed great freedom, making the compositions feel less arranged. After his work in *The Long Goodbye*, actor Sterling Hayden remarked how much he enjoyed the freedom this approach allowed the actor. He was not constantly annoyed by having to hit the marks that are required in a more structured approach.

The style of films like these can be quite engaging, though it never gained wide acceptance by audiences. Jean-Luc Godard was systematic in his theoretical and filmic assaults on the shackles of the old, highly choreographed style. In the United States, Dennis Hopper's *Easy Rider* (1969) was a key work in paving the way toward a less structured approach. However, Gordon Willis's shooting in Francis Ford Coppola's *The Godfather II* (1974) and John Alonzo's in Roman Polanski's *Chinatown* (1974), among others, marked a return to formal, structured imagery. The impulse remains, but the revolutionary fervor has diminished. With his ability to integrate both formal and informal styles, Martin Scorsese is one of the few directors to effectively incorporate this trend over the long term.

Notes and Suggestions

One critical thing to remember is that there is a big difference between just looking through the camera and "shooting." Anyone can look through a camera. Shooting is an art. Many young camera operators bring to shooting too much of their experience of viewing film. When looking at a shot, the eye is generally drawn to a specific area of the frame, and awareness of the rest of the frame is limited. If it is a shot of a person, the viewer's eyes are generally drawn to those of the performer. In a classroom exercise several years ago, I asked a student camera operator for an MS of an actor. A crew member hit the slate that marks each scene and stepped to the side. I thought he was standing too close to the actor for the composition I had called. I assumed the camera operator was doing the right thing. When we got the film back, there was the guy with the slate, standing a few feet away, smiling and enjoying the performance. Everyone ribbed him mercilessly until I pointed out that this was really the operator's responsibility. The camera operator was shooting like a movie viewer. He zeroed in on the performer's eyes, completely unaware of the rest of the frame. He was watching content when he should have been watching form. A camera operator needs a whole-frame awareness when shooting film.

A good camera operator is going to find a way to make the composition arresting and interesting *at all times*. It is not a matter of coming up with a decent composition occasionally. If you set up a camera on a busy street, a decent composition will wander by every once in a while. But this is not filmmaking. The tension between the edges of the frame and its contents is of paramount importance. There needs to be a symbiotic relationship between the contents of the frame and the "rightness" of their arrangement.

Again, the primary responsibility is an awareness of whether what is being shot will cut together. It is clearly the director's responsibility to make sure that what is shot works, but the DP monitors exactly what the pieces will be and should be able to extrapolate to an edited finished product. Many students have heard the famous story of Orson Welles's encounter with a balky DP. While shooting a scene, the DP was constantly interjecting his opinion about what shots would cut and arguing about shots he felt would not cut. In exasperation, Welles told him that they were filming a dream sequence. By Welles's account, the DP was putty in his hands from that moment on. Whether or not this story is true (anyone familiar with the day-to-day practical aspects of production would have to be dubious), it is repeated too frequently by people who do not have the experience and, potentially, vision that Welles had. The knowledge that a good DP has about cutting should be seen as an asset, not a source for confrontation. There will always be technical people who are overbearing and overly schematic in their approach. But there are an equal number of directors who should be listening when they are about to make a mistake. As suggested, a DP with some editing room experience is often a real ally.

PART III

Lighting and Exposure

8

Concepts and Equipment

The Importance of Lighting

One shock for aspiring filmmakers is the high percentage of films that make extensive use of artificial light for both interior and exterior shooting. The necessity for interior lighting surprises no one, but the number of lights and the complexity of their implementation often does. Beautiful exterior light—natural light—has always been found by still photographers, but it occurs too unpredictably and changes too rapidly to be a good ally of filmmakers. On his film *Ran* (1985), it is said that Japanese director Akira Kurosawa kept a cast of thousands standing by for several hours, waiting for just the right cloud formation. Most filmmakers do not have that luxury. Because the light in any situation may not exist in the volume or with the highlights desired, a filmmaker must know how to evaluate existing lighting situations and become completely conversant in the uses of artificial light.

Just as a painter starts with a blank canvas, a filmmaker starts with an unlit space. Light is the filmmaker's brush and palette. Phrases such as "painting with light" or the "painterly qualities" of light suggest the power of light, dark, and color to establish mood, suggest psychological states, and communicate the tactile qualities of observed objects. Lighting can accomplish much more than this, but it is nevertheless a key building block of the photographic image.

Despite the fundamental importance of light and lighting, industry professionals often express frustration with the poor preparation students receive in the area of lighting, a distressing situation given that many entry-level positions are on lighting crews. Although there are a number of reasons for this, the major one is that students cannot possibly duplicate the Hollywood model for lighting. Limited in financial resources, schools cannot afford the sophisticated equipment that makers of features and commercials use on a daily basis. Even if the equipment were available, the complexity of setup would stymie even the most ambitious student. To achieve the *production values*, an umbrella term that refers to the amount of resources devoted to the image, of commercial features requires a commitment of time, equipment, personnel, and access to locations beyond the means of any one individual, particularly an inexperienced individual.

The last reason is probably the most decisive. While the story and content elements will always be the hardest parts of making a film, a mastery of lighting and exposure is one of the most difficult things for students at all levels to achieve. The novice lighting person is going to make many mistakes. Without knowing a few tricks of the trade, it is hard to get the lights to create the effects that one wants and sees so apparently easily achieved in other films. There are many technical specifications to learn. The equipment is heavy and bulky and, without compassionate and strong friends, it can be a struggle just getting it from here to there.

The key to this is control. Every beginner sweats through that seemingly interminable period between turning the film into the processing lab and getting it back, vexed by the question: Is the film going to turn out the way I want? What this chapter addresses, and what you will have as a long-term goal, is the elimination of that query. Lighting is presented here in a systematic way that, albeit technical, does not intimidate the reader. The first step before beginners can usefully move to advanced technical lighting manuals is to understand some key concepts clearly and unambiguously.

What is provided here is a simple, step-by-step introduction to how to think about lighting. That is not the same as teaching you how to light. The only way to learn that is by actually doing it. There are no quick fixes, no way to be there without the process of getting there. The getting there part is what not only teaches you the craft of lighting but is central to the process of maturing as a creative individual. And, besides, getting there is all the fun.

Basic Three-Point Lighting

This basic lighting setup is so fundamental that people have a tendency, when it is first presented to them, to dismiss it as too simplistic. It is the textbook approach to figure (character) lighting, and most everyone knows that lighting is generally more complicated than this. To some very small degree, they are right. Most lighting is far more complicated, with many more lights used than in the three-point setup. But it is still the starting point for most lighting. Whatever else you are doing, you almost always have to consider these points. **SEE 8-1**

8-1

The basic three-point setup is the textbook approach to lighting.

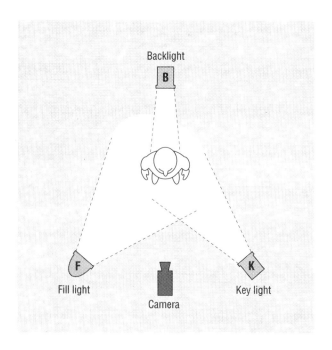

Key Light

The *key light* is usually the major source of illumination. It is generally a bright, hard beam of light that casts harsh shadows. It will create a deep nose shadow on the side of the face away from the light. The rest of that side of the face will also be dark. It is usually the main *source* of light in a shot. The viewer identifies it, though probably unconsciously, as the direction from which the light is coming. When we are outside during the day, the key light is, of course, the sun. At night it might be the moon or some artificial source. Indoors it may be a window, a lamp, or a ceiling fixture. You can think of the key light as the "source" light or the "main" light, but it is usually referred to as the "key." Some lighting people prefer the term *point source*. The key light is frequently, though not always, the light that is used to determine the *f*-stop.

Fill Light

The *fill light* is generally on the opposite side of the camera from the key. It is generally softer than the key light and, as its name suggests, it "fills in" the harshness of the shadows created by the key. To a large extent, the intensity of the fill light in relationship to the key light controls the dramatic quality of the shadows. If the fill light is close in terms of intensity to the key, the shadows will be light. If the fill light is much lower than the key, the shadows will be deeper.

Backlight

The *backlight* is often considered to be the least essential of the three points. Its presence is open to a certain amount of debate, as it is often difficult to determine what its source is. The backlight is generally above and behind the subject, shining down and hitting the subject on the back of the head. Its use can be more general than this, hitting a more substantial part of the body. In recent years, though, the term has come to identify what used to be called a "hair" light. It provides texture and definition to the hair and will also help to separate the subject from the background. The lack of a backlight will often leave the subject's hair shapeless and looking like a single mass sticking straight up out of the head.

If you think about it, these points, particularly the first two, are very logical and are going to exist in some form or other in most images. All light has a source, and we can think of that source as the key light. A cinematographer friend likes to use the example of "sun and sand." Sunlight hits a person and casts harsh shadows on the side away from it. This light continues through to the sand, which reflects the light back to fill in the harsh shadows the sun has created. The same is true indoors. The source light reflects off other surfaces in the room, such as the walls and the ceiling, filling in the side away from the source. Generally, we refer to this bounced or reflected light as *ambient light*. Not only does the key light have a source (it *is* the source), but the fill light has a source that can be identified as well.

This is where the backlight becomes somewhat controversial: there is often no identifiable source for it. Many people who light for film like to think of a light's source in terms of there being some *justification* for a light hitting a subject from a specific direction. Sometimes DPs are every bit as careful about establishing where the source of light is as directors are in establishing the spatial characteristics of the scene. There are DPs who will not use backlights for this reason. For the many who do, however, the major justification is photographic. Without it, the hair can look characterless and flat. This idea of justification is a significant one and is discussed further in this and subsequent chapters.

It was stated that one of the controls of the dramatic quality of an image is how intense the fill light is in relationship to the key light. But why is it necessary to have a key side and a fill side? It is essential to have a shaded side of the face (or object) because it aids the perception of depth in an image. The film image is two-dimensional, and achieving a sense of dimensionality requires some work. If the key light and the fill light are even in terms of intensity, facial features will be flattened—the nose will appear to be pushed flat against the face.

Using a key and fill does not necessarily mean that one side of the face must be in shadow. In several scenes of Ivan Passer's *Cutter's Way*, cinematographer Jordan Cronenweth essentially exposed for the traditional fill side, allowing the key side to overexpose dramatically. **SEE 8-2** The effect is the same, but with the bright side being responsible for dimensionality.

Eventually you may not even think about lighting in terms of these discrete points, but the key/fill/backlight system will remain central to the process of lighting. These concepts are so basic that people either tend to be too dogmatic with their application or disregard them altogether. The latter is by far the greater sin. Invariably, I get at least one student per semester who wants to skip over this dry, textbook stuff and get on to the real exciting stuff. Get out the fog machines. It is somewhat like jumping into trigonometry before you learn how to add. You must have a starting point, and the three-point system is just that, in terms of learning not only how to light but also how you are going to approach many of the other elements in the scene.

The key/fill concept works because, just as in daily life, there has to be some source of light. This does not mean there is just one source of light or just one key light; there may be many. There may not be just one fill—there may be two or twenty. There may not be a backlight as we have defined it. There may be a light used for that function as well as others. But these basic lights are going to exist. Not necessarily all of them on every shot, but the concepts are nevertheless fundamental.

I once worked on a film in which a group of characters walked down a carnival midway at night. What would be the source of light? Obviously there was more than one source. As they passed every hotdog stand and ring toss parlor, we created some kind of light to expose them the way we wanted. Sometimes the light from the hotdog stand was filling while the ring toss keyed. Occasionally the characters passed through a darkened area. And this was only the starting point.

When you approach the lighting of a shot, you generally have something in the frame that you consider to be the most important. Often you want that subject, let's say it's a person, to be normally exposed—and if you do *not* want them normally exposed, the same reasoning applies. The amount of light you

8-2

Exposing for the fill side overexposes the key side
Ivan Passer's *Cutter's Way*

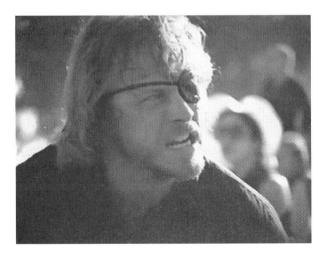

have on the person you want normally exposed is then going to become the dominant light value. Thinking of the key light as being this dominant value helps us plot out all the other values.

In other words, once you have set the key, you have established the value for which you are exposing the scene. If you key someone to $f/5.6$ and want them normally exposed, you are going to shoot at $f/5.6$. This may seem like backward logic, but once the f-stop has been determined, you can then decide where you want all the other values. If you have another area or object that you want normally exposed, you will light that to the established value, and so on. Once you figure out what you want normally exposed, all the other values will fall in line. How do you want to fill it? What do you do for backlight?

High-key and Low-key

The first terms you will hear when learning about lighting are *high-key* and *low-key*. These refer to types of lighting and have standard definitions.

High-key

This is even, fairly flat lighting. One could call it nonjudgmental lighting. There is little contrast between the darks and the lights in the image. A large part of the image exists within a fairly neutral range. Writers on film usually associate high-key lighting with musicals and comedies. It is used when we do not want the quality of the light to dominate what is occurring in the image or to imply judgments that are not associated with the subject. In other words, we do not want the lighting to contradict what the image is doing. Some might call this lighting Rockwellian, because it gives an even sense of well-being and normalcy, like the works of the American painter Norman Rockwell.

Low-key

This is the opposite of high-key lighting. It is moody and atmospheric and might be considered judgmental. There is contrast within the image and therefore a significant play between the lights and the darks. **SEE 8-3** Low-key lighting is often associated with horror films and mysteries, psychological dramas and crime stories. The German filmmakers of the 1920s were pioneers in their experiments with the expressive qualities of light in film. Certainly, the apex of low-key lighting in

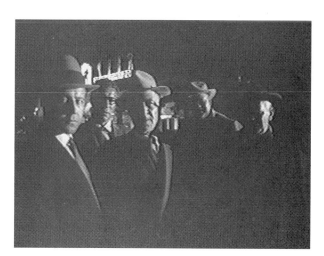

8-3

The contrast between light and dark in a typical low-key image

Orson Welles's *Touch of Evil*

American film came in the 1940s and 1950s with a group of films called film noir (see following section).

Again, these are basic definitions. They are the conventions, and their use has become somewhat cliché, from the moody lighting of Dracula's castle to the sunny atmosphere of a standard love story. Still, at least in terms of conventional narrative films, high-key and low-key are the choices, and nearly all variations at least recognize these limits. More adventurous directors will stretch the conventions—witness many of the family scenes from Alfred Hitchcock's *Shadow of a Doubt* (1943). The high-key images of uncomplicated small-town life are undermined by both the viewer's, and eventually one of the character's, knowledge that the beloved Uncle Charlie (Joseph Cotten) is a killer. One scene that takes place on the family's sunny front porch could be an image from any typical Norman Rockwell tableau. **SEE 8-4** In Hitchcock's hands, the scene is invested with a dark undertone. The parameters of the conventions are being played with. It is not so much whether the conventions exist as what you do within them and how you manipulate them.

European cinematographers often break down light into three distinct categories, rather than the two that Americans use. Low-key remains the same, but what Americans call high-key is referred to as normal-key. When Europeans use the term *high-key,* they are referring to overly bright, termed *overexposed,* images. Ingmar Bergman's *Persona* (1966) uses this approach to great effect. Virtually the entire film is shot slightly overexposed. This gives the film a very unrealistic tone, and the characters, as well as the audience, always seem to be squinting, almost overwhelmed by the act of trying to see. The final sequences of Stanley Kubrick's *2001: A Space Odyssey* (1968), in which the aged astronaut wanders around his brightly lit living quarters, is another example of a very expressive use of an overexposed image. The last shot of Oliver Stone's *Platoon* (1986), in which the main character is lost in the sun as the helicopter flies away, is also a good example.

Given American filmmaking's fascination with realism, overexposure has not found wide acceptance. On the other hand, **underexposure**, dark areas in the shot, replicates common perceptual experience and is employed frequently. Overexposure does not mimic routine perceptual experience, an exception being the painful adjustment to strong light after emerging from a dark space (such as a theater). As such, overexposure's strongest association is probably with pain, and its exclusion is probably understandable if not entirely justified.

In discussing low-key and high-key lighting, we in some sense return to the key/fill relationship. How intense the fill light is in relationship to the key light goes a long way toward determining the general character of the image. If the fill is close to the key in intensity, the shadows will be light and the shot will be high-

8-4

Stretching the conventions of lighting
Alfred Hitchcock's
Shadow of a Doubt

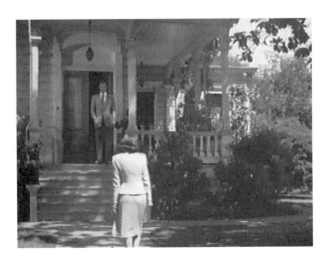

key. If the fill is much less intense than the key, the shadows will be darker and thus the shot more low-key. The distinction suffers somewhat because key and fill are generally discussed in relationship to figure lighting whereas high-key and low-key are used in terms of the whole image. Still, the relationship of all light values, particularly the fill, to the dominant value is a factor in determining the overall character of the image.

Some Notes on Lighting Styles

Lighting styles are difficult to categorize. The possibilities are so limitless that even within a single film there may be many different approaches. Certainly such terms as *high-key* and *low-key* are helpful. Terms like *texture* and *mood* can also be brought to bear. Depth and dimensionality play a role in a film's overall approach to the subject it is covering. Lighting can also be used to direct viewer attention to bright areas of the frame, and focus them on specific parts of the image.

The most significant trend in lighting has probably been *film noir*, a style that advanced the use of an expressive image in American films. Noticing a trend in the films that flooded their screens just after World War II, the French coined the term *film noir*, roughly translated as "dark film," to describe a body of films that were very dark and pessimistic in both their content and their low-key look. **SEE 8-5** These films created a claustrophobic, nightmarish universe, filled with guilt, hysteria, and moral ambiguity. Film noir's use of dark and foreboding visuals and stark, unorthodox compositions put Hollywood film in the same arena, albeit belatedly, with many of the radical formal concerns of modern art.

Highly influenced by the detective fiction of Dashiell Hammett, Raymond Chandler, and James M. Cain, film noir has been identified as a style and trend that appears in a wide variety of genres. In films ranging from Michael Curtiz's *Mildred Pierce* (1945) to Joseph H. Lewis's *The Big Combo* (1955), noir represents Hollywood's first extensive experimentation with an expressive image. What was being expressed was much stronger on a visual level than the stories, which were still bound to a certain extent by the Hollywood tradition of the happy ending. The grim visual and moral world they created largely negated any neat narrative closure or cheerful conclusion.

Film noir is possibly the most chronicled of Hollywood's stylistic and thematic trends. It has also been of great interest to modern cinematographers, particularly after a period of generally bland productions in the 1950s and early 1960s. Many cinematographers, in both American and international films, have

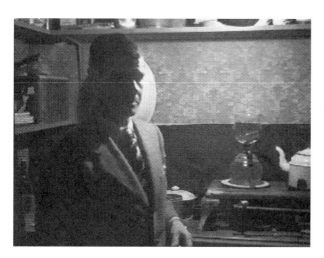

8-5

Classic film noir created a dark, claustrophobic visual environment
Edward Dmytryk's *Crossfire* (1947)

8-6

Modern color film noir cinematography

Jack Nicholson in *The Postman Always Rings Twice*

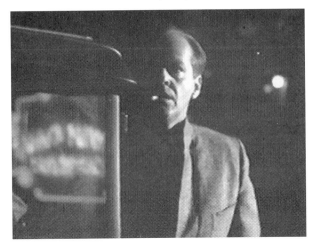

been greatly influence by noir stylistics, because the approach allowed them to do their most challenging work. The image in classic Hollywood film prior to noir, while in its own way being a different high point in the art of cinematography, was still generally a vehicle for performance, setting, and action. In film noir, the image became such an integral and expressive part of the presentation that it often overpowered content elements. The interest in noir and the expressive image on the part of a new generation of cinematographers produced what might be called the "great age of modern cinematography," a period in films that stretched from roughly the late 1960s to the early 1980s.

Previously mentioned for compositions, Bernardo Bertolucci's *The Conformist* has examples of some of the most adventurous images in color cinematography. The film's dark tone gave a nightmarish visual representation of Fascist Italy of the late 1930s. Cinematographer Gordon Willis has also been responsible for great modernizations of noir stylistics, particularly in Alan Pakula's *Klute* (1971) and Francis Ford Coppola's *The Godfather* films.

Sven Nykvist's cinematography for Bob Rafelson's *The Postman Always Rings Twice* (1981) has many exceptional examples of noir color cinematography. **SEE 8-6** Although many have considered the film a disappointment on a content level, it is probably one of the greatest explorations of modern film noir stylistics.

This trend toward modern noir interpretations seems to have been followed by an equal interest in color and design, as represented in films such as Ridley Scott's *Blade Runner* (1982) and television shows like "Miami Vice." The pursuit of an expressive image remains consistent and fuels much of the work of the lighting crew and the DP. The light that you create will always be an important factor in defining the content and the character of your image.

Types of Lighting Instruments

A tour of a lighting equipment rental company would probably leave you struck by the size and variety of lights available. In the industry, lights are called *instruments*, to distinguish equipment that produces light from the light itself. Although there are many specialized instruments, only a few need to be known from the outset. Generally speaking, lighting instruments are either *focusable spots* or *floodlights*, a distinction that parallels the difference between two types of light, specular and diffuse. *Specular light* is direct light and is produced by focusable spots; *diffuse light* is indirect and is produced by floodlights.

The best example of specular light is the sun. Light rays from the sun are parallel, and on a clear, bright day create harsh shadows with well-defined edges. Diffuse light, on the other hand, is light that has passed through a medium, such as clouds, or that has bounced or reflected off a textured surface. Some hard surfaces, of course, do not diffuse light. If the light hits a uniformly smooth and reflectant surface, such as a mirror, it will remain specular. If the surface is rough or absorbent, the light will be diffused.

The DP is responsible for determining the type, size, and quantity of lights needed. In this, he or she is assisted by the *gaffer*, a key crew member who heads the lighting crew and is responsible for the technical implementation of the lighting plan.

Focusable Spots

There are two types of focusable spots: open-faced and lensed. Lensed instruments have a glass lens through which light passes whereas open-faced instruments do not. Focusable spots of both types have a single bulb called a *lamp*, seated usually in a ceramic base. The lamp and its base are mounted in a spherical reflector coated with a polished silver material. Most open-faced and lensed focusable spots come with *barn doors*, black metal doors on a frame that are mounted on the front of the instrument. They are used to cut and shape the light as well as eliminate unwanted *spill*, a term you will hear quite frequently which refers to excess light from an instrument.

Both open-faced and lensed focusable spots are called focusable because the operator has the ability to *spot* and *flood* the light's beam. In spot, the energy of the lamp is focused in the center of the beam where it is narrow, intense, and hard. Away from that intense center, the volume of light drops off very rapidly. This drop in intensity, from either the center of the beam or the instrument itself, is called *falloff*. In flood, the energy of the lamp is spread out more evenly—wider, not quite so intense, and softer than in spot. A knob on the instrument, usually on the back, controls the movement of the ceramic base and lamp against the reflector. Turning the knob back and forth controls whether the light is spotted in or flooded out. As the lamp moves away from the reflector, the instrument floods out. As it moves closer to the reflector, it is spotted in. A small number of instruments employ the opposite strategy. In some designs both the lamp and reflector move. **SEE 8-7**

Spot and flood are important ways of manipulating both the quality and volume of light from a focusable spot.

8-7

Basic mechanics of lighting instruments

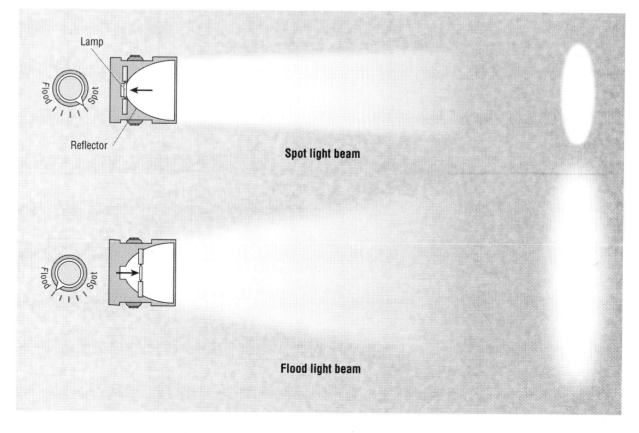

Spot light beam

Flood light beam

Open-Faced Focusable Spots

Open-faced focusable spots are characterized by a bare lamp with no lens. **SEE 8-8** The light they produce is a little more difficult to control than that from a lensed instrument.

A minor drawback of the open-faced design is that direct light from the bulb mixes with light bouncing from the smooth, hard reflector. **SEE 8-9** Light thus hits the subject from several different directions, creating shadows that are not hard enough for some applications. A subject lit by an open-faced instrument has a harsh

8-8

Open-faced lights produce a big, hard, fairly general beam

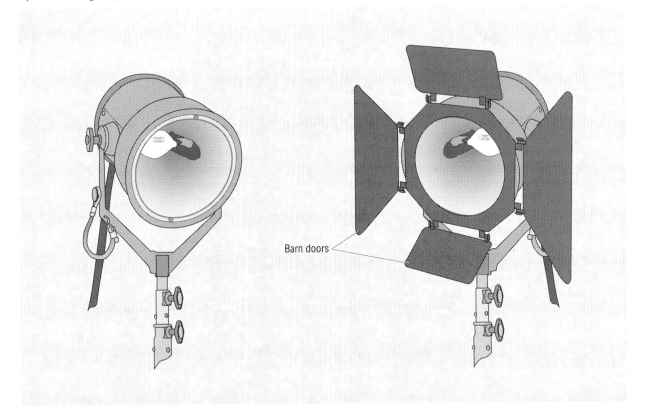

Barn doors

8-9

Reflector causes light to come from multiple directions, creating indistinct edges to the shadows

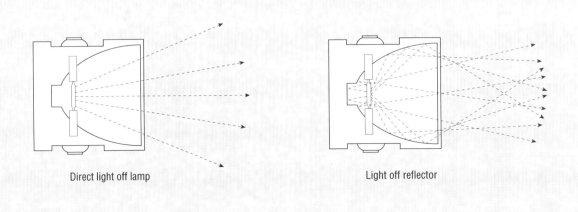

Direct light off lamp   Light off reflector

shadow mixed with less distinct shadows caused by light from the reflector. Light appears to bend and wrap around objects, though it actually does not. Open-faced lights produce harsh shadows, but without the hard edges associated with light from a single source.

Open-faced instruments create a big, hard, fairly general beam of light and are often used when precise manipulation of light is not critical. They are difficult to use, however, when the goal is to cut out part of the light for a shadowy or low-key effect. In such cases, open-faced instruments require a great deal of work for the desired effects.

On the other hand, open-faced instruments are less expensive than lensed instruments, both in original outlay and in continued operation (the lamps are less expensive). The weight of the glass lens and the attendant instrument housing design means that lensed lights are heavier and need sturdier stands. Open-faced lights are generally more compact, and a number of companies make very good lightweight, portable kits. These kits are used in many schools, particularly in beginning and intermediate classes.

Lensed Focusable Spots

Lensed focusable spots are generally more desirable than open-faced instruments because they are easier to manipulate. The most popular type of lensed instrument has a *Fresnel* (pronounced "fre-NEL") lens, which employs concentric ridges of glass in the lens. **SEE 8-10**

8-10

The most popular lensed focusable spots use a Fresnel lens

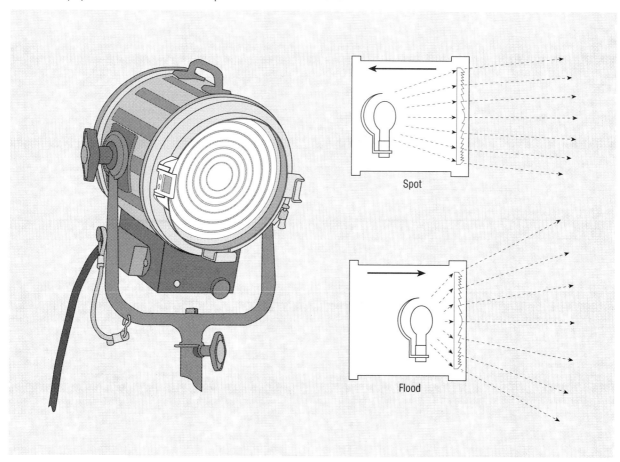

Spot

Flood

Lensed lights have the same bulb and reflector design as open-faced instruments, but the lens redirects the light into a single specular beam. The Fresnel lens eliminates the multiple sources and the indistinct shadows of the open-faced instruments, allowing easier manipulation for hard shadow effects.

Open-faced kits are usually satisfactory for many general lighting requirements. Lensed instruments, however, are relatively inexpensive to rent, and obtaining a few of them for the more discriminating effects can be a good approach, using open-faced instruments to light peripheral areas if necessary.

Floodlights

Floodlights, so called because they produce diffuse, indirect light, are of three basic types: scoops, broads, and softlights. Scoops and broads have only limited uses in filmmaking, whereas the softlight is popular and can be used very effectively in location shooting. One important characteristic of floodlights is that they create indistinct shadows or no shadows at all. This may be helpful in situations where ceilings are not high enough to shoot shadows into the floor.

Scoops

Big instruments with large parabolic reflectors, *scoops* have a single bare lamp but present so much reflecting surface that the light emitted has no single source. **SEE 8-11** Scoops produce a big, general "piece" of light that is difficult to control. Because they are large, heavy, and difficult to manipulate, they are not very popular in location film production. Scoops are often quite useful as permanently mounted lights, especially in studios.

8-11

Scoop lights incorporate such a large reflecting surface that the emitted light has no single source

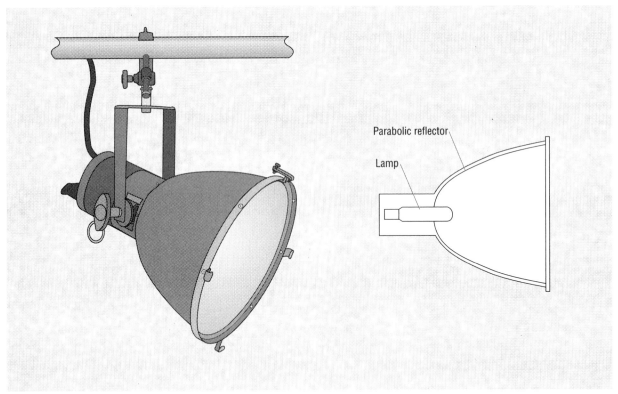

Parabolic reflector

Lamp

Broads

Broad lights are somewhat more common than scoops in film production. *Broads* are characterized by a long, bare, cylindrical lamp seated in a shallow reflector. **SEE 8-12** Although this design would seem to produce direct light, broads actually create diffuse light because the filament is long, creating many sources. Focusable spots, in contrast, have a pear-shaped lamp with a single filament, creating a single source. Many broadlights diffuse their light further with a frosted glass lamp or a textured reflector.

Of all the lights, the broad is probably the least controllable—it just creates a large, diffuse piece of light. Yet it is more popular than the scoop because of its small size—usually less than a foot long—and because it can be shot into a variety of reflectant surfaces. Used in that way, a broad light can create a nice general fill for a shot. Broads are much better for bouncing than focusable spots because they distribute their heat across the length of the lamp. Focusable spots concentrate their light and heat in the center of the beam, and if the instrument is spotted in all the way, materials can actually catch fire. By comparison, the broad has proved itself very effective and safe in shooting into a variety of materials.

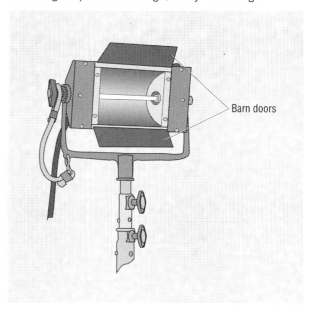

Broad lights produce a large, fairly diffuse light

Barn doors

Softlights

By far the most popular of the floodlights for filmmaking applications, the compact size and portability of *softlights* make them ideal for location work. Softlights are similar to broads in the design of the lamp housing—a long, cylindrical lamp mounted in a shallow reflector. But unlike a broad, the lamp of the softlight is hidden from view in the base and it shoots light from below into a spherical white or silver reflector, called a shell. **SEE 8-13**

8-13

Softlights emit a very soft and even, almost shadowless light

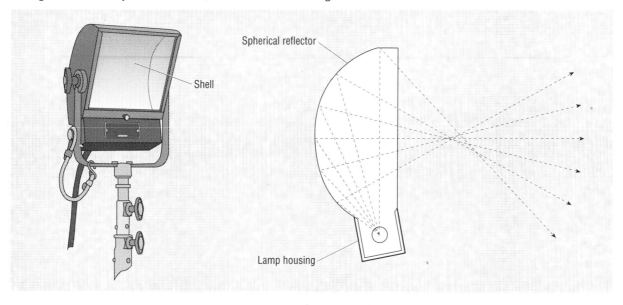

Shell

Spherical reflector

Lamp housing

Light from the softlight comes from reflections off the shell and is very diffused. Softlights produce a very even, very soft, almost shadowless light, which can be handy when trying to avoid the multiple shadows that plague lighting crews.

Applications: Key and Fill

Focusable spots and floodlights thus have characteristics that make them useful for establishing key and fill. Key light has been defined as a strong beam of light casting harsh shadows, and fill light as a soft piece of light brought in to fill those shadows. Focusable spots are frequently used as key lights, and softlights as fill lights, but these are traditional roles, not hard-and-fast rules. There are many situations in which a filmmaker might use a softlight as a key because that is the quality of light desired. So, while the key/fill distinction between spots and floods is useful, remember that it does not *have* to be that way. Be flexible.

Other Types of Sources

Three other light sources—ellipsoidal spots, practicals, and reflectors—are not as common as focusable spots and floodlights but can prove quite useful.

Ellipsoidal Spots (Lekos)

Commonly referred to as lekos, *ellipsoidal spots* are barrel shaped and are often, though not always, equipped with Fresnel lenses. Due to their lamp housing and reflector design, ellipsoidal spots produce hard, specular light, creating highly defined shadows. **SEE 8-14** Even Fresnel instruments create shadows with slightly diffuse edges, but the leko allows virtually no diffusion. Lekos are difficult to use on foreground subjects, however, because the light they produce is hard and unattractive, at least for people or objects of interest.

8-14

Ellipsoidal spotlights (lekos) produce hard, specular light and highly defined shadows

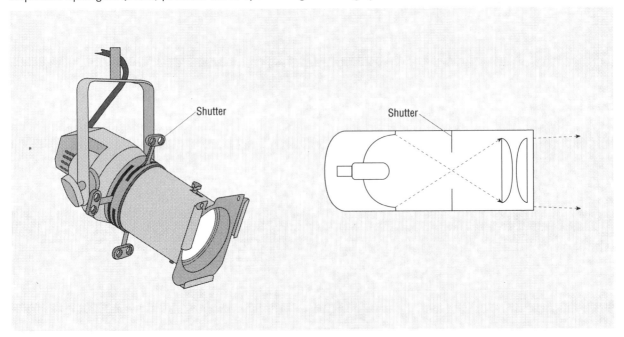

Lekos are generally used to create hard-edged lighting effects, particularly patterns and designs on backgrounds, such as prison bars and venetian blinds. To accomplish this, there is a slot just behind the shutter for inserting plates with cutout designs. With filters in the pattern slot, lekos can also produce color effects. Ellipsoidal spots get more use in television studios and traditional stage productions than in film, but there are many applications for them on location.

Practicals

Practicals resemble standard light bulbs in shape and function but are bigger and more powerful than their household counterparts. There are several types of practicals; most are in the 250-watt to 500-watt range, with the bigger ones usually the bell-shaped photoflood type.

Practicals are screwed into standard household sockets, such as table and floor lamps and ceiling fixtures, and are used to duplicate the light emitted, for example, by a typical living room lamp or other ordinary fixture. Practicals are necessary because household bulbs are redder than standard motion picture lights; without them, matching the color of other instruments would be problematic (see page 277).

Although they are most often used in lamps, practicals are also handy for screwing into fixtures outside the frame for general fill in a scene. If there is a ceiling fixture in a room, a DP can screw a practical into it to give a certain level of light in the room. They can be employed for a variety of purposes, particularly in location shooting.

Reflectors

Not really instruments, *reflectors* are used frequently, especially in exteriors. The most sophisticated are called *reflector boards*, which pivot in a U-shaped holder. **SEE 8-15** One side of the board is a hard surface that reflects hard light; the flip side is often divided into sections or textured to provide a softer fill.

8-15

Reflector boards are two-sided, to provide both hard and soft light

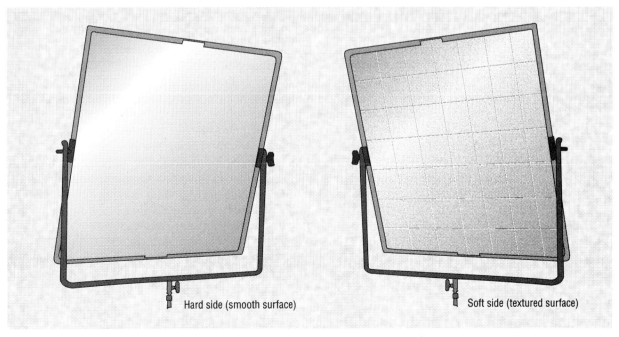

Hard side (smooth surface)   Soft side (textured surface)

Reflectors are most often used to reflect sunlight into shadows when shooting outside. They are particularly handy for producing fill light for characters, especially when the actors are walking through shaded areas. Small reflectors are popular for many situations, and there are some very large ones that are generally used on bigger projects.

There are other types of reflectors, including handheld boards. *Foam core*, a material used in picture framing, is one of the most popular inexpensive "bounce boards." On location it is common to see a grip following a scene with a board in hand; light coming from the board punches the characters up just a little bit. Reflectors can be very handy for saving the time and bother of setting up an electrical instrument to accomplish a simple goal.

These are the types of lights available to most small projects. Again, if you go to a rental house you will see a number of other types as well. As your projects become more sophisticated, you will use more specialized lights, although most of them are either so specialized or so big that you will not need them while you are learning the field. The bigger lights usually have a substantial electrical draw, requiring a trained electrician and/or a powerful generator.

Light Meters

There are two approaches to light measurement: one measuring incident light and the other measuring reflective light. In measuring *incident light*, a light meter is held at the subject and pointed toward the camera. From this position the meter determines how much light is falling on the subject. In measuring *reflective light*, the meter is held at the camera to determine how much light is being reflected from the subject back to the camera lens. Many cameras, particularly still cameras and Super 8 models, have light meters built into the viewing system; these internal meters are called *through-the-lens (TTL)* metering systems and they read reflective light. As we will see, TTL metering systems, and reflective light meters in general, have shortcomings that make them of limited use to film professionals.

Except for the TTL systems, light meters are handheld and can measure either reflective or incident light. Meters typically come with both a white bulb for reading incident light and an interchangeable flat grid for reading reflective light. You insert either the bulb or the grid, depending on which kind of light you need to measure.

The Sekonic L-398 is a commonly used light meter, shown here with the incident bulb. **SEE 8-16** Other makes have similar displays and, although occasionally employing different strategies, are used in the same ways. The white bulb measures light in a 180-degree radius, the bulb simulating the shape of a human face. Many light meters, the Sekonic included, also have a white, flat incident disc for measuring individual light sources.

The scale in the middle of the meter displays the measurement of the amount of light present in the scene we are metering. The button in the center of the dial activates the needle, which renders the amount of light in *foot-candles (fc)*. The word *foot-candle* refers to the amount of light that falls 1 foot in any direction from a standard plumber's candle. A foot-candle is a standard unit of measure, like an ounce, a pound, a foot, or a mile, measuring a standard volume or amount of light. If the light meter reads 20 fc, it means there is twenty times the amount of light as can be found 1 foot from a candle. People sometimes have a hard time grasping the fact that light is measurable, but measuring the light in a room and finding 20 foot-candles is just as certain and objective as measuring the width of the room and finding it to be 12 feet across.

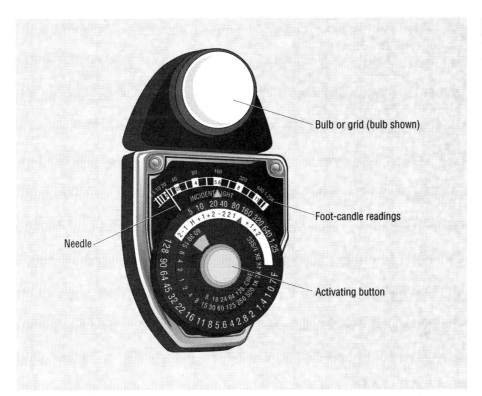

The Sekonic L-398 is a typical, commonly used light meter

Shutter Speed

The term *shutter speed* refers to how long each individual frame is being exposed to light. It is referred to in terms of fractions of seconds, say ⅓₀, ⅟₅₀₀, and so on. Those with experience in still photography know that shutter speed, along with the *f*-stop, is a major control of how the image is exposed. In film, shutter speed is not so critical a factor because, unless you are going for some specialized motion effect, it is a constant. It is dependent on the number of frames per second at which you are running.

Shutter speed is calculated by a simple, straightforward formula:

$$\frac{1}{2 \times fps}$$

Recall that the shutter allows light to reach the film plane during half of its rotation. **SEE 8-17** If the camera is running at 24 fps, how much exposure is each individual frame of film getting? Each frame has ⅟₂₄ of a second devoted to it, but it is actually being exposed only half that time—the other half of the time the light is being blocked by the rotation of the half-moon shutter—so it is being exposed for one-half of ⅟₂₄ of a second. The actual shutter speed would be ⅟₄₈ of a second, usually rounded off to ⅟₅₀. Thus the formula makes sense. Whatever fps you have chosen for the camera, the frame is getting light half the time of its possible exposure.

The variable that is not addressed in this simple formula is the size of the shutter. Most shutters are the half-moon configuration or close to it (most are actually a little smaller). But if for some reason you need to use a different size shutter, which is very rare, you have to know the complex formula:

$$\frac{Degrees\ of\ shutter}{360\ (\text{total degrees in a circle})} \times \frac{1}{fps}$$

8-17

The shutter allows light to reach the film plane during half its rotation

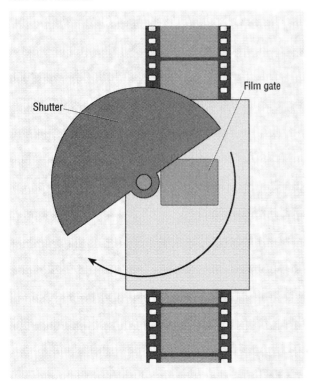

Shutter

Film gate

If the camera shutter has the half-moon configuration, which is 180 degrees of the circle, the first part of the formula will simply reduce to one-half ($^{180}\!/_{360}$). With a normal shutter, the formula is always going to be simple one—one over two times your fps. Again, the only time you need this complex formula is when you are dealing with a shutter that is not the standard half-moon configuration. Other than this, shutter speed becomes an issue only when you change running speeds (that is, fps) for slow- or fast-motion effects. If you change speeds, you have to make the necessary adjustments (see page 285).

On still-photography cameras, the shutter speed is variable, and not having a variable shutter speed can be a real shock for people with a photography background. I often use Kodak Tri-X black-and-white film for outdoor still photography. Because it has such a high EI, I can shoot at a high shutter speed and a high f-stop; that would stop fast-moving action and give tremendous depth of field. In motion picture photography, you just cannot do that. Without substantial filtering, a stock with an EI like Tri-X (400 in still photography) would be unusable on a bright, sunny day. Without the ability to get less light from the shutter speed, you would get an f-stop higher than anything on the lens. It makes for a whole new set of considerations.

The Computer

The first function of a light meter is to measure the amount of light. The second function is to translate the foot-candle readings into an f-stop, usually one that will produce a normally exposed image. The dials on the bottom of the light meter are used to set the EI, the shutter speed, and, eventually, to determine the f-stop. Some manufacturers call this the light meter's computer, used to compute the f-stop. Many newer light meters actually have on-board computers that display digital readouts rather than the moving needle. Digital readouts will probably replace the older needle design, even though it can be quite instructive to watch the needle physically respond to different volumes of light.

The most significant variable in the translation of a foot-candle reading into an f-stop is the film stock's EI. It is the first thing to set on the light meter. The meter usually has a window that displays the range of EI numbers, and you simply dial to the number that the manufacturer has recommended. **SEE 8-18**

Light meters are also used by still photographers and thus have a scale with the full range of shutter speeds. Because shutter speed is determined by frames per second in motion picture photography, a small scale with fps numbers, generally called the *cine scale*, will be interrelated with the still-photography numbers. The numbers pictured here are fps rates commonly used in filmmaking. **SEE 8-19**

To find the f-stop, the computer will have a moving scale to set the foot-candle reading that the light meter has given. As this is set, the cine scale moves against the f-stop scale. Once set, the f-stop that will produce normal exposure for that foot-candle value is straight down from the fps. **SEE 8-20**

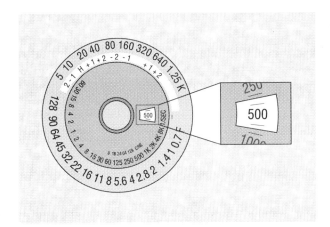

8-18

The film stock's EI is the first thing to set on a light meter

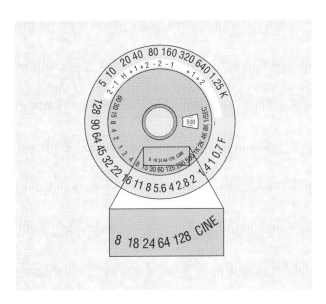

8-19

The cine scale gives the fps rates commonly used in filmmaking

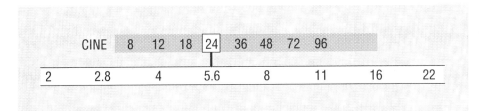

8-20

To find the *f*-stop, set the foot-candle reading, and the cine scale moves against the *f*-stop scale to yield the value for a normal exposure

Although this gives simple *f*-stops, the process of metering and determining *f*-stops is far more complicated than this. The goal, which is developed in the following chapters, is to be able to evaluate and control a complex image that has a wide range of lights and darks.

Manipulation of Lights

Manipulating the lights means changing the *volume*, the *pattern*, or the *quality* of the light to suit your purposes. A common example of a situation in which you might want to manipulate the light is when you want to soften or diffuse a hard light without going all the way to a softlight. Another is when you want the light to have a different feel, say, warmer or multifaceted. The most common is when you simply have too much or too little light to achieve the desired effect.

The primary way to manipulate light is in your initial choice of instruments. You will be working with the two basic types—focusable spots and floodlights—which produce two different kinds of light—direct and indirect, respectively. Once you have the instruments, you still will be constantly changing or adjusting them to create the exact effect you want. Taking an example of an instrument that is producing too much light for a scene is a good starting point.

Problem

Let us say you set up an instrument and get a reading of 160 fc but want 40 fc. (Potential reasons for desiring specific volumes of light are covered in the next chapter.) In this case, you want to *back off* the light, that is, make it less intense. How would you deal with this situation?

There are many options and materials you can use to manipulate the instruments. Seven potential solutions are listed here, but there are many others. The first three solutions are probably the most common; the last four can create a variety of side effects, the severity of which is discussed. If you want to *bring in* a light rather than back it off, simply do the reverse of what is suggested. Either way, this is called *trimming* the instruments. Trimming can be much more complex than simply backing off and bringing in, but these two terms are a good starting point.

Solutions

Simply move the light back.   This is straightforward. Have an assistant stand at the subject with a light meter, keeping the activating button depressed. As the instrument is moved back, the needle will respond to the lower volume of light. Just move the instrument back until you achieve the desired foot-candle value.[1] This is most easily accomplished with an assistant, as most things in lighting are. If you try to do it alone, you will find yourself running back and forth from light source to subject. It will be physically wearing and unnecessarily time-consuming.

Flood out the light.   If you are using a focusable spot, it will have a spot/ flood capability. In spot, the greatest amount of light is concentrated in the center. When you flood the light out, you widen the beam and, consequently, have less light in the center. Keep the activating button depressed as you flood the light out, and the meter will tell precisely how much the light falls off. Just flood it until you get the reading you want.

Use modifying material in front of the light.   Modifying materials come in many forms and work in various ways, from simply cutting down the amount of light to significantly altering its quality, which most manufacturers call redistributing the light. Commonly used modifying materials include:

- **Spun** This is an artificial spun glass–like material. *Spun* is one of the most popular modifying materials for beginners; it cuts down the light as well as diffuses it. Lighting crews use clothespins to attach spun to the barn doors, and it can be used to cover all or part of the light.

---

1. Most crews actually communicate in *f*-stops (or, more accurate, *t*-stops—see page 239). Learning foot-candles is recommended, because it helps you think about light in terms of volumes.

- **Scrims** These are made from a metal screen–like material. Scrims cut down the amount of light without significantly diffusing it. Usually these are designed for a specific make of instrument and slip into a holder in between the barn doors and the light itself.

- **Silk** This white artificial material looks like its namesake. *Silk* cuts down the volume of light and strongly diffuses it. Coming in a variety of sizes, silks have metal frames and are usually set in front of the instrument on a Century stand *(C-stand)*, one of the key pieces of equipment used to set things in front of lights. Silks made out of real silk are available but are very expensive and require careful handling.

- **Nets** This material looks like mosquito netting. Nets are similar to scrims but diffuse the light only slightly. Constructed like silks, nets are also used on C-stands. **SEE 8-21** They come in different sizes and shapes that have exotic names of their own, for example, fingers and dots.

- **Frost and tough-white diffusion** These are milky-looking diffusion *gels* (a cellophane-like material). The use of 216—one of the *tough whites*—is very common. Both 216 and *frost* are popular ways of softening and giving a warm feel to the lights. They are used quite frequently in what is often referred to as glamour cinematography.

- **Opal diffuser** This type of diffusion softens the light and is also quite popular. An *opal diffuser* is similar to frost but gives a slightly harder feel to the light, as if it were broken down into the facets of an opal gem.

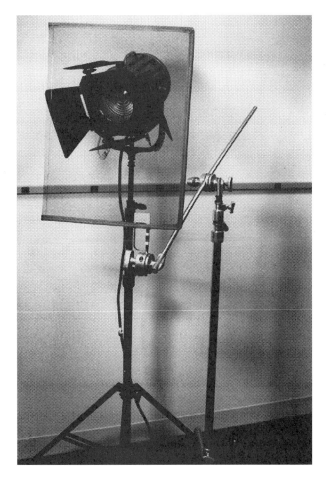

8-21

A C-stand rigged with a net, used to cut down the volume of light and lightly diffuse it

- **Rolux** Denser than opal, this material cuts down the light tremendously and can make the light source very indistinct. This is effective when you want an unlit feel to the image. It is used mostly on very large lights because it cuts the volume so dramatically.

- **Shower curtain** A material called *shower curtain*, which looks similar to its namesake, is less dense than Rolux but affords the same soft feel. It should always be put a short distance away from instruments, not right on them.

- **Tracing paper** Also called *trace*, *tracing paper* is used for many purposes but particularly on backlights to diminish the harsh quality of the shadows they create.

- **Flags** Made of black opaque material, *flags* are similar in design to silks and nets. Flags are not true modifying materials because they *cut*, or block, the light from individual instruments. Nevertheless, flags are used in much the same way as many of the other materials, and their role in manipulating light is quite important. Like nets, flags come in a variety of shapes and sizes that have names of their own, such as cutters and solids.

- **Cookies** Short for *cukaloris*, *cookies* are similar to flags, but with cutout designs that break up the light. A cookie, also called a *kook*, is generally used to lend texture to a background. They are difficult to use on foreground subjects because shadows from their cut-outs would be noticeable, but they are very effective in breaking up flat and uninteresting light in other areas of the frame. Like flags, cookies are not true modifying materials but, again like flags, are used in enough situations to warrant their mention.

Change the wattage of the bulb.   Within the limitations of the manufacturer's recommendations, almost all lighting units will accept different wattages of lamps. Lamps with lower wattage produce less light. This strategy is less attractive to many users because taking apart hot lights on location consumes valuable time. It is better to think about this in planning a lighting setup. A competent gaffer will think out what kind of space the crew is working in and plan out in advance the lamp sizes needed in the instruments. It is not unheard of to switch lamps on location, but efficient use of time advises that such decisions be made earlier rather than later.

Bounce the light.   This is a possible solution, but it carries its own liabilities in that the quality of the light is so different from what you started with that it significantly changes the shot. There are many surfaces that serve as good vehicles for bouncing, from white walls and ceilings to specially designed aluminum reflectors; one of the most popular is foam core. The practice of bouncing light is very common, but more as a source than a modification. If your goal is to modify a light from 640 fc to 320 fc, bouncing the light could create a more radical change than you want, in terms of both volume and quality.

Use a neutral density filter.   A gray gel that cuts down the amount of light passing through it, *neutral density (ND)* does not change any color quality, nor does it diffuse the light—it just cuts the *amount* of light from the unit. It is available in filters rated at .1, .2, .3, and so on. Each tenth represents one-third of an *f*-stop. Thus, a .3 equals one stop, a .6 equals two stops, and a .9 equals three stops. Usually, people just drop the point, so a .3 filter is called an ND3, and a .6 an ND6.

Although a few professionals use ND on lights, it is much less useful than may first appear. One general rule of lighting is that the more you put on an instrument, the harder it is to use other modifying materials on it. Neutral density can be cumbersome, and its use as something put on or in front of an instrument is infrequent. Some specialized instruments, lekos for example, have little slots where you can just slide in the gel. ND has many other important applications, such as in window gels (see page 275) and as front filters on lenses, but its use on instruments is limited.

Focus the light so the subject is off-center. By closing the barn doors or panning the light, you can position the light so the subject is not in the center of the beam. This is often the first thing people want to try yet it is the least viable solution of all. In both cases, a lower reading is produced by narrowing or changing the point where the light shines. Most often, the subject looks unlit—as if the light is just shooting past it or it is sitting outside the beam of light. This is the kind of effect that calls attention to lighting and can appear to be very artificial.

Another technology that comes up is theatrical *dimmers* and, though they may seem useful for backing off lights, their application in film is somewhat limited. The big problem with dimming is that when voltage to the instrument is reduced, the color of the light—the color temperature—changes. On occasion filmmakers use instruments on dimmers very successfully to create peripheral light, that is, light on the background. But if dimmered light is used on foreground figures, particularly people, unwelcome effects may result. You need to know your way around color temperature to work with dimmers effectively.

Many modifying materials discussed here were developed specifically for film to replicate what can be achieved quite easily on stage with theatrical dimmers. In film, because you generally need consistent color temperature, you have to put something on the light to reduce the foot-candles rather than simply reduce the voltage to the instrument.

These are some of the main options available for manipulating light. Once you get the instruments up, the object is to adjust them until you get the values and quality of light you want. Keep working with the instruments and the materials. Experience will be your best teacher.

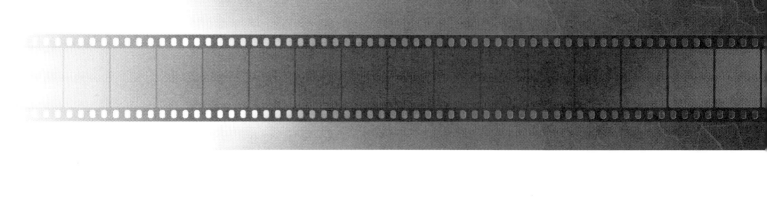

9

Exposure and Latitude

Exposure Index, Foot-candles, and *f*-stops

Although there are a number of considerations in choosing a film stock, ***exposure index (EI)*** is often the determining factor for beginners and independents. It harkens back to the key distinction made earlier—use a film stock with a high EI when filming in low light and, conversely, a stock with a low EI in high light. However, given the ability to manipulate light in almost any way imaginable, experienced DPs can use whatever film stock they want and simply light for it. Using low-rated stocks outdoors is consistent through all levels of production, but filmmakers with marginal budgets, forced to work with the smaller instruments in interiors, often use higher-rated stocks to achieve at least some depth of field. One must often be completely arbitrary in this choice, eliminating many factors, such as image quality and color rendition, that will eventually become a much bigger part of the decision-making process.

As may have been surmised, the key variable in the relationship between a given amount of foot-candles and an *f*-stop is the EI of the film stock that was chosen. Once the film stock is determined and the EI on the light meter has been set, the translation of specific foot-candle readings to *f*-stops becomes automatic. With this in mind, a chart can give the foot-candle–to–*f*-stop relationship for a number of different potential film stocks. **SEE 9-1** These exposures are the manufacturer's recommendations, all made with normal exposure as the stated goal. There are, of course, many other possible EIs.

If you are shooting with a film stock that has an EI of 500 and your light meter gives a reading of 320 fc, you would shoot at *f*/11 to produce normal exposure. If you are shooting with 100 EI film and get a reading of 160 fc, an *f*/2.8/4 would produce normal exposure; that is read as "2.8 slash 4," and you set the *f*-stop ring between those two stops. If you were to use two different film stocks to film the same lighting setup, this would become readily apparent. A film stock with a low EI will yield one *f*-stop, lower numerically, say, an *f*/2.8, while a film stock with a higher EI will yield another *f*-stop, higher numerically, say, an *f*/5.6.

As suggested, you should probably use the manufacturer's recommended EI. You will eventually find out that this number is not written in stone. DPs often rate the film stock differently, because they know they will achieve a specific effect if

217

9-1

The foot-candle–to–
f-stop relationship for
potential film stocks

Foot-candles	EI				
	32	**100**	**125**	**250**	**500**
5				*f*/1	*f*/1.4
10			*f*/1	*f*/1.4	*f*/2
20		*f*/1/1.4	*f*/1.4	*f*/2	*f*/2.8
40	*f*/1	*f*/1.4/2	*f*/2	*f*/2.8	*f*/4
80	*f*/1.4	*f*/2/2.8	*f*/2.8	*f*/4	*f*/5.6
160	*f*/2	*f*/2.8/4	*f*/4	*f*/5.6	*f*/8
320	*f*/2.8	*f*/4/5.6	*f*/5.6	*f*/8	*f*/11
640	*f*/4	*f*/5.6/8	*f*/8	*f*/11	*f*/16
1,280	*f*/5.6	*f*/8/11	*f*/11	*f*/16	*f*/22
2,560	*f*/8	*f*/11/16	*f*/16	*f*/22	*f*/32

they do. If you rate a film stock higher or lower numerically, you are just building in a consistent level of over- or underexposure. If you go too far, though, you could totally over- or underexpose your film. There are some limits.

Using the Light Meter

The choice between an incident and reflective light meter represents different approaches to metering a scene. Each approach has its own advantages and disadvantages. For film applications, however, the incident meter is far more useful than the reflective meter.

A hypothetical situation with a person standing in front of a window can illustrate the difference between the two types of meters. Outside the window in the background, there is a street awash in sunlight and a building in the shade. Inside the room on the table there is a lamp which is turned on. The room itself is not receiving any direct sunlight, but the left side, that is, the person's back and the bookcase, is receiving strong ambient light. **SEE 9-2**

Given the assumptions of the situation, you should see an immediate problem: there is a wide range of light values in this scene, a relatively dark subject against a brilliant background. Because the reflective meter can be pointed only at the scene as a whole for an average, its readings will not indicate the various amounts of light in different parts of the scene. If you shoot at the *f*-stop suggested by the meter, whatever is lit to that value will expose correctly, but everything else will come in at a different and potentially unacceptable exposure.

So the problem is not how much light is present in the scene as a whole, but how much light is on each subject or area. Furthermore, as subjects move in a composition, they also move through exposure. Does the subject get too dark over here? Is the backlight more than we want over there? These questions suggest why the incident light meter becomes not only the tool of choice but the tool of necessity.

With the *incident light meter*, as suggested earlier, you can go through a scene and measure the light in specific areas. The meter can indicate precisely how the light is increasing or falling off. If you walk through the scene with the activating button depressed, you will actually be able to see, as the needle

9-2

A wide range of light values in a given scene necessitates the use of an incident light meter

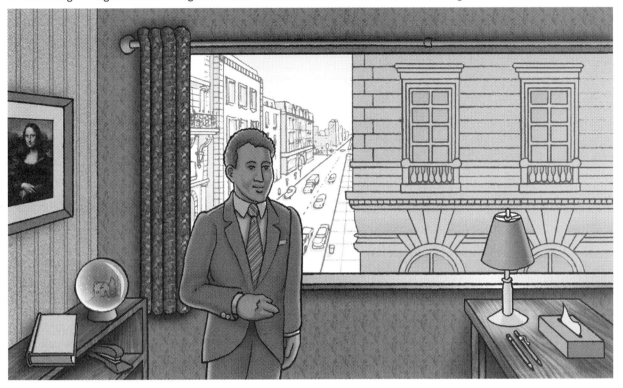

responds, where the light is above or below the desired amount. Steps can then be taken to compensate.

People who have shot with Super 8 cameras will recall that they have reflective meters with an automatic exposure option. In other words, the camera automatically sets the *f*-stop for the user. Very few professional cameras have this option, and few professional camerapeople use it when they do. Automatic reflective meters are too random in evaluating the information they collect. They may work for basic still photography, but do not perform to the exacting standards necessary in most filmmaking applications. Automatic exposure meters do have their uses, particularly in documentary filmmaking, but their value is limited and they should not be used beyond formative efforts.

The example of the person in front of the window provides an instance where training in the use of light meters pays off. To show some simple metering techniques, consider the previous example but eliminate the window. The image is by no means simple, however. Even here it is easy to make some basic mistakes. Again, the lamp is turned on. **SEE 9-3**

With the incident light meter, you measure how much light there is in any one spot. Remembering what has been said about the key and fill, go to the person and take individual readings on each side of his face. **SEE 9-4** The side toward the lamp is going to be the key side, and the side away from the lamp is going to be the fill side. With the activating button depressed, move the meter around; let's say that the readings shown in the figure are found. In this case, point the meter toward the source rather than toward the camera as was suggested earlier. Generally, when trying to find out what a specific instrument is accomplishing, point the meter right at the source.

As suspected, the reading on the fill side is very low because it is getting no direct light. When you measure an individual instrument as you have measured the fill here, you have to be careful that the reading is not being confused by another

9-3

A single source may not provide the light levels required for a usable exposure

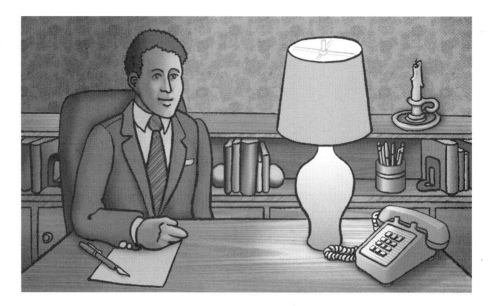

9-4

To take readings on the key and fill sides of the subject's face, point the meter in the direction you want to measure

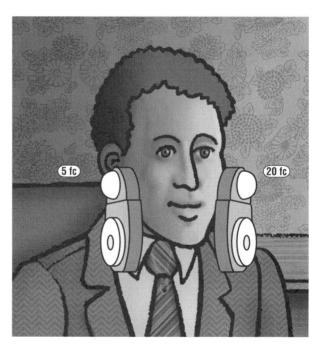

instrument. Sometimes just blocking the offending source with your hand or a card is all it takes to eliminate the problem. In many situations you can just turn off the instruments that you don't want confusing the reading. Since the lamp is the sole source in this instance, you will not be able to do that here.

The readings around the lamp are also significant. **SEE 9-5** You do a general reading and find 320 fc right under the lamp. Let's say you find 640 fc halfway between the lamp shade and the table. The light is stronger as you move toward the lamp and weaker as you move away.

Going back to the foot-candle chart in figure 9.1, translate these readings into *f*-stops. If you are shooting with a film stock with an EI of 500, the reading at the top of the lamp base (1,280 fc) translates to an *f*/22. That is, if you shoot at *f*/22, the top part of the lamp base will be normally exposed. The 320 fc on the table translates to an *f*/11, which would give normal exposure there. It is literally an *f*/22 at the top of the lamp base and an *f*/11 on the table.

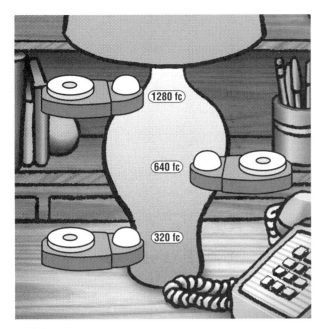

9-5

Light levels are measured by moving the meter through the scene

It is important to note that this is not an evaluative process at this point. It is a measurement process. It does take experience and skill to do it correctly, but once you are aware of the pitfalls, this is essentially no different than checking the dipstick of your car or weighing yourself on the bathroom scale. If there is x amount of light in an area, there is x amount of light. That does not mean it will not or cannot change. It just means that at the time the measurement is taken, there is x amount of light. Once you get these readings, you are faced with some decisions.

The ability to evaluate, of course, precedes the ability to control, or manipulate, the light. Clearly, if you can find out what a specific light source is reading, you can also introduce an artificial light source and manipulate it to a specific value.

A cinematographer friend tells the story of a mistake he made on one of his first big jobs, lighting a convention hall for a political figure whose speech was getting network coverage. The advance men told him they wanted the hall lighted to an $f/5.6$. With an incident meter as a guide, one can go through and manipulate the lights to an even $f/5.6$. The cinematographer came into the huge convention hall and proceeded to light the podium. On the evening of the speech, two Secret Service types showed up, took one look at the hall, and, in unison, reached inside their trenchcoats. Suddenly, the cinematographer had visions of his career coming to an abrupt and violent end, but rather than producing the anticipated instruments of destruction, the agents produced... light meters.

The two men then proceeded to go through the entire hall, reading all the light values. Aha, a 2.8 here. Here we drop all the way down to an $f/2$. The cinematographer was mortified but immediately realized the misunderstanding. They had wanted an even $f/5.6$ throughout the entire hall, and he had left areas at less than that. In a sense, the $f/5.6$ was the plateau he was supposed to achieve, and anything less was a valley. And by falling into the valley, the shots would fall into underexposure. **SEE 9-6**

My friend lived to light again, but with more instruments he could have easily accomplished what was wanted of him. With the incident meter, he could determine where the exposure dropped below an $f/5.6$ and set up additional instruments to bring those areas up to the appropriate level. **SEE 9-7** He could literally fill in the holes. In the areas where he found an $f/4$, he needed a relatively small amount of light. Where he found a large area lit to an $f/2$, he would have to bring in a number of instruments.

9-6

Anything less than the "plateau" level (*f*/5.6 in this case) can be thought of as a "valley," and areas falling into a valley will be underexposed

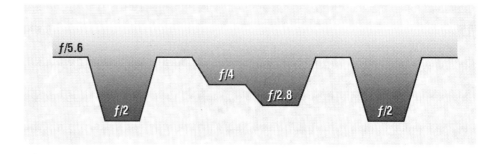

9-7

Additional instruments can illuminate the valleys, bringing those areas up to the appropriate level

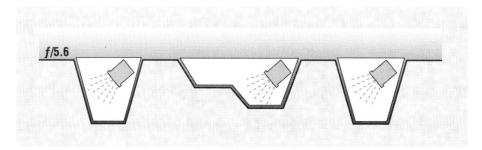

You will rarely want lighting that is this even. This is television news lighting, what's referred to as illumination. The point is that you need to go through any scene and determine all the lighting values present. Second, and of much greater importance, the incident meter is your best guide for manipulating the instruments to achieve the levels of exposure desired. A reflective meter can give only an average of a complex situation, but an incident meter allows you to check every source and determine how much light is there.

The incident light meter allows you to be reasonably precise. It gives you more control not only in evaluating but eventually in manipulating the values that will create the dramatic quality of your images.

Halving and Doubling

So far, the light meter readings used in the illustrations have been either halves or doubles of each other. This has been deliberate in order to illustrate another important concept.

▶ **RULE:** *Virtually everything to do with the measurement and transmission of light is based on halves and doubles.*

The reason that the numbers that have been presented are *the f*-stops is that each one represents the discrete and identifiable point at which the light halves or doubles from the previous stop. **SEE 9-8**

Reciprocally, every doubling or halving of foot-candles represents a one *f*-stop change. If you get a foot-candle reading in a specific area and then find either half as much or twice as much light in another area, there is a one–*f*-stop difference between those two areas. This means that there is a one–*f*-stop difference between the 320 fc of the table and the 640 fc halfway to the lamp shade. There is a two–*f*-stop difference between the 20 fc of the key side of the face and the 5 fc of the fill side of the face.

The concept of halving and doubling pertains not only to the light in front of the camera, but also to the *f*-stops. Assuming a consistent amount of light in front of the camera, every sequential change from one *f*-stop to another represents a halving or a doubling of the amount of light reaching the film plane. Thus, if you are shooting at an *f*/4 and change to an *f*/5.6, half as much light is reaching the

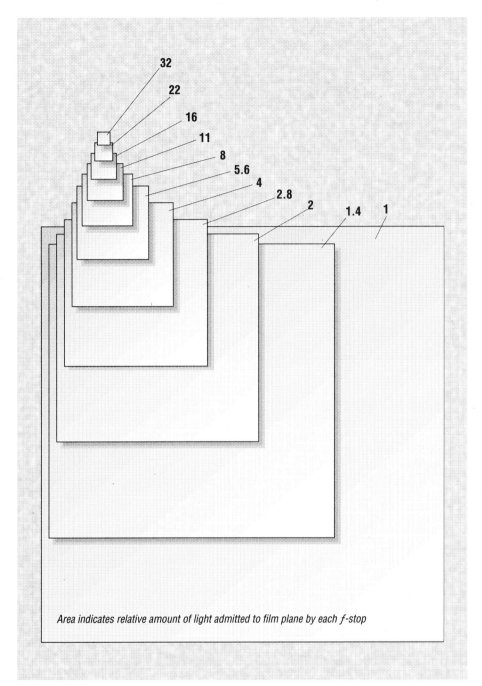

9-8

Each *f*-stop represents the discrete and identifiable point at which the light halves or doubles from the previous stop

32

22

16

11

8

5.6

4

2.8

2

1.4

1

Area indicates relative amount of light admitted to film plane by each f-stop

film plane as before. If you change to an $f/2.8$ from an $f/4$, twice as much light is reaching the film plane.

As you may have noticed from figure 9.2, this doubling and halving also includes the EI.

▶ **RULE:** *Every halving or doubling of EI represents a one–f-stop difference.*

If you are shooting with a film stock with an EI of 160 and getting an $f/5.6$, what would happen to the *f*-stop if you reloaded (and DPs do *not* make arbitrary changes like this) with a film stock that has an EI of 320? You could, theoretically, reset the *f*-stop without remetering. What would the new stop be? Would you ***open up***, that is, choose a lower-numbered *f*-stop? Or would you ***close down***, that is, choose a higher-numbered *f*-stop?

Because the EI is going up numerically and the film stock is more sensitive to light, you need less light to expose it. You would close down to an $f/8$. If you were to change to a film stock with an EI of 80, you would do the opposite: the film stock is less sensitive to light, so you need more light to expose it; you would open up to an $f/4$. In both examples, you need to either double or halve the volume of light provided by the f-stop to produce a normal exposure.

Halving and doubling the light may sound drastic, but it is actually a relatively small change in terms of the image. The primary goal at the outset is to achieve a usable image, and a deviation of one f-stop is relatively minor. It *is* a noticeable change, however, and the difference can be significant when shooting scenes where matching the lighting from one shot to the next becomes critical.

How this relates to the concept of normal exposure is explored in following sections, but you can see that already you are presented with a choice. When there are so many f-stop values present in the scene, how do you expose the image? Or, more to the point, what foot-candle value do you choose to expose for in this, or any, complex image? Although the rule of halves and doubles may seem like a trivial detail at this point, it is crucial to remember it when evaluating the different exposure levels in any image.

f-stops: Two Applications

Up to this point we have referred to light and f-stops in two different senses. Earlier it was shown that higher f-stops on the camera mean less light reaching the film plane. But higher f-stops also mean *more* light, it being $f/22$ closer to the lamp and $f/11$ farther away. Clearly we use the term *f-stop* in two different ways, and the difference needs to be clearly understood before one can proceed to advanced lighting techniques.

Put simply, the term *f-stop* is used to refer to *both the light in front of the camera and the actual setting on the aperture ring.* It refers to light in two different places, at the subject and in the camera. Up to this point we have measured the light in front of the camera in foot-candles. So far so good, but once we have the EI, we can convert our readings into f-stops. So, for example, if we get a reading of $f/8$ at A and then go to B and get an $f/11$, which area has the most light? B must have more light, because we need to use a smaller diaphragm opening to get a normal exposure. Areas with greater volumes of light require smaller openings, that is, higher f-stops. Areas with smaller amounts of light require wider openings, that is, lower f-stops.

Of course, *f-stop* also refers to the diaphragm on the lens. If we get a reading of $f/8$ at the subject and set the lens to an $f/11$, less light is going to reach the film plane than if we set the diaphragm to an $f/8$. Smaller openings allow less light to reach the film plane and are the appropriate response to greater volumes of light.

We have, then, two different ways of talking about the same thing. One is the amount of light at the point of metering. The other is the amount of light reaching the film plane. Getting a reading of $f/2.8$ at a subject by definition means that there is a small amount of light there. That same $f/2.8$ on the camera means more light reaching the film plane than a higher f-stop. Conversely, getting a reading of $f/11$ at a subject means there is a large amount of light there. That same $f/11$ means less light reaching the film plane than, say, an $f/2.8$.

These less-and-more distinctions may baffle you for a while. It can be quite confusing to hear people talking in f-stops all the time on the set. Until you learn the language, listening to people speaking in f-stops can be just like listening to people conversing in an unfamiliar tongue. But the language of light is a fundamental part of filmmaking, and the sooner it is understood, the sooner you'll be able to communicate with the rest of the crew.

Evaluating Existing Light

Now the big question: How do you determine your *f*-stop? The answer is not necessarily an easy one, but the starting point is measuring and evaluating the amount of light present in the scene you want to shoot. This ability to evaluate a shooting situation is essential to predicting what your image is going to look like. The fact that you evaluate a scene, though, does not mean that you are not going to change things. The process of evaluation, by its nature, precedes manipulation.

Not only are there different volumes of light in most scenes, but these volumes of light are sometimes changing, and always changeable. If you go into a room that is too dark, you turn on a light. When you do this, you change the physical amount of light in the room. Hence, there is more light. If there is a window in the room and it is sunny outside, the situation becomes more complicated. When we return to our original scene of someone in front of a window on a sunny day, this becomes evident. **SEE 9-9**

With the light meter, you can determine most of the light values within this scene. Let's speculate that you find the foot-candle values shown in the figure; the numbers used here behave nicely—all relating to specific *f*-stops. In real life, the values you find would presumably settle in at many different levels—full stop, half stops, and such. For the sake of simplicity, the numbers given here will not complicate the issues.

For evaluation purposes, you can go through this scene and group the objects and areas in terms of the amount of light falling on them. **SEE 9-10** That is, you can group together all things lit to 640 fc, all things at 80 fc, et cetera. As you examine the scene, you find that there are nine different exposure values—10 fc through 2,560 fc. (By exposure value we mean simply that this value of light, as we have measured it, exists within our proposed frame.) There are then nine different choices for exposing this image, each exposure value relating to an *f*-stop that is yet to be determined.

The variable in how all this relates to the *f*-stop is, of course, the EI. For this example, we will choose a color film stock that has an EI of 500, a stock that is presently manufactured by a number of companies. Keep this film stock in mind;

9-9

To evaluate a scene, use an incident light meter to measure the light falling on different objects and areas

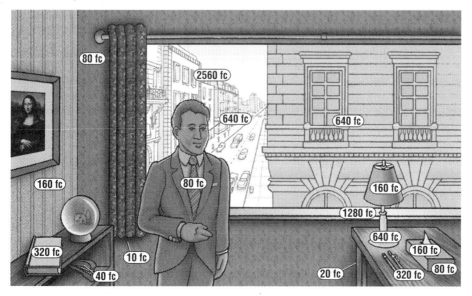

9-10

For evaluation purposes, objects and areas can be grouped in terms of the amount of light falling on them

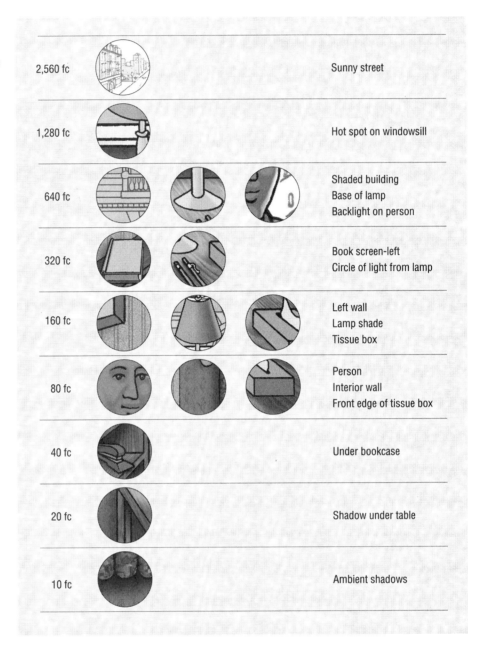

2,560 fc	Sunny street
1,280 fc	Hot spot on windowsill
640 fc	Shaded building / Base of lamp / Backlight on person
320 fc	Book screen-left / Circle of light from lamp
160 fc	Left wall / Lamp shade / Tissue box
80 fc	Person / Interior wall / Front edge of tissue box
40 fc	Under bookcase
20 fc	Shadow under table
10 fc	Ambient shadows

9-11

When evaluating existing light, the first step is always to set the EI on the light meter

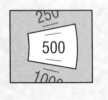

it will be our example throughout the text. Step 1, as always, is to set the EI on the light meter. **SEE 9-11**

Once you have decided on the stock and thus the EI, you've established a constant relationship between foot-candles and f-stops. By looking at the chart in figure 9.1, you see that the 640 fc of the shaded building converts to an $f/16$. If you want the shaded building to expose normally, you would shoot at $f/16$. Anything at 2,560 fc is going to translate to an $f/32$ at 500 EI. The 80 foot-candles on the person in the room translates to an $f/5.6$. If you wanted the person to expose normally, you would shoot at an $f/5.6$.

This is straightforward. If you want something normally exposed, you shoot at the f-stop that corresponds to that foot-candle value. It is also important to note that when you shoot at a specific f-stop, only the things that are at that foot-candle value will expose normally. Everything else will come in at some level of over- or underexposure. These deceptively simple statements are the key to understanding how to produce almost any lighting effect.

9-12

Shooting the objects at 80 fc at *f*/5.6 produces a normal exposure for that group

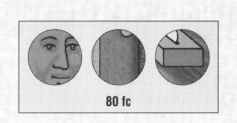

80 fc

9-13

By deciding on the fps, shutter speed becomes a constant, and can be plugged into the formula

$$\frac{1}{2 \times 24}$$

When you decide to shoot at a specific *f*-stop, you have in effect chosen a specific group to be normally exposed. If you decide to shoot at an *f*/5.6, to normally expose the person, you have also chosen to normally expose the other elements in the 80 fc group. **SEE 9-12** Hence, choosing the objects at 80 fc and shooting at *f*/5.6 means that all the variables we have been suggesting come together to produce a normal exposure. You have already chosen your EI (500), so that is one variable out of the way. Another variable is the shutter speed. If you decide to run at 24 fps, the shutter speed also becomes a constant. **SEE 9-13**

There is a third variable that we will, at least for now, posit as a constant—the final exposure. All that has been discussed so far is normal exposure, but the possibility remains that you are often pursuing something else. In fact, you will eventually come to see normal exposure as only a part of the goal, as one part of the entire image. Eventually you will come to regard normal exposure as somewhat of a mythical beast, nice to scare and teach the children with but being only part of a rich and multifaceted image.

The next two variables are the ones over which you have the most control: the *f*-stop and how much existing light there is in the proposed frame. The *f*-stop is clearly a key variable. At this point you are just evaluating an existing situation, so you will not be changing the amount of light on anything. (This is artificially imposed on the discussion and will change soon.)

Given the group of objects you have chosen—the ones at 80 fc—the following figure shows the elements you are combining to achieve a normal exposure. We will call this a formula, though the + and = signs are somewhat misleading. It is not so much that you add these elements together to get this result, as it is that when these elements are present you get a specific result. **SEE 9-14**

9-14

The elements that when taken together produce a normal exposure

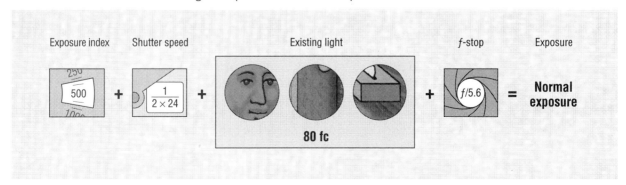

| Exposure index | Shutter speed | Existing light | *f*-stop | Exposure |

500 + $\dfrac{1}{2 \times 24}$ + 80 fc + *f*/5.6 = **Normal exposure**

9-15

Because the first three elements are constants, changing the *f*-stop affects the final exposure

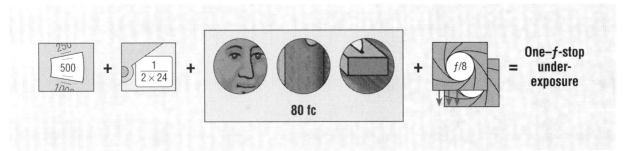

9-16

When the *f*-stop is set to normally expose the 80 fc group, the 160 fc group is one–*f*-stop overexposed

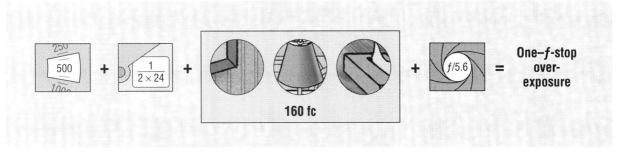

What would happen if you shifted the *f*-stop in this formula? If you shift the *f*-stop, say, to an *f*/8, things would change—something has to give somewhere else. Because you have established the first three elements as constants, the place where the line gives has to be in the result. **SEE 9-15**

When you decide to expose at a particular *f*-stop, it is going to affect what happens to objects and areas that have different foot-candle amounts falling on them. What would happen to objects lit to 160 fc? Because 160 is twice 80, there is a one–*f*-stop difference. **SEE 9-16** Elements at 320 fc would overexpose by two stops. Elements at 40 fc would underexpose by one stop, and elements at 20 fc by two stops.

As suggested, the result can also be considered a variable. In that case, you would just look at the formula in a slightly different order. If you wanted to underexpose for an effect, you would change the result variable first, and something else in the line would have to change. In this case, the *f*-stop would have to change to get the desired result. Although this seems to just be a case of inverted logic, this is an important point: if you want something in the scene to be dark—underexposed—the result is indeed the starting point.

This suggests that the formula may be a helpful concept. While as a metaphor it is somewhat problematic because you are not actually adding things, it does suggest a method of evaluating virtually everything in the frame. There are five variables here: EI, shutter speed, amount of light on subject, *f*-stop, and exposure. If you lock in four of the five, and remember that two are constants given certain preliminary determinations, the fifth has to be where the change is going to occur.

At this point the formula has just five variables. These are *the* basic variables for any image. The line will not necessarily be this short, however, as many things can complicate your considerations. As new topics are introduced, the list will get longer and more complex. We have demonstrated how to determine what is happening in terms of how specific elements in the image are exposing. The next step is understanding how this affects the way the film stock is going to render the image.

Latitude

The concept of latitude is absolutely crucial to an understanding of how light, and the image, is registered on the film. *Latitude* can most easily be defined as the "seeing range of the film." It is the amount the film stock can accept under- or overexposure and still render objects with detail. The best way to explain this is to compare it to the human eye. The eye can take in a wide range of lighting values and average them so you see all aspects with detail. If a person is standing in front of a bright light source, you have no trouble seeing detail in any area in which you look.[1] The film stock cannot do this. It can see only within a relatively narrow range of lighting values. That is, it can render objects only to a certain level of under- or overexposure before it renders them completely black or clear, respectively.

Latitude varies from film stock to film stock. It can be quantified, and the manufacturer includes a graph in the product information, called a *characteristic curve*, that tells you how the film stock performs. **SEE 9-17** The characteristic curve plots the density of grains on the negative against rising exposure. It shows the gradual consistent rise of exposure, called the *straight line portion*, while also showing the precipitous drop-offs to under- and overexposure, called, respectively, the *toe* and the *shoulder*. Characteristic curves are quite difficult for beginners to interpret, and simple discussions with a knowledgeable source should tell you what you need to know. A working filmmaker or someone at a processing laboratory should be able to give you a good idea. The majority of film stocks have latitudes ranging from two stops to three and a half. That is, most film stocks produce detail anywhere from two to three and a half stops on either side of normal exposure.

---

1. The eye also has an iris that facilitates taking in a wide range of values.

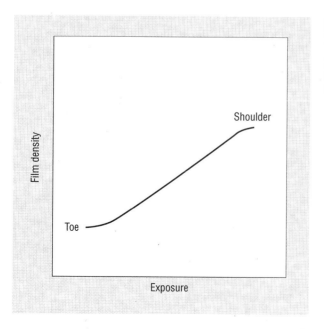

9-17

The characteristic curve plots the density of grains on the negative against rising exposure

When learning exposure technique, many people find it useful to think of latitude as the mistake factor. In other words, how badly can I miss on the *f*-stop and still get a usable shot? How badly can I be off and still get some detail in the subject? This is okay for starters, but eventually you will have to think of it in the more complex terms presented in this section.

To apply the concept of latitude to our example, you have a light meter reading of 80 fc (*f*/5.6) off the person in front of the window. There is substantially more light outside (2,560 fc). In just looking at this scene, your eyes have no trouble taking in these two extreme values and rendering a composite image. The film can see only within a relatively narrow range of values. And, more to the point, it will expose normally for only one value at a time. What would be the likely result if you did shoot at *f*/5.6? Obviously, the person in front of the window would be rendered normally, and the outside would be totally overexposed (blown out). The only other areas that would be normally exposed would be those also lit to an *f*/5.6. Everything else would be lit, and respond on the film, to some degree of over- (+) or underexposure (–). Your immediate response might be "I do not want that." If you think about it further, though, remember that you usually do want some form of gradation in terms of light in the image. If everything is normally, that is, evenly, exposed, the image will look flat and characterless. We expect areas to look shady (–) and bright (+). The point is that with a knowledge of latitude, you can begin to control what areas are over- and underexposed and to what degree. The film stock renders detail in the shaded and highlighted areas only to a certain point. The varying degrees of detail in over- and underexposed areas depends on how radically different the values are from the *f*-stop at which you are shooting.

Today's color negative film stocks have a latitude of roughly three to three and a half stops; that is, they render detail anywhere from three to three and a half stops on either side of normal exposure. If you shoot at *f*/5.6, with your proposed stock, the film will see objects that are lit to the values in roughly this range. **SEE 9-18**

An area that is lit to an *f*/11 (320 fc) will be two stops overexposed, and an area lit to an *f*/32 (2,560 fc) will be five stops overexposed. An area that is lit to an *f*/4 (40 fc) will be one stop underexposed, and if there were an area lit to an *f*/1.4 (5 fc), it would be four stops underexposed. Now, positing the latitude described, you can predict with a fair amount of accuracy what will happen in these four areas. An area at 320 fc will be two stops overexposed; but, because it is within the latitude of the film, it will be bright but rendered with at least some detail. The sunny street in the background (2,560 fc) will be five stops overexposed and, being outside the latitude of the film, will be totally overexposed. Areas at 40 fc will be one stop underexposed but rendered with substantial detail. Anything at 5 fc or less would be totally underexposed.

A good example of the interrelationship between latitude and exposure is a streetlight. (It is a hypothetical example because you may never find a streetlight that gives you readings like these, even though we might sometimes wish that one would.) Let's say that your shot will be of a person walking from right to left under the light. With the activating button depressed, you just walk through the scene. The meter will respond as the light gets stronger and falls off again. To simplify things, go ahead and translate the foot-candle readings into *f*-stops. Again, there

9-18

Color negative stocks have a latitude of roughly three to three and a half stops

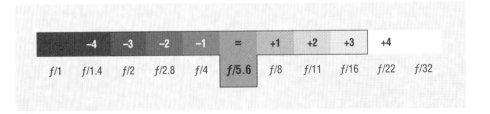

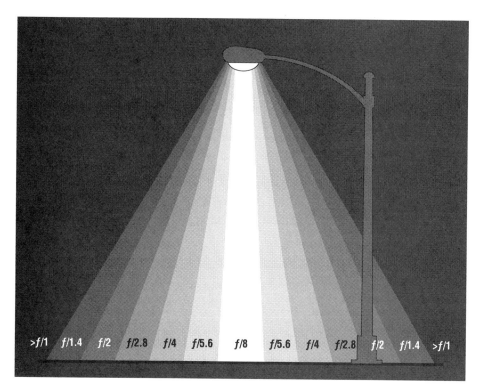

9-19

A hypothetical streetlight is a good example of the interrelationship between latitude and exposure

would be gradations, half stops, and so on, between these readings, but we'll just show the full stops, assuming that the brightest spot is directly under the center of the light. **SEE 9-19**

If you shoot at $f/8$, what is going to be the likely effect? The subject will be exposed normally only for that very brief point in the center of the light. With a knowledge of latitude, you can also predict where the subject is going to drop off to underexposure. The following figure delineates the final exposure, given the various light readings of the different areas. **SEE 9-20**

Although you can see to the edge of the light with your eyes, you will find that the subject is lost much earlier on the film.

What would happen if you decided to expose this scene at an $f/5.6$ instead? Now you get a larger area of normal exposure but it overexposes by one stop in the

9-20

The subject exposes differently at different f-stops

When the subject moves into an area where the light reading is:	The person is:
$f/5.6$	one stop underexposed
$f/4$	two stops underexposed—the subject is getting dark, but you still see detail
$f/2.8$	three stops underexposed—the subject is almost completely dark, nearly on the edge of the latitude
$f/2$	four stops underexposed—positing the three-to-three-and-a-half–stop latitude, the subject has gone entirely to underexposure

very center. It also extends the area of exposure one more stop at the edges. Where you lost the subject just above $f/2$ before, you now keep him to just above $f/1.4$. The subject, in a sense, traverses more area of exposure. Would that one stop of overexposure be acceptable in the center? That is always your decision, but if there is a strong top light, you can almost always expect its effect to be more amplified in the center. You can speculate that it would not only be acceptable, but you might like the effect more than the previous shot.

What would happen if you shot at $f/4$? By following this method of evaluation, you can make what might be called an "exposure pyramid." With it, you can predict what will happen at virtually any f-stop at which you choose to shoot. **SEE 9-21**

Are any of these possible exposures—that is, results—usable? Any of them might be usable, depending on what you want to achieve with the image; the emphasis is on *depending*, because that is the key. If realism is the goal, the $f/8$

9-21

With the "exposure pyramid," you can predict the outcome of virtually any f-stop at which you shoot

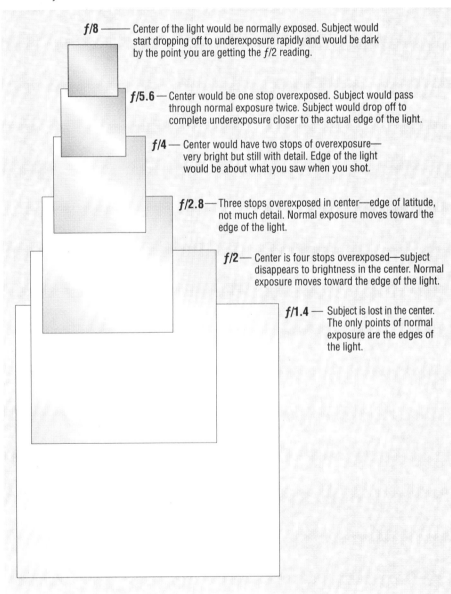

$f/8$ —— Center of the light would be normally exposed. Subject would start dropping off to underexposure rapidly and would be dark by the point you are getting the $f/2$ reading.

$f/5.6$ — Center would be one stop overexposed. Subject would pass through normal exposure twice. Subject would drop off to complete underexposure closer to the actual edge of the light.

$f/4$ — Center would have two stops of overexposure— very bright but still with detail. Edge of the light would be about what you saw when you shot.

$f/2.8$ — Three stops overexposed in center—edge of latitude, not much detail. Normal exposure moves toward the edge of the light.

$f/2$ — Center is four stops overexposed—subject disappears to brightness in the center. Normal exposure moves toward the edge of the light.

$f/1.4$ — Subject is lost in the center. The only points of normal exposure are the edges of the light.

shot might be acceptable. As suggested, with a realistic shot still your goal, the one stop of overexposure at $f/5.6$ might be preferable. Would you accept the two stops over in the center that you would get with an $f/4$? That has to be your decision. Lower stops yield an effect that would be decidedly less realistic ("Beam me up, Scotty"), but might fit into some dramatic contexts. Remember the example of the astronaut's brightly lit quarters in Stanley Kubrick's *2001: A Space Odyssey*.

The question of exposure is dependent on what the filmmaker wants to achieve with a given image. If the image serves to provide dramatic context for the narrative (or maybe we should say that if the image is at the service of the narrative), that may be the determining factor. If you want something more expressive or subjective, then that becomes the determining factor. The effect you achieve should always be the effect that you want for the particular situation.

Armed with an understanding of latitude and an ability to evaluate a given situation, you have the ability to predict what will happen to any image at any exposure. You can meter any situation and set up an exposure pyramid. Then you have some decisions to make, each yielding an image that is a little different and has a different dramatic impact.

With a wide range of volumes of light in front of the camera, the f-stop must be used so that these volumes expose at the levels at which you want them. Think of this in terms of the filmmaker (you) using the f-stop as a response to a volume or, more accurate, volumes of light. The f-stop controls the light so that the correct amount of light for the desired exposure reaches the film plane. The choice of f-stop thus becomes one more creative tool in that its selection involves decisions as to the character and dramatic context of the image you are creating. If you do not treat exposure as a major consideration, you are saying—and I have heard it from people who should know better—that the image is unimportant to you.

If we return to the original example of the person in front of the window (figure 9.9), some significant points become evident: As you evaluate shooting at different f-stops, you know what is going to happen to objects lit to the stop you are considering. Then, with a knowledge of latitude, you can predict with accuracy what is going to happen to objects lit to other stops. Are they within the latitude of the film?

If you can peg specific exposures to objects that are lit a certain way, you can make a graph of the relationships among a given f-stop, objects lit to that f-stop, and side effects of other things being over- or underexposed. Again, you are shooting with the same film stock, EI 500. The following figure represents what will happen if exposure is decreased. **SEE 9-22** The lengths of the vertical lines represent the suggested three-to-three-and-a-half–stop latitude. To see what and where things will fall into the latitude, extrapolate from the line to the left side of the chart.

Again, if you decide that you want the subject normally exposed, you would choose an $f/5.6$ and would select the group shown in the following figure. **SEE 9-23** Areas at 640 fc, the shaded area on the building, the backlight on the person, and the base of the lamp, would be three stops overexposed. This would put you in the unenviable position of having a shaded area three stops overexposed on the edge of the latitude. Would this be an effect you like?

If you think about how you might perceive a scene like this normally, you might expect a person standing in front of a very bright background to look slightly dark, as if she were in the shade. How could you achieve this effect? If you want to see something as being dark, you underexpose it; so, rather than $f/5.6$, what would happen if you shot at $f/8$? The subject would be one stop underexposed and look more as though she were in the shade. Doing this, however, would change how all the areas lit to other values respond. In effect, you would shift the whole exposure range to the right on a standard f-stop scale. **SEE 9-24**

When you shot at $f/5.6$, the objects lit to $f/2$ were at the bottom end of the latitude. As you can see, they fall off the bottom when exposed at $f/8$. All the

9-22

The vertical lines represent the latitude at each individual exposure

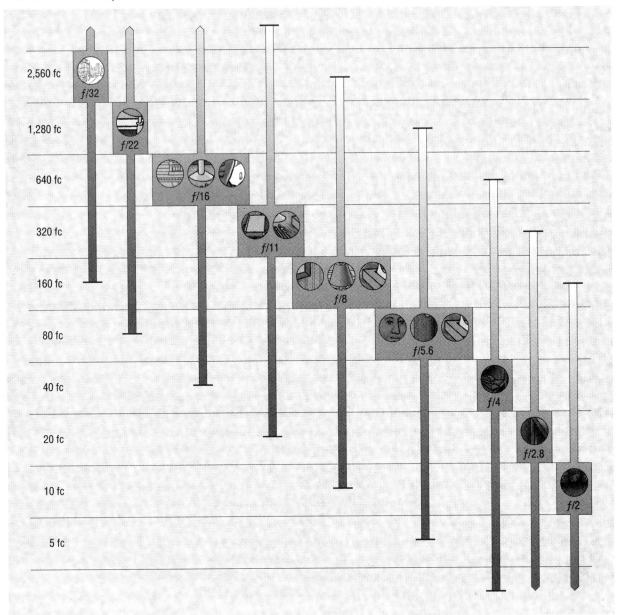

2,560 fc	f/32					
1,280 fc		f/22				
640 fc			f/16			
320 fc				f/11		
160 fc					f/8	
80 fc						f/5.6
40 fc						f/4
20 fc						f/2.8
10 fc						f/2
5 fc						

9-23

When an *f*-stop is chosen, everything lit to other values will come in at different levels of exposure

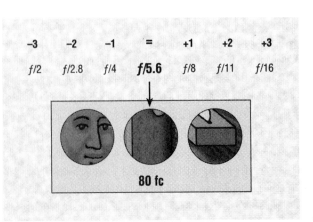

−3	−2	−1	=	+1	+2	+3
f/2	f/2.8	f/4	**f/5.6**	f/8	f/11	f/16

80 fc

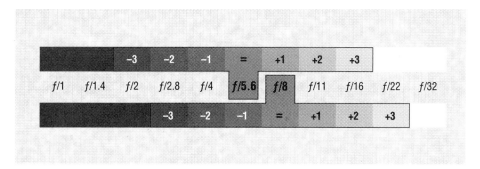

As the *f*-stop is changed, the parameters of the latitude change

objects lit to *f*/16 were three stops overexposed when you shot at *f*/5.6. They are only two stops overexposed when shot at *f*/8. It begins to appear as though exposure were a structure imposed on a space, imposed on the scene you are shooting. When you expose at *f*/5.6, you are imposing a structure on the scene that will bring a specific result on the film. If you change to an *f*/8, you in a sense pick up that whole structure and just move it to the right. If we were to shoot at *f*/4, you would move it to the left.

You will often hear people talking about lenses in terms of how they "collect" light. When you expose at a specific *f*-stop, you are collecting what is in front of the camera in a certain way. If you expose at a different *f*-stop, you are collecting in a different way. And when you choose one *f*-stop over another, you are making a choice as to what you consider important in the image, what you value.

After postulating a possible lighting scenario, people often ask the question, "How would you expose this?" Or, worse, "How *do* you expose this?" I answer the question with a question: "What do you *want?*" You are not after some abstract, one-size-fits-all, perfect image. You are going for what you want.

Try thinking about latitude being like a table: You can think of the range of exposures in the scene (that is, the range of light readings you have found with your meter) like objects spread out across a table. Call the center of the table "normal exposure," because normal exposure can be thought of as being halfway between total underexposure and total overexposure. One edge of the table represents underexposure, and the other overexposure. As you near either edge of the table, you get closer to total over- or underexposure until you drop off the edge. One should recognize this table analogy as a representation of the characteristic curve, the toe and shoulder being the edges of the table.

If your film stock has a latitude with a total of seven stops (three and a half stops on either side of normal exposure), the table is seven stops long. If your film stock has a total latitude of roughly five stops (most black-and-white reversals would fall into this category), the table is five stops long.

If you shoot the person in front of the window at an *f*/8, the objects that read 160 fc are in the center of the table, normally exposed; *f*/8 is also right in the center of the exposure values for our hypothetical scene. In this example, the ambient shadows and sunny street fall off the edge of the table. **SEE 9-25** If you shoot at *f*/22, different objects or areas are going to fall off the table. In this case, a large part of your exposure range is dropping off the latitude table. **SEE 9-26**

With enough people and equipment, you could light any proposed image, including the person in front of the window, to the center of the table. In fact, that was precisely the goal in the "Secret Service" story recounted earlier in this chapter. There are many reasons, most of which have already been discussed, why you would not want to do that. The image would be flat. This is why normal exposure is referred to as being a mythical beast. We talk about normal exposure, and it remains central to the discussion, but most of the images you see in films encompass a wide range of exposures. Yes, there will usually be areas that are normally exposed, but most images—and this is just common sense—have a wide

9-25

The latitude "table"

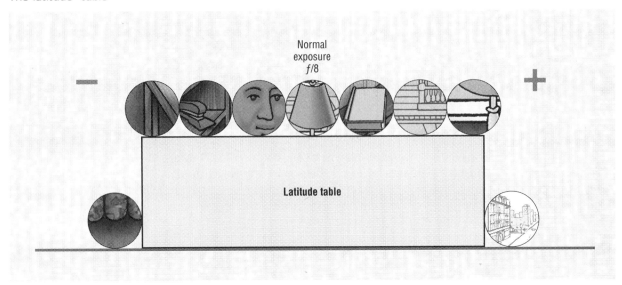

9-26

Shot at $f/22$, many areas fall off the edge to underexposure

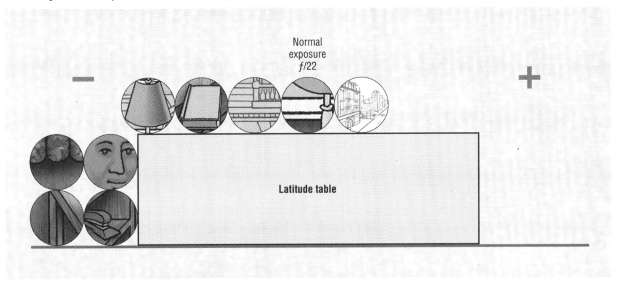

range of values. As a beginner, you may develop an abject fear of the edge of the table, but this is where you will want to learn to live. It is, simply put, where the texture and character of the image lives.

The scenario of the person in front of the window is an image that essentially has nine different exposure possibilities, $f/2$ to $f/32$, and nine distinctly different outcomes, again leaving out the fact that the readings have been simplified so they fall on the f-stops. Obviously, real life is not so cooperative.

If you can look among these results and find one of those many exposures that does precisely what you want, you are fine. The discussion, at least in terms of this image, can end here. But if your goal is to produce something that looks roughly like what you would see with your eyes, one can safely predict that none of the choices here would be acceptable. This pursuit of producing an approximation of human perception is generally referred to as **realism**, a concept that keeps the film world scrambling and thousands employed. Ahhh, realism. One might think that with all the interest in modernism and postmodernism things would be different. But now, oddly enough, realism's hold on film is probably stronger than ever. However much artists and critics may rail away at it, realism remains the stuff that fuels the engines of a substantial percentage of films, both American and international.

This part of the discussion can be concluded by saying that if your goal is realism, the person in front of the window represents an image with uncompromisable extremes. There are simply too many differing values to get an acceptable compromise. The obvious answer to the problem is to use artificial light and/or manipulate the existing light.

Reflectant Quality

The way objects and materials reflect light and how film responds to that light is referred to as **reflectant quality** or **luminance.** Most people know that lighter objects reflect a high percentage of the light that hits them, and dark objects reflect a small percentage. This, of course, is why we perceive them as light or dark. It stands to reason that objects that are highly reflectant, light objects, are going to photograph differently from objects that are not.

If you have ever worked with a monochrome monitor on a computer, you probably know that all objects can be measured and categorized according to the **gray scale**, which represents discrete points in how surfaces reflect light. The gray scale represents all the possibilities, from the smallest amount of light—black—to the most amount of light—white. The gray scale starts from black and goes through all shades of gray before it gets to white. **SEE 9-27**

The relationship of the gray scale to exposure, and the general issue of how objects reflect light, is of critical importance. If you take a gray scale and light it to an $f/5.6$, what will be the result if you then set the lens to $f/5.6$ and film it? It will be a normal exposure and you will see the scale as you see it here. But what happens if you over- or underexpose the gray scale? If you underexpose it, you essentially take the whole scale and move it to the right, the darkest grays shifting over into the black area. Medium and light grays, as well white, shift to grayer tones. **SEE 9-28** A similar shift occurs with overexposure as it does with underexposure. This time the scale shifts to the left. **SEE 9-29**

It should be noted that the gray scale will not respond this way at five stops of under- or overexposure, latitude being the complicating factor.

When you change the f-stop, you shift all reflectant values on the scale. With the gray scale lighted to an $f/5.6$, if you racked the f-stop all the way from an $f/1.4$ to an $f/22$, the whole scale would shift from overexposure to normal exposure to underexposure. Simply stated, this means that darker subjects will drop off to

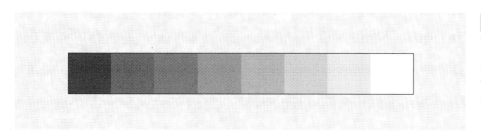

9-27

The gray scale consists of a sequence of discrete reflecting tones, from black through shades of gray to white

9-28

If you underexpose
the gray scale,
you essentially shift
the entire scale
to the right

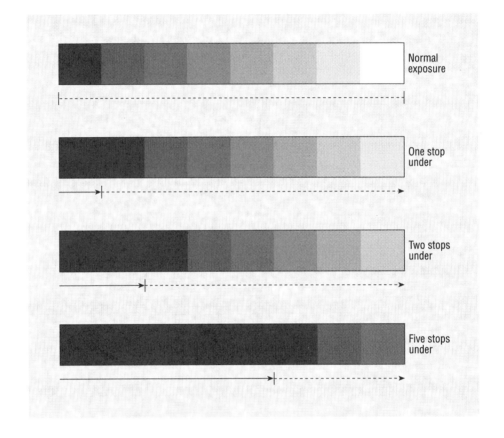

9-29

If you overexpose
the gray scale,
you essentially shift
the entire scale
to the left

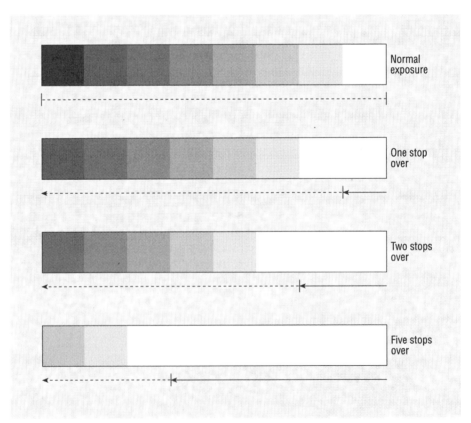

underexposure much more quickly than lighter ones. The same is true of lighter subjects on the overexposure end.

Thus, reflectant quality obviously complicates any discussion of exposure. It should also be evident that latitude is not written in stone. Latitude is a general guide, and different subjects are going to respond differently to over- or underexposure. To a certain extent, an understanding of reflectant quality can be gained only through experience. You have to film a lot of different materials to be able to predict how things are going to respond.

The way this issue affects exposure decisions has wide-ranging implications. This is particularly true when filming subjects with dark skin tones. You will quickly find out that most technical recommendations for exposure and light were, at least to a certain extent, calculated with the Caucasian face in mind. This is explored further in chapter 11.

t-stops

The term *t-stop* has appeared several times and, though their use is relatively simple, it requires explanation. The *t* in *t*-stop stands for transmission. It might be useful to think of it as meaning the "true" stop. What a *t-stop* does is take into account the light that is lost passing through a lens. Almost all lenses lose light due to lens complexity and something called aberrations—the failure of a lens (or any refracting surface) to produce exact correspondence between an object and its image. In a perfect world, an f-stop, let's say an $f/5.6$, is going to let in a specific amount of light under given lighting conditions. But in our less-than-perfect world, if some light is lost in the lens, you are not getting a "true" $f/5.6$'s worth of light to the film plane. If not compensated for, this results in a slight underexposure. The *t*-stop compensates for the lost light by using a slightly larger aperture.

The manufacturer calibrates *t*-stops for each individual lens. Virtually all professional lenses are calibrated in *t*-stops rather than f-stops. They are simply the point where a true f-stop's amount of light reaches the film plane. You use them just like you do f-stops. If you get a reading of $f/5.6$ and your lens is calibrated in *t*-stops, you simply set it to $t/5.6$.

Most film crews communicate in *t*-stops. So far you've been encouraged to think of light either in foot-candles or f-stops, and we will continue to use these measurements so as not to needlessly complicate the discussion. As you begin to work on larger productions, you will hear people using *t*-stops with more frequency.

By their definition *t*-stops provide a wider opening, but none are as much as a full stop wider. This occasionally prompts the question of why one would bother to compensate when a single stop is well within the latitude of most film stocks. Just so you are forewarned, I've been on film sets where the DP was talking about light in terms of fifths of a stop. Needless to say, DPs are very exacting in determining how the film is exposed. This is partly an issue of maintaining consistent photographic quality, but it is mostly because different exposures produce different effects. Eventually, it will be you who is making the choices.

10

Planning the Lighting

Thinking Out the Process

From this exposition of basic principles, we can move into some pragmatic examples of specific lighting setups. We can start by reiterating that when you are exposing an image, that is, choosing an f-stop, you are exposing for something, such as a value, a person, an object, an area, or a dramatic effect, that is important to you. Cinematographer Vilmos Zsigmond has made an interesting observation in this regard.[1] He states that beginners mistakenly set up their lights and then stick out their light meter to get a reading. They then shoot at what the light meter tells them. This is a backward method. What most DPs do, particularly those involved in making narrative films, is start with the light meter reading; they start with a value, in terms of an amount of light, that they want to achieve, and all subsequent decisions flow from that one piece of information.

On a less pragmatic level, you will hear many claims about the kinds of effects lighting can achieve. Lighting produces feeling. Lighting produces mood. Lighting creates visual text and subtext. You will hear many a cinematographer waxing philosophical, and sometimes a bit romantic, about all the things that lighting can do. This is as it should be. You have to be a bit of a romantic to want to express yourself with light, particularly when there are so many other attention-grabbing elements of film. But, on a gut level, *lighting is achieving the image that you want.*

This is both a technical and a creative process. It is a matter of knowing what you want and how to manipulate the materials to get it. The processes are inseparable. You cannot get one without the other. It is what has been referred to as *technique*, that application of the technical to produce the desired effect. At this point it is a matter of using the lights and meters to achieve the effects you want. Eventually you will probably be able to do much of your lighting to your eye. For now, however, it's wrestling with those lights to get them to do what you want.

Lighting: A Basic Strategy

Before getting into an extended discussion of lighting it should be stated, in all honesty, that thinking out the lighting of a scene is essentially an easy process. Albeit

---

1. Salvato, Larry, and Dennis Schaefer, *Masters of Light: Conversations with Contemporary Cinematographers* (Berkeley: University of California Press, 1984) p. 337.

dissembling, there is a certain amount of truth to this statement. The following strategy constitutes an easy way to think out your lighting.

1. **Start with choosing an *f*-stop.** There are many reasons to choose a particular *f*-stop, such as depth of field, lens resolution, quality of light, ease of achieving other values in the frame, and so on, but choose one that makes sense to what you are trying to achieve. Once you have this fundamental piece of information, everything else falls into place.

2. **Ask the question: What areas or objects do I want to be normally exposed?** Then light those elements to your desired *f*-stop. Remember, you rarely want everything normally exposed. That would make for a flat and uninteresting image.

3. **Then ask yourself: What areas or objects do I want underexposed? And, How *much* do I want them underexposed?** Light the areas you want underexposed, including the fill side of faces, to values less than your chosen *f*-stop. How *much* less is determined by how dark you want them to be, always remembering that eventually they will slip outside the latitude of the film.

4. **The last question is, of course: What areas do I want overexposed?** You light those areas to values greater than the chosen *f*-stop. As with the previous example, the amount of overexposure depends on how much you want, remembering again the latitude of the film.

With both underexposure and overexposure, you may want to exceed the latitude of the film for effect. The important consideration is to know where all your other light values are registering in relation to normal exposure, keeping in mind the limits of the film.

That is it in a nutshell. It sounds easy but of course it is not. The pragmatic part of executing a lighting setup is hard enough, but there are all kinds of side issues—such as quality, continuity, and coverage, to name just a few—that complicate the task. But as a starting place, this is as good a one as I have found.

Lighting Applications

Some of these basic principles can be demonstrated if you start with some simple tests that involve the key light and the fill light. Go ahead and load up a camera and shoot this. Before you shoot, though, there are a few general guidelines with which you should become familiar.

Guidelines

☑ **There are two basic movements used in trimming the instruments: panning and tilting.** These terms are used in the same way as with the camera. When you move a light from side to side, so the beam is sweeping horizontally, you are *panning* the light. When you move a light up and down, so the beam is sweeping vertically, it is called *tilting*. These movements are done frequently as you set up and make choices.

☑ **When using a focusable spot on your subject, always find and use the center of the light.** If you aim one of these lights at a wall, you will notice that it throws a round pattern. You should be able to discern its center—it's where it is the brightest. It is easiest to find the center of the pattern when you have the light spotted in. Put it right on whatever you are lighting. Nine times out of ten, you'll get yourself in trouble if you start some other way. If you pan the light off the subject or area to get a lower reading, it will just look like they are not in the light, like the light is going past them.

☑ **Lighting is a very time-consuming process.** You will often be working with people who have not worked on films before. Be sure to prepare both crew and talent for the kind of time that you are going to have to take. Lighting is a deductive process in which you keep creating and solving problems until you get what you want. You just have to be patient and go through the necessary steps. The most time I have ever seen go into lighting a single shot is about three hours but, in comparing stories with other film people, that is pretty tame. A friend loves to tell the story of the time a crew he was on took eight hours to light a potato chip bag. The client did not like anything they set up. An efficient film crew can light a simple shot in ten to fifteen minutes, but, the more complicated the shot and/or scene, the more time it takes. To get the result you want, the preparation and time have to be invested.

☑ **Take notes.** Without a guide for analyzing your test, you may have a difficult time reconstructing all the things you did. A sheet with columns for the foot-candle readings of all your lights is probably the best approach. Have a column for the key, fill, backlight, and so on. Also have a column for the f-stop. Most of these tests should be shot at the f-stop you get for the key. This is the usual, though by no means uniform, approach. It is also recommended that you try shooting some of the setups you create at different f-stops. It can be instructive to see what happens when you expose for the fill light or the backlight. Experiment.

Learn these basic terms and practices because, if you get on a lighting crew, you will be expected to execute some basic tasks. Fellow crew members have little patience with anyone who slows them down.

Tests

Start the test by setting up a key light to 160 fc, which translates to an $f/8$ with a 500 EI stock. We are choosing 160 fc for several reasons. First, it is a relatively easy value to achieve with the kind of lights you will probably be using. Also, there is lots of room on either side of it for experimentation with overexposure and underexposure. Light meters, particularly inexpensive ones, do not always read small amounts of light with the kind of accuracy needed for an effective test. We will use values that you should be able to reproduce and measure with ease and accuracy.

If possible, use a focusable spot for the key. To achieve 160 fc, it is easiest to have an assistant move the light while you are at the subject with a light meter. Holding the meter at the subject, point it at the key and have the assistant move the light toward or away from the subject. Stop when the meter shows the desired value. Using the spot/flood capacity of the light is another easy method of getting the value you want.

Nose shadows receive significant attention. DPs generally try to have the light above and to the side of the subject so the shadow will go down into the lines to the side of the nose. **SEE 10-1** Other light positioning can make this shadow go strange and irritating places, such as into the mouth, straight across the face, or even into the eye.

Next, set up the fill light and move it until you get an $f/5.6$ (80 fc). This is easiest to do with the key light switched off. Before shooting, check the total by taking another reading at the subject toward the camera. Sometimes the fill can add to the total, and you may have to back off the key light to reestablish your 160 fc. What will be the result if you shoot at an $f/8$? The fill light will underexpose by one stop—well within the latitude of the film, so the fill side of the face will be

10-1

When the fill is underexposing by one stop, lighting will be high-key

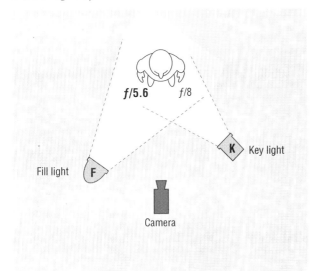

10-2

As the fill is drawn back, shadows on the fill side will become deeper

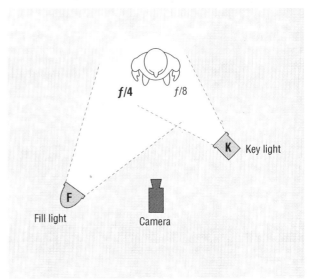

slightly darker but will be rendered with a fair amount of detail. Thus, the shadows are not very harsh, so you have an even, high-key image.

This relationship between the key and the fill is called a ***lighting ratio*** or ***contrast ratio*** (see page 267 for the specific formula). Remember that the intensity of the fill light in relationship to the key controls the dramatic quality of the image, and a ratio between the key side and the fill side of the subject can be calculated.

What happens if you walk the fill light out to an $f/4$ (40 fc)? Remember to recheck the total for 160 fc before shooting. The fill light is now underexposing by two stops. **SEE 10-2** Again, the shadow areas are well within the latitude of the film but darker than in the previous shot. It is not quite as flat as the previous image, but is still high-key. Continue backing off the fill light in this manner, always rechecking the total.

When backed off to an $f/2.8$ (20 fc), the fill light is underexposing by three stops and, while still being within the latitude of the film, it is getting close to the edge of the table from our earlier analogy. At this point you have moved into lighting that would be considered low-key. **SEE 10-3** The shadow area is very dark though still having some detail. It is an image with much more contrast. If you continue and back off the fill to an $f/2$ (10 fc), you are going to fall off the edge. **SEE 10-4** The fill is going to underexpose by four stops, and at this point we can predict—and this is all about being able to predict results—that it will have virtually no effect on the resulting film. In fact, you might want to try switching the fill light on and off to see if there is any effect at all. Remember that latitude is not an absolute. There may be some effect, but you can be assured that if there is, it will be small.

Try to keep a visual record of how you see what you are shooting. When the fill is at an $f/2$, it is definitely producing an effect visible to the eye. The point is that the film will not see it. With this in mind, consider the following basic rules of lighting which, at first glance, appear to be contradictory.

▶ **RULE:** *If it does not look good to your eye,*
it will not look good to the film.

This is common sense. If you are getting ready to film a shot and there is something about it that just doesn't look right, it is still not going to look right when you get the film back. Are there are too many shadows? Can the viewer see everything that

10-3

At 20 fc, the fill is underexposing by three stops—still within the latitude of the film, but very low-key

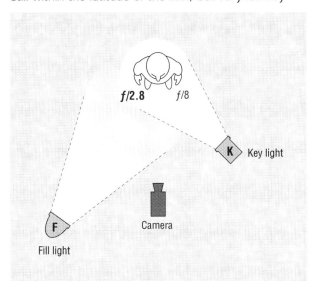

10-4

At 10 fc, the fill will underexpose by four stops and will have little or no effect on the film

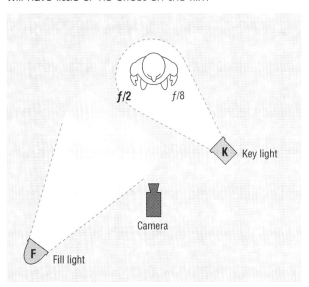

is important? Are there shadows in the eyes that make the subject look like a raccoon? Is it just ugly light?

▶ **RULE:** *Just because it looks good to your eye, does not mean it is going to look good on film.*

Again, these two rules appear to contradict each other. This is clearly a question of latitude. Your light values have to fall within a relatively narrow range in order to show up on film. As you look at the last test with your eyes, the one filled to an $f/2$, you might say it looks fine, but the film sees only a segment of what we see. The light meter and a knowledge of latitude are the keys.

Essentially, you treat all the rest of the lights as you have the key and fill. To start, try introducing a backlight. The light is usually set up above and behind the subject, pointing directly at the crown of the head. **SEE 10-5** How do you use the light meter to read it? The meter, in this case, should be pointed directly at the light, not toward the camera.

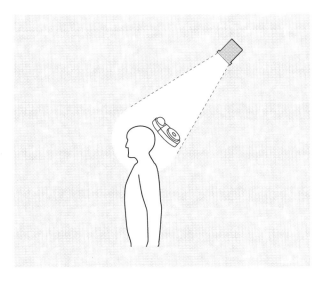

10-5

The backlight is measured by pointing the light meter at it

10-6

Trimmed to *f*/16, the
backlight overexposes
by two stops

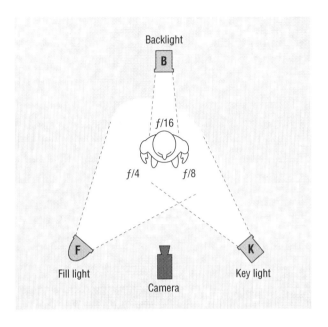

The light meter will be used in this fashion with more and more frequency. In many cases, we are not so much interested in how much light is being seen from the camera position, as we are in how many foot-candles are being produced by a particular lighting instrument. *Each instrument is set up to accomplish a specific purpose*—to light a desired area or subject, to create a certain effect—and its intensity is set to achieve a specific level of exposure. The goal may be as general as to give an overall fill to a large area or as specific as highlighting a glass on a nightstand.

The intensity you want for the backlight depends somewhat on the color of the subject's hair. These are very general guidelines, but if the subject has brown hair, many DPs like to keep the backlight the same number of foot-candles as the key light. If the subject has black hair, they go higher; if the subject is blond, they go lower.

To make the test interesting, trim the backlight to an *f*/16 and walk the fill light back to an *f*/4, so it is having an effect. **SEE 10-6** As you set up the backlight, try to make sure that its beam is hitting only the back of the subject's head and not spilling onto the face.

If the backlight is at *f*/16 and you are still shooting at an *f*/8, the backlight will overexpose by two stops, which will create a halo effect. Is this something you might want on occasion? Of course.

At this point there are three different values in the shot: *f*/4, *f*/8, and *f*/16. What would happen if you shot at different *f*-stops? If you shot at an *f*/16, you'd be exposing for the backlight. The only thing that would expose normally would be the subject's hair.[2] The face would be two stops under. Could this be interesting? You may want to do something with the fill light, which is now out of the latitude of the film, but the overall answer is probably yes. What would happen if you shot at *f*/11? The possibilities are pretty much limitless, but you can continue to manipulate volumes of light and exposure to create differing effects. Try shooting some different exposures and intensities on the three lights, as well as setting up other lights for other areas of the frame, the background for example.

Remember that lighting is a very deductive process, particularly when you are just learning it. You can start with a question: What are the central points of

---

2. Technically speaking, trimming the backlight to an *f*/16 would make it the key light. The key light can be thought of as the source of light and it does not necessarily have to come from the front.

interest in this image, and where do I want the viewer's attention focused? These are usually, though not always, the areas that you want keyed and normally exposed. Set up key lights for these points. Once you've done that, you will see that you have some problems. You don't like the shadow created by this key or whatever. Manipulate the lights until those problems are at least superficially solved. Do not overdo it—the other lights will cause problems, too. Once all the keys are set up and reading the foot-candle values you want, you then decide what you want to fill and how you want to fill it. Set up the appropriate lights. Again, this will create problems. Solve them. Then do the same thing with the backlights and other lights. You just keeping trimming the lights and adjusting for their side effects until you get what you want. Remember the methods for trimming instruments: repositioning, moving spot/flood, using modifying materials, and so on.

Clearly character movement complicates these simple tests. Have your subject turn his or her head to the left and right, turn to see what the fill side looks like, and so on. Characters rarely look directly at the camera, so position the subject however you like. I generally prefer to have the key on the camera side of a subject's face, although this is more apt to leave the subject's shadow in the background of the shot. Many cinematographers take the easy way out and make the key side away from the camera, although the nose shadow can stand out.

Sometimes the hardest thing to do is to get started. You have all these lights and may not have a clear conception of what to do with them. These tests should give some basic direction. Be forewarned, learning lighting is an experiential affair (isn't everything). As a gaffer friend likes to put it, the best teacher is just spending a few years "putting it up, shooting it, and taking it down."

Problems and Solutions

The approach so far has been essentially evaluative. We have looked at several situations, such as the person by the window, the streetlight, and the table lamp, with one question in mind: What can I do with what exists here? While evaluation is clearly part of the process, the approach has to be much more active in terms of changing things. The way to look at a shot or a scene is not to say, "What can I get?" but rather, "What do I have to do to get what I want?" The only reason a DP will walk through an unprepared location with a light meter is to find out what has to be changed to create the desired effect.

Shooting an Existing Situation

We will start with several relatively simple situations and, for now, talk less in terms of specific instruments and in the more general terms of keys and sources. Let's say you're shooting in a room that has natural illumination from windows. You want to do a camera pan from person A to person B. **SEE 10-7**

With your light meter, you find that person A has 40 fc falling on him. Using the stock with an EI of 500, that is an $f/4$. Person B has 320 fc and an $f/11$. Consider the possibilities and make some determinations. If you shoot at:

$f/4$ Person A will be normally exposed and person B will be +3, three stops overexposed.

$f/5.6$ Person A will be –1 and person B will be +2.

$f/8$ Person A will be –2 and person B will be +1.

$f/11$ Person B will be normally exposed, and person A will be three stops underexposed and will be rendered with only a small amount of detail.

10-7

Setup #1: using natural lighting from the windows

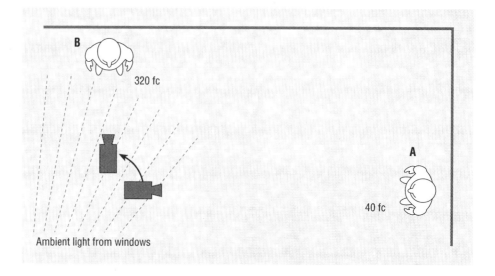

B

320 fc

A

40 fc

Ambient light from windows

If any of these choices represent the effect that you desire, you can go ahead and film. If your purpose is different, and it usually is, you have to bring in lights.

Let's say that you decide you want normal exposure on each person. The question always comes up: Could I simply rack f-stops? That is, rotate the f-stop ring from an $f/4$ to an $f/11$ as you are executing the pan, just as one would with a rack focus. That way you would get normal exposure on each person. If you did this, though, you would have an unwanted by-product. Think back to the discussion of reflectant quality and the gray scale. You are crossing over the wall as you execute the pan. If you change the f-stop, you shift where the wall is read on the gray scale. If the wall is white, as you close down you are shifting the white into the gray area, and the quality of the white wall will become darker. This effect can be very pronounced, depending on how radically different your values are.

Because there is the three-stop difference between the two people, one must assume that there is also a shifting amount of light on the wall. Attempting to calibrate an f-stop rack to the changing values on the wall, however, would be an exercise in futility; it would be virtually impossible to execute.

So again, given the desired result, you find uncompromisable extremes. If you want a normal exposure on both people, the best solution is to use an instrument to light person A to 320 fc.[3] There are other possibilities (and complications), but this is probably the most straightforward solution. So set up a light and modify it to 320 fc. **SEE 10-8** That will even out the two extremes and you shoot at $f/11$.

Another example of the problems involved with several different exposure values is shooting in a car. Several years ago I was involved in a film that had many daytime shots inside a car. Step 1 was to read the exposure values already present in the scene. First the DP metered outside and got a reading of 640 fc ($f/16$). Then he went inside the shaded backseat of the car and got a reading of 40 fc ($f/4$). This presented him with several choices. If he shot at $f/4$, the subject in the car would be normally exposed, and the outside would be, what? Overexposed, but by how many stops? $f/5.6$ is +1, $f/8$ is +2, $f/11$ is +3, $f/16$ is +4. Positing the latitude of three to three and a half stops, the outside would be totally overexposed.

If we shot at $f/16$, the outside would be correct but the subject would now be four stops underexposed and merely a silhouette. Each solution might be acceptable given the dramatic approach of the scene, but in this case the director wanted detail in both areas. He essentially wanted a realistic look, even though the subject being filmed was a rather bizarre character. As much as people discuss

3. This recommendation is complicated by the color temperature of artificial lights (see page 274).

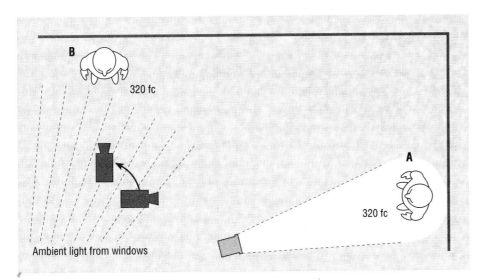

10-8

Setup #2: lighting person A to 320 fc

breaking out of realistic modes of representation, it is amazing how often we find ourselves discussing pictorial realism.

Without manipulating the situation, what were our other choices? We could shoot at:

f/5.6   The figure would be one stop underexposed, and the exterior would be three stops overexposed, on the edge of the latitude.

f/8   The figure would be –2, and the outside +2. A possibility, but, in my opinion, the worst of all possible worlds—neither one nor the other.

f/11   The figure would be –3, on the edge of the latitude, and the outside would be +1.

None of these seemed like very acceptable solutions, given the desire for a realistic image. The obvious solution was to bring artificial light into the car. In a film with a larger budget, there probably would have been a generator that the car could tow. But with the limited budget on this project, we simply wired some small lights onto the car's battery (you have to know what you are doing to do this). The temptation might be to pump the interior light up to *f*/16. This would be a real trick in pragmatic terms. Even if we could have done this, what would be the result? A normal exposure inside and out, and it would look as though the sun were shining not only outside but also next to the subject in the backseat of the car! I have seen this done, and the results are spectacular—spectacularly bad.

The idea here is to manipulate the lighting values so there is gradation, gradation that maintains the viewer's visual expectations. If you will, it maintains our visual stereotypes. We perceive light and shadow in life; the absence of it on film makes the image unrealistic. The solution was to light the person in the car to an *f*/8 (160 fc), which is pragmatically much simpler. We then shot at *f*/11. The interior of the car and the subject were one stop underexposed, thus looking somewhat shadowed. The outside was one stop overexposed, giving it a bright, airy feel. **SEE 10-9**

For all intents and purposes, the foot-candle value that translates to an *f*/11 (320 fc) may not have even existed in this image. It probably did somewhere, but that is not what is relevant here. The point is that we expose to achieve a specific effect. If there were no points at 320 fc (*f*/11) in the image, the final image simply would not have had any elements of normal exposure. Again, we were exposing less for the mythical beast, normal exposure, than for a specific effect. We exposed the image, knowing how all the areas were going to fall into the latitude. Again, the

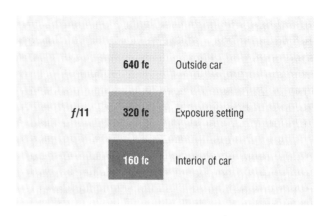

10-9

Manipulating values to produce gradation maintains the viewer's visual expectations—a bright exterior and a more shadowed interior

f/11

640 fc	Outside car
320 fc	Exposure setting
160 fc	Interior of car

worst thing that could have happened would have been to light the scene so that all the exposure values were equal and exposed normally.

Averaging

The example of the car scene illustrates a concept that many people with a background in still photography may recognize as averaging. It is similar, but we are accomplishing something slightly different here. With ***averaging***, when confronted with a range of *f*-stop choices, many still photographers choose a stop somewhere in the middle. That way they will have detail in all areas. If things are not precisely the way they want them on the negative, they can make printing adjustments in the darkroom stage.

Although averaging can be a reasonably good approach for still photographers, it has major drawbacks for most types of filmmaking. Films, of course, are made up of tens of thousands of individual frames, and it would be virtually impossible, without it becoming prohibitively expensive, to give them all individual attention. Each shot is analyzed before a final print is made, but it is analyzed for color and exposure corrections in the entire shot, not problems in small areas.

Even then, films are printed in reels, not in shots. In 35mm, reels are 10 minutes long; in 16mm they are 45 minutes long. You cannot take a couple of printing tries to get an individual shot right and then move on to the next shot. If one shot is wrong, the entire reel has to be reprinted. You occasionally have to make a number of tries to get a whole reel right, with each try being very expensive. You do have control over individual shots. Without getting too far into the science and art of printing, the lights in the printer can be programmed to change every shot. You just can't print each shot individually and start again if you get it wrong. You make your best analysis of every shot and then print the whole reel.

This reinforces the importance of getting exposure and lighting right on location. This is true for virtually everything in terms of picture, particularly composition. Once you have the picture, it is almost written in stone, at least for those who work with small budgets. There are ways, optical printers and such, to correct mistakes and manipulate preexisting footage, but they can be expensive and lead to a whole new host of matching problems. The more you get right on location, the fewer messy and expensive corrections you have to make in postproduction.

Again, people ask me, "In such and such situations, should I just average these different exposures?" My answer is an emphatic, *"No! You should be choosing an exposure for some reason!"* Averaging can be useful in some situations. Documentary shooting in particular has many situations in which you are unable to control the light. Finding an average can help you out of some complex situations. But, in general, the answer is no.

Working with Artificial Light

A good example of an exposure problem comes from a film that I directed several years ago. It called for two actors to come around a corner, stand in front of a door, and exchange dialogue. Then, still in the same shot, they approach the camera, stop, and exchange some more dialogue. The action took place in a dingy furnace room and was to initiate a segment of the film that was dark and mysterious.

I wanted the characters to enter a strong, narrow beam of light and have their first discussion. Still in the same shot, they exit the beam and approach the camera and have a second discussion in the darkened area of the furnace room. Setting up the beam of light was relatively simple. The problem became the darkened area outside the beam. The following figure illustrates what the proposed action looked like from overhead. **SEE 10-10**

We set up the beam and trimmed it to the foot-candle readings shown in the next figure. **SEE 10-11** Once we had the beam, we were able to check all the other areas and see how all the other values settled out. The areas outside the beam—

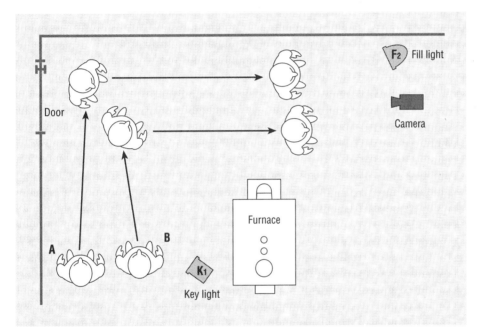

10-10

Proposed character movement for the furnace-room scene

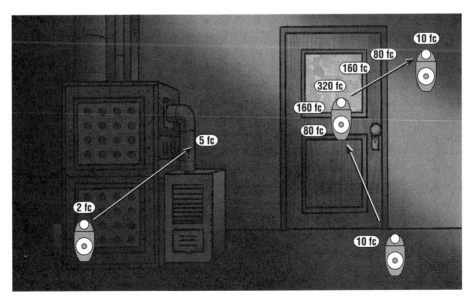

10-11

The foot-candle readings after setting up the single light source

and we were just measuring ambient and bounce light because the only light was the beam—were at 10 fc and less, mostly less.

I wanted the center of the beam to overexpose by one stop because it would intensify the slash effect. We decided to shoot at the f-stop we got for 160 fc, an $f/8$ with our 500 EI stock. The areas at 10 fc translate to what f-stop? $f/2$. Areas below 10 fc range below an $f/2$. Even though the maximum aperture on the lens we were using was an $f/2.3$, the light exists at these levels and can have an effect on the film. In this case, however, this is four or more stops less than $f/8$, outside of the latitude of the film. I wanted the characters to have detail but still look as though they were in the darkened area, essentially a realistic image.

The solution was to set up a small light (setup #2 in figure 10.10), that filled in the front area. I wanted a look that replicated the indirect quality of the ambient light, so we used a softlight. The question was: How strong did we want it to be? We wound up trimming it until we got 30 fc right by the furnace. That is two and a half stops less than the stop at which we were shooting. Always thinking in terms of what the film is going to register, that was within our proposed latitude. We could predict that the characters would be rendered very dark but still with some detail when they reached their final position. This was precisely the desired effect. It is not quite so clearcut as the example with the car but, again, the areas of normal exposure in this image are exceedingly small—the edge of the beam. Think *effect*.

Consider one final example before we move on to more complicated approaches. In another film, a scene required two characters to come into a darkened apartment and turn on the lights. **SEE 10-12** (Again, the three lights shown represent only general sources; the actual setup probably involved as many as a dozen lights.) Two things of concern to me were that a strong hall light be established and that the room not be entirely black when the characters enter. The first step was to light the apartment for when the lights are switched on. From instrument #2, we lit the room to 80 fc ($f/5.6$). Because I wanted a normal exposure in the room, this was the stop at which we were going to shoot, the stop on which all subsequent decisions were based. Now we could figure what values we wanted the other lights to be.

As suggested, I wanted a strong hall light on the characters as they entered the room. What would the effect be if we took instrument #1 and threw 80 fc on the doorway area? The light would normally expose, and the hallway effect would be just the same as the front effect once the lights were turned on. In other words,

10-12

The three basic sources each create different levels of light

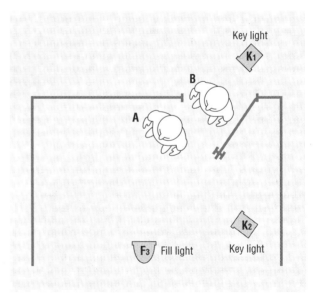

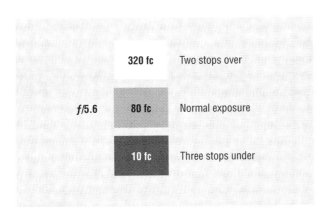

10-13

This complex exposure incorporated a range of six stops

it would not stand out. We wanted a pronounced effect, so we lit the area to 320 fc (*f*/11). The light that streams in the open door is going to overexpose by two stops.

Now we turned our considerations to the darkened room. You almost always have to use some light to represent a darkened space. If there are no lights at all, the shot will have an opaque photographic texture. Also, and probably more important, we do not associate darkness with blackness, because there is at least some element of light in most of the night or dark settings we encounter. We rarely experience a complete absence of light, and it is quite disorienting when we do.

I wanted the effect of ambient city light coming in through the window. This goes a little beyond what we have been talking about, but what color is generally associated with night? Blue. The first thing we did was put some blue gel on instrument #3—the light which we used to create the night effect. What kind of foot-candle reading do we want off this light? It has to be less than 80 fc because that matches what happens when the light gets turned on. But how much less? We wanted dark, so the decision was to light the room to 10 fc, three stops underexposed.

The first time I tried this kind of effect years ago, it took a lot of courage. I counted a few new gray hairs while I was waiting for the film to come back from the lab. In a sense, what you are doing with this effect is plumbing the edges of your latitude. Occasionally, particularly as a beginner, you cross your fingers, hoping you have not fallen off the edge.

In the example of the man in front of the window, it was suggested that the range of light values represents uncompromisable extremes for a realistic image. But here there is a range of six stops—10, 20, 40, 80, 160, 320—that are put together for a complex exposure. **SEE 10-13** Actually, there were more than six stops, because the fill for the dark segment of the shot was not a flat 10 fc across the whole space. It would have looked abnormal if the darkness was totally even. So, here we see a very wide range that works in the particular situation we created.

The Setup: Decision Making

The big question is: How do you work with individual lights? What follows is a lighting-plan walkthrough. As stated, lighting is a very deductive process, and this discussion will elaborate on as much of the reasoning process as possible. You start with a basic premise about what you want the scene's lighting to accomplish and then go from there.

Knowing just what it is you want to accomplish is one of the hardest hurdles to get over. There is just no single answer and, regardless of what is said here, the

10-14

The starting point for the lighting walkthrough

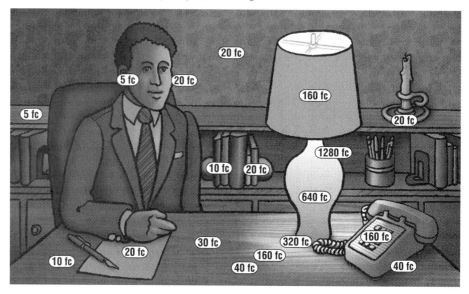

answer has to come from you. Every scene is going to be different. It is not as simple as saying that you have to do the right thing for a specific scene or that the material is going to determine the light. That leads to cliché and stereotypical answers. Sometimes you have to play against type or create some kind of visual subtext. Sometimes you want to highlight specific subjects or areas. Maybe you want to hide something. Sometimes you just want to cheat conventional expectations.

Still, the effect should be appropriate to the context. I have a friend, an experienced director who closely supervises the lighting in his films, who was filming a scene in an all-night restaurant. The scene had a number of offbeat characters and ambiguous action. He had the scene lit in a very atmospheric, low-key way. A couple of months later, I noticed him hunched over the editing table with his head in his hands. He was looking at the scene and all he could say was, "How could I have done this? It's a @*#&%! all-night restaurant, not the Film Noir Cafe."

Our walkthrough will start with the person and the table lamp. **SEE 10-14** The lamp is on, and the bookcase is about five feet behind the person. This is still a complex image. We will see many early mistakes with an image like this, particularly when using the automatic meters in Super 8 and video cameras. Let's say that we went through the scene and got the readings shown in the figure.

Notice the area just on the edge of the circle of light from the lamp, showing readings of 40, 160, and 320 fc. This represents someone moving the meter along the surface of the table with the activating button depressed. **SEE 10-15** This response is very common when there is a strong light with a hard edge. You get a strong reading in the center, which drops off a little toward the edge; then you see a precipitous drop outside the circle. This is quite straightforward—we are just doing the necessary measurement of what is plain to see with our eyes. What is important to remark is that there is a four-stop difference between the first and last positions.

With this four-stop difference in mind, it is easy to see why so many beginners make mistakes when using the automatic meter on a camera. Again, the automatic meter does not know what to read in this image. Undaunted by the fact that he is getting no reading when the camera is pointed at the face, the novice will pan over to the light. The needle will respond with some kind of exposure, let's say an $f/8$. He will lock the f-stop, shoot the scene at $f/8$, and be disturbed when it returns looking like the following figure. **SEE 10-16**

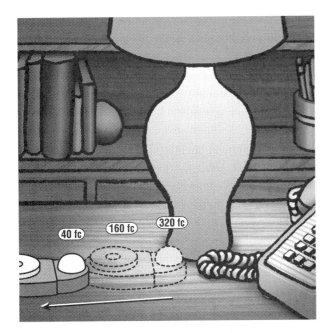

10-15

The range of readings represents someone moving the meter along the surface of the table with the activating button pressed

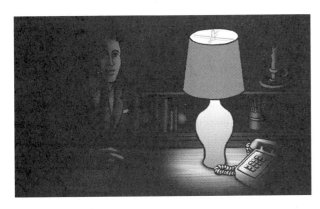

10-16

The result of basing the readings of this scene on an automatic light meter pointed at the light

What happened is fairly obvious. The meter responded to, and the scene was exposed for, one of the brightest values. When the latitude of the film takes over, you are left with nothing. Looking at the scene with the naked eye, everything probably looked fine. Even through the camera everything probably looked fine. But there was a rude awakening when the film came back. This kind of mistake is one of the most common exposure errors, and automatic light meters will do it to you with a fair amount of frequency. It is a prime example of the second rule of lighting: Just because it looks good to your eye...

Using more-accurate metering methods, you can determine that there are a number of possibilities for exposure in this example, none of them good. As with the first example, if pictorial realism is your goal, what you see here represents uncompromisable extremes. If you expose to get one thing right, something else in the frame is going to be at an unacceptable level. If you expose the person's face correctly, the lamp is going to be totally wrong, and so on.

Applying the method described earlier in this chapter, you should first determine the exposure at which you want to shoot. Looking over all the values, what would you choose? We will go with *f*/8, which is what we get for 160 fc at 500 EI. Sometimes you want to choose values that are read from sources that pose problems. Part of the reason we are choosing *f*/8 is because it is the reading off the lamp shade. Lamp shades are very difficult to manipulate to other values. You could put in a lower-wattage bulb, but this could create color problems and would change all the other readings in the scene. Another possible method is to wrap the interior of the lamp shade with spun and tape it in. This is a relatively simple solution, but it must be done carefully, or seams and tape will show through the shade. Probably the most effective method is to bring your own lamp shade, one that allows the amount of light that you want to pass through it. I have a number of lamp shades around that I use for just such purposes.

With all that said, the reading off the lamp shade is fairly reasonable, so there is really not much cause to manipulate it. I can look at that 160 fc (f/8) and feel comfortable with it. The lamp is one element that you might fear would jump out at the viewer if you shot at f/8, but it is actually the one thing you are going to leave alone. When you shoot at f/8, the ring of light on the table will overexpose by one stop. The base of the lamp will overexpose by two stops. The very top of the lamp base will overexpose by three stops. This may seem to call for some attention on your part, but you will be surprised how normal it will look on the film. In a sense, we expect these areas to overexpose and we expect them to overexpose in this way. If you were to manipulate all these values to an f/8, the effect would look pretty silly. Lamplight is not flat.

For simplicity's sake, let's say you want a fairly even feel to the image—not flat, but not deep low-key. You already know what would happen if you shot at f/8 without changing anything else. Where do you start with the actual lights?

As suggested, start with the key(s). Set up an instrument, and light the person to 160 fc. Even here there is some room for maneuvering. If a person is sitting some distance from a lamp, might you expect him to be a little dark? Rather than lighting our subject to 160 fc, you could light him to 120 fc, a half stop less. You would still shoot at f/8, and the subject would underexpose by a half stop, looking slightly dark. This is not a bad option, but we will stay with 160 fc.

All the light on the subject is coming through the lamp shade, so you can safely assume that it is fairly soft light. To duplicate that soft, warm light, we are going to put a piece of tough white diffusion (#216) in front of the key light. You can still get 160 fc by spotting in the light or moving it forward. **SEE 10-17**

You have to be very careful that the light from the key does not hit the lamp shade. You should be able to accomplish this with the barn doors, though you could bring in a flag on a C-stand. If light from the key does hit the lamp shade, there could be a shadow of the lamp on the table, an effect that would look very peculiar. Another reason to be careful of light hitting the lamp shade is that it would actually boost the foot-candle reading on the lamp shade, which would then expose differently. You also want to control the spill off the bottom of the instrument onto the table. Light spilling onto the table could ruin the circle of light from the lamp. You should be able to accomplish this, again, with the barn doors.

10-17

To duplicate the soft light coming through the lamp shade, use tough white diffusion in front of the key light

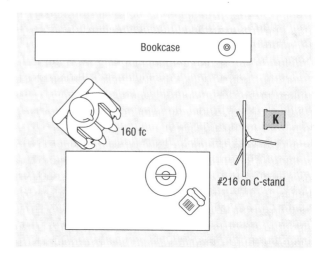

The Setup: Fine-tuning

Next, you have to set up the fill light and the other lights. Once they are up, it is a matter of fine-tuning, what people call *tweaking*, the lights. You want an even feel to the image, so the fill should be relatively close to the key light in terms of intensity. Again, the lower it is in relationship to the key, the more contrast there will be in the image. I have found that having the fill light one stop less than the key creates an image that is too flat; it does not have enough texture and definition, even when I am going for a high-key image. Use a softlight and set it to 40 fc, two stops less than the key. **SEE 10-18** You still want a slightly darkened-room effect, and this should give the image some character. Occasionally, the shadow from the fill can cause a problem, even though it is very diffuse and soft. You can generally put the light up high or move it until the shadow is hidden or out of camera range.

Next comes the backlight. **SEE 10-19** Because the person has medium brown hair, you probably want about 160 fc on the crown of the head. You have to be careful with spill coming off the backlight. You may want to use either aluminum foil or *black wrap*, a material specifically designed to wrap around the barn doors of lighting instruments.

People occasionally get the impression that spill from the backlight can or should be used to illuminate the background as well. Generally speaking, this is a bad idea. You will find that spill is hard to control, because you are attempting to use what is spilling off the bottom of the light. It is a good idea to keep the beam fairly narrow and just have the backlight do what it is supposed to do. If the background needs something, which it often does, supply it with other lights, called *set lights*.

This pretty much settles the lighting on the person. If you like it, you are done... with this part. Now it's time to take a look at the scene and see what else needs to be done. Since you have changed a number of things, check the ambient background light again. Let's say you meter and get a range of low readings, 30 fc being the highest; 30 fc is going to underexpose by two and a half stops. This is getting toward the edge and may be darker than you want, particularly if it is a dark bookcase.

10-18

Adding the fill constitutes the first step in fine-tuning the lighting setup

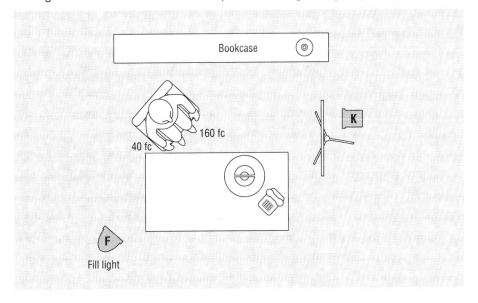

10-19

The backlight beam should be fairly narrow and aimed at the crown of the head

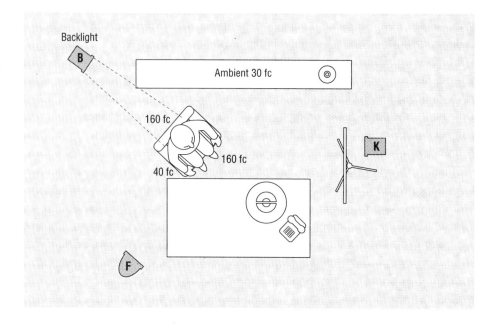

One solution would be to use a set light to throw an even 80 fc across the back wall. A softlight could be used if the goal is for the light to be diffuse and relatively even. What is the best position for this instrument? The fill for the person has been from frame-left, but is that the correct place for this fill? No, because the light from this softlight is designed to appear as though it is created by the lamp; it should come from the lamp's direction. Set it up fairly close to the key light. **SEE 10-20**

The instrument is positioned close to the wall so that its throw will not affect the person. In doing this, the right-front corner of the instrument is too close to the background. A net set up to cut down that side of the light is one potential solution. If you position it expertly, you should be able to get an even 80 fc all

10-20

To boost the ambient background light, use an instrument positioned near the key, so the light appears to come from the lamp

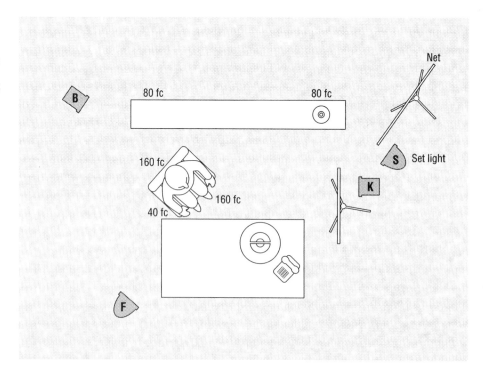

across the background. Spun is also handy for cutting an instrument in the manner described; it is frequently used to cut a corner of a light or knock out some unwanted spill.

Are you done? Again, step back and look. My guess is that your criticism will be that it looks too even, too flat. The lamp is the major source, and the light should fall off as you move frame-left. Now you could move the net and fixture so the light will fall off from 80 fc on the right, to 50 or 60 fc on the left. Even with this, my guess is that it would still look too uniform. It would lack character. The execution here was right, it was just the idea that did not work.

Do not hesitate to abandon an idea when you determine that it is just not going to work. Every filmmaker will have the experience of sitting in a screening room shaking his or her head, wishing that just a little more time had been spent to get it right. You cannot go in and do a little housekeeping without incurring major expenses.

So, what do you do? My recommendation would be that rather than junk the fill arrangement you had set up, just move it back. **SEE 10-21** It could still serve as a low-level fill, say, 40 fc. Then I would set up several small, direct lights that would have either a very narrow beam or be trimmed so that they could throw some highlights on the background. The books behind the person might be a nice place for a little slash of light. The clock might be a good place as well. Might I even dare to bring a few small areas up to 320 fc? Having these discriminations in the background will help give a sense of depth to the scene.

Putting these lights up on stands is one possibility. Another, and probably better one would be to set up some kind of rigging and hang the lights. **SEE 10-22** More and more sophisticated poles and portable lighting grids are being developed so everything does not have to be from the side and on cumbersome stands. I frequently run a 2 by 4 with holes drilled in each end between two C-stands: the tops of the stands go into the holes. The instruments would be in a position very similar to the backlight, only pointed in the opposite direction.

The specifics of what we did with the lights here are not so important. It is not the only approach. As suggested, if you were to give this problem to twenty

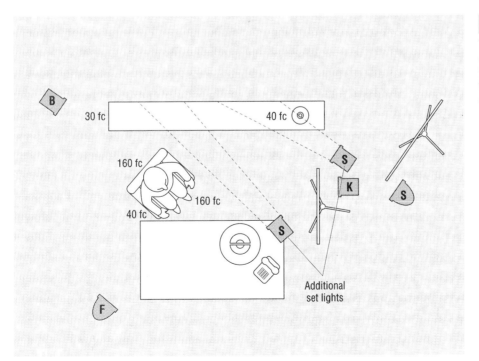

10-21

To add character to the otherwise uniform background, move back the fill arrangement and add several highlights

10-22

Accent lights can also be suspended from rigging

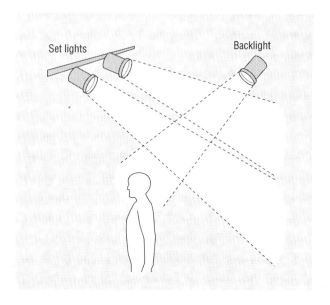

different lighting crews, you would get twenty different solutions. What is important is the approach, the process. What questions are being asked. What problems are being solved. You decide on a goal, you put up an instrument to achieve that goal, and then you trim that instrument until you get what you want.

There are other options and other lights. It is possible that you might want to use a kicker. The *kicker light* is always on the fill side and behind the subject. It comes in and brushes or rims the cheek when the fill is not covering the area as adequately as you would like. It also helps to separate the subject from the background. There are *eye lights* that come in to highlight just an actor's eyes. You will hear many other lights mentioned—rim, side, underneath, *special effect,* and so on. These lights tend to characterize direction or achieve specialized goals, rather than identify overall function (for example, an instrument creating the glow from a cigarette). *Underneath light* is usually key light. *Rim lights* and *side lights* are just types of key or backlight. Oddly enough, there are not that many identifiable overall functions of lights. This simplifies things somewhat, but a useful starting point can be boiled down to four important ones: key, fill, backlight, and set. Don't worry, you'll have your hands full with these.

It is not only a matter of problem solving for specific setups, it's a matter of being able to reflect on the context of what you are shooting and come up with the appropriate response for a given situation. Remember what my gaffer friend said about learning to light: "You just have to put it up and take it down for a few years." This means the ability not only to manipulate the technical aspects, but also to develop a vision of what you want things to look like. Your influences in this area are numerous: other films, painting, still photography, graphic design, or a variety of other media. Learning the technical and pragmatic aspects of working with lights is not an end in itself. You need to learn to do something with them.

That said, learning the technical side of lighting is an essential first step in learning the process of producing images. In the final analysis, that is all that is up there on the screen—light. You will not be served by ignorance about the tools available to you. A lack of knowledge necessarily limits your understanding of what is possible, much like a painter who has only two primary colors on a palette. Without a full understanding of and access to the range of technical possibilities, you can never reach the fullest expression of your ideas. If a painter has all the colors and still produces works of little interest, it is the *artist* who is lacking, not the materials.

Get out there and light. Too many people put it off. "The equipment is too heavy." "I'm not interested in the technical stuff." "I'm afraid I'll make mistakes." "I want to be a director." I've heard all the excuses. A fundamental, incontrovertible truth about filmmaking is that it is a process of producing images. To produce the images you want, you have to know what you are doing.

Direction and Shadow

Refer again to figure 10.20. Why did we put the key where we did? The instrument is set up to the screen-right side of the subject because the shot establishes the table lamp as the source of light. If you were to put it to the left of the subject, the shot would not make any sense. If the light is not justified, the shot can have an unconscious feel of something being wrong or out of place.

This issue of justification is a central concern. Reynaldo Villalobos's cinematography in Eugene Corr's *Desert Bloom* (1986) has an excellent example of light that creates a dramatic effect and is also justified. A scene involves a father (Jon Voight) having a confrontation with his daughter (Annabeth Gish). In the master shot, we see light streaming through the window, creating a bright pool of light right in front of where the father is standing. **SEE 10-23A** When we see the close-up, the father has very ominous, Halloween-style lighting from underneath. **SEE 10-23B** This eerie light makes sense to the viewer, however, because we have seen its source.

You will hear substantial discussion on sets regarding shadows. Some crews devote an inordinate amount of time to trying to get rid of them. Sometimes a shadow can draw attention to itself and detract from the image, but the point is not that a character should have no shadow, but that the shadow should be in a logical place, *and there should be only one*. A hallmark of low-budget films is that when characters move, multiple shadows wander over every wall in the shot. Start watching how films treat shadows. I have seen beginning filmmakers run themselves ragged trying to get rid of each and every one of them. Except for multiple shadows, it is often time and energy wasted. You will have to decide about how to handle these constant companions, but beware of shots that are unintentionally otherworldly because the characters do not have shadows.

Never solve a problem created by one light with another light. Trying to kill an unwanted shadow with another light is a tempting solution. The reasoning

10-23

The dramatic underneath lighting of the close-up was justified by the master shot, showing the source
Eugene Corr's *Desert Bloom*

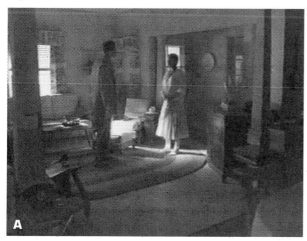
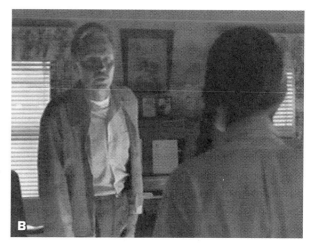

appears clear enough: if you don't like the shadow, just overpower it with another light, usually an instrument down low or up high. The effect is an image that looks like somebody tried to overpower a shadow with something down low or up high. Solve the problem by either redirecting the light (setting the light higher is sometimes a good solution) or, often more to the point, changing the background. Faced with an ugly shadow on a wall behind a character, you can simply put something dark on the wall to cover or soak it up. Find a poster or a plant—something that will break up the background and make it easier to work with the wall.

Natural Light

Beginning filmmakers often choose to shoot outdoors, wishing to avoid the issue of lighting altogether. They quickly find out that they have made a big mistake. The sun is not as loyal a friend to the filmmaker as might at first be imagined. If anything, shooting outdoors can be more complicated than shooting indoors. The foremost concern is understanding light well enough to know when what you are shooting is going to provide the results you want. Again, this is a process of evaluation. You will often hear of film crews "waiting for the light," and you will have to develop the skills to understand just what it is they are waiting for.

This is also an issue of being able to evaluate the quality of light. A good example of the quality difficulties you can experience is filming when the sun's rays are the most direct. From roughly 11 A.M. to 1 P.M., the light is very harsh, and you can get extremely dark shadows. Let's say that you are filming a medium shot of a person in bright sunlight. You want the image to read "nice sunny day," so you want a pleasant, bright feel to the image. You take a light meter reading and find you have an $f/16$ in the direct sun. The immediate concern is the quality of all the shaded areas, particularly the fill side of the subject's face. How dark is it going to be? You meter in a shaded area, or just shade the incident bulb with your hand, and get a reading of $f/2.8$. You do the standard computation: $f/11 = -1$, $f/8 = -2$, $f/5.6 = -3$, $f/4 = -4$, $f/2.8 = -5$. The nose shadow is going to be five stops underexposed and, thus, totally black. Will this be a pleasant effect? No. The darkness of the nose shadow, as well as all the shadows in general, will probably be too harsh for an appealing image.[4]

One solution is to bring in artificial light to fill in the shadow. Bouncing existing light off foam core or a reflector also works quite well. Obviously, you don't want to bring up the shaded areas to an $f/16$ because that would be flat and textureless. How far you bring them up depends on what you want the image to look like. Another solution is to just shoot at a different time of day when the sun's rays are not so direct. We all know the dangers of sunbathing during these hours, and you can get burned, in a figurative sense, filming then, too. Only mad dogs and Englishmen go out in the midday sun. Filmmakers, even when unhindered by budgetary and scheduling concerns, generally try to stay away from it as well. Being totally unhindered, of course, is rarely the case.

Another equally important issue is continuity. Just as you have to think about objects and body position within the frame, you must be conscious of the consistency of light from one shot to the next. Still photographers and filmmakers less interested in conventional narrative scene breakdowns sometimes have the luxury of waiting a long time to get the right light. But when you have to execute a number of shots and you want them to appear to be occurring in real time, the activities of the sun and the sky can make you jump through a lot of hoops. Of

---

4. Cinematographers will "light for black" to stay away from this peculiarly unpleasant phenomenon. That is, they will light a dark area to just outside the latitude of the film so that they get a richer black.

course, we do not usually think of the sun and sky as having activities, but there are times when I have thought of them as unruly crew members whom I would fire in a minute if I could.

The sun has a nasty habit of rising in the east and setting in the west. If your subject is facing north or south, the fill and key sides will change from morning to afternoon. If the subject is facing east, the sun will go from being in front of the subject to being behind. Things change so rapidly that you can have substantial problems matching the light of individual shots.

Even more difficult are the vagaries of weather and clouds. California is the home to a substantial percentage of the film business because of the quality of light and the consistency of the weather. For those of us who work frequently in distant locations, a partly cloudy day can wreak havoc, making scenes that should have been shot in a few hours take double the time. A rainy day can put you behind schedule, disrupt continuity from a previous day's work, and, in extreme cases, even change the environment in which you are working, such as growth of underbrush. I once worked on a film in which we had to hand-dry a rain-soaked wooden wagon with hair dryers so it would match shots from the previous day. Another time a location was completely flooded out. Snow, wind, haze, fog, and smog can all work their special magic to make your life miserable.

There are all kinds of ways to cheat the elements, from bringing in instruments, to shooting from a high angle to exclude the sky, to moving people so they face different directions. Sometimes you have to just sit down and wait it out. This happens to everyone, but larger-budget films are able to handle delays more easily than those precariously close to the financial edge. For lighting continuity, you have to know and understand the materials that are going to help you work despite the elements.

Finally, these issues of light quality and continuity can be interrelated. If there are very harsh shadows at noon, the shots will not match those taken at a different time of day when the light was less direct. For anyone who has seen production stills from films that are largely shot outside—a John Ford western is a good example—it soon becomes apparent why there are often banks of lights and reflectors on the hills above the location. A high percentage of the time, the shadows that the sun creates and the fill necessary for a good photographic image do not go hand-in-hand. John Wayne needed some consistent fill light in some of those famous rides through Monument Valley.

Natural light can obviously be extraordinarily beautiful. There are two important points, though. First, you have to know enough about light to understand when it is going to photograph the way you want. Second, you have to be able to add to it when necessary to match individual shots to other shots. When working "in continuity," consistency of light is an issue whether you are working indoors or out. And it is particularly difficult to achieve lighting continuity when the quality of light can change unpredictably.

Night Shooting

In the golden age of the Hollywood studios, much night shooting was done in a process called *day for night*, in which black-and-white film was shot with a combination of underexposure and red filtering to create a dark effect that represented night. Day for night is a lovely curiosity; some people love it and some people hate it, but it has rarely been seen in recent years. It does not really work in color, and newer, faster film stocks have made night filming quite practical.

The key to night filming is understanding that even at night there has to be a source of light. Darkness, as we generally experience it, and an absence of light are not the same thing. When there is an absolute lack of light, you cannot see your hand in front of your face. Night shooting must establish or incorporate some source of light. It might be a simulation of the moon. It might be from a storefront or streetlight. Once you have determined the source, it becomes a matter of deciding how you want the elements to expose, just as in any other situation. Here, though, being willing to work on the edge of the table can produce remarkable effects.

Of course, the movement that fully explored night cinematography was film noir. The dark city streets and their claustrophobic interior counterparts fully incorporated all the shades from white to gray. Bob Rafelson's *The Postman Always Rings Twice* (Sven Nykvist, DP) has numerous examples of what can be achieved in color night cinematography. The sequence in which Cora (Jessica Lange) and Frank (Jack Nicholson) first try to kill her husband shows exceptional mastery of both interior and exterior shooting. Frank is outside talking to a policeman who happens by as Cora paces nervously through the dimly lit restaurant. The exterior shots have two strong side sources, one established from a sign and the other from instruments by the gas pumps, which give both characters shape and definition while maintaining the logic of what night "should" look like. **SEE 10-24** The slight amount of detail that can be seen on the fill side of characters' faces (particularly the policeman's) is evidence of the careful approach. This low fill would not be there had someone not wanted it there. The interior has Cora turning off the restaurant's lights as she builds up her nerve. Small sources inside have her passing from light to dark areas, emphasizing the indecision and heightening her dilemma, while light from outside casts stark patterns on the background. **SEE 10-25**

Night shooting, much like any shooting, entails determining the sources and, given the latitude of the film, how all the other values are going to fall in. Some boldness on your part is necessary, because many of the effects have to be around the edge of the latitude, with the idea that cinematographers often "light for black" complicating the job. It takes some experimentation with underexposure to achieve truly exceptional effects. Often, early experiments wind up having a too-bright foreground subject against a too-dark background. Do not let this deter you. Working with low values can be intimidating, but effective night shooting incorporates many different levels of exposure.

10-24

The strong side sources give both characters shape and definition while maintaining what night "should" look like

Bob Rafelson's *The Postman Always Rings Twice*

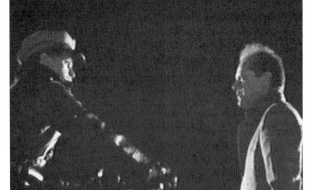

10-25

The character of the light emphasizes the subject's indecision

Jessica Lange in *The Postman Always Rings Twice*

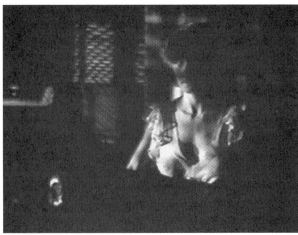

11

Executing the Lighting

A Checklist

To aid in lighting a scene, we can start assembling a checklist of questions you can ask yourself about every image. Everyone involved in lighting asks all or most of these questions for every shot, whether on a conscious level or not. Eventually, you will internalize all these concerns, but in the meantime do not hesitate to simply go down the list before every shot. (You can be flexible in the sequence in which these issues are addressed.)

What fundamental questions can be posed from the topics that have already been covered?

- ✔ *What do I want to achieve or accomplish with the image?*

- ✔ *What is the source of light? What direction does the viewer expect the light to be coming from?*

- ✔ *How am I going to expose the subject(s)? Am I going for normal exposure? Overexposure? Should the subject be darker, a little underexposed?*

- ✔ *What quality of light do I want? Do I want it to be soft? Hard? Should it be diffuse?*

- ✔ *What goal(s) is each individual instrument accomplishing?*

These questions have all been addressed in preceding chapters. More questions will be listed as we take up the general issue of executing the lighting.

Lighting Continuity

As suggested previously, you'll find that it's not necessarily difficult to create beautiful and arresting images. Learn a few basics and you can do some great things. What is difficult is creating beautiful and arresting images that cut to other similar images. If your wish is to create a seamless sense of continuous time and space, the hallmark of conventional narrative film, the burden is even greater. This goal is referred to as *lighting continuity*.

If a shot that looks like it was done in the early morning is followed by a shot that appears to have been done at another time of day, the resulting images will

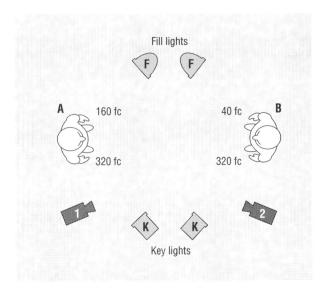

11-1

A standard shot/reverse shot setup illustrates the importance of lighting continuity

not maintain the fiction of continuous time and space when edited together. Given the lengthy amounts of time required to execute shots, lighting for continuity is less the exception than the norm that has to be wrestled with every day.

Early in his career, one cinematographer shot a scene that had two characters sneaking up on a house as the sun was rising. The scene took about two hours to shoot, and the light was changing so rapidly that the first shots had an entirely different look from the last shots. The edited scene proved challenging to print due to the inconsistent quality of the light. The lab was able to fix it somewhat, but all DPs have to be able to come up with solutions in such situations.

The issue of lighting continuity has to be confronted not only when you are subject to the whims of the sun, but also when you work in interiors with artificial lights. A good example is a simple shot/reverse shot sequence, the most common way to treat a dialogue scene between two characters. **SEE 11-1**

The foot-candle values below the two subjects (both 320 fc) represent readings off the key lights. The values above (160 and 40 fc) represent readings from the fill lights alone. Again, reading the instruments individually is the most effective way of finding out what each one is accomplishing. With a hand or a card, you can block out the instruments that confuse the reading. Turning off the intrusive instruments can be equally effective.

As this scene is set up, you should immediately see a problem that is central to lighting continuity. The lighting on person A is even, with 320 fc key and 160 fc fill. The fill is one stop less than the key, thus underexposing by one stop. The fill side is rendered with a fair amount of detail and would be considered high-key. Person B has the same 320 fc key, but is filled by only 40 fc, three stops less. This is just on the edge of the latitude, and the fill side would be very dark and the image low-key. When the two images are cut together, they will have such different visual qualities that the people may appear to be in two totally different places. The difference may be something like trying to cut from a claustrophobic film noir to a romantic comedy. The two characters may not appear to inhabit the same universe.

It should be fairly obvious now that if you simply match the two fills, depending on which universe you want, you will be much closer to a continuous sense of space; the "ratio" between the key and the fill would be the same in each shot, and the look would be similar.

Comparing the key and fill is what has been referred to as lighting, or contrast, ratios. This ratio is obtained by measuring the lights and plugging the foot-candle readings into the following formula. (Do not do this in *f*-stops because the answer you get will not make any sense.)

$$\frac{key + fill}{fill\ alone}$$

Take a light reading at the subject with the key light and the fill light turned on. Then turn off the key and measure the fill alone. Divide the first figure by the second figure. We did this with person A and got the readings shown: 320:160 = 2:1, a two-to-one ratio. The ratio on person B (320:40) is eight-to-one. The lower the ratio, the more flat the image (high-key). The higher the ratio, the more contrast in the image (low-key). A four-to-one ratio is generally considered the rough dividing line between high-key and low-key.

What is at issue here is how much the fill light is underexposing. In a two-to-one ratio, it is underexposing by one stop. In an eight-to-one ratio, it is underexposing by three stops. It should be evident that this can be done with other instruments. How much is the backlight overexposing? How is the set light underexposing? Most of the time, however, you will hear ratios discussed in terms of key and fill.

Some variation in the ratios can be tolerated. An audience, unless it is composed entirely of filmmakers, is not going to catch minor errors or deviations. Audiences generally do not perceive this kind of thing on a conscious level. But if foot-candle values and exposure deviate very much, spatial continuity is going to suffer.

Lighting ratios are valuable for continuity, but they also can be helpful when you want to light a character consistently throughout a film. What would happen if you wanted the villain of a piece to be consistently filmed with low-key shadows? If you were indoors, you might consider the setup shown in the following figure. **SEE 11-2** Later in the shooting, you are outdoors and want to be consistent with previous shots. The sun gives 2,560 fc. How would you fill the subject to get the light to match? **SEE 11-3**

In the first example, the fill light is underexposing by three stops. What do you need off the fill to get it to underexpose by three stops? 1,280 fc is one stop under;

11-2

A low-key lighting setup

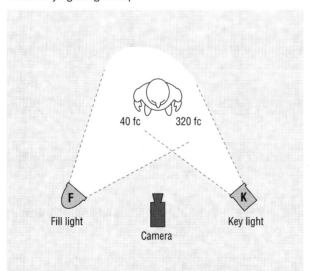

11-3

A lighting setup for the same low-key effect outdoors

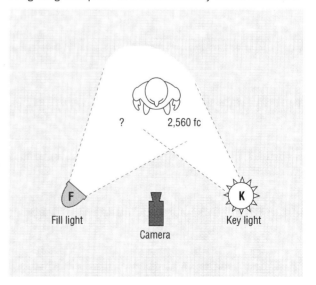

640 fc is two stops under. 320 fc is three stops under and is your answer. When you shoot at the appropriate *f*-stop, the fill light is underexposing by three stops in each shot. This leaves the quality of the light out of the quotient, but you have achieved at least some level of photographic consistency between the two images.

Lighting continuity, and the more general issue of photographic consistency, is not the goal in every film, but films that employ it are more numerous than one might imagine. Even films that deconstruct conventional narrative structures, such as Maya Deren's great experimental film *Meshes of the Afternoon* (1943) and Luis Bunuel and Salvador Dali's surrealist film *Un Chien Andalou* (1928), incorporate lighting continuity extensively.

> ☑ *Is lighting continuity important to what I am doing? Do I need to match the shot I am executing to other shots?*

f-stops and Consistency

I frequently hear the question: "Should I always shoot at the same *f*-stop within a scene?" My answer, which I then go on to qualify, is yes. It is yes because I have seen too many mistakes from people who are not aware of the limitations. There is room for maneuvering, but you really have to know what you are doing.

A good example of this is a scene from a student film made several years ago. It was a relatively simple scene, a woman crosses a room and stands by another woman sleeping in a bed. **SEE 11-4**

11-4

Initial setup for streetlight effect

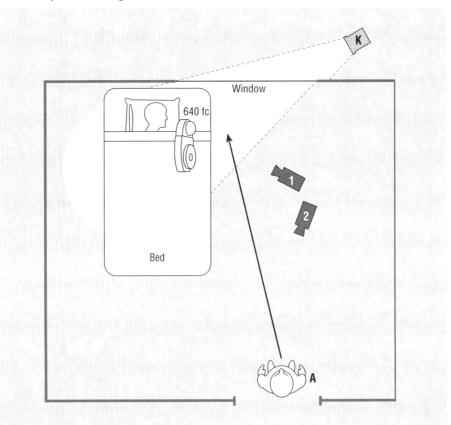

It was a night scene, and the filmmaker wanted to simulate a strong beam of light from a streetlight illuminating the bed. To accomplish that effect, he set up an instrument outside the window, throwing a big beam of hard light.

The filmmaker wanted the beam to overexpose by one stop, so, given his reading of 640 fc on the bed, he decided to shoot at f/11. He then metered the rest of the room. The only other light was the ambient light created by the instrument he had set up for the streetlight effect. As you might expect, the readings were quite low, 20 fc and lower. Given the f-stop at which he wanted to shoot, he anticipated that everything lower than roughly 30 fc was going to drop off to underexposure. He wanted the room dark but not black, so he decided to put in a low-level fill. In a corner, he set up a bounce card and shot an instrument into it. **SEE 11-5**

From this, the filmmaker got a nice, even fill of about 40 fc throughout the room, three stops underexposed. Dark, but not entirely lacking in detail. So far so good. All the material of the woman in bed was shot from setup #1. Then he turned around to shoot from setup #2 the other woman approaching the bed. He already had a meter reading of 40 fc in the area through which she was moving. That translates to an f/4 at 500 EI, and he proceeded to shoot this part of the scene at that stop. Therein lay his big mistake.

Let's consider this scene. We have established that the woman is passing through a dark area. If we shoot her at an f/4, how will she expose? She will be exposed normally. But she is supposed to be dark. You might actually be able to get away with some slipperiness in the way she is exposed. Viewers might accept, if

11-5

Adding low-level fill by bouncing a beam off a card

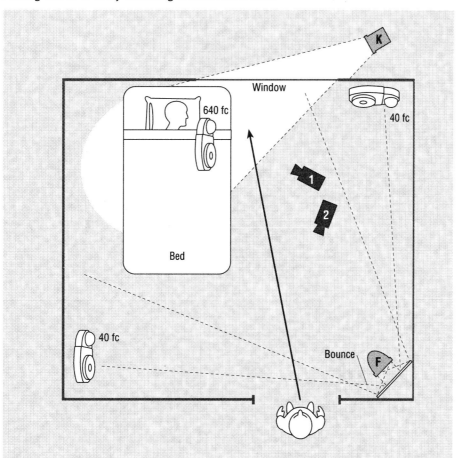

11-6

Different light levels in a scene from *Days of Heaven* illustrate a common exposure problem

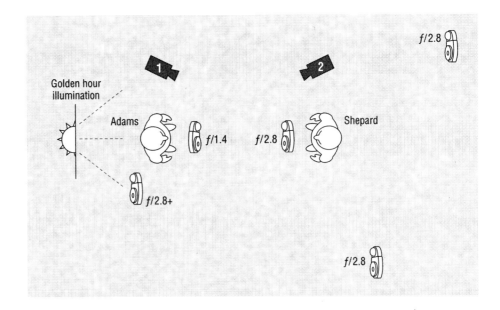

not demand, a slightly higher exposure in a close-up or a reverse angle than they did in a wider shot. The woman crossing the room is the main focus of the shot, so we expect to see her in more detail than in a shot where we see only her back. What happens to the character, however, is not the major problem. What is?

As is so often the case in situations like this, the problem is the background. In shot #1, we established that the walls are very dark, underexposing by three stops. If we expose at *f*/4, what happens to the walls? They are suddenly at, or are very near to, normal exposure. The walls in this particular example were light blue. From the exposure the student did at setup #1, the walls were underexposed and thus a deeper blue. At the higher exposure of setup #2, the walls were a very light and airy blue, almost normally exposed. When he later attempted to cut the two pieces together, it just did not look like they were shot in the same room at the same time. The pieces did not look continuous, and the student had to reshoot that side of the scene.

Academy Award–winning cinematographer Nestor Almendros, in his excellent book *Man With a Camera*, relates a story that further illustrates this principle.[1] While working on Terrence Malick's *Days of Heaven*, Almendros was shooting during what is commonly called "golden hour"—the time between when the sun sets and when it actually gets dark. The light is very soft and nondirectional at this time, and it is a favorite of many cinematographers. He was filming a shot, discussed in chapter 7 for its composition, with actors Sam Shepard and Brooke Adams. Shepard was facing west toward what was left of the sunlight, and Adams had her back to the setting sun. **SEE 11-6**

Almendros does not recount actual readings, but one can assume that they were fairly consistent and probably close to the *f*/2.8 depicted here. Everything, that is, except Adams's face. With her back to the sun, there was very little light on her face, probably somewhere in the neighborhood of an *f*/1.4. Now, none of this has anything to do with worries about achieving normal exposure. If the object was a normal exposure on Shepard's face, Almendros would have shot him at an *f*/2.8. He could also have achieved a normal exposure on Adams by shooting at an *f*/1.4. What, though, would be the problem? As with the last example, the problem would be with the background. If he had shot Shepard at an *f*/2.8 and his background is roughly an *f*/2.8, the background would expose normally. If he had

1. Almendros, Nestor, *Man With a Camera* (New York: Farrar, Strauss, and Giroux, 1984), pp. 181–182.

shot Adams at an $f/1.4$, what would happen to the background? It would overexpose by at least two stops and, because that area is closer to where the sun has set, probably more. If it were shot this way, we would be asked to accept as continuous a cut from a shot of Shepard with the background normally exposed to a shot of Adams with the background two or more stops overexposed.

What are some possible solutions? The first one that comes to mind is to bring in an instrument and light Adams to an $f/2.8$. This is not a bad solution, but several problems present themselves. The first is that it would be very difficult to match the quality of light in the two shots. Producing an $f/2.8$ can be done relatively quickly, but that takes care of only the quantitative part. Getting the qualitative part right is difficult, and fiddling with it could take long enough that the light completely changes. The light changes so rapidly at the golden hour that by the time you have gone through all the hoops to get the light up and trimmed, everything may have changed to the extent that what has been done is no longer right. A good gaffer and crew can plan for such circumstances, including electrical needs and setting up the shot beforehand. If no one on the set has extensive preplanning ability, however, the beginner can watch the approach of twilight's last gleaming with the sense of desperation that accompanies not getting all the desired shots.

If properly prepared, you could feasibly use artificial light, but Almendros came up with a different solution. He simply took Adams to another part of the field, faced her toward the sun, and shot her at an $f/2.8$. The backgrounds did not make any difference because it was a generic wheat field. The viewer, given time to think about it, might question whether it was possible for her to have that much light. "Could there be a world with two suns?" asks Almendros. Most people would accept it fairly readily.

The more experienced and confident you become, the more you should be able to shift f-stops without making mistakes. A normal exposure is a normal exposure, whether it is shot at $f/2.8$ or $f/22$. One filmmaker was shooting in an office building on a late winter afternoon and began losing the exterior light as evening approached. He could see on the meters that the light was dropping a half stop every fifteen minutes or so. Because the outside was in the background of all shots, he just had to trim each instrument (about six altogether) the same half stop every fifteen minutes. He started at an $f/5.6$, and by the time the shoot was over, the exposure was an $f/2.3$, the lowest stop on the lens.

If shifting your f-stop becomes unavoidable, you too can simply manipulate the light to the appropriate value. All experienced DPs know how to shift values around to match what has happened in other shots. Given a choice, however, a DP would probably opt to keep things at the same value just to prevent unnecessary complications.

A final point: Most DPs will go into a scene with an f-stop already in mind. This stop is not based on a value that they know is in the scene, as we demonstrated in chapter 10. Rather, it is based on the fact that most DPs have an f-stop of choice, a *preferred* f-stop. The choice of f-stop has to do with their personal preference for the quality of light and the way the lens resolves at specific stops. Different DPs have different preferred stops, but they usually fall in a range from $f/2.8$ to $f/5.6$. There are situations, say, outside on a sunny day, where they may not be able to achieve their stop of choice, but when full control is theirs, they will almost always light to that particular stop.

There are two major reasons for this. Simply stated, the quality of light needed to achieve an $f/2.8$ is different from that needed to achieve an $f/8$. Most DPs, after years of experience, simply prefer certain qualities of light. Given scenes that do not need dramatic extremes, they will go with what they like. The second reason is more complicated: the image is sharper, with higher resolution, at lower f-stops. Even though there is greater depth of field at the higher f-stops, a smaller

11-7

The modified formula after changing the *f*-stop from a variable to a constant

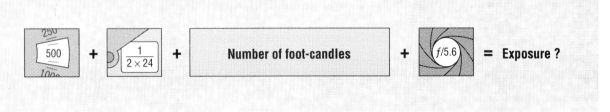

amount of the surface area of the lens is being used. This small area physically cannot transmit as much information as a larger lens opening. The light also refracts against the closed-down diaphragm, reducing sharpness. Overall sharpness and depth of field are different issues, and many DPs will sacrifice some depth of field for greater image clarity.

The idea of lighting for a specific *f*-stop seems to depart from the calculations presented earlier. Beginning with a given *f*-stop removes the *f*-stop as a variable. But eventually you will come to see that the true variables in the formula are the amount of light in front of the camera and the desired exposure.

The idea of a given *f*-stop casts a different light on our decision-making process, particularly when considering the basic strategy of lighting proposed in chapter 10. It was suggested that determining the *f*-stop is the starting point, and having an *f*-stop of choice makes this part of the decision-making process appear more arbitrary. If we go into a scene with a predetermined *f*-stop, the emphasis shifts to the manipulation of other variables in the formula—most specifically the amount of light present. The *f*-stop may not be quite as much of a constant as the shutter speed and the EI, but there are many professional cinematographers who treat it as a given.

Thinking of the *f*-stop as a constant changes our formula somewhat. **SEE 11-7**

So most DPs will light for the *f*-stop of their choice. Many people on the West Coast love *f*/5.6. Other filmmakers will shoot only at *f*/2.8. A DP's *f*-stop of preference can vary depending on the format—16mm, 35mm, and so forth.

Some DPs are extreme enough about wanting a specific *f*-stop that they will control situations that appear uncontrollable. If you are shooting exteriors and get a reading of *f*/16, is there any way you can shoot at a preferred *f*/5.6? Could you use neutral density as a front-filter on the camera to get there? The permutations become dizzying.

The question of lighting continuity does not have to be posed solely in terms of a preferred *f*-stop. It can be posed in a way that has already been suggested in the discussion of the lamp shade and table lamp. Is there something in the image that is going to be difficult enough to manipulate that you are better off just shooting for that stop? For example, neon exposes well at *f*/4 with 500 EI film. If there is going to be a neon sign in a shot, you can base how you light everything else on that fact.

The specter of consistency will haunt you in almost everything you do. Exposure can be understood, though not mastered, relatively quickly. Matching shots is the tricky part. It is recommended here that as a beginner you try to shoot at the same *f*-stop in a given scene. It can possibly save you from some very difficult matching problems, and it is also good discipline to manipulate instruments to specific values.

☑ *Is there a particular f-stop at which I want to be shooting?*

Controlling Focus

The *f*-stop is a major variable in the production of the image, but it is also a major variable in depth of field. It is often necessary to light in order to achieve a specific depth of field. When you plan out a scene and do storyboards, you can begin to anticipate difficulties presented by specific shots. If there is a shot with two people on opposite sides of the room, you will have to consult the depth-of-field charts if you want them both in focus.

One film several years ago had a good example of this problem. One shot called for a man to be sitting on the edge of a bed while a woman in the background sat at a dressing table. Owing to the dimensions of the room and action that had to occur, the closest they could be to each other was just under 20 feet. The man needed to be as close to the camera as possible. The DP was working with a lower-rated stock (EI 100) as well as small instruments and limited electricity. Thus he had to light the shot with a relatively low amount of foot-candles.

To maximize depth of field with focal length as a variable, the DP chose the widest angle lens available—12mm. This lens did not have the perspective characteristics he desired, but he needed the depth of field. He consulted a depth-of-field chart and found that his best option was to shoot at an *f*/4 and focus at 6 feet. This would bring everything from 3 feet 5 inches to 27 feet into focus. He planned to put the man a little less than 4 feet from the camera, just for some margin of error. The woman would be about 22 feet from the camera.

Thus, the DP needed to produce an *f*/4 on location. You essentially read the light meter backward to find out how many foot-candles you need. Start on the bottom of the meter with the *f*-stop, match the frames per second to it, and go up to see the resulting number of foot-candles. In this case, the DP needed 250 fc. That became the base foot-candle value on which he planned the lighting of the entire scene.

Anticipating specific shots, you know you are going to need a certain *f*-stop to produce the necessary depth of field. Although all levels of production deal with lighting for depth of field, the complications described in this scenario, such as inadequate space, too short focal length, limited electricity, and so on, are common on smaller projects. Filmmakers with more resources are less likely to paint themselves into corners. The solutions devised are typical of the kinds of compromises that often have to made when you don't have complete control, compromises that effect the visual quality of the film.

☑ *Am I lighting to achieve an f-stop that will give a specific depth of field?*

Matching Color Sources

Matching the color temperature of light sources can be an almost overwhelming aspect of location shooting. As stated, it is an issue only when shooting color film, a not insignificant reason why students often choose to shoot black-and-white film.

The man in front of the window is an excellent example of a situation in which there are different light sources. **SEE 11-8** We have not actually put any artificial light on the person yet. We most certainly will, but for now we have only the lamp and its area of illumination. Assuming the use of tungsten-balanced film, what will the result be if we shoot this scene without an 85 filter? The area under the lamp will be normal, and the outdoors will be blue. If we shoot with the 85 filter, the area under the lamp will be red and the outdoors will be normal.

11-8

There are two commonly used ways of matching color temperature when mixing daylight and tungsten sources

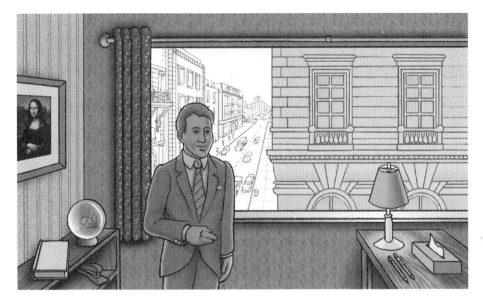

The problem is: How do we match these two sources? There are two ways to do it. The first takes substantial experience to do correctly, is quite costly, and is the better approach. The second method is less expensive, requires fewer skills, and is less preferred. However, the second way is probably the approach most students will take, at least at the outset.

The first method is to put rolled 85 gel on the window, the same material that you use in front of the camera lens. It comes in large rolls and can be laid smoothly against windows. The 85 adds a red component to the light coming into the room from outside, as well as to the exterior light the camera sees. The tungsten film then reads this red light as white light. **SEE 11-9** Do you use the 85 filter on the camera in this situation? No. What you are doing is bringing the color temperature of the daylight down to the color temperature of the tungsten instruments. Thus, it will read correctly on tungsten-balanced film.

These filter rolls are quite expensive. To do a standard-sized picture window could cost $100 or more, including labor. Experienced people are required to put up the 85 material because if it's not applied properly, you can be plagued by reflections, glares, and bubbles.

The second method is effective, but slightly more cumbersome. Rather than adding a color component to daylight, you can add one to the tungsten instruments.

11-9

Reddish gel on the window brings the daylight color temperature down to match that of the tungsten instruments

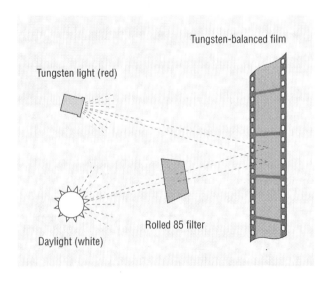

Tungsten-balanced film

Tungsten light (red)

Rolled 85 filter

Daylight (white)

The material is called *tough blue* gel, and you will put a piece on each of the instruments. The tough blue gel also cuts the instrument down by one *f*-stop. In terms of color, the gel adds a blue component to the red tungsten instruments, bringing them up to daylight color temperature. Do you use an 85 filter on the camera? In this case, yes. **SEE 11-10**

This is getting complicated, but here you take the red of the tungsten light and add blue to match it to the white daylight. You then take this white light and, with the 85 filter, turn it red again so the tungsten-balanced film will then see it as white. Confusing? Perhaps, but it does make sense.

If it sounds as if the light is getting digested one too many times, you see at least one reason why the first method is so attractive. A general rule of lighting is: Do not junk up an instrument unnecessarily. Often enough, you will be doing other things to it, and putting on blue gel makes other adjustments more difficult. Along these lines, whenever you put something on an instrument that cuts the light in half (one stop), you are not using the instrument to its full capacity. You do not always want or need the full capacity of the instrument but, again, you don't want to impose limitations before you even start. There are always plenty of constraints built into the process without unnecessarily creating new ones. Anytime you want to do something with the instrument, such as pin spun on a corner, you have to deal with the blue gel as well. The blue gel just complicates your task.

You also have to use the 85 filter. As stated, it cuts out two-thirds of a stop, so you use the lower EI. You will be getting less light through the lens as well as less light from the instruments. The smaller output from the instruments makes matching light levels between the interior and exterior more difficult. All these factors only complicate your task and place an unnecessary limitation on your work. It will make achieving any significant depth of field difficult as well.

Having stated these negatives, we can reiterate that for the time being the blue gel method is probably the way you will match the color temperatures. The expense and experience that it takes to use the first method may be beyond your means at this point. It also takes substantial preplanning to use the first method. The gaffer and *grips*, the jacks-of-all-trades on the set, are well served by being early for the shoot. Setting aside the evening before or the early morning to put the materials in place will allow you to make better use of actual shooting time.

Given what has been said, you might consider it a toss-up between the two methods. The detail that tips the scale toward the "85 the window" method is that it also provides the ability to use mixed gels. This is where neutral density (ND) filter really comes in handy. Like 85, it also comes in large rolls and can be applied to windows. More significant, it can be mixed with 85 in a single gel.

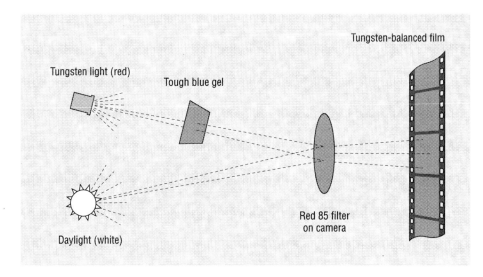

Tungsten-balanced film

Tungsten light (red)

Tough blue gel

Red 85 filter
on camera

Daylight (white)

11-10

Blue gel on the tungsten instruments brings their color temperature up to match that of daylight

11-11

The original formula for the shaded building in the example of the man and the window

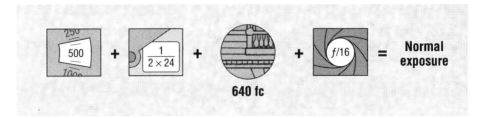

Going back to the example of the man in front of the window, you not only have to solve the color temperature problem, you still have a major exposure problem. Assuming you want a realistic image, it would not be feasible to set up enough light to bring the foreground close, in terms of exposure, to the background. The solution is to bring down the background with ND.

A roll of 85ND3 gel would change the color temperature to tungsten color temperature (85) and cut out one stop (ND3) of light. If it is an 85ND6, it cuts out two stops. Also remember that the 85 cuts out two-thirds of a stop, so the total light cut on an 85ND6 would be two and two-thirds stops. There are many other mixes; these are just a few examples.

To go back to the example of the formula, the ND and 85 filters become another variable. The figure above depicts the configuration you originally had on the shaded building (640 fc) of the man-and-the-window example. **SEE 11-11**

You will not always think of it like this, but when you put an 85ND6 on the window, you are reducing, at least from the camera's perspective, the foot-candle readings you found outside. Obviously, the actual readings on the shaded building and the street remain unchanged. You are simply putting a block between the filmed object and the camera, cutting down these areas by two and two-thirds stops. This can be treated as a subset within the equation: −1 = 320, −2 = 160, −3 = 80. The new reading would be about 100fc. **SEE 11-12** Although normal exposure may not be your goal here, changing the amount of light reaching the camera means that you have to change the *f*-stop for a normally exposed image. You consult the EI chart and find that 100 fc is a little over an *f*/5.6.

You can do the same thing with the street, taking into account the 85ND6 on the window. **SEE 11-13**

It becomes evident that neutral density filters give you substantial control of the light outside and coming through windows. The material comes in enough gradations that you can even keep up, at least to some degree, with changing volumes of light as a day progresses. The ND approach allows you to bring down the values into a reasonably narrow range, eliminating the uncompromisable extremes identified earlier.

A friend tells the story of a scene that was being shot in an abandoned warehouse, one of those old ones with many windows. Wanting to achieve some effects with their lighting and to reduce the light coming in the windows, the DP

11-12

The change in foot-candle readings caused by the filter can be treated as a subset within the original formula

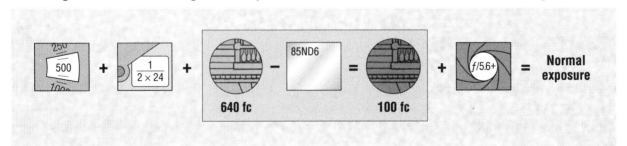

decided to 85ND6 all the windows, of which there were about 160. It was, or soon became, a film with a large budget. A whole crew of carpenters and grips came in and replaced all the windows with a Plexiglas 85ND6 material, rebuilding the windows, frames and all.

Tearing down and rebuilding is only one possible solution for a tough lighting situation. You obviously have to have the budget to support it, but changing the set gives you a measure of control that the blue gel method does not. The blue gel method actually cuts down the tungsten instruments, making matching light with exteriors even more difficult. Keep rolled window gels in the back of your mind, because you will want to use them someday.

The major point to take away from this discussion is that color temperature is an issue that you will continually have to confront. Many people who have worked in video recognize that, at least on the surface, it is a slightly simpler issue in that medium. Video cameras can be white balanced to just about any source, so front-filters for color correction have largely been eliminated. Despite all that's been said, this is somewhat true of film as well. An increasing number of camerapeople have discarded their 85 front-filters and are just letting the lab take care of any color differences in prints or transfers to video. If you shoot outdoors without an 85, you simply have the lab filter out (subtract) the extra blue.

This may eliminate the need for an 85 on the camera, but it does not solve the problem of matching color sources. Whether for video or film, color temperature remains a consideration. You can white balance your video camera to fluorescent lights, but if you introduce a tungsten instrument for additional illumination, you will have a problem. There are a bewildering array of sources, from mercury vapors to sodium vapors to cool white fluorescents, that are fueling an increasingly sophisticated array of responses. Filter companies have produced a wide variety of materials to solve these problems, and it takes an extensive knowledge of the possibilities just to keep up. Even with this know-how, careful planning and preparation are necessary to deal with the problems you will encounter.

A *color temperature meter* is an aid to sorting all this out. It resembles and is handled just like a light meter, and with it you can measure the color temperature of any light source. Most color temperature meters will also have a chart or on-board computer that tells you what kind of filter is required to get a given light source to the color temperature you want. Color temperature meters are complex and expensive tools, but are a necessity when you get into professional production.

Another advancement that has made dealing with color temperature easier is the development of *HMI lighting*. This is a relatively new line of daylight color temperature instruments. Their use by professional crews has increased dramatically in recent years in spite of the fact that they are complicated and expensive to use. Most of them run on 220 volts and can be used only with crystal cameras. Although you probably won't have a chance to use them as a novice, you should be aware of their existence.

11-13

The change caused by the 85ND6 filter on the window

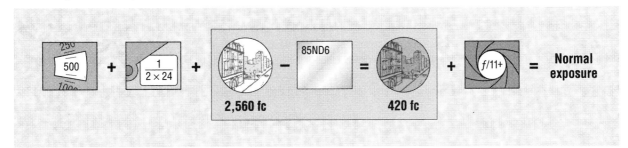

Again, this entire discussion applies solely to color film, as color temperature is not an issue with black-and-white. Pay attention to it, though, because even the most ardent black-and-white enthusiasts will eventually find some circumstance in which they want, or need, to shoot color.

✓ *Will I have to make adjustments in order to match color temperatures? If so, what materials and skills will I need?*

Electricity

Knowledge about electricity, how to use it and respect it, becomes a must when you start working with motion picture lights. Even the smallest instruments draw a substantial amount of electricity, so you will need to know how to evaluate your power requirements.

When the subject of electricity comes up, it's amazing how many people admit to sheer terror at even the simplest of applications. It seems as if everyone has, or has heard of, at least one horror story. We treat electricians as though they are bearers of some mystical, dangerous secret, when it is actually something quite accessible.

In terms of electricity, it is not necessary to become a highly trained professional electrician. You do need to exercise common sense, however. Specifically, you need to be able to determine your power needs and identify their source.

Access to electricity will always be an issue. At this point it means learning how to evaluate standard wall power—household outlets. Large-budget productions invariably bring large noiseless generators or go through a process called "tying in." Tying in requires the gaffer to use clamps that look like standard automotive jumper cables to tap into the main power of a building. This job should be handled only by qualified technicians,[2] but it eliminates the time-consuming process of identifying the outlets and running extension cords all over the place. Identifying outlets is the approach that, at least for now, you will have to take.

Every house or commercial building has multiple series of outlets referred to as *circuits*, which are tied to the main **breaker box**, often found in the basement or near where the electrical service enters the building. Most people have seen a breaker box, as found in most newer or rewired homes. Older homes often have fuse boxes instead, with the old screw-in style of round fuses. Breaker boxes and fuse boxes essentially amount to the same thing. The term *breaker* is used here. A typical breaker box is shown in the following figure. **SEE 11-14**

Each breaker represents a circuit. The numbers—15 or 20—on the breakers refer to the amount of **amperes**, or **amps**, that can be drawn from the circuit. Everyone knows that if you overload the outlets, you blow a circuit breaker. If you blow a breaker, you go to the breaker box, find the blown one, and put it back in service. In the type shown in the figure, the breaker simply snaps to the off position and you have to flip it back on again. For the older, screw-in fuses, you must replace the fuse, which means that you should plan for that possibility and have spares on hand.

Obviously, you don't want to be constantly blowing fuses as you are filming, so you have to apportion the instruments to the outlets so that too much power is not being drawn off any one circuit. To do this, you have to know how many amps each lighting fixture draws. There is a simple formula for this:

---

2. In many localities, tying in is highly regulated or, in some cases, illegal. Failure to check pertinent electrical codes may result in stiff fines or problems with insurance holders.

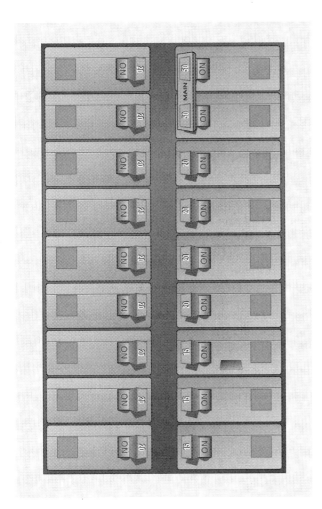

11-14

A typical electrical breaker box

$$\frac{\text{Watts}}{\text{Volts}} = \text{Amps}$$

In all standard household circuits, **volts** are a constant: 110. Virtually everything you plug in is based on 110 volts, except for some large appliances that have special plugs and receptacles and are 220 volts. **Watts** vary according to the specific lamp or appliance. Everyone has heard of 60-watt bulbs. If you had a motion picture instrument with a 1,000-watt bulb, and that is a pretty standard small lamp, you would use the formula to find out how many amps it required.

For a much simpler figure with which to work, 110 can be rounded off to 100 and used in a formula that is much easier to remember:

▶ **RULE:** *For every 100 watts, you need 1 amp of power.*

This is just a simplification of the complex formula. For your 1,000-watt lamp, you need 10 amps (1,000/100 = 10). A 15-amp circuit cannot support two 1,000-watt lamps; you'd blow a fuse. Eventually you will want to use the complex formula shown above, but the simpler formula will yield the information you need; it also gives you a small margin for error.

So how do you go about determining what outlets are on what circuits? You have to go to the fuse box and do some simple testing. It is a fairly simple matter, but for some reason this is where people start to get cold feet. You turn off one breaker and see which outlets are no longer working. It is important that you turn off only one breaker switch at a time. If you are lucky, someone will have written on the facing plate which rooms each breaker controls; it might say "bathroom" or "east bedrooms," for example. If there is nothing written, you'll have to go through the whole house.

Once you have turned off one breaker, you can use a circuit tester to find out which plugs are not working. *Circuit testers*, also called "pigtails," have two prongs with an LED (light-emitting diode display) on the end. You can buy one at any hardware store for about two dollars. You stick it into an outlet, and if the LED does not light, the outlet is on the circuit you have turned off. Most *multitesters*, which are multifunctional battery testers, also have a position to test AC (alternating current). Other functions of the multitesters come in handy for other applications. If you have neither, you can use a small appliance, such as a radio, to identify which outlets are "hot."

By this method, you can go through the entire structure and determine which outlets are on which circuits. As you do this, you should make a map, an overhead similar to that used for planning shots, that details the location of circuits and where the sources might be for the instruments you want to use. This is a time-consuming, albeit necessary, process.

Once you've determined where everything is, you can apportion the instruments to the outlets so that you never draw off more than a circuit can hold. If you find that a room has a 20-amp circuit, the most that you can plug into that room's outlets is a total of 2,000 watts; if two rooms are served by a 15-amp circuit, the most you can plug in is 1,500 watts, and so on. By the end, you may have a tangle of extension cords running from many different sources.

Several tips can give you some direction in evaluating power on a location:

- Rooms that tend to have lots of circuits include bathrooms, workrooms, laundry rooms, and kitchens. Kitchens can be most valuable, often having two or more 20-amp circuits. Underpowered rooms include bedrooms, living rooms, and recreation rooms. If you think of what kind of appliances take a lot of power, this makes sense. Things that produce heat are the biggest users: toasters, hair dryers, and the like. Air conditioners are also heavy consumers of electricity. Televisions, clocks, house lamps, computers, and many other appliances are not really significant users. Rooms where people generally use a specific type of appliance are usually going to be powered accordingly.

- Apartments and rental units often have what are called distribution boxes, individual fuse boxes in each unit. These are not to be confused with the main fuse boxes, particularly by someone intent on tying in. There is still a main fuse box, again probably in the basement, from which the power is being distributed to these smaller boxes. This is to give all the users individual access, and billing, if they blow one of their fuses. Older buildings will often have a distribution box for an entire floor or group of units. All this, of course, can be quite bewildering.

- If there are people who might have more knowledge of the space than you, consult them. Building managers and maintenance personnel can be great allies.

- Be aware of other demands being placed on the circuits. A number of appliances, such as refrigerators, dehumidifiers, and space heaters are demand appliances, turning on when they are needed. This not only can cause circuit overload, it can also cause a momentary dimming of the lights. This will play havoc with the intensity of the lights and the color temperature as well. When you are doing synchronous sound, you will probably shut off these appliances anyway. But you should be aware of them.

Considering all these potential problems, you can see why generators are so popular. A generator can provide one seemingly limitless source of power. Moreover, you will eventually be working with instruments that are bigger than anything household circuitry can handle. In the industry, the size of instruments is spoken about in terms of **k** *(kilowatt)*. This should not be confused with the K in degrees Kelvin. A 1k lamp is a 1,000-watt lamp; a 2k is a 2,000-watt lamp, and so on. It is not uncommon, particularly when working in large spaces, for commercial productions to use 10k lamps and larger. If you plug 10,000 watts into the formula, you will find that you need 100 amps for a 10k lamp. It is clear that no standard household circuit, or even the whole house for that matter, can meet those power requirements. In fact, the use of any instrument larger than a 2k necessitates an alternative power source.

Power limitations are an important issue because they force the novice to work with smaller instruments. Crews on bigger-budget films use large instruments—4k, 5k, 10k, and so on—fairly regularly, but it's virtually impossible for beginners to use them. This is probably fortuitous, for it takes a good bit of knowledge to deal safely with larger instruments, considering their heat, weight, voltage requirements, and so forth. This should never be used as an excuse or seen as a limitation, because you can do some wonderful things with small instruments.

That said, you can also do some things with big instruments that you just can't do with small ones. If you shoot a 1k through a silk, you just won't have much light left to work with. If you want to add a deep color, you have the same problem. If you want to achieve a certain depth of field with a certain lens, you may not be able to create enough light to get the stop you want.

A substantial part of evaluating electrical requirements should occur in preproduction. As you become more secure with lighting, you will be able to anticipate the size, type, and number of instruments you will need. In fact, you should be prepared to the extent of knowing where almost every instrument will be placed. Drawing a map of your overall lighting design can be incorporated into the overhead that indicates the location of all the circuits (see page 293). Planning may be hard at first, but keep it as a long-term goal.

✓ *Have I determined how much electricity I need and identified the source?*

Printing, Processing, and Exposure Manipulations

There are a number of ways to manipulate film images and these, of course, have a direct bearing on light and exposure. Techniques include under- and overexposure, color effects, and actually manipulating the film stock and the processing. While most of your effort should be toward mastering basic exposure, you can still create some interesting effects, and you may want to start experimenting with some of these. In any case, it is important that you learn how to communicate to the processing lab what you have done.

Chip Charts

The *chip chart* is the main way of communicating any changes to the lab. It is a series of colors on a chart and is the photographic equivalent of color bars in video. You should shoot this chip chart at the beginning of every roll. Often the chart has a gray scale. When your film is processed, you will always request a workprint, a one-for-one duplicate of your camera original. To make the workprint, lab people analyze the chip chart and use it as a guide in exposing the workprint.

11-15

Setup for creating a
blue moonlight effect
by putting tough blue
gel on the instruments
and omitting the 85
filter on the camera

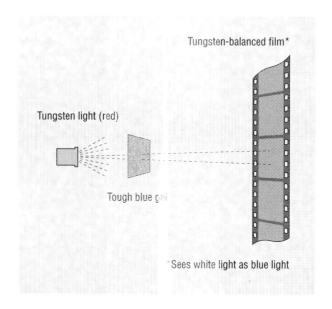

Tungsten-balanced film*

Tungsten light (red)

Tough blue gel

*Sees white light as blue light

When your shooting is straightforward in terms of exposure, the chip chart is
not so important. The lab will look at your shots and should be able to give you a
reasonably good print. When you are trying for a difficult exposure or color effect,
however, it is crucial that you have a chip chart and that it is shot correctly. Without
a good chip chart, the lab may have no idea how to print your film.

Several years ago one student was shooting an exterior scene at night. It was
mentioned earlier that people tend to associate the color blue with night. The
student decided to try for a blue moonlight effect by putting the same tough blue
gel that corrects for daylight on the instruments, omitting the 85 filter on the
camera. **SEE 11-15** If there is no filter, the film will read the light as blue.

He sent the film to the lab, justly pleased with creating an interesting, albeit
relatively common, effect. The people at the lab took one look and said, "Too blue,"
so they filtered out the extra blue. He got his film back and hit the ceiling. The lab
had murdered his beautiful blue effect. He made noises about never using that lab
again until he was pulled aside and told what had happened. It was not "the lab's
fault." It was his for not communicating to them what he was doing. All was not
lost, of course, because the student's blue effect was still there in his camera original.
When he went to a final print, the lab brought out the blue effect as they could
have from the beginning.

If the student had shot a chip chart at the head of the roll, he would have
been all right. In this case, you just throw some light on the chart and shoot at the
f-stop that the light meter tells you. You might ask if the student should have put
the same blue light on his chip chart, because that was the effect he wanted. The
answer is no. The lab dials the lights on the analyzing machine until the colors
appear as they should be on the chart. If there is blue light on the chart, the lab will
dial out the blue to get normal colors. This will be exactly the opposite of what you
want. If you shoot the chart normally, no changes will be dialed in, and your blue
makes it to the workprint.

Many exposure manipulations bring up similar questions. One student
wanted to do a number of underexposure effects. She knew that if the lab saw this
without being informed, they would overexpose it, or print it up, in the printing
process and take away the effect. So the filmmaker exposed the chart normally at
the beginning of the roll. The lab set their printing lights normally, and the
underexposure effects made it to the workprint. Conversely, another student
wanted the grainy effect of underexposed film printed up to look normal. She had

underexposed her whole role by one stop. If she had shot her chip chart normally, the workprint would have been one stop underexposed, which was not what she wanted. Instead, she underexposed her chip chart by that same one stop. The lab looked at the chart, dialed their lights up, and pumped more light through the entire workprint. This was exactly what she wanted.

▶ **RULE:** *If you want the lab to preserve your effect, shoot the chip chart normally. The lab will set the printer lights to normal exposure and your effect will be printed.*

▶ **RULE:** *If you want the lab to manipulate your print, shoot the chip chart with whatever modification you are attempting. The lab will make the necessary adjustments to correct the color chart, and you will get the correction you desire.*

There is certainly a lot more to this, but these are some good general rules. If you shoot a chip chart, be sure to write on the packaging in big letters: "PRINT TO CHIP CHART AT HEAD."

Force Processing and Flashing

There are several other types of manipulations, the most common two being force processing and flashing.

Force processing, also called *pushing,* is the more common of the two. The easiest way to explain this is, if you find yourself in a situation where you don't have enough light, you can underexpose the film and ask the lab personnel to "push" it. They would then leave the film in the developer longer, overdeveloping it. Most labs have substantial experience with this and can be quite precise in how they match up what you have done with how they process the film. However, care must be taken when you do this, because the quality of the image will change from the film that has been normally exposed and normally processed. The film will have a different look. Leaving the film longer in the soup, slang for developing chemicals, generally reduces contrast and creates more visible grain. As always, you have to think about how the pieces will match up with other things you are shooting.

In fact, most DPs push film because they are trying to achieve a specific effect. It is great for producing a grainier, more abstract image. In cases like this, you build that one stop of underexposure into your filming by changing the film's EI. This relates to the concept of halving and doubling that was discussed earlier. Every doubling or halving of EI represents an *f*-stop, and you change your EI rather than make the mental computation each time. If you have a film stock normally rated for 500 EI and you want to push it two stops, what would your new EI be? One stop would be 1,000, and two stops would be 2,000. If you rate the film stock at 2,000, you will automatically be building two stops of underexposure into everything you film. You then tell the lab to push the film two stops, and they compensate for what you have done by leaving the film in the soup longer.

A couple of notes of caution: First, consult the lab before you attempt any experiments. They will have limits and recommendations on how much you should push specific film stocks. If you exceed these limits, you might not like what you get or the lab may flat out refuse to process it. Second, shoot tests. This is the only way to find out if the effect is what you want, before you commit a lot of time and footage to the concept. Third, it costs more to push film. Labs have specific charges for pushing, generally additional cents per foot. Make sure it is in your budget. Fourth (and this should be obvious), if you want your film pushed, you have to do the effect consistently for the entire roll. A lab cannot push part of a roll or a single shot; it's the whole roll or nothing.

It is also possible to *pull* film, that is, build overexposure into your filming. In this case, you "underprocess" the film. Most labs will tell you that the resulting film will be flat and characterless, not worth the effort. I have seen people do a lot of odd things to their films, but the effect of pulling film is consistently unpleasant, and I have never seen anyone who was pleased with the result.

Flashing is somewhat more complicated and not quite as common as force processing. It is a procedure that the lab does to your unexposed film stock before you take it on location and shoot. At your request, the lab runs the unexposed film past a low-intensity light on one of its printers. This light builds an increment of exposure into the film. It is not quite this simple, but you add a small number of foot-candles to your total. That increment of exposure brings up the shadow areas, while not significantly affecting the highlights. If you add 5 fc to an area that has 10, that is a half stop. If you add that same 5 fc to 160 fc, the change is marginal. Again, DPs do this for effect. It gives the image a washed-out, foggy feel, makes the dark areas look milky and gray, and makes the light areas wash out.

Vilmos Zsigmond, on Robert Altman's *McCabe and Mrs. Miller*, flashed everything that was shot. The resulting film has a washed-out, old look that is central to the elegiac tone of the film's action. He did similar work on the same director's *The Long Goodbye*. Another good example of flashing is Hal Ashby's *Bound for Glory* (Haskell Wexler, DP). The film is the story of Woody Guthrie in the 1930s, and the effect gives the film a worn-out, old feel that adds immeasurably to the texture of the film. More accurate, these films were preflashed because the exposure was done before shooting. You can also postflash film, that is, flash it after you have shot it, but the former is more popular.

Again, manipulating the EI of the film stock builds the desired exposure effect into your filming when force processing. This can be a dangerous piece of information, but the EI that you find on a film's packaging is only the manufacturer's recommendation. The number basically states that if you have a certain level of light, a specific *f*-stop will usually produce the best results. Many cinematographers, after years of shooting a specific film stock, will simply rate it slightly differently. By doing this, they build in some level of underexposure or overexposure, at least in terms of what the manufacturer says. They rate it differently because they like the way the film stock exposes at that EI. Some cinematographers will rate the film stock differently and have the lab process it differently. They will rate a 100 EI stock at 150 and have the lab process it for 150 EI. You may be scratching your head at this, and for good reason. To understand this, you have to have substantial experience with labs and film stocks. The important thing to remember from this discussion is that all those things that we earlier established as constants start to have more indistinct boundaries.

That said, you should treat the EI as a constant until you feel confident that you fully understand it. As stated, pushing and flashing are done to achieve a specific look. These are only two ways of doing what DPs like to call "torturing" the negative.

Characteristically, beginners often want to get right out there and apply their own thumb screws. Remember, as a novice, it is incumbent upon you to master basic exposure before anything else. One student, after reading some Martian film book, baked his film in the oven for several hours. He then proceeded to go out and misexpose the whole roll. Not only did this experience give him nothing to work with, it failed to communicate to him what a terrible idea the whole thing was to begin with. Before you try out all the settings on your microwave, figure out what exposure is all about. Then you can start playing with it.

> ☑ *Am I doing anything for an effect, in terms of exposure, color, or stock manipulation, that I should communicate to the lab?*

Slow Motion and Fast Motion

We have questioned the EI as a constant and now it is time to turn our attention to shutter speed. This is not as slippery a topic as the previous one. Shutter speed is tied to frames per second (fps) and it changes only when you change the fps. You do not change the fps arbitrarily—only when you want slow or fast motion. Recall from chapter 1 how frame rates slower than 24 fps produce fast motion and how those faster than 24 produce slow motion.

Consider the example of the man in front of the window. What would happen if you decided to shoot the scene at 48 fps? In this case, you would change your shutter speed variable. If your desired result was still normal exposure on the person, how would the formula have to change? Something would have to give in the f-stop. Most light meters have a function that will tell you, but remembering that everything is expressed in halves and doubles, you should be able to figure it out arithmetically. **SEE 11-16**

In this example, an $f/5.6$ produced normal exposure when running at 24 fps. If the film is running faster, there is less light reaching it. But how much less? Plug 48 into the shutter speed formula. The new shutter speed is $1/96$ of a second, as opposed to the normal running speed of $1/48$. So you are getting half as much light from the shutter speed. What shift in the f-stop will yield twice as much light? Wanting twice as much light, you change one stop. Which direction? If you want more light, you open the diaphragm (lower numerically). You open up one stop, which would be an $f/4$. **SEE 11-17** If you go the opposite direction to, say,

11-16

The modified formula after changing the shutter speed

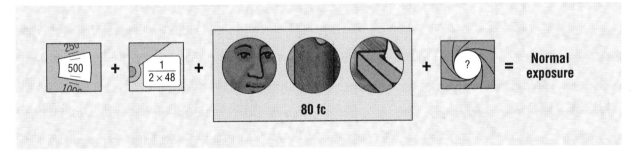

11-17

To yield twice as much light, you open the diaphragm one stop

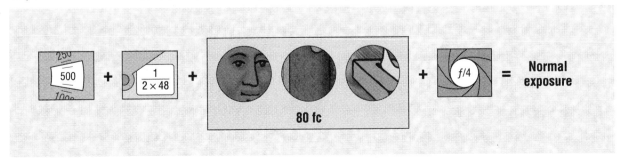

11-18

To yield half as much light, you close the diaphragm one stop

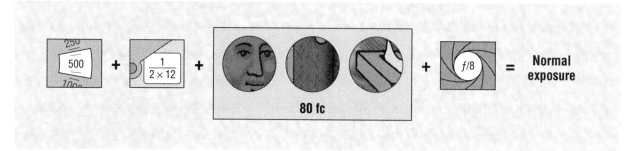

80 fc

Normal
exposure

12 fps, you would have to close down one stop. **SEE 11-18** Again, the light meter will tell you. But if you can do fractions, you should be able to figure out the *f*-stop for any fps.

> ☑️ *Am I shooting at standard sound running speed, 24 fps? If not, have I made the necessary adjustments?*

Filming Various Skin Tones

Filming people of varied skin colors presents several issues that have to be addressed. Although this concerns people of many races, it is especially pertinent to filming African Americans and other people with dark skin, who will probably not have the facial detail you want if you use conventional exposure recommendations. Dealing with this issue will provoke a fair amount of discussion in the coming years. There have been brief references here and there but, to my knowledge, there has yet to be a definitive discussion. Experienced DPs have certainly learned to deal with this issue, but well-meaning novices, particularly when experimenting with latitude, can make mistakes that may have implications they do not want. The solution I recommend is on the simplistic side, but what follows here is not meant to be definitive. It will be helpful if it leads to a long-overdue discussion that could give beginners some direction in this area.

As stated in the section on reflectant quality, dark subjects respond to underexposure much more quickly than light subjects. This is obviously true of people as well. Without pointing fingers or laying blame, we can say that most photographic recommendations were designed considering surfaces that reflect an average amount of light, which includes the white face. This makes a modicum of sense because most things in nature and many things that humans create fall within this range. At the manufacturer's recommended EIs and *f*-stops, white objects are white, gray objects are gray, and black objects are black. The problem is that photographic black represents a lack of detail and, unless you are going for some effect, you always want detail in the face.

This will require some clarification, but to create normal exposure on a dark-skinned person, open up one stop more than standard recommendations; that is, overexpose by one stop. If the conventional translation of 160 fc is *f*/8, expose at *f*/5.6. This does not mean that you set up your instruments, get a reading, and shoot at a lower stop. It is not that you should choose a lower exposure, but that you manipulate light values to create higher levels of exposure.

Once again, using the example of the person and the table lamp, it is not that you shoot at *f*/5.6 rather than the recommended *f*/8, for that would change how

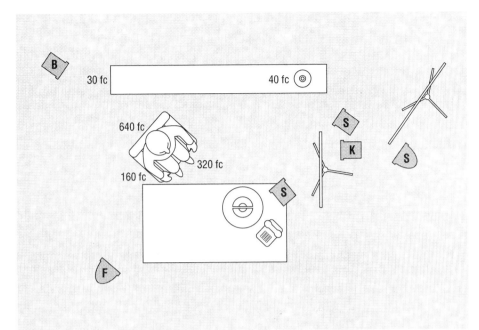

11-19

For better facial detail in a dark-skinned subject, set the key light one stop higher than standard recommendations

the lamp and everything else exposes. Rather, you still shoot at $f/8$, but just manipulate the light to create more exposure on the person. **SEE 11-19**

Rather than the 160 fc that you keyed the subject to earlier, you key to 320 fc. You will notice that the fill and backlight values have changed as well. In general, dark hair needs more backlight, so don't hesitate to go as much as two stops higher than the exposure. The fill is actually at the recommendation for normal exposure (160 fc).

This discussion is complicated by the obvious fact that dark-skinned people nevertheless have a tremendously wide range of skin tones. Again, experience will teach you, but try varying levels of overexposure. An African American with very dark skin will take the full stop that I have recommended. A person with lighter skin might respond well at a half stop. There are some people with very light skin for whom the standard exposure recommendations will work just fine.

This becomes a bigger issue when you have a number of people with a variety of skin tones. A film on which I worked as the gaffer called for the staging of a discussion group. Persons A and D were African Americans with very dark skin. Person B had somewhat lighter skin. Persons C and E were white. The room was quite large, so the scene presented many challenges, particularly for the wide shots. **SEE 11-20** There was a drop ceiling, so I started by pushing away some of the panels and rigging several broad lights shooting into foam core. This gave me a general fill of 80 fc in the area where the table was. I decided that this would be a nice level of fill if we were shooting for the f-stop that translates from 160 fc ($f/8$). We set up three instruments to serve as keys for the five participants. Persons A and B were keyed by instrument #3. I wanted person A to have 320 fc. I wanted person B to be a half stop less. This was accomplished by positioning the instrument in such a way that person B's distance from the instrument accounted for the difference. Person C had his own key (instrument #2) trimmed to 160 fc. Persons D and E were keyed with a single instrument (#3). In this case, we put a half scrim on the right side of the instrument to cut the intensity on person E. Because the instruments that were rigged in the ceiling did not illuminate the back walls, we rigged set lights to get the back wall up to 80 fc. We used several other instruments to accomplish specific purposes, but this was pretty much it.

11-20

Lighting setup for a discussion group that featured panelists with a wide range of skin colors

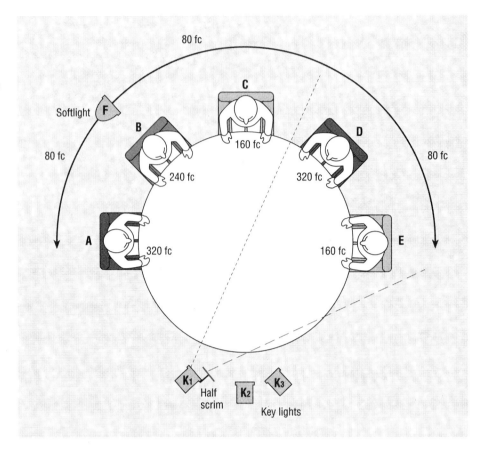

In this setup, persons A and D were overexposing by one stop, person B by a half stop, and persons C and E were exposing normally. When we moved in for close-ups and medium shots, we did a little more with backlights. We also used a traveling softlight on a rolling stand to give us the same consistent 80 fc on the background that we had previously accomplished with set lights. In setting up the entire shot as we did, we accomplished different levels of exposure without an overall change in the f-stop. Unless you are in a documentary situation, you do not accomplish this overexposure technique by simply getting a reading and opening one stop. As with everything, it is a matter of manipulating the lights to get the levels of exposure that you want.

Again this is not meant to be definitive, but it is an approach with which I have had good results. It comes from using conventional exposure recommendations and having been disappointed with the results. Anyone with substantial experience filming African Americans will probably find this somewhat formulaic and simplistic; there are many other considerations, including the use of color gels. Be aware, though, of the issues identified here and the general guidelines provided.

Clearly, this has ramifications beyond the filming of people. When underexposed, dark objects lose definition much more quickly than lighter objects. A black shirt is going to be lost much faster to underexposure than a white shirt. How people and objects reflect light also has a direct effect on any notion of high-key and low-key. If you attempt a traditional low-key situation with an African American subject or, for instance, a character in a dark leather jacket, the results may not be to your liking. This discussion goes back to reflectant quality and gray scales. From experience, you start to learn how different subjects and materials read on film. This is an issue with color film, but even more so with black-and-white. If you were able to go back to an old Hollywood studio shoot, the color of the costumes and sets might surprise you. The colors were often chosen because they read a certain way on the film stocks being used. Very few people with this kind of knowledge of black-and-white film remain. For financial and creative reasons, many students like to shoot black-and-white, but some of the biggest mistakes in exposure occur when shooting black-and-white film.

✔️ *Are there any subjects, objects, or areas in the shot that are going to require adjustments in light levels or exposure?*

Safety

There is one question you must constantly ask yourself: Is it safe? Maybe we should take on the same menacing demeanor of Laurence Olivier and his dentist's drill when he asked that same question of Dustin Hoffman in John Schlesinger's *Marathon Man.* You have to hold yourself to a high standard, and it has to be a tough question with a thorough answer. Work-site accidents are a problem in any field, and beginners rarely notice, if even think about, some of the potential hazards they face.[3]

When working with instruments and on films in general, you are routinely exposed to the following hazards.

✔️ **Enough heat to cause fires.** Shooting instruments into walls, boards, or other materials can cause buildup of heat that can cause problems ranging from serious burns to spontaneous combustion. Most materials made specifically for film work are designed to be nonflammable, but if used improperly many can still catch fire. You also never know what is inside a wall. On one film, I was shooting an instrument into a wall until I was told that a previous owner had used shredded newspaper for insulation. We recommend using broad lights, because they distribute the heat across the length of the bulb. Focusable spots concentrate their light and heat in the center of the beam and, particularly when spotted in, can burn many materials. I have been on a number of sets where clothespins or foam core have started smoldering. *Keep a fire extinguisher handy!*

Always wear leather gloves when working with lights. They protect your hands from the heat. I have gotten burns that required first-aid treatment and a few that even left scars. *Always keep a first-aid kit around.*

Be aware that heat will melt the glue on many adhesive tapes. Gaffer's tape is an indispensable aid on the set. You can use it to fix or put up anything. But if you put it on or near something that produces heat, it will lose its bond and not hold. Some companies make "tape-up" brackets which have *spuds* (the mounting piece on most small light stands), and you can tape them to a wall and hang an instrument. If this is not done correctly, the tape can loosen and the instrument can fall. I was on a set where the gaffer taped up a backlight that fell and missed an actor by about a foot. This does not endear the crew to the talent—or the crew to the insurance company. *Be careful.*

The sprinkler systems in many modern buildings can also present a problem. They can be triggered by heat, and if you place an instrument too close to one, you are really in for trouble. I was on a shoot where a system triggered, and they put out a tremendous amount of water. Some gaffers will tape Styrofoam cups around them. I don't know how effective this is; I just try to keep my instruments at least 3 or 4 feet away from any sprinklers. This constrains your lighting design, but the consequences of not taking these precautions can be worse.

---

3. Even very small shoots should be insured against accidents and any other potential legal complications.

☑ **Enough electricity to cause potential harm.** It would be impossible to go into all the potential hazards associated with electricity, and it is assumed that everyone has a healthy respect for what it can do. Suffice it to say that electricity should be dealt with only by trained technicians. Don't let anyone who thinks they know what they are doing do anything foolish.

Use common sense. Don't fiddle with a light or change a bulb unless the instrument is unplugged. If you are unsure if it is hot, turn it on to find out. Always wear rubber-soled shoes. If somehow the worst happens and a crew member is getting a dose of electricity, never touch the person. Grab something that does not conduct electricity—a 2 by 4 will do quite nicely—and knock the person or the offending source away. Don't worry that doing so might hurt the person. That person is already getting hurt, and you just may be saving his life. If you are working with lights around water, take precautions that the two do not mix. Students thinking about shooting around swimming pools or in bathrooms should either be admonished to be extremely careful or discouraged entirely.

☑ **Heavy instruments on high, potentially unstable stands.** Many lighting instruments are heavy and, when you get them up high on a stand, they can be unstable. Put sandbags on the base of the stand for stability. You can find them at any lighting rental house or you can improvise. Never put a heavy instrument on a stand that is inappropriate for its weight. Never build something with C-stands and extension arms that has the potential to fall over. Secure everything so it cannot fall accidentally or be tipped over by a careless crew member. You will hear the term *balanced weight* quite frequently on a set. Whenever you have uneven weight on a stand, be sure to use something to balance it.

When shooting outdoors, be prepared for weather-related problems. On one shoot, we were filming a family sitting around a table eating lunch. As is so often the case, the beautiful natural light flooding through the windows was being provided by two 10ks outside. As we were shooting, some nasty-looking thunderheads appeared on the horizon. Always prepared for something like this, the gaffer and the key grip rigged up a tarpaulin to protect the lights from rain. As the thunderhead approached, the wind picked up. With ropes and tent stakes, they secured the instruments to the ground; this was done anyway—they just reinforced it. As the storm drew nearer, it became obvious that it was not going to be an average downpour. The gaffer advised the director that they had better strike the exterior lights. Not wanting to lose a moment's shooting time, the director asked if it was absolutely necessary. When apprised of the potential danger, she ordered the lights struck immediately. The storm was short and violent, and we were back shooting within twenty minutes of its conclusion. We later heard that a tornado had touched down several miles away. *Do not take chances and be prepared for the worst.*

☑ **People working up high on ladders, grids, and genie lifts.** Ladders are standard equipment on film sets, and you must learn how to be comfortable and work safely on them. Have someone steady the ladder and assist you with moving heavy equipment. I have seen people standing on all kinds of silly things to reach instruments. Be sure to stand on something stable that will hold your weight and have someone steady you. Location work can require numerous skills, from mountain climbing to the ability to do what almost amounts to high-altitude heavy construction. Learn how to work cooperatively in difficult situations.

Studio work also requires care. Most instruments are hung from grids and, though many studios have the traditional theater catwalk, most grids require ladders or genie lifts to access them. A genie lift is similar to a crane, but it has extensions that send its operator straight up. With this you can reach instruments from below. Genie lifts are handy, but they can tip over if not properly secured. They should be used only by people trained in their operation.

☑ **So many extension cords and stands on the floor that the potential for tripping or stumbling is a constant danger.** Lighting crew loves to make what they call "grip jungles," where stands and modifying materials are so thick that you feel as though you need a machete to get through. I have seen setups that make it hard to get from one side of the room to the other. Everyone on the set must be sensitive to the fact that they have to be careful. That said, you should attempt to limit potential hazards. Gaffer's tape can be used to tape down extensions or any other cords. If you are not taping cords, try to at least get them out of the way of high-traffic areas. Keep open walkways. Do not have head-bangers sticking out into areas that people are going to be moving through. Again, use common sense.

Do not take shortcuts. Filmmaking requires a measured and careful approach that includes making sure that everything you have set up is properly secured. Watch how experienced crew members do things. Everything is done for a reason. Putting a heavy instrument on a stand is a two-person job and is done a specific way, which is probably the easiest and, more important, most predictable way—both people understand what they are supposed to do. I have seen some Three Stooges imitators drop a 10k and they were just lucky it did not land on anyone's head. Know your limits and learn how to work cooperatively.

☑ *Is it safe?*

Planning and Preparation

It should be evident from these discussions that a substantial part of the battle is won or lost in the planning and preparation. If you know what the challenges are and what is going to be asked of you, you can be equipped for, and do, virtually anything. If it happens to you only once you will be lucky, but it is all too easy to back yourself into corners. You do a really beautiful shot that establishes a specific quality of, or direction to, the light. When it comes time to do the shots that have to match, you don't have the proper materials to create what is needed.

Early in my career, I worked on a scene that was being shot in a kitchen/dining room. The director wanted the scene to have a sunny feel and, as always seems to be the case, the day turned out to be overcast. The improvised plan was to have a 2k outside the kitchen window, supplying the sunlight—the key for the scene. We set this up and proceeded to fill in all the areas that needed it. We shot all the material from setup #1, which was character A standing at an open refrigerator talking to character B. This all went fine. We had a 2k behind B, again to simulate strong morning light, and did some OTS shots from setup #1. **SEE 11-21**

The problems started when we turned around to shoot character B. Because we had established a strong morning light creating a nice backlight on B, the background from setup #2 had to be bright. It would have been impossible to light the entire exterior background, so the DP intended to draw the curtains in such a way that we saw only a single shrub just outside the window. We could then light the shrub with our tungsten lamps, thus simulating sunlight. We got everything up and then noticed an untenable problem: the bright light for the exterior was causing the backing of the curtains to reflect in the window. The reflection was large and unattractive, surely a distraction to anyone viewing the finished product. We scrambled while the talent waited. And waited.

Our solution was to tear down what we had done to the shrub, set up a large silk behind character B, and blow a lot of light into it. This also blew out the reflection. The character then had a very bright background that completely lacked detail. The director convinced himself that this solution would be adequate.

And that is all it was—adequate. The real problem was that by the time we had a solution, our time with the talent was limited and we had to rush through

11-21

The reverse of setup #1 posed significant lighting problems

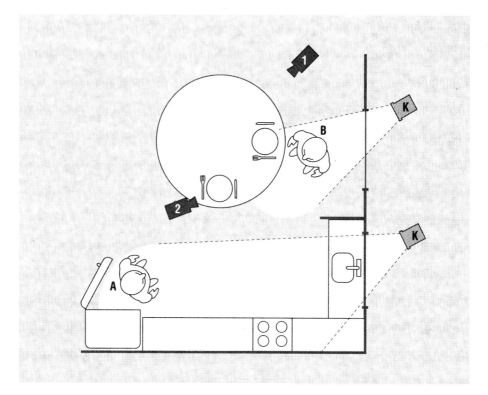

the shots. Almost invariably, you do your worst work when you are rushing. People are hired and money spent to make sure that directors have the appropriate, but by no means limitless, time to accomplish the task at hand.

In working with the footage later, the questionable quality of the image and the difficulties in editing the scene together reflected the conditions under which it was produced. Had the execution of the scene been completely thought out, we could have anticipated and dealt with the problem in a timely manner. Since the second setup was the more difficult of the two, it probably would have been better to shoot the material from setup #2 first. If we could not have found a workable solution to the background problem, we could have done different lighting for setup #1. I suppose the director and DP didn't even consider the possibility that what they had figured out for setup #2 would not work. Remember Murphy's Law: Anything that can go wrong will go wrong. Part of becoming adept at the craft of filmmaking is learning how to negate that law. If something can go wrong, you have to anticipate the problem and cannot let it stop you dead in your tracks.

On a more pragmatic level, you have to be able to anticipate all your equipment needs. Clearly you have to know what instruments you will be using. This sounds more difficult than it is. One rule is to always bring more instruments than you think you are going to use. This anticipates malfunctions and, more to the point, you will always have that one little instrument necessary for perfecting the image.

Not only do you need to anticipate the instruments, you need to know how you are going to rig them. If they will all be on stands, you need those as well. If you are going to hang them, you need the right kind of clamps. There is a great array of **grip equipment** to aid you in this task. From simple C-clamps with spuds to very sophisticated specialized clamps, there is something to help get that light just about anywhere you want. Sometimes they have very exotic names, such as mafer clamps or baby Matth pipe clamps. On occasion, it almost appears as though all the complex names are a foreign language designed expressly to exclude you. Just do everything you can to learn the lingo.

Not anticipating all your needs can slow you down or, in some cases, stop you altogether. Even the lack of something as simple as a cheater—the plastic adapter used to insert a three-prong plug into a two-prong outlet—can delay or even shut down a shoot. Working quickly and efficiently is crucial because your time with talent and locations is almost always limited. Again, experienced camera and lighting crews are able to anticipate and be prepared for just about any contingency. Many productions, particularly those with adequate budgets, will rent a *grip truck*. These are trucks that rental houses have outfitted with virtually everything you need: instruments, grip equipment, heavy-duty extension cords, and *expendables* (such as spun, gel, cheaters, and so forth). Usually you are charged both by the day and for what you take off the truck.

DPs often have longstanding working relationships with specific gaffers and key grips; they come as a team. If you are working with people who know what they are doing, they are thinking about more than the shot being done at that moment. They are thinking down the line to the shots that have to cut to what you are doing now. Is this light right for the emotional content of the image? Will the lighting continuity be correct? They should know all the right questions. They should know some answers, too.

All these pragmatic considerations are related to what is probably the most important aspect of lighting a scene: *having a plan*. Always visit a location before the day of the shoot. As suggested, draw out an overhead of the positions of outlets and circuits. The overhead can serve a dual purpose to plot out an overall lighting plan as well. In conjunction with the director and the DP, sketch out where the action is going to occur and how the instruments will be set up. At this stage, figure out electrical requirements, justification of light source, depth of field, modifications for color temperature—in other words, just about everything.

The following question is presented last because having a plan includes consideration of all the previous items on the checklist. You will find, however, that frequently it is the appropriate starting point.

☑ *Do I have a plan? Am I prepared for all contingencies down the line, in terms of both equipment and thinking? Am I asking the right questions?*

A Typical Scene

How do lighting and all the other components of production interlock? What follows is a replication of an overhead plan for a scene that was shot in a bookstore. The scene involved one character following another around the store, offering suggestions for buying specific titles. As our time with location and talent was limited, we had to work at maximum efficiency. The director blocked out the action and planned to cover the scene from a total of twenty-one camera setups. **SEE 11-22**

The space was served by a distribution box that had six circuits. The building owner would not allow us in the basement to the master breaker box. The first three circuits were 15-amp circuits and, because they were wired many years before, nongrounded (two prong). Two grounded (three prong) 20-amp circuits had been added more recently. The sixth circuit was for the overhead lights, large fluorescent fixtures that were turned on with pull chains. We did not want the ugly fluorescent light, but the fixtures had grounded outlets also controlled by the pull chains. We removed the fluorescent bulbs and, with C-clamps, rigged broads that effectively reproduced the overhead lighting. We could use these to create general fill and a couple of effects in which the characters turned on lights for dark areas of the bookstore, particularly for setups #19, #20, and #21.

11-22

Overhead plan for the bookstore scene

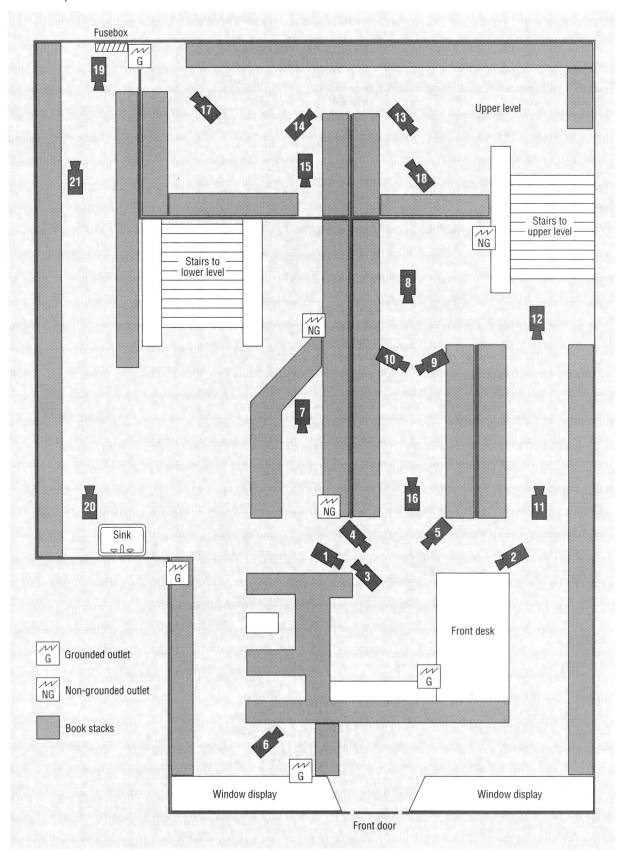

11-23

Lighting plan for setup #1 of the bookstore scene

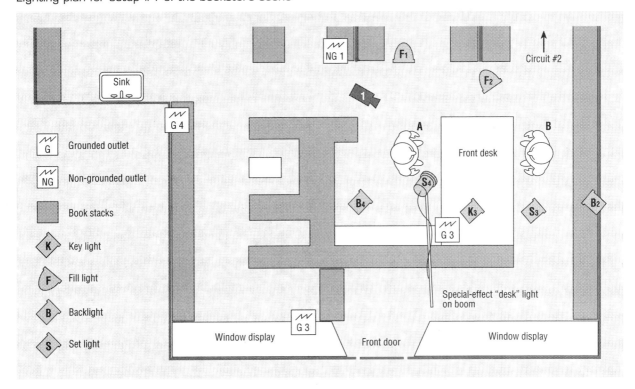

With this information, we could then plan out where we would put the instruments and what was going to be accomplished with each one. We could also determine what outlets we could use. Setup #1 was an over-the-shoulder shot of character B. The numbers in the squares refer to the circuits we used. The keys and fills were 1,000 watts. The backlights and set lights were 650. **SEE 11-23**

The backlight for character B had to be up quite high to be out of camera range. The scene took place in daytime, so the key was from the window side, and the direction of the instruments was based on this. We also had to be careful to light the shoulder of character A. We measured a number of the aisles in the store so we could plan for the depth of field that we needed for specific shots. The more you have figured out before you actually shoot, the more efficient you can be on the set.

Setup #2 was not an OTS, so we didn't have to consider character B. **SEE 11-24**

In this example, we determined where we wanted the people, where we wanted the camera, what action was going to be covered from each camera, what order we were going to shoot in, and how we were going to light it all. Issues of sound were also considered. Shooting is a matter of determining what you have to accomplish, what shots you want to capture on film. You then determine what elements are needed—talent, cameras, lights, and so on—to accomplish that purpose. Planning the implementation of these elements is the next step, with shooting being the culmination of the process. All that is left now is editing.

It is difficult to communicate the special atmosphere of a film shoot. Sets can become extraordinarily tense, given the narrow focus of the area being filmed and all the attendant people doing their utmost to make it as visually interesting as possible. The process can be all-consuming. There is at once the tension involved in getting the shots right and an almost childlike focus on an intensely small area in front of the camera.

11-24

Lighting plan for setup #2 of the bookstore scene

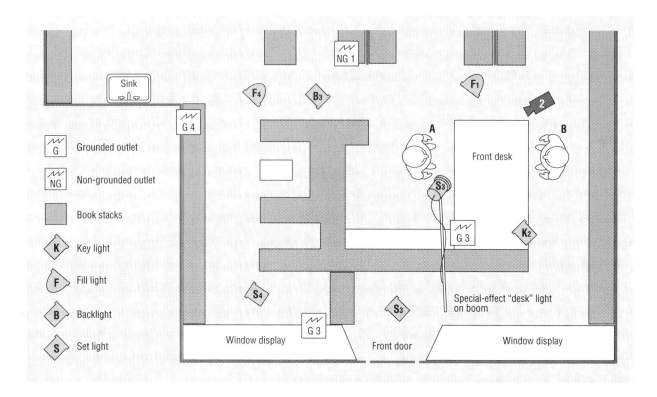

As suggested, Murphy's Law is always in effect or, in the best of situations, it is being kept from exerting its defeating influence by the slightest of margins. Chaos is always just one small step away. A large measure of production is putting yourself into a position where being successful is possible. It's that little thing called preproduction, or preparation. You have to think of all the factors that will complicate your task and make your goal more difficult to achieve. The most successful technical/creative people in the field are those who can anticipate virtually any eventuality and have a contingency plan to go ahead and get things done.

The Checklist Revisited

Lighting is about posing and answering questions. Addressing these questions will eventually become almost automatic for you—they are all issues that have to be considered. Until the day when they forever become part of your subconscious, do not hesitate to just go down the list before you shoot. Be flexible in the sequence in which you address the questions. Different concerns will jump to the top of the list in specific situations. This list is not meant to be all-inclusive. You will certainly find many other things that demand your attention.

✓ *What do I want to achieve or accomplish with the image?*

✓ *What is the source of light? What direction does the viewer expect the light to be coming from?*

✓ *How am I going to expose the subject(s)? Am I going for normal exposure? Overexposure? Should it be darker, a little underexposed?*

☑ *What quality of light do I want? Do I want it to be soft? Hard? Should it be diffuse?*

☑ *What goal(s) is each instrument accomplishing?*

☑ *Is lighting continuity important to what I am doing? Do I need to match the shot I am executing to other shots?*

☑ *Is there a particular f-stop at which I want to be shooting?*

☑ *Am I lighting to achieve an f-stop that will give a specific depth of field?*

☑ *Will I have to make adjustments in order to match color temperatures? If so, what materials and skills will I need?*

☑ *Have I determined how much electricity I need and identified the source?*

☑ *Am I doing anything for an effect, in terms of exposure, color, or stock manipulation, that I should communicate to the lab?*

☑ *Am I shooting at standard sound running speed, 24 fps? If not, have I made the necessary adjustments?*

☑ *Are there any subjects, objects, or areas in the shot that are going to require any adjustments in light levels or exposure?*

☑ *Is it safe?*

☑ *Do I have a plan? Am I prepared for all contingencies down the line, in terms of both equipment and thinking? Am I asking the right questions?*

Some of these questions, particularly the first one, will be real head-scratchers. If you do not have all the answers right now, don't be intimidated. Experience is the key. The more lighting you do, the more solutions will suggest themselves, not only in the pragmatic aspects but in what happens in your head as well, the creative part. The process will be frustrating, time-consuming, and expensive. But you will never learn it unless you get out there and do it. It all leads to the most rewarding part—creating images of value and expressive power.

f-stop Recap

The checklist should be helpful, but one topic bears further emphasis: what factors make you choose a specific f-stop.

- A preferred f-stop gives you the lens resolution and quality of light desired.

- There is an existing light value to which it would be expedient to conform.

- There are shots that require a predetermined amount of depth of field.

- There are situations in which a specific value is easy to achieve and simply makes sense. This could be because of the type of instruments you are using, the size of the location, the way instruments that are going to be balanced against the key can be set, or a number of other reasons. There is simply some value that makes common sense given the situation.

The checklist topics included here should eventually become internalized to the extent that you consider them automatically, or your approaches become so sophisticated that the basic language becomes almost obsolete. In a recent conversation with some colleagues, when I mentioned the three-point system as a starting point, one DP remarked that she didn't think in terms of key and fill any longer. She went on to talk about lighting with a 5k and shaping and feathering the instrument with flags and silks and other modifying material. Still, she had a source and needed to create detail in the shadows. On further questioning, she admitted that she still worked with all the same issues, it was just that her language had changed. In addition, you are not going to have access to 5ks, much less any way to power them up. You have to face the fact that you will be working on a more limited scale than the "bigs." Use your creativity and ingenuity to find ways to be productive on that level.

Again, the key to lighting is not to look at a given location and say, "What can I get here?" but rather, "What do I have to do to get what I want?" Once you start to understand how light and exposure interrelate, you find that there are many things, small and large, you can do to improve the image in a substantive way. To produce on a high level with limited resources and time, you need to analyze a situation in advance, create a workable approach, and then develop a plan to implement your ideas quickly and efficiently. Quick, however, does not mean instantaneous. Lighting takes time, and you need to allocate enough to do it right. Still, if you can envision the end product and work toward it logically and cooperatively, you can be productive without wasting time. Martin Scorsese's most significant early feature, *Mean Streets* (1973), was shot in about three weeks. Richard Linklater's *Slackers* (1991) was shot in a similar time frame. Given a creative and organized approach, producing shots of weight and value is both a worthy and achievable goal. You can create tremendously beautiful images with a few well-applied resources. Moreover, the crucial concept to grasp is that virtually all images of character and interest are composed of complex levels of light and exposure.

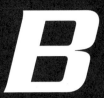
Lighting

Video Versus Film Lighting

Lighting principles in video are generally similar to those in film. *Key, fill,* and other related terms remain as part of the language of light. The same instruments, modifying materials, and tools are used for the same purposes. Despite this, the video image responds slightly differently to light and has a different look. Filmmakers find that lighting principles learned in film adapt well, but video brings a number of new considerations. From a filmmaker's perspective, there have been three basic charges against video:

- Video cannot be shot in low-light conditions.

- Video does not have as much latitude as film.

- Video does not perform as well in the shoulder and, particularly, the toe of the tape's latitude.

Although there is some validity to all these claims, they can all be responded to in kind.

Video and Low Light

Older video cameras indeed did not perform well in low light. For example, a moving object that was not lighted to a certain minimal level would leave an almost ghostly trail, called lag, behind it. Needless to say, the most recent cameras have addressed these shortcomings. The video camera's ability to respond to light is based on the number and design of pixels in the chip(s). Many of the newer designs have very impressive light-gathering potential. This complaint about video is also a very reactive one. It is a question of "What can I do with this situation?" as opposed to "What do I need to do to this situation?" It avoids the need to create lighting that achieves the desired effect, although there are certainly situations in which this is not feasible.

Video and Latitude

The most significant rap against video is that it does not have as much latitude as film. This is clearly a matter of concern, but the argument itself is largely specious.

As the preceding chapters have demonstrated, you position the values of your instruments to the available latitude. If you are working with a medium that has a shallow latitude, you just have to light in a narrower range. Although this may pose difficulties because the discriminations between different light values have to be closer together, videographers rapidly determined that they could light "film style." The only arena where this shallow latitude can be problematic is when you don't have control of the light. These situations include documentary and newsfilming, ironically two approaches in which film was doomed from the moment video became portable.

Video and the Characteristic Curve

The last charge, that video responds poorly in the toe and the shoulder of its latitude, is the most difficult to dismiss. The toe and shoulder are parts of the characteristic curve described in chapter 9. They are those areas in a frame just before the image drops off to complete over- or underexposure, the edges of the metaphoric table. In video, the information in the toe and shoulder areas can become muddied. This is particularly true of the toe, that is, underexposure, resulting in a grayish, almost milky tone to the shadow areas. Although this is a significant complication, much as with latitude, crews have simply had to take it into account when lighting. Values are either placed within the straight line of exposure or outside of the latitude altogether. This clearly relates to the first concern listed, where low-light situations are by definition going to be in the toe of exposure. You simply have to view it as one of the characteristics of video and come to appreciate it as part of the look of the medium. The only alternative is to add light or . . . shoot film.

The Video Monitor

Another significant difference between film and video lighting is that video cameras have a monitor that represents the image. The quality of that monitor, however, is an issue. The small black-and-white liquid crystal display (LCD) monitors on most video cameras can represent only some simple parameters of basic exposure. To get a good idea of the lighting, you need a *field monitor*, a high-quality color monitor. Even then, the monitor needs to be adjusted for brightness, color, and various other aspects. A monitor that is not correctly adjusted will give an inaccurate representation.

With a properly adjusted video monitor, the process of video lighting is more analogous to painting than it is in film. In representational painting, you can look at a subject, put a brush stroke on the canvas, and look back at the subject to see how well the two match. Using the monitor like a canvas, you can put down a "brush stroke" of light and compare the video image with the subject. In film, predicting the final image is a highly informed guessing game replete with occasional nasty surprises.

While the ability to see the lighted image in video is useful, it does not solve all problems. Given the intense schedules, one generally does not have the time to apply each brush stroke individually. Having a monitor also does not necessarily eliminate continuity problems. Sometimes glaring problems do not show up until the actual editing of the pieces. It is necessary to develop an eye for these kinds of things, just as in film.

Other Video Issues

☑ Video's shallower latitude can be addressed in shooting, but it becomes a concern again when film is transferred to video. If video has a shallower latitude than the film stock, as is almost always the case, detail in the darkest and brightest areas of the film will be lost in the transfer. Experienced film shooters often find that their darker shadow areas, in particular, are lost. The visuals in Francis Ford Coppola's *The Godfather* (Gordon Willis, DP), which explored the deepest valleys of underexposure, are not quite as powerful when video represents its darkest elements poorly. It takes experience to determine what kinds of things will make it through the transfer.

☑ Whereas a light meter is absolutely essential in film, the ***waveform monitor*** is the most important lighting tool in video. It is an oscilloscope-style device through which the video signal is fed and analyzed. **SEE B-1** It creates a readout of the quality of the video signal, giving a visual representation of all the black-through-white elements of the signal. A video engineer can analyze the signal for anything from color saturation to the presence of sync pulses. Despite their importance, waveform monitors are often not available to students due to their expense and the logistical difficulties of using them with small, inexperienced crews. Much of the general quality of the signal is thus monitored by eye.

Light meters can be used in video, but they are most useful for calculating the balance between the lights and are not effective for determining exposure. As stated, the relationship of the *f*-stop to exposure is based on the design of the chip. The whole system—the relationship of the light in front of the camera to the *f*-stop

B-1

The waveform monitor is the most important lighting tool in video

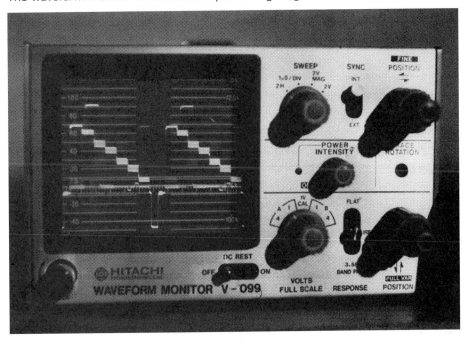

to exposure—that we have so carefully developed for film becomes much less concrete in video. This may have less to do with technical factors than with the ease and immediacy of the monitored video image. Used film-style, however, the light meter can have applications, particularly in maintaining continuity.

✓ As with consumer-grade film cameras, many video cameras come with an automatic iris. These are fine for initial projects, but mastering and eventually controlling exposure is as much a goal in video as it is in film.

✓ Color temperature remains a significant issue, with the white balance function of the video camera helping only in uncomplicated situations. You still must deal with matching the color in front of the camera. If you have a mix of light sources of two different colors, as in the example of the man in front of the window, the ability to white balance does not eliminate the need to match the sources. All matching is done in the traditional film approach, although the need to match to the color balance of the film stock is removed. You could match all your sources to fluorescent, for instance, and then white balance the video camera to that color. This matching would be done in film as well, but then you have to use a front-filter on the lens to get the light to match the balance of the stock.

✓ As cameras that create a digital image get closer to becoming a reality, traditional approaches to lighting may come under some pressure. Though the efficacy of this is yet to be tested, there is the potential that some lighting will be done in paintbox-style software in postproduction. Much as some films are colorized, a lighting scheme could be applied to an image that was lighted flat on the set. While this concept may be too futuristic for some, the notion of manipulating the plastic quality of the image in post will certainly have at least some effect on how films are shot and edited.

PART IV

Shooting

12

Crew Organization

THIS **chapter details** some of the general principles behind organizing a film crew. By its nature, this includes some discussion of the practical aspects of preparing a script for shooting. Although independents and students may not be employing all of the crew members described here, it is important to become familiar with all the roles and their attendant responsibilities. The organization and sophistication with which a project is approached has a direct bearing on the final product. As with so much else, just because there is no specific person on board, the job they are responsible for nevertheless has to be done. It's simply one more thing for which you, the filmmaker, must be responsible.

The Sequence of Events

Although all three phases of a film's production have legitimate claims to being *the* critical one, a film that is not properly prepped is a disaster waiting to happen. Even films that appear very improvisational require input from key creative personnel. The first step is coming up with an acceptable script. Scripts can come from many sources, ranging from original scripts, to adaptations of acquired short stories or novels, to simple story ideas that a producer wants a screenwriter to develop. However advanced the script is, the producer generally engages writers to either rewrite, adapt, or develop the project. After the writers, the producer's next hire is usually the director, although talent, stars usually, may also be brought on board at earlier stages. The director then starts developing the script in terms of casting, locations, general visual style, and dramatic approach.

Once funding, script, and director are in place, the sequence of events is fairly straightforward. Putting a film together in preproduction has become something of a science. Very early in the process, the producer hires a *production manager (PM)*, who is responsible for all the practical planning and scheduling of the film. Along with the director and the DP, the PM is critical to the day-to-day management of a film shoot. Responsibilities of the PM are detailed in ensuing sections, but a good PM can break down a script and estimate costs to within a few percentage points.

The next step is usually to hire the other key personnel: the DP, a production designer, and anyone else whose input may be needed during the initial stages. Crew that is specific to actual shooting—sound engineers, props, makeup, and so on—can be hired closer to actual shooting, although almost everyone needs some prep time to anticipate the needs of a given production.

Once these central people are in position, the following tasks have to be undertaken, and personnel to assist in these stages must be hired as well.

Casting is a crucial aspect of any narrative film, conventional or unconventional. A good measure of the failure or success of a film is determined in this stage. There are films that do not rely heavily on the performers, like certain types of action and horror movies, but most rely on the creation of credible characters in believable situations. Whereas casting can be quite informal for independent and student projects, it is a major undertaking for commercial films. Just as so much else, casting has also become specialized, with agencies coming forth to play a key role in auditioning. The casting crew can even separate into groups for casting main roles, peripheral roles, and even extras.

Union rules are a critical consideration in casting. Many actors are members of the Screen Actors Guild (SAG) or the American Federation of Television and Radio Artists (AFTRA), which have stringent rules about participation in films that don't pay the talent or that defer payments until later. You need to become familiar with these rules. Many independents choose to work with nonunion performers, although this obviously excludes many talented people.

Auditions are a must. For independents and students, this generally means putting an *audition call* notice in the want ads of a local newspaper. Major urban newspapers have a specific section for these, referred to as "cattle calls" by the insensitive, which actors frequently consult. It is also worthwhile to put up notices at local theater companies and at university drama departments. The notice can be general, although you may want to list the number of roles, the gender and age, and such issues as controversial subject matter. When scheduling auditions, be very up-front about what the actors' time investment will be, the subject matter, and the payment they can expect. If an actor finds anything objectionable, it is better to find out at this stage and not waste either your or the actor's time. In this initial phase, roughly fifteen minutes should be allotted for each audition.

Actors are usually asked to do a *cold read* of a short section of the part for which they are being considered. A good approach is to explore the actor's ability by asking for different interpretations of the chosen selection. Find out how responsive the actor is and how sensitive to trying out different approaches to character. In auditions for stage plays, actors are generally asked to perform a monologue from a play of their choice. Beginning directors may find these useful to evaluate how animated a performer is and to get an example of their overall ability, although monologues are generally not required in film auditions.

The director must bring thoughtful, interpretative skills to the casting session and be able to look at a script and think out character, motivation, and the nuances of every role. This is as true of a main character who is in every scene as it is of a bit role in one small scene. It takes an experienced eye to be able to evaluate individual talent for specific roles. The biggest mistake beginning directors make is evaluating performance in terms of an actor's interpretation of a part. This is usually because the director has not defined the character clearly in his or her mind before the casting session starts. It is imperative that the director do an interpretative session with the script, virtually writing a brief analysis of every character. Again, asking actors for different interpretations of the part is a clue to their general ability.

Sometimes an actor will show up at an audition and appear to be perfect for a specific part, perfect as you have visualized that particular character. Though this works occasionally, don't let superficial appearances determine character. Type is certainly important, but if the performer cannot be successful in the role, the approach is defeating.

The first auditions should produce a number of potential candidates for each role. *Callbacks* may be needed to make final decisions. In these, spending more time and working with a larger section of the script should help identify the performers you want for the roles. As casting decisions are narrowed down, try to find some measure of the talents' commitment to the project. If you sense hesitation or a condescending attitude on an actor's part, those feelings may become magnified when shooting commences. Inexperienced performers often do not understand exactly what they are getting themselves into and, if maturity level is low, can cause problems, such as tardiness, lack of concentration, and so on. Although someone's attitude cannot be dictated, commitment is simply a requirement of performance. Once filming has started, disaffected talent is usually impossible to replace without starting over from scratch. Rather than struggle with a talented but balky actor, hiring a slightly less talented performer may make sense if he will be there for you.

Arranging as much time for *rehearsals* as possible is a good idea, but in reality they are rarely afforded as much time as the talent and director would desire. This is particularly true when actors work for free, as is often the case in independent situations. A stage play is often rehearsed for months before it is seen by the public. In film, the actors must give a usable performance from the first day of shooting. Any rehearsal time is a bonus; but if none is possible, be ready to start producing at a high level right from the start. When preshooting rehearsals are not feasible, set aside time on the set to walk through the entire scene before commencing to shoot. This gives the actors a sense of the shape of the scene prior to breaking the scene down into the individual pieces.

In conjunction with the director and cinematographer, the production designer begins preliminary work to determine the overall *design* approach of the film. Many major decisions have to be made prior to shooting. One of the first has to do with the amount of studio versus location shooting. Certain scripts demand studio shooting whereas others clearly require location work. Most films, though, fall somewhere in the middle, where locations and studios have to be weighed in terms of costs and a variety of other factors. A common approach is to shoot the exteriors on location and then shoot all interiors on matching sets created on soundstages. Independents and students, unable to absorb the costs of renting expensive studio space and creating sets, frequently do all work on location. While locations do have cost advantages, they also frequently need some preparation, whether it be as complicated as painting and sophisticated interior design or as minimal as bringing in a few props and moving furniture around.

Location scouting is the responsibility of the location scouts and includes searching for and assessing locations for specific scenes. Familiarity with the script is generally required, although some location scouts are armed with just a list of needed locations and their desirable features. Once suitable possibilities are found, the director, the DP, and in some instances the production designer will visit the locations and evaluate their visual and technical appeal. With the input of the DP and the designer, not to mention the financial people, the producer and director make the final decision.

Permission to use locations must then be secured. Public spaces require contacting the appropriate authorities. Use of private property must be cleared. Most states have film boards, and many large cities have a liaison to facilitate film- and videomaker's needs in these regards. Cities where filming is common may require permits, location fees, insurance binders, and other guarantees. Security precautions may be stipulated as well. In smaller markets, local people are generally more enthusiastic about the movies, often letting students and independents use locations for free. This can be a great opportunity unless something happens, such as damage to property or an accident resulting in injury, which makes liability an issue. Industry practice is to have all bases covered when shooting on location. Many young filmmakers are tempted to grab locations without prior permission, being in and out before anyone knows they are there. This is a bad idea. The entire shoot is spent looking over your shoulder to see if anyone is coming to throw you out. It invariably colors how the scene is executed.

Be honest with people about how long you expect shooting to take. Commercial features have the budget to take over spaces for the appropriate periods. Substantial sums are spent to make the use of locations as simple and hassle-free as possible. They can simply clear everyone out and shoot in peace. For independents, shooting around the comings and goings of the rest of the world can be very trying. Independents frequently find themselves "relying on the kindness of strangers" to let them use locations, particularly when needing public spaces or businesses such as restaurants or bars. When a shoot that is sold as taking a couple of hours becomes an all-day ordeal, goodwill can go right out the window.

Independents are often compelled to conform their needs to a convenient location whereas commercial features can manipulate existing spaces to conform to their needs. A colleague tells the story of how he had a location scout scouring a city for a professor's office, with nothing left in the budget for location fees. After days of searching, the scout turned up at my friend's office with the news that he had found the best possible spot—they were standing in it. It was the best possible spot because the price was right—free. My friend was stuck with a location forced upon him, rather than one that may have better suited his purposes.

Such are the decisions made in the independent world. For *The Long Goodbye,* Robert Altman shot several scenes at his own beach house. Having a crew in your home is something akin to having scouts set up camp in your living room for a week. Moving heavy dollies and lighting instruments, rearranging furniture, and the constant parade of crew members can take its toll on any space. Set building on a soundstage has many advantages; the biggest factor against it for independents is the cost of space rental and the materials and labor involved in building. Despite this, studio work should be carefully considered. Extended work in a single location can become stressful, with the disruption to neighbors and local businesses becoming an increasing source of irritation.

The Production Crew

Most film crews are put together from scratch with skill positions being filled from a pool of experienced freelancers. In the studio days, all the crew members were in-house employees. The costume department may have been working on a half-dozen films at a time. The music department had an in-house orchestra that worked hand-in-glove with composers, songwriters, and the film editors. The grips were assigned to specific soundstages and worked on dozens of films a year.

To a certain extent, putting together a film crew today is like putting together an entire orchestra to perform an original composition one time. Many people have to be brought on board and their efforts coordinated toward achieving a common goal. Freelancers are known by their reputations and are sought out and hired for each new film. People who are fast, understand the needs of a set, and bring creative decision making to their craft are always in demand. In general, being fast may be the most valued aspect. Many newcomers to the process are seduced by stories of people who have started at the top, but most people start in entry-level positions: production assistants, cable pullers, or as the new guy on the grip crew. Some stay there, others slowly work their way up to positions in which they are most able to bring their skills to bear. Most successful craft professionals tell of how humbly they started and what they had to go through to get where they are.

Established craft people frequently turn down work, while the newcomer struggles to get name recognition and nail down a few paying jobs. It is the old catch-22: you need proof of your ability to get work, but no one will give you the opportunity to prove yourself without a list of credits. Newcomers often have to work for free to get recognition, although one should be wary of abuses. Many film companies love to get this free labor, and newcomers should put strict limits on how many freebies they are willing to do. The more you work for free, the more people tend to take advantage. After one or two projects, if you have not proven your worth so that someone is willing to pay you, you may want to look for another company.

Crew members generally have no more job security than the project of the moment and the network of employers who know and trust their work. Freelancers have to handle deductions for things like taxes, Social Security, health insurance, and retirement on their own. All the ramifications of being self-employed need consideration.

The Team Spirit

Although sports metaphors can be irritating, team spirit is essential to making films. In the early 1960s, the "auteur theory" became popular in the United States. Derived from the writings of François Truffaut, Jean-Luc Godard, and other contributors to the influential French journal *Cahiers du Cinema*, the major tenet was that the director is the "author" of the film, the key motivating force in the creative life of the work. While the theory gave much-deserved attention to such directors as Alfred Hitchcock, Howard Hawks, and John Ford, it has led to a significant misunderstanding about the role of the support crew members. It would seem unnecessary to repeat the cliché that filmmaking is a collaborative art, except that few people truly understand what it means: Every crew member is faced with decisions large and small that contribute many elements to a film. If they do not bring some measure of creativity to these decisions, the project as a whole will suffer.

Particularly in independent settings, the key to putting together a crew is to assemble a group that is basically compatible and, more important, committed to finishing the project. Nothing is more destructive than having people around who clearly want to be elsewhere, for whatever reason, be it immaturity, ignorance of their role, or other excuses for being unproductive. Film crews tend to be an amalgamation of iconoclasts and eccentrics, individualism and ego seemingly a necessary attribute to successfully staying in the field. Despite this, responsible crew members understand the need to move forward as a unified whole. They also do not make the mistake of over- or underestimating their contribution. Chronic complainers can poison the atmosphere on a set and make everyone wish they were somewhere else. If someone on the set does not want to be there, do yourself a favor and grant their wish.

A crew that is committed and harmonious is, of course, the ideal. However, anyone remotely involved in the business has endless war stories about the stresses and personal frictions that occur. The creative process involves the clash of temperaments and visions that strong personalities bring to any venture. In addition, the amounts of money involved have become so astronomical that the whole enterprise can be suffused with the tensions produced by needing to get it right under intense pressure. I have been on sets where the bickering was constant. Despite this, the goal of producing the necessary material was never lost. Those who are unproductive or hinder productivity need to be shown the door.

The crew is there to maximize efficiency. An inefficient set results in inadequate footage, leaving the editor without enough to work with. In the final analysis, all the crew members exist to relieve the director of some of the decision-making pressure. Crews that force the director to focus on minutiae are not doing their jobs. The director must be able to focus on the important issues: performance and the camera. This is a major concern for independents, with the overwhelming technical considerations frequently detracting from what is occurring in front of the camera.

Crew Responsibilities

What follows are brief descriptions of some of the key positions in a film crew. Feature films have many more credits not covered here, including guarantee companies, bonding agents, and assistants to the stars. While these people are important players in making a commercial feature film, many independent shoots may consist of just camera and sound, some talent, and a location. The job descriptions below represent the skill positions needed during actual shooting. Although the duties of a number of positions may fall to a single individual on a small crew, all these jobs need to be done. The effectiveness with which they are carried out has an impact on the overall quality of your work. For lack of an adequate crew, beginners may find themselves in the role of gaffer/grip/boom operator/sound mixer/part-time script supervisor, or some similar outrageous combination. This is discouraged, certainly, but it represents the reality of working with limited resources.

Although credits for modern films have grown to exaggerated lengths, they still do not encompass all the people who work on a film. Crew sizes vary, but are generally dependent on how logistically ambitious the scene being shot is. A scene between two people in an easily manageable location takes a relatively small number of people, by feature film standards. Bigger scenes require hiring additional crew members for a day or even a week. Carpenters, crowd control specialists, security guards, and a host of others may be needed for a few specific shots. Day workers with specialized skills, such as Steadicam operators or animal handlers, get into the credits because they must market their specialty to other productions. Individual films have unique needs that are generally easy to visualize from the credits, for example a "horse wrangler" in a western or a "prosthetics" person in a horror film. One film listed a "pigeon wrangler," which might appear absurd except that whenever an element that is difficult to control has to perform on cue, professional services are a must.

With crews as with performers, unions are highly developed and have a major impact on the parameters of many of the positions covered here. Union rules often dictate the boundaries of a particular crew member's responsibilities, with other crafts being barred from doing specific jobs. These rules occasionally seem ridiculous, but the delineation of responsibilities clarifies who does what. When division of responsibility is not clear, important things can slip through the cracks. Time spent haggling over who is responsible for what on a set is better devoted to productive pursuits.

Most independent shoots are nonunion, and the boundaries often blur into a "let's pitch in and get it done" approach. The sound crew helping strike the lights is unheard of on a union shoot but not uncommon with a small crew. As suggested, the parameters of some positions can be fluid even within union rules. The moment someone says "a director does this," someone else interjects their own experience where there was an entirely different crew structure. General responsibilities of crew positions are outlined in the following discussion, and significant deviations are considered where appropriate.

Crews are broken down into departments—the art department, the grip department, and so on. Three key positions, the *sound mixer*, *boom operator*, and *script supervisor*, and their crafts and responsibilities are explained in appropriate chapters. Some of these roles, the director's for instance, have already been described, though a brief summary is in order. All editing personnel are discussed in the final three chapters.

The Producer's Team

The producer's job is to shepherd a film from beginning to end, although that role can vary with the size and complexity of a project. "Supervisor" is probably the best description, although the job can range from the customary role of being the pivotal figure in a film's entire life, to being a figurehead, to being the director's right-hand aide. On most commercial features, the producer ushers the film from initiation through to the editing, exhibition, and the film's residual economic afterlife. Usually there from before it starts to long after it ends, the producer may be involved in hiring other decisive personnel, such as the DP, the production manager, the production designer, the assistant director, and so on. In many situations, the producer hands this responsibility to the director, respecting the director's need to create a production team with whom he or she feels comfortable.

With a writer/director frequently initiating independent projects, the director often winds up being the producer as well, until the pressure makes hiring someone else necessary. This new person often is called the producer but winds up as some manner of production manager, helping the director with many responsibilities. On commercials, the producer may be the ad agency executive who developed the ad concept. The director may be a hireling whose sole job is to execute a highly developed storyboard.

In the traditional Hollywood path, the producer is the major organizing and capitalizing force in preproduction. Although there are numerous exceptions, the producer is generally not involved in the day-to-day logistics of shooting. A film produced by George Lucas or Steven Spielberg may have as much of their imprint on the film as the person's who directed it.

Production Manager

As stated, the PM is responsible for initial budgeting and logistical planning and, once shooting starts, for managing the pragmatic aspects of a film's production. The PM works mostly out of the production office, the hub of communications for the entire shoot. Much of the work is done with the assistant director, both being responsible for scheduling the daily operations of the film crew. Responsible to the producer, the PM also controls the production company's purse strings, approving most major cash expenditures.

Production management has been boiled down to a science of how to most effectively manage all the disparate elements it takes to create a film. Any film can be broken down into manageable tasks. The PM analyzes the script and subdivides the individual scenes into elements needed for their execution. This includes main players, locations, props, extras, vehicles, and anything else the script requires. The producer, director, and in particular the assistant director help the PM devise the most efficient schedule for shooting the film. From this, they create a master plan in the form of a chart called the *production board* (see page 361 for a description). On union shoots, the PM must consider overtime, night shooting, remote locations, and other factors to minimize costly crew holdovers. The PM's goal is to maximize production resources while maintaining cost efficiency.

When scheduling shoots, particularly with exteriors, the weather and acts of God can make the PM's job very demanding. Most PMs could probably write a dissertation on the accuracy of the weather-prediction industry. When a shoot depends on such factors as weather, the production manager must consider what other scenes can be done instead if the weather does not cooperate. The job is a constant juggling act, marshaling talent and resources to be at the right place at the right time.

A film I was involved with that was highly reliant on exteriors coincided with the rainiest month in the history of the film's location. This left intended locations flooded and made photographic matching of one day's shoot to the next difficult. Every rainy morning found the production manager scrambling to put together an interior shoot on obviously short notice. On overcast mornings, she had to consult the DP to see whether the light matched previously filmed scenes and then formulate a plan. Eventually she ran out of alternative interiors to shoot, and it was still raining. Rather than keep the full crew standing by, we wrapped and then returned with a smaller crew once the weather cleared.

Craft Services

The notion that a film crew runs on its stomach is well worth remembering. Some directors can work a whole day without eating, running just on nervous energy. The crews' stomachs are not so forgiving. The student who gets all the pieces of the puzzle into position but forgets to feed the crew is courting dissension and possible rebellion. Small amenities like coffee can make the difference between a productive crew and a snarly one.

The time and expense involved in rounding up the required items needs to be anticipated. Although this would never happen on a commercial shoot, time is not being spent wisely when the director has to stop somewhere before the shoot to get coffee and rolls for the rest of the crew. Someone who enjoys feeding other people may be interested in the job. Have this person poll the crew for any special dietary needs or preferences, such as vegetarianism. Get a sense of preferred beverages and provide as wide a range as possible. The crew is important, but the talents' needs should be particularly considered. A thirsty performer is one who is not focusing on the appropriate concerns.

The Director's Team

The people included herein report to the director personally. Their major role is to take some of the pressure of the routine pragmatic decisions off the director's shoulders. Again, the director is one of the key forces in almost every phase of a film's production. The extent of his or her involvement in postproduction depends on contractual obligations. In the golden age of the studios, after shooting concluded, many directors did not see the film again until it was on the screen. Contemporary directors generally have more power, though it is still a matter of the director's reputation. Directors such as Woody Allen and Spike Lee are strong presences in the editorial process; there are obviously others who cannot exert similar influence. Directors rarely do any actual cutting, because it is so time-consuming and painstaking, but will generally look at rough cuts of the film periodically and make suggestions.

First-time crew members are sometimes surprised at how unapproachable directors often are. Some are brusque to the point of being rude. It was only when

I started to direct that I understood this; there are so many details the director has to consider that it is not rudeness but simply the blinders of intense concentration. There is a story of a famous director who was re-creating a World War II conflict over a river bridge. Because it was the only bridge for miles, he was able to use it for only one morning. In the frantic preparations on the day of the shoot, a battery of assistants buffeted him with questions to which he answered with a perfunctory "yes," assuming that most details were inconsequential in the grand scheme of things. But when he was asked if all the extras in the German uniforms were supposed to be on the near side of the bridge or the far side, he decided he had better stop and think for a moment.

Assistant Director

The *assistant director (AD)* is the conduit and buffer between the overwhelming technical preoccupations of the crew and the director's need to focus on performance, action, and camera. The AD is the director's right hand and is responsible for communicating with all the departments, making sure that the production is progressing. The AD also works hand-in-hand with the production manager in scheduling all the needed elements for each scene. A good AD often has a reputation for toughness, being the one who comes down on crew members who are not producing at the level or speed expected of them. "What are we waiting on here?" is a question often heard on the set and it frequently comes from the AD.

The AD's major responsibility is to make sure that all crew members are on the same wavelength, pursuing the same goals. This may not appear to be critical, but any exposure to an incompetent AD will quickly disabuse anyone of that notion. The AD must let every crew member know what the next shot is and what is expected of them or things can deteriorate quickly. The AD must also make the crew aware of what is coming down the line. Certainly much of the ability to anticipate needs is left to the initiative of the individual crew members and departments, but they need to be told the essential blocking of the scene and camera angles. The farther ahead each department plans, the more prepared they are for all eventualities.

However important the AD's communication to the crew is, it depends on the director's ability to communicate with the AD. A disorganized director leaves the AD impotent in terms of knowing what is going to be shot next. The goal is always forward movement. When people are donating their time, which is often the case on independent and student productions, it is crucial that their time be thoughtfully and productively spent.

Talent

Working with *talent* is one of the most challenging areas for inexperienced directors. The director's role is to guide the actors cooperatively in the evolution of an organic performance. In the best situation, this is a team effort in which the actor works out a suitable approach within the director's interpretation of the story. The most important thing a director can do is allow performers to find the characters on their own. If the director can create the conditions where trust is a given, talented actors will be able to find their characters. If young directors err, it is on the side of underdirection, leaving performers without firm footing in creating a consistent approach. Actors bring a tremendous amount to their roles, but it is the director's responsibility to help them shape a coherent performance.

The question is how to translate the words in the script into recognizable human behavior. What language does the director use to describe emotion? How is a response qualified? If a character is told that the bank is going to foreclose on his home, what are the possible responses? Desperation? Passive acceptance? Rage? How many different ways are there to express rage? Is it quiet steaming, uncontrolled yelling, or throwing things? Clearly, the choices are many, and each defines the character in a distinct way. Think of Orson Welles's *Citizen Kane* and the way the title character destroys his wife's room.

In the final analysis, the actor must be responsive to the director's interpretation of the part, although an actor might balk at this. Both theater and film abound with stories of actors who have their characters clearly thought out before the director is even on board or have clashed with directors about interpretations. This usually represents the actions of a professionally secure actor and can in many instances yield productive results. Despite attendant tensions, this does not diminish the need for directors to forcefully state their ideas.

The inability to pay actors often forces young, inexperienced directors into a marriage of convenience with young, inexperienced talent. Even though there are young actors who are as talented as established ones, they are still in the process of developing their craft and, as such, their life experiences are often not broad enough or rich enough to offer a thoughtful and compelling performance. One can tell when a performer is emulating the common stereotypes they think typify a specific group. Portrayal requires empathy and empathy requires insight. When empathy is not present, acting takes on the character of impersonation. A performer must be capable of crawling inside the character's skin. Although the responsibility for an inorganic performance is usually laid at the actor's feet, it is equally, if not more so, the director's responsibility.

Two key issues need to be addressed when working with either stage-trained or untrained performers. The first is the often remarked-upon difference between stage and film acting. On the stage, the performer has to act for audience members in the back row. If this is done in film, the performance will be too intense and overblown for the intimacy of the camera. Almost invariably, performers from stage backgrounds are asked to give less. Broad facial expressions and gestures must be subtle so the performer does not "knock the camera over." Second, the pace of performances often looks much slower on the screen than when shooting; screen time is quite remarkable in how it makes normally timed events feel drawn out. To avoid slow sections on-screen, performance often needs to be delivered a little faster than what at first appears normal.

If possible, it is better to use professional talent for even the most peripheral roles. Inexperienced production crews often try to get friends, family members, or significant others to do small roles. This is generally a mistake. People unfamiliar with the process often don't understand the timing necessary to create shots that are appropriately paced. Talent that can follow instructions and perform peripheral actions the same way every time minimize delays and allow the director to focus on foreground action.

During shooting, there should be a limit to how many people are communicating with the talent. Sound problems should be funnelled through the AD. Discussions of continuity problems should probably follow the same route. In complex shots, a ***stand-in*** will be useful for working out the pragmatic aspects of the shot. For beginners, the technical elements of film often take over and become overriding forces that have to be dealt with. Those technical factors can so overwhelm inexperienced directors that actors often get left to their own devices. Although it has been suggested that the crew is there to take pressure off the director, eventually you will realize that everything is there for the performers—so they can do their job with as few distractions as possible. To a certain extent, the crews' major responsibility is to keep all the chaos of a film set in control so the actors can perform unhindered.

Production Assistants

Production assistants (PAs) do all the general running around on the set and behind the scenes. They are responsible to the assistant director and do all the inevitable last-minute tasks that come up. They can be made available to other departments, but only at the direction of the AD.

Although PAs are not pivotal players, the assistance they provide is indispensable. The position warrants discussion because it has traditionally been where many beginners get their start on crews. These are excellent entry-level positions in which you can gain a vantage point, albeit an active one, on the inner workings of a film crew. Be aware, though, that in recent years beginners have been forced to compete with a growing group of professional PAs. The position has evolved to the extent that an experienced and knowledgeable PA can be a valuable asset on a set.

The Camera Crew

In most commercial productions, the DP does not actually look through the camera as the shot is being executed. All actual shooting is done by the *camera operator*. The DP calls the composition and relies on the operator to execute that framing. This distinction between job descriptions is the product of union rules. International cinematographers who have to conform to these working relationships often find them stifling. Nonetheless, the operator/DP relationship has evolved to the extent that it works relatively well.

The camera itself requires several highly skilled technicians. This crew is led by the *first assistant camera person (1st AC)*, whose responsibility is the organization, handling, loading, transportation, setup, maintenance, and cleaning of everything having to do with the film, camera, and lenses. This includes all tripods and other camera support equipment, although the grips will help, and additional personnel will be brought in for complex setups—cranes, aerial mounts, and the like. On large projects, there will be a *2nd AC* as well as several other positions dedicated to the camera. The 2nd AC is responsible for filling out *camera reports*. The *clapper/loader* is responsible for marking the scene and loading magazines. For a detailed explanation of the responsibilities of the AC and attendant assistants, see chapter 15.

On a set, the 1st AC and assistants constantly attend to the needs of the camera, going to seeming fastidious extremes to make sure the camera is clean and operating properly. If you are working by yourself, it's up to you to take care of all these concerns. Whether on your own or with a full crew, the camera is no small responsibility; if the camera does not perform as it should, you will not be successful. Ignoring the double negative, the commonly heard phrase is "if you ain't got the camera, you ain't got nothin'."

The Director/DP Relationship

Many directors have a very clear conception of the photographic aspect of a film, in which case the DP is there to implement that vision. Other directors may hand over the entire visual approach of the film to the DP. In the first case, the DP still brings rich talent and experience to the visuals. Alfred Hitchcock had an extremely clear visual sense, and yet you can see stylistic differences among his many cinematographers, particularly when looking at films shot by his longtime collaborator Robert Burks. The directors who turn responsibility for composition and lighting over to the DP—and this is more the case with contemporary than classical Hollywood directors—tend to see their role more as working with actors and story.

Very few directors shoot their own films, a fact that surprises many newcomers until they understand the complex demands of each position, each discipline requiring competing sensibilities. Despite their far-ranging responsibilities, directors must focus on the subject in terms of performance when the camera is rolling. Rather than watching performance, DPs tend to treat the entire field of camera vision as an abstract space, focusing on the movement of form and shape. The DP who focuses on the talent may miss other elements in the frame, such as background movement, lighting problems, mic boom shadows, and so on. While not mutually exclusive, each approach requires treating the frame in different ways. Shooting and directing at the same time is more common in commercials, where more attention is paid to each image and less to issues of performance, continuity, and marshaling the many resources that it takes to make a feature.

Grip/Electric

Outside of the ACs, the other major camera support crews fall into two distinct departments: grip and electric. These departments, which are often lumped together under the general heading of grip/electric, work closely together on lighting, although the grip crew is also responsible for all rigging involving the camera, from dolly and tracks, to camera mounts on cars, to setting flags for lens flares. The *gaffer* is the head of the electric crew, and the *key grip* is the head of the grip crew, although the grips' work with the instruments is generally at the direction of the gaffer.

The gaffer is responsible for locating all sources of electricity and directing the setup of the instruments. The name comes from the hooks, resembling those used by fishermen, that old-time electric company workers used to climb poles. The electric *best boy* is the gaffer's right hand. A number of *electricians* fill out the crew. The *grips* are the jacks-of-all-trades on the set. The name comes from the suitcases full of tools that the ancestors of today's generation of grips used to bring to the set every day. The skills needed by the grips range from basic carpentry, to metal working, to knot tying. Problem solving is an essential part of filmmaking, and the grips are the great practical problem solvers on the set.

A gaffer friend likes to joke that the electricians are the forces of light and the grips are the forces of darkness. The electricians erect the instruments and "fire them up." The grips then cover the light, shaping and manipulating it to create the details and shadows necessary for a complex image. Although the division is never quite so clear, the grips take care of everything in front of the instruments, and the gaffer and his crew take care of everything at and behind the instruments. If it is electric and produces light, the electricians do the work. If it needs rigging or is not electric and needs setting on a stand—silks, flags, and so on—it's the grips' job.

While the two crews work together on lighting, they have very carefully delineated responsibilities. More than other positions, these distinctions tend to break down on small independent shoots. The grips do just about everything under the sun. The general job of both the grip and electric departments is to do everything possible to facilitate shooting. Having a few people around who can troubleshoot and rig setups will expedite filming greatly.

The Art Department

The art department is technically aligned with the camera, but its responsibilities are different enough to warrant separate discussion. The production designer is responsible to the director, but they often work most closely with the DP. The production designer is the nominal head of the art department, which is an umbrella for a wide range of related skilled people. The key personnel responsible to the production designer are those involved in the building and decoration of the set or location. The *art director* is an expert in materials and building and is responsible for executing the production designer's plans. Carpenters, painters, and other specialists assist in the actual creation of the set. The *set decorator* plans the small items on the set—the details that make the space look realistic. The *set dresser* executes the set decorator's conceptions. Loosely associated with this group are the *costume designer*, the *props master*, the *hair stylists*, the *makeup* people, and everyone involved in the nonphotographic content of the frame. On commercial features, each skill position has a battery of assistants.

When outside the comfort of the soundstage, most locations need prepping. The art department generally works several days ahead of the shoot, although assistants are present during the shooting to respond to the inevitable last-minute needs of the talent and set. They are all responsible for the myriad activities necessary to produce the kind of look that is desired.

Films vary dramatically in terms of how much the art department contributes to the process. A film with a contemporary setting shot largely in exteriors or locations may require modest prepping, ranging from painting to hiding, cheating, or changing the elements that are present. On films that are design heavy, particularly period pieces and futuristic or fantasy projects, the production designer is on board early in preproduction and can have a substantial impact, participating in discussions with the director and the DP to determine a general approach to the look of the film.

13

Sound

SERIOUS consideration of sound often gets postponed to the end of the filmmaking process. Students usually do not get to the subject until later in their academic careers, and independents often lack the resources or support staff to give it consistent attention from the beginning of a project. Even many professionals often give it little attention until late in the editing phase. No matter how strong the visuals, sound is a critical component of any film and it is often one of the glaring weaknesses in student and independent projects. Alfred Hitchcock is often referred to as a visual director, and yet his films were never meant to be played without sound. Small segments of his films, such as the museum and cemetery scenes from *Vertigo* or the cornfield sequence from *North by Northwest* (1959), work without words. These scenes, however, are still highly dependent on music to achieve their effect. And there are certainly equal stretches in his films that are dialogue driven. The often observed fact that many works, particularly episodic television programs and soap operas, can be followed just as easily with your back turned to the picture may speak to a weakness in conception. But there are also few films that can be equally powerful with their sound shut off. Even the pre-1927 "silent" films had titles and were designed for and always accompanied by music.

Just as with the picture, the controlling factor in recording sound for later use in film is determining and producing what the editors need in order to cut the sound tracks. Nothing is more instructive in grasping recording mistakes than trying to cut sound that is inadequate in quality, insufficient in length, or conceptually flawed in terms of continuity. As with so much else, understanding the hows and whys of generating material that meets the needs of the editing room is the goal of learning good audio-recording technique.

Toward a Final Film Track

It is necessary to have a clear understanding of the path the audio takes to the finished product before you can effectively discuss recording sound for motion pictures. The medium for recording location sound for film is generally conventional audiotape: a quarter-inch reel-to-reel or a professional cassette recorder, with the new DAT (digital audiotape) format making inroads in this domain. The sound that the *sound mixer,* the person who operates the tape recorder and is head of the sound crew, records on location, as well as all anticipated sound effects and music, is then transferred to the mag stock (see chapter 4).

During the editing process, the editor creates multiple rolls of edited sound, called mixtracks, layering effects on top of each other to create the complexity of sound desired. If you foresee needing the sound of a dog barking mixed with trains rumbling by in the distance, you would never record the two sounds together. Premixed sound, sound that is already combined on one piece of film, is generally too inflexible for the elastic demands of the editing process. If sound is premixed, the timing of the audio elements tends to dominate how you cut the visuals to match, an approach that usually compromises optimum picture efficiency. You would record the train and the barking dog on separate pieces of mag stock; then they can be moved against each other on separate mixtracks as well as against the picture. You want to be able to move any piece of sound against other sound to facilitate optimal positioning.

All these separate mixtracks are eventually mixed down to produce the final sound track for the film. To this end, the edited film and mixtracks are taken to a commercial mixing facility, where each individual mixtrack is assigned to a *channel* on a *studio mixing console*. Here, the loudness of all sound in the final sound track is set with the volume *fader*. In addition to this simple volume control, each channel has, or can be patched into, various signal processors—equalization, reverb, echo, delay, and so on—that offer many opportunities to manipulate the quality and character of the sound. If the original recordings are of sufficient quality, these options can create virtually any desired effect in the sound. For this reason, *the goal in initial recording is to record every sound at the optimal quality, no matter what it is supposed to sound like in the final film.*

To a certain extent, you do what works to create the desired sound. If you find a multilayered piece of sound that suits your needs, you would never hesitate to use it. But if any effect needs to be manipulated against another effect, that is, needs to change positions against other sound, it must be recorded and transferred to mag stock as a separate entity. Thus, it is imperative to collect sounds individually and to have each one be as clean as possible, meaning that it is optimally recorded and free of interfering recording-system and background noise.

Applications

There are two distinct approaches to collecting sound for films: sync and nonsync. *Sync* sound is recorded as the camera is rolling on location or on the soundstage; it is referred to as *production sound* and is generally, though not exclusively, dialogue. *Nonsync* sound is recorded at other times, ranging from effects that the location recordist collects, to effects recorded later in a sound studio, to library effects, to music that was prerecorded or specifically designed for a film. Nonsync sound eventually appears to be a misnomer, because all sound is ultimately precisely positioned against the picture and thus is eventually in sync. But in the actual production, nonsync sound is recorded at a different time than the picture.

A distinction is often made between recording production sound in a studio and on location. As with virtually everything else, doing sound is much simpler in the studio, although the recording crew may have to contend with some of the contraptions (such as fog machines and fans) that are required for the picture, as well as with their operators. Locations can occasionally be a real nightmare. With the goal being clean dialogue and effects, responding to horrible acoustics, traffic noise, airplanes, refrigerators, heating systems, and a host of other complicating factors can make recording on location an estimable challenge. A measure of a good sound mixer may well be the ability to deal with difficult situations.

Due to considerations like this, the production sound is often replaced in editing, particularly on features and episodic television shows. *Postdubbing*, re-recording the dialogue and replacing it later, is a relatively frequent reality, although it takes a healthy budget to support the needed studio time and additional time with talent. Independents and students should be encouraged to get it right on location, even though they often have limited control over locations precisely because they have limited funds.

Single- and Double-System Sound

Single and double system refer to methods of achieving sync sound. For a generation brought up on confrontational video journalism, the idea that achieving lip and picture synchronization requires some effort may catch many off guard. Sound became a viable commercial entity in film only in the late 1920s. Any student of film history knows that the early sync-sound cameras were very big, requiring their own soundproof closets. These early limitations were actually overcome quite quickly, although the cameras used to make feature films during the early years were far from portable. Sync sound on location could be supported only by sound trucks carrying cumbersome sound-recording equipment.

Outside of instructional filmmaking, sync-sound equipment did not come into the hands of non-Hollywood filmmakers until the early 1960s, with the introduction of lightweight, portable sound and camera equipment. Just as video has created its own revolution, the introduction of the lightweight crystal camera and portable sound recorders also revolutionized the way films were made. These developments, along with more light-sensitive film stocks, allowed makers to film in almost any situation.

These developments occasioned documentaries made in the *cinema verite* style, an influential approach characterized by handheld camera and a sense of immediacy. From the on-location concert films such as Michael Wadleigh's *Woodstock* (1970) and Albert and David Maysles and Charlotte Zwerin's *Gimme Shelter* (1970), to the simple interview techniques of "60 Minutes," to the intrusions of the tabloid journalism programs, there has been a wave of films that were not even possible due to technical limitations prior to the early 1960s. Of all the documentaries made before 1960, one rarely sees sync-sound location work, and then only in situations where it is painfully obvious that the situation is very controlled. The great documentaries of the 1930s and 1940s, including Pare Lorentz's *The River* (1937) and Willard Van Dyke's *The City* (1939), were all shot wild—narration, music, and effects being added later. Most World War II combat footage was shot without sound, with most sound effects created in the studio.

It would seem at first that the most sensible solution to the problem of how to incorporate sound would be to put the sound along the edge of the film. That is how sound is handled in projection prints and logically is an appropriate place for location sound as well. While it has drawbacks, this is indeed one approach—the single-system sound method. Film chambers are outfitted with a record head, and the microphone is connected directly to the camera. The sound is then recorded on a magnetic stripe along the edge of the film. **SEE 13-1** Rather than the double-perf configuration described earlier, single-perf film is used, with the area normally devoted to the second set of perfs taken up by the sound. Called striped film, it is available from several manufacturers.

13-1

In single-system sound, audio is recorded on a magnetic stripe along the edge of the film

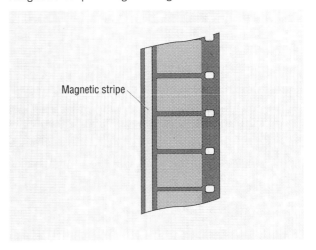

Magnetic stripe

13-2

Because the movement of the film image must be intermittent and that of the sound must be continuous, the record head is positioned below the gate area and controlled by the sprocketed rollers

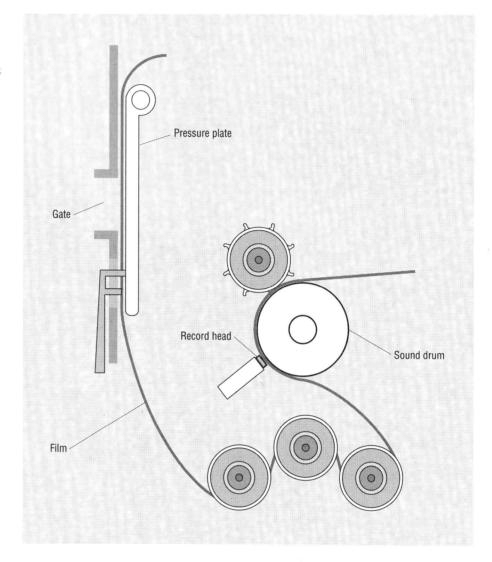

Pressure plate

Gate

Record head

Sound drum

Film

As suggested, there are major drawbacks to this approach, the most significant having to do with the different types of movement needed to both record and reproduce the two media. The film image requires intermittent movement at the gate and, as everyone knows, sound must move continuously across the heads. The two movements cannot be recorded at the same place, so the record head has to be displaced from the gate. **SEE 13-2** The record head is thus positioned below the gate area, where it is controlled by the continuous movement of the sprocketed rollers. It records the sound as the corresponding picture is being photographed at the gate. The sound is displaced by twenty-eight frames, thus reconciling the two movements. Projectors also employ this displacement and have since the optical track was universally adopted in 1932. As the sound is being played back on a projector, the corresponding image is in the film gate being projected.

This is fine for recording and projecting, but is untenable in editing. If you cut the picture at a particular frame, you are affecting a different part of the sound track. Thus, critical editing is impossible with single-system sound. In addition, adding sound, such as music or effects, to a film is impossible because the recorded sound occupies the track. The whole system is too inflexible for anything but the crudest editing.

In the days when television news was shot on film, a receding memory at best, single-system sound was very common. The film was shot for immediate broadcast, with no intention of editing. This approach was also quite popular with consumer Super 8 cameras, being a practical way for amateurs to get sound for home movies. Single-system sound is no longer used extensively, although it has made somewhat of a comeback as a portable medium that gives a film image when the intention is to transfer to and finish on video.

These drawbacks are why double-system sound is the more accepted method. In the double-system approach, the camera and sound recorder are separate entities. The problem is synchronizing the two media. When you set a wild camera at 24 fps, it does not run at precisely 24 fps—it will run at some percentage above or below 24, with no visible difference in the reproduction of movement until you get 3 or 4 frames away. When you set a tape recorder to 7½ inches per second, it will have some fluctuation as well. When you add in the variable of inexact projectors and sound playback systems, the possibility of sound and image playing back at the same rate is statistically improbable.

Crystal cameras are the image part of the solution because they run at precisely 24 fps[1]—precise at least to the extent that their fluctuations amount to at most a one-frame variance every ten or so minutes. This was accomplished by outfitting the camera with a crystal oscillator that produces a perfect tone. This tone is then referenced against a variable tone that is produced by and dependent on the speed of the camera's motor. When the two tones match, the camera is running at 24 fps.

Finding an audio recorder that could interlock with the camera was slightly more difficult. There is no such thing as a crystal tape recorder, at least in terms of conventional magnetic audiotape. Conventional tape recorders cannot run a precise amount of tape across the sound heads because of capstan slippage and tape stretch; if the tape stretches, it would run a different amount of tape past the head. The solution was to design the recorder with a crystal oscillator that, like the one in the camera, produces a perfect tone. This tone is recorded on a small area of the tape, usually down the center. When these production sound tapes are brought back into the studio, the recorded tone is played back and slaved to the 60-cycle tone in standard 110-volt electrical current. The mag stock recorder is also slaved to this tone and thus a "real-time" transfer is achieved. In editing, the slate is used to manually match picture and sound.

The most familiar recorder with this function is the *Nagra*, although there are certainly others, Stellavox and Arri/Tandberg are two, that employ similar strategies, and new digital technologies are putting pressure on this market. **SEE 13-3** Nagra is a product name, but this recorder was so central to the development of portable sync-sound filmmaking that it has become virtually synonymous with sync sound. The Nagra and its emulators would be considered just standard top-of-the-line recorders were it not for this one distinguishing feature: they record sound that can be synced to picture.

Lightweight and portable, the Nagra is designed to be either carried on the shoulder or set up in convenient spots on location. The *channel locks* on the recorder's tape spindles keep the take-up and feed reels from disengaging if the sound person is on the move. The Nagra employs a shorting plug, often referred to as a *crystal pin*, that, when inserted, makes the machine generate the tone down the center of the tape that is the basis for synchronization. Check for both of these items when picking up the machine at the rental house or school equipment room.

Another issue with double-system sound is the noise created by the camera. The generation of crystal cameras introduced around 1960 was either *self-blimped*, that is, padded against noise, or designed to be relatively noiseless. The blimped

---

1. A second method, which used an umbilical cord between the sound recorder and a noncrystal camera, was also a player in early portable double-system rigs. This system has largely fallen into disuse.

13-3

The Nagra recorder has become virtually synonymous with sync-sound recording

The Nagra 4.2 recorder

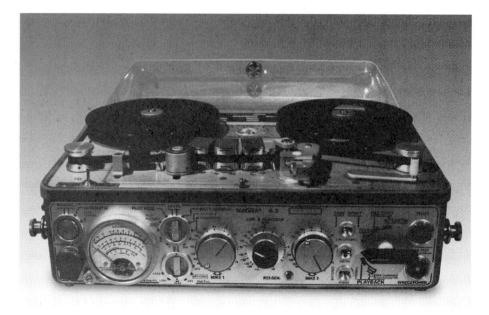

cameras, such as the Arriflex BL, can be cumbersome because of the additional housing needed to deaden sound. Today's soundproofed cameras, the Arriflex SR and the Aaton, are quieter than their predecessors and have become the standard in 16mm production cameras.

There is no such thing as a completely noiseless camera, and noise, particularly when working with older cameras, can be a significant problem. If you are in a space with live acoustics, camera noise can render the location sound unusable. Many camera manufacturers offer a padded hood, called a *barney* or *blimp*, to further dampen unwanted noise. If you don't have a barney, a heavy jacket will significantly deaden the noise (big, fluffy down jackets are particularly useful).

Synchronization

With the picture and sound being recorded separately, synchronization becomes a key issue. Beyond considerations of sound alone, shooting, transferring, editing, and playback must all be controlled. As you go through the circuitous routes of production and postproduction, any equipment that is not designed for sync can cause problems down the line. With video transfer thrown into the mix, the scenario becomes even more complicated.

This slaved-tone approach was the standard for many years. It is still a key player, but video technologies have introduced other methods of producing speeds that are perfect or can be duplicated. Actually, with the appropriate sideboard equipment any stereo recorder, whether cassette or quarter-inch, can be a sync recorder. A tone from a separate oscillator can be recorded onto one of the two stereo tracks, with the mono microphone signal being recorded on the other track. With the appropriate equipment, this tone is used to produce a sync transfer. There are also companies that can build the oscillator into existing recorders. The ever-increasing quality of professional cassette recorders has made this a popular modification, although there are sound people who still refuse to use cassette players for dialogue or music.

Original recording on a sync recorder is not absolutely essential for effects and music. They are generally fitted to the picture, and production sound is the only thing that must be sync. Even so, recording everything sync, particularly music, can avoid potential difficulties in postproduction. Many people will transfer music to the Nagra first and then to the mag stock, because the Nagra provides a sync transfer that can be duplicated. Whereas a quartz turntable or a disc player plays back at a perfect speed, the mag stock recorder is slaved to the wall power rather than creating a perfect 24 fps. Unless transferred from the Nagra, a piece of music will be slightly different each time it is transferred. This approach pays off if more than one copy needs to be made or if the mag stock being used in the editing process must be replaced due to damage.

The Character of Sound

Extensive knowledge of sound and its reproduction is not necessary to make simple recordings, but the more complex the challenge, the more a lack of knowledge will cause inadequate sound. Therefore, some basics about the character and recording of sound are presented here.

Sound emanates from a source and becomes the vibration of elements in a transmission medium, usually molecules in the air. Sound is air molecules compressing and separating, generally represented as a wave. **SEE 13-4**

The *frequency* with which the signal fluctuates above and below normal air pressure is called cycles per second (cps) or, more common, *hertz (Hz)*. Hertz represents the pitch of the sound, that is, whether it is a low, midrange, or high tone. Sounds with rapid rates of fluctuation are higher, such as a soprano or flute. Sounds with slow rates of frequency are low, such as a bass singer or tuba. *Frequency range* refers to the spectrum of audible and inaudible sound, represented in hertz. The average adult human ear hears from roughly 20 to 16,000 Hz. Sound exists above and below these parameters but is inaudible. The distance of variance from normal air pressure represents amplitude; the more the air is disturbed, the louder the sound.

Musical notes are at specific frequencies measured in hertz, with the audible spectrum easily divisible into octaves. Middle C is about 260 Hz. Someone singing bass would be in a range roughly from 60 to 200 Hz; a soprano would be around 200 to 1,000 Hz. Despite the general accuracy of these last two statements, wherever in the audible spectrum a particular human voice is, that voice has elements of other frequencies in it. Even if a person has a very low voice, there are elements of high frequencies in it. Conversely, a high voice has elements of low frequencies. This is true of all sound, from distant thunder to the piccolo. When one starts manipulating the sound with equalizers and other signal processors, this becomes a significant consideration.

Frequency response refers to how evenly and completely a specific recorder or playback format reproduces the audible range. High-quality recorders reproduce

13-4

A sound wave is a representation of compressing and separating air molecules

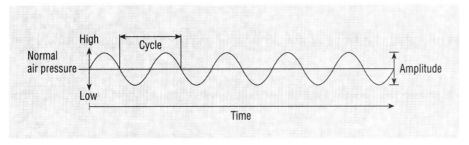

almost the entire spectrum of human hearing. Consumer recorders may record only within a relatively narrow range. Some recorders have poor low-frequency reproduction and others fail on the high end. A recorder's frequency response can be checked in the machine's "specs," a listing of its technical specifications. Find a recorder that reproduces as much of the spectrum of sound as possible.

Frequency response is based on technical considerations, most notably quality of electronic circuitry, tape speed, and area on the tape devoted to the signal. Quality of audiotape is also a contributing factor. Due to the nature of photographic reproduction, sound on 16mm films is notoriously poor—reproducing the range of frequencies from about 70 to 7,000 Hz. Sound for 35mm is significantly better because it is running at a faster rate and has a larger area devoted to it.

The following terms and concepts are necessary to understanding some of the basic potential of sound.

Decibels   A *decibel* (dB) is an increment of measurement of the amplitude, that is, loudness, of sound. Decibels are logarithmically based and defy any simple explanation, as their parameters are defined by the invisible structure of the sound wave. Suffice it to say that most recorders represent dBs as either a unit of amplitude in the recording of an audio signal or as a percentage or increment away from an optimal recording.

Mixing   There are generally two types of mixers available: the previously mentioned studio mixing consoles and field mixers. A studio console is a large board with a varying number of channels for individual signals. A *field mixer*, also called a mic mixer, is a simple unit with a small number of mic inputs and, on some models, a few signal-processing options. A field mixer is not a requirement for location recording, but is used when a particular setup requires more than the standard two mic inputs on most professional recorders. A field mixer converts the *mic signal* to a *line signal*, which is then fed to the recorder.

Signal processing   The idea that an audio signal can be changed and shaped is important. When dealing with sound coming from a microphone, you are faced with an electrical, or possibly digital, signal that can be altered as desired. Signal processors, like equalizers, are frequently used to "clean" or "brighten" sound that was recorded in less than optimal conditions. Other signal processors, such as reverb units and echo chambers, can add specific character to sound.

Signal path   The route an audio signal travels is important to understand, to be able to both troubleshoot and determine what processes the signal is going through. The microphone converts sound into an electrical signal that is directed by the microphone cord toward the record head. The signal goes into a microphone input on the recorder, where the weak microphone signal is boosted by a *preamp*. In a simple recording system, the signal is then fed to the record head. In a complex recording system, the signal may be routed through a number of internal circuits.

Virtually all audio equipment—recorders, mixers, signal processors, and so on—come equipped with *line inputs* and *outputs*. The audio signal can be routed through a *line out* to the *line in* of another machine. You might choose to route the signal through a variety of sideboard signal processors. If you send it to an equalizer, it has to come out again. If you send it to a field mixer, you should be able find out where it is and how to send it where it needs to go. With some basic knowledge of how signals travel, you should be able to route the signal wherever you want.

As a sound person, you should also be able to follow the often labyrinth-like path of virtually any signal in any setup, including the path of a video signal. When the path of the audio signal for a specific setup is understood, the various things that affect the signal become less mysterious. There are also many points in the chain where the signal can get waylaid, and understanding the concept of how a path works can be helpful in audio troubleshooting, a skill all too frequently needed on the set.

Ambience   This is the quality of the underlying sound in any given location. The acoustics of any space give a distinct character to the sound, whether it is the muted sound in a plush bedroom, an echo-filled school gymnasium, or the cavernous sound of Grand Central Station. This *ambience* "colors" the dialogue and effects you are recording as well, and will have a specific character in even the briefest silent stretches in a scene. Even if there is no discernable audio occurring, every space has distinct acoustic characteristics. One generally attempts to exclude as much ambient sound as possible. Ambience is distinguished from *background noise*, such as distant traffic, heaters, fans, and similar interfering sources, all of which need to be addressed as well (see chapter 14 for a further discussion of both concerns).

Generation   The term *generation* refers to the "family tree" of an image or piece of sound. In the context of sound, it relates to how the quality of recorded sound deteriorates as it is transferred from the original to various levels of copies. Successive copies of sound eventually noticeably degrade from the original. Remember from chapter 4 that a recorded sound has to go through a number of generations to get to a final product. Although sound holds up well through this process, this is another reason why the original recording must be as high quality as possible. This has been a difficulty in conventional audiotape recording, but one of the major benefits of digital reproduction is that the number of generations is not an issue.

Recorders

This discussion centers around conventional recorders because they are mostly used by students and independents, although the new DAT recorders have come down in price enough to start having an impact. They may someday take the place of the humble, conventional recorders.

A key to recording quality sound is to have as strong a system as possible. As important as such things as mic position are, all pieces must be equal to the task. Do not use an inexpensive consumer recorder or, more important, an inferior microphone. The sound is going to be only as good as the weakest link in the chain. You can go almost anywhere with a good strong signal, but a weak or inferior signal leaves you with limited options. Although there are methods for improving signals, a bad signal generally gets worse as it goes through the generations necessary for transferring and mixing.

Magnetic recording tapes are composed of a magnetic oxide solution applied to a polyester or acetate backing. The electrical signal created by the microphone is arranged as patterns in the magnetic oxide at the record head. The most commonly used conventional audio recorders are the quarter-inch reel-to-reel and cassette formats. For production sound, quarter-inch reel-to-reel recorders such as the Nagra are the norm. Although cassette recorders are associated with consumer use, there are high-quality models that can be useful for collecting film sound.

The conventional head configuration on a professional recorder includes an erase head, a record head, and a playback head. **SEE 13-5** Most consumer cassette recorders combine the record and playback heads in a single head. Occasionally you find professional decks that do this as well, though having separate heads is

13-5

The conventional head configuration on a professional recorder includes three heads: erase, record, and playback

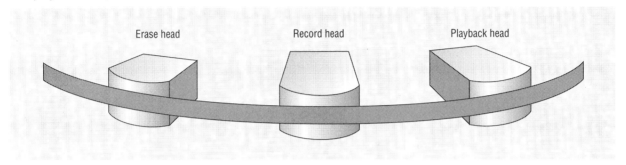

Erase head   Record head   Playback head

13-6

Recorders designed for sync sound have a fourth audio head that lays the reference tone

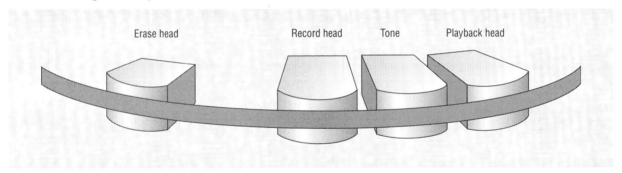

Erase head   Record head   Tone   Playback head

the norm. Recorders designed for sync, such as the Nagra, have a fourth audio head that lays the tone needed to generate a reference on the tape for sync. **SEE 13-6**

Beyond sync recording, there is usually an extensive campaign for recording effects and music. This can be as simple as someone with a cassette recorder and mic, recording a local band or whipping up funky effects in the kitchen, or it can be highly sophisticated audio studios recording a full orchestra or producing complex effects in a *Foley* studio. This phase can also involve narration sessions and the replacement of bad or inadequate dialogue. (See page 351 for a discussion of effects creation and dialogue replacement.)

Microphones

Microphones are classed by their *pickup*, or *polar*, *patterns*, terms that refer to how a mic picks up sound from different directions in relationship to where the mic is pointing. The two types of mics that are generally available to students are omnidirectional and cardioid.

Omnidirectional mics pick up sound in a spherical pattern, that is, equally in all directions. **SEE 13-7** This approach is not particularly useful because of the more focused recordings required for sound in motion pictures. These mics do, however, have occasional applications. They can be useful for picking up the general sound, the ambience, of a scene or location. When held close to the mouth, they can also be used for voice in a reporting or interview situation. The ElectroVoice (EV) 635a is a typical example of an exceptionally durable omnidirectional mic used in field recording.

Unidirectional, or *cardioid*, *mics* pick up sound in a heart-shaped pattern, hence the name. They pick up sources in front of the microphone to the general

13-7

An omnidirectional microphone picks up sound in a spherical pattern

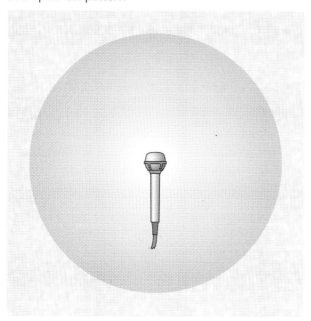

13-8

Unidirectional, or cardioid, mics pick up sound in a heart-shaped pattern

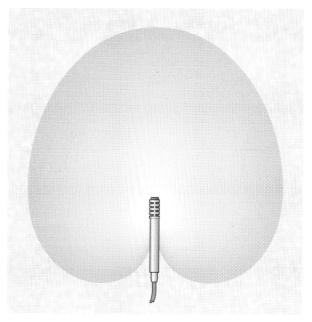

exclusion of sources behind. **SEE 13-8** In the familiar "shotgun" variation, cardioids are designed to pick up sound in a narrow angle. Because of the need to focus on specific sound, these short cardioids *(short shotguns)* and supercardioids *(super shotguns)* tend to be the mics of choice for location recording. **SEE 13-9** Sennheiser, AKG, and a number of other companies make high-quality shotguns that are in common use.

Many different types of microphones are used in film production, but mics with narrow pickup patterns have obvious advantages. Traditional voice mics, such as the ones used by a rock band, are not suitable for film applications. They are meant to be put close to the mouth, which is unfeasible in most filming situations. The long shotguns, while being physically impressive, are usually too much for interiors, their weight and size making them difficult to use in the often tight quarters of locations. Using a short shotgun indoors and a long shotgun outdoors is a common approach.

Shotgun mics are also used because their narrow pickup pattern excludes some amount of unwanted ambience or background noise. However, this has led to certain misunderstandings. Just because a sound originates from behind a microphone does not mean that the sound does not exist in some form in front of the mic. Sound is like water, or light for that matter: it flows into any area not completely blocked to it. If a sound is emanating from behind a microphone position, elements of it will be recorded no matter how

13-9

Mics with narrow pickup patterns, such as super-cardioids, have obvious advantages in film production

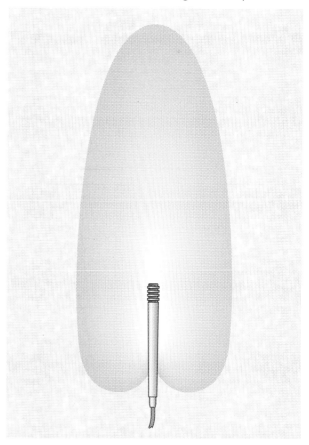

dissipated. Shotgun mics do not eliminate unwanted sound, they simply lessen the impact of these sounds.

Lavalier mics (lavs) are small clip-on mics that are frequently used for interviews, although they have a wide variety of applications in film. Lavs are not truly a class of mics, as they can be omnidirectional or cardioid, although most of them pick up in a cardioid pattern. One complication of using lavs in many film applications is that they have to be hidden. Many filmmakers leave them out in plain view in interview or documentary situations, but they must be concealed in other circumstances. This can lead to problems of muffling and the rustling of clothes.

Wireless mics, also called *radio mics*, have become increasingly popular in recent years. This mic is usually a lavalier plugged into a radio transmitter, which is clipped onto the back of the performer's waistband, taped to the body, or placed in a pocket. The radio signal is sent to a receiver that feeds it to the recorder, usually into a mic input. These mics can be handy for long shots where effective conventional miking is impossible or when the subjects are moving through tightly confined spaces.

Radio mics are useful for many applications, but their convenience must be balanced against their recording capabilities. The quality of the signal they produce is arguably lower than that produced by a conventional mic, mostly because of the clothes rustle and muffling previously mentioned. Their use is also complicated by the interference of other radio signals. Many places are so saturated with radio frequencies (RF) that other signals, such as radio stations, CBs, and cordless phones, can get thrown into the mix. The higher-end mics have many of the bugs worked out, but the rental costs of these may be beyond many independent shoots. With miniaturization, microphone designers have been able to create mics that look like jewelry or lapel flowers, but again these are frequently beyond the means of independents.

While there are a number of other approaches, *dynamic* and *condenser* microphones are the two most common types found in schools and arts centers. In a dynamic mic, the current—the *mic signal*—is produced by movement within a magnetic field. The moving air created by sound hits a membrane in the head of the mic, and the resulting vibration generates the signal. Condenser mics, also called capacitor mics, require a source of power, usually a battery, that supplies the microphone head with a consistent electrical signal. In this case, the consistent electrical signal is altered by the movement of air against a similar membrane.

A common method of powering condenser mics, as well as several other types, is the phantom powering system. *Phantom mics* provide a good, clean signal and are powered by the batteries in the recorder rather than an internal battery. Microphone cords have to be specially wired with the polarity reversed for the current to reach the mic. The phantom design is one you will encounter frequently.

Sound people tend to find a small number of mics with which they are comfortable. They can be very opinionated about microphones, with arguments about what constitutes the best mic getting emotional and vehement. You need to get past the hype to pick the right mic for a given situation. Try out as many mics as you can. Listen to mics side by side to get a sense of which one produces the cleanest and highest-quality signal. Remember that the recording chain is only as strong as its weakest link, and a good microphone is essential to a high-quality recording.

Audio Connectors and Microphone Cords

There are four basic types of audio connectors used in the United States: quarter-inch, mini, RCA, and XLR. You will occasionally find others, but they are generally associated with foreign-made, mostly European, pieces of equipment or specific brands of equipment. Japanese and American recorders tend to conform to the same standards.

Audio connectors and cords are all based on a simple connection. Most connectors have simple positive-to-positive and negative-to-negative contacts. On the standard plug-style connector, the tip of the pin is the positive, or "hot," contact and the shaft is the negative, or ground, contact. **SEE 13-10** Microphone cords are equally straightforward. A simple cable has a single *conductor* surrounded by *shielding*—a metal mesh that encases the conductors for the length of the cable. The single conductor is connected from one hot contact to the other, and the shield is used to connect the grounds. All connections are soldered. The plug end of a connector is traditionally referred to as the male end, and the input end is referred to as female. While some may find this usage of language peculiar or uncomfortable, it nevertheless remains the terminology of choice among audio people.

13-10

All audio connectors and cords are based on a simple negative/positive connection

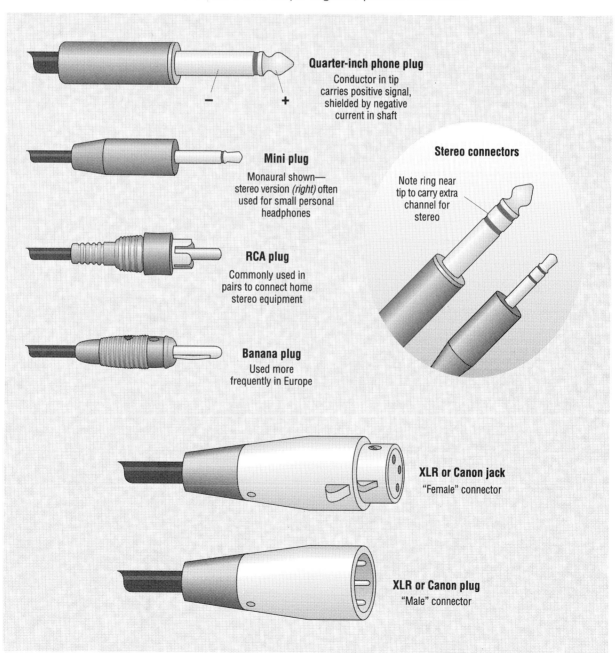

Quarter-inch phone plug
Conductor in tip
carries positive signal,
shielded by negative
current in shaft

Mini plug
Monaural shown—
stereo version *(right)* often
used for small personal
headphones

Stereo connectors
Note ring near
tip to carry extra
channel for
stereo

RCA plug
Commonly used in
pairs to connect home
stereo equipment

Banana plug
Used more
frequently in Europe

XLR or Canon jack
"Female" connector

XLR or Canon plug
"Male" connector

There are two types of audio inputs in general use in filmmaking applications: microphone and line. Mic inputs, of course, accept the signal from the mic. A line signal is of higher voltage and is exchanged either internally or between two machines. All the connections between recorders, mixers, and signal processors are line connections.

Mic and line connections are differentiated by the voltage level of their signal. Inputs are rated by their ***impedance***, which refers to the designed resistance to voltage in the line. Low-impedance microphones and thus inputs are standard. Line inputs are generally high impedance. Mic and line connections are not interchangeable. You cannot plug a mic into a line input or vice versa, unless you use an impedance transformer. These are usually available for circumstances when gear does not have the output or input needed. In filmmaking applications, however, most inputs are used for the purpose for which they were designed. The only other signal impedance of interest is with speaker connections.

Quarter-inch or phone plug   The durable and heavy *quarter-inch*, or *phone*, plug receives extensive use as both a mic connection and a line connection. Professional headphones are also usually equipped with quarter-inch plugs. The input requires quite a bit of dedicated space in the interior of the record deck, a possible reason why it is not as popular as it might be in consumer equipment.

Mini plug   A *mini plug* looks like a smaller version of the quarter-inch plug. It is generally used as a microphone input on consumer cassette recorders and video cameras. Its major drawback is that it is not very durable, particularly on the input end, which is on the recorder or camera. It is also prone to being accidentally pulled out of the recorder. The mini is also a common headphone jack, though rarely found on professional equipment.

RCA plug   The *RCA plug* is used almost exclusively as a line connection and is probably the most common type. It is found on everything from consumer stereos to VCRs. The center pin is the positive connection and the sleeve is the negative connection. The sleeve also allows for a tight fit on the line input.

XLR or Canon   The *XLR* (X=ground, L= left, R=right) plug has a three-pin configuration and is the standard mic connection on most professional equipment. It is also used for line connections in high-end studio gear. It is the norm because the three-pin configuration incorporates a second conductor to connect the grounds and uses the shield to protect the signal from electronic interference. The hot contact carries the signal, and the ground carries its opposite.

Banana plugs   These are used more frequently on European-produced equipment, particularly the Nagra. In a banana plug, the two leads are separated out into individual plugs. The plug has a flexible sleeve that constricts when inserted into the line input, thus holding it in place. The banana configuration is one of the key connectors used with the Nagra, although it does not show up that frequently on other equipment.

There are a number of other specialized pins, Tuchel pins and DIN pins to name two. Tuchel pins are used with the Nagra and often come with a "threaded sleeve"—a loose-fitting sleeve on the connector that screws into the body of the recorder. The DIN pin is a European connector found on older equipment, including the Uher recorder which was used extensively in sync recording, particularly in Super 8.

Adapters convert one type of plug to another, from a male mini to a female RCA, for instance. Anticipating all needs is always the goal, and having a good selection of adapters on hand can get you out of many tight situations.

Stereo and monaural (mono) are also important issues. The separate channel configuration of *stereo*, which consists of two separately recorded tracks on the same tape played back simultaneously, has become such a standard in home audio systems that the old single-signal *mono* has almost been forgotten by the consumer. Until recently, recorders designed for films recorded in mono because all individual sounds are treated separately in editing and the final product is usually mono. Advanced theatrical sound systems and transfers to video have complicated this issue, but sound for film is still frequently recorded in mono. Given that so much audio equipment is set up for stereo, this can cause problems matching equipment so that the signal is both transferred and monitored properly.

In line connections, the stereo signal is handled by two separate conductors, particularly the familiar, paired *stereo RCA* cords. There are single cords designed to carry the stereo signal, particularly quarter-inch and mini headphone plugs. As with a mono connector, the tip carries one channel; the shaft of the connector has a band just below the tip which is the contact for the second channel. The stereo cable has a separate conductor connected to this second contact. Stereo headphones plugged into a mono headphone jack will produce sound in only one ear. Adapters that convert the mono signal so it can be heard on stereo headphones are handy to have when different pieces of equipment are being used.

Stereo recorders have seen increased use in professional production in recent years because there is a growing feeling that a stereo recording allows more options in the editing. The mono system remains an adequate approach, although a wide release on video requires a stereo signal. If stereo separation is an issue, it can always be part of the audio design in the final mixdown. Nagra produced both a stereo and mono machine, and many schools have the older, traditional mono machines.

Recorder Features and Accessories

Sound recorders come with a variety of features, all designed to aid the sound person in creating the highest-quality recording possible while on the set. Although these features aid in controlling and manipulating the technical quality of the audio signal, your ear should be the final arbiter of the sound. You can make everything look fine on the recorder's displays, but if the mic is too far away, the result will be inadequate sound. If it doesn't sound good to your ear, it won't sound good when you try to plug it into your film. However, the same is true of the ear as was of the eye in lighting: just because it sounds good to the ear does not mean that you are getting the best recording possible. It has to be happening with both the ears and the displays. Being sensitive along with attentive to the evaluative tools is one mark of a good sound person.

Running speeds   Most professional recorders give a number of options for *running speed*, measured in *inches per second (ips)*. A typical professional quarter-inch recorder might offer speeds of 3¾, 7½, and 15 ips. Cassette players run at 1⅞ ips, with many professional decks offering a higher speed as an option. Higher running speeds produce higher-quality sound. The major reason for this is that a higher speed devotes more magnetic material to the sound per second. Another major consideration is consistent speed and stable transport across the head. Slower recording speeds are harder to keep constant, and the tape tends to wobble on the heads, causing "wow" and "flutter." Higher recording speeds are generally used because they afford greater stability. In fact, when sound was introduced to motion pictures, camera running speeds were bumped up from 16 fps to 24 fps, because the audio fidelity was unacceptable at the slower speeds. This is why films of the silent era look speeded up: they are being projected at the wrong speed.

Most recording is done at 7½ ips for dialogue scenes. The 15 ips speed runs through tape at high rates, and the extra speed does not translate to higher-quality sound in terms of the human voice. The difference, however, between 7½ and 3¾ is substantial, so the slower speed is rarely used. For the most part, the slow speed is present on professional recorders to facilitate non–film-related disposable recordings, recordings of meetings and similar events that may not even be saved much less destined for a final product. Music is usually recorded at 15 ips, as the reproduction of extended tones and notes requires the highest quality possible. Sound effects are usually recorded at 7½ ips, although they are the least needy in terms of perfect reproduction. Some consumer cassette decks offer an optional slower speed, ¹⁵⁄₁₆ ips, which should not be used for film under any circumstances.

Mic inputs   Professional recorders generally employ the XLR plug. Occasionally you will find a professional deck with quarter-inch inputs. Stereo machines have separate mic inputs, with each mic signal being fed to its own individual track. The older mono Nagras also have two mic inputs, with the signal being mixed internally. Some recorders have switchable mic inputs that can change to other impedances or microphone-powering methods.

Line inputs and outputs   Line connections are an important feature on any recorder. When recording subjects that are being amplified or require multiple mics, such as a rock band or someone speaking at a meeting, it is preferable to patch into the sound system being used. This should give good, clean sound, avoiding the acoustic effects of the amplified signal.

Record level adjustments   Recorders generally have twist knobs to control the record level of the sound. These are also called *potentiometers (pots)*, faders, or *gain controls*. A *fader* is the sliding control found on most mixing consoles. Stereo machines have a pot for each channel, as does the mono Nagra.

VU meter   The *VU (volume unit) meter* monitors the level of the audio signal being fed to the record head. It is the familiar scale on the front of all but the most rudimentary recording machines. **SEE 13-11** The microphone turns sound into electrical energy, which triggers the VU meter's needle. The needle registers the high—the peak—and low-amplitude points of the audio signal as it is expressed in

13-11

The VU meter shows the level of the audio signal being fed to the record head
Stereo VU meters on a Sony TC-D5M cassette recorder

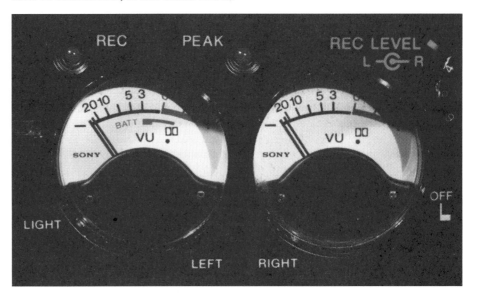

the electrical current. ***Zero VU (0 VU)*** is often presented as the point the signal should not exceed because of distortion, although this is not a completely accurate assertion. VU meters are imperfect tools because they are peak-averaging meters—they do not show all the high points of the recorded signal, only an average so that they are in position to respond to the next signal. This has led designers to leave **headroom** in the meters, that is, room above 0 VU where the recorder still reproduces an undistorted signal. Although there are different theories for recording various sounds, suffice it to say that professional sound people frequently record certain sounds substantially above 0 VU.

Peak program meter or modulometer   The *peak program meter (PPM)* is an improvement over the VU meter. It is featured on many high-end machines, most notably the Nagra, on which it is referred to as a ***modulometer.*** The *ballistics* of its needle are delicate enough to respond to all fluctuations in volume, giving an accurate reading of the signal at all times. Modulometers do not have a 0 VU point like standard VU meters. They have instead a 0 dB point that displays how far off an optimum recording you are. There may be slight headroom, given that distortion is not an absolute concept, but, unlike 0 VU, the 0 dB point on a modulometer is the effective limit past which distortion occurs. Sound people generally keep the signal slightly under this point to give room to respond to minor fluctuations in the signal.

While zero on either meter represents an important point in the consideration of distortion, it also represents an important qualitative point. It is roughly the point at which the recorded signal best covers the inherent noise of the recording system, better known as *hiss*. Many beginning sound mixers are so terrified by 0 VU on the meter that they tend to underrecord the signal, assuming anything is better than the dreaded distortion. If the recorded signal is too low, the sound may be overwhelmed by what is called the "noise floor" of the recorder and can eventually become unintelligible. Although the effect of system noise on the tape may not be immediately audible, sound has to go through a number of generations to reach a final sound track. Any hiss on the tape will be magnified in this process. Underrecording is actually worse than having the signal occasionally go above peak levels.

Effective recording can be done with either the VU or the modulometer, although the latter gives a more accurate depiction of the sound. The key is to know the capabilities of each.

Tape/direct   Most professional recorders offer a choice of how to monitor the sound as it is being recorded. Recorders with separate record and playback heads have a toggle switch that allows you to choose between monitoring the sound as it comes to the record head (*direct*, which is labeled "source" or "input" on some machines) or off the playback head *(tape)*. When monitoring in the *tape* position, the sound is recorded at the record head and then played back next to it at the playback head. Because of this, you will hear a slight delay between the actual live sound and the playback sound. This echo can be quite disconcerting for beginning recordists but, because there can be some difference between the microphone signal and the signal that is actually recorded, many recordists monitor in the *tape* position. They get accustomed to the delay and can feel confident in the quality of the final product. On a more mundane level, it also lets you know when you are out of tape. This is handy when you are on the move, working on documentaries or in difficult locations.

Headphones   Be sure to obtain a pair of headphones that give a complete representation of sound and isolate any confusing external noise. This means getting the padded, cup-shaped isolation headphones rather than cheaper pad or flat consumer models. Do not hesitate to pay for a high-quality set of headphones.

There are few things more foolish than using a $15 pair of headphones to monitor the recording of critically important sound on a $10,000 tape recorder.

Use headphones for all film applications, whether recording key production sound or seemingly innocuous background effects. The internal speakers on most production recorders, including the Nagra, are not of sufficient quality to monitor sound, and you probably won't have the time to go back and listen to something you have just recorded anyway. There is no effective way to detect minor flaws in the recording without headphones.

Two pairs of headphones are needed for the sound crew: one for the person recording and one for the person handling the mic. A simple Y adapter that splits the signal at the headphone jack is generally used, although you have to be careful that the signal fed to the headphones is not adversely affected.

Headphone volume controls and headphone jacks   These are relatively straightforward parts of the recorder but warrant a few comments. While recording on a set, be careful not to overcrank the headphone volume. The sound can bleed through and disturb the recording, particularly if you are monitoring in the *tape* position with the delay. This extra sound may render location recordings unusable; even if the bleed-through is quiet enough that it is not recorded, it may be disconcerting to the talent. Set the volume to a level that is both comfortable for you and an accurate reflection of the sound, without being audible to other people on the set.

When organizing the equipment for a shoot, check to see if you need stereo or mono headphones. Mismatched headphones and recorders will leave you with sound in only one ear and may cause volume level problems. Adapters are available to convert a mono output signal to stereo headphones, and having a few on hand is helpful if you need to plug into various pieces of equipment.

Automatic gain control   Referred to as the *automatic level control (ALC)* on the Nagra, **automatic gain control (AGC)** is available on many recorders, although it generally gives disagreeable results. The AGC reads the signal being fed to the record head and automatically adjusts the record level appropriately. The drawback is that AGCs tend to overrespond to peak and low signals, with frequent wide and seemingly uncontrolled swings of the record level, particularly with complex sound. The result can have a mechanical sound to it. It is somewhat like automatic exposure on a camera. You want to control the record levels just as you want to control the exposure. A number of high-end recorders have very sophisticated AGC features that anticipate these difficulties and minimize negative side effects. Even so, they are not used extensively. A good AGC feature can be useful in documentary situations, when you are working with a small crew and may have to leave the recorder unattended or cannot keep your eyes on the meter (a situation that generally should be avoided).

Limiters   A *limiter* adjusts peak signals that are liable to be distorted. It is used while manually setting the record level and kicks in during the occasional peaks that you cannot anticipate or respond to adequately. It is something like a cap that will not allow the signal to be recorded above a certain level, usually 0 VU or 0 on the modulometer. If used carelessly, it can lend the same mechanically manipulated quality to a recording as the AGC. When the levels are being carefully monitored, however, it can knock the top out of a signal that would otherwise be distorted.

Equalizers   An *equalizer* is commonly used to manipulate the quality of the sound, cutting or boosting it at specific frequencies. Equalizers are used to either clean up sound that has unwanted elements or add brightness or character to the production sound. While the goal is to record perfect production sound, conditions

13-12

An equalizer divides sound into bands, each of which centers on a specific frequency

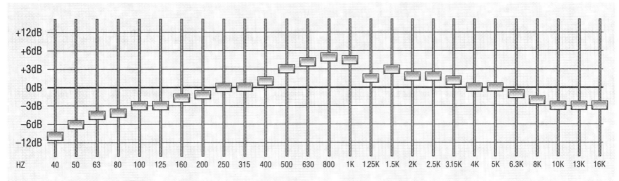

often make this virtually impossible. Equalization can add dimension to the sound that was impossible to obtain in the location recordings, although there are limits to what can be done.

An equalizer consists of controls that either boost or cut the amplitude of frequencies at specific Hz. The equalizer divides the sound into **bands**, each of which centers on a specific frequency that is controlled by either a fader or a twist knob. **SEE 13-12** The unit portrayed above equalizes the sound at twenty-seven different frequencies. Just as with the spectrum of audible sound, equalizers can be, and frequently are, broken down into octaves.

While the faders control amplitude at a specific frequency, those on either side of the selected frequency are also affected. Equalizers with more bands offer finer discriminations in affecting individual sounds and are generally more useful in film as well as most other audio applications. The equalizer shown in figure 13.12 separates the audible spectrum into many increments. Each band thus controls a narrow range of frequencies, having a relatively small effect on adjacent frequencies. Equalizers that separate the sound into a small number of bands affect an often unacceptably wide range of adjacent frequencies at each band.

Equalization is an important tool in transferring production sound to mag stock and in the mixing stages of a film. If you have an unwanted low-frequency sound, traffic rumble in the background, for instance, you could equalize certain low frequencies and limit or eliminate the sound. If there was an unavoidable high-pitch hum from fluorescent lights, you might be able to make it less objectionable by equalizing some high frequencies. These problems can be partially or completely eliminated in the transfer and then further addressed at the mix if necessary. Equalizers are often brought on location but, even then, it is a good idea to save most signal processing for postproduction. Conditions are generally not optimal for effectively monitoring sound, and thus it is difficult to be consistent with how the sound is manipulated. Like a DP's eyes, a sound person's ears can change over the course of a long day.

Although the transfer houses and mixing personnel can do amazing things, there are of course limits. Sound people occasionally get into the bad habit of depending on equalization later to eliminate blemishes that may be addressable in the recording. If the offending sound is too loud or covers too wide a range of frequencies, equalization may be a small Band-aid on a big wound. When you equalize at a specific frequency, you not only affect the desired sound but all other similar sound as well. If you have an actor with a particularly deep voice, for example, equalizing low frequencies to eliminate traffic ambience may create an unwanted change in the voice. Remember also that a wide range of frequencies exists in some form in any sound, and excessive equalization will change the character of a sound even when you are working on entirely different frequencies.

Bass voices devoid of high frequencies may sound muddy and unintelligible. High sounds are less affected by the absence of low frequencies, although voices can sound tinny and shrill.

Keep in mind that the equalizer, and the sideboard equipment in general, can be used to add specific character to the sound in the final stages of the film. Attempting to slavishly create the desired audio effect in the original recording is one of the biggest mistakes a mixer can make. A certain amount of this is all right, but the mixer must first and foremost produce a usable recording. If you want someone to be speaking from the other side of a closed door, the sound should be recorded clean. If the sound is recorded through the door, it may not be intelligible by the time it gets to the final sound track. As suggested at the beginning of this chapter, if the recorded sound is good, you can go almost anywhere with it, that is, make extensive adjustments in the mixing process. If the recorded sound is poor, the ability to manipulate it will be severely limited.

Having unaltered sound can be disconcerting for uninitiated viewers of the dailies and rough cuts. For this reason, sound mixers occasionally find themselves recording sound "for the dailies." This approach reflects an understandable fear of those unfamiliar with the process, often clients or potential funders. A friend tells the story of being called on the carpet by an inexperienced producer and client "to explain himself" for a clean recording of a sound that would be manipulated later. When he launched into a lengthy technical explanation, he was cut off and told to do better next time. Most people on the production team do, however, understand the technical requirements of sound.

Filters   The term *filter* has several connotations. The controls on equalizers are often referred to as filters, although they are used primarily for controlling the amplitude at desired frequencies. When spoken of outside of this usage, *filters* refer to options on the recorder that affect a wide range of frequencies above or below a certain point. Recorders often come with a few filtering options. The following are common choices, each cutting out a certain range of frequencies. Where exactly they start cutting the signal is dependent on how the individual filter is set by the manufacturer.

- *High-pass filters* filter out low frequencies, allowing high frequencies to pass through to the tape.

- *Low-pass filters* do the opposite, allowing low frequencies to pass while cutting high frequencies.

- *Low-frequency attenuators (LFAs)* cut low-frequency signals, *attenuation* being a common technical term for cutting.

- *High-frequency attenuators (HFAs)* cut the sound above a preset level.

Most location sound mixers do not do much filtering while recording sync takes. Filters affect quite a bit of the audio signal, changing the character of a wide range of sounds. They tend to be coarse controls, used as broad remedies for big consistent problems in the sound, such as traffic, fans, heating systems, and the like, that cannot be addressed by other means. However, if you can get to the source of the sound and shut it off, that is far preferable to filtering.

14

Recording Strategies

The Production Sound Crew

The sound crew has one of the more frustrating jobs on a film set because sound is rarely afforded the attention the camera and lighting receive. Because so many fellow crew members are devoted to the picture—camera crew, gaffer and grip crews, design people, makeup, script supervisor, and so on—the sound crew can feel substantially outnumbered and overwhelmed by picture people. There is a saying in the business: "An hour for picture, a minute for sound"—an accurate assessment of the weight given each endeavor in shooting a film. Because of this attitude, the sound crew may have to occasionally assert the importance of their endeavors in the general scheme of things.

Although this lack of attention can be exasperating for the sound crew, there is a certain amount of justification for it. If the sound recorded on location is not good, there are a number of viable remedies. If you do not get the picture, however, you have nothing. As suggested, location dialogue recording is often done with the knowledge that it will be replaced. Many sound effects are also done in post-production. Despite all this, everything should be done to get high-quality location sound, particularly for filmmakers with small budgets. When working with limited resources, dealing with inadequate sound can be an expensive, messy, and time-consuming process. Whenever you find yourself saying, "I can get that sound later," it is frequently easier to get it right then and there.

The sound crew is usually asked to do their job without disrupting the set. As shots are set up, the sound crew cannot expect the lighting crew to arrange the instruments in a way that facilitates their work, nor should they. If lighting makes it virtually impossible to boom, usually lighting from above, the sound crew may have to try a different approach to miking. However, all this does not mean that the sound crew should not be assertive when elements are conspiring to make recording high-quality sound next to impossible. There is a certain "deal with it" attitude on the part of many picture people that occasionally requires some forceful behavior modification.

The sound crew is generally composed of two people: the previously mentioned sound mixer and the ***boom operator***. On larger commercial productions, the sound crew may have the luxury of a third person, who is generally listed in the credits as a ***cable puller***. The cable puller helps with setup, keeps the microphone cords out of the way during the shot, and occasionally takes care of the ***sound logs*** (see page 359).

The mixer has four primary responsibilities: determining microphone positions for the best sound reproduction, addressing any excess noise that is interfering, determining how to best work with the acoustics of the shooting space, and monitoring audio levels for optimal recording. At the direction of the mixer, the boom operator generally handholds the mic on a boom above the heads of the talent. If characters are moving or if there is more than one person being recorded, the boom operator may have to incorporate substantial movement of the mic during a shot. As one might suspect, booming can be physically demanding, requiring stamina and good upper body strength. The physical stress is somewhat mitigated by the boom needing to be in position only for the generally short duration of the individual takes. The microphone cord should be cradled gently in the hands, making sure that cable noise does not become a problem.

It is the sound mixer's responsibility to formulate a miking strategy for each shot. Pursuing the primary goal of miking sound for motion pictures makes the sound crew's job appear easy. Although there are clearly other significant considerations, the three keys to successful miking are the same as those to a successful restaurant: location, location, and location. Get the microphone as close to the subject as possible. Given the complexity of many shots, this can be quite a trick. If the subject is far from the microphone, the mixer has to crank the record level. When the mixer has to crank the volume, the acoustics of the space and unwanted extraneous noise become an element. The closer the mic is, the more the recording can be focused on the subject.

The AD lets the mixer know what the next shot is going to be and what setups are being considered for the near future. As the scene is being blocked for the camera, the mixer should determine where the boom operator can stand and what mic movement will be needed. An experienced boom operator will have worthwhile input into this planning. The mixer may need to plant mics in the scene to catch characters at certain positions. Essentially, the mixer observes the entire shot and designs the miking so that the subject is always optimally recorded.

The boom operator needs to be aware of two problems of which he or she may be the source: casting boom shadows on the scene and allowing the boom to drop into the frame. The sound crew should handle as much of this as possible on their own, but these concerns frequently require consultation with the camera crew.

Boom shadows in the shot are unacceptable, and their presence demands that alternative miking positions be found. In conjunction with the mixer, the boom operator should pay attention to the lighting of a scene so the "path of least resistance" to the subject can be found, that is, where can the boom be positioned without casting shadows. Frequently, the boom operator's best path is going to be to come in from around the fill light. This keeps the mic out of the path of the key light, staying near the softest and most diffuse light.

The boom will always cast some shadows, and it is the camera operator who will identify which ones are in the shot and which ones fall harmlessly outside the frame. Be aware that there are many elements in the frame that demand the camera operator's attention; subtle shadows may be missed. If concerned about a shadow, the boom operator should tell the camera operator, who will check the shot or do an entire *walk-through*, an initial rehearsal in which the technical personnel and the actors walk slowly through a shot to identify potential problems, in this case looking specifically for errant shadows.

Boom mics dropping into the frame are a staple on late-night talk shows but are unacceptable in film applications. The boom must be positioned just outside the top of the frame. With the goal being to get the mic as close to the subject as possible, the boom operator needs to know exactly where the top of the frame is and have the mic hover just above it. Knowing some basic compositional principles helps in this regard. Individual DPs generally have consistent approaches to headroom. If you know what that approach is, you should be able to determine boom position without too much consultation. Inexperienced boom operators may be tempted to hold the boom so high that it could not possibly be in the shot. This mistake amplifies room ambience and compromises the quality of the sound. Simply find out what the limits of the frame are and stay just outside of them. In my booming days, I became so familiar with one DP's shooting style that we rarely spoke to each other on the set except to determine where to go to relax after the shoot.

In the final analysis, it is the camera operator's responsibility to identify both boom shadows and encroaching mics in the shot. It is the boom operator's responsibility to eliminate them. Both concerns are complicated by the shifting frame and the necessity to follow moving subjects with the boom. The shot has to be checked from beginning to end to ascertain that the boom is not presenting a problem anywhere. The camera crew will of course expect minimal interference from the boom operator but, in the pursuit of as high quality sound as possible, be assertive if the need arises.

Riding Gain

Riding gain refers to shifting the record level during each recorded take in order to respond to changing levels of sound. Whether it be an actor's voice or an effect, the volume of sound within a shot will most likely change. The mixer must constantly adjust the potentiometer (pot) to keep the meter's needle as close to zero as possible. **SEE 14-1** The modulometer, or meter, is the guide, and the mixer's attention should be completely devoted to the meter during takes. If you can see a mixer's eyes during rehearsals or takes, he or she is not doing the job properly. By constantly adjusting the pot, the mixer is able to obtain an optimum recording at all times. Learning the parameters of what needs to be done here is one of the first and most important goals for the inexperienced sound mixer.

14-1

Riding gain means shifting the record level during each take to respond to changing audio levels
The meter and needle on the Nagra

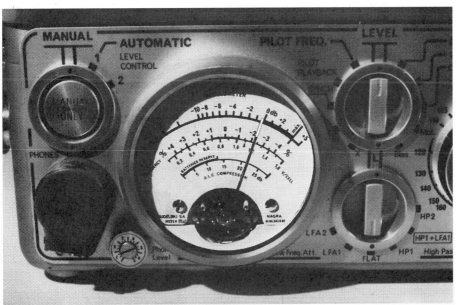

Just as there are rehearsals for the actors and the camera, recording of the sound needs practice as well. After getting a description of the shot from the AD, the mixer uses the first walk-throughs to ascertain what is occurring in the sound. In conjunction with the mixer, the boom operator develops a plan for booming the scene and then must be ready for the rehearsals. Just as the mixer has a plan for miking each setup, he or she must formulate a strategy for riding gain as well. During rehearsals, the mixer should practice all the movements of the pot. By the time shooting starts, the mixer should have all adjustments finalized and be able to anticipate all fluctuations in amplitude. Obviously there can be differences in individual performances by the talent, but the mixer should be able to keep the meter within accepted tolerances.

Most volume adjustments require only small movements of the pot, but occasionally there are times when a more dramatic response is needed. I was once recording an actor who whispered a line and then broke into a loud laugh. Even though I could get quite close with the mic, I had to turn the pot up almost all the way to obtain a usable recording of the whisper. When the loud laugh came, I had to turn the pot almost 180 degrees to get an undistorted signal. After several rehearsals, I had a sense of the actor's timing and was able to shift the pot at the right moment. The boom operator helped me by moving the mic slightly away from the actor just before the laugh came, although this response to a louder sound is not always the best one. If the movement of the boom is too big, it can cause problems with the different quality of sound created by a different mic position.

The approach to riding gain is very similar to that of anticipatory camera, except that the boundaries are less distinct. There is no frame line to watch through the viewfinder; the representations of the needle are the only guide, one that can start to feel quite abstract even though it represents something very real. Just as the camera leads subject movement, the recording of the audio should lead the fluctuating levels of sound. As with many elements, proper audio recording goes largely unnoticed; the listener recognizes that the sound recording has not been done properly only when there is a glaring error or something is unintelligible.

Keep in mind that the goal is always an optimum recording. Fear of distortion, again, often causes beginning mixers to mistakenly underrecord. Always keep the needle as close to zero as possible for all dialogue and effects. Occasional peaks above zero will not render the recording unusable, and a good limiter will soften any potential distortion. While the needles and meters give an accurate depiction of the technical quality of the signal, your ear should be the final arbiter of the sound. If it does not sound good on location, it will not sound good when you start trying to incorporate it in your film.

The biggest challenge in recording sync sound in conventional filming situations is the issue that has complicated so much of the task: continuity. Producing a clean signal clearly serves the requirements of continuity, and a "dirty" signal causes problems. Beyond that, if mic positions are wildly different or record levels fluctuate, consistency will suffer and production sound may prove uncuttable. Again, ensuring that the pieces are going to cut together becomes the determining factor.

Recording a Scene

As with everything else in film production, creating usable sound for a scene takes careful preparation and a measured and thoughtful approach. There are many things that complicate what appears to be, but of course isn't, a simple task.

Complicating Factors

Effective recording of a scene requires an understanding of how all the individual elements of sound are going to interlock. There are a number of complicating factors that need to be addressed before achieving this goal. With the exception of perspective and phasing, the following discussion outlines problems associated specifically with location filming, the controlled atmosphere of studio shooting eliminating many of these potential headaches.

Ambience concerns the sound crew in two different ways. The mixer generally wants to exclude as much ambience as possible in the original recording. The less ambience present in a take, the less likely it is to interfere with consistency. Ambience can always be added, but it is problematic to take it out. The second concern is that even though we have attempted to eliminate as much ambience as possible, the editors need some recorded ambient sound to cover silent or empty spots in the sound track. As suggested, every place in which you shoot will have its own distinct sound characteristics. Just as darkness is not the absence of light, silence is not a total absence of sound. Any gaps in the dialogue tracks, and there will always be some, must therefore be covered by recorded silence matching the ambience level that is under the dialogue. Variously called *presence* or *room tone*, several minutes of uninterrupted silence should be recorded by the sound mixer in each location.

Background noise is of even greater concern, often causing substantial problems with the consistency of the sound in editing. On location, problematic background interference is relatively common. The sound crew must locate and eliminate anything jeopardizing the recording. Sometimes this simply requires finding the source and shutting it off. Other problems may cause lengthy delays while the source gets out of hearing range. Some unsolvable problems may force replacement of the dialogue during postproduction. A location as free of unwanted sound as possible is particularly important when postdubbing is not a realistic option, whether for financial or other reasons.

Air-conditioning and heating systems frequently cause problems as do fluorescent lights, which make a highly undesirable hum, another reason to avoid shooting under them. Shooting in a restaurant or a kitchen requires turning off refrigerators and other noisy appliances, noisy neighbors may need to be quieted, and the guy down the street mowing his lawn may need some incentive to wait for another day.

More permanent problems can impose even greater demands. Shooting near heavy traffic areas or airport approaches can ruin sound takes and cause lengthy delays. As a sound such as an airplane recedes, the mixer lets the crew know that the sound has diminished enough to try a take. Given the odd path reflected sound can often take, this can be a risky proposition. Like the vagaries of the sun described earlier, such circumstances can turn four-hour shoots into eight-hour shoots. As suggested, postdubbing sound may be a foregone conclusion when working in completely untenable locations.

Camera noise can also be problematic, particularly when working with older cameras. The new generation of sync cameras, such as the Aaton and Arri SR, are generally not a problem, although in the pin-drop quiet of a set even they can be picked up on a sensitive microphone. Noisy cameras can be muted by modified blimping. Unfortunately, the camera lens tends to act like a megaphone for camera noise, shooting it right out in front of the camera which, as luck would have it, just happens to be right where the subject you are recording is. Although my suggestion of putting a sock over the lens has always fallen on deaf ears, the glass filters used to protect the front element of the lens can help with sound problems as well.

If the camera is noisy, it must be recorded with the space's ambience. Recording room tone without the camera noise is meaningless if it is contributing significantly to the sound in a space. And it must be recorded with the camera loaded, because a camera running empty does not sound the same. Some camera crews will go so far as to bring dummy loads in anticipation of camera noise. Barring this, recording sound during shots that do not require sync sound can be a good source for this sound. With this sound, the editor can then make the offending source consistent rather than having it irritatingly dropping in and out.

The need to cope with unwanted sound is the common thread. As you edit the film, you tend to find that the presence of unwanted sound in itself is not so much the problem, rather, it is the inconsistency of that sound. The variety of different mic positions and record levels employed will mean that each of these three problems—ambience, background noise, and camera noise—will sound different from one setup to the next. Listeners may accept some background noise, but when its amplitude and character jump at every cut, it becomes very unnatural and noticeable. Many of these problems can be covered by music or some other consistent effect. But when music or effects are employed to cover things rather than to follow some internal logic in the script, they can be distracting as well.

While unwanted sound must be addressed, remember that some sounds, particularly consistent ones, can be equalized in the transferring and mixing stages. A huge generator at a carnival once caused me major headaches. I recorded the generator by itself for a minute and from this the transfer house was able to isolate the frequencies and eliminate most of the problem. Similarly, camera noise is usually isolated around a specific frequency and is consistent enough that it can often be equalized out in the transfer to magnetic film stock. Transfer house personnel must be alerted to problems in the production sound. This is done on a sound report and by clearly marking the tape's packaging. However, do not depend on repairing problems in later stages. As suggested, there are limits.

Wind noise is a slightly different type of unwanted sound that is frequently problematic. Wind is similar to sound in that it is moving molecules in the air. If not taken into account, it can play havoc with microphones, causing such a strong signal to be fed to the recorder that distortion is unavoidable. A ***wind zeppelin***, also called a ***wind shield***, has a baffle design that cuts much of the interference from wind. **SEE 14-2** Many zeppelins have an additional ***windsock*** that fits around the exterior for high-wind situations. Moving air in interiors can be an issue as well, mostly through air-passage systems associated with heating or air conditioning. Using a zeppelin or a simple slip-on foam wind shield to protect against moving air is common. Be particularly careful of wind noise in spontaneous shooting situations, documentary shoots for instance, where you cannot monitor the recorder's meter. In the *direct* position, the distortion caused by wind noise will often go unheard, although it does show on the meter. Be sure to monitor in the *tape* position, hearing the actual signal that has been recorded, when wind is an issue.

Acoustics refers to the way sound travels in a given space and particularly to how it reflects off surfaces before arriving at the microphone or ear. **SEE 14-3** It is one of the greatest challenges to the sound crew. Spaces are frequently referred to as being either "live" or "dead." A live space has many hard surfaces off which the sound bounces. The sound thus comes to the microphone at different rates and from many different directions. Although the sounds reaching the mic are only milliseconds apart, this accounts for sound that has a boomy, echolike character. School gymnasiums and museum exhibit rooms are classic examples of live spaces, as are bathrooms and tiled kitchens. Dead spaces usually have many absorbent surfaces, such as plush couches, bedspreads, and particularly carpets. This substantially reduces reflected sound arriving at the microphone.

14-2

A wind zeppelin, or shield, has a baffle design that cuts much of the interference from wind

Rycote™ wind zeppelin

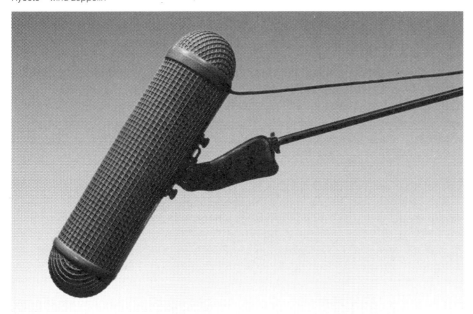

    In most instances, the mixer wants the space to be relatively dead. Like ambience, some liveness can always be put back into a recording but it cannot be effectively taken out. To this end, acoustic characteristics can be altered. The sound mixer supplies sound blankets or other acoustic material to deaden live spaces; the grips frequently help put the blankets up on C-stands. Put up as many as possible, but if you have only a few, putting them directly in front of the speaker is the most effective position. Hardwood floors are notoriously difficult surfaces. If the floor is not in camera view, laying down blankets or spare carpet can be effective. Miking as tightly as possible is also important. The resultant lower record level will lessen the recording of the lower-amplitude reflected sound.

14-3

Working with acoustics is one of the greatest challenges to the sound crew

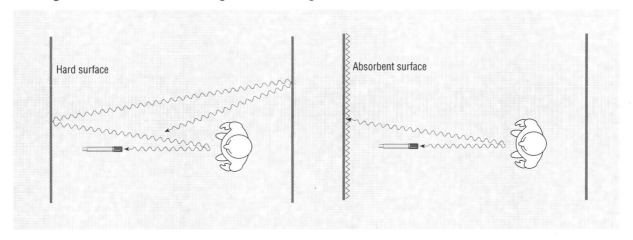

Changing the acoustic characteristics of a location depends on the space, your resources, and how much the sound crew is expected or allowed to do. To effect a change in a small space is within reason. Changing the acoustic characteristics of Grand Central Station might be possible, but not when sensible alternatives exist. Suffice it to say that acoustics complicates recording clean location sound.

Clearly, this issue involves expectations. If a scene takes place in a school gymnasium, an audience would expect the sound to have a boomy acoustic character. However, although the signal you record in a gym will have that quality, it may not be usable. If there is too much confusion on the tape, a poor signal is just going to get worse. Producing an intelligible recording may require a different strategy.

Sound perspective refers to the way we expect to experience sound at specific proxemic positions. In a close-up, the viewer expects to be very near to the sound. When a character is in a long shot, the expectation is that the voice will sound more distant and the ambient sound of the location will be a more significant factor. The voice of a character speaking from the other side of a door will have a specific character.

The key is to remember that the sound should always be recorded cleanly, whatever the perspective characteristics desired for the final product. Excessive distance from the mic may produce an unusable recording. Having some perspective in a recording, however, is unavoidable and is not necessarily negative. Long shots often have more headroom than close-ups and, barring using wireless mics, getting a mic the same distance away as the close-ups may not be possible. Just plan to get the mic as close as possible, and slight differences in perspective will probably be acceptable.

Phasing is a complex phenomenon in which specific frequencies are canceled out and thus not recorded. It can affect sound waves before they strike the microphone or, when using more than one microphone, the electrical signal as it passes through the recorder's circuitry. In the first case, when a sound wave is met by a wave of the opposite shape, they balance out movement in the air pressure thus negating each other. This kind of phasing, from the source to the microphone, is uncommon in most film recording and is difficult to control anyway. The second case, phasing in the electrical signal, occurs when signals from separate microphones meet in the recorder's circuitry and cancel each other out. This is dependent on how microphones are positioned in relation to each other. Though there can be a sophisticated science to phasing, trying the mics in different positions is a solution whenever a problem is heard.

Phasing is one reason why mixers try to use a single microphone whenever possible. Using two microphones with similar pickup patterns, particularly the shotguns, can create some of the most baffling phasing effects. Phasing is not always a bad thing. Highly skilled sound technicians can position microphones to set certain frequencies, such as those associated with ambient traffic sounds, "out of phase." But for the beginner, phasing is generally a negative factor, eliminating important frequencies that can dramatically alter the character of the sound. With the goal being consistency, anything that changes the character of the sound poses a problem.

Any one these concerns can cause major headaches when trying to produce usable production sound, so potential problems must be addressed before effective recording can occur.

Sync Recording

Like the lighting crew, the sound crew must be prepared for all eventualities. Although not always afforded the luxury, the mixer can evaluate a location and plan out an approach that will ensure optimal sound. If this preparation is possible, the mixer should be able to deal with acoustical problems, quickly identify and eliminate unwanted sound, and determine a strategy for miking the scene. And though there are as many miking strategies as there are setups, a few common approaches should give direction.

Again, the primary goal in sound recording for motion pictures is to get the microphone in the optimum position for recording the source. In practice, this presents many complications and roadblocks. The more complicated the shot, the more difficult the boom operator's job is. As suggested, the sound crew will mic each setup with a single mic on a boom whenever possible. Avoiding phasing is a major reason for this, but a single high-quality mic simply produces a cleaner, less complicated signal. The mixer will try to employ just one mic for entire scenes as well. Using mics from different manufacturers or with different pickup patterns to record different setups in the same scene can cause consistency problems. If another mic needs to be incorporated, it is generally done with the first mic kept slightly open to give the sound the same character as the rest of the scene.

Booming from above is preferred. It gives the cleanest, most natural sound and, with the mic pointed down, excludes excessive noise from the background of the shot. Booming from below is an alternative when lighting or location interference force it, but this position usually amplifies bass frequencies. *Plant mics*, which are "planted" in the shot, can be useful; wireless mics are also occasionally employed.

Barring difficulties with unwanted sound, booming and recording a single, stationary subject is relatively simple. Just as the camera operator needs to adjust for body position, the boom operator must be prepared for the minor movements conducive to a fluid performance. The boom should be held above the talent's head, and the mic brought in as close to the mouth as possible. To avoid clicking and swallowing sounds, the mic should be pointed several inches in front of the talent's mouth rather than straight-on. Sound "flows" out of the mouth, and the mixer should receive a good strong signal no matter how loud the talent's delivery.

When movements or multiple characters are introduced, the challenge increases. If characters are in close proximity to each other, pivoting and swinging the mic back and forth between them for each line of dialogue is usually the best approach. **SEE 14-4** To facilitate movement, the mic is cradled in a *shock mount*, a

14-4

Pivoting a single mic back and forth between two characters is usually the best approach

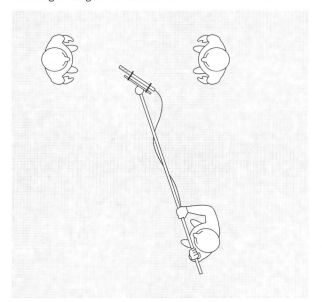
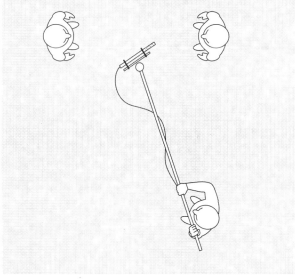

suspension system that absorbs any moderate shaking of or shocks to the boom. Even with a shock mount, move the mic gently to reduce excessive rattling of the mic and thus the likelihood of producing unacceptable sound. Be careful of windlike noises as well. If the mic has to be swung so fast that it creates noise, a different miking arrangement should be tried. A wind shield may help with quick movements, but there are limits to how fast you can go. The mic cable must be gripped so it does not rattle against the boom, but it should not be tightly stretched across the boom—it should be loose, but not so loose that it flaps around.

When characters are separated by some distance, which oddly enough does not occur that frequently, it may be necessary to use two mics. Using shotgun mics together is generally a mistake, so two booms would *not* be employed. Putting one character on the boom and the other on a plant mic is one viable solution. Hide the plant mic where it can pick up the needed dialogue. Boundary layer microphones (BLMs) are expressly designed for this purpose, although they are quite expensive. These small, flat mics can be set on a piece of furniture or taped to the ceiling. High-end versions have interchangeable mic heads that control the shape and direction of the pickup pattern. In lieu of a BLM, a simple lavalier planted at a specific location of the set can accomplish roughly the same thing.

Subject movement requires the boom to follow or, more accurate, lead the subject through a space. **SEE 14-5** Just as with anticipatory camera, boom operators use the rehearsals to monitor subject movement and find a way to always have the mic in front of the performer(s). Except for minor adjustments, as a boom operator you should never react to anything that happens; you should always lead the movement. You may be able to mic small movements from a single position by simply extending your arms. Larger movements require you to move along with the situation. When a character moves from one point to another, you have to lead

14-5

Subject movement requires the boom to lead the subject through a space

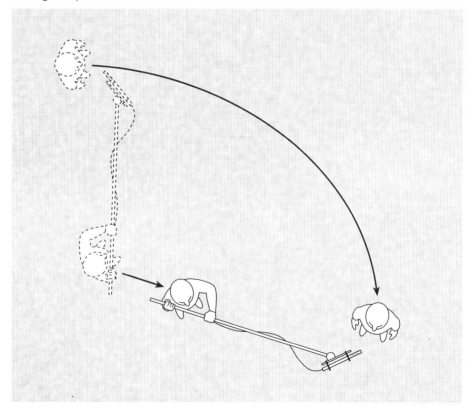

the subject from one point to the next. This is easiest when you can incorporate a swing of the boom with your own small movement.

Boom operators generally try to lead as much of the movement as possible by swinging the boom, keeping their own movement to a minimum. To maintain the correct mic position, you must keep your eyes on the performers as the shots are being executed. Given the "grip jungles" that are often created, planning your footing so you don't trip or run into things is a necessity. In walk-throughs, as a boom operator you must quickly determine where you are going and how to get there.

If the movement is broader, for instance characters moving in front of a dollying camera, you will have to walk backward or sideways when leading. **SEE 14-6** Cabling can be tricky on shots like this. The slack created during the move can trip you. A cable puller is in charge of coiling the cable as the shot is being executed, making sure that no one gets fouled up in the excess. Barring that, the mixer may have to pull the cable with one hand while riding gain with the other.

Despite the need for some fancy footwork, these movements are still relatively straightforward. However, subject movement can occasionally put the actor in a position where effective booming is impossible. One scene I mixed began with a character saying several lines of dialogue in a standard medium shot. He then turned away and started shouting while pounding his fists on a table, venting his anger. The table was up against a window, and the shouted lines were delivered directly into the tabletop, making booming impossible. My solution was to hide a lav on the windowsill, positioning it so it was pointing directly at the actor's mouth. The boom handled the first lines, and the lav, with the pot turned very low, handled the shouting. In a situation like this, the pot for the boom is turned down as the lav is brought up. In this particular case, the boom mic was left partially open to maintain a consistent quality in the ambience.

14-6

For broad movements, such as characters moving in front of a dollying camera, the boom operator has to walk backward or sideways when leading

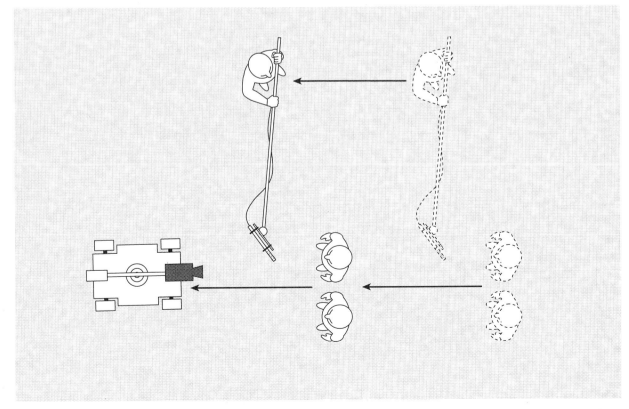

I once boomed a scene that provided a good example of this. **SEE 14-7** The scene took place in a hospital room and involved a woman talking to her ailing husband. To portray the tension, the actor playing the wife wanted to have full freedom to pace around the set. The director wanted to shoot the entire three-minute scene in master (an irritating habit of first-time directors that places heavy physical demands on the boom operator). The whole scene could be boomed with some movement on my part, except for a brief segment in which the actor nervously fiddled with a plant as she spoke. With the woman's back to the mic and her face virtually buried in the plant, the boom was unable to pick up her dialogue. We ran a lav under a window curtain and pushed it right up the middle of the plant. The actor was told not to be too rough with the plant, and her lines were picked up perfectly.

These are just a few representative examples. Many setups are easy to boom whereas others will test all your skills. Steadicam has made life more difficult for the humble boom operator. The ability to follow characters from room to room or even floor to floor with the camera means following with the mic as well. Going through doorways presents a significant challenge. In this situation, two booms might be used, with the signal from the mics being "handed off" in a cross-fade when moving from one room to another. Wireless mics are often the only solution when movements are more involved.

Recording and miking is about anticipation and problem solving. The sound mixer has to determine the best way to mic a scene and then practice the best way to record it. The mixer is generally not as vocal as the DP, but will on occasion have to speak up. If, for instance, the latch sound from a door closing is interfering with a line, be sure the door is muffled in some way. If the door's hinges are squeaking, have them oiled. If an actor's shoes are making too much sound on a hard floor,

14-7

In cases of complicated movement, a subject may need multiple mic setups

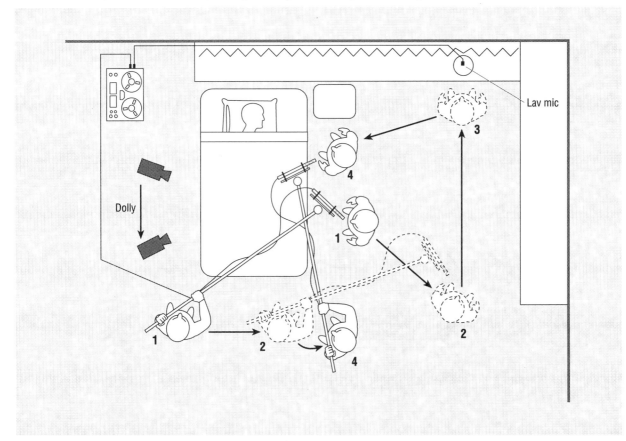

have the shoes removed or lay down a blanket. Anything causing a problem with the sound must be addressed.

Automated Dialogue Replacement

Automated dialogue replacement (ADR) is a method of creating and replacing dialogue in postproduction, a process that used to be referred to as *looping*. This is done when recording high-quality production sound is not possible or when a better reading is desired from the actor. The shot or shots that need this treatment are cut into a loop with a set of visual cues. The actor sits in a soundproof booth with the loop projected on a screen. The actor has a set of headphones that play back the original sound preceded by three short tones that correspond to the visual cues. With these cues, the actor can anticipate the visual and time the reading of the lines to the film. The actor does as many readings of the line as the director of the session feels are necessary. Each reading is dropped onto a synced tape, and the editor can later choose the desired take.

If ADR is not feasible, the sound mixer should have the talent read the dialogue in a quiet place. The director may want to be present to ensure that the delivery conforms to expectations. The editor will later position this new sound against the appropriate visuals. Although this is the hard way to approach it, a talented editor can generally make it work. Whether using ADR or the latter method, recording a *scratch track* should be done on location. This means that the mixer records a conventional sync track, even though it will not be used in the final film. It is recorded to serve as a guide for the actor in postdubbing or for the editor, who positions specific words and effects against the picture.

A number of years ago, I worked on a film in which a lovely spontaneous shot happened during a lull in shooting. In the film's story, a young boy was stranded on a broken Ferris wheel. As we were in one of the often unavoidable delays, the AC asked the boy if he knew any songs, and he launched into "Help Me Rhonda"— the Beach Boys standard. He was much too far from my mic to get any usable sound, but I recorded it anyway, knowing it would be useful. I later took the boy aside and had him sing the song into the microphone. The editor was able to use the barely audible scratch track as a guide to matching the words of the song with the words recorded later.

All this said, it is important to get high-quality production sound, particularly when working on independent or student projects. Replacing dialogue is expensive and can be difficult for inexperienced talent. The experience of being in an ADR booth can be somewhat akin to spending a day in a sensory deprivation tank. There is no input except seeing and hearing the same lines repeated over and over. When the actor starts having out-of-body experiences à la *Altered States*, you know that that is all you are going to get done that day. Recording usable production sound at the outset reduces costs and unneeded hassle in the editorial process.

Sound Effects

The number and employment of *sound effects (SFX)* is, of course, up to the postproduction team. Some situations require sparse, minimal sound whereas others demand highly dense and layered sound. Sound effects often go virtually unnoticed by the viewer, but most films would seem empty without them. Hampered by limited time and experience in editing rooms, sound effects studios, and mixing houses, student and independent films often have sound that is "thin," particularly when compared with the dominant trend of lush sound tracks in commercial feature films. Although individual films call for different approaches, creating sound that is full and natural is frequently the goal.

The selection and cutting of sound effects is an integral part of the entire effect of a film, both in terms of augmenting indifferently recorded sync effects, such as doors opening, footsteps, and so on, and in adding dimension to the texture and flavor of a scene. Mics are usually positioned to record dialogue, often leaving sync effects dull or inadequately recorded. Frequently, the actual sound the actions produce is not particularly interesting. Being prepared to replace effects recorded on location is common, with going into the studio to improve something almost the norm. In addition, virtually all off-screen effects—those that are not generated by some action in the shot—are recorded later and positioned by the editor in the appropriate place against the visuals.

Recording Effects on Location

On large commercial projects, the producers may be planning a sophisticated sound-effects campaign, and the need to consider sound effects may be limited. On smaller films, it is sensible to get the effects then and there, when you have all the elements needed to produce the sound assembled. Planning to record effects later or using sounds from an effects library is a perfectly good approach if the resources and personnel are there to do the work. However, creating sound in post is a difficult process with limited resources, and sounds from effects libraries can require extensive searching and often do not have the feel of being designed for specific situations.

Often, the perfect effect is right in front of you on location. For one scene, we needed sounds of a crowd milling about in a barn. I suggested to the AD and director that we take a few minutes and get the needed sound, but they felt we were too far behind schedule to devote time to getting an effect that could be recorded in post. Once we got into post, finding and creating a sound that had the appropriate acoustic characteristic became a major headache. I finally had to get a bunch of people together and drive back to the barn. I am sure the producer had some choice words for me when he saw my bill.

The sound mixer should be familiar with the script to anticipate and record needed effects. As shooting proceeds, the mixer should make a list of all the effects. The sound crew is rarely afforded the luxury of stopping the whole production to collect sound. Some effects can be done during a lull in the shooting, or just after a shot as the camera crew is checking the gate. Gathering part of the talent or crew after the day's shooting can also be effective. I once worked on a film that was supposed to take place in the 1840s. It was plagued by the sounds of a nearby modern urban center. All kinds of effects from ax chops to footsteps in the forest were on my list. We simply set our alarms for three in the morning and went out and got all we needed while the city slept. To go back later and re-create these effects would have meant the investment of substantial time as well as creating the potential for delays in the editing process.

Foley

The Foley room is similar to the ADR room, but with more space for the active process of creating effects. The activities of the Foley room surely resemble the efforts of crews for the old radio programs, a variety of voice artists and sound-effects people banging garbage can lids and running in place. The Foley room is outfitted with a variety of surfaces to re-create footsteps on carpet, gravel, tile, and so on. There are also numerous objects available to create different sounds, from creaking doors to broken glass to squeaky chairs. The Foley artists watch the projected picture and create an appropriate effect at the precise moment. What they produce is recorded on a synced tape that is easily dropped into the film. They also have access to a variety of prerecorded effects, which can be tested against the looped picture.

While commercial films may achieve effects through Foley, many filmmakers just go out and create the effects needed. In the absence of a soundproof booth, it may be hard to find a quiet place to do the effects. Again, recording effects at three in the morning when passing traffic is limited is not a bad approach. It is amazing what tasty effects you can whip up in your kitchen late at night.

The sound-effects campaign in independent and student films is often neglected and left for last. In many situations, someone, often the editor or an assistant, goes out with a recorder and tries to drum up a few quick effects. It is no surprise that these effects are often inadequate. Get someone who understands the requirements involved in successfully creating and competently recording sound effects. If you are in a city with an active professional filmmaking community, you may find a Foley artist who will cut you a deal. The services of a competent professional could be the difference between effects that are bland and effects that add flavor and character to your film. Just like the backgrounds of shots, this underlayer of sound often constitutes the difference between a one-note, single-dimension film and a rich and complex work.

Sound Transfers

Recording to magnetic stock is a specialized process that can be done only with the appropriate equipment. This transfer is usually made at a professional facility, often the same one that will do the final audio mixdown. The mag stock recorder is set up like the camera, a set of sprocketed rollers feeding the mag stock across the record head just like the film and the gate minus the pull-down claw. **SEE 14-8** Mag machines run at 24 fps, although they are not set up for a true crystal 24. Sync is provided by an electronic interlock of the tone recorded down the center of the tape on the Nagra. Mag stock is available in 35mm, 16mm, and, though seldom employed, Super 8.

An audio signal from virtually any source can be transferred to the magnetic stock. Traditionally, cassette, quarter-inch, LP, or compact disc are the source media; however, any equipment with an audio line output, from a video deck to a

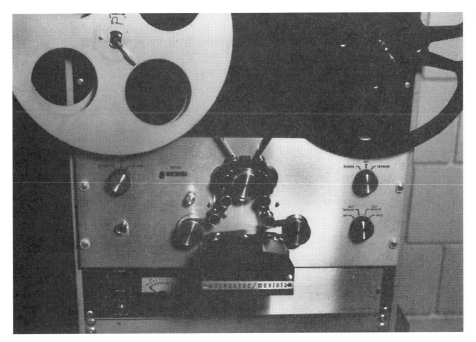

14-8

The mag stock recorder is set up like the camera, a set of sprocketed rollers feeding the mag stock across the record head—just like the film and gate

Moviola/Magnasync mag stock recorder

synthesizer, could be used. Record original narration, effects, and music on audio-tape first rather than straight onto the mag stock.

Again, each sound is transferred individually to the magnetic stock. Transferring everything except the clearly unusable recorded sound is standard procedure. This leaves the selection of individual sounds to the editor. Although it means transferring quite a bit of material, the selection process is done only once rather than twice.

Many schools and media arts centers have individual transfer machines, which can save substantially on transfer charges. However, be aware that most of these machines cannot be serviced and maintained at a level comparable to a professional facility. With sound that requires the best reproduction possible, dialogue and music in particular, it is generally better to spend the money for a professional transfer.

Cleaning and Repair

As important as cleanliness is in other realms, it is crucial in sound as well. The biggest concern is keeping the record head and the other heads clean. There are commercial cleaning solutions that can be applied with a cotton swab. This should be done before shooting every day, and maybe once more on a busy day. These solutions should not be applied to the rubber capstan roller, as they will eventually dry the rubber out.

Demagnetizing heads should also be done frequently. The constant tape movement can make the record head develop a magnetic charge that must be removed with a demagnetizer, which is available commercially. The recorder must be turned off during this process. The demagnetizer is turned on several feet from the recorder and brought in to the heads without touching them. It is then pulled away from the recorder and turned off when it is at least four or five feet away.

Mic cables must also be kept clean, and connections must have integrity. The dust on dirty mic cables can actually build an electric charge that can disturb the signal. Connections are equally important. Being able to troubleshoot audio takes a basic knowledge of signal paths. The theory behind a mic cable is quite simple. The cable can be checked with a multimeter, an inexpensive meter that tests batteries as well as having other important functions. Using the meter function for testing *ohms*, you can check for resistance in a line, that is, whether or not you have a connection. This function can be used to check virtually any electric or electronic connection that needs testing. When touched together, the ground and hot leads from the meter give a reading on the display. By touching the leads, you complete a circuit. To test any other circuit, you simply put the connection to be tested in sequence with the ground and hot leads. Touch one tester lead to the hot on one end of the audio plug and then touch the other tester lead to the hot on the other end of the cable—from the tip of one quarter-inch plug to the tip of the other end, for instance. You can find adequate multimeters for around twenty dollars, although good ones cost four to five times that much.

It is not uncommon to set up the recorder on location and get no signal on the meters, particularly when you are just learning the vagaries of sound. Being able to follow and test the logic of the signal path will help you go into the chain and identify the problem. A kit with jeweler's screwdrivers, a soldering iron, and solder is useful if a connection has gone bad. Always bring extra cords for quick testing and replacement.

15

The Setup

THE execution of the setup is a complex process of solving the many problems with which you will be confronted. Many concerns regarding the overall quality of the image have to be resolved before the camera can roll. This chapter delineates some of the necessary considerations for individual setups.

The setup generally represents hours of preparation which includes the devotion of extensive resources, both human and monetary. Conventional theatrical films usually evaluate a day's work by the number of script pages completed, but they also evaluate their efficiency in terms of number of setups executed. A crew on a *feature* film—anything above roughly seventy minutes and intended for commercial release—that averages twelve to fifteen setups a day will generally be considered acceptably efficient. Episodic television crews must work much faster. Given the small number of shots and the intense expectations invested in each of them, crews shooting television commercials often work much more slowly. Independents, due to restricted budgets and limited time with locations and talent, often have to average twice as many setups per day as a standard feature.

Just as a day's work can be measured in terms of setups, an entire film can be similarly measured. Psychological dramas with slow, contemplative editing might average somewhere around 800 setups for the entire film. An action film with fast-paced editing can easily have double that number. Robert Rodriguez's *El Mariachi* (1993) reportedly had almost 3,500 setups, an extraordinary number given the film's minuscule budget. Woody Allen's *Annie Hall* employs slightly fewer than 400 individual shots in its final form. Although Allen reportedly shot much more material than this (more setups), the figure illustrates much about his working method. Some of the film's most famous scenes—the film critic in the ticket line, Alvy and Annie chasing lobsters in the kitchen—are done in single, extended shots. Jim Jarmusch's *Stranger Than Paradise,* in which every scene is done from a single camera position with no cuts, consists of roughly 70 setups.

A setup does not necessarily cover just one part of the script. Like the master shot from the diner scene in Jonathan Demme's *Something Wild,* the material from one setup can be spread out throughout a scene. The material generated can even be used throughout an entire film. *Intolerance* (1916), D. W. Griffith's classic study of persecution throughout the ages, is regularly interrupted by shots of Lillian Gish rocking a cradle. This represents one setup from which all the shots of this action were obtained. Gish stated that she spent less than one afternoon completing her entire part in the more-than-three-hour film.

The Take

Scenes in a script are broken down into shots, which translate to setups for shooting. These setups are numbered so they can be marked and then logged. Each setup is then covered in *takes*, the number of attempts at each shot needed to produce at least several usable versions.

The Slate

The slate is used for organization in shooting, easy identification of the shots in editing, and matching production sound and the picture. It consists of a board for writing pertinent information and a striped bar across the top that is slapped at the beginning of every sound take. **SEE 15-1** This hit of the slate, referred to as marking the scene, is the reference point for syncing the sound.

There are two common methods of numbering the scenes on the slate. The first is to number all shots sequentially from the first day of shooting. Slate numbers would run from #1 for the first shot on the first day of filming to the last shot on the last day, the final number depending on how many individual setups the film had. This method is perfectly acceptable, although it can become difficult to manage for those inexperienced with dealing with many days of shooting. The second method is to use the scene numbers as listed in the shooting script combined with letters designating the position of the shot within the scene, probably a more logical system for novices. The opening master for scene #80 might be listed as #80A. A close-up in the middle of the scene might be #80F. The closing master might be #80R. Whatever the numbering method used, the shot is identified by both scene and take when the clapper/loader marks each scene. "Scene 80C, Take 5" would denote the fifth take of scene #80C in the shooting script.

The science of slates and slating has advanced dramatically in recent years. Time-code (see page 472) slates are common, with LEDs providing a constant, rolling readout of time. The rolling clock stops for a moment when a time-code slate is slapped, freezing on a number that is later used to sync picture and sound. Tie-tack or lapel slates are also popular. Worn by the sound person, they emit a light when a button is pressed, with a matching tone being sent to the recorder. The old-fashioned slap-style slate, however, remains popular.

15-1

The slate is used for organization in shooting, easy identification of shots, and matching production sound and the picture

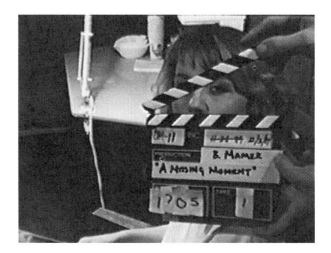

Executing the Shots

The sequence of events to initiate a shot may vary slightly from set to set but is usually something like the following. The director, or the AD on some sets, will call for sound. The sound mixer turns on the recorder and, upon seeing the speed indicator on the recorder (the "Speed & Power" butterfly on the Nagra), will yell out, "Speed." The director will then call for camera. The 1st AC hits the trigger and will call out, "Rolling," once the speed indicator flashes (a red light on many cameras). The director will then call for the slate. The person with the slate, the 2nd AC or clapper/loader, will call out the numbers and hit the slate. The director will then call for action. Each scene ends with a "Cut" from the director.

The sequence is a set of calls and responses:

Sound: Speed

Camera: Rolling

Mark it: Scene one, take one, hit of slate

Action:

Cut.

Hollywood tradition dictates that the scene and take numbers be said before hitting the slate, but it is recommended here that this information be stated after the hit. This is a slightly unorthodox approach, but it makes syncing sound and image a little easier, particularly for the novice (see page 411).

Marking a scene appears to be a straightforward matter, but a number of factors must be considered to make sure that the appropriate people can see the slate. The entire slate should be recorded, but it is the hit of the bars is the crucial piece of information from the camera operator's perspective. This is what the editorial staff needs to match sound and picture. All the issues that are important to the shot itself are essential here: exposure, proximity to camera, focus, framing, and so on.

If the scene has a dark film noir tone, the slate could potentially be held in an area too dark for adequate exposure. In this situation, the gaffer will set up a slate light, the sole purpose of which is to illuminate the slate as the scene is being marked. The light is switched off before action is called.

Having the slate numbers large enough to be read is also an issue. The general rule is to keep the slate 1 foot from the camera for every 10 millimeters of lens length. The slate should be 5 feet from the camera for a 50mm lens and so on. This can lead to focus problems when the action is some distance from the camera, but is usually resolved by having the AC rack focus from the slate to the action after the scene is marked.

Most of all, the framing must include the bars at the top of the slate. This is usually a simple matter, but mistakes are often made in tight close-ups, where there may not be room for the entire slate in front of the subject. It may also be a problem when you are "running and gunning," shooting quickly due to lack of time or because of involvement in a spontaneous event. In the first case, this may require a pan from the slate to the subject after the scene is marked, often requiring a rack focus in the process. In the second, taking a few seconds to get the slate right will prevent headaches for the editors. Whatever is necessary, the bars must be visible.

The clapper/loader should be in position, ready to hit the slate when the camera is rolling. Trying to find the correct position while the camera is running wastes precious film. The camera operator uses hand signals to guide the clapper/loader into position before the take starts, spoken directions being superfluous for two people facing each other. Once the scene is marked, the clapper/loader should know where to go and get there quickly. In exiting, casting a shadow on the scene or walking in front of the camera is discouraged, as is making excessive noise while moving.

Some shots require different methods of slating. *Tail slates* are useful in certain situations. Because the slap of the bars can be disconcerting for inexperienced talent, particularly documentary subjects and children, the tail slate is done at the end of the shot. Sometimes it is simply more convenient. The clapper/loader inserts the slate at the end of the shot and marks it there. The slate is held upside down and bar is slapped up to denote the tail position.

Sync and MOS

All shots are done either sync or MOS, that is, with or without sound. The legend for the term *MOS* is that, shortly after the introduction of sound, a German director replying to a question about mic placement said something to the effect of, "Oh, no, vee do dis vone *m*itt *o*ut *s*ound." Thus *MOS* became the acronym for shots that are done without the sound recorder rolling. A surprisingly high percentage of shots are done MOS, from reaction shots to action shots that will have sound added later.

MOS shots are slated similarly to other shots except that the bars on the slate are not hit. The clapper/loader will simply insert the slate, and the 1st AC will "squeeze off" a few frames of it. The shot will then be initiated with a simple "Roll camera" and "Action."

Camera Reports

Camera reports, or logs, provide a daily chronology of shooting. They are indispensable as a record of all the shooting activity on the set but are most valuable in keeping the many rolls of film organized in the editing process. The 2nd AC is usually responsible for filling them out after every take.

Blank camera report forms are available from commercial sources, but you can work up a simple camera report quite easily by simply providing places for the key information. **SEE 15-2**

The main headings are used to list the particulars of the shoot. Manufacturer and stock numbers are written in the middle. Emulsion numbers are taken from

15-2

A basic camera report form should include all the key information

Date			Scene #		Title			
Film stock			Emulsion #		Director			
Processing instructions					Camera			
Scene	Take		Remarks	MOS/Sync	Begin footage	End footage	Camera roll	Sound roll

the label on the raw stock. The first two columns are for the scene and take numbers. These come from the shooting script or storyboard and are provided by the script supervisor. They are also replicated in the lined script.

Beginning and ending footage is recorded to keep track of where specific shots are located on the rolls. Barring any camera runs for testing, the ending-footage number is transposed to the beginning footage for the next take. Beginning and ending footage is important for **spot printing**, a common practice on feature films in which only the desired takes are printed. These takes are circled on the camera report, and the lab personnel then refer to it to find them on the rolls. Lab personnel also need to be able to read the slate on the negative when searching for circled takes, another reason why the slate must be very cleanly photographed. Filmmakers working on short films and in 16mm usually have workprinted all the film that is shot.

Remarks generally pertain to the quality of the take, with deviations from other takes—different positioning of performer, different line readings, slightly different camera strategies, and so on—also noted. *NG* (*no good*) obviously designates spoiled takes.

The sound mixer keeps a **sound log** as well, with all the same information except beginning and ending footage. Some form of designation for all camera and sound rolls is very important. At the beginning of a project, the 1st AC and sound mixer will start a numbering system, usually numbering rolls sequentially from the first day. The camera roll number is written on camera tape and is kept both on the film's packaging and on the magazine itself. This helps the 1st AC keep the rolls organized for appropriate marking for the lab (see page 370). As suggested, camera reports are equally important for keeping track of rolls in the editing room. If the editor wants to try another take of a shot, the assistant editor can consult the camera report, determine the appropriate roll, see if it was printed (if applicable), and find it among all the **outtakes**, the unused shots. Beginning and ending footage is important here as well for determining exact locations on the rolls. Although footage on the sound rolls cannot be recorded, similar logging allows for easy location of individual pieces.

The camera report is also used to keep track of the camera's performance. The AC will indicate in the remarks column when the gate was last checked and if problems were found, any irregularities on the camera's part such as excessive noise, and any other problems that may be noticed.

Organization on the Set

Once preproduction is concluded, a film moves into *principal shooting*. When preparing a film, it seems like there are always things left undone prior to shooting. This is just the nature of the beast. Shooting can be seen as series of tasks, replete with obstacles and rewards, all requiring a measured and thoughtful approach. It is almost impossible to anticipate all eventualities, but with experience comes the ability to visualize all the potential problems and take preemptive steps. It is essential to put yourself in a good position. I always tell aspiring filmmakers that they can put themselves in a position where success is possible. Conversely, people can put themselves in a position where failure is not only possible, it is virtually guaranteed. Preproduction is where it all happens.

As suggested, the preparation for shooting has become somewhat of a science. Although some departments work from the script or talk to the director, many crew members simply consult the overheads or storyboards to determine what each scene will require of them. Beyond that, these tools are useful in creating an order for shooting and determining all other practical aspects of daily activity on the set.

Storyboards and Organization

Storyboards are not only important conceptual tools, they are also essential organizational tools. Scenes—and indeed entire films—are not shot in chronological order. They are shot in the order that allows the crew to be most efficient. All sections of the script that are to be shot from a specific setup are thus grouped together and shot at the same time. The scene can then be organized so that setups are shot in a sequence that makes sense for all the departments, particularly the lighting crew. Relighting an area that has already been struck will cause lighting continuity problems no matter how carefully the plan is reconstructed. Cost of talent and extras is also an issue. The setups can be sequenced so that time with talent is efficiently used and there is as little duplication of effort as possible.

The storyboard can thus be interrelated with the idea of the shot list to produce a snapshot of a day's work. Refer back to the overhead and storyboard example from chapter 6. **SEE 15-3** All the material from setup #1 would be shot at once. The camera's gate would be checked, and then you would move to the next logical setup. The camera positions would not necessarily be shot in numerical order, with setup #3 probably being the next logical choice in this instance. It was not necessary to light the background for setup #2 for the master, and you would shoot setup #3 first because, though you might make some adjustments, it is essentially lighted. The shots would be filmed in the most logical order, again with lighting and efficiency with talent being major determining factors.

In addition, when the frame and its contents are essentially a matter of public record, individual departments can anticipate almost any need. This is true of both preproduction and daily shooting. Many productions will post storyboard sheets in a prominent place, either in the production office or on the set, where the crew can consult them whenever needed. The camera department will know if any special camera mounts are needed; the lighting crew can be prepared to match color temperatures and respond to potential differences in the volumes of light if windows are in a shot during daytime interiors. If a painting of the exterior is more appropriate, the art department would be consulted. The props people can evaluate what is expected of them in terms of providing elements for each scene, and so on through the departments. The storyboard may not completely eliminate the need for consultation with responsible parties, but it does assist in individual initiative.

Because the storyboard lays out what shots are supposed to cut together, it is also of particular assistance to the script supervisor, who can thus be aware of what elements in the frame require attention. Nothing can be more frustrating for a script

15-3

Rather than shooting this scene chronologically, all the material from setup #1 would be shot first, followed by that for setup #3, to make use of the existing lighting

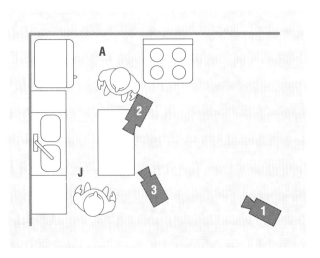

supervisor than being unable to understand the director's ideas about how a scene is supposed to cut together.

The Production Board

Effective organization of a film shoot is crucial, and the ***production board*** is a key factor in creating an efficient approach. It is a huge chart kept by the PM in the production office. It dominates the film crew's efforts, being an overall flow chart detailing all the elements, both human and material, needed to make a specific film. It is an ever-present entity—the visual record of how the shooting is proceeding. It can easily fill up an entire wall in the production office, although many production managers are using new computer software designed specifically for the purpose.

The production board lists the scenes and all the elements needed for them: characters, props, vehicles, and the like. **SEE 15-4** The individual scenes are on long, removable strips across the horizontal axis. All the elements that the script requires are listed down the vertical axis. The strips for the scenes are put in the order in which the production manager foresees shooting them. Script pages are broken down into eighths for logging and shooting.

15-4

The production board comprises long, removable strips representing individual scenes across the horizontal axis; all the elements that the script requires are listed down the vertical axis

Scene	8	49	37	9	34	78
Day/Night	N	N	D	N	N	D
Interior/Exterior	I	I	i	I	I	I
Location/Studio	L	L	L	L	L	L
Number of Pages	1⅞	⅔	6⅝	1⅝	1⅛	⅞
Title: THE WOK	KITCHEN	KITCHEN	KITCHEN	THEATER	THEATER	THEATER
ANDREA MARTIN	X	X		X	X	
JOHN MARTIN	X		X	X	X	X
THEATER MANAGER				X	X	
PROJECTIONIST				X		X
CLEANING SUPPLIES	X		X			
WOK	X	X	X			
MONEY BELT W/BILLS				X		

The major purpose of the board is to assist the PM and AD in organizing the most efficient approach to shooting an entire film and to know at a glance what resources are needed for each scene. The PM will be able to organize the shooting around the availability of talent, major props, specific locations, and any other resource. The use of talent and expensive props can be scheduled for the smallest number of days possible, thus maximizing efficiency and limiting costs. All the scenes to be done at a specific location are grouped together, regardless of whether they occur close to each other in the narrative. Everything is organized so it is both cost efficient and logistically practical.

As an example, both the beginning and concluding scenes from Jonathan Demme's *Something Wild* take place in and just outside the same New York City restaurant. In both scenes the shots are similar, though significantly not the same, with only the lighting and the actors' wardrobes changing. One can presume that both scenes were shot in the same time frame. When the material from the first scene was completed, the same setups—with lighting and wardrobe changes—from the final scene were then done.

The production board starts as an apparently unwieldy mass of information. After each scene is completed, the corresponding strip is removed. As the film is shot, the board becomes smaller and smaller. The removal of the last strip can occasion huge sighs of relief, wild partying, and submissions to exhaustion.

The Lined Script

The *lined script* is the script supervisor's responsibility and is a visual record of how a scene is being shot. Similar to one of the methods of working out coverage in the script (described in chapter 6), the script supervisor will draw a vertical line through the dialogue that is being covered from a specific setup. **SEE 15-5** If you were covering the first three lines of the script in the master, you would draw a line through those three lines of dialogue. If you were shooting everything except the first line in a medium shot from setup #2, a line would be drawn accordingly. If the last two lines were covered from setup #3, the appropriate line would be drawn. If you shot the fourth line in close-up, it would be marked as well. Different-colored pencils are used to denote the different types of shots. Scene numbers are also listed on the lined script, with camera roll and footage numbers often recorded as well. There are many other potential markings on this version of the script, but the general idea is to show what material has been covered from what angle.

The lined script is indispensable for keeping track of how much coverage is being done. The director and script supervisor can refer to it at any point to determine if the appropriate footage is being generated. As important as the lined script is on the set, it is also essential for the editorial staff. They use it to quickly determine if specific angles have been shot. For instance, if a close-up of a specific character would work well at a certain point in a scene, the lined script is first consulted to see if it was shot. If the close-up was shot, the scene number will appear on the lined script. The editor will then consult the camera reports to find exactly where the shot is on the many rolls of outtakes.

Production Forms

Sophisticated written record keeping is necessary both in the production office and on the set. Over the years the commercial film industry, and episodic television in particular, has developed production forms and notation sheets that help in the preparation and shooting of scenes. The phrase "verbal orders don't go" applies here. With the myriad elements that must be in the right place at the right time, all instructions must be in writing. As with storyboard sheets, the forms suggested herein are available commercially, and there are software programs that

15-5

The lined script, denoting setups, shot types, scene numbers, and often camera roll and footage numbers, is a visual summary of how a scene is being shot

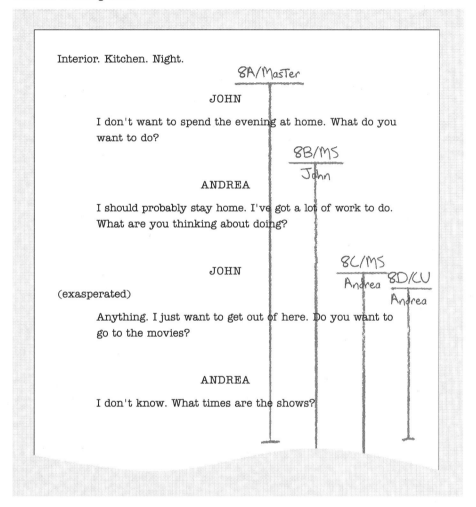

Interior. Kitchen. Night.

8A/Master

JOHN

I don't want to spend the evening at home. What do you want to do?

8B/MS
John

ANDREA

I should probably stay home. I've got a lot of work to do. What are you thinking about doing?

8C/MS
Andrea 8D/CU
Andrea

JOHN

(exasperated)

Anything. I just want to get out of here. Do you want to go to the movies?

ANDREA

I don't know. What times are the shows?

can generate them as well. Individual forms from different sources may vary somewhat in detail but request the same basic information. Almost every department is expected to do some written record keeping, and only a few key forms are described here.

Budget forms   Budgeting is essential in the creation of a workable shooting plan. There are a multitude of detailed forms that list areas of potential cost. Many of these are nonissues for independents and students, although many costs are unavoidable, including those for raw stock, processing and printing, sound, finishing, and so on. Still, becoming familiar with the filming expenses that are easy to identify as well as those that are hidden will help avoid much painful recalculation down the road.

Script breakdown forms   Prepared by the AD or PM, script breakdown forms precede the production board and represent all of an individual scene's needs on a single sheet. The sheet is generally broken down into a grid, each square requesting information about specific needs, such as cast, extras, props, wardrobe, special effects, animals, and so on. A modified version is often used in actual production.

Call sheets   Again the responsibility of the AD or PM, a call sheet is just what its name implies; it informs the talent of when they must be on the set and how much time is given to makeup, hair, and the like. It also details for crew members when they are supposed to be where, and what will be needed from them.

Continuity logs   These are kept by the script supervisor for records about specific elements in the frame. Some forms have an area for a rough sketch of the scene, but most require written information.

Script note forms   Also filled out by the script supervisor during shooting, these list all the technical details of the shots, including *t*-stops, filtering, lens length, duration of shot, and so on.

Although the specific materials for organizing a shoot will be unfamiliar to the beginner, you should make every effort to establish and maintain organized work habits. The tools discussed in this section should provide guidance. It is difficult to realistically communicate the kinds of pressures you will find on the set. Suffice it to say that shooting a scene with a full crew is an intense experience. While shooting, it may seem as though chaos is but a short step away. If you can keep chaos at arm's length, your time and efforts will be spent more productively.

Things will undoubtedly change on the set, no matter how carefully a shoot is planned. Unanticipated problems will require changes in some shots and render others impossible. This is particularly true for beginners, who lack the experience to be able to visualize every eventuality. Crew members who can look at any shooting situation, anticipate problems, and deal with them in advance are greatly valued resources. Part of learning is understanding how to anticipate problems.

The Camera Assistant

Many of the 1st AC's duties have already been covered, but there are several other considerations essential to producing a clean product as well as general efficiency on the set. Although this section details advanced production practices and magazine-loading cameras, ambitious learners will want to take them into account from the start.

Camera Preparation

The AC's first responsibility is to pick up the camera package and get it ready for use. Whether picking up a camera from a friend, a school equipment room, or a rental house, it is imperative that you check to make sure that the camera package has everything you require. Failure to have necessary pieces or to check key features can result in a canceled shoot or unpleasant surprises when you get the film back.

In addition, practice threading many times before attempting to load that precious celluloid gold. Use a dummy load—a ruined roll of raw stock; labs, schools, or rental houses are potential sources. As you practice loading, try not to let the film become too loose on the feed reel. The longer you struggle with a roll, the looser the top few winds will become and the more light is going to penetrate into the reel. Become completely conversant with the camera's loading procedures as you practice. Mistakes in threading account for more ruined footage than any other single cause.

Magazines and Loading

Each camera has its own unique magazine design and threading pattern. Most are threaded manually. A knowledge of the basic mechanism should make every camera an open book to you, although one should never be arrogant when learning a camera. Finding either a manual or a person to walk you through loading is, again, the best approach.

Because all cameras have at least slight differences, it is impossible to give specific loading instructions. Despite this, a few general principles will be helpful.

☑ When working with core loads, a changing bag—the photographic darkroom bag—is used to load the film. Using the bag can be disconcerting at first. Become familiar with what is supposed to happen in the bag and how to respond to any problems that arise. Individual magazines have their own idiosyncrasies: the lighttrap might be very tight on one magazine, the counter arm may not be locking out of the way on another. Learn to anticipate all difficulties. Practice both outside and eventually inside the bag.

☑ Once you feel completely comfortable with threading procedures from practicing in the light of day, you are ready to use the bag. The traditional changing bag is black and rectangular, although a tent-shaped bag, which keeps the folds of material off your hands and is quite popular with ACs, has recently been introduced. Changing bags have two compartments, each with a separate zipper, to make sure no light gets in. The bag has two armholes with elastic that makes the sleeves tight against your arms. Once the film is out of its packaging, you cannot remove your arms from the holes without risking ruining the film. If you have to get out of the bag, put the film back in its packaging or in a closed and locked magazine.

☑ Core-loaded film comes packaged in a metal can. Inside the can, a black plastic bag acts as an inner layer of protection from light. This plastic bag is *not* designed to protect the film outside the can, and *a can should never be opened outside of the changing bag*. A piece of blue tape secures the unexposed roll. After loading the magazine, save the can and plastic bag for **recanning** the exposed film. The piece of tape that secures the roll should be carefully preserved inside the bag; make sure it is not left in the magazine, where it could cause a camera jam. Bring extra cans with black bags in order to recan any partial rolls of film, called **short ends**. Short ends are what remains in the magazine at the end of the day or is leftover when a change to different film stock occurs.

☑ In the changing bag, feed the film through the lighttrap before you mount the load on the spindle. Once this is done, close the film compartment and lock it shut. Most magazines need only the feed side set up in total darkness, so the mag can be removed from the bag and the take-up finished in the light. Tape the feed side of the mag immediately after removing it from the bag.

☑ Always test the threading with the inching knob and then run the camera to make sure the loops remain consistent. Run the camera and, if the camera's design allows it, check to make sure that the take-up core is operating correctly.

☑ When you load the camera, the emulsion must be facing the front. This is obvious, but it seems like just about everyone makes this mistake once in their career. If the antihalation backing is toward the front of the camera, something has been done wrong.

✓ The diameter of the hole in the center of a core is larger than that of a daylight spool. The spindles in the magazine require *core adapters* to make up the difference. Core adapters mount and lock on the spindles. They can be accidentally removed when downloading and sent off to the lab. You will also need a core for take-up. Be sure the magazine has all its core adapters when you take the camera on location. You won't be able to shoot if one is missing and you are unable to cannibalize one from another magazine. Sometimes the smallest things can bring a shoot to a standstill. Be sure to bring extra cores, as you may have to download unfinished rolls. The extras will be needed when you reload a new magazine. Use only 2-inch cores because larger ones do not allow room for take-up of the entire 400 feet of film.

Become completely familiar with as many cameras and magazines as possible. A person who knows cameras and can load them quickly, accurately, and cleanly has some very marketable skills. Many entry-level positions in film are on the camera crew, which is a good way to get some experience on the set. It can also pay bills as you pursue other interests. You may have to work into it slowly, because no one is going to be hired to load magazines without proven ability. Loading appears to be a small cog in the system, but it is far too critical a cog to be left to someone with limited knowledge. I knew an aspiring AC who scratched several thousand feet of film on a project because he did not know a specific loading peculiarity of one camera. He had a hard time finding work for quite some time thereafter. Know your camera.

Racking Focus

As with so much else, racking focus is something that is worked out and rehearsed in advance. The AC stands by the camera and physically rotates the focus ring as the shot is being executed. To set up a rack focus, you need a roll of *film tape*, also called white paper tape, a permanent marker, and some gaffer's tape. Film tape is available at motion picture supply stores and no substitute should be used. You put the film tape on the barrel of the lens. The gaffer's tape is used on the floor to mark the talent's position.

Using a character moving toward the camera as an example, the AC has to ascertain and mark on the floor the talent's position at the beginning and end of her move. **SEE 15-6** If it is a long move, the AC also measures several arbitrary points in between. A piece of the film tape is placed on the movable part of the focus ring—across from the distance settings. If distances of 15, 10, 8, 6, and 5 feet have been measured, a mark is put on the film tape at the appropriate distances. These marks will be lined up with the hatch mark by turning the focus ring as the shot is being executed. **SEE 15-7** During performance and camera rehearsals, the AC will practice the focus move as well, hitting the specific focus points as the talent hits the corresponding marks on the floor.

Note: If you are measuring to the actor with a standard hardware-style metal tape measure, have the casing at the camera and the end of the tape toward the actor. If you do it the other way, a tape that slips out of an AC's hand can snap back toward the actor and put an eye out. Most ACs use the cloth, hand-winding tapes.

Marks are used in dolly movements as well. **SEE 15-8** Though dolly moves can incorporate both subject and camera movement, we will use the example of the camera moving in on a stationary subject. Rather than measure to points in the subject's movement, the AC bases the measurements on the distance from the

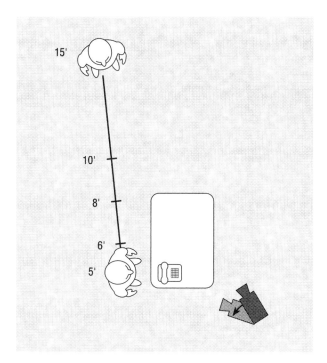

15-6

When a character will be moving toward the camera, the AC marks the talent's beginning and ending positions, as well as several in between

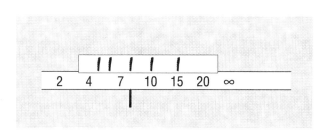

15-7

Marks on film tape corresponding to measurements on the floor are aligned with the focus hatch mark as the rack focus is being executed

15-8

When marking dolly movements, the AC bases the measurements on the distance from the subject to the dolly

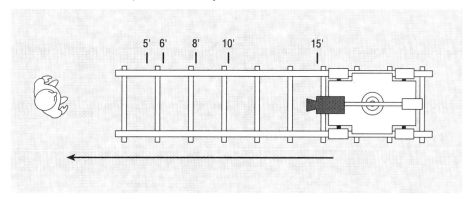

subject to the dolly. The measurements are the same as in the previous example (15, 10, 8, 6, and 5 feet), so these distances are marked on the floor with gaffer's tape along the path of the dolly. As the dolly shot is being executed, the AC will rack focus to the appropriate distance as the dolly passes the marks on the floor.

All planning for focus racks takes time and effort during a shoot. It is important that racks be accomplished as quickly and unobtrusively as possible. I have been on sets with inexperienced camera crews where the shot is rehearsed and ready to go and the AC announces that he has to set focus marks. He then takes ten minutes to measure and set marks and practice the move a few times. This, of course, would be unacceptable. Once an AC has ascertained the action of a shot, he should quietly do some measuring, set up the tape, and be ready to go by the time camera rehearsals start. It does engender discussion with the talent and the camera operator, but this should be worked out as quickly as possible. An AC who is efficient and does not make mistakes is going to get a lot of work.

The idea of setting up marks and racking focus is clearly most applicable to highly controlled situations such as narrative and commercial shoots. In many documentary situations, things are happening too quickly to do any extensive preparation. The zooming-in method is the approach of choice when stopping to measure is impossible. One well-known documentary cinematographer has actually rigged up a little dentist's mirror that reflects the focus setting to his nonviewfinder eye.

Racking focus can sometimes be an inexact process. Most complex camera moves are done with wide-angle to normal lenses because long lenses amplify even the slightest imperfection in movement. Because of this, it is difficult for the camera operator to recognize soft focus. When working in video, the camera operator can see if the shot drifts out of focus. Even if a potential problem is missed, the camera operator can go back and check the videotape. Being unable to see immediate results in film can leave one unsure as to the accuracy of any given focus rack.

Good ACs become very sensitive to how to move the focus ring and keep the subject in focus, though even they make occasional mistakes. Actually some of the great shots with rack focuses, such as the crane shots in Alfred Hitchcock's *Notorious* and *Vertigo,* drift slightly out of focus toward the ends of their movements. It just shows that it was made by human hands.

Racking Focus and Depth of Field

The 1st AC must be aware that the depth of field changes when racking focus. As the focus point shifts farther from or closer to the camera, the depth of field is also going to shift. If a character moves from 10 feet to 5 feet from the camera, the depth of field is going to change as you do the attendant focus rack.

The example from Mike Nichols's *The Graduate* discussed in chapter 3 illustrates this point. Dustin Hoffman's long run toward the camera clearly incorporates a substantial rack. **SEE 15-9** While the 1st AC is racking focus, the depth of field travels toward the camera, becoming increasingly shallow. Focus your attention on an object in the background as you watch the shot. By the time Hoffman reaches the turn, the background is completely out of focus. The numbers in the figure are purely speculative.

You will notice that objects, the car in particular, go soft slowly at first. As Hoffman approaches the turn, the rate at which the car becomes soft increases. By the time the camera pans, the car is a completely abstract shape. In the final position, we are dealing with at least two elements that are minimizing depth of field: long focal length and close focus. Because it was a sunny day, one can presume a high *f*-stop, bringing to mind the potential problems of doing a similar shot in low light. Significantly, when the zoom out is executed, we suddenly see all the elements that maximize depth of field. The shot now incorporates a wide-angle lens, a high *f*-stop, and, one would presume, a relatively far focus point.

Although this event may not be noticed by the average viewer and cannot be categorized as any kind of aesthetic effect, it clearly must be considered while shooting. You can tell that it is a technical by-product of attempting to achieve another effect.

15-9

During the rack focus in this scene, the depth of field becomes increasingly shallow
Mike Nichols's *The Graduate*

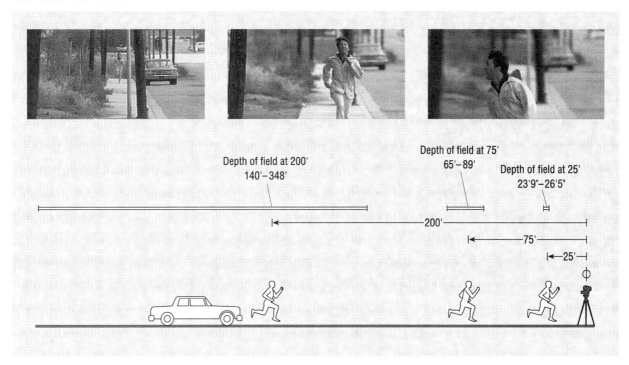

Depth of field at 200'
140'–348'

Depth of field at 75'
65'–89'

Depth of field at 25'
23'9"–26'5"

200'

75'

25'

Lens Flares

The AC also needs to check for lens *flares*, which are produced by light shining directly into the lens, causing either washed-out areas or multifaceted patterns on the image. Backlights and the sun are particularly notorious for causing flare problems. Flares can be seen as small points of light, called **kicks** or *hits,* on the front element of the lens. The effect can sometimes be seen by the camera operator, but just as often it will not be visible when looking through the viewing system. Thus, potential problems are identified by standing right in front of the camera and looking straight "down the throat" of the lens. Flares are tricky because not all kicks cause a problem.

The 1st AC is responsible for checking the front of the lens. If a problem is seen, something must be set up to block the offending light source from hitting the lens. Identifying which instrument is causing the problem can be tricky, with turning off or blocking the suspected culprit being the best method. While the offending ray of light can occasionally be cut at the instrument, the flare is usually cut by a flag on a C-stand at the camera. This is the AC's call and a grip sets it.

Moving shots present more complex problems. Flares might be eliminated at the beginning position but then appear at a later point in the camera's movement. This requires at least one run-through devoted to the AC walking in front of the camera, watching for problems. Obviously, a stationary flag on a stand is useless in this situation. A ***French flag***, a small flag on an articulated arm that mounts on the camera, is particularly helpful with these kinds of flares, as is a matte box or sunshade.

The multifaceted patterns, usually caused by the sun, are occasionally incorporated into shots as stylized effects. However, most flares are unacceptable and require some effort to eliminate them on the set. The AC does this as a matter of course, disrupting the set as little as possible in the process.

Scratch Tests

Scratched film is a significant problem, particularly when working with older cameras. It is usually caused by dirt, improper loading, or a problem with the camera. Whenever possible, the AC breaks off the first few feet of film that are run through the camera while loading is being checked. Left on a core, the piece is labeled with the camera roll number and stored for future reference. If there is any scratching, the scratch test can be processed to see if it was a camera problem or a processing problem.

Lab Instructions

The 1st AC is also responsible for marking all the film cans and getting them to the lab. The film is often either shipped to a distant lab or left in a late-night drop-off box, so accurately marking the cans is essential to avoid any misunderstandings at the lab. Even if the AC drops off the film in person, verbal instructions need written reinforcement. Mistakes in communication can have disastrous results and are almost always the filmmaker's fault for giving poor or inadequate instructions. The film cans should be labeled with:

- **Production title and camera roll number**: These are necessary to keep all footage organized in editing.

- **Production company and billing information**: The lab likes to know who is going to pay. Advance payment is generally required from customers who do not have a credit history with the lab.

- **Stock number**: Even if the film is in its original packaging, write the stock numbers in prominent places. Leave no room for error.

- **Footage**: Write down the amount of footage in each can. Shooting less than a full roll is common, and the lab needs to know approximate totals to plan its processing runs.

- **Printing and processing instructions**: Writing "Process and print normal" is often all that is required, but beyond that the lab needs to be alerted to any special requirements such as force processing or any of the other "tortures" that have been suggested. This may require a separate sheet if there are complex instructions. The AC often turns in a copy of the camera report that lists any desired lab manipulations and any spot printing to be done. Make sure these instructions are explicit, making the lab aware of any special effect—such as color, exposure, and so on—done on the film.

- **Phone number**: If there are any questions about exposure or printing instructions, the lab may need to get in touch with you on short notice to facilitate quick turnaround on the job. You will want to answer any questions they have.

The rolls should be clearly marked and the instructions unambiguous. An AC on one shoot was labeling two rolls of film that were being pushed one stop for effect. He carefully labeled the two cans, put them on top of two other cans that were to be processed normally, and taped them all together to ship to the lab. The lab saw the labeling on the top two cans and force-processed all four cans. The film was not completely ruined because exposure was well within the latitude of the film, but there were heated denunciations of the lab among crew members when the news of the error arrived. However, in a private moment afterward the DP castigated the AC for packaging the film in a way that left the potential for misunderstanding. Clarity is absolutely essential in all communications with the lab.

Equipment

Having the necessary equipment on location is essential. Forgetting important pieces of equipment can slow down or, in extreme cases, terminate shoots. Always delineate who is responsible for bringing what. I have seen inexperienced crews arriving on location missing everything from tripods to the film itself, because someone thought someone else was going to bring it. On professional crews, this virtually never happens, because responsibility has been delegated in very clear channels. The AC always brings the tripod. The key grip handles anything to do with dollies. The gaffer is responsible for determining and obtaining the necessary gear to rig the lights.

Equipment Checklist

The time to be focused on equipment needs is when you are preparing for and picking up the gear at the equipment room or rental house. Know what you need and be sure you leave with it in hand.

The lists shown in the figure on the following page include the equipment often available at schools and media arts centers. **SEE 15-10** An experienced AC or gaffer could list several dozen other useful items. Some things, such as cleaning and repair kits, a beginning professional may want to start acquiring. Virtually every experienced crew member seems to have accumulated at least several cases full of the tools that are commonly used in their specific jobs.

Do not hesitate to think big in terms of obtaining equipment, but be prepared to make do with what you can get. Rental houses are often beyond the means of noncommercial producers. However, the fact that your primary time with busy talent is often on weekends may be in your favor. This is the rental houses' slow time, when much of their gear is sitting on the shelf. Get to know people at the rental houses and try to impress them with your knowledge and responsibility. If you make the right impression, rental houses will on occasion cut deals, particularly if you are working on the weekend. On the other hand, if they perceive you as someone who neither understands nor is concerned with the care of equipment, they will do anything to avoid letting you use their gear.

A Note on Movement and Efficiency

Intricate moving shots are very attractive to first-time directors. However, both the time devoted to them on the set and the internal pacing of the shots themselves pose significant challenges. Movement is essential to a film, but specific camera moves need to be weighed in terms of their value in the script versus the time taken to execute them.

Activity on the set slows down whenever you start moving the camera, particularly with inexperienced crews. Focus marks have to be set, dolly track may have to be laid, and the movements have to be practiced. The talent must be thoroughly drilled on what the boundaries of their movements are. Lights and the microphone boom have to be carefully considered so they are not problems in the shot.

Timing and pacing of the shot is also a critical concern. What is on-screen should always be interesting visually. If it takes too long to move from one key composition to the next, the "travel" time will slow the pace of the finished product. Thus, material that should logically occupy a few seconds of screen time occupies

15-10

These checklists include equipment essential for a location shoot

Camera package

- ☐ Camera
- ☐ Lens & lens cap
- ☐ Film
- ☐ 2 to 3 magazines
- ☐ Core adapters
- ☐ Cores
- ☐ 85 filter
- ☐ Neutral density filters, .3, .6, & .9
- ☐ Proper filter ring adapters
- ☐ Sunshade
- ☐ Batteries (check for charge)
- ☐ Battery cables (one backup)
- ☐ Changing bag
- ☐ Extra 400' cans (with black plastic bags)
- ☐ Camera tape & white film tape
- ☐ Slate
- ☐ Tape measure
- ☐ Light meters
  - ☐ High slide
  - ☐ Incident disc
  - ☐ Reflective disc
  - ☐ Flat disc
- ☐ Chip chart
- ☐ Pens & permanent markers
- ☐ Log sheets & clipboard
- ☐ *American Cinematographer Manual*

Tripods

- ☐ Head & legs
- ☐ Tri-downs
- ☐ Quick release
- ☐ Bushing for mount adapters
- ☐ Lens-cleaning tissue and fluid

Lighting

- ☐ Complete kits—barn doors & stands
- ☐ Extra bulbs for each light
- ☐ Extension cords
- ☐ Cheaters
- ☐ Clothes pins
- ☐ C-stands and arms
- ☐ Modifying materials
- ☐ Blue gel
- ☐ Gaffer's clamps
- ☐ Gaffer's tape
- ☐ Electrician's tape
- ☐ Practical bulbs
- ☐ Shims
- ☐ Leather gloves
- ☐ Gel cutter
- ☐ Electrical tester
- ☐ Rope
- ☐ Sandbags
- ☐ Spare fuses, if applicable

Repair kits *(camera & sound)*

- ☐ Pocket knife
- ☐ Flashlight
- ☐ Flat- & Phillips-head screwdrivers
- ☐ Jeweler's screwdrivers
- ☐ Solder & iron
- ☐ Scissors
- ☐ Set of Allen wrenches
- ☐ Battery tester with ohms meter
- ☐ Needle-nose pliers
- ☐ Wire cutters & strippers
- ☐ Tweezers
- ☐ Electrician's tape

Sound

- ☐ Recorder & supplies
  - ☐ Audiotape
  - ☐ Spindle locks
  - ☐ Crystal plugs
  - ☐ Extra take-up reels
- ☐ Microphones (plus backups)
- ☐ Mic cords (plus backups for every mic)
- ☐ Boom
- ☐ Shock mount (with adapter)
- ☐ Wind zeppelin
- ☐ 2 headphones (monaural)
- ☐ Y adapter for above
- ☐ Headphone extension cord
- ☐ Log sheets & clipboard
- ☐ Extra batteries
- ☐ Gaffer's tape

Cleaning kits

- ☐ Denatured alcohol
- ☐ Q-tips
- ☐ Compressed air
- ☐ Camel-hair brush
- ☐ Orange stick
- ☐ Small flashlight

Miscellaneous

- ☐ Pens & pencils
- ☐ Permanent markers
- ☐ Notebooks
- ☐ Polaroid camera & film
- ☐ First-aid kit

double or triple that. Editing allows you to condense time, eliminating the less interesting aspects of getting a subject from here to there. If the camera covers action that would otherwise be eliminated, the viewer is forced to watch action that is not germane. Many carefully planned and painstakingly executed moving shots wind up being cut into pieces in the editing room because their dead spots kill the pace of the film.

The flip side of both of these drawbacks is that if you do not move the camera, the film will usually be flat and static. Also be aware that movement is the lifeblood of the actors' performance. Deprived of the ability to move, performers can become stilted and unnatural. It is one of the great paradoxes that the movement that is so essential to the performer is a complicating factor for the camera crew.

The beauty of movement is that you can cover significant portions of the script from a single camera shot. The eight-minute opening shot from Robert Altman's

The Player presumably covers action for about eight pages of script, potentially taking dozens of setups to cover. Despite this, be careful of movements that are peripheral and slow you down. With inexperienced crews, time-consuming moves that do not cover at least a modicum of script can kill a shoot.

One novice director had to film a scene in which one detail was a boy getting up to answer the phone. The phone was in the foreground of the shot, and the boy was in the background. To recompose for the movement, the director decided to dolly right and pedestal up. The crew, all beginners as well, got the dolly set up and practiced the move without the camera. Then they measured for focus and planned the pedestal. At the end of the dolly, they found that the camera saw part of the room that had not yet been lighted. Three hours after starting, they had a few usable takes. After the shot was finished, I took the director aside and pointed out that he had spent almost half a day shooting one-eighth of a script page. At that rate, this ten-minute film would have taken forty days to shoot. Weigh carefully whether the material in the script warrants the kind of time devoted to the proposed shot.

This is one of the fundamental albeit subtle differences between commercial features and low-budget independents. The previous example might take a professional crew about an hour to work out and as such may have been worth the time devoted to it. Independents are often stuck in the position of accomplishing more script pages with a less experienced crew, a primary reason why independent films do not have the production values that commercial features have.

Editing

16

Principles, Procedures, and Equipment

The Future of Film Editing

Nowhere has the impact of the video revolution been more apparent than in the editing process. In conjunction with emerging exhibition patterns, digital video-editing options have developed to the extent that, outside of the feature film market, very few projects are edited and completed in film. The more common approach when film is being shot is to transfer to and finish on video, particularly in commercial, industrial, and music video work. Even when finishing on film, many of the techniques suggested here have been radically altered by analog and digital video technologies, as well as digital audio technologies. Despite this, the techniques presented in this and subsequent chapters are both the genesis for similar approaches in video and are still being used in traditional filmmaking. Until the new digital editing technologies become affordable for schools and independents, the limitations of simple analog video editing leaves the student unaware of the potential transformations possible in the editing process. Learning film editing remains the most comprehensive and intensive introduction to visual-media editing.

The Purposes of Film Editing

The inevitable clichés about editing are all true: This is where the real magic of filmmaking happens. This is where the film comes alive. The old folk saying that you can't make a silk purse out of a sow's ear applies to film, yet stories abound of films botched in their conception and shooting that were made substantially better in the editing. The flip side of this is the film that had great potential but was edited indifferently. Editing is the process of selecting the parts of the shots that are good and serve the needs of the film, with the rest eventually being discarded. To edit with facility and authority takes an extensive knowledge of the mechanics of cutting, an initially daunting though eventually easily mastered undertaking.

While this is a simplification, there are essentially three decision-making areas in cutting a film: cutting picture, cutting sound, and determining optical effects (dissolves, fades, and the like). For the picture, editing is going through and determining the specific order of shots and then deciding on the precise transition point from one shot to the next. The order of the shots may be predetermined in a narrative film, though that order may not be as rigid as first assumed. In documentary and experimental film, you may have to devise the order yourself. Cutting sound includes a number of approaches, from cutting sync tracks in conjunction with the picture, to determining the relationship between music and picture, to building complicated, layered sound effects after the picture is mostly cut. Optical effects are discussed in a following section; these choices relate to planning the available range of visual effects.

In his book *Cinema: Concept and Practice,* film director Edward Dmytryk has a chapter that should be required reading for all aspiring filmmakers, titled, "About a Forgotten Art."[1] In it, Dmytryk puts forth the notion that anyone who wants to direct a film should spend time as an assistant in an editing room. No one learns better what kind of material is necessary to edit a film than those who actually have to make the film work. If a director failed to get a significant close-up or botched a camera angle, the editor is the one who both understands the problem and has to struggle to find a solution.

Thus it is imperative you start editing your images from the start. The production of images is a meaningless enterprise without the process of trying to fit them together. You can create beautiful images, but if there is no plan to their organization and employment, the outcome will generally be flat and uninvolving. To paraphrase a famous line from Orson Welles's *Citizen Kane,* it is not hard to produce beautiful images if all you want to do is produce beautiful images. It is hard to create beautiful images that cut in an intelligent and cohesive manner to other beautiful images. A friend is fond of saying that editing is "the process of falling out of love with your footage and into love with your film." I have found no better summation of the editing process.

The beauty of film is that it can take the chaotic and random nature of human perception and give it shape and form. The great Russian documentarist of the 1920s, Dziga Vertov, was fond of making grand emblematic statements on this subject.

> The starting point is: use of the film camera as a cinema eye, more perfect than the human eye for fathoming the chaos of those visual phenomena which evoke spatial dimension.[2]

> . . . Freed from the frame of time and space, I coordinate any and all points of the universe, wherever I may plot them. My road is towards a fresh perception of the world. Thus I decipher in a new way the world unknown to you.[3]

General Editing Principles

A number of key principles that influence both shooting and editing, the 180-degree rule, dramatic emphasis, and so on, have already been addressed, but a few additional topics bear discussion. As suggested, these concerns have such a strong impact on shooting that they need to be considered from the very start.

Parallel Editing

Parallel editing is the intercutting of two separate events to suggest they are occurring simultaneously. Cutting from shots of a raging blaze to fire engines racing

1. Dmytryk, Edward, *Cinema: Concept and Practice* (Stoneham, MA: Butterworth Publishers, 1988), p. 144.

2. Vertov, Dziga, "Film Directors, a Revolution," *Screen* 12 (Winter 1971–72), p. 52.

3. Vertov, Dziga, "'Kinoks Revolution' Selections" in *Film Makers and Film Making,* Harry M. Geduld, ed. (Bloomington: Indiana University Press, 1970), p. 86.

to the rescue is a typical example, the association making the actions appear to be happening at the same time. This simple effect is generally traced back to Edwin S. Porter's *The Great Train Robbery* (1903), though evidence suggests that it had been used before. Porter's film cuts from a scene of a trussed-up railway station manager trying to escape his bonds to a band of train robbers making their getaway. Though hardly appearing revolutionary today, the effect was a major step forward in the development of cinematic resources. The approach was further refined by the ever-active D. W. Griffith, particularly in the effective though odious scenes of the Ku Klux Klan's charge to rescue the main characters in *Birth of a Nation.*

Parallel action can achieve much deeper associations. Bob Fosse's *Cabaret* has an excellent example in which an upbeat dance number on the cabaret's stage is intercut with the club's owner being savagely beaten outside by the Nazis. The juxtaposition of the gaiety and decadence of the cabaret with the undercurrent of something going dreadfully wrong is inescapable. Jonathan Demme's *Silence of the Lambs* (1991) has a clever twist on this common ploy. The scene has the film's killer hearing the doorbell ring as the viewer sees dozens of agents surround a house, preparing for an arrest. The impatient agents move into position as the agitated killer prepares to open the door. When he finally opens the door, we see Clarice (Jodie Foster) rather than the expected battery of agents. This is followed immediately by a cut to the agents breaking down the door of an empty house. When we see actions cut together in this manner, we assume they will be associated in a straightforward fashion. These actions are indeed associated, but in a way that is completely unexpected.

Transitional Devices

Shots that bridge one setting to another or mark the passage of time are called *transitional devices.* This covers a wide range of approaches, but often transitional shots have the added burden of being establishing shots as well. The common approach is to show a setting, establishing both the place and, by extension, the time of day. If a scene that takes place in a dilapidated cabin in the mountains at night needs to be established, the approach can be very general or very specific. The scene might start with a shot of mountains at dusk, rather than of an individual cabin. A cut from the mountains to the interior of an appropriately appointed cabin would be accepted.

This long shot can be useful, but it can also become predictable. Several years ago, I was hired for a day to camera assist on a feature film that had finished principal shooting several months earlier. We started the day by shooting the exterior of a warehouse. We then shot the exterior of a hospital. Next came a shabby bar. It soon became clear what we were doing. We were collecting transition shots for a film that was not connecting well. I saw a rough cut of the film several weeks later, and the establishing shots were not helping. There was a shot of a shabby bar and then there was a scene in the shabby bar. There was a shot of a hospital, and then its interior. After a while, this sequence became painfully predictable. The film's problems were in the script, and no amount of transitions were going to make it more coherent. There was no apparent logic to the sequencing of the film's scenes, and no amount of establishment was going to change that. The film needed major surgery.

Transition shots establishing location can be useful, but frequently the elements of a scene can speak for themselves. There are many ways to establish a shabby bar or a hospital without going outside—from planting some rationale in the script, to focusing on details, to employing wider interior shots. There are many ways to handle transitions, and you should find those that are effective but not predictable.

Economy and Pace

Economy and pace are very difficult to quantify. Each individual film, scene, and shot demands its own pace. Often this refers to employing each of the individual shots for the shortest time possible while still allowing them to achieve their purpose. This is generally controlled by the physical lengths of the shots, though there are many other elements that effect the sense of a film's internal rhythm. Usually, it is a question of the editor consciously deciding how long each individual piece of film should be held. While cutting, you can almost start an internal rhythm by snapping your fingers when shots are getting too long.

Pace also has cultural determinants. Mimicking the culture from which it emanates, the hallmark of American commercial film is that all the parts and the whole itself are exceptionally efficient in the way the material is presented. Any useless or redundant shots, scenes, or sequences are trimmed down or eliminated altogether. American commercial features rarely hold shots longer than absolutely necessary, and scenes are played to their maximum efficiency. This attitude implies that if a point cannot be made in two seconds, it is certainly not going to be made in ten seconds. Occasionally, subtle nuances of performance are sacrificed to moving the narrative forward.

The efficient approach has long been the hallmark of American films, but it has been effectively challenged by numerous filmmakers, films from other cultural backgrounds often having a more leisurely pace. A slower pace forces the viewer to contemplate the meaning of the material more, particularly when coupled with an ambitious use of proxemic effects. Michelangelo Antonioni has been one of the most adventurous directors in this regard, exploiting both a slower pace and the psychological intensity of the close-up. In *The Red Desert* (1964), he employs long, lingering, some might say too long and too lingering, close-ups of the main character (Monica Vitti), forcing the viewer to identify with her intense isolation and alienation. **SEE 16-1** Antonioni is quite remarkable in that he purposefully holds his shots well past what would be deemed their natural ending points by traditional American standards.

In Antonioni films, notably *The Passenger* (1975), scenes take two or three times longer than they would in conventional American films due to the inclusion of extensive visual detail and lengthy pauses between lines of dialogue. The approach has a much more contemplative and "environmental" effect. The longer we are forced to linger, the more we must contemplate the state of mind of the protagonist and the more the character's environment becomes a factor in the drama. The approach emphasizes the spaces between the conventional vehicles of meaning—the dialogue. In uninterrupted viewing, we must confront and create meaning in a subject.

16-1

Lingering close-ups of the character force the viewer to identify with her isolation and alienation
Monica Vitti in *The Red Desert*

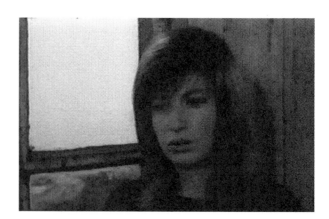

Keeping a film lean and efficient brings up the concept of visual shorthand. *Visual shorthand* refers to accomplishing an action visually in a minimum of images, again as economically as possible. It is an idea similar to the old "Name That Tune" television show. Rather than naming a tune by listening to a small number of notes, we can attempt to communicate an idea in the smallest number of shots. John Huston's *The Maltese Falcon* (1941) is often used as an example of the efficient "Hollywood classical style." Its terse pacing is key. The second scene of the film is an excellent example of this. It depicts the murder of Sam Spade's partner, Lew Archer, an action represented by a few sentences of description in the script. As always, this simple action can be thought of in terms of choices. It could be covered in an infinite number of ways—into one shot or thirty—all depending on the desired visual presentation and the amount of weight the scene should have in terms of the rest of the film.

The scene opens with a shot of a street sign (Bush Street), the setting having been mentioned in the previous scene. **SEE 16-2A** The next shot is a medium long shot of Archer walking into the frame. A gun, held by an unseen hand, comes up in the right corner and Archer is shot. **SEE 16-2B** The next shot is of a body crashing through a barrier and rolling down a hill. **SEE 16-2C** The entire scene is composed of three shots. The first shot serves to establish location and approximate time, the second is the action, and the third is the result of that action. The scene could have been drawn out to heighten suspense or emphasize other elements, but none of that was necessary. The action is a minor albeit significant plot point. More attention would give it more weight than it deserves.

Terrence Malick's *Days of Heaven* also has many excellent examples of this concept. The film attempts to make all communication as indirect and visual as possible, cutting away from conventional climactic points in many scenes. All potential conflict is left either for the viewer to imagine the resolution or with a strong visual symbol. One sequence has several characters escaping after the murder of another character. They travel by car but soon trade it for a boat, continuing their escape downriver. This sequence of events could be treated in many different ways but is handled in four highly effective shots. The scene has a segue from a shot of the trio driving away from the scene of the crime in the victim's car. The next shot pans from a boat moored at a dock to a group of people gathered around the car. **SEE 16-3A & 16-3B** An elderly man kicks one of the tires, a commonly accepted visual symbol of people haggling over a car. The next shot is a close-up of the elderly man inspecting some jewelry that the viewer can assume is also part of the deal. **SEE 16-3C** And then, with remarkable efficiency, the next shot is of characters on the boat on the river. **SEE 16-3D** Not a word is spoken. The entire transaction is handled visually.

16-2

The terse pacing of this scene establishes, initiates, and completes the action in three quick shots
John Huston's *The Maltese Falcon*

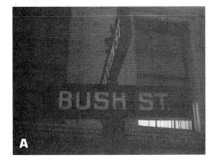
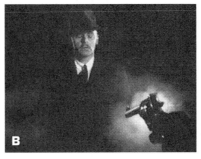
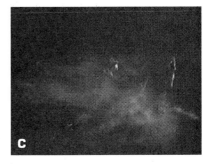

16-3

In this scene the purchase of a car is handled completely visually in only three shots

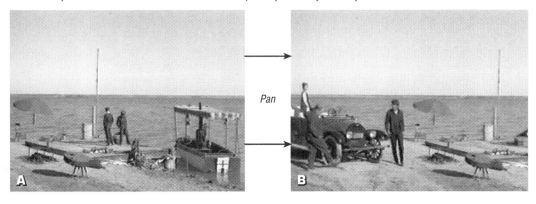

Pan

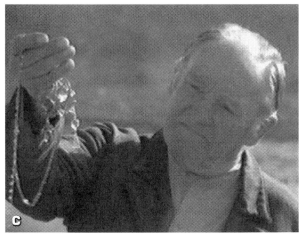

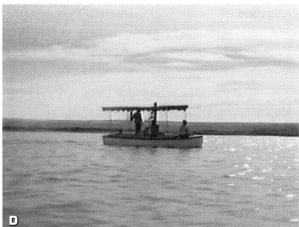

The notion of choice is critical. There are infinite ways to visualize either of these scenes described in a script; each could be broken down in many different ways. There could be dialogue, more atmosphere shots, or shots that further developed character or the meaning of the scene in the context of the film. But both scenes are minor though necessary links in the scripts; they do not warrant extensive development, and the efficiency with which they are presented gives them the appropriate weight in the general scheme of things, conveying simple, relevant information in a straightforward and efficient manner.

Alfred Hitchcock's *Psycho* (1960) has a shady transaction similar to the one in *Days of Heaven,* in which Marion Crane, in flight after embezzling money, stops to buy a car. In this case, the scene is broken down into almost fifty shots. The entire 7-minute scene is played and developed much more extensively than in *Days of Heaven,* where the sequence of shots simply serves to get the characters onto the river. In *Psycho,* the scene has a very important function in developing Crane's mounting paranoia caused by the intrusiveness of the people she meets on her journey. This handling of the scene suggests that it has more weight in the general scheme of things than the one described from *Days of Heaven.*

Visual shorthand is clearly a film-specific concept, although the idea of economy and pace exists in most media. Writers frequently speak about the necessity of presenting their ideas in as efficient a manner as possible. It is a matter of getting straight to the point. Filmmakers such as Antonioni purposefully challenge that style. Although experimenting with any convention is always recommended, you should first understand and then master the conventional efficient approach to pacing.

Structuring the Editing

The vast majority of American films are cut so that their editing is as seamless as possible. This has been referred to as *invisible editing*. In this approach, any cut that is abrupt or calls attention to itself is considered a bad cut. All the rules that follow have their genesis in this conventional approach. As always, these rules apply not only to editing but also to how you approach shooting a scene. It is difficult to call some of these topics "rules." As with most rules of art, each demands to be broken at times. It might be better to call them suggestions.

Even so, these "suggestions" represent years of acquired folk wisdom by many talented editors. As such, they should be clearly understood. How they are applied is your business. An acquaintance once told me that her editing ability had almost been ruined by her being forced to learn conventional editing techniques. Being polite, I held my tongue. If you consider yourself to be "ruined" by learning other people's approaches, you may be shutting off some important creative avenues. Listen to and learn from other people's experience. Rather than instantly treading new and exciting ground, most young editors unfettered by conventional techniques wind up simply reinventing film editing.

The Basic Rule

Before going into specific concepts, the primary axiom of editing bears discussion:

▶ **RULE:** *There has to be a reason for a cut!*

This is the great overriding, unbreakable rule. When you cut from one image to another, there has to be a purpose for that choice. Often it is a narrative reason, a response has to be shown or an action must be emphasized. But do not get locked into the notion that a cut necessarily needs narrative justification— something that moves the story forward. Often the reasons are kinetic, to keep the shots from being too long or too static. Sometimes, as in many experimental films, a cut explores an element of film technique or an aspect of a character's subjective experience. Whatever the reason, when you are looking at a piece of film in the editing room, there has to be some reason why you feel one shot should end and another should come next.

Cutting on Action

A term that you will hear frequently is "cutting on action." This refers to match cuts and basically states that when choosing to cut from a long shot to a closer shot, or vice versa, the cut can best be masked by cutting on a character's movement. This, of course, is the conventional approach of invisible editing. If a sequence requires a cut from a wide shot of a person taking a seat to a closer shot of them speaking when seated, the point to cut would be during the action of the person sitting. Cutting on movement usually occurs on emphatic rather than subtle character movements.

Once alerted to this technique, you will see it in almost everything you watch. In the scene from Alfred Hitchcock's *Notorious* mentioned in chapter 5, the cut that leads to the lengthy two-shot is an excellent example. **SEE 16-4** In a long shot, Alicia comes out on the balcony and is talking to Dev. The problem is how to get from this LS to the two-shot. The cut is masked by cutting on the action of Alicia throwing her arms around Dev. If the shots were cut anywhere else, the cut would not appear as fluid as this particular choice makes it.

Cutting on action dominates invisible editing. Editors consistently cut on a movement of an actor to create a fluid transition from one shot to the next. They generally cut toward the beginning of the movement rather than the end. Editors

16-4

The cut from the long shot to the two-shot is masked by cutting on the action

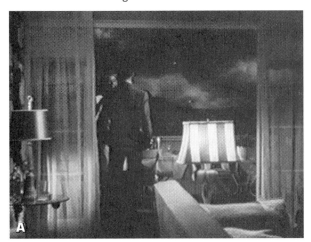 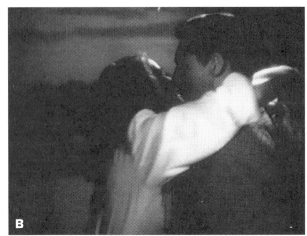

usually try to leave a little overlap (two frames or so) between actions, to let the viewer adjust to the incoming shot. Cutting without this overlap leaves a slight gap in the action.

The 30-Degree Rule

The 30-degree rule is tangentially related to but not nearly as rigid as the 180-degree rule, which is known by virtually everyone who has considered directing a narrative film. The 30-degree rule is less well known. It is more a matter of common sense than of the diagrammed schematic associated with the 180-degree rule. Simply stated, it says that if a subject is shot from one angle, the next shot should be at least 30 degrees off an axis drawn from the original camera position to the subject. If you use a camera position that is on the same axis toward the subject, the possibility of a disagreeable jump is great.

When you shoot a master shot, it is always recommended that you then move in for closer shots. The mistake comes when people move straight into the subject. The major point of the 30-degree rule is that you should not move the camera in on a straight line to a subject. This is difficult to visualize and may best be explicated by an example. **SEE 16-5**

If you are doing a master shot of two characters, do not cut from setup #1 to setup #2, or it will look as though you are "leapfrogging" toward the subject. The problem is compounded if you repeat the sequence. If you jump in and then jump back out again, it will look even more as though the camera is leaping forward and backward.

The other key issue is continuity. If a character has his hands at his side in the long shot and at his waist in the close-up, the jump will stand out in a same-angle cut. Because so much else changes—the background, the character's position within the frame—when the angle is shifted by 30 degrees or more, minor continuity flaws like this are much less noticeable. Small differences in body position during performance are unavoidable because things like hand position are bound to change from take to take and setup to setup. Any attempt to make performance consistent on this minute level would certainly be counterproductive. The implication here is that if you can just get the continuity right, a same-angle cut will work. However, most editors would maintain that it would still be a poor cut, even if the continuity matched.

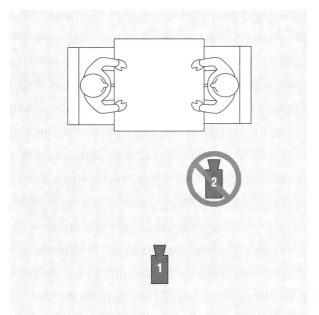

16-5

Cutting from setup #1 to setup #2 would look as though the camera was leapfrogging toward the subject.

A more common sequence of cuts is to go from the master, setup #1, to setup #3. **SEE 16-6** The background and position of character within the frame change enough so that minor differences in body position will go largely unnoticed. Another application of this concept is a cut from an over-the-shoulder shot to a closer shot of the same individual. Cuts between setups #1 and #2 of figure 16.5 are rarely attempted, although both setups are frequently shot for scenes. When you intend to insert something between the two pieces, shooting and using the closer angle is appropriate.

Looking at the breakdown of the scene from *Something Wild,* you will notice that the overhead appears to have camera positions that specifically break the 30-degree rule. **SEE 16-7** The close-up of Ray (#3) is at the same angle as the over-the-shoulder of Ray (#2). The same is true of both Lulu (#4 and #5) and Charlie (#4 and #6). But as you analyze the scene, you will see that at no point do they ever cut

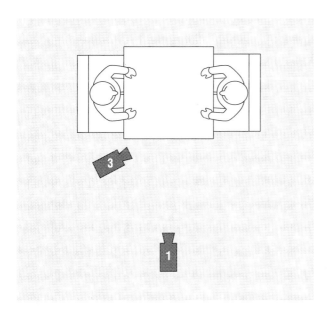

16-6

In a cut from setup #1 to #3, background and character position change enough that minor continuity issues would go largely unnoticed.

16-7

Although several camera setups are at the same angle to a character (#2 and #3, for example) cuts are never made between them without an intervening shot from another direction

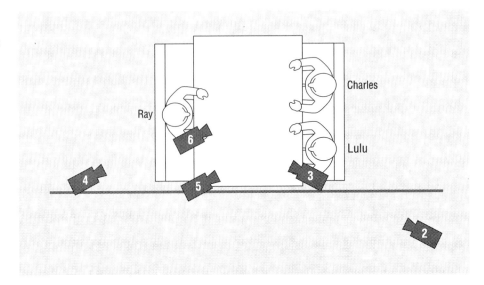

16-8

A sequence of straight-on shots of a laterally moving character will cause the camera to appear to be leapfrogging alongside the subject

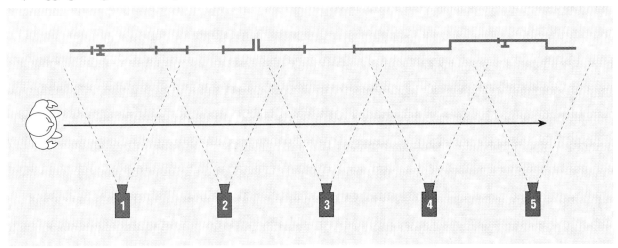

from an over-the-shoulder shot to a close-up of the same subject. If we see a shot over Ray's shoulder (#4), the next shot we see is from another direction.

The 30-degree rule also applies to lateral movement of a character. If a character is walking down a street, you have to vary your angles. If you use straight-on camera positions all the way, it will look as though the camera is leapfrogging down the street. **SEE 16-8** Clearly, this is an exaggerated example, but the same is true if you use any other angle consistently. The solution would be to vary the camera angles, with some shots from the front and back included.

Emphasis

Cutting on a subject or action exaggerates the significance of that subject. In essence, the implicit message is that this subject is important enough to warrant more than a single perspective. If there is a shot of an object on a table, say a knife, followed by a cut to a close-up of the knife, the implication is that the knife is an important element.

Similarly, when a simple action is broken down into a number of different views, the attention given it exaggerates its importance. Sergei Eisenstein explored this idea in his landmark film *The Battleship Potemkin* (1925). The sequence has a dissatisfied sailor responding to rancid food on the ship. He looks at a plate inscribed with the motto "Our Daily Bread." Angered, he smashes the plate against a table. Clearly, this action could have been shot from one angle and been reasonably effective. But Eisenstein wanted the action to achieve much greater significance. He did a number of shots from the same camera angle of the plate being broken. He then started the motion in one shot and cut to the same action from another shot. Under normal circumstances, the resulting cut would simply match. What he did differently was to start each new shot at a substantially earlier point in the movement than he had left it in the previous shot. This created overlaps of movement, exaggerating and intensifying the action.

I once had a student who, given the assignment of creating several matched action cuts, decided to have some fun. She took the action of a car coming down a street and pulling into a driveway. She broke it down into about twenty separate setups, each covering a small part of the movement of the car. That this simple movement was given so much attention created the assumption that it was an immensely important part of the film. The anticipation was so great by the time the car finally came to a stop that when the occupants just got out and walked into the house, the letdown was comical.

Visual Interest

You have to go through the unedited footage to find the meat of the shots. What you have shot will inevitably have stretches that are not visually interesting. If you film a dance rehearsal, for example, there will be parts in which the dancer is turned from the camera, framed poorly, or the action is just not engaging. Select the segments in which what was in front of the camera interrelates with the film frame in a visually exciting way. You should find moments when the physical makeup of the frame, the arrangement of shapes, the kinetic elements, the tension created by the parameters of the film frame, make a shot speak.

In the best shots, not only is the subject exciting, but *the way it is filmed* increases visual interest. Find these points. As a beginner the infrequency of these moments can be discouraging, but they should increase as you gain experience. The goal of a cinematographer is to have exciting moments happening all the time. Great cinematographers have the ability to find the frame that gives the material an edge. As both an editor and cinematographer, you must be able recognize those moments when something is "happening" in the film frame.

Variety

Your shots must employ a variety of approaches; vary between close-ups and long shots, low angles and eye-level shots, images with different balances of compositional interest, moving and static camera, and so on. In other words, use the camera resources available to you.

If a film is composed entirely of long shots, it risks becoming visually dull and predictable. If the area of interest in all the compositions is in the same part of the frame, the same problems can occur. Obviously, there are exceptions. Several films that were done largely in long shot are examples of successful films, such as Jim Jarmusch's *Stranger than Paradise* and Chantal Akerman's *Jeanne Dielmann: 23 Quai du Commerce, 1080 Bruxelles* (1974). There are also films shot almost exclusively in close-up. But these are the exceptions; they do not represent the kind of explorations and experimentations that provide useful learning experiences for beginners.

As with almost every facet of editing, camera perspective requires consideration during shooting. If you have not used a variety of perspectives, options in editing will be very limited.

Continuity Problems

While cutting, you will occasionally find continuity mistakes that were made in shooting, from minor problems to ones that will make you want to tear out your hair. If you have two shots with a bad continuity jump, for example, it may be possible to cut in a shot between them that would mask the problem, such as a reaction from another character. This has the potential to work, but it can also have unfortunate by-products. The first is that you can often destroy the pace of the scene. Extra shots frequently slow down a scene and, though you may improve the individual cut, the overall shape of the scene suffers. The second problem concerns the logic of the visual presentation. It often just does not make dramatic sense to slip in a reaction shot or, more significant, some detail of the set. By cutting to it, that reaction or detail takes on an importance that it may not warrant. In both cases, the operation is a success, but you lose the patient.

Sometimes you simply have to brazen your way through some of these minor continuity difficulties. Just make the cut. In the rush of frames, the dislocation for the viewer will be momentary, and new shots will quickly take center stage. As an editor, you look at a cut with poor continuity over and over, in slow motion and frame by frame. It grates on all your sensibilities. But you must realize that the viewer is going to see it briefly only once, and, unless it sticks out like a sore thumb, it will generally go unnoticed.

Specific Cutting Concepts

Film editing takes a single-frame consciousness. As insignificant as a single frame is in relation to the whole film, it can make the difference between a good cut and a bad cut. Although these differences may not be apparent to the average viewer, editorial attention to the importance of individual frames can make the difference between a scene that is flaccid and unstructured and one that is tight, dynamic, and efficient. As a learner, it is good practice to generate some footage and start editing it. Advanced editing equipment may not be available for some time, but you should start using simple equipment as soon as possible, so you can be wrestling with the images from the outset. As has been stressed from the start, a knowledge of basic editing considerations must inform the way you go about shooting the action.

Each cut is the result of a conscious decision on the part of the editor. I like to say that every cut is an adventure, an idea that will become clear as you spend more time in an editing room. It is always a matter of trying a cut, and if it doesn't work, going back and trying something else. You may have to try many different options for each transition until it works the way you want. Once you have the cuts working individually, you must make sure that it all works as a whole. This usually requires further changes.

The following principles refer more to the specific mechanics of editing—those specific decisions you have to make when looking for the transition points from one shot to the next. These are all things you should try to avoid, things that will make your cuts awkward and noticeable. Editors like to inquire if awkward cuts were made with a chainsaw. The following are ways to avoid "chainsaw" cuts.

☑ **Do not cut to similar compositions.** Our eyes are drawn to specific areas of the projected film image. If an image draws attention to part of the frame, do not cut to an image that is balanced in a similar way. A key objective in conventional editing is to keep the eye moving and interested. If all compositional weight is in one part of the frame, the mind's eye will become disinterested.

Objects will also tend to pop into each other. If a shot of a character in the left part of the frame is followed by a shot with a plant in the same part of the frame, the character will appear to pop into the plant. When exploited for effect, this technique has intriguing possibilities. Referred to as the *pop-on* or, its opposite, the *pop-off*, its first use is generally credited to the French film pioneer of the 1890s and early 1900s, Georges Méliès. The story goes that Méliès was filming on a Paris street one day when his camera jammed. He was able to fix it without ruining any film, and continued filming. Unbeknownst to him, a bus had left while he was attending to his camera, and a hearse had come and taken its spot. When he projected the film, the bus suddenly popped into a hearse. The effect intrigued him and he based many of his effects on this principle. The popping effect still gets widespread use, particularly in comedy films; it can be effective when used for a purpose, but can be quite disconcerting when unintended, creating associations that are far from what you want.

If you cannot edit for a variety of points of compositional interest, your film will be visually dull. Several years ago, a student with a background in still photography shot a film on mountain climbing. It was amazing how much terrain he covered to get his shots, but every shot had the mountain climber right in the center of the frame. After a while the film became difficult to watch because the climber kept popping into himself. This need for variety will influence your approach to shooting. Varying compositional interest helps you avoid visual dullness.

☑ **Do not cut to similar angles.** This is similar to the previous idea but warrants separate attention. When you cut to a new view of the same character or characters, the composition must change enough to warrant this new view. In other words, do not cut to virtually the same view of the same thing. This goes back to having a reason for every cut—each cut should have new information or be significantly different enough to warrant its inclusion. If you have a full shot of a person from head to foot, what would be the point of moving slightly closer? Go to a medium shot. Go to a close-up. Make it different enough to justify itself as a new view of the subject.

The biggest mistake I ever made as a director was during my first narrative film. It was a simple scene of two men talking; one was seated on a couch, the other in a chair. I wanted to keep the action moving at the beginning of the scene without ever getting too close to either character, saving the close-ups for later in the scene. As scenes are shot out of sequence, two of the shots I had planned included both characters from setups #1 and #2. **SEE 16-9** The problem was that these two pieces do not cut together. Clearly, any two pieces of film can be joined, but this is simply a poor cut. Why move the camera ten feet when you are producing virtually the same shot? **SEE 16-10** The camera is jumping around unnecessarily.

☑ **Do not cut to dissimilar tones.** This involves photographic consistency. If you cut together shots that have very dissimilar tones, say, very bright shots with very dark shots, the cut will shock the viewer. The viewer's eyes will need time to adjust, just like when going from a dark space to a bright space or vice versa. On the other hand, although the discomfort this can produce in the viewer may be generally undesirable, it can also have intriguing possibilities. A cut like this is referred to as a *shock cut*, and it can give a film an edgy atmosphere. It can be used to wake up the audience, get their blood flowing faster. Shock cuts can also be achieved with sound, movement, and many other elements.

16-9

The two setups are too similar to warrant a cut between them

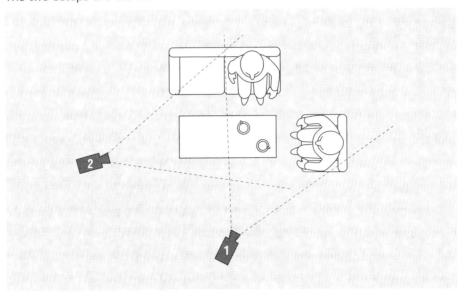

16-10

Although camera position has changed between these two shots, they are too similar to produce a seamless transition when cut together

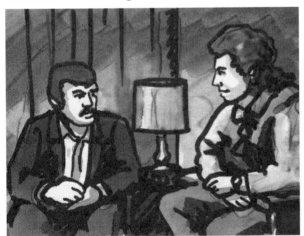
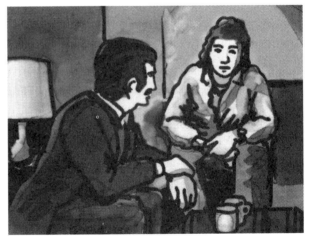

☑ **Do not start what you cannot finish** and, conversely, **do not finish what you cannot start.** Not a bad rule to apply to filmmaking in general, this applies to all cutting in which you are *not* creating match cuts (noncontinuity cutting). The former generally applies to when you are going to cut out of a shot, and the latter applies to when you are going to cut into a shot. Simply stated, the two rules mean that you should not cut while a dominant element in the frame is just starting or ending an action.

In a match cut, you finish the action of one shot in the following shot. If, however, you are not matching the action, the viewer expects completion, resolution of the action. Without continuance in a second shot, the action seems incomplete.

Completeness can be difficult to grasp and is highly subjective. A simple example is a shot of a bird sitting on a tree branch and then flying off. The question is, How much of the shot should be used? This answer can only be generalized, but the point *not* to cut would be a split second after the bird has started flying. Either cut before the bird flies or retain enough of its flight to give some sense of completion. This is the "do not start what you cannot finish" part. Again, it is usually an issue when you are contemplating when to cut away from a specific shot.

I once had a job cataloging footage from a university's basketball program. To make a highlight film, someone had gone through the footage and removed all the parts of the shots that had the basketball going through the hoop. A player would put up the ball and, midway through its flight, the shot would end. It was one of the most frustrating things I have had to watch. We expect resolution, completion. Clearly, this is a heightened example, because there is suspense when the ball is put in the air, and though most examples of this are not so dramatic, they still leave the viewer with a sense of incompleteness.

The reciprocal "do not finish what you cannot start" applies when you are deciding when to cut into a shot. It means that you should not pick up a shot at the end of a preceding movement. If the shot has the bird returning to the tree branch, you would not cut in as the bird is landing. Either include the whole movement or exclude it entirely.

Use these general concepts for guidance when you are actually cutting film. They are not to be applied rigidly. As stated, every cut is an adventure. You have to work on each transition until it looks right. To make that decision you have to depend on your own taste and judgment, although that should be informed by some consensus of what constitutes a good cut. I like to tell people that there is not one right place to cut between two shots, but there are many wrong places. Keep working at each individual cut until all the cuts in your film are good cuts.

Basic Terms and Procedures

The following terminology applies to the basic principles and procedures of editing film. Refer also to the glossary at the back of the book. Many of these effects can be created "in camera," but the norm is to plan them in editing and have them executed by the lab in the final print (see chapter 18). This gives greater control in positioning the effects and avoiding the inexactness that comes with being created by hand.

Fade-out and Fade-in A *fade-out* is simply where the picture fades to black. A *fade-in* is the opposite, where the image comes up from black. Fade-outs and -ins are generally used as transitional devices, to either get from one location to another or to signify the passage of time. Occasionally filmmakers fade to shades and colors other than black. Ingmar Bergman fades to a brilliant red in *Cries and Whispers* (1972), amplifying the film's concerns with the symbolic aspects of blood. Films also occasionally employ a *fade to clear* or *fade to white*. These can be popular, though they tend to have a very stylized effect.

Dissolve A *dissolve*, also called a *lap dissolve*, is a common technique in which one shot is faded out while the next shot is faded in on top of it. Similar to the fade-out, this is often used to signify a change of time or place.

Although dissolves are immensely attractive to the novice, they are not used as frequently as you might imagine. There is an old put-down among editors, "If you can't solve it, dissolve it." As this suggests, the dissolve is frequently used to soften an otherwise terrible cut. Despite this, they are also used to extraordinary effect, such as in Basil Wright's great British documentary *Song of Ceylon* (1934). The film dissolves between long tracking shots across temple ruins to create a poetic vision, emphasizing the timeless quality of setting and place.

Superimposition   Also called a "super," a *superimposition* is composed of two shots laid on top of each other. This effect is not common in feature films, but it has long been a staple of experimental films. Supers can be achieved in the camera while shooting or in the editorial and final printing processes. In the former case, the camera must have some backwinding capability. You make one pass on a section of film, wind the film back, and make a second pass on the same section. Each pass must be underexposed by roughly one stop, so the overlay does not result in overexposure. Tests should be shot to determine exact exposures, as different situations can present different problems.

Opticals   This umbrella term indicates a graphic effect that is created at the lab. *Opticals* include *split screens*, *keyholes*, *freeze frames*, *spins*, *wipes*, and a host of other effects. Opticals are executed by the lab at the filmmaker's instructions and are done prior to the final printing. They are difficult to get right and may take several tries to obtain the precise effect.

Most of these effects are produced on an optical printer. **SEE 16-11** Used to rephotograph existing footage, the *optical printer* is essentially a projector that has a camera shooting straight into it. Both the camera and the projector can be advanced one frame at a time. The camera can also be repositioned to focus on specific parts of the projected frame. The projected image can be manipulated in terms of both coloration and the speed the film is going through the gate. If you wanted to create a slow-motion effect, you could shoot two camera frames for every one projector frame. Any more than two frames creates a staggered effect between the individual frames, which can also have applications in creating time and image distortions. If you shoot seven or eight camera frames for every one projector frame, the result will be a staggered, almost balletlike distortion of the original movement. Ernie Gehr's *Eureka* (1976) uses this effect on a piece of film originally shot in 1908, in which the camera was mounted on the front of a trolley car. The effect created

16-11

The optical printer is used for rephotographing existing footage

Maritex JK-105 optical printer

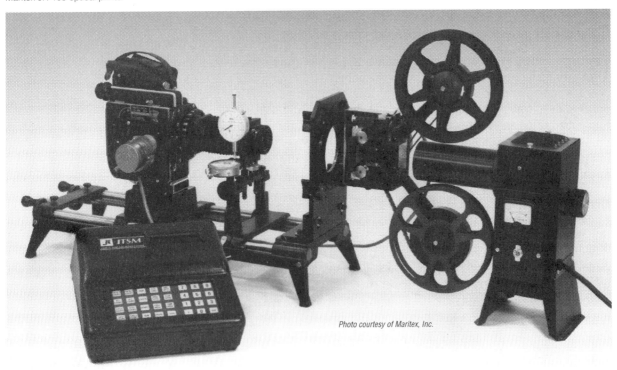

Photo courtesy of Maritex, Inc.

by the optical printer turns the content abstract, making it a play of shapes and form in stylized movement.

Optical printers are used most frequently to create optical effects, special effects, and titles in the editing stages of film. A complicating factor is that film produced on a printer looks slightly different than the original film because it is one generation away. If footage from the optical printer is mixed with first-generation footage, the difference will probably be apparent to even undiscerning viewers.

Many of the effects that are painstakingly produced on an optical printer can now be produced at the touch of a button on many video-editing systems. Freeze frames, which take extensive planning and calculations on an optical printer, can now be executed in video in a few minutes. The new digital setups also completely eliminate generational problems. Although use of the optical printer has diminished, it is still instrumental in creating many visual effects and can be an exciting tool for beginning filmmakers, particularly those interested in formal experiments.

The Editorial Staff

The head of the editorial staff is, of course, the editor. Though there are many different working relationships, the ***editor*** is generally responsible to the producer to create a workable version of the film. Depending on how powerful they are, directors are often integral parts of the process as well, taking editorial supervision from the producer. In the Hollywood studio days, directors often handed over what they shot to the editor and that was the last they saw of it until it was finished. Today, such directors as Woody Allen, Martin Scorsese, and Robert Altman have their hands in virtually every editorial decision.

The editorial staff can be large, with many members performing specialized or limited roles. The assistant and apprentice editors work most closely with the editor. The ***assistant editor*** is responsible for the overall organization of the editing room and all the materials of the film. The ***apprentice editor*** is responsible for many of the routine procedures that the editor does not do, such as syncing up, stringing out, configuring mixtracks, and so on. Beyond that, there may be a wide variety of specialists, including sound effects editors, music editors, Foley editors, and ADR editors, among others. Each of these jobs is very specialized. British films frequently have a credit for a "footsteps editor," an individual whose sole responsibility is to edit in the sound of characters' footsteps.

Even if they have power in the editing stages, directors rarely spend much time in the editing room. Editing is too painstaking and laborious to be effectively supervised, or even watched, by an uninvolved second party. The editor generally is given the footage and then trusted to do the best job possible. The producer and/or director will occasionally be shown rough cuts of the film, and they will usually make detailed suggestions. The editor will generally give a rationale for any questionable sequences, and some compromise will be reached. Those with decision-making power thus negotiate the best possible cut of the film. Though film history is replete with examples of abuses of this process, this collaboration is generally the wisest path. A director must realize what a talented editor can bring to a project.

Having people critique the work is a crucial part of the process. Even if you are editing a film that you have written and directed, nothing is created in a vacuum. The person who thinks that anyone else's opinion dilutes his work is usually the person who is intent on producing one more trivial piece of self-indulgence. Watch out for the myth of the lone genius. There may have been a few in the history of art, but to assume that one is at that level is more than a touch pretentious. Even van Gogh had Cezanne.

Organization

Organization in the editing room is essential. Students generally start working on short films without sound. Because the films are brief, organization is not too complicated because the footage is limited. Working without sound simplifies organizational concerns as well. This is a good discipline that gives valuable experience in telling a story visually. The spoken word can be a crutch, easily dominating the visual. When many beginners get their hands on sync equipment, they wind up just photographing the dialogue. They film head shots of actors conversing, derogatorily referred to as "talking heads." This is not by definition bad, but it can deny the power of visual storytelling.

All the material to be used in the film has to be extracted from the rolls of uncut footage, called *raw footage*, and be kept track of until it is incorporated in the edited workprint. All the outtakes and *trims*—frames trimmed from the shots you are using—must be stored so they can be found if needed at a later date.

There are many ways to organize when working with a small amount of material. One method is recommended here, or you can determine one that is workable. You should develop good habits from the beginning. However you proceed, be aware that there are accepted industry practices that you will learn if you ever assist in an editing room. But for now, it is important to just save everything and know where to find it.

Project your unedited footage many times and make as many preliminary determinations as possible about the choice of shots. With the viewer or on the flatbed (editing table), go through the raw footage and take out the shots you want to use. Generally, you want to extract the entire shot from first frame to last frame (unless there are parts of the shot that are absolutely unusable). In most 16mm and 35mm applications, the beginning and end of each shot is easily identified by a series of flash frames. A *flash frame* has more exposure—it looks thinner—than the rest of the shot. This is because while shooting, it takes a split second for the camera to get up to speed at the beginning of each new take as well as to come to a complete stop when shut down. In these brief periods, the entire mechanism is moving slowly, thus giving the first and last frames more exposure from the slower rotation of the shutter. There are generally several flash frames at both the beginning and the end of takes. Although at first appearing to be an irritant, these flash frames can be useful in identifying the beginning and ends of takes both in the workprint and the original.

Professionally equipped editing rooms have *trim bins*, which provide a safe and clean place to hang the shots you intend to use. Outtakes should remain on the roll of raw footage. In the absence of a trim bin, you can make something on which to hang the shots. Set up a clean garbage bag in a large trash can. Put a rod across the top and hang the film from it. Or you can simply tape the film up on a wall (be careful if you have a cat). Whatever system you decide on, the film should be hung with *film tape*, also called *cloth tape* or *white paper tape*, which is available from film-supply retailers. Do not use any other types of tape, because they will leave a gummy residue both on the film and whatever you hang it on. This residue on the film will attract dirt and may cause problems in editing machines and projectors. Film tape also won't pull the paint off your wall.

Start a numbering system on the film tape. Cross-reference these numbers on a sheet of paper or, more convenient, on 3-by-5 cards, describing the type of shot (CU, MS, LS) and its contents. A simple list is all that is required. If you were making a film on a violin maker, the list of shots might look something like this:

1. CU, violin maker's hands

2. CU, glue being applied

3. LS, work area

And so on.

After all the shots are hung and numbered, the order can be determined by evaluating the list. If you are working on a nonstory film (uncontrolled event, self-portrait, impressionistic documentary), determining how the shots should be ordered will require significant thought. This is where 3-by-5 cards come in handy. You can arrange the film by ordering the cards and splicing the shots back together. I had a student once who just threw the cards in the air, and the order in which he picked them up was the order of the film. It was an awful film.

The next step is to cut all the pieces of film together in the order you have determined. The result of this process is called a *first assembly* or *string out*. Once the shots are in order on a reel, you can start working on the individual transitions from one shot to the next. If two shots are not working together, do not hesitate to go back to the outtake rolls to look for help. Sometimes a shot that did not seem useful, or a snippet from a bad shot, can get you out of major difficulties.

The first cut of a film is called a *rough cut*. From there you identify any superfluous material and work toward a *fine cut*. You start with the raw footage and keep rearranging it and whittling it down until you have a thoughtfully ordered and fluid piece of work.

Equipment

The flatbeds and uprights are the top of the editing-equipment pyramid, and even under the best of circumstances, access to them is often limited. Students rarely get their hands on them until late in their educational careers, generally making do with more rudimentary, though perfectly adequate, equipment. With film, you can do experimentation with some very simple pieces of editing equipment. All you need is a film viewer and splicer, as well as access to a projector. Armed with these, you can work for quite a while.

Projectors

Whereas Thomas Edison and his assistant W. L. K. Dickson are generally credited with creating the first motion picture camera, the Lumiere brothers, Auguste and Louis, resolved the dilemma for an appropriate presentation device. In Paris on December 28, 1895, they projected a motion picture to a paying audience for what is generally recognized as the first time. As significant a part of twentieth-century experience as it has been, Edison apparently never even considered the idea of showing film to a large audience prior to the Lumieres' screening.

In design, the *projector* is very similar to the camera. The film is driven by sprocketed rollers, each frame is pulled in front of the gate by the pull-down claw, and the shutter hides the movement of the next frame as it is moved into position in front of the gate and then allows us to see that next frame. Just like the camera, the film must form top and bottom loops for the reciprocation between the constant motion of the sprocketed rollers and the intermittent movement of the claw. The biggest difference is obviously that a projector generates light whereas the camera captures it.

The other major difference is that most projectors have a sound playback assembly through which the film generally needs to be threaded. Some projectors have a means of bypassing this sound head, but it is often a good idea to thread through the sound path to take advantage of the loop-restoring capabilities. Be sure to turn off the sound if you are analyzing workprint. The sound head will pick up the shape of the sprocket holes and make a machine gun–like popping sound.

Many of the newer projectors are channel loading, an automatic-threading feature. You slip the film into a slot, and the projector is closed on it. These projectors are generally not acceptable for viewing an edited workprint, because they tend to chew up films with splices. Try to get a manually threading projector, such as the Kodak Pageant, as it will be gentler on your film. **SEE 16-12**

All tips for cleaning a camera apply to a projector. Be sure to keep the projector free of dust and dirt. Even when you are handling a workprint, keep the film as clean as possible. The dirtier the film gets, the more difficult the evaluation of the overall quality of the project becomes. Projector cleanliness is particularly relevant when you finally get a projection print of your film, be it an answer print or a release print. Projection prints are very expensive, and one scratch can render the print unwatchable.

Projectors are the most fragile, bulky, and expensive part of a basic editing system. Despite this, it is essential to view your raw footage many times before starting to cut. Rather than find a projector for personal use, it may be more sensible to secure access to a screening room. When you get the film back from the lab, the original film should be rolled emulsion out. Workprints should be wound emulsion in for correct projection. If the image is flipped side-to-side, it merely needs to be given a half-twist right before it runs through the top sprocketed roller.

During the first screening of the footage, the condition of the workprint, and thus the original, should be thoroughly checked. The further the film advances in the editing process, the more it will show wear. You may begin to wonder when the damage occurred if the film is not checked at the start. If scratches or dirt are seen in the first screening, their source needs to be identified. It is possible they are in the workprint, so check it first. If you do not find the problem, have the lab check the original. Damaged or dirty film is generally discarded and reshot, so be

16-12

Older, manually threading projectors are useful in editing stages

Kodak Pageant 16mm projector

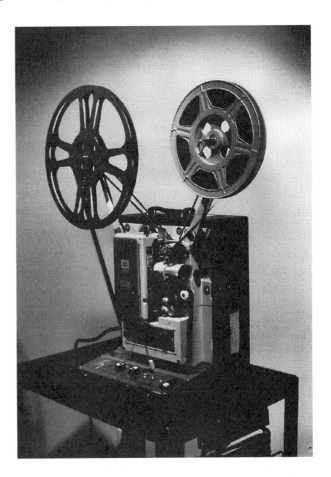

completely conversant with any flaws and know whether they are in the workprint or the original.

View the uncut footage repeatedly before you actually start to cut. Take extensive notes about what shots you want to use and how you want to cut the film. Evaluate the quality of your shots from a purely "plastic" standpoint, that is, quality of camera movement, efficiency of timing, overall composition, lighting, and so forth. Minor defects are often difficult to see on the editing tables and particularly on Super 8 and 16mm viewers. Lack of awareness about flaws in shots can lead to unpleasant surprises when you get a final print back.

Keep in mind that the projector is *the* presentation medium for a film. The editing process may leave the film dog-eared and hard to evaluate. A clear memory of the raw footage's initial impact may buoy your spirits during some pretty dark days.

Viewers

A film *viewer* is a standing viewing machine on which you can analyze the film a single frame at a time or at any other speed you desire. Viewers are usually a little less than a foot tall and sit on a tabletop. **SEE 16-13** Super 8 viewers have arms to hold the film reels. The greatest use of the viewer is in determining editing points— analyzing the shots and deciding on the beginning and ending points of the segments of film that you intend to use. The film can also be hand-cranked at roughly 24 fps, reproducing normal movement.

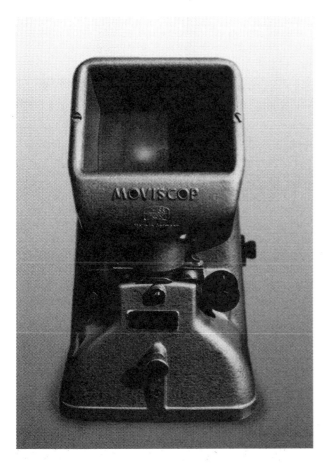

16-13

Viewers are used to analyze shots frame by frame

Zeiss Moviscop film viewer

Although viewers are good for analyzing shots frame by frame, they're no substitute for repeated screenings with a projector. They're also not the best place for determining the overall quality of your shots. Speed and timing are difficult to analyze because you are hand-winding through the viewer. Shaky camerawork and slight focus problems may be very difficult to discern as well. As suggested, you don't want to be noticing a shot's bad elements for the first time when you are looking at an answer print.

The Bench

The *editing bench* is essentially a less expensive and more cumbersome version of the flatbed editing table. **SEE 16-14** Unlike Super 8 viewers, 16mm and 35mm viewers do not have arms, necessitating a pair of *rewinds* for hand-winding the film. **SEE 16-15** The rewinds have long shafts to mount more than one reel at a time and are spaced roughly 4 feet apart with the viewer in the middle. A *gang synchronizer* is not required for simple picture cutting, but is necessary when working with sound. The synchronizer consists of interlocked rolling drums with sprocket teeth. **SEE 16-16** Sound and picture rolls can be locked to individual drums, called gangs, to be fed through the synchronizer in sync. With an amplifier/speaker, called a *squawk box*, and a sound head mounted on a gang, sound can be read and locked to the picture. With this equipment, it is possible to outfit a workable and inexpensive editing room. Though flatbeds are preferable, when resources are limited you can do a substantial amount of effective work on an editing bench.

16-14

The editing bench is a table that comprises rewinds, a viewer, a synchronizer, and other pertinent editing equipment

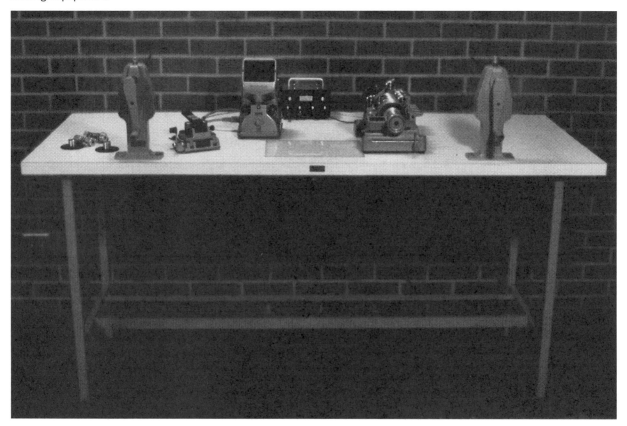

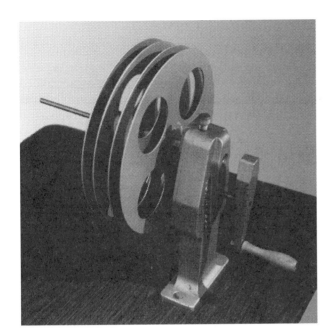

16-15

Rewinds are used to hand-wind the film

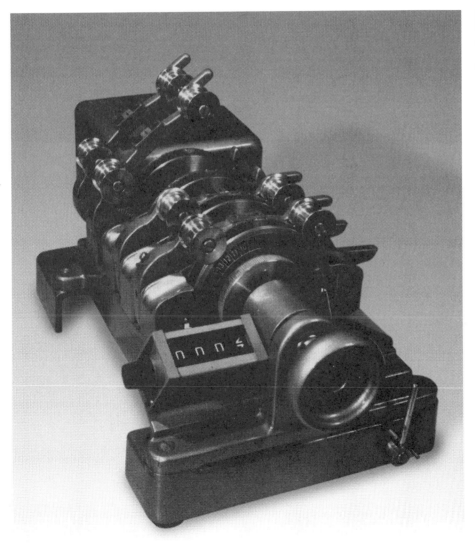

16-16

A synchronizer is necessary when working with sound

Moviola gang synchronizer

Splicers

The *splicers* in general use for 16mm and 35mm are the Guillotine splicer and the Rivas splicer. **SEE 16-17** Inexpensive splicers that use precut splicing tabs are also available, but are (or were, because of video) more for individuals and organizations that repair only a few home movies and institutional film prints. In terms of both the time they take to use and the durability of their splices, they are not adequate for extensive use.

Both the Guillotine and Rivas splicers have a setup block with a series of sprocket pins. When the film is set up on the pins, they ensure that it will be cut on the frame line and that it will line up correctly when the splicing tape is applied. Both models have blades that cut the film. Guillotine splicers use rolled tape, which is pulled across the film. A recessed, two-bladed knife trims off the excess splicing tape when you press down the handle; pins also come down and clear out the sprocket holes. The Rivas splicer also uses rolled tape, but the holes for the sprockets are precut. The tape is lined up and applied on the sprocket pins of the setup block and then cut with a blade. The precut rolled tape is more expensive than the Guillotine's unperforated tape, but there is less waste.

Guillotine splicers have both a straight cutter for the film and an angled cutter for the sound. The angled cut "cushions" the splice as it crosses the sound head and makes it less apt to pop. Despite this, many editors do not use the angled cutter, having determined that they can just cut the sound with the

16-17

On both types of splicer, the film is set up on pins, which ensure that it will be cut on the frame line and that it will line up correctly when the splicing tape is applied

Guillotine splicer   Rivas splicer

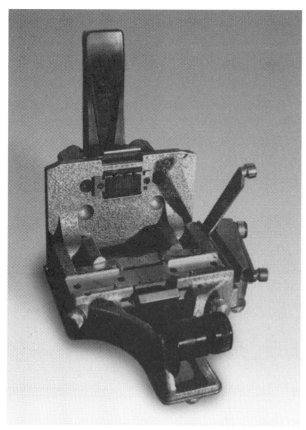
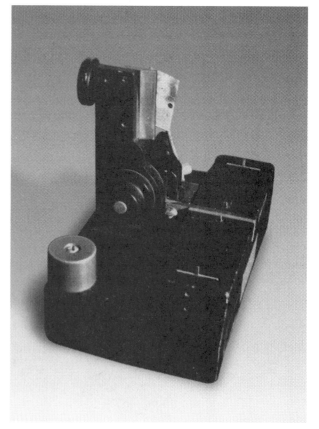

straight cutter without experiencing any difficulties. With the Rivas splicer, doing angled sound cuts requires using a second splicer, one equipped with the angled blade. Many editors use *white opaque tape* for sound splices, as opposed to the clear tape for the film. The white tape is stronger and keeps splices from pulling apart during the rigors of editing.

The Super 8 splicers commonly used are of the guillotine variety. They are slightly different from 16mm and 35mm splicers in that the double-bladed knife leaves a tab of extra splicing tape, which is folded over to cover the other side of the film, creating a splice that will run through a projector. Super 8 splicers have four pins to clean out the sprocket holes, rather than the two of 16mm. Two of the punches are in the tab, so it will not cover up sprocket holes when it is folded over. The fold-over tab is not quite the complete width of the film, allowing for the magnetic sound stripe that is often employed in Super 8.

The frame line runs between the sprocket holes on both 16mm and 35mm, so the cut is right at a set of sprocket holes. In Super 8 the frame line occurs halfway between two sprocket holes, so the cut does not come at the sprocket holes. When editing 16mm or 35mm, put splicing tape on only one side of the film so you can try different options for each transition between shots. If you try one cut and don't like the way it looks, peel off the splicing tape and try another possibility. If you put tape on both sides of the film, you have to peel it off with a fingernail, a process that is both time-consuming and hard on the film. Editing is about trying different options until you find the desired cut. The tape splice method affords the best opportunity for experimentation.

Editing machines are designed to accept splices with one side taped, but be careful with projectors. If you are unfamiliar with a projector, run a test with some junk footage to see how the projector accepts splices. Sometimes, making the top loop very big will help a spliced workprint run through a projector.

Another type of splicer should be mentioned here. The *cement splicer*, also referred to as a *hot splicer*, works on a principle of welding the film together and, unlike a tape splicer, creating a permanent splice. Cement splicers are used largely for preparing rolls for printing, repairing projection prints, and, most important, in the negative-cutting process. Specifics about cement splicing are covered in the section on A & B rolling the negative in chapter 18.

The Guillotine and Rivas splicers are the two choices for editing workprint. Each has pluses and minuses. On the Guillotine splicer, the pins that punch out the sprocket holes must be clean; if they're not, the sprocket holes may not be cleared out properly and the film can jam or get chewed up—get "eaten" in film parlance—in a projector or on an editing machine. Uprights, in particular, love to dine on messy splices.

Supplies

The following supplies are necessary for basic editorial procedures. Many of these items are available only through labs, rental houses, or film-supply retailers. Always get more than you need.

Split reels   All editing in 16mm and 35mm is done with the film on cores. Reels are too bulky for effective storage, as well as hard on the editing equipment. A split reel is used when film has to be projected or set up on a bench. A *split reel* has the two flanges of a regular reel with a threaded center so they can be detached. One flange has a pin to hold the core from spinning in the reel. The core should be set on the threaded center of this flange, and the second flange is screwed down on top of it.

Regular reels   Regular reels are used for take-up on the bench. These are simply the familiar reels used in projection that do not have detachable flanges.

Spacers   Donut-shaped plugs that are slid down the shafts of the rewinds, *spacers* replicate the distance between the gangs on the synchronizer so the reels do not turn flange-to-flange and the film does not come off the reels at an angle.

Clamps   Clamps are also slid down the shafts of the rewinds to lock the reels together so they spool in tandem.

Splicing tape   There are two types of splicing tape available: clear tape for the picture and white opaque tape for the sound. The clear tape tends to pull apart if used on the sound, causing damaged or lost frames. The only other difference is the perforated tape for the Rivas splicers and the uncut tape for the Guillotines. Do not use any substitutes, particularly, heaven forbid, Scotch tape; these leave a gummy residue, creating problems in projectors and editing equipment.

Grease pencils (china markers)   Grease pencils are used to mark whatever information is necessary on the picture.

Permanent markers   Permanent markers are used for identifying leaders and making all marks on the sound. Do not use a grease pencil on the sound; the marks will rub off on adjacent layers and cause sound dropouts.

Film tape   Film tape should be used to close rolls, mark them, and hang up film in the trim bin. Again, use no other tape; anything else will leave a gummy residue on the film.

Hole punch   A hole punch is used to mark the starting point of every roll, a reference to line up the film and mixtracks in the transports.

Extra cores   For editing, you will need many cores to store outtakes and trims. Have a good supply handy. Although 2-inch cores are used almost exclusively in shooting, they are not used extensively in editing. The tight wind of the inner layers can damage the film's emulsion and be particularly hard on sound stock.

Small trim container   It will be useful to have something to keep trims that are small, particularly those without edge numbers. Egg cartons are handy for storing frames, with identification written above each section.

Slug   Also referred to as sound *fill*, *slug* is leader or junk picture that is simply used to fill in the empty spots on the sound rolls. The positioning of sound against picture is controlled by where it is cut on its individual mixtrack (dialogue, narration, music, sound effects, and so on). If there is nothing occurring in the intervening time between two sounds on a mixtrack, several sound effects for instance, slug is used to create the distance between the two pieces. Unrecorded mag stock is not used to make up the gap between sounds, because even when blank it will give the sound a certain quality. Commercial films generally buy clear or colored leader for this, but picture from old projects can be used, or discarded prints can be purchased from film-supply stores. Any film with even a slightly complicated sound track will go through many feet of slug.

   Unused negative from past projects is very good for slug rolls because it keeps its shape and dimension well. Film prints and workprint that are very old should be avoided, because often the material has shrunk, causing the pitch to become smaller. Older film tends to be brittle as well, and as you run the mixtracks through the transports, the sprocket holes can tear and chip. If the slug makes clicking sounds while running, it will probably cause substantial problems that will entail many time-consuming repairs. This should be avoided even if it means ordering expensive slug from a commercial source.

Bad slug can cause damage to the actual pieces of sound as well. When the slug breaks or slips out of the sprocketed teeth in the transport, the mag stock will run through the sprocketed rollers out of line with the teeth. This tends to punch a new set of sprocket holes or tear up the existing sprocket holes to the extent that they will no longer run through the transports. The sound can always be retransferred, but this can cause delays as well as an unnecessary expense.

Footage Counters and Frame Rulers

Virtually all editing equipment comes with footage counters. Although their usefulness may not be apparent at first, everything in a film is counted and organized in footage and frames. Flatbeds have a button or switch to "zero the counter." You can then make counts from that zero point. This is helpful for timing effects and getting lengths on sequences. Toward the end of cutting, footage counts are used to communicate specific needs to the lab, such as identifying shots that need attention when printed.

On a 16mm synchronizer, the gangs have 40 sprocketed teeth per rotation—40 being the number of frames per foot in 16mm. The front gang has an indicator running from 0 to 39. Thus one spin of the synchronizer passes 1 foot of film through it. The rotation of the drum of the synchronizer is interlocked with a counter that keeps track of feet. If there is a specific frame you want to count from, you must lock it into the synchronizer at 0.

Frame rulers help determine the length and thus the running time of individual shots. You will learn the multiples of 24 very fast. In lieu of an actual ruler, you can lay out a piece of film on a page and put a small pen mark in each hole. Number each frame on the paper, and it can then serve as an easy reference. Frame rulers are helpful, but much of the actual counting of frames during cutting is done by matching pieces of film side by side.

Edge Numbers

Edge numbers are an aid to managing your footage and are the guideposts for conforming the original film to your edited workprint. They are latent code numbers that each manufacturer photographically imprints between the sprocket holes on all raw film stocks. As the image is processed, the numbers will develop as well. When the lab makes workprints, the edge numbers are printed through to the workprint; most labs do this automatically, although it must be requested at a few. Be sure to check.

Edge numbers come every twenty frames (6 inches) in 16mm and every sixteen frames in 35mm. **SEE 16-18** Super 8 does not have edge numbers, a fact that complicates the format's employment as a professional medium. The first set of letters and numbers (KJ63 on figure 16.18) refers to the date produced and the emulsion batch. The other two sets (0646 and 6104) are part of a sequence of ascending numbers that go from the head to the tail of the film. The frame twenty frames toward the tail would be identified as 0646, 6105. Twenty frames farther on would be 0646, 6106, et cetera. The frame with the • on it is called the *zero frame*— the frame from which all frame counts are made during conforming (see page 447 for a discussion of this process).

16-18

Edge numbers are used primarily as guideposts for conforming the original to the edited workprint

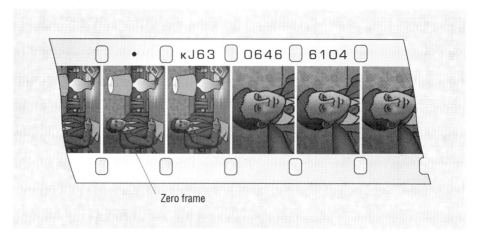

Zero frame

The newest wrinkle in the edge number picture is the introduction of magnetic edge coding, a bar-code–style method of referencing between videotape and film. Most film stocks now come with these bar codes. Along with the still-present edge numbers, they are located between the sprocket holes and provide an electronic output of the corresponding edge numbers. For many years, digital editing was not really an option for films destined for theatrical release, because there was no good way to get back to the edge numbers of the film for conforming. The bar-code numbers can now be referenced with the tape in the process of transferring the film to video. Once a video edit is completed, the bar-code numbers can be translated back to edge numbers and given to a negative cutter, and a film print can be made. This new approach has been a big step in the growing interface between film and video.

Edge numbers are helpful in organizing the workprint and avoiding mistakes in editing. In the process of trimming frames, storing them, and then trying to find them later, things can get very confused. If it is not clear if there are frames missing in a cut you are attempting to restore, checking to see if there are twenty frames between the edge numbers will answer any questions. If there are not twenty frames, further searches are necessary. If the frames turn out to be lost (an unacceptable outcome in a professional situation though an occasional reality for inexperienced editors), they can be slugged in with black leader, because the frames still exist in the original. The number of needed slug frames can be determined using a frame ruler.

17

Cutting Picture and Sound

COVERING **the mechanics of editing** presents a number of pitfalls. Clearly, the practical aspects of editing must be introduced before going through the detailed finishing processes of a film. And yet, the details of finishing a film must inform all decision making as the cutting is done. This chapter presents the traditional chronological sequence in which films are edited, but you should familiarize yourself with the specifics of finishing in chapter 18 before starting to cut. Understanding how frames are lost in the negative-cutting process is essential, and awareness of the requirements of dissolves, fades, and similar effects helps avoid problems later. Sound tracks have specific requirements and must be configured in standardized ways. All the steps in the editing process require knowledge and skill.

The crucial concept to understand is that all relationships between sound and picture are controlled by the frames. Once the tracks are threaded and locked together on the flatbed editing table, the picture frame has a corresponding sound frame on every mixtrack. Each frame on a sound head is theoretically in sync with the one that is in the picture gate. The relationship of each frame can be easily changed, but the goal is to create the relationships you desire. On the bench, looking across the top of the synchronizer is just the same as looking at the film on the individual heads of the flatbed editing table. The obvious difference is that on the flatbed, the frame is right there on the screen for you to look at, but on a bench it must be rolled out to a viewer in order to be seen.

Much of the mechanics of the cutting suggested here may appear complex at first, but these methods are relatively easy to master. The goal here is to describe some of the mechanical processes of cutting so you can refer to them during the actual process. Some descriptions may not become completely clear until you actually sit down and start trying some cuts. The terminology of the more popular flatbeds, such as *transports, locks,* and so on, are used, although effective editing can also be done on the bench, as well as on the older uprights.

Flatbeds

Although the video revolution has forced many manufacturers of film equipment out of the market, there are still a number of different flatbeds in common use, specifically Moviolas, Steenbecks, and KEMs. The six-plate, so named because it has two plates for each transport, one for feed and one for take-up, is the table commonly available to students and independents. The more versatile eight-plates are preferred because picture and sound are interchangeable on the fourth transport, giving the option of either picture searching or running a third mixtrack. Two-plates and four-plates are also available, both having been used extensively in television when news was shot on film; they receive limited use now. Several tables have interchangeable transports so the table can be switched between 16mm and 35mm. For a more complete view of flatbeds, see chapter 4.

The Control Panel

The knobs and buttons on the control panel control the movement of the film and what tracks are interlocked to what other tracks. **SEE 17-1** Manufacturers employ a number of approaches to how a control panel works, but the general theory is consistent from one table to the next.

Transport controls Each twist knob, called a pot (potentiometer), controls an individual transport, allowing you to run sound and picture independently. These hand controls can vary speed from creeping frame by frame to more than 100 fps; the maximum fast-forward speeds vary with manufacturers. The transports can be run in forward or reverse.

Sound-1 and sound-2 locks The lock buttons do what their names suggest. By depressing sound-1 lock, the first sound track is locked to the picture. Sound-2 lock does the same for the second sound transport. When lock buttons are depressed, all rolls are fed at precisely the same rate across the sound heads and picture gate, thus providing sync. The sound tracks are said to be slaved to the picture pot. When a lock button is depressed, the corresponding pot no longer functions. This lock is electronic on some tables, mechanical on others.

17-1

The transport controls and locks control the movement of the film and what tracks are interlocked to what other tracks
The control panel of the Moviola M77-AH

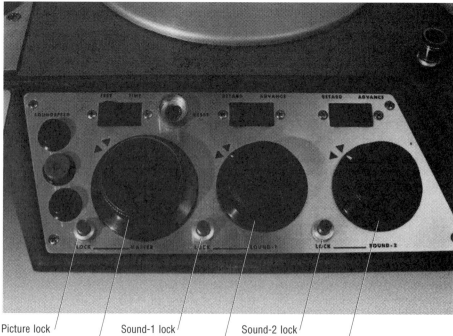

Picture lock
Picture transport control   Sound-1 lock   Sound-2 lock
                            Sound-1 transport control   Sound-2 transport control

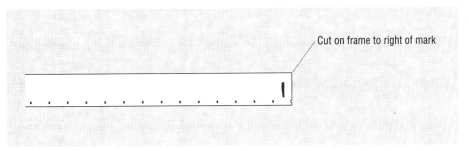

Cut on frame to right of mark

17-2

When marking a frame, put the mark right in the middle of the frame

Picture lock and soundspeed Depressing the picture-lock locks the picture pot to the soundspeed buttons at the left of the control panel. With this button, the picture and any sound tracks locked to it are run at soundspeed (24 fps).

Practical Cutting Considerations

Almost all cutting is done to the left of the transports. When you set up hole punches and pass the film and mixtracks from left to right through the transports, you are in effect "committing the act of sync"; that is, any tracks that are locked together are in sync as they are fed through the transports. Clearly, there is no permanency in this description of sync. You merely need to unlock the tracks or cut in different frames to vary the relationships between picture and sound. But the goal is to create and finalize the relationships between sound and picture that you want.

The process of cutting sound requires frequent marking of the magnetic stock, both designating cut points and identifying specific events in the sound. When marking a frame, put the mark right in the middle. **SEE 17-2** If you mark on the frame line, it might be unclear later which frame was being identified. In the context of this chapter, *cutting at the mark* means cutting at the first frame line to the right. You may eventually work out other methods but, for now, consistency and clarity is the key.

The terms *head* and *tail* are both used frequently in these discussions. *Head* is the beginning of a shot or a roll; *tail* is the end of a shot or a roll. As a film is set up on the bench or flatbed, the head is on the right and the tail is on the left. Although this is a natural left-to-right movement, it forces the dialogue and other audio information to be represented in reverse in the illustrations.

While editing, care should be taken to keep the workprint clean and trouble-free. The dirtier it gets, the harder it is to evaluate. In commercial situations, clients or funders may view the film, so you will want to have a clean product to impress them.

Preparing to Edit Sync Sound

Although many film programs justifiably have students start editing to sound effects and music tracks, the logical starting place for understanding the relationship between sound and image is with the production sound, the sync tracks. For those with experience in basic video editing, handling synchronous sound in film may appear cumbersome. The editorial staff must perform a number of procedures to prepare the film for viewing and cutting. A typical film takes days of prep work before you can start making any creative decisions.

Of the many things that should be done, two processes cannot be avoided: syncing up and creating the first assembly. *Syncing up* refers to matching the production sound, which has been recorded separately, with the image. Creating the first assembly, also called ***stringing out***, is choosing the desired takes and then putting them in the order called for in the script. Two other processes are optional but highly recommended: edge numbering and A & B rolling the sound tracks. Both can save beginners many headaches. Though A & B rolling can be done at this time, the practical and theoretical aspects of this process are discussed in the section on actual dialogue cutting, later in this chapter.

Syncing sound and picture is often done on the flatbed, although it is also easy to do on the bench. Given limited resources, working on a bench may be an excellent option to save costly table time. If you are going to sync up on a bench, make sure that the sound and picture rolls are carefully organized and logged during shooting. Any irregularities will be much more difficult to iron out on the bench. Whether on bench or flatbed, the logs themselves are indispensable for all cutting; any discrepancies should be easily cleared up by consulting them.

The methods of syncing, preparing rolls, setting up leaders, and cutting all sound is very standardized in a professional editing room. This standardization maximizes efficiency when the editing crew is going through massive amounts of footage. It also sets up cues so that everyone involved in cutting, printing, and sound-mixing procedures will understand how the rolls are to be threaded in the various machines. All the procedures, codings, and markings could not be detailed here, and several of them may not be that efficient for inexperienced editors working with a small amount of footage. Some general approaches are covered, and what is presented here should guide you through the initial stages and get you into some good habits as well. That said, you should start becoming aware of what will be expected of you should you ever find yourself in a professional editing room.[1] The rationale behind the specific procedures and the general way in which editing is approached is organization. Without an organized approach, the creative aspects of cutting can and will be defeated.

Syncing Up

The editorial staff starts with the production crew's work from the previous day. The film is picked up at the lab and the mag stock transfers of the production sound, called ***sync rolls***, are picked up from the transfer studio. Because the sound and the image are recorded separately, there are always different amounts of each. The assistant or apprentice editor must go through and manually match them up. The sound is transferred to the mag stock, and all sync is controlled by the sprocket holes. As stated, the hit of the slate is the reference point used to match the visual and audio.

When you sync a roll of sound to a roll of picture, there are two different basic procedures. The first sets up the rolls and puts the first shot in sync. Once the first shot is done, you employ the second procedure for every subsequent sync shot throughout the roll.

The first procedure is straightforward and logical. Thread the workprint into the picture transport and the sync-sound roll into one of the sound transports. With the transports *not* locked together, run the picture until the slate is hit. With some practice, you will be able to control the transport to move the picture frame by frame and stop on the exact frame where the slate hits. This frame is easy to discern. The shot will start with the clapper/loader holding the slate bar up. You will be able to see the frame where the bar starts to come down and then the exact frame where it hits. The diagonal white lines of the bar and the board itself are designed so that you will be able to find the exact point where the two meet. **SEE 17-3**

---

1. The responsibilities of and procedures used by the assistant and apprentice editors are detailed in Norman Hollyn's *The Film Editing Room Handbook* (Beverly Hills: Lone Eagle Publishing Company, 1990).

17-3

The hit of the slate is the reference point used to match the visual and audio

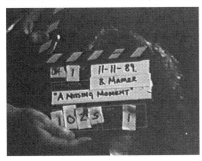 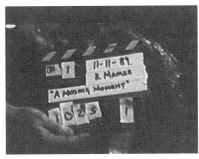 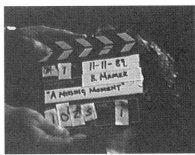

With this frame resting in the picture gate, run the sound up to the hit of the slate. Play the sync track at roughly normal speed until you find the sound of the slate. It will be easy to find as it is accompanied by all the starting instructions and the verbal identification of scene and take by the 2nd AC or clapper/loader. Once you locate the slate, find the exact first frame of its sound.

Although the sound is not visible, it can be graphically represented. **SEE 17-4** You can determine this first frame, called the *attack*, by moving the stock very slowly across the head. The attack will be loud and raspy as distinct from the silent frames before it. For future reference, use a permanent marker to indicate the exact frame where the slate starts. Lock the sound transport to the picture, and you are set to go. At this point the first shot, and only the first shot, is in sync. Once the picture and the sound are set up, the second procedure will be used to sync each subsequent take.

It is imperative that you find the exact first frame where the slate hits on both the sound and the picture. If this is handled carelessly, the shots will not be in sync. Once the slates are removed in the actual editing, the mistake will not be caught and the shot will be wrong until the very end. If you are lucky enough to catch the problem at the mix, correcting it will be very costly. If you do not catch it at the mix, it will be on-screen in your final print. A mistake of a single frame may be difficult to see on a table, but when the film is magnified 300,000 times in a theater, it will be noticed by many. Mistakes of more than one frame will be visible to all.

There is one more thing that needs to be done before rolling on to the next shot. With the transports still locked, roll back several feet toward the head and mark a picture frame and its corresponding frame on the sound roll. Roll these marks out and put a hole punch on each mark. This will be used as a reference point to load the rolls. Their positioning is somewhat arbitrary, because these punches will soon be replaced with the familiar countdown leader (see page 414).

Once you have completed these setup procedures, roll on to the second shot. Nothing has to be done to the tail end of the first shot. The beginning of each new shot is always easy to identify because of the *flash frames*, the overexposed frames at the beginning of every shot. With the second shot, you will start the procedure

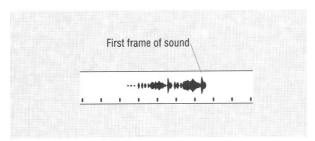

First frame of sound

17-4

You can determine the first frame of sound—the attack—by moving the stock very slowly across the head

that will remain consistent for all subsequent takes. It is broken down into simple steps, outlined below, that are relatively straightforward. These steps will eventually be complicated by a number of issues that are important when working as an assistant or an apprentice in a professional setting. These complications are easily surmountable once you understand the basic theory.

The following steps outline the second phase of syncing up and apply to all subsequent sync shots on the roll.

1. Find the hit of the visual slate and mark on the audio straight across from it.

2. Find the actual audio slate and mark it.

3. Roll the film out of the transports, cut from the first mark to the second mark, and splice the remaining pieces together.

Find the hit of the visual slate   The visual hit of the slate will be found in the manner previously described. Once you have the exact frame in the picture gate, mark the frame straight across from it on the audio track. **SEE 17-5** The positioning of this marked audio frame on the mag stock will be random, but it should occur in the start-up sequence ("Speed," "Camera," "Rolling," "Mark it").

Find and mark the audio slate   With picture and sound still locked, roll to the actual audio slate. There is almost always more sound than image for each individual take, because the sound recorder is started before the camera in the sequence to initiate takes. So you will roll forward to find the audio slate. Find it in the manner described earlier and mark the exact frame. **SEE 17-6** You now have two marks on the audio: one marking the frame that corresponds to the visual slate and the other the actual audio slate.

Roll out, cut, and splice the pieces   Roll your marks out to the *left* of the transports. Cut from the *right* of the first mark to the *right* of the second mark. **SEE 17-7A** Then splice the remaining pieces together. **SEE 17-7B**

17-5

Step 1: Find the hit of the visual slate and mark on the audio straight across from it

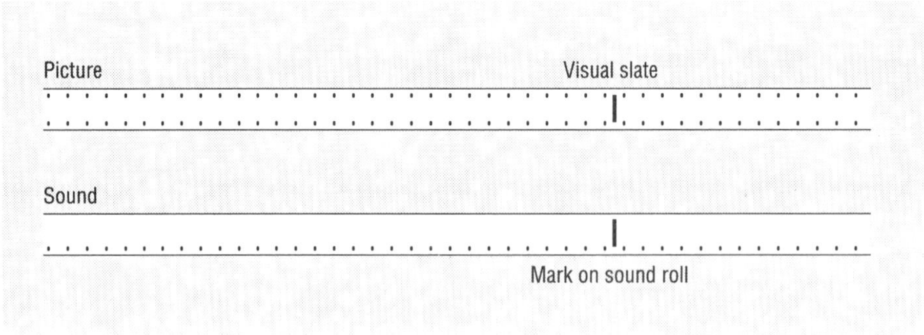

17-6

Step 2: Find the actual audio slate and mark it

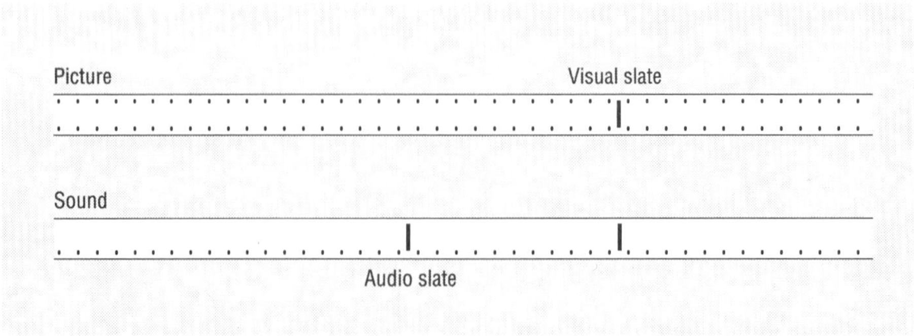

17-7

Step 3

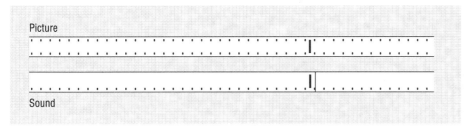

A. Roll the film out of the transports, cut from the first mark to the second mark...

B. ...and splice the remaining pieces together

This simple process has to be repeated for every sync take throughout the entire roll. Before attacking the remaining slates, however, there are a number of ground rules to keep in mind. First, as with virtually all other sound and image cutting, all the splicing in the syncing-up process is done to the *left* of the synchronizer or transports. Any cutting to the right will disturb shots that are already synced, causing the rolls to go out of sync. Second, once you have locked the picture and the sound together in the setup procedure, keep them locked. If you unlock either picture or sound, you take them out of sync. Although picture and sound are relatively easy to get back in sync by going back to the last synced scene or the hole punches at the head, unlocking the tracks can lead to errors and consequently time-consuming repairs of sync. When you clearly understand what you are doing, this may not be important. Until then, *keep the tracks locked.* Third, close counts only in horseshoes and grenades. You have to find the *exact* first frame of the slate on both sound and image. If you make a mistake of a frame or two, it will follow you all the way through editing, mixing, and the final print. A mistake of one frame may not be perceived on a conscious level, but you want to be dead-on all the time.

Fourth, the sound slate almost always follows the picture, but on the rare occasion when it does not, the tracks require special handling. The visual slate would follow the audio slate if there were camera runs for cleaning and checking camera functions. The easiest way to deal with this is to insert a piece of slug at the head of the sound take. **SEE 17-8** This will back up the audio slate so it is behind the picture slate. Once you have done this, you continue the normal procedure.

With the exception of MOS shots, the picture should be kept intact and all cuts should be on the sound. Even the botched takes should be synced and left on the roll. All MOS shots and nonsync sound effects that the sound mixer recorded on location should be removed from the rolls and rolled onto separate cores. The most effective way to remove an MOS shot is to mark the first frame and then roll to the tail of the shot, as always with the picture and the sound locked. You will hear the next sync take as you do this. Mark the last frame of the MOS shot and roll this marked frame out to the left. Cut at the mark, remove the

17-8

On the rare occasions when the sound slate precedes the picture, insert a piece of slug at the head of the sound take to back up the audio behind the picture slate

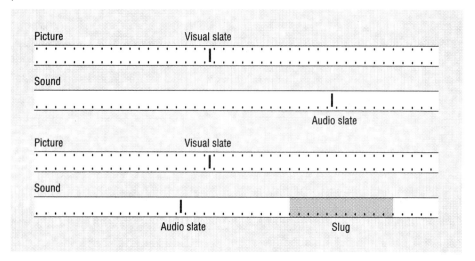

picture roll from the plate, and then attach the tail of the MOS shot to a new core. Roll the entire shot back onto the core, cutting it at the first frame, which is the first mark. Remove the new core with the MOS shot, and splice the picture roll back on. The next sync picture will be against its sync sound, and the original procedure can be resumed. The process is identical when removing sound effects. Occasionally, the editor may want you to leave the MOS shots on the roll. In this case, you use slug against the picture.

All MOS shots and sound effects should be clearly labeled once they are removed from their original rolls. On the film tape used to close the rolls, write the scene and take numbers. To cross-reference with the pieces of film themselves, the assistant will also make lists with brief descriptions of both effects and MOS shots. Keeping this material organized is important to efficient editing and one of the primary responsibilities of the assistant editor.

The aforementioned complications deal with cutting on the exact frame of the audio slate. Frequently, there is information in front of the slate that needs to be kept for the editor, particularly scene and take identification. This is why it was recommended that the numbers be said *after* the slate. Also, if you cut right in front of the slate, you risk accidentally cutting the slate itself if you have made a mistake identifying the frame. If the sync looks wrong later, you cannot go back to check it because the piece between has been discarded. The solution is to move the cut away from the slate itself. In this process, you make the first and second marks as described previously. Then you make the cut an equal number of frames, 8 frames for example, toward the head from each mark. Preserving verbal information that precedes the slate is handled in the same manner. Find the beginning of the verbal identification of the slate and mark just in front of it. Cut at this third mark. The third mark will be displaced a certain number of frames from the second mark, 60 frames for example, and you just cut that same displacement (60 frames) in front of the first mark. To avoid all that messy frame counting, the cut is made by stretching out the already cut piece of film against the piece yet to be cut.

Edge Numbering/Coding

Edge numbering is going through the synced-up film and physically transferring all the edge numbers on the picture onto the corresponding frames of the sound.

Many labs provide a similar service called *coding*, in which the lab inks an entire new series of numbers on both sound and picture. This latter approach is vastly preferable, relatively affordable, and is the professional norm. For the low-tech filmmaker with limited resources, edge numbering is easily done by hand with a permanent marker. Independent filmmakers occasionally bypass edge numbering or coding the film, although the time it will ultimately save for an inexperienced editor is substantial.

Whichever approach you choose, the purpose is to provide a reference for sync. Once actual editing is started, you will obviously be cutting out the slates. Without the slate as a reference, the code or transferred edge numbers allow you to reestablish sync when you make the unavoidable errors in removing sound or picture. The more experienced you become, the less this will be an issue. Mistakes should diminish, although it is still crucial to have a reference if any questions arise. The numbers can be used to correct everything from big errors to questions of individual frames. There is nothing more frustrating than looking at a shot and not knowing if it is in sync; and nothing is quite as time-consuming as going in and shifting frames to see if it is correct.

Edge numbering by hand is easiest on the synchronizer. Before starting, double-check the rolls to make sure that all slates are in sync. Mag stock has a base and emulsion just like film, and the film must be set up so you are writing on the base. If you write on the emulsion, the entire production sound will have to be retransferred on fresh stock and resynced. Set up the film so it is running the opposite way on the synchronizer, that is, from right to left instead of left to right. Set up the reels so they run off the top rather than from the bottom. This will put the sprocket holes in the appropriate position for the teeth on the synchronizer and the base facing up. Write each edge number on the precise corresponding frame on the mag stock. Do this for all rolls.

Obviously, this approach to edge numbering is time-consuming. As suggested, the coding method should be discussed with the lab to see if it fits your budget. On a feature or complex documentary, the amount of footage may make edge numbering by hand less feasible. Going to the lab may be the only option. But to avoid costs, writing the numbers by hand is a viable alternative. It is not as painful as it appears, and whatever time is expended initially will be saved many times over when you start the actual creative part of editing.

First Assembly

Creating the *first assembly*, or *string out*, is arranging the film in rough order. One end product of the syncing-up stage is that the sound and picture for each shot are exactly the same length in terms of frames. Stringing out is taking out the desired shots, organizing them, and then putting them back together in order. On a short film, the entire piece may be strung out in this stage whereas a feature may be done a scene at a time. Don't worry about every subtlety—all you are creating is a rough sequence.

The first step is to evaluate the synced film and pick your *selects*—the version, the take—of each shot that you consider the best for your purpose. There are several deciding factors in evaluation, most notably performance, continuity with other shots, overall compositional integrity, and sound quality. In conventional narrative films, performance tends to be the overriding factor, though shots with poor formal qualities, such as sloppy camera movement, are generally eliminated out of hand. Do not remove these selects during this evaluative process, but circle the chosen takes in the logs. Pulling them out is a separate procedure.

Beginners will find it advantageous to do the first assembly on a bench rather than on the flatbed. On a synchronizer, the relationship between frames is exceptionally clear and, as with every other stage, precision is a must. Any errors in removing the shots will cause major headaches in trying to reassemble the film both in order and in sync. The film should be strung out with all the slates and other information still intact. When you pull the selects, pull them from the beginning flash frame to the ending flash frame.

To cut out the identified select, roll to the flash frame at the head of the shot. Mark the flash frame and the corresponding frame on the mag stock. Roll the film out to the *right* of the synchronizer and cut at the marks (the first assembly is one of the few stages in which you cut on the right). Roll to the tail of the shot, hanging the head of it in the trim bin. Mark the first flash frame of the next shot and the corresponding frame on the sound. Roll the marks out to the right and cut. You now have two pieces—one sound and one picture—representing the entire take, each piece being precisely the same length, frame for frame. With film tape, label the scene by its number. Keeping the material organized when it is hanging in the trim bin is essential.

In this manner, pull each desired shot out of the sync rolls. It is imperative that what you pull out has an equal number of sound and picture frames. Any error will mean that the entire film will be out of sync that number of frames from the mistake on. Do not hesitate to check the shots by measuring them against each other. Stretch the two pieces out side by side and match up the sprocket holes for the length of the shot. **SEE 17-9** Sometimes the mag stock might be slightly smaller, requiring constant adjustment to make sure you are going frame by frame. If the two pieces are not the same length, you have made a mistake which must be corrected. Although this method may at first appear odd and cumbersome, measuring sound and image against each other is the central approach to controlling and maintaining sync in editing. When you have completed pulling the selects, they should all be numbered and hanging in the trim bin. It is now a matter of putting them back together in order, creating two new rolls—one picture, one sound—made up entirely of the selects.

Before putting the film back together, standardized leaders should be set up with reference points, called **head start marks**, for cueing up the separate rolls. This is done with **SMPTE Universal leader** (*SMPTE* stands for Society of Motion Picture and Television Engineers). It is also referred to as *Academy leader* or **countdown leader**. The leader is made up of the sequence of descending numbers familiar to most readers. **SEE 17-10** The sequence starts with 8 and descends to 2. Each number lasts for twenty-four frames (one second), with the exception of the 2, which is a single frame. This frame with the 2, the *Academy 2*, is used to sync up all the other elements in the printing process. The frame right before the actual

17-9

Measuring sound and image pieces side by side is the standard approach to controlling and maintaining sync

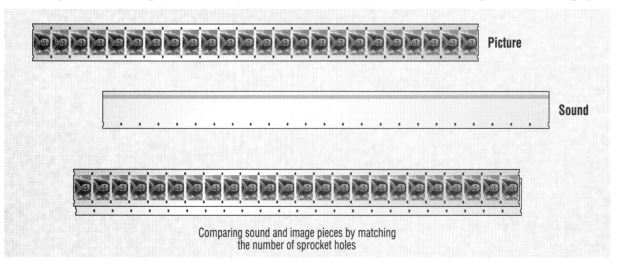

Comparing sound and image pieces by matching
the number of sprocket holes

17-10

Standardized countdown leader is set up at the beginning of the edited workprint

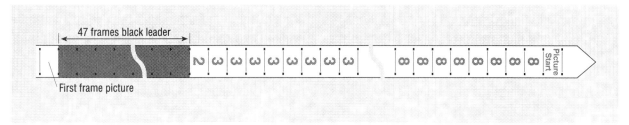

countdown sequence—the frame before the first 8—should also be noted. Labeled "picture start," it is the point from which all shots are identified for the technicians who are part of the process of creating a final print. The footage counter is zeroed on the synchronizer, and picture start is set up on the zero frame of the gang. If a shot needs special attention, it is identified in footage and frames from this point (see chapter 18 for further discussion). Countdown leader can usually be bought at a lab or a film-supply store.

Set up a countdown leader in one of the gangs of the synchronizer. There will be an arrow symbol with "splice here" printed underneath it forty-seven frames after the 2. **SEE 17-11** Cut your first shot in here, leaving its corresponding piece of sound in the trim bin.

For the sound, set up 10 to 15 feet of white leader in the gang across from the countdown leader. On this white leader, mark the frame corresponding to the first picture frame and cut in the piece of mag stock for the first shot. Now the first shot, picture and sound, is attached to these leaders in sync. In order to cue up the separate rolls, the frame corresponding to the Academy 2 must be indicated on the white leader of the sound roll. To this end, mark the frame corresponding to the Academy 2 and replace it with a *sync beep* or *sync pop*—a single frame of mag stock cut out of a longer piece with a constant tone recorded on it. **SEE 17-12** When it runs across the sound head at 24 fps, it provides the familiar beep at the head of all film reels.

It is now a matter of taking the shots hung in the trim bin and cutting them onto these rolls in order. If the scenes have been properly numbered and organized

17-11

Cut in the first frame of picture where indicated

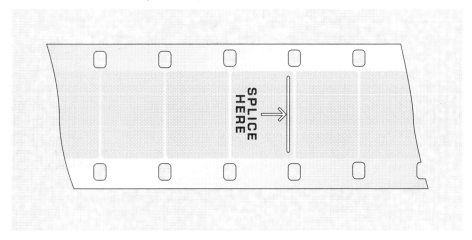

17-12

The sync beep is a single frame of mag stock that provides the beep tone at the head of film reels

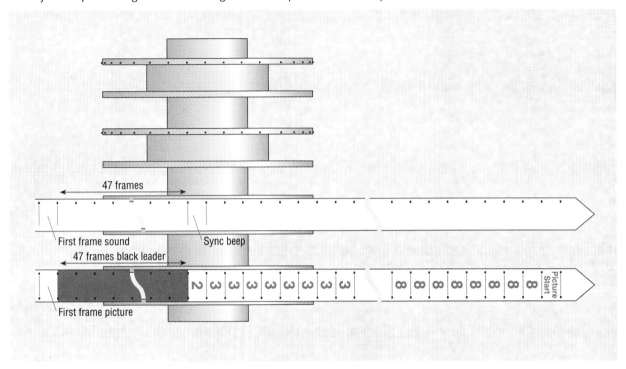

47 frames

First frame sound

47 frames black leader

Sync beep

First frame picture

2 3 3 3 3 3 3 3   8 8 8 8 8 8 8 8   Picture Start

on the set, this should be a simple process of following the scene numbers. However, have a copy of the script handy to make sure that the sequence is correct.

If you have been accurate in pulling the scenes out frame for frame, you should be able to put all the shots back together without the synchronizer. It is recommended, however, that you use the synchronizer to double-check your work. All first assembly cuts should be straight across from each other when you roll them into the synchronizer. If they do not correspond, you have made a mistake. When you have reassembled the takes, you should have one roll with the film in order as well as a number of outtake rolls.

Handling MOS shots is also an issue. If MOS shots are designed as inserts into longer shots, I tend to leave them on their cores to be cut in later. If they are key pieces that drive the narrative forward, I go ahead and string them out with slug against them.

Once you have chosen a take, do not assume that you are locked into that decision. With the take in the context of the other shots, you may notice a problem, say, continuity or timing, that makes the shot unsuitable. Do not hesitate to go back to the outtakes to see if there is anything that better fits the specific situation. Another take may have shortcomings but better continuity characteristics. If the shot you have to discard has better line readings, it is possible to drop the better dialogue onto the preferred shot.

Avoid the temptation to mix any of these processes or make creative decisions in these stages. Keep your parameters focused. It is important to see the raw material in each stage before effectively making decisions about the next stage. You also get into a groove with each process, becoming very efficient. Trying to make decisions prematurely will draw straightforward activities out to painful lengths.

Dialogue Cutting

The statement that "every cut is an adventure" could not be truer than in dialogue cutting. Getting each individual transition to work is challenging enough, but the shape of the entire scene has to be considered as well. It is possible to get the cuts to work well on an individual basis and still find that the scene is slow or awkward. As suggested, although there is no single correct place to cut between any two shots, there are myriad wrong places. The goal in conventional dialogue cutting is to find the *cut point* where the natural rhythms of human speech are maintained, the movement matches appropriately, and the pacing in relationship to other cuts is right.

The first cut discussed will be the straight cut, a cut that tends to be abrupt. Although this is a good starting point, the fundamental approach to all dialogue cutting is the overlapping dialogue cut. This simply means that the picture cuts come in the middle of lines of dialogue. In many cases, we see a character responding before the speaker has finished speaking. While we look at a film, we are rarely aware that someone has made a conscious choice between different shots and transition points, and, particularly, that these choices affect our response and interpretation of what we are seeing.

Straightforward shot/reverse shot sequences are used here for basic examples. Dialogue cutting obviously becomes much more complex than the simple examples used here, but the principles presented are the starting point for even the most advanced cutting. In a sense, these simple cuts act as a window into the more complex cutting that can be learned only by doing.

Here is a fundamental principle of the mechanics of editing:

▶ **RULE:** *Whenever you make a cut in one roll—sound or picture— there must be an equal and reciprocal cut in all other rolls.*

If twenty frames are cut out of the picture, the sound roll is now that same twenty frames out of sync. To get back into sync, you have to cut out the twenty frames of sound that correspond roughly with the picture frames. This undoubtedly brings up a host of questions, but keep the idea of cutting equal amounts of picture and sound in mind.

Straight Cuts

A *straight cut* is one in which a character finishes a line of dialogue, and you cut to the next shot with the second character delivering his or her line of dialogue. It is simple to execute, although there are some complications with the sound. Eventually you will find that most cuts are more complicated than the simple, arbitrary straight cut demonstrated here.

An example is the exchange of two lines of dialogue suggested in the section on storyboarding. In shot #1 John asks: "Do you want to go to the movies?" In the second shot Andrea responds: "I don't know. What times are the shows?" The first assembly still has the entire shot, including all the verbal and visual directions: the director's "Cut" on the outgoing shot and the start-up calls, the mark of the slate, and the "Action" on the incoming shot. **SEE 17-13**

The first step in making a straight cut is to determine the length of the pause desired between the two lines of dialogue; that is, how much time do you want to elapse between the end of the first line and the beginning of the second. Generally, the goal is to re-create the natural cadences and rhythms of human speech. Experienced editors cut to the inherent pace of the scene. For our purposes it is helpful to think of a pause as a specific number of frames. When you cut the mag stock, you are dealing with increments of $1/24$ of a second. If there are 24 frames

17-13

The first assembly still had the slate and all verbal directions

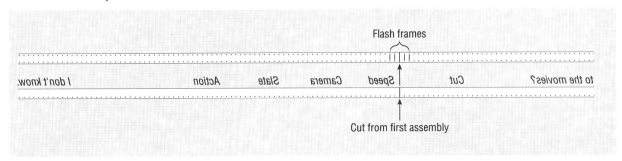

17-14

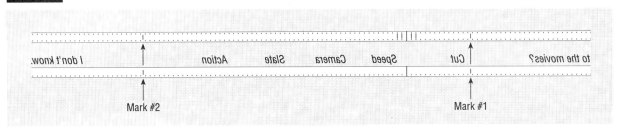

A. To establish a 1-second pause, you cut out all but 24 frames between the two lines of dialogue...

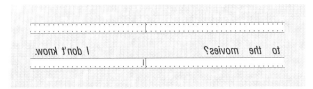

B. ...and splice the pieces together

between two lines of dialogue, the pause will be 1 second long. An 18-frame pause will be ¾ of a second, and so on.

If you want the pause to be 1 second long, you need to plan 24 frames between the end of the word *movies* and the beginning of the word *what*. While this represents a somewhat arbitrary approach, it nevertheless illustrates the process. To start, find the **decay**—a term that describes how sound trails off and reverberates—of the word *movies*, count 12 frames toward the tail, and mark on the both the audio and the picture. Then find the attack of the word *I*, count 12 frames toward the head, and again mark both audio and picture. Then cut from mark to mark on both rolls. **SEE 17-14** As always, check the two pieces against each other to make sure that you are removing the same amount of sound and picture.

The two 12-frame extensions add up to the 1-second pause desired. Taking 12 from one side and 12 from the other is, of course, completely arbitrary in terms of the example. You just need the total to add up to 24. That we have paid little attention to the picture's content suggests how arbitrary an example this is.

Pauses are shorter than one at first expects. When you start cutting, you begin to appreciate just how much time one second can be. Screen time is much more intense and concentrated than real time. If one second feels long, five seconds can feel like an eternity. Normal conversations generally have pauses of a little less than one second. Characters engaged in a heated exchange would have even shorter pauses in the dialogue. A scene with two characters engaged in a contemplative discussion might have a much different rhythm.

If the pauses are too short, the lines will seem stacked on top of each other and unnatural, and if the pauses are too long, the dialogue will sound stilted or mannered. Very quickly, you will internalize this and not think about specific times of pauses. You will just cut it until it sounds right. The performers themselves often provide the pauses in situations where the camera covers lengthy exchanges of dialogue. As with the visual example from Michelangelo Antonioni's *The Red Desert* in chapter 16, cadences can be delayed or accelerated to create stylized effects. For now, it is helpful to think out the pauses in specific numbers of frames.

Always cut the shot long before cutting it short. Cut the pause slightly longer than you think will be appropriate. You can then listen to the transition and cut it down if necessary. It is much easier to trim the shots down than add removed frames back in. Inexperienced editors tend to fiddle too much with cuts, adding frames in and taking them out, leaving both picture and sound frames prone to damage. Trying to cut in one or two frames is an exercise in frustration. They are hard to line up on the splicing block, frequently resulting in frames at slightly skewed angles. This can make a picture cut hard to evaluate, because it will jump at the gate. It also increases the possibility of the film tearing on editing tables and in projectors. The sound is even more of a problem because tight cutting on frames can increase glitches and dropout as the pieced-together area crosses the sound head. Keep in mind that the mag stock you are cutting is the mag stock that you will be taking to the final audio mix. Any imperfections will be difficult to keep out of the sound track.

As stated, this type of cutting tends to feel very abrupt. It can be useful for interruptions and dialogue that needs a punch, but if all cuts are straight cuts, a scene can start to resemble a Ping-Pong match, with the perspective abruptly flipping back and forth. Oddly enough, straight cuts work better on television than they do in films. Given the financial limitations and brutal deadlines of the medium, their greater ease makes more sense. Editors who can make a cut quickly are valued in television. This does not mean that the shows could not be cut better and that overlaps would not be appropriate, but the straight cuts do not look as abrupt on TV as they do on the big screen.

Overlapping Cuts

The overlapping cut is the bread and butter of narrative dialogue cutting, both conventional and otherwise. An *overlapping dialogue cut* is one in which the transition from one shot to the next occurs during a line of dialogue. In simple shot/reverse shot sequences, a common example is to cut from the speaker to the respondent before the speaker has finished the line of dialogue. A step-by-step approach to this type of cut is given below, although eventually it becomes internalized to the extent that it is simply the natural way to cut a film.

The opening scene from John Huston's *The Maltese Falcon* (Thomas Richards, editor) has often been used as an example of the efficient Hollywood commercial feature. The use of shot/reverse shot, the way the camera leads the action, and the use of the camera to establish narrative space epitomizes the traditional approach. However, many of these studies have not recognized the unique contribution of the cutting, with a number of key relationships and character traits established through editing. The scene involves private detective Sam Spade (Humphrey Bogart) and a potential client, Miss Wonderly (Mary Astor). **SEE 17-15**

As you look at this breakdown, a simple pattern emerges. Spade is virtually always cut to in the middle of one of Wonderly's lines, and Wonderly is always cut to just as she begins her lines. This tends to make the cuts to Spade very smooth and natural, as well as emphasize his response to Wonderly. The cuts to Wonderly, on the other hand, are abrupt, emphasizing the skittish aspects of her character. Also notice that the sole MOS shot in the scene belongs to Spade as he studies Wonderly suspiciously.

17-15

The editing pattern in this scene establishes a number of key relationships and character traits

John Huston's *The Maltese Falcon*

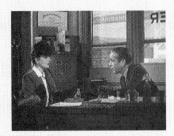

SPADE

Won't you sit down, Miss Wonderly?

WONDERLY

Thank you. I inquired at the hotel for the name of a reliable private detective. They mentioned yours.

SPADE

Suppose you tell me about it from the very beginning.

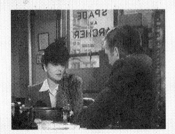

WONDERLY

I'm from New York. I'm trying to find my sister. I have reason to believe that she's here in San Francisco with a man by the name of Thursby—Floyd Thursby. I don't know where she met him. We've never been as close as sisters ought to be. If we had been, perhaps Corrinne would have told me that she was running away with him. Mother and Father in Honolulu would kill him. I've got to find them before they get back home....

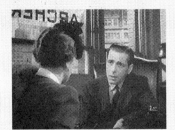

...They're coming home the first of the month.

SPADE

You've had word of your sister.

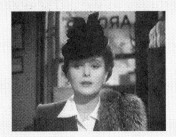

WONDERLY

A letter from her about two weeks ago. It said nothing except that she was all right. I sent her a telegram, begging her to come home. I sent it "general delivery" here. That was the only address she gave me. I waited a week and no answer came, so I decided to come out here myself. I wrote her that I was coming....

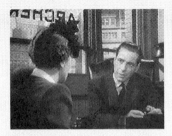

...I shouldn't have done that, should I?

SPADE

It's not always easy to know what to do. You haven't found her?

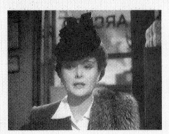

WONDERLY

No. I told her in my letter that I'd be at the St. Mark and for her to meet me there. I waited three whole days. She didn't come—didn't even send a message....

(continued)

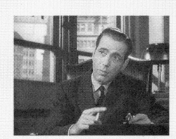

...It was horrible...Waiting....

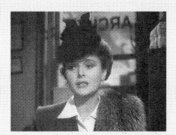

...I sent her another letter through "general delivery." Yesterday afternoon I went to the post office. Corrinne didn't call for her mail, but Floyd Thursby did. He wouldn't tell me where Corrinne was. He said she didn't want to see me. I can't believe that. He promised to bring her to the hotel if she'd come this evening. He said he knew she wouldn't. He promised to come himself if she didn't. He didn't...

(sound of door opening)

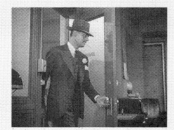

ARCHER

Oh, 'scuse me.

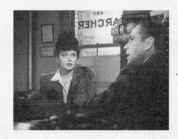

SPADE

It's all right, Miles. Come in....

Through this editing pattern, Spade is subtly established as someone who is both in control of his environment and distrustful of virtually everyone. Screenwriters frequently talk about "whose scene it is" when they are writing a script. This refers to defining what character is the central focus of a given scene and then structuring the scene accordingly. The editing of this scene from *The Maltese Falcon* accomplishes a very similar goal. By emphasizing Spade's response and Wonderly's agitation, the cutting subtly establishes who is in control. Eventually we find out that Miss Wonderly is putting on an act and has lied about everything including her name, but the scene is still Spade's. Miss Wonderly, while being an important and well-established character, is a foil that motivates the action. She both initiates and complicates the action in what is essentially a character study of Sam Spade.

As with everything else, there is nothing random or accidental about the cuts. As you analyze the way scenes are cut, imagine an editor evaluating the material and making conscious choices. The precise cutting points are thought out and made with a specific purpose in mind, be it for dramatic (as in this example from *The Maltese Falcon*), kinetic, or formal reasons.

17-15

(continued)

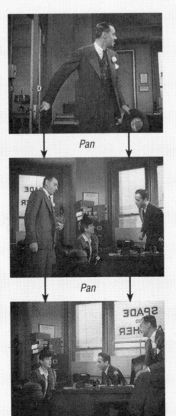

…Miss Wonderly, my partner, Miles Archer. Miss Wonderly's sister ran away from New York with a fellow named Floyd Thursby. They're here in San Francisco. Miss Wonderly has seen Thursby and has a date to meet him tonight. Maybe he'll bring the sister with him. The chances are he won't. Miss Wonderly wants us to find the sister, get her away from him and back home. Right?

Pan

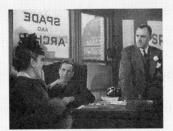

WONDERLY

Yes.

SPADE

Now, it's simply a matter of having a man at the hotel this evening to shadow him when he leads us to your sister. If, after we've found her, she still doesn't want to leave him…well, we have ways of managing that.

Pan

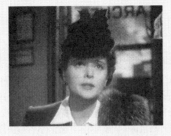

ARCHER

Yeah.

WONDERLY

Oh, but you must be careful. I'm deathly afraid of him…what he might do. She's so young, and his bringing her here from New York is such a serious…

…Mightn't he… mightn't he do something to her?

SPADE

Now, just leave that to us. We'll know how to handle it.

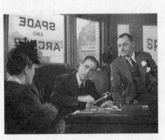

WONDERLY

Oh, but I want you to know he's a dangerous man. I honestly don't think he'd stop at anything. I don't think he'd hesitate to…to kill Corrinne if he thought it would save him.

ARCHER

Could he cover up by marrying her?

WONDERLY

He has a wife and three children in England.

SPADE

They usually do, though not always in England. What does he look like?

17-15
(continued)

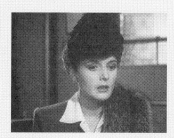

WONDERLY

Has dark hair and thick, bushy eyebrows. Talks in a loud, blustery manner. Gives the impression of being a violent person....

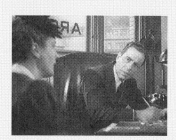

...He was wearing a light gray suit and a gray hat when I saw him this morning.

SPADE

What does he do for a living?

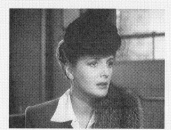

WONDERLY

I haven't the faintest idea.

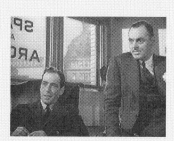

SPADE

What time is he coming to see you?

WONDERLY

After eight o'clock.

SPADE

All right, Miss Wonderly, we'll have a man there.

ARCHER

I'll look after it myself.

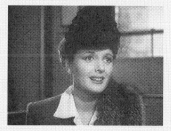

WONDERLY

Thank you....

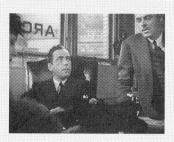

...Oh, yes....

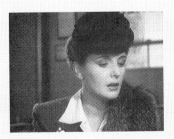

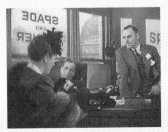

…Will that be enough?…

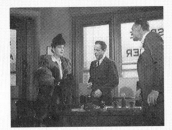

…Thank you.

SPADE

Not at all.

WONDERLY

Oh, it'll help some if you'd meet Thursby in the lobby.

ARCHER

You don't have to look for me. I'll see you all right.

There are two basic steps to making an overlap between two shots. Eventually your cutting will become complex and sophisticated enough that these simple steps will appear overly schematic, but they should be helpful for starters.

1. Make the audio cut.

2. Make the picture cut, displaced from the sound cut.

Make the audio cut   The rhythms and cadences of human speech are again the determining factors in making this first cut. Decide what pause you want between the lines and cut, paying no attention to the picture. This will leave the next shot out of sync, the removed piece of sound representing the exact number of frames the following shot will be out of sync. **SEE 17-16** To restore sync, you will remove an equal number of frames from the picture.

Make the picture cut, displaced from the sound cut   Using the removed piece of sound as a guide, make the reciprocal picture cut, only displace it from the sound cut you made in step 1. If you were to cut the picture at precisely the same place as the sound cut, the result would simply be a straight cut. A good approach for determining the displacement is to find where you want to exit from the first speaker. If you decide that you want to exit during the word *movies,* you would mark on the picture across from the word. **SEE 17-17A** Cut at the mark and stretch the sound against the picture toward the tail, cutting out an equal number of picture frames. The resulting cut will exit speaker A during the word *movies,* overlapping speaker B over the word. **SEE 17-17B**

17-16

Step 1: Make the audio cut

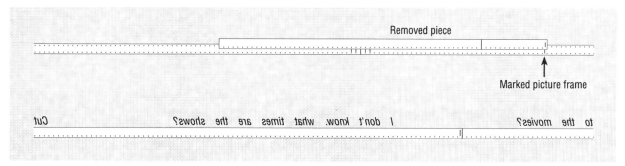

A. Make the picture cut, displaced from the sound cut...

B. ...resulting in an overlap

The opposite approach would be to evaluate the cut in terms of where you want to enter the second person's dialogue. In this case, you would find where you want to enter the second shot and stretch the film toward the head of the film. Obviously, you must plan the removal of the picture so that the cut eliminates all the frames with the slate and otherwise unusable material. When you have finished, there should be an equal number of sound and picture frames in the two removed pieces.

Both the straight and overlapping cuts described here are examples of simple cuts. Most films are shot in such a way that the choices are somewhat more complex. Still, the general principles presented here apply.

As suggested, the overlapping dialog cut is the mainstay of conventional film editing, particularly cutting that attempts the invisible style associated with realism and the Hollywood commercial film. The cuts are masked by being put in the middle of the dialogue, where they are least likely to be noticed. The technique also fits into the great tradition of dramatic emphasis, with focusing on responses frequently being more important than showing the speaker. Avoiding the overlapping cut can produce a stylized or unrealistic effect. The great Japanese director Yasujiro Ozu rarely employed overlaps in the editing of his films. His objective style is famous among film critics and theoreticians, many of whom fail to discern some of the key practical aspects of his editing style.

As suggested, the straight cut tends to look better on television than it does amplified many times on the big screen. This fits into the economics of the system, given the tight deadlines of editing episodic television. It simply takes longer to wrestle with a cut to get the perfect overlap than it does to determine a straight-cut transition and do it. This also may be the result of the straight-cutting options available in analog video editing. What is called *cuts-only video* makes it very difficult to do overlaps. Although editors for episodic television have the highest-quality equipment, prior to digital editing, overlaps were time-consuming and cumbersome. When I edited video for the first time, my initial question to the video engineers was, "How do you do overlaps?" Their resulting blank stares tipped me off that video editing had a long way to go as both a learning and a creative tool. The digital domain will change all that.

Cutting Nonsync Sound and Picture

Effects, music, and narration editing makes up most of the rest of the editor's work. The sequence on a commercial feature is as follows: The editor edits the picture with dialogue until an acceptable cut of the film is produced. The picture is then locked, denoting that the picture is done and all subsequent cuts will be in the sound. Picture and sync-sound rolls are then turned over to the sound-effects and music editors. All their work is done on separate rolls, not cut into the sync rolls, to facilitate effective final sound mixing. Although the division of labor may not be so structured on an independent film, nonsync cutting is generally kept separate from dialogue cutting.

Effects, music, and narration are generally cut into *slug rolls*—rolls of junk picture or leader into which the nonsync sound is cut. Some source for long, uninterrupted stretches of quality slug will have to be located. All the rolls used need to have reference points that correspond to the Academy 2. To do this, set up a slug roll in the unused sound transport. Roll the Academy 2 on the countdown leader right in front of the gate. With the lock control, lock the slug roll to the picture and mark the frame straight across from the 2. Roll out the locked tracks and put a punch on the frame you just marked on the slug track. This punch is now lined up with the Academy 2 and is the reference for all future cueing of the rolls. A more formal leader will be set up later in the process (see page 443). What is referred to here as a slug roll would probably just be called a mixtrack in a commercial situation. However, these rolls need to be distinguished from the sync rolls.

Cutting Sound Effects

A film on which I was the sound mixer can serve as a good example of some of the hows and whys of effects cutting. It was a period piece, taking place in the 1840s, and featured several shots of a man chopping wood. Usable production sound was impossible because the location was near a four-lane highway as well as being at the end of an airport runway (I think all locations are). For this reason, all affected scenes were shot MOS and the individual sound effects collected later. This audio was transferred to mag stock, the result being a large roll of sound effects.

There are a number of approaches to cutting an effect like this, but one standard way is to find the desired effect in the sound-effect roll and cut it out. This entails running the effects on the flatbed at normal speed while listening for

17-18

Cutting a few frames before the actual sound allows the rerecording mixer to soften the cut if necessary

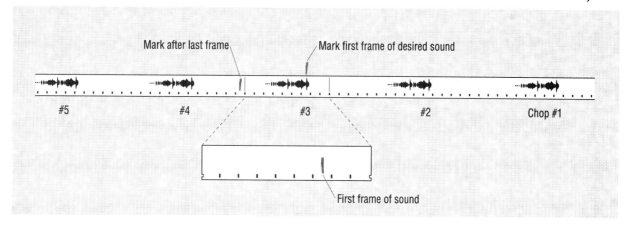

Mark after last frame

Mark first frame of desired sound

#5   #4   #3   #2   Chop #1

First frame of sound

the appropriate sound. Once you have determined the effect you want, find the frame that has the attack and mark it with a permanent marker. This is similar to finding the attack of the slate. Generally, it is a good idea to cut a few frames before the actual sound. **SEE 17-18** These few frames of ambience before the effect will allow the rerecording mixer time to soften the cut if necessary. Mark the last frame of the piece you want to take out as well. Be careful not to cut the decay too soon. It will sound incomplete, an outcome that will cause problems at the mix. A problem like this may not necessarily be unsolvable, but it will require expensive time to fix.

When the effect is cut out, you will have a piece of mag stock—nine frames in this example—with a single mark on it. Hang this in the trim bin, being careful to label it clearly by writing directly on the mag stock with a permanent marker or using film tape.

The next step is to find the picture frame that you want the sound to be set up across from. This can be done by moving the film very slowly through the viewer or editing table. The individual frames will show a sequence of the movement. In the wood-chopping example, you would find the frame with the ax up in the air. The next frame might show the ax coming down. Then you can find the exact frame where the ax hits the wood. Mark this frame and the frame directly across from it on the slug roll. **SEE 17-19A** Once the slug roll has been marked, splice the effect into it so that the mark on the effect replaces the original mark on the slug roll. To accomplish this, cut on the slug roll the same number of frames before the mark, two frames in this example, as are on the effect to be cut in. **SEE 17-19B**

This approach can be streamlined on a six-plate, combining the process of searching for the appropriate effect with the cutting. Lock the picture together with a synced slug track in the first transport; the slug roll should be punched as described in the previous section. Use the second sound transport for the unlocked sound-effects roll. Find the exact visual frame where you want the effect and leave it in the picture gate. Then listen to the unedited sound effects on the unlocked second transport. You can line up the desired effect with the visual, lock the second transport, and see and listen to it in sync. Once you find something you like, simply cut the sound effect from the unedited effects roll to the locked slug roll in the first transport.

The cutting of sound effects is generally a painstaking operation. Much of the extra sound heard in films is cut in individually. A representative example of the nature of effects cutting is the work of the footsteps editor—a credit frequently seen in British films. The footsteps editor literally goes through the entire film, cutting in the sound of footsteps as the characters move. While recording

17-19

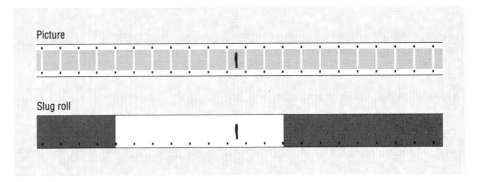

A. To incorporate a sound effect, mark the frame on the picture roll and the corresponding frame on the slug roll...

B. ...and splice in the effect

production sound, microphones are generally positioned to record the voice, so the sounds of footsteps are either too soft or completely nonexistent. The footsteps that are cut in are usually so subtle that they are not recognized on a conscious level. Their absence, however, can leave a scene with an otherworldly feel.

Cutting to Music

Cutting to music has always been a popular starting place for students learning how to cut picture to sound. With the advent of music videos, it has become an even more significant part of the field. In the heyday of the Hollywood studios, music was generally timed to already edited footage. The composer, a full-time studio employee who produced multiple film scores a year, would score to the length of shots, complete scenes, or sequences (twenty-four picture frames corresponding to one second of time in the composed music). The studio's orchestra would perform while viewing the edited film. The conductor could thus control the pace of the music to conform to the elapsed time of a given section of film.

Although this method has not been discarded completely, the norm today is to use a prerecorded piece of music and manipulate the picture to conform to its timing, pace, and rhythm. There are no house orchestras; that role is now performed by established orchestras hired for contract work. The old approach is still occasionally used but not with the same frequency, with the facilities designed to time performance to projected picture being few and far between. As even the most casual viewer knows, music videos are prerecorded, and the song is played back as

17-20

With sound broken down to specific lengths of stock, you can cut an image to the music to create very specific relationships

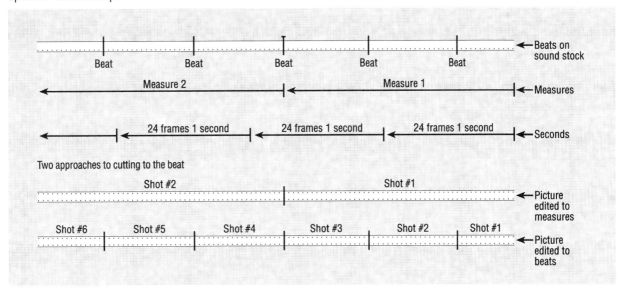

the performers lip-sync the lyrics. The prerecorded track is used as the guide to the timing of all performance.

The key to success in cutting to music is to think of the sound as a specific length of magnetic film stock. A song that is, for instance, five minutes long will be represented as roughly 185 feet of film. Punch a frame in the beginning of the transferred mag stock, setting it to 0 feet and 0 frames on the frame counter. Specific events in the music, the singer hitting and holding a high note, for instance, can then be located and logged as occurring at specific footage and frames. You might find, for instance, that the first notes of the song start at 1 foot, 12 frames. The singer might start singing at 3 feet, 6 frames, and so on. Once you have these lengths, specific images can be cut against the sound.

The music can be further broken down into measures and even beats. Most music is in time signature, ¾ and ¼ time being two standards. Taking a song that is in ¾ time as an example, you can make some determinations about the timing in frames. You might find that a specific measure is, for instance, 45 frames long or roughly 1.9 seconds. In ¾ time, each beat then occupies 15 frames. If the tempo increases or decreases, these measurements change as well.

With the sound analyzed, you can cut the image to the music to create very specific relationships. There are two lines of picture at the bottom of the illustration above to represent two possible approaches to cutting to the beat. **SEE 17-20**

If you wanted a shot to correspond to the precise length of a measure, it would be trimmed to 45 frames and cut to the beginning of the measure. If instead you wanted each new image to come at a beat in the music, each shot would be 15 frames long and started with the first beat. Persistent cutting on beats and measures would undoubtedly become schematic and predictable, but the approach can be applied in a less rigid manner.

Cutting Voice-overs

Voice-overs and narration are handled in a fashion similar to the one for music. Once the recorded voice is transferred to mag stock, the text is represented as a specific length of film. Just as in the discussion of cutting to music, visuals can be positioned against specific events in the sound. Voice-overs generally offer more opportunity to be manipulated than music does and, in many cases, they can be cut and conformed to the visuals as desired. There are, of course, limitations, depending on the size and length of the text being spoken.

The first step is to get a good, clean recording of the speaker. The audio medium is your choice, be it quarter-inch cassette or any of a variety of audio machines. Be sure to use a high-quality recorder and, more important, a high-quality microphone. Consumer cassette players, particularly those with internal microphones, should be avoided. Choose a speaker who has a strong, clear voice. Many people do not have broadcast-quality voices, and there may be intelligibility problems. Any weak link in the chain will cause difficulties down the road. In addition, do everything in your power to obtain as clean a recording as possible. Use a sound recording booth if one is available. If not, find an acoustically dead room and record at a time when there will be little or no interference.

Transfer this audio to mag stock. If there are particularly good takes, you can skip all the bad material and spot-record the good ones. Pauses and line muffs can be changed or eliminated altogether through cutting the mag stock. For those familiar with editing conventional magnetic tape, it is not a good idea to cut original audiotapes. Transfer to the mag stock and then do the cutting. If a sound take gets ruined, it can always be retransferred.

The following illustration gives a representation of the transferred mag stock. **SEE 17-21** Just as with music, the shots can then be cut to the desired length and positioned against the track. If you identify certain events in the voice-over that you want to have specific images against, they can be located and the picture cut to match. One approach, which also works with music, is to slug black leader against the sound and cut in the images you know you want against the appropriate events. If you determined that you wanted shots 1, 2, and 3 to be against events A, B, and C, respectively, you could position them and then worry about all the interim material later. **SEE 17-22** Again, pauses in the speech can either be shortened or lengthened by cutting the mag stock. If anything is lengthened, the interim space should be filled with slug. Unless there is music or some other covering sound, this will require some ambience to be cut on another track to fill the hole.

In the studio newsreel days, the picture was often cut first, and then a narrator came in and read his spiel in a soundproof booth with the picture projected in

17-21

Narration is transferred to mag stock and can either be manipulated to match picture or have the picture matched to it

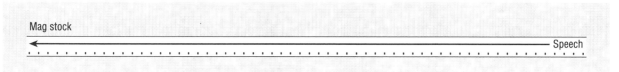

17-22

To match specific images against certain audio events, you can slug black leader against the sound and cut in the appropriate images

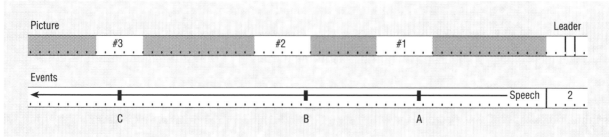

front of him. Given the way the documentary form has evolved, the trend has been to record the narration first and then fit the picture to it. Although this has become the preferred method, it sometimes entails compromising visual efficiency to fit proscribed verbal timing.

MOS Inserts

Cutting shots that were executed without recorded sound takes on a variety of forms. In the most straightforward manifestation, MOS shots are used to break away from a character who is speaking. Called **reaction shots** or *inserts,* they are used either to show a reaction or to transit from one take to another, much like in the earlier example from Leo McCarey's *Ruggles of Red Gap.* This is similar to the cutaway, but MOS inserts tend to have much more specific purposes. A cutaway is often used as a repair or filler shot, but a well-placed MOS shot can be an important element, giving a flash of the eyes, a nod of the head, or some similar response as much weight as a line of dialogue.

The MOS insert of Humphrey Bogart from the opening scene of *The Maltese Falcon* is an excellent example. In this case the cuts are very uncomplicated. If the goal is to cut to a character responding to someone's speech, you have to replace the frames removed from the sync take with the same number of frames from the MOS shot. One approach is to look at the sync shot and determine and mark where you want to exit and reenter the speaker's picture. Cut the piece out; then identify an equal number of frames from the MOS shot that you want to use and insert them in place of the removed section. Again, use the removed piece as a guide for the length of the piece needed from the uncut MOS shot. **SEE 17-23** If you cut out 72 frames of sync pictures, you need to replace them with an MOS piece 72 frames long. The speaker will pick up the speech in sync because the eliminated sync frames have been replaced with an equal number of MOS frames.

The only question is whether the length of the insert is determined by what you want to take out of the sync shot or by the length of the MOS piece that you want to insert. This depends on what you want to accomplish in a given situation. You may want to be away from the speaker for a specific period, for pacing reasons or whatever. In this case you would conform the length of the MOS insert to this requirement. On the other hand, you may have a good reaction shot that is a specific length, in which case that determines how much you take out of the sync shot.

Although this example suggests the employment of an unmolested sound track, the cut to an MOS insert affords the editor the opportunity to manipulate the audio. If an actor gives a perfect performance for the first part of a take but then muffs the second part, you can cut between it and a take with a better second half. The jump that would result from the cut between the two different

17-23

For a reaction shot, you replace the frames from the sync take with the same number of frames from the MOS shot

takes can be covered in the manner just described. The same is true if the performance has a pause that is either too long or too short. In the former case, the offending frames can be trimmed out and again covered by a cut to another character or object. In the latter case, slug frames would be cut in with attendant ambience cut on later mixtracks. Use this technique judiciously, however, as it is often obvious that reaction shots are being placed to cover mistakes or soften awkward visual transitions.

What is being described here is easily recognized as an approach to cutting interviews and general documentary footage. In an interview, the subject is filmed for a long period of time and is then excused. The crew turns the camera around and films a few minutes of the interviewer nodding in agreement and posing some of the key questions again. When the subject's unavoidable uninteresting sections are eliminated in the editing process, the resultant jumps in the footage are covered with shots of the interviewer. **SEE 17-24**

Eventually the approach to MOS will become more complex, with planned cutaways from a speaker being only a small part of the handling of MOS material. Many special photographic effects are done without sync sound. The timing and execution are so complex that the presence of a sound mixer would be an unnecessary complication. Many shots and scenes have the sound built completely from scratch, particularly when the execution of the shot is complicated enough to require extensive communication among crew members.

Responses that are pulled out of sync takes can be handled like MOS shots. Many of the wordless pieces in the diner scene from Jonathan Demme's *Something Wild*, simple shifts of sightlines and nonverbal responses, were not designed as MOS shots. They are clearly fragments of longer sync takes, removed and put to good use. Although this represents a very straightforward use of shots, trims and

17-24

When undesired material is edited out, the jumps in footage are covered with inserted reaction shots

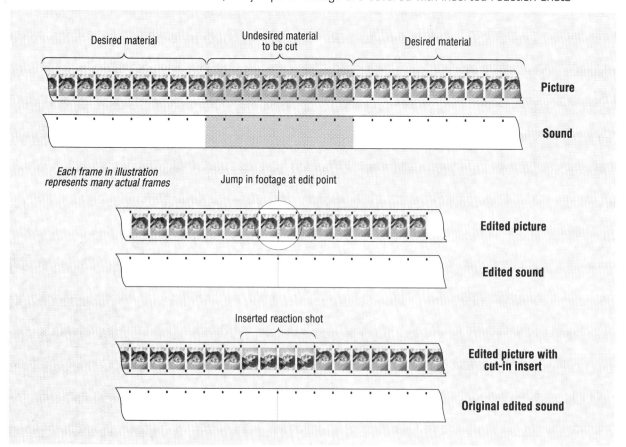

heads and tails of sync shots can provide important cutting material when scenes have not been covered adequately.

Mixtrack Configurations

When you take your film to a mixing house, the tracks must be laid out in a logical way, one that makes sense to the mixing-house personnel (see page 444 for details of the final mixdown process). As you are editing, you can be informal about what mixtrack each sound is on. You generally want the sounds where they are most convenient, particularly in order to view the film with the sound as complete as possible. However, the different types of sound should be segregated onto separate tracks before going to the mix. This allows the mixer to both find specific sounds quickly and group together sounds that are to be treated similarly. This makes the mix simpler and faster. The mix is a substantial budgetary concern, so it should be as streamlined as possible.

Many mixing houses, especially those accustomed to commercial features, are very particular about how the mixtracks are set up. If you do not have the film set up appropriately, they may send you back to the editing room, while charging you for the time it took them to load and unload your mixtracks. Mixing houses in smaller markets might be a little more forgiving, but mixtracks not set up in a straightforward manner will require costly time to figure out. Once mixing is understood, the logic of creating tracks that facilitate mixing is inescapable.

In setting up the mixtracks for the mix, two requirements need to be emphasized. The first is this:

▶ **RULE:** *There should be no sound-to-sound cuts anywhere in the mixtracks.*

That is, the mixtracks should be cut in such a way that all pieces of sound are cut to slug rather than to other pieces of sound. The main reason for this is to allow the rerecording mixer room to do sound manipulations. If one sound effect follows right on top of another, it should be put on a different roll. Minimum slug length between any two pieces of sound will vary from house to house, but is around four or five seconds. This seems quick, but it generally gives the mixer enough time to make discreet changes. If your sound is dirty and needs substantial manipulation, you should plan on longer gaps. This will require spreading the sound effects through more mixtracks. Some labs require lengthier gaps between sounds. Be sure to check.

▶ **RULE:** *There should be no place in the film where there is only slug on all the mixtracks.*

There must be some recorded sound on at least one of the mixtracks, even if it is just silence. What the listener perceives as silence is not the same thing as an absence of sound. If there is only slug on the head, the track will sound flat and empty. Mixing houses will generally be able to provide something, such as white noise or open-mic room ambience, to cover the gap if you make a mistake. Still, you should consider the quality you want for any quiet moments and provide the appropriate track.

A & B Rolling

In configuring the mixtracks, A & B rolling the sync mixtracks is one of the key considerations. *A & B rolling* refers to *checkerboarding*, or alternating, the original sync mixtrack on separate sound rolls to facilitate the final mixing process. Thus, you create two rolls for the sync tracks instead of the single strand that has been demonstrated up to this point. All the odd-numbered sound takes would be on the first sound roll, and all the even-numbered takes on the second roll, although

17-25

The A & B–rolled sound alternates from one mixtrack to the other

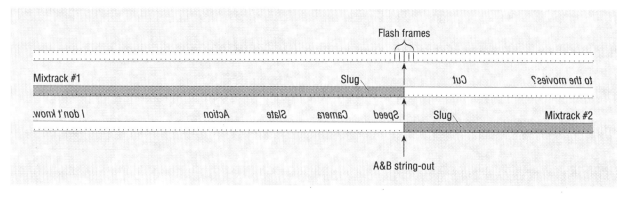

it does not always work out quite so cleanly. In the string-out, A & B–rolled sound tracks would resemble the following illustration. **SEE 17-25**

Like edge numbering, A & B rolling the sync sound before the actual editing is optional, although highly recommended for the beginner. However, it is not so much a matter of *if* as it is of *when*. The process of separating your sound has to be done before you go to the mix anyway, it is just a question of whether you do it in the beginning stages of editing or in the last few days before the mix. If done at the beginning, A and B rolling would be done after the first assembly is completed but before the creative part of editing—the actual cutting—starts.

Four important rationales for A & B rolling the sound are listed below. The first two must be considered in sound cutting at all levels of production, whether you have been cutting for one week or twenty years. The third and fourth rationales are more considerations for inexperienced editors working on smaller projects. Commercial films generally have sophisticated resources to address these last two issues.

1. To facilitate volume control, equalization, and signal processing in the mix.

2. To allow interruptions and blending of dialogue.

3. To create ambience overlaps.

4. To avoid damaged splices and the problems associated with them.

Volume, equalization, and signal processing   In the mix, each track is assigned to an individual channel on the mixing board. This channel will have a fader to control volume, as well as having limited equalization capability. Each channel can also be assigned to sideboard signal-processing equipment, allowing for further equalization, reverb effects, echo effects, and other audio manipulations.

Thus, each and every sound in your film will have the volume set for it in the mix and, if necessary, can be equalized or otherwise processed. If the sound for a shot is cut to the sound for the next shot, the rerecording mixer could not shift volume levels in the split second that the cut crossed the sound head, much less create any complex equalization. The slug between each take allows the rerecording mixer time to anticipate and shift all necessary controls.

Interruptions and blending   It is impossible in the single-strand method to have an actor "step on" another actor's line of dialogue or to create any kind of blending, or layering, of dialogue. A & B rolling allows dialogue to be dropped on top of other dialogue. Robert Altman is famous for using this style of layered dialogue cutting. The frontier barroom scene that opens his *McCabe and Mrs. Miller* (Louis Lombardo, editor) has snippets of conversations underlying all foreground action. While the cutting in this film includes other approaches to sound layering, sync tracks are frequently held and extended into surrounding shots.

Ambience overlaps　When executing any dialogue cut, you want to maintain as much of the ambience that follows or precedes the voice, overlapping it between shots if possible. This allows the rerecording mixer to soften any potential harshness of the cut. If there is substantial difference in the quality of ambience in any two shots, the sound may jump between the two levels if they are cut directly together. Despite efforts to avoid it, there will occasionally be gaps in the ambience where there is not enough audio to cover the pause. This is when the room tone that the sound mixer recorded on location comes in handy, with an ambience mixtrack created to cover any holes.

Damaged splices　As stated, editing film consists of trying different cuts until you find the one that works perfectly. You may like a cut one day and come back the next and wonder where on earth your mind was when you made that decision. If you decide the cut is slow, you trim it down. If you decide a cut is too short, you add frames back in. Getting a cut right may take many attempts. This cutting and recutting can cause problems in the single-strand method. The cut becomes choppy with several one- or two-frame cuts pieced together. With the picture, this is not a significant concern because you will be going back to the original.[2] But since this is the actual mag stock that will be used in the mix, too many quick cuts in a row can significantly affect audio quality. With the sound on alternating rolls, all trims and additions of frames made after the initial audio edit are cut in the slug, thus avoiding further splices in the mag stock. With limited time and resources in the editing room, it is better to keep the sound "mixable" all the way through the project.

Most of these rationales can be generalized to the other mixtracks as well. Sound effects need to be separated so their volume and quality can be shifted.

In configuring the mixtracks, you should apportion the sound to tracks composed of similar effects. The dialogue is always on the first two mixtracks, although there are circumstances in which more would be appropriate. If there is any narration, it would be on one or two separate mixtracks. Music would be on one track, a second required if there are any cross-fades between songs. Sound effects will occupy a number of tracks, potentially a high number, depending on the complexity of your sound. Ambience may take several more tracks. Different mixing houses may ask for slight variations, but the following is a general guide. Be sure to check with your rerecording mixer before making final decisions. The tracks should look something like this:

Mixtrack 1—Dialogue

Mixtrack 2—Dialogue

Mixtrack 3—Extra dialogue and narration (if necessary)

Mixtrack 4—Music

Mixtrack 5—Additional music (if necessary)

Mixtracks 6 through 10—Sound effects

Mixtrack 11—Ambience

Mixtrack 12—Additional ambience (if necessary)

---

2. This can actually pose a problem in compromising one's ability to evaluate the cuts as well as affecting how projectable the film is. When going to the mix or when working with clients or backers, you want to be able to have as clean and trouble-free a version as possible.

Again, the number of sound effects and ambience tracks is fluid, depending on the complexity of your sound. Ambience tracks can be handled in a number of ways. Many editors will go to the mix with a loop of ambience for each individual scene. A *loop* is a piece of mag stock with the head end cut to the tail end. It is loaded on a playback machine and runs continuously underneath a scene to provide ambient fill for any gaps in the dialogue tracks.

Again, the only real decision here is whether you separate out all the sound before editing or just prior to going to the mix, particularly the A & B sync tracks. To a certain extent, you can cut the sounds anywhere you want while you are doing the actual editing, but they must be separated out to facilitate full control of their quality and volume before the final mixdown. Editors on most commercial films will cut the sync mixtracks single-strand and then have the assistant or apprentice A & B roll the tracks just before they are mixed. In order to ensure optimal sound quality, theatrical films will frequently replace the sync tracks with fresh tracks that have not gone through the rigors and manhandling of the editing process. This entails transferring and edge coding two sets of mag stock, one as a "workprint" of the sound and the other to replace it. Any needed ambience can thus be reclaimed in this stage, although there are other methods of dealing with the issue of matching ambience between shots. Given that commercial films will be shown on high-quality Dolby systems, the added time and expense of this approach makes sense. Independent filmmakers, as well as television producers, generally mix the sound that has been cut throughout the process, a perfectly adequate approach given the less patrician presentation options.

Appropriate separation of the mixtracks is essential for an efficient mix, where the full potential of the sound can be fully explored. If your mixtracks are a mess when you go to the mix, be prepared to have either an unpleasant mix or your project unceremoniously handed right back to you. A mix that is inappropriately configured is a clear sign to a mixer that the job is going to be one long headache.

A Typical Scene

A scene from an independent feature that I worked on several years ago can serve as a good example of the way tracks are built and separated out. The scene involved a taxicab driver and his passenger caught in a traffic jam. In a single take, the passenger gets out and runs past the cars stalled in front of them to insert her business card under the windshield wiper of an arguing couple. Still in the same shot, she runs back to the taxi and starts yelling at the driver and honking the horn. As the sound mixer, I was on the floor of the cab, miking and recording the dialogue between the cab driver and the woman. It was senseless to jump out and record sound for the middle of the shot, given the phalanx of camera crew members, dolly and lighting grips, and sundry other personnel who were chasing after the action. As the actor and I waited in the cab, I continued to roll sound because turning off the recorder would have disrupted sync. When the woman returned, I had her hit the steering wheel next to the taxi's horn, faking the car honk. The horn may have covered key dialogue and would have been too hot for the volume levels I had set for the dialogue.

As I watched rehearsals, I started to compile a list of sound effects needed for the scene. After shooting, I took the actor aside and had her run in place to get the clacking of her heels on the sidewalk. I also had to record the sound of the taxi's horn being honked to fill in where I had her fake it. For stylistic reasons, the traffic jam was made up of classic cars. I went to each of the cars and recorded the distinctive sound of its horn. I asked the director if he wanted the sound of the engines idling, but he did not see that as part of the overall sound design. There were several other effects on the list that I knew could wait until postproduction.

17-26

Mixtrack 1: the unwanted sync sound is replaced with slug

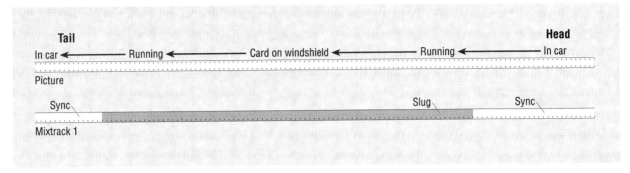

17-27

Mixtrack 3: the couple's argument fades in as the woman approaches the car, and fades out as she leaves

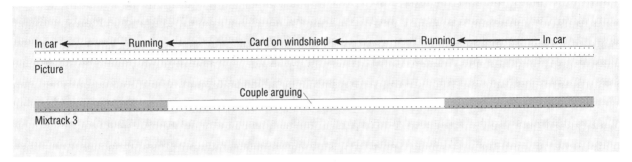

The editor's first concern was the long, dead middle stretch of sync sound when the woman and camera were elsewhere, the remaining actor and I having filled the time with idle chatter. With the aid of the second transport, he simply measured out the piece of sync sound that he wanted to remove and replaced it with slug. As we were not intercutting sync sound, mixtrack 2 went unused. So the sync track (mixtrack 1) looked like the illustration above. **SEE 17-26**

As there was narration and voice effects in other parts of the film, the editor used the third mixtrack for the arguing couple in the lead car. We never really see the actors' mouths, so we took them into the studio after shooting and just had them improvise an argument for a while. They are not heard until the woman is close to their car, so their voices occupy the center part of the scene. To achieve the appropriate sound perspective, the rerecording mixer was instructed to start this track with the fader down, bringing it up as the woman approaches the car and bringing it back down as she runs back to the taxi. **SEE 17-27**

Next came the footsteps. The editor found a section that sounded appropriate and cut them in from the door slamming at the beginning to the end of her run. There was also a brief pause in the middle as she put her card on the windshield. **SEE 17-28**

Since the main focus in location recording had been on the dialogue, the sound of the car door as the woman entered and exited needed some attention. The camera was outside the car, and the recording inside made the sound perspective wrong. Something like this is usually, though not always, easiest to address in postproduction. I went around and recorded the opening and slamming of the door on a number of older cars. As everything between the two sets of dialogue was being removed anyway, the sound of the car door being slammed was also then completely replaced. In both cases, it was the combination of several

17-28

Mixtrack 4: the woman's footsteps to and from the couple's car

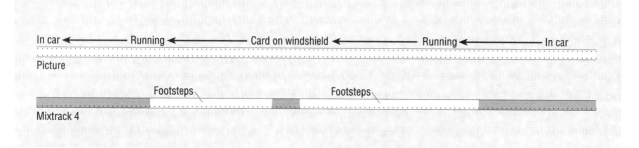

17-29

Mixtracks 5 & 6: the car door slamming, mixed from several takes

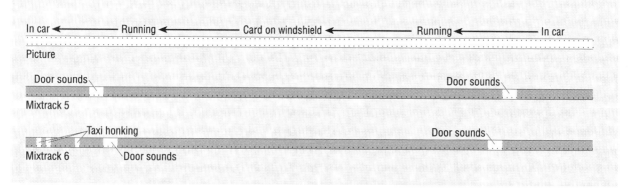

17-30

Mixtracks 7 & 8: car horns recorded on location

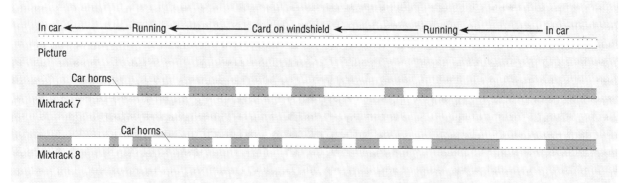

sounds, the creak of the opening from one recorded door being mixed with the swing and slam from other takes. This took two tracks. **SEE 17-29** Another two tracks were built out of the car horns recorded on location. **SEE 17-30**

Last, the editor needed some light city ambience to fill out the overall sound design. This proved to be quite tricky to record, but the appropriate track was eventually found. It was cut uninterrupted into an ambience track. **SEE 17-31**

Just as we created an overview of an exposure in the lighting section, we can create an "exposure" of the way sound can be built. Although this leaves out several unused mixtracks, second sync, music, and so on, all the mixtracks can be viewed together. **SEE 17-32**

17-31

Mixtrack 9: an ambience track to fill out the overall sound design

In car ◄────── Running ◄────── Card on windshield ◄────── Running ◄────── In car

Picture

City ambience

Mixtrack 9

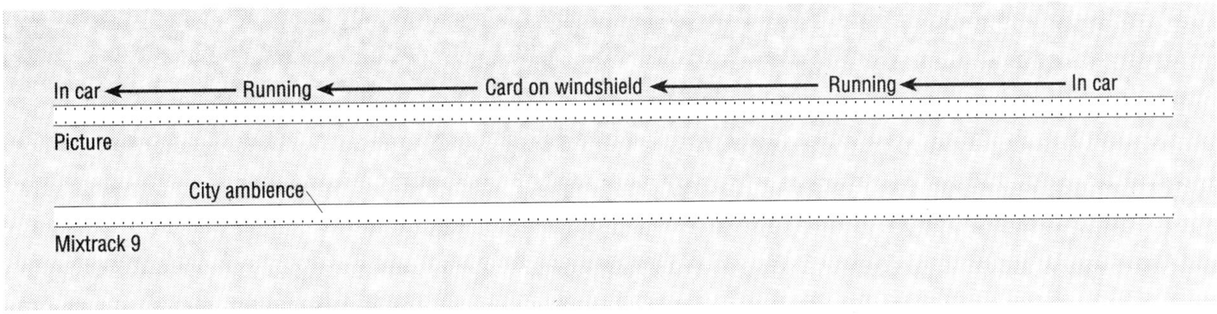

17-32

Mixtracks 1–9: the overall sound design

Tail   **Head**

In car ◄────── Running ◄────── Card on windshield ◄────── Running ◄────── In car

Picture

Sync   Slug   Sync

Mixtrack 1

Couple arguing

Mixtrack 3

Footsteps   Footsteps

Mixtrack 4

Door sounds   Door sounds

Mixtrack 5

Taxi honking   Door sounds

Mixtrack 6   Door sounds

Car horns

Mixtrack 7

Car horns

Mixtrack 8

City ambience

Mixtrack 9

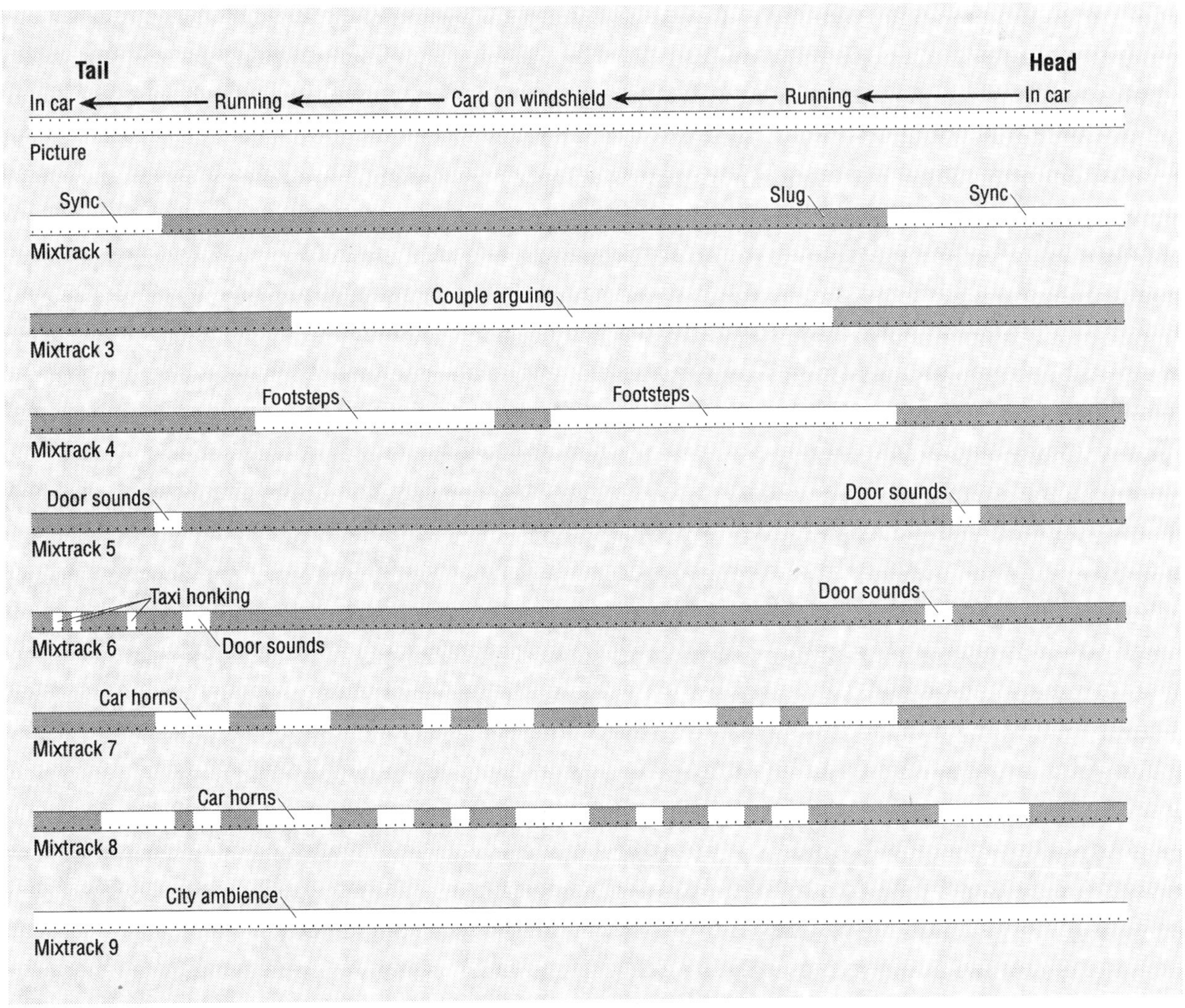

This chapter may at times have appeared to be recommending dense sound, but it is simply illustrating how to create a multilayered track. There will be situations in which you find one sound that is absolutely perfect for a scene or sequence. The point again is to do what is good for the given situation. Determine what kind of effects will give the scene the flavor, the ambience, the lushness, you desire.

18

Finishing the Film

FINISHING involves the three previously mentioned processes: audio mixing, negative cutting, and final printing. These processes are generally performed in this sequence, although there is modest debate among film professionals as whether to mix first or conform first. The audio mix is done at a commercial mixing house specifically designed for the purpose. Negative cutting is generally done by a professional, although students strapped for cash and willing to take risks can do it themselves. Refer to chapter 4 for an overview of terms and processes.

These first two processes generate the *elements*—sound rolls and picture rolls—needed to create the final print. Final printing is done by a motion picture processing laboratory. The first print—the answer print—is essentially the lab's best shot at creating a print that you like. Although the goal is to get it right the first time, it occasionally takes the lab several attempts to produce an answer print that satisfies you. Once you have one you like, all subsequent release prints are made using the satisfactory answer print as a guide.

As with processing, it may take some searching to find a lab that both has all the services needed to finish a film and will do it at a reasonable price. Due to the shifting landscape involved in finishing a project, many labs have diversified their services. With video finishing becoming the commercial standard, labs have reoriented themselves to this new reality and as a side-effect have had to reduce their film-related services. Many labs continue to process and workprint film but have eliminated making final prints. This is particularly true of smaller labs between the coasts. Some labs have gone to processing only, with transfer to video replacing conventional workprinting. You may have to search to find a lab that will do everything you want at a reasonable price.

It is essential that these processes be executed at the highest level possible. An indifferent mix can ruin the most visually interesting film. Sloppy negative cutting can leave the film damaged and dirty and even out of sync. Unless you are attempting some specialized effect, you want the film to be as clean and polished as possible. Remember, there is no better advertisement for your talents and abilities than your work. Informality may be a desired aesthetic effect in certain circumstances, but generally viewers are left unimpressed by work that appears crudely executed.

This chapter describes the steps for finishing a film on film, the path that many features as well as student and independent projects still follow. Even the traditional path of finishing a film "on film" has been permeated by video and digital sound technologies. The rounded aspiring filmmaker will want to understand as much about both film and video processes as possible.

Titling

In professional situations, *titles* are generally shot on an animation stand, an arrangement with the camera mounted on a column designed to shoot fixed artwork. In the absence of this stand, shooting quality titles can be more difficult than one might at first anticipate, and nothing announces an amateur project quite as effectively as sloppy, crooked, misspelled, or out-of-focus titles. A good film may never recover from a slipshod start. Obviously, professional titles do not mean a quality film, an observation that is endlessly proven, but at a beginning level they say something about the filmmaker's attention to detail.

Generally, the first step is to build your titles on a card or paper stock. The title cards are then photographed on a large, high-contrast *sheet negative*, a standard film negative often referred to as a *Kodalith*. For independents and students, a standard way of building title cards used to be with the press-on lettering available at office-supply stores. This painstaking and time-consuming approach has largely been replaced with generating the titles on a computer. Titles must be output on a printer that produces completely opaque lettering, or there will be problems with the sheet negatives. These negative sheets are set up with strong backlighting and filmed, sandwiching gels if color effects are desired. It is possible to just shoot the cards themselves, but it is difficult to find an exposure that does not represent the blacks and whites as grays.

Anticipate all the titles you will need before creating and shooting them. Negative cutters, mixing houses, and the labs that produce the final print are frequently credited in films. Just as with crew members, postproduction personnel use a carefully crafted film as a résumé item, and it takes preplanning to determine who will do this work.

Common Problems with Titles

- **Creating level titles.** You can set up the titles so they look level to your eye, than get a rude surprise when you get the film back. Even the slightest discrepancy will be magnified many times in the resulting film when screened.

- **Solving exposure problems.** Titles generally require *bracketing* the exposure, shooting the subject at what the light meter tells you, plus at least one stop over and one stop under.

- **Focusing.** The logistics of shooting titles means that you will be working with factors that minimize depth of field. Measuring is by far the preferred method, although the camera must be perfectly adjusted to get good results.

- **Eliminating misspellings.** Check the spelling of all words in the titles. Verify proper names of cast and crew as the film is being shot. Trying to track down the sometimes gypsylike crew members when you are rushing to meet deadlines can lead to mistakes.

- **Framing.** Be sure that all titles are composed within the TV safe frame. Video is such a common form for submission of work, whether for grants, festivals, or job applications, that you will almost certainly be transferring your film to video. Also be sure that you are not lining up the edges of the film frame right on the edge of your cards or sheet negatives. Cameras, particularly those in multiple-use school situations, may frame slightly differently than what the viewfinder targets show. This may go completely unnoticed in live-action shooting, but the closeness of title shooting will amplify the slightest discrepancies.

Keep in mind that the titles act as a representative of your film. While an audience may forgive an error, those considering hiring you or funding and exhibiting your work will take a dim view of what can only be chalked off as carelessness. Take the time to make sure that everything is perfect.

Preparing Leaders

The Academy 2 on the countdown leader has been the sync mark during editing, but it is necessary to incorporate a more complex set of leaders for the final mixing and printing phases. These leaders provide critical information to the mixing studio and lab about how all picture and sound rolls are synchronized. They must be set up correctly. Final leader configurations are standardized among labs, the accepted setup being represented in the figure below. You will need several hundred feet of white leader and enough one-frame beeps—the sync beep—for all mixtracks. **SEE 18-1**

18-1

The configuration required for final leaders is standardized among labs

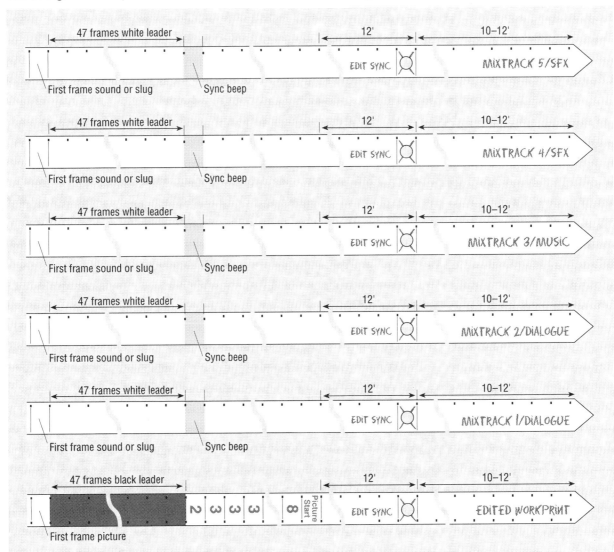

Set up the picture and all mixtracks in a synchronizer—do not attempt this process on the editing table. Set the picture start frame on 0 feet, 0 frames on the gang. Remove all old leaders from the punched mixtracks and cut 15 to 20 feet of white leader on the head of all rolls. If there are more mixtracks than gangs on the synchronizer, which is frequently the case, set up as many as you can and do the others after the first ones are done. From the leaders created before stringing out, the picture has the countdown leader, and your first mixtrack has the sync beep that corresponds to the Academy 2. Cut in a sync beep on the corresponding frame on all tracks. This beep will be recorded on both the master mix and the optical master. It will then be used at the motion picture lab to sync the sound for the final print.

Once the appropriate beeps are cut in at the Academy 2 on all leaders, the rest of the head leaders can be set up. Using the footage counter on the synchronizer, roll back, toward the head, into the white leader exactly 12 feet from picture start. Additional white leader will be required in front of the SMPTE Universal (countdown) leader as well. With a permanent marker, draw an *X* on this frame, 12 feet from picture start, on the edited workprint and all the mixtracks. Put a punch in the center of all of the *X*'s. Write *edit sync* next to the punched frame on all rolls. This punch is used by the mixing house personnel to line up all the rolls on the projector and playback machines at the mix, so it must be accurate and clearly marked. It is also used by the negative cutter. There should still be another 10 to 12 feet of white leader prior to the edit sync punch on all rolls. This beginning leader is necessary to thread the playback machines and projector at the mix.

Some mixing houses require standard tail leaders, again Universal SMPTE leader, on the picture and mixtracks as well. Be sure to adhere to whatever requirements they have. If they do not require Universal tail leaders, be sure there is at least 20 feet of white leader at the end to prevent the film from spooling off the feed reel while mixing the end of the film. Nothing is more irritating for the mixer than constantly having to jump up, at your expense, to rethread the tails of your mixtracks.

Clearly, these leaders can be, and in many situations are, set up right from the start or at any point during the process. I tend to set them up at the end so they don't get dirty or damaged. Be sure that they are set up in the standardized way and that all the cuts and punches are accurate. Double-check everything you have done. Any mistakes will cause sound synchronization problems at the mix and potentially worse problems during printing.

Final Sound Mixing

Many of the general principles of the mix have already been detailed, but the procedures at the mixdown itself warrant a few notes. Commercial mixing houses for motion pictures provide a specialized service that cannot be duplicated in other contexts, although with digitized sound this is changing. The key requirement is the interlock of mag stock playback machines, the projected film, and the sound's destination—the mag stock machine that records the master mix. The finished sound is on one uninterrupted, uncut piece of mag stock. The mix is necessary only when you are combining two or more sounds. When you have all your sound on one piece of mag stock from the start, the mix can be bypassed. This is the case in films that have only a music or premixed effects track, with music videos being a good example of the former.

The mixing studio is a screening room with a mixing console at the rear. **SEE 18-2** In a booth separate from the screening room, the edited workprint is loaded into a projector that is electronically interlocked to a bank of mag stock

18-2

The mixing studio is a screening room with a mixing console at the rear

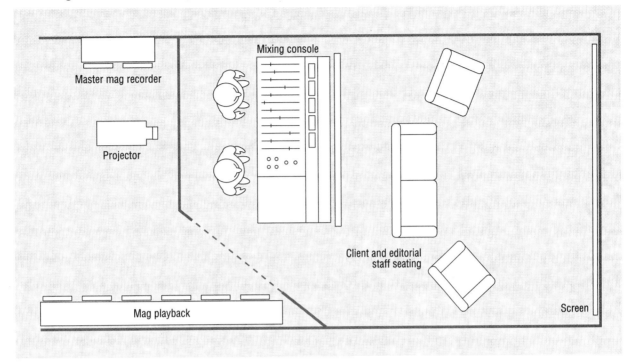

playback machines. The film is projected into the screening space, and the sound playback is routed through the mixing console. Each individual mag stock playback machine will be fed into its own channel on a mixing console.

When you go into the mix, the position of all sound has been determined by your cutting. What is being finalized is the volume and character of the sound—the final product. The mix is always done with the film's editor present, although the mixing board is run by the studio's rerecording mixer. A good rerecording mixer can contribute much to a film. Although the original recording is presumably, though not always, of good quality, the mixer can "clean up" or "sweeten" your sound, bringing it to its full potential. No matter how good you think your location recordings are, the magnificent sound reproduction of a mixing studio will unmask some heretofore unheard imperfections. Editing tables, particularly those in school situations, do not necessarily reproduce sound perfectly. Be prepared for a few surprises. Hopefully there are no problems that the mixer cannot eliminate.

Mixes at smaller houses range from $150 to $200 per hour, while the most advanced mixing facilities run in the $700-per-hour range. A mix on an uncomplicated five-minute film would probably take about an hour. Complex features can take a month or more.

The Mix

The mix is usually the first time you get to see your sound and picture together on a big screen. The experience usually produces that giddy feeling one gets when watching all the elements converge to finally create a finished product. This is where all the work and preparation start to come to fruition. However, the process is not without its tensions. This is the sound that your film is going to live with for the rest of its natural life. The pressure to get it right can be intense, particularly if the preparation has been incomplete or the sound problems that have gone unnoticed in the editing are severe.

Mixing equipment is set up so you can run back and forth on short stretches, scenes, and sequences of the film, working on the sound until you are satisfied. With **punch-in recording**, the mixer can lay down one section of sound on one pass and then record over it if it needs to be redone. The mixer will make one pass on a section just to listen to what sound is there and see where it is located on the mixtracks. Then the film and all the interlocked mixtracks are backed up, and if the mixer feels ready, he or she may try recording it. If the recording is not right, the film will be backed up again and the mixer will take another shot at it, recording over the first attempt. Again, the mixer is determining volume levels, at your direction, and doing everything possible to maximize the quality of the sound. It usually takes a number of passes to get it right.

Because the mix entails all this running back and forth on individual sections of the film, it is essential that your edited workprint and mixtracks are in good shape. Any broken sprocket holes or ripped picture should be replaced with black leader (see "Marking the Workprint" later in this chapter), and damaged mag stock should be retransferred and replaced. Lost loops and broken film can cause costly delays at the mix.

Many mixers require *cue sheets*, or *mixing logs*, that detail where all the sound is. The cue sheets have the mixtracks listed numerically across the top, and footage and frames down the side; the assistant or apprentice editor lists what sounds are at what footage and on what roll. This used to be obligatory, though mixers are increasingly discarding the practice. Many mixing houses have positioned the playback machines so the mixer can just turn and see which heads have sound on them, an approach that can be faster than asking the editor to find it on a complicated log. Many mixing houses still require logs, so be sure to ask when arranging a mixing date.

The master mix itself has the shortest life span in the life of a film (see page 113). It is quickly transferred to the optical master, which is the photographic record of the sound and is the printing source for all answer and release prints of the film. Occasionally you will find a mixing house that can produce the optical track, but they are becoming rare. Usually the motion picture processing lab produces the optical master.

The mix is such a daunting expense that there is a great temptation to find ways to bypass it. In the "guerrilla days" of independent filmmaking, many producers outside the mainstream would search out any conceivable way to avoid the costly, conventional finishing processes. After years of puttering around the edges, most independents realized that this was a mistake. There are perfectly good reasons why things are done certain ways, and established finishing technologies are designed to produce the highest-quality results possible. While informality and roughness may be valuable aesthetic alternatives, the trade-off for trying to get by cheaply is often unintelligible sound.

I once assisted a young animator who had completed editing his first feature, a painstakingly executed puppet animation that had taken him more than a year to shoot. He was about to go to a mix, and I questioned him on how prepared he was. It turned out that he did not have the tracks appropriately separated and was going to mix at a rudimentary setup at a local college. I implored him to take some time to reconfigure the tracks and mix them professionally. He needed to meet a deadline and claimed complete poverty. I begged him to do anything to find the time and the money, but to no avail. At the premiere of his film, the sound was virtually unintelligible. There are many false savings between the beginning and the end of a film. It struck me as tragic that someone could take a film that far and not nail it down.

The recommendation is to go with a commercial mixing house. Alternatives have drawbacks, the most significant being that it is impossible to obtain the quality of sound achievable at a commercial mix. Go into the mix with an open mind. A good mixer looks like an octopus, with hands moving all over the mixing board, twisting knobs, patching equipment, and tweaking volume levels. The more mixes you go to, the more you will be able to penetrate the mystery of all the things the mixer is doing.

The first mix of my work as a location sound mixer left me scratching my head. I went with a certain amount of cockiness, knowing I had done a thorough and competent job on a difficult location. However, it is not possible to get back into the editing room without flaws. I was amazed by the dimension that the mixer was able to bring to improve the audibility of my already high-quality tracks. He was also able to identify and correct some flaws—cable noise, unwanted background noise, and so on—that were inaudible in the editing process. The more you understand the process, the more you can be an active participant in it and the more you will understand how to create mixtracks that give your film a rich and dynamic sound.

Negative Cutting

Negative cutting is the process of conforming the camera original to what the editor has done in the edited workprint. Essentially, it is making an entirely new film out of your original, using the edited workprint as a guide. This process is not undertaken until the picture is "locked," that is, until you are absolutely sure that the picture is exactly the way you want it. The old adage of "measure your cloth a dozen times because you can only cut it once" is applicable: Once you cut your original, there is no turning back.

Students often conform their first one or two films, but the job is usually handed over to an experienced professional, because careful handling of the film is so critical. The *negative cutter*, called a *conformist* until the term's connotations occasioned the name change, is generally independent of the editorial department. This individual is brought on board after the editing staff has completed all their work, although projects that anticipate complicated printing jobs may require consultation with the neg cutter early in the editing process. The negative cutter's activities facilitate the lab's work, so a professional negative cutter is completely conversant with what material the lab needs to make a print of your film. Complicated cutting, supers, mattes, fast cutting, mixing black-and-white and color, and so on generally require that the original be laid out in a specific way. A good negative cutter will be able to give you guidance through the process.

The latent edge numbers are the reference points for replicating all cuts. Cement splicers are used exclusively to create splices that will be clean and durable in the printers. The original film is not cut into a single strand but into two rolls, called A & B rolls, although there are instances where more than two rolls are needed. Cutting A & B rolls is also called checkerboarding and is discussed in detail in ensuing sections.

Negative cutting is the least creative, and least romantic, of these finishing processes. The negative cutter never looks at the film and is completely uninvolved with sound. On the surface, it is a dull and mechanical process demanding little or no thoughtful involvement. And yet, the process is extremely exacting, and any mistakes in handling or cutting the film can have serious repercussions. The negative cutter is dealing with a precious commodity—your original. Handling of the original in this stage must be scrupulous. With it damaged or destroyed, you have nothing.

The Clean Room

A professional negative cutter will have a *clean room*—a room designed to be kept as clean and dust-free as possible. The rooms often have double doors to limit dust from the outside world and have air-transfer systems to clean and purify the air. The room is cleaned before every job, more often if it is a lengthy project. Cleanliness is essential to a quality negative-cutting job. Any dirt or dust that gets on the film will show up as spots on subsequent prints. If the dirt works its way into the film's emulsion, it can cause scratches and even worse damage. Fingerprints on the film must also be avoided. The negative cutter wears lint-free cotton gloves to minimize contact with the film.

The room generally has two pairs of rewinds. One set is used for the A & B rolls whereas the other is used to search for shots in the original. There is also a spool for the black leader needed to slug in the shots. A synchronizer and, of course, the cement splicer are also required items. Other equipment includes a trim bin, a pair of scissors, film tape, and a good supply of split reels, regular reels, spacers, and clamps.

How carefully and cleanly films are handled is the determining factor in a negative cutter's overall reputation. If the work consistently has dirt, fingerprints, or torn sprocket holes, no one is going beat a path to their door.

Cement Splicing

Negative cutting is done with a cement splicer, because all the splices must be permanent; the three final processes all have permanence as their final goal. Printers are designed to be gentle on the film, but tape splices will eventually pull apart, leaving a clear gap that will show on the film. Tape splices can also show bubbles and collect hair and other debris. Cement splices are permanent, strong, and will hold up in the contact printers. **SEE 18-3**

18-3

A cement splicer is used to create a strong, permanent splice that will hold up in the contact printer
Maier-Hancock cement splicer

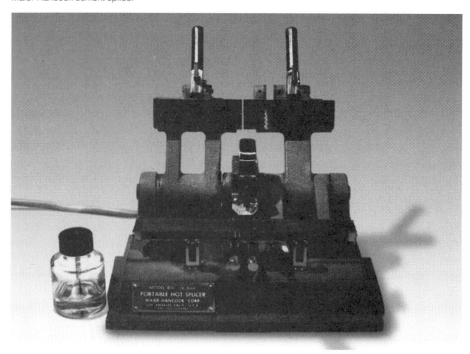

The ***cement splicer,*** also called a *hot splicer,* works on the principle of overlapping and cementing the first frame of a shot on a small part of the last frame of the preceding shot. The splicer has two film cutters, one for the head of the incoming shot and one for the tail of the outgoing shot. The head cutter does not cut on the frame line, but about an eighth of an inch into the bottom of the preceding unwanted frame. **SEE 18-4**

The negative cutter then scrapes the emulsion off this overlap with a small tool on the splicer. This scraped area allows the two pieces of film to bond together, which would not be possible if the emulsion were left on. A small amount of ***film cement*** is applied to the scraped overlap to create the bond. The previous shot is then laid on top of the overlap. **SEE 18-5**

When two shots are cut together, this overlap will be visible as the film is projected, a small blip appearing on the bottom of the frame at every cut. The A & B process masks this by overlapping the cut on black leader. The cement splicing destroys the frames that are used for the overlap, an important

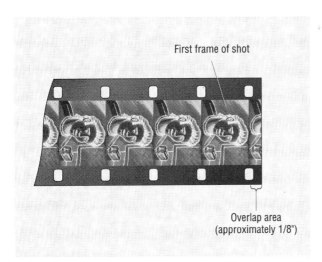

18-4

The cutter cuts about an eighth of an inch into the bottom of the preceding frame, rather than on the frame line

First frame of shot

Overlap area
(approximately 1/8")

18-5

The previous shot is laid on top of the overlap

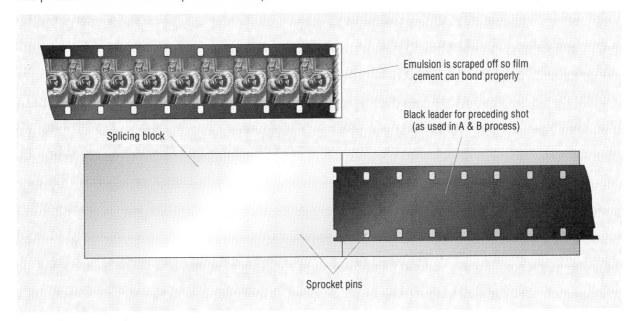

Emulsion is scraped off so film cement can bond properly

Black leader for preceding shot
(as used in A & B process)

Splicing block

Sprocket pins

consideration while cutting your film (see "Notes and Cautions" later in this chapter for a discussion of these issues).

The cement splicer has a small heating element in its base that keeps the splicer warm. This heat reduces the time it takes a splice to bond from about one minute to roughly fifteen seconds. The two pieces of film are not glued together—they are welded together. The splices should, if anything, be stronger than the film itself.

Marking the Workprint

Before being sent to the negative cutter, the edited workprint must be carefully marked with a grease pencil so the negative cutter clearly understands everything you are intending to do. Every actual cut from one shot to the next has to be clearly identified for the negative cutter. All *unintentional splices,* that is, splices where you tried a cut but decided to put it back together again, must be identified as well. If there are standard effects (fades, dissolves, and so on), they must be communicated to both the lab personnel and the negative cutter. When you are done marking, there should be a grease pencil mark on every splice in the entire edited workprint.

The most important thing to keep in mind as you are preparing the workprint for the negative cutter is that everything you want in the final film must be in the edited workprint. Freeze frames and all optical effects have to be created by the time you get to this stage. Conversely, if you do not want something in the final print, it had better not be in the workprint. Flash frames or lightstruck footage must be weeded out unless they are wanted for effect. All markings are done on the base side of the film, that is, rolled out on workprint.

All actual cuts in the film are marked with the letter *C.* **SEE 18-6** All unintentional splices should be marked with an equals sign (=). **SEE 18-7** This is essential to avoid any potential misunderstanding on the negative cutter's part.

Labs execute *fade outs* and *fade-ins*—where the picture fades out to or up from black, respectively—at a number of standard lengths, called *fade rates*. The standard options are fades of 16, 24, 32, 48, 64, and 96 frames. Fades of 16, 24, and 32 frames are the most commonly used lengths. Although it may be hard to imagine, anything longer than that tends to look very slow on-screen. Slow fades have their uses, but they tend to call attention to themselves and are frequently used in a stylized or mannered fashion. Fade-outs and fade-ins are literally drawn on the workprint. In both cases, write a description of the effect next to the marking with a grease pencil, "16-frame fade-out" in the first example. **SEE 18-8**

18-6

All markings are done on the base side of the workprint, actual cuts being indicated with the letter *C*

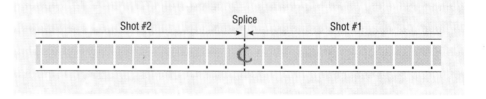

18-7

Unintentional splices must be marked with an equals sign

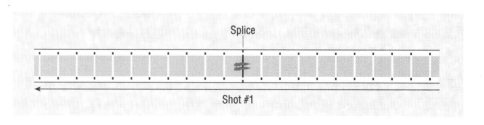

Whenever you have a fade-out followed by a fade-in, be sure to cut in some black leader between the two shots. If a fade-in is called for with no pause after the fade-out, the screen will never achieve a complete black. The length of the black depends on what you are attempting, but anything more than about a second will feel lengthy. Again, periods that seem brief can be an eternity in screen time. Rather than going to or coming from black, you can go to colors or "fade to clear" for a more stylized effect. Check with your lab and negative cutter about executing specialized effects like these.

Labs have the same standard *dissolve rates* as are available for fades. Also like fades, dissolves of 16, 24, and 32 frames are the most popular, with longer ones again taking up substantial screen time. The effect of a dissolve can be only suggested in a workprint, because you cannot sandwich film stock. The workprint must be cut so that the splice represents the "center" of the dissolve between the two shots; that is, the point when we are seeing an equal amount of each shot. The lab and the negative cutter will not understand other configurations.

If you are doing a 24-frame dissolve, you count 12 frames from the cut toward the head for the beginning of the dissolve. For the end of the dissolve, you then count 12 frames (for a total of 24) from the cut toward the tail. The following figure shows how they are marked on the workprint. **SEE 18-9** Again, write a description of the effect with a grease pencil just before the marking.

The technical requirements of dissolves are explained in the following section, but suffice it to say at this point that they must be completely planned before they are called for in the workprint. You cannot go through your film and capriciously decide that you want specific cuts to be dissolves. Both shots of the dissolve will be extended in the negative cutting, so there has to be more usable footage than represented in the edited workprint.

Another frequent need is to mark footage that was replaced during editing. During the lengthy and painstaking editing process, it is not uncommon to spoil or lose sections of shots. After running through projectors and editing machines,

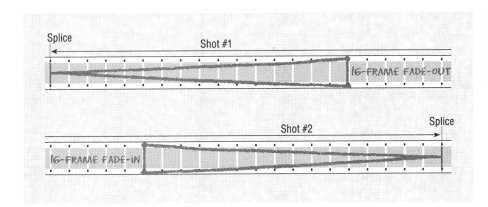

18-8

Fade-outs and fade-ins are drawn on the workprint as well as indicated in writing

18-9

To indicate a dissolve, the workprint must be cut so the splice represents the midpoint between the two shots

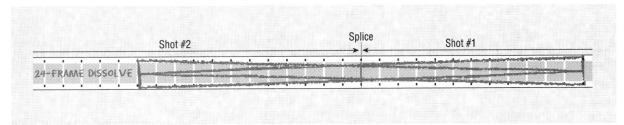

18-10

Replace missing frames with black leader and indicate the resulting splices with equals signs

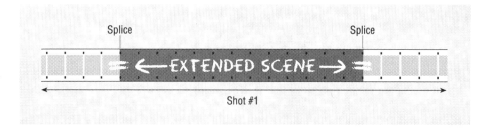

18-11

The *C* indicates which shot the missing frames belong to

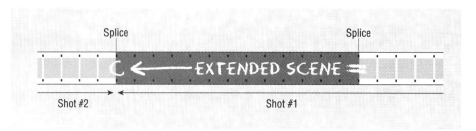

18-12

When damage occurred at the splice of two consecutive shots, the cut is indicated on the black leader

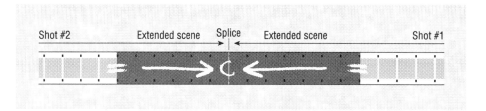

the much-traveled workprint often gets ripped sprocket holes or otherwise damaged sections. When workprint is damaged or destroyed, keep in mind that the corresponding frames in the original are still intact. If you are confident that the contents of the frames are good and you want them, you can still plan to use them in the final film. The common method of dealing with this situation is to replace all damaged or lost sections with black leader.

Any questions of how much black leader to insert can be determined by consulting the edge numbers. There are always twenty frames between every set of edge numbers, and you should check the shot on a frame ruler if there are any questions. Since these are essentially unintentional splices, the splices are marked with the equals sign. Write "extended scene" on the black leader and draw arrows, as shown. You should replace any length that is missing. If the piece is too small to write on, draw the arrow and write next to the shot. **SEE 18-10** If the damage occurs at the end or beginning of the shot, this too is marked on the workprint. **SEE 18-11** And damage at both the beginning and the end of two consecutive shots is indicated as shown in the figure above. **SEE 18-12** When the damaged section runs up to or includes a cut, your intentions must be marked clearly, since the negative cutter will have no idea which shot should have the extra frames.

These are the basic markings. There are a few others, such as supers (a squiggly line), which should be discussed with your negative cutter. Again, there should be a mark on every splice when you send the edited workprint to the negative cutter. Unclear markings create the potential for a mistake in the conforming process. If the mistake is a result of sloppy marking, it is no one's fault but your own.

A & B Rolling Picture

The latent edge numbers are used as the guides for the entire process of cutting the original. The negative cutter goes through the film and records the beginning and ending edge numbers of each individual shot, counting from the edge numbers

18-13

In the A & B–rolling process, alternating shots are placed on separate rolls, with shots on the opposing roll replaced with black leader

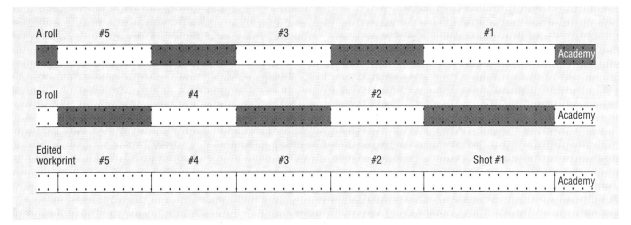

to the actual frame where the cut is. If the first shot runs from, for example, edge number 3247 minus 9 frames to 3291 plus 17 frames, the neg cutter will go to the original and pull out that piece. For technical reasons, a little more is actually taken out. This is an important issue to consider while cutting (see "Notes and Cautions" later in this section).

Rather than creating a single strand, the original film is cut into two separate rolls, called *A & B rolls.* A & B rolling, also referred to as checkerboarding, places black leader between alternating shots. This process is done on the synchronizer, with the edited workprint set up in a gang to act as a guide. The Universal leader is put on the B roll, and the first shot is on the A roll. **SEE 18-13** Although it does not always work out this precisely, the A & B configuration puts all the odd-numbered shots on one roll and all the even-numbered shots on the other. This leaves the original film with no image-to-image cuts. All shots are cut to black leader at both the head and tail. The black leader between shots is the same length, frame for frame, as the shot on the opposing roll. As one might suspect, the reasons for doing this are similar to those used when preparing for the mix.

To understand the rationale for A & B rolling, it is necessary to jump forward to what the lab does with these rolls prior to the printing process. With a virgin piece of raw stock, a contact print from the A & B rolls is made in separate passes on a lab's printer. The A roll is generally printed first, printing all the odd-numbered shots. The raw stock is then rewound to the appropriate marks on the standardized leaders, and the B roll is then printed. This second pass drops in all the shots missing from the printing of the A roll. The optical master is printed at a separate gate that exposes just the edge of the film. It is run at the same time as one of the A & B rolls.

The following are what A & B rolling allows the lab to do. Be aware that the negative cutter has no control over these elements, although he or she can usually answer many questions about the printing process. These are aspects of finishing that are facilitated by the neg cutter's efforts.

- Facilitates color and exposure corrections.[1]

- Facilitates optical effects: fades, dissolves, superimpositions, and the like.

- Creates "invisible splices."

---

1. Color is not an issue in black-and-white, so exposure correction is the important control.

Color and exposure correction. The printer affords extensive opportunity to manipulate the character of the film's shots. Each light valve in the printer breaks down the transmission of each primary color of light into a series of ***printer points***, each representing an increment in the intensity of the individual color (see page 108). There are 50 points represented on a dial that controls the valve. Theoretically, a perfectly exposed and colored image will fall right in the middle of the points. That is, the perfect setting for exposure would be 25-25-25. It must be emphasized that this is theoretical, because individual labs set their printers for different standards or norms. It rarely works out precisely as 25-25-25, though the lab's standard numbers rarely deviate too far from 25.

Prior to printing your film, the A & B–rolled original is put on an analyzing machine, where each individual shot is evaluated. The machine used for this is generally a *Hazeltine*, though there are other companies that produce equipment designed for this purpose. The A & B rolls are loaded separately into the Hazeltine, which shoots light through the original and gives a video representation of the image. Just as on the printer, this light is broken down into the three primary colors of light. A lab employee, the *timer*, or *grader*, goes through the entire film and analyzes each individual shot for color and exposure.

The printer lights, the actual volumes of red, green, and blue, are determined in this process. If a shot was underexposed on location, the lights can be dialed to compensate. If a shot is too blue, the blue light could be dialed to contribute less, and so on. The timer looks at each shot and uses his or her best judgment for both the appropriate color and exposure level. This process is called *timing*.

These dials clearly allow substantial control over the image, but only over the entire shot. The timer cannot manipulate specific elements in the frame, such as a blown-out window, without affecting the rest of the scene. Think back to the example of the man in front of the window: if the window area is overexposed, you cannot bring it down without bringing down the exposure of all the interior elements. Nor can you change the color in just one area of the frame without affecting other elements. If you had not corrected for the exterior color temperature with filters or gels, you could not subtract the resulting blue cast without affecting the interior. To do so would, for instance, make the lamp much redder.

If there is enough information in the image, almost any difficulty can be corrected. Material that cannot be corrected is that which is so overexposed or underexposed that there is no detail. If part of your image is overexposed, ***printing down*** the image will darken any normal or underexposed areas. Conversely, ***printing up*** dark images will lighten normal and overexposed areas.

Although modern printers can "fire on a frame," the A & B–rolling method is necessary because the printer lights work most effectively when given time to adjust. If the original was cut in a single strand, the printer lights could not be changed from the last frame of the outgoing shot to the first frame of the incoming shot without a change in the image. The black leader between each shot allows the printer lights time to adjust to the printing needs of the upcoming shots.

Exposure on location is a tricky beast. As with the sound, your images frequently need to be tweaked for exposures that are slightly off. Labs do the bulk of their work with commercial clients and thus go for photographic normal. They will try to make facial tones accurate and generally push for realistic representation. If you have color or exposure effects built into your shooting, you will want to alert the lab to that fact. Individual timers have their own preferences, and experienced DPs will find timers they like, working closely with them throughout all the printing-related aspects of a film.

Beginners tend to see this final printing phase as an opportunity to correct mistakes, as it most certainly is. However, experienced DPs are highly conversant with printer lights, and the roll these lights play influences their plans before the first instrument is set up on a set. In fact, much of the discussion of lighting in part

III can be tied to the theory behind printer lights, but mastering basic exposure technique precedes these considerations.

Optical effects. The A & B method allows the lab to execute the optical effects that were planned in the editorial process. Dissolves, as well as superimpositions and matte shots, clearly require two shots to be printed together. This would be impossible if a single roll of conformed original were used. The A & B method allows images to be on both rolls concurrently and thus printed together.

As the color and exposure are analyzed and recorded on the Hazeltine, the effects indicated on the marked workprint are similarly logged. In the path of the light in a printer, there is a master shutter, the ***fader unit*** (see page 108), which is opened and closed to create the overall effects. All fades and dissolves are created by this fader. A 24-frame fade programmed into the printer instructs the fader to close in one second at the appropriate point. A dissolve has a fade-out start at the programmed point on one roll. When the second roll is printed, a fade-in is started at the same point. The result of the fade-out on top of the fade-in is the dissolve.

In the workprint, a dissolve is marked in the manner described in the previous section. The cut in the workprint always represents the center of the dissolve, that is, the point where there is an equal amount of each image. The negative cutter extends the shot past the center point represented in the workprint. If it is a 24-frame dissolve, the negative cutter will extend each shot an extra 12 frames in the appropriate roll. **SEE 18-14**

There are two issues that must be clear in order to understand the requirements of dissolves. The first is that the frames at the splice in the workprint are in the same position in the A & B rolls. Some people make the mistake of thinking that because the shots are being extended that the film somehow becomes longer, thus requiring some adjustments in the mixtracks. As figure 18.14 suggests, the dissolve occupies the same area, that is, number of frames, in the final film as its corresponding straight cut does in the workprint. The overlap portions of the shots simply are extended in the A & B rolls.

The second consideration is that there must be more usable frames than are represented in the edited workprint. In a one-second dissolve, the negative cutter will be employing the twelve frames after the cut on the outgoing shot. They must be frames that you want to be visible. The same is true on the head of the incoming

18-14

The dissolve occupies the same number of frames in the final film as its corresponding straight cut does in the workprint; the overlap portions simply are extended in the A & B rolls

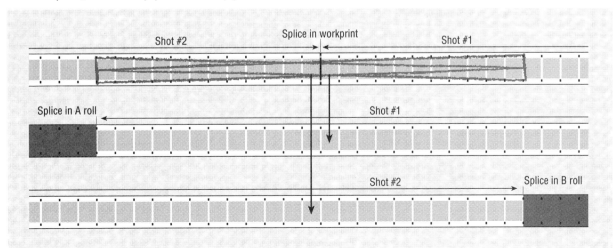

shot. You cannot cut on the last frame of a shot and then call for a dissolve in the edited workprint. If you did, the extended part of the dissolve would overlap into the next shot.

Superimpositions and matte shots are also printed together in the A & B method. A super is created by putting images in the same place on the A roll and the B roll. The lab will have to adjust exposure to compensate for two pieces of film being printed together. Similarly, mattes are generally made of two or more components printed together. One part of the frame might be blocked off on one shot while the opposite side is blocked off on another piece of film. The two are printed together in the A & B method to produce a composite shot. Mattes and supers may have other requirements that should be checked with both the lab and your negative cutter.

Numerous situations come up in which more than two images need to be combined, thus requiring the addition of more rolls—C rolls, D rolls, et cetera. Special effects and matte shots are the clearest examples of this. Ivan Reitman's *Ghostbusters* (1984) has an excellent example of this in the scenes of the giant marshmallow man coming down the street to confront the ghostbusters.[2] The shot consists of three elements: an animated miniature of the marshmallow man walking down a city street, a painted backdrop of the cityscape at night, and the ghostbusters on a roof with their backs to the camera. This would presumably mean the addition of a C roll to accommodate the third element. Many special-effects shots and animations are even more complicated. A shot from George Lucas's *Star Wars* (1977) is reported to have had more than seventy separate elements.

Invisible splices.   This refers to a method of masking the glitches inherent in the process of cement-splicing the film together. As stated, the cement splicer works by overlapping a small piece of the incoming shot on the outgoing shot. Left uncovered, this tab is visible when the film is projected. In the A & B method, this scraped tab is always covered by black leader laid on top of it and cemented. The picture is scraped and then covered by the outgoing frame of black leader.

Cutting the Original

Negative cutters have their jobs broken down into efficient systems. Although there may be some minor differences in approach, the following is generally the sequence of events. The first step is to go through the edited workprint and log the beginning and ending edge numbers of all the shots. The next step is to go through the uncut original and find what sequences of edge numbers are on the individual rolls. The negative cutter will then have some idea of where all the pieces will be found. Given the huge amount of footage, longer films are often conformed a scene at a time.

The next step is to set up the appropriate leaders. The edited workprint is set up in one of the gangs of the synchronizer with the leaders for the A & B rolls set up next to it. The beginning of the A roll consists of white leader. The B roll has the Universal leader preceded by white leader. The frames corresponding to the edit sync on the edited workprint are punched and marked on both the A & B rolls. On the A roll, the frame corresponding to the Academy 2 is also marked.

Once the leaders are completed, it is a matter of starting with the first shot and building both the A & B rolls from the original. The negative cutter gets the edge numbers off the first shot and determines on which roll of original it can be found. The neg cutter then winds through the appropriate roll until the shot is found. While winding through the original, the negative cutter rolls the film gently but not to the point of it being loose on the reel; any snapping or undue stress that

---

2. This scene is detailed in the June 1984 issue of *American Cinematographer,* one of the most effective discussions of the matting process available.

will cause the layers of film to grind against each other is to be avoided. The shot is carefully cut out of the original with a pair of scissors, pulling the piece indicated in the edited workprint. The negative cutter actually pulls out an extra one and a half frames on either end of the shot, which are needed for handling and the area to be scraped on the cement splicer.

This first shot is then cut onto the A roll at the place indicated in the workprint. The B roll has black leader across from this first shot. Black leader is cut to the end of the first shot with the second shot being cut onto the B roll, and so on. By this method, a new version of the film is built out of the original.

Commercial feature films rarely cut the original. It is always kept intact, and all cutting is done with duplicates of the original, often the beginning of a complicated family tree of interpositives and internegatives. The film that you see at the theater may be many generations removed from that original piece of raw stock that was exposed in the camera on location. Strapped for cash, many students decide to conform their own original. This is an acceptable route, although there are considerable risks. The more you get into film, the more the idea of touching the original becomes an issue of substantial concern. Any handling involves risk. When you start conforming, be as prepared as conceivably possible. If any element of the process gets confused or messy, the whole effort can start on a downward spiral, which at this stage jeopardizes all the time, effort, money, and, most significant, emotion you have invested in the project. This is why most people turn the process over to a professional.

Notes and Cautions

Whether you intend to go to a negative cutter or do the conforming yourself, there are some basic considerations that should inform the process.

☑ All communication about specific shots, with both the negative cutter and the lab, is done in footage and frames. The "picture start" frame in the Universal leader is used as 0 feet, 0 frames, and everything is counted from there. If you have a shot that needs special attention, you would tell the lab or negative cutter that a shot at such and such a spot, say, from 125 feet, 12 frames to 128 feet, 32 frames, needs something done to it. Usually this refers to alerting the lab to a shot that needs exposure or color correction, but there are also concerns that need to be relayed to the negative cutter.

☑ You should never be scraping black leader. Cement-splicing the tail of each shot presents a problem. The head of each shot feeds into the left of the splicer, so you are always cutting and scraping picture. However, when you cut the tail of a shot, the last frame would theoretically be dropped onto the scraped head of the black leader of the next shot. This scraped part would create a glitch that would be visible. To avoid scraping black leader, you have to orient the film so that you are still scraping picture when you cut the tail of all shots. Usually this means bringing the tail of the shot from the right so it feeds into the left of the cement splicer. **SEE 18-15**

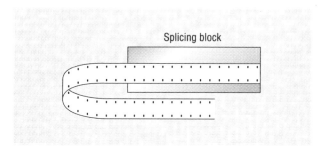

Splicing block

18-15

To avoid scraping black leader when splicing the tail of a shot, orient the film so you are always scraping picture.

This much handling of the fragile original justifiably makes some people nervous. Rather than twisting the film around, you may want to turn the splicer so it faces away from you and move to the opposite side of the table to make all your tail cuts. You will get a lot of exercise this way.

☑ The *lost frames* constitute one of the most difficult mechanical editing concepts to understand. It concerns how the requirements of the negative cutter affect the way you cut your film, specifically how you need to account for the frames that are ruined in cement splicing.

All frames of the unedited workprint have precise corresponding frames in the original. Thus, if you have to cut and scrape frames when cement-splicing the original, the ruined frames correspond to real frames in the workprint. These corresponding frames must be identified, catalogued, and set aside. If they are used elsewhere in the edited workprint, the negative cutter will be faced with a problem. Looking at a piece of workprint and its corresponding original should clarify this. **SEE 18-16** If you were to pull section A from your raw footage and use it in your edited workprint, the negative cutter would go to the original film and pull that piece, plus an extra one and a half frames on either side of A, piece B in the original. Frames 2 and 3 are needed for the scraped emulsion overlap required by the cement splicer. The negative cutter also pulls frames 1 and 4 because they provide safe handling of the film. *Frames 1, 2, 3, and 4 in the original are thus destroyed in the negative-cutting process.*

Therein lies the problem. These ruined frames are intact in the workprint and could potentially, but wrongly, be used elsewhere in the edited workprint. If these workprint frames are used later in the film, the neg cutter will not find them when attempting to pull the shot. The shot in the original must be the same length as the one in the edited workprint or there will sync problems with the sound. The negative cutter has to do some fancy footwork to fix your mistake, usually pulling the necessary number of frames from the tail of the shot or lengthening the next shot. Although these solutions can work, they can alter sync for individual shots and cause cuts to be less fluid.

A mistake like this represents poor planning on the editor's part. You must take into account that these frames are going to be destroyed and simply discard two frames, rounded up from one and a half, at the beginning and end of every shot which will be used in your film. Do not throw them away; mark them so that if you consider using them later you will know they are off limits.

As with dissolves, this invariably leads to confusion about whether this makes the film longer. "If I have to add a frame and a half, doesn't that affect my sound?" The answer is no. The piece that is represented in the workprint coincides with the

18-16

Always keep in mind that two frames on either side of a shot must be sacrificed when making the A & B rolls

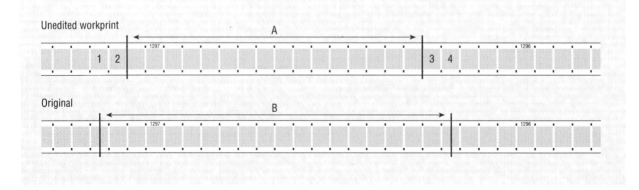

piece that will be in the conformed original frame for frame. The lost frame pertains solely to what is in your outtakes. The frames the negative cutter will need for cement splicing must remain intact in the unused portion of the workprint.

This rarely becomes a problem but does require attention to avoid mistakes. Shots have flash frames at the head and tail, and sync shots have all the starting and finishing information that make mistakes almost impossible. It becomes a problem only when you want to use different sections of the same shot at different places in the edited workprint.

☑ In the negative process, creating fades and stretches of black requires special handling. Using black leader on both the A & B rolls does not produce black on the resulting film print. Because everything is reversed, black leader produces clear film or thereabouts. If you are working in color, you need to use *orange mask* in the A & B rolls to create black in an answer print. Color negative, whether still or motion picture, has an orange cast to it, which is simply the shade that creates black in the resulting prints. A black stretch is created by cutting orange mask on one of the A & B rolls. Fades require unusual treatment, with the two shots to be faded uncharacteristically cut together and the orange mask on the opposing roll. **SEE 18-17** The fader is closed on the picture during the pass on that roll. For the orange mask on the opposing roll, the fader is opened to produce black. A & B–rolling negative requires knowing how the negative gets printed. Be sure to check everything with your lab if you are conforming your own film.

☑ Special care must be taken when doing fast cutting—cutting of shots less than one second long. Any piece shorter than twenty frames has the potential to not have an edge number, which would leave the negative cutter without a clue as to where the piece came from. As you are cutting, pieces that do not have an edge number must be identified and logged for the conformist. There are a number of ways to do this. The best method is to lay the film that you intend to take the piece out of on a sheet of white paper. Put a pencil mark in each sprocket hole of the intended piece from one edge number to the next. Transfer the edge numbers to the page as well. **SEE 18-18** When you are done, you will have a line of more than twenty dots with the edge numbers indicated. Draw a line on the frames that are being used in the shot. This page is given to the negative cutter, with a note saying that this is the shot at this location in the film. Again, the location of the shot is indicated in the footage and frames from "picture start."

18-17

Fades require the two shots to be cut together with orange mask on the opposing roll

Fade-out and fade-in in workprint

Cut in one original role

Orange mask in opposing roll

18-18

Film pieces that do not have edge numbers must be identified and logged on paper for the negative cutter

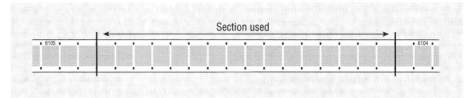

☑ Nothing in the editorial process requires more practice than cement splices. Considering that you are working with the original, it behooves you to become completely comfortable with them before tackling the job. Scraping the emulsion on the overlap without damaging the frame is tricky. Try scraping many test frames, practicing not ripping sprocket holes or weakening the film. Practice applying the film cement so it does not spread onto the adjacent frames. These splices should be tested by gently twisting them to see if the edges separate. Holding the film in both hands and snapping it is the final test. The splice should be stronger than the rest of the film. Be absolutely comfortable with splicing before attacking your original.

As stated earlier, there is modest debate among film professionals about whether to mix first or conform first. Most filmmakers mix first. If there are any structural problems with the film, they will show up as you watch it in all its glory in the mixing studio. Though it may be costly, you can always terminate the mix and return to the editing room. This would not be possible if the film was already conformed.

The counterargument is that if there are any errors or miscalculations in the negative cutting, the mixtracks may need adjustments to compensate. If you have already mixed, all sound remaining in sync depends on the film being conformed frame for frame to the edited workprint. Given the complications of the process, lost frames, and so on, mistakes are occasionally made. However, if all guidelines have been followed and the negative cutter is an experienced professional, this should not be an issue.

Again, negative cutting appears to be mechanical and dull, but it is a critical process that must be done meticulously. Mistakes in conforming can be disastrous. Any errors or carelessness will result in ruined shots, difficulties in synced sound, or dirty, scratched prints. I worked on a film in which the negative cutter misread the numbers on one shot, a rare but costly occurrence. **SEE 18-19** Rather than pulling piece A, he pulled piece B and spliced it into the roll.

When the wrong piece is pulled, what resulting problem is immediately noticeable? Sync. When the otherwise perfect answer print was projected, we were

18-19

Misreading the edge numbers on a shot while conforming—pulling piece B rather than piece A, for example—results in irrevocably lost frames and a disruption of sync

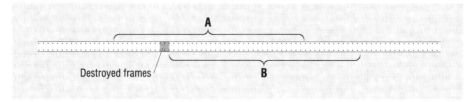

stunned to see one shot in which the dialogue and the picture were completely mismatched. As the piece used was in front of the piece we wanted, correcting the head of the shot was no problem. However, the incorrect tail cut occurred in the middle of the desired shot, thus causing substantial problems. The one and a half frames already pulled and destroyed were frames intended for the film. There was no getting them back. We were left with the unenviable choice of either finding another shot with sound timed similarly to the already mixed sound or accepting a slight (two-frame) jump in the footage and a disruption of sync for the length of the shot. No suitable replacement shot worked, and the latter solution was reluctantly agreed upon. Though many viewers do not even notice it, I still flinch when I see the jump.

The Final Print

With all the elements created, it is time to produce an *answer print*—the first attempt at making a final print of your film. The lab you choose needs a minimum of four elements to make a print: the A roll, the B roll, the optical master, and the marked edited workprint. If it is a complicated job, printing may require C rolls, D rolls, or more.

In many ways, this last process is the most exhilarating. It is when you finally get to see a project that you have put so much into come to fruition. Be prepared for some disappointments as well. Too often, beginning filmmakers expect the lab to magically create perfect exposures and correct all deficiencies in shooting. Making an answer print involves many variables, and there may be trade-offs between what the filmmaker desires and what the lab can actually do. The lab workers make their best attempt to produce the print you want; however, the lab cannot work miracles.

There is a certain irony in that the more ambitious you have been in lighting, filtering, and exposure, the harder the job is for the lab and the timer. A flat image is easy to time. When there are exposure gradations and color effects in an image, the timer may legitimately become confused about what you are attempting to achieve. Communication is the key. Let the timer know what you have done and what you want. Frankly, the biggest variable in printing is how well you have executed the shots. If the negative is exposed properly and the lighting volume and quality is consistent in continuity scenes, the timer's job should be easy. If the shots are a mess, the potential for problems multiply.

There is an old joke among filmmakers about fixing films. When presented with problems in preproduction, the saying goes that "we'll fix it in shooting." Problems in shooting will be "fixed in the editing room." Problems in the editing room? "We'll fix it in the mix." And problems at the mix are "fixed in the answer print." This takes on a certain aspect of gallows humor, but the buck stops with the final print. There is no place to fix the film after this. There is a certain painful finality to going to a print.

You need to be aware of some of the pressures involved in finishing. Like the birth of a child, it is a joyous occasion. And, similar to a child's birth, there can be both a sense of separation and nervous fretting over what this wrinkly, squalling thing will look like to other people.

Reversal Versus Negative

Before discussing printing theory, the different approaches necessary for negative and reversal must be addressed. Reversal film is very straightforward. If a film is underexposed, you pump up the light to get a better exposure. If there is too much red in the original, the lab simply reduces the amount of red in the final print. If there is a light area on the original, it will be light on the print.

However, in negative film everything is the opposite. An underexposed negative is very "thin," that is, almost clear. It would thus need less light from the printer. An overexposed negative is very dense, or thick, thus needing more light for the printer. In addition, when the lab increases a color, the result is less of that color in the final print. Thus if there was too much blue in a print, the lab would need to, paradoxically, increase the amount of blue. This last part is the most difficult to understand, and the novice may not have much immediate need to apply this knowledge. As with everything, though, the long-term goal is to understand every element of the process. And the process of printing, that is, creating the final version of your film, is clearly one that demands significant attention.

The Printing Program

As stated, the timer analyzes each shot for color and exposure. The resulting decisions are fed into a computer-generated decision list, called a ***printing program***, which will "run" the printer lights as the A & B rolls are printed. The timer also checks the marked edited workprint for all cuts and effects and encodes all ***printing cues***—instructions to the printer lights and fader unit—into the printing program. This decision list comes in a number of forms, but is usually an old-fashioned punched computer strip. Whatever the form, the decision list controls all the values at which the red, green, and blue printer lights will be set for each individual shot. It also instructs the fader unit to open and close for dissolves, fades, and any other printing effects.

The following figure shows the beginning of a typical printing program. It represents a simple, short film employing just an A & B roll. It had no dissolves or fades and was shot on negative. **SEE 18-20**

18-20

The beginning of a typical printing program for a short film employing an A & B roll

```
                              PRINTING PROGRAM

                  JOB NUMBER:       DATE:       SCENES:  73

                  EFFECTS  CUES    MIN CUE    LAST CUE    MAX FPM

          A ROLL            36     4   00     357  00    2000

          B ROLL            37     5   00     357  00    2500


SCENE  FEET  FRAMES  A ROLL  RD  GN  BL   B ROLL  RD  GN  BL

       0000    25      ZC    00  00  00

0001   0008    03                          LC    10  13  06

0002   0013    08      LC    22  18  13

0003   0014    20                          LC    16  16  09

0004   0060    25      LC    22  18  13

0005   0073    05                          LC    16  16  09

0006   0074    15      LC    24  16  11

0007   0077    05                          LC    24  16  11

0008   0080    25      LC    28  27  34
```

The numbers under the *RD, GN,* and *BL* headings represent the red, green, and blue printer light settings for each individual shot. This film had 73 shots, with the cue total being slightly higher (75) because of head and tail leaders. A feature with, for example, 1,200 shots would have 1,200 settings. That some numbers are duplicated suggests that material from certain setups was used more than once, a shot/reverse shot in this case.

One of the first shots was evaluated at 22-18-13. Although the precise meaning of these numbers would not be consistent from lab to lab, this suggests that the shot was slightly underexposed and was a little too red. Because it is negative, less light is needed to get through the less-dense negative. The higher number on the red is what suggests that the red component in the image had to be pumped down. When the red is pumped down, it affects overall exposure. This explains why the green and blue numbers are lower. The fact that the green light is set higher than the blue suggests that the red being eliminated had a little bit of yellow in it, the mix of red and green producing yellow. Remember, more is less in negative. The shot evaluated at 24-16-11 is similar to the shot just described. The shot at 28-27-34 would suggest slight overexposure but with too much blue. Indeed, it was tungsten-balanced film shot in daylight without an 85 filter.

When the A roll is printed, the computer decision list created by the timer controls these settings on the light valves in the printer. The transition from shots #6 to #8 is a good representation of what occurs. The printer lights are set for 24-16-11 for shot #6. In the time that the black leader corresponding to shot #7, 140 frames, or almost six seconds, is masking the gate, the printer lights are instructed to change to 28-27-34.

This particular program had no fades or dissolves, so there are no effects cues. If there had been, the computerized printing program would have had instructions to the fader unit to create effects. Both the fader unit and the light valves require some response time to be able to either reopen or adjust to the programmed values. Short shots may not allow the fader unit or light valves the time to adjust to new settings. Individual labs may require different response times, but it is generally less than one second. If your shots are very short, you may have to put some of them on a C roll.

The First Answer Print

The first answer print should be looked at and evaluated in terms of your standards. Although labs generally do a highly professional job, the print is rarely perfect—perfection being virtually impossible to achieve with so many variables. Sometimes you have to look at a print and decide whether it is worth the effort and cost to correct a few minor mistakes. If it is good enough, the lab makes all subsequent release prints from the printing program that has been created. If there are problems, you may have to negotiate with the lab as to the cost of another answer print. If you can demonstrate that the mistakes were the lab's fault, they should absorb the cost of or cut a deal for the next print. If the mistakes are a matter of poor preparation or communication on your part, you will probably have to foot the bill for the next answer.

The key complicating factor is that the lab tries to make the best print according to their established standards. Effective communication with the timer takes experience and a clear understanding of all the variables. Many times, what the timer sees and what you are hoping to see may be two completely different things; it may be that what you are hoping to see is not possible. More often than not, it is that you have not communicated your desires effectively. In the final analysis, it may be that printing as well as shooting is an inexact art. There are situations in which even the most capable cinematographers are stymied by elements that are beyond their control.

In chapter 11, there was a story about a scene involving two people sneaking up on a house as the sun rises (see page 266). The character of the shots was different enough that the filmmakers placed their hopes on the answer print. Their first step was to alert the lab of a potential problem. Not being familiar with a scene's context, the timer would have no possible way of knowing that it had problems. Once alerted, the timer can use only personal judgment to get the scene close. Although there are undoubtedly timers out there who can look at a negative and predict the look of a film perfectly, most mere mortals do not know precisely what a sequence is going to look like until it is printed. Once you see how close you have gotten, you can take another shot at it. In the sunrise story, it took three tries to get the printer lights set appropriately for the scene.

Again, be aware that most labs do the bulk of their work with commercial clients and thus are generally geared toward a straightforward photographic normal image. That is, flesh tones are normal, colors are true, exposure is within a certain range, and so on. If you want to create unorthodox images, this is simply a reality that you have to learn to accept. If you have any special desires in either correcting or not correcting a shot, they must be clearly communicated to the lab both verbally and in writing. As stated, all communication is done in footage and frames. All footage and frames are counted from the "picture start" frame in the Universal leader as 0 feet, 0 frames in the synchronizer. If a shot is too red in the workprint, you need to tell the lab that a shot at such and such a spot—say, 125 feet, 12 frames to 128 feet, 32 frames—needs some red eliminated. Or that another specialized effect should *not* be corrected.

The finality of all these processes should be reemphasized. Corrections to a print are very expensive and in some cases completely impossible. In a film about chemical contaminants, a director absentmindedly, and foolishly, used a 20-frame shot that included an identifiable product name. He had secured a well-known narrator and made multiple prints, anticipating wide interest in the film. When company representatives saw the film, they threatened legal action if the shot was not immediately removed. There was some unsubstantiated evidence that the company had produced the contaminant, but the director could never have afforded the protracted lawsuit that the company threatened to bring.

His options were all bad. On a final print, the picture and optical sound track are printed side by side. There is no way to replace one without affecting the other. He could go to every print and cut out the twenty frames, but the problem is that he would eliminate twenty frames of sound. Because of the displacement, it would not even be the corresponding sound. He could go back to his A & B rolls and cut out the offending shot, but then he would have to remix the sound and replace all the existing prints, both expensive propositions. He could replace the shot in the A & B rolls, but would again have to reprint everything. Someone recommended that he could take a permanent marker and blot out the offending shot, a wisecrack proposal until we noticed his expression, suggesting he was actually considering it.

He finally decided to cut the twenty frames out of one print, a radical action given the cost of an individual print. Mercifully the sound that was cut turned out to be unimportant, and he cut the twenty frames out of the rest of the prints. While bemoaning his fate over a few beers, another documentary filmmaker pointed out the obvious: the shot should never have been there in the first place. If you are going to take on a corporation, go ahead and do so straightforwardly. Do not let twenty frames endanger an otherwise untouchable $80,000 project.

For most students and independents, a final print is just that—final. Commercial feature films can experiment with different versions because most producers never cut the original. High-quality intermediate prints of the film are generally the source for prints. For those of you who have to cut the original, everything must be exactly the way you want it before you embark on any of these processes.

Despite all the possible headaches that have been described, the creation of the answer print is the most exciting part of the filmmaking process. You finally have something you can hold in your hands. This is what all the effort has gone toward. With all the hurdles that had to be jumped and the mountains that needed to be climbed to reach that moment, there is nothing as satisfying as seeing a project, no matter how complex or simple, come to fruition. And the more you understand the requirements of each individual step, the more those hurdles and mountains will become surmountable.

Once you have an acceptable answer print and begin making release prints, your film starts to take on an entirely different life: distribution and exhibition. In certain ways, it can be a life that is even more demanding and draining than the actual production itself was, particularly for independent filmmakers. Although venues for nonmainstream films are becoming more plentiful, it is still a challenge to get one out there and seen. Festivals offer opportunities to get attention. There are also the "markets," conventionlike events where "indies" can screen work for potential distributors. The direct-to-video market may hold possibilities, although the film you are making may not conform to the product commonly found on the shelf at your local video store.

While independents scramble to be recognized, we hear about only the successes. The story behind Robert Rodriguez's *El Mariachi* is generally well known. Studio executives saw it, snapped it up immediately, and offered the maker opportunities for future work. We rarely hear about the films that languish in some netherworld because they are not good enough or are perceived as unable to command a wide enough audience to attract a distributor. Despite all the pitfalls, the growing number of successful films—both independent and commercial—is greatly encouraging. Somebody has to make them, and it might as well be you. But all this is a different story, one that goes far past the one being told here. For students and novice independents, the key is to work and get experience. You have to make them before anyone is going to come to see them.

C

Editing

FIRST **and foremost,** all video editing is done electronically. Film is a wonderfully tactile medium, with images being handled, held up to the light, and physically cut together. Video editing is a matter of choosing edit points on a monitor, programming those points into a computer or controller, and sitting back and watching the machines perform the edit.

As suggested, as this book is being written, the video-editing situation is taking some consistent shape. For years there were competing systems with varying claims, producing a sometimes bewildering set of options. Most systems had their own set of shortcomings, at least from the perspective of a film editor coming to the field. With the advent of the new digital video-editing systems, many of the drawbacks of the old analog video editing have been overcome. The flexibility of these new systems has broken down many of the last pockets of resistance of editors who clung to their flatbeds and uprights. For that reason, outside of students, independents, and the feature film market, very few projects are edited and finished on film. Learning the alternatives in video editing has become imperative for all those seriously interested in the field.

Analog and Digital

The terms *analog* and *digital* have very specific definitions regarding how information is encoded on a recording medium; it is easiest to understand the concepts with a simple example. A conventional typewriter (analog) and a word processor (digital) provide a good illustration of the difference. If the following sentence is typed on a sheet of paper (analog), the sentence occupies a specific amount of space on the page.

I could not anticipate all the problems.

If you decide to replace the phrase *could not anticipate* with the more informal *couldn't foresee*, you can use whatever erase function is available to eliminate the first phrase, but it isn't possible to plug in *couldn't foresee* without there being extra space—the video parallel would be a blank space on the tape.

I could not anticipate all the problems.

I   all the problems.

I couldn't foresee   all the problems.

To eliminate the extra space you would have to erase everything after the word *I* and retype the entire sentence from that point on. If you want to lengthen the sentence, say replace *anticipate* with *possibly foresee,* the problem is even clearer. On a word processor, digital storage allows you to eliminate or change whatever you want while drawing all the succeeding information forward or pushing it back.

Linear and *nonlinear* are terms that get thrown around with some abandon, and are sometimes mistaken as being the same as *analog* and *digital,* respectively. **Linear** simply means that information is stacked end to end in a line, film frames for instance; **nonlinear** means the arrangement of information is fluid. Although there are similarities, everything that is analog is not by definition linear, and everything that is digital is not by definition nonlinear. Film is analog and yet its editing is nonlinear. Digital audio- and videotape record a digital signal and yet do so on a linear medium.

Conventional videotape is linear, with each shot laid end to end and filling up a specific amount of space on the tape. One cannot go into an edited tape to shorten or lengthen pieces. Different shots can be substituted, but only ones of the same length. As in the typewriter example, changing the length of a shot in the middle of an edited program would require reediting everything after that point This is generally regarded as a significant drawback, particularly by editors trained in film, because it eliminates much of the flexibility in editing the image. Through the early years of analog video editing, many editors continued to work in film because of its nonlinear capabilities. Any piece can be shortened or lengthened. All pieces can be moved against each other as desired.

Digital editing has brought video into the nonlinear world. A digital editing system is simplicity itself, working in a way not unlike a word processor. The ability to drag images and sounds to wherever you want with the click of a mouse, shortening and lengthening them as needed, is highly efficient. Though many film editors were frustrated by analog video, they rarely return to film once they have entered the digital domain.

Off-line and On-line

The distinction between off-line and on-line concerns the working methods in finishing a project. An off-line system is used to make all the editorial decisions, and an on-line system is used to finish the project. This all relates back to the issue of broadcast quality (see page 117), the question being whether the project measures up to objective, and frequently subjective, broadcast standards. Off-line systems employ a lower-quality image, a video workprint or low-resolution digitized version. Off-line edit systems are less sophisticated, lacking the equipment and software designed to manipulate the image and create optical effects. Their primary advantage is that they provide a low-cost place for the time-consuming process of making editorial decisions. The intention is to return to a higher-quality image and finish on a more sophisticated system. Some percentage of production companies, particularly television stations, have on-line facilities, but more often than not finishing means going to a professional studio similar to a film audio-mixing studio. And with similar prices. Working off-line saves the time with the expensive gear for when many of the decisions have already been made.

While the idea of not working on a finished product may seem peculiar, it is worthwhile to remember that film editing is essentially an off-line process. You are editing mixtracks and workprint that must be taken to the mixing house and lab to create a finished product.

Video-Editing Applications

As the ways that a film or video project can be finished become more diverse (film, analog video, digital video), you need to recognize that there are a number of different applications of editing. The basic question is whether the final destination of your project is going to be a movie screen or a television screen or both. The answer to this question dictates many aspects of your approach.

Film editing is a process in which the product is very tightly controlled. It is the product of a person, or persons, making conscious decisions about what piece should be attached to what piece, and what sound or sounds should go with what picture. There is nothing accidental or arbitrary about what happens in film editing. It is, of course, controlled by what footage is produced on location, but what is done with it is up to the film editors.

In video editing, there are three significantly different types of editing—on tape, live, and what is referred to as live-on-tape. In the first instance, editing of already-shot footage can be just as tightly controlled as film editing. Any show that is done live, a baseball game for instance, is edited as it happens, using a piece of equipment called a *switcher*. Live-on-tape is a mix of the first two approaches.

In a typical live situation, a number of cameras are routed into the switcher in a control room, where each camera has its own monitor. The director watches these monitors and selects which camera's signal will be fed to the live broadcast feed. The switcher has simple touch buttons that the operator uses to select the camera the director has called. If there are six cameras, there are six buttons in use. The selected signal is called the *program feed*.

While there are often prearranged shots, everything occurs spontaneously. The camerapeople wear headsets, and the director calls the shots, though often camera operators have a specific responsibility, such as covering the pitcher or the man on first base, or are called on to use their best judgment. If the director wants a close-up, the instructions are given over the headsets. In a baseball game, nothing can be anticipated once the pitch is thrown and, although there are a limited number of options, the cameraperson has to be constantly improvising. Live shows such as awards ceremonies are also spontaneous, although as many shots and ideas as possible are worked out in advance.

Many live programs actually mix these different types of editing. Television news is a good example. Like a live show, TV news has a multiple-camera setup in the studio. There is a control booth, where a director watches the monitors and gives directions to the camerapeople. A technician sits at a switcher, taking the director's calls on-camera. The difference is that playback of already filmed and/ or edited news footage can be incorporated into the broadcast. Similar to news programming, sportscasts show replays, and talk shows use film clips. In contrast, there is no such thing as "live" film. Film, by its nature, is a very mediated process. Video, on the other hand, can be live and improvisational.

Live-on-tape means that the program was shot and switched live but delayed before broadcast—talk shows, for example. If there are any technical problems or unusable material, the tape can be adjusted in a conventional edit.

Cuts-Only Editing

Most beginning videomakers usually start with the half-inch VHS or Super VHS cuts-only systems, because they are generally the most affordable. **SEE C-1** A cuts-only system is simply where the only options are straight cuts—no dissolves, no

C-1

Cuts-only editing systems utilize straight cuts—no dissolves, fades, or complex audio manipulations
JVC BR-S series Super VHS cuts-only video-editing system

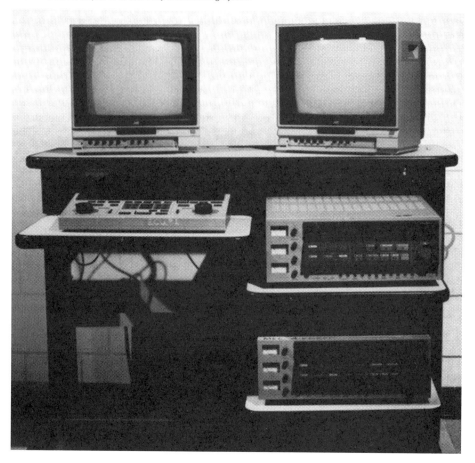

fades, and no complex audio manipulations. While there are ways to finesse some subtlety in the audio tracks, the audio-cutting options are relatively simple.

The video suite consists of a ***source deck***, or *playback deck*, and a ***record deck***. All tapes used to create the program are called ***source tapes***, and the tape you are creating is called the ***master edit***, or just *master*. There is also an ***edit control unit (ECU)*** which has hand controls, called ***shuttles***, that allow the editor to go through the tape at any speed desired, from frame by frame, to fast forward or reverse. **SEE C-2**

The edit control unit has LED readouts of time and frames, with the pulses in the control track—the pulse track recorded on all videotapes that regulates consistent playback—used to create reference points for editorial decisions. Each pulse represents a frame and, read in sequence, they produce a rolling time clock, which displays hours, minutes, seconds, and frames—1: 29: 46: 08, for instance. This clock can be reset to identify new points. Although the reset feature is useful, it has some major drawbacks. The video frames have no consistent way of being identified and logged for later use. When the clock is reset, or the editing machine turned off or the tape ejected, the reference points are gone. This is the problem time code was designed to address (see following sections).

There are essentially four edit functions on a cuts-only system, though mixing the latter three provides several other options. These functions are outlined below.

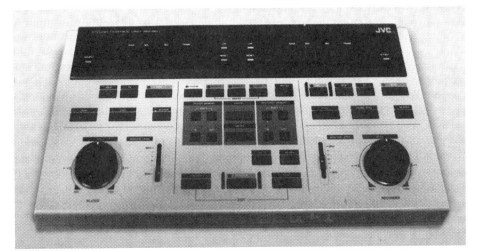

C-2

The ECU is used to program the source and record decks
JVC BR-S 622 edit control unit

Assemble   The assemble edit is the standard way of building a videotape from start to finish. The editor identifies the beginning of the first shot of the program to be transferred to the master. This is done by designating a specific frame on the source tape, determined by using the LED frame counts. The shot is then laid down on the master. When enough of it has been put down, the edit is terminated by the editor. The next step is to determine an out-point on the freshly recorded tape and an in-point on the next shot you want to use from the source tape. The editor programs the machines to exit the outgoing shot at a chosen frame and enter the next shot at another chosen point. A note of caution: You cannot assemble-edit in the middle of an already edited videotape. If you do, the control track will be broken at the end of the shot you are attempting to put in. A broken control track is essentially irreparable, and there will be significant glitches whenever the tape hits the damaged spot in playback.

Insert   The insert function allows you to insert image wherever desired. This function can be done only on a tape with a control track already laid down on it. Inserts can be done either MOS or in conjunction with one or both of the following audio functions.

Audio one   Different camcorders and VTRs have different strategies for laying down the sound recorded on location. Consumer camcorders often record a mono signal on track one; VTRs generally allow the operator to choose. Whatever track the location sound is recorded on, often remains the track of choice in editing.

Audio two   This usually leaves audio two for effects and music. The employment of this track, however, should remain fluid.

While having two audio tracks may be adequate for some projects, it is generally considered a drawback to the cuts-only system. The small number makes it difficult to do the layering necessary to create a complex sound track. There are ways to mix sound to the tracks, but synchronization of the tracks to each other as well as to the picture requires either expensive sideboard equipment or equally costly professional studio time. It is best to transfer additional sound—music and effects—from an audiotape to a blank videotape before editing the sound onto the videotape. It is possible to hook an audio cassette straight into a video-editing system, but then start and stop points can be done only by pressing *play* and *stop* on the tape recorder. Having the sound on a videotape allows exact positioning.

Thus, in editing, the editor uses the shuttles to find the outgoing points on the edited master tape and the incoming points from the source tapes. ECUs have *preview* and *perform* functions that allow you to first analyze and then finalize editing decisions. The *preview* function allows you to see the cut on the monitors without actually committing the edit to tape. You can program the in- and out-points, preview the cut, and, if it is not quite right, reprogram the points. Once you have a cut you like, you can punch *perform edit* and commit your decision to tape.

A tape is thus built from the beginning. Although this is certainly a viable approach, the major drawback is that you can get all the cuts right and yet miss the whole. One key, at least for the beginner, is to be able to go into a tape and improve pacing and overall editorial design by shortening or lengthening shots. Again, in analog cuts-only editing, you can replace shots with ones of similar length, but if a tape is 20 minutes long, it will always be 20 minutes long. If you look at the tape and know intuitively that it should really be 15 minutes long, the only option may be to start over from the beginning.

The most significant advancement in this analog approach has been A & B rolling. This is simply where you have two source decks instead of one. Both decks are interlocked, allowing the machines to roll together, creating effects between shots, particularly fades, dissolves, and other optical effects. A & B–roll editing requires a *time base corrector*, which puts new timing information on the tapes to slave two machines together for consistent operation.

Time Code

Designed to address the failings of the simple control track, *time code* is simply a perfect-time rolling clock that is recorded on the videotape. Like the time assigned to a control track on an ECU, time code reads in hours, minutes, seconds, and frames. You can base this rolling clock on the hours of the day or determine an individual start point for each tape. Unless removed for some reason, the numbers are consistent throughout the life of the tape. The advantage of this is that when a frame is identified, it can be returned to at any point during editing. If time code has not been recorded during shooting, it can be introduced by *striping* the video, recording externally produced though equally functional reference times. In the editing suite, time code is output to LED readers and it can be logged and stored in an analog or digital list.

The Digital Frontier

There are essentially two approaches to editing that incorporate digital information, the first working with analog videotape that is digitally encoded and the second with video information that is itself digitized and stored on a hard drive. The latter approach is preferred professionally, although the former is a viable and more affordable alternative. The first system is more accurately called computer-assisted editing, and is not completely digital.

Computer-assisted editing can employ either conventional or digital videotape. With either format, the tape generally has time code so the editor can log the individual frames where edits and effects are to occur. You analyze and make decisions similar to the way you do on a cuts-only system, except that the decisions are not committed to tape. While going through this process, you create a list of time-code numbers, referred to as an *edit decision list (EDL)*, designating the beginning and ending points of all shots. In computer-assisted editing, time-code numbers are input into the computer and used to give commands to editing decks. The systems are all software-based, and you can program in any optical effect available in the system. Once the list is completed, you then push a *perform* function, and the system will build your tape from the beginning. An uncomplicated five-minute project might take twenty minutes to build (while you go have a cup of coffee). Although the finished product is linear, the EDL can be changed, and new versions can be made at any time.

Time code can also be printed in a small box at the lower right of the video frame. Called a ***window burn****,* this allows you to analyze your source tapes on any deck, even a consumer deck, and create an EDL composed of all the time-code numbers. You can type the EDL into the editing system's computer at some later point, thus helping to maximize efficiency in the costly editing suites.

Although some companies incorporate attractive design features, a digital video-editing setup looks like a standard computer operator's station only with more monitors. **SEE C-3** The starting point with most digital editing systems is to input, that is, digitize, the image from an analog or digital videotape. The image can be input at different resolutions, which refers to the visibility of the individual pixels. When input at a high resolution, hard drives store only a small amount of unedited footage. One frame of digitized video can require as much as 1 MB of memory, an amount of information that requires huge hard drives and is difficult to retrieve in the split second needed. At a low resolution, much more material can be stored and easily retrieved.

As suggested, in true digital editing, images and audio can be moved in a way similar to text in word processing software. Both image and audio tracks are represented on a computer monitor. **SEE C-4** The parameters of a shot or a sound can be identified by time code, or the tape can be built from the beginning with the computer identifying the shots internally. Digital systems are almost in a

C-3

Digital editing stations resemble an advanced computer system

ImMIX VideoCube digital editing station

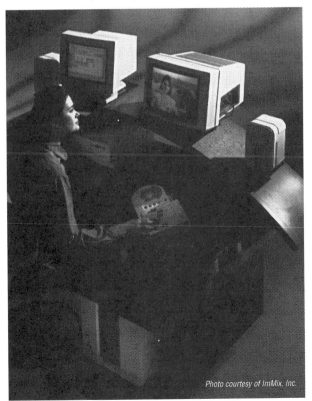

Photo courtesy of ImMix, Inc.

C-4

In digital editing, you can drag images and sounds to wherever you want with a click of the mouse

Avid Media Suite Pro

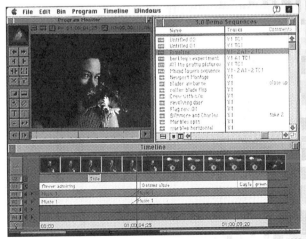

Photo courtesy of Avid Technology, Inc., copyright 1995

permanent preview mode. You can see what you have done at any time, but it is not committed to a final copy, either digitized or on a tape. As you are viewing your rough-edited project, the system retrieves each desired shot, no matter where it is on the hard drive, as it is demanded by the EDL. A final version can be produced, but most people use the digital editing systems for off-line decision making before an on-line edit.

At this writing, the digital systems and the hard drives that store digitized images are very expensive. New affordable equipment and particularly software are on the horizon, although such issues as the interrelationship with time code have yet to be worked out. These new systems will start the movement of bringing all the systems down in price. Affordable digital editing systems are the next big step in the video revolution. Though it is impossible to predict, there may be some sense of finality to the seemingly endless evolution of video editing when these systems are completely in place. There will always be improvements, but the production of equipment that is not obsolete within a year or two may be the real next step in the video revolution.

Getting Back to Film

For makers who still wanted to create a film print, the earliest off-line video-editing systems did not offer an efficient way to return to the edge numbers. This problem has finally been solved. With the new bar codes on film stocks, edge numbers can be electronically read on the film and then recorded on the videotape in the transfer. Striped time-code numbers are also generated in the transfer process, allowing an interface between the two sets of numbers to be created. The time-code numbers are then used during the video edit to create the EDL. When the project is finished, the time-code numbers from the EDL can be translated back to edge numbers. Another list can then be generated to designate the beginning and ending edge numbers of all shots. This list can then be given to a negative cutter, who initiates the traditional path to an answer print.

As suggested, this has had a profound impact on the process of making films. Many companies that resisted video technology have switched, or are in the process of switching, to digital editing. Despite all this, there are still many projects, particularly features, edited and finished on film. Producers have found that digital editing is good for shorter projects, such as commercials and music videos, where there is a manageable amount of footage. The notion of digitizing and storing all the footage involved in a feature, however, can overwhelm even the biggest system. Moreover, film will remain an exhibition medium for at least the foreseeable future, so the need to get to a final film print will remain. On many commercial projects with limited budgets, there is a sense of "why fix it if it ain't broke." The support system to make films is still in place and very sophisticated. In addition, many independents, lacking the resources for and access to elaborate video finishing, cling to film more tenaciously than ever. If they cannot compete aggressively in the video arena, why not make a good old-fashioned film? As the cost of digital editing comes down and the capacity for digital storage goes up, this may change. There is still a commendable desire among some film editors to hold on to a craft for the worth and beauty of it, much as people remain interested in calligraphy. But as most technology is eventually replaced by better and more efficient technology, traditional film editing will remain viable for a while and eventually go the way of the many technologies, from zoetropes to riffle books, that have preceded it. The oft-envisioned image of an editor surrounded by strips of film draped over the shoulder and hanging from the walls may drift slowly into mythology, but the tactile joys of putting one image right up against another, and remembering all the sweat and effort that went into creating them, will remain with us for the foreseeable future.

Glossary

⅓-⅔ rule   States that one-third of the depth of field is in front of the focus point and two-thirds is behind.

1st assistant cameraperson (1st AC)   The crew member responsible for everything to do with the cleanliness and operation of the camera.

16mm   The midsized format used in many independent film projects and most intermediate and advanced film production classes.

35mm   The format in which the bulk of professional work is shot.

180-degree rule   The principle used to create an understandable sense of the space in which the action is occurring. Also called *axis of action*.

A & B rolling   Checkerboarding the original on separate rolls to facilitate the final print.

Academy 2   The 2 at the end of the countdown leader.

action   The interrelationship of pull-down claw, shutter, and the other elements of the basic mechanism.

ambience   The character of the underlying sound in any given space.

ambience loop   Ambience on a piece of mag stock with the head cut to the tail, used to provide ambient fill for any gaps in the dialogue tracks.

ambience overlaps   The overlapping of ambience between sync takes that allows the rerecording mixer to soften any potential harshness of the cut.

American Society of Cinematographers (ASC)   Publishers of the *American Cinematographer Manual*.

amperes   Rating of the load-bearing potential of individual circuits. Also called *amps*.

animation   A single framing technique that puts inanimate objects in motion.

answer print   The first attempt at creating a final print of a film.

anticipatory camera   Rehearsed, highly choreographed camera movement that leads rather than responds to subject movement.

antihalation backing   The antireflectant coating on a film stock.

aperture   The place where each individual frame is exposed. Also called *gate*.

apprentice editor   Responsible for many of the routine procedures that the editor does not do, such as syncing up, stringing out, configuring mixtracks, and so on.

arm   A crane-style device that has a suspended camera controlled electronically by a remote.

art department   The crew members involved in the design elements of the image.

aspect ratio   The film frame's width-to-height relationship.

assistant director (AD)   The crew member primarily responsible for organization and efficiency on the set.

assistant editor   Responsible for the overall organization in the editing room.

attack   The first frame of an individual recorded sound.

audio mixing   The mixdown of the mixtracks created in editing.

automated dialogue replacement (ADR)   A method of replacing dialogue in postproduction.

automatic gain control (AGC)   The function on a sound recorder that reads the audio signal and automatically adjusts the recording to an appropriate level. Also called *automatic level control (ALC)*.

automatic threading   Mechanism on some cameras designed to feed the film unassisted.

baby legs   Short tripod legs used for low-angle shots.

background noise   Distant traffic, refrigerators, fans, and similar interfering sounds.

backlight   Generally positioned above and behind the subject, it provides texture and definition to the hair and separation from the background.

backwinding   A function that allows the basic mechanism of the camera to be driven backward with a hand crank.

ball joint leveling   Design used for leveling the tripod head.

banana plugs   Used frequently on European-produced equipment, the banana plug has the leads separated out into individual plugs.

barney   A padded hood used to further dampen unwanted camera noise. Also called *blimp*.

base   In the construction of the film stock, it is the acetate vehicle for the emulsion.

bellows   An accordionlike attachment that is mounted on the front of the lens.

best boy   The gaffer's first assistant.

bird's-eye view   A shot from directly above that tends to have a godlike, omniscient perspective.

black wrap   A material designed to cut light by wrapping around instruments.

blocking for the camera   Refers to staging action for the camera.

boom operator   The crew member who holds the mic on a boom.

bracketing   Shooting your subject at what the light meter tells you, plus at least one stop over and one stop under.

breaker box   Generally the main fuse box in a building.

breathing   Created by the moving front element of the lens, a slight zooming effect that is a by-product of a rack focus.

callbacks   Used to take a closer look at talent after general auditions.

call sheets   Informs the talent and crew of the time they must be on the set, how much time is devoted to makeup and hair, and the like.

camera mounts   Umbrella term that includes tripods, dollies, cranes, Steadicams, and many other specialized camera mounts. Also called *camera support systems*.

camera noise   Problematic sound created by the camera during sync takes.

camera obscura   A phenomenon in which light passing through a pinhole creates an upside-down representation.

camera operator   On most commercial films, the person who does the actual shooting.

camera package   Umbrella term for the camera, lenses, magazines, batteries, battery chargers, tripod, and any other camera needs specific to a shoot.

camera reports   The daily record of shooting kept by the 1st or 2nd AC.

cement splicer   Cements shots together, used mainly in preparing rolls for printing. Also called *hot splicer*.

characteristic curve   A representation of a film stock's latitude that plots the density of grains on the negative against rising exposure.

cheating   Shifting elements in the composition to balance the frame, thus improving an otherwise problematic shot.

checkerboarding   Another term for cutting A & B rolls.

chip chart   Used by the lab to set printer lights, a series of distinct colors on a chart that are shot at the head of every roll.

circuit   A series of outlets which are tied to a breaker or fuse in the main power box.

clapper/loader   The crew member responsible for slating shots and loading magazines.

clean room   A space that is designed to be clean and dust-free for cutting original film.

close-up (CU)   Essentially a head shot, usually from the top button of a shirt up. Variations are the extreme close-up (ECU) and the medium close-up (MCU).

coaxial   A magazine design that has the feed roll in a chamber on one side and the take-up in a second chamber on the other side.

coding   A set of numbers printed on both the picture and sync-sound rolls, used as a reference for sync.

color balance   The way film stocks are designed to respond to different colors of light.

color temperature   The distinct color of a given light source, measured in degrees Kelvin.

color temperature meter   Measures the color temperature of light sources.

composition   The arrangement of shapes and forms within an artistic frame.

continuity shooting   The creation of shots that when cut together appear to be continuous, creating a real-time relationship between the shots.

contrast   The play between light and dark in the photographic image.

core   A circular plastic piece on which film is wound.

core adapters   Used in the magazine to compensate for the larger centers of cores.

core loads   Raw stock loaded on cores.

countdown leader   The leader with descending numbers at the beginning of films. Also called *Academy leader* and *SMPTE Universal leader*.

coverage   Shooting action from more than one angle in order to provide options in the editing room.

crane   A camera support on a rolling vehicle with a single elevating arm.

critical tightener   Bar beneath the screw head on a tripod head that can be turned so the camera is tightly mounted.

crosshairs   Two intersecting lines in the center of a camera's viewing system.

C-stand   Short for Century stand, a commonly used stand for setting nets, flags, silks, and so on.

cue sheets   The log of mixtracks that assists the mixing process. Also called *mixing log*.

cutaway   A shot that the editor can cut away to.

cuts-only video   Basic video-editing system that performs only straight cuts between shots.

dailies   The footage from the previous day's work. Also called *rushes*.

daylight (D)   Photographic white that is 5,500° K.

daylight spool   Camera load that allows film to be loaded in subdued light.

decay   A term that describes how sound trails off and reverberates.

decibels (dB)   Increments in the measurement of the amplitude of sound.

deep focus   A theoretical approach that keeps all elements in the frame in sharp focus.

depth-of-field tables   Charts of the near and far parameters of focus for the common focal lengths.

detent   A click stop at a position on a moveable ring.

digital audiotape (DAT)   Digital sound-recording technology.

diopter   An adjustable glass element in the eyepiece which allows operators to adjust the viewing system to the peculiarities of their eyes.

director   Usually the key decision-making force in all stages of a film.

director of photography (DP)   Responsible for all things photographic for the film. Also called *cinematographer*.

dissolve   Technique in which one shot is faded out while the next shot is faded in on top of it. Also called *lap dissolve*.

dissolve rates   Standard rates of dissolves available at labs; 16, 24, 32, 48, 64, and 96 frames are the standard options.

dolly   Wheeled vehicle with a camera mounting device on it.

dolly track   Specially built track used for fluid movement.

double perf   Perforations on both sides of the film. Also called *two row*.

downloading   Unloading the film.

dramatic emphasis   Use of the camera to show the action in the order and with the amplification desired.

dummy load   A ruined roll of raw stock used for practice loading.

edge numbering   The process of transferring edge numbers onto synced mag stock.

edge numbers   Latent numbers encoded in all film stocks by the manufacturer. Also called *key numbers*.

edit sync   A hole punched at the head of rolls, used to sync the rolls.

edited workprint   The workprint version of the film that is created during editing.

editing bench   A table with rewinds, viewer, synchronizer, and any other pertinent editing equipment.

editor   Head of the editorial staff, responsible for creating a workable version of the film.

electricians   Lighting-crew members responsible to the gaffer.

elements   The sound rolls and picture rolls used to create the final print.

emulsion   A gelatin bath that contains the silver halide crystals used in exposure.

equalizers   Audio equipment commonly used to manipulate the quality of the sound, cutting or boosting it at specific frequencies.

expendables   Supplies used while shooting such as spun, gel, gaffer's tape, and so on.

exposure index (EI)   A numerical rating of a film stock's responsiveness to light. Also referred to as *ASA* (American Standards Association) or *ISO* (International Standards Organization).

extreme long shot (ELS)   Shot in which the subject is far away from the camera.

eye-level shot   Shot taken with the camera near the eye level of the subject.

eye light   Light used to highlight an actor's eyes.

eyeroom   Compositional space given in the direction a character is looking. Also called *looking room*.

fade-in   Where the picture fades up from black.

fade-out   Where the picture fades out to black.

fade rates   Standard lengths of fades that labs will do; 16, 24, 32, 48, 64, and 96 frames are standard.

faders   Name for the sliding amplitude controls found on a studio mixing console.

fader unit   A valve in the printer which is opened and closed to create the overall effects (fades, dissolves, and so on).

feature   A film roughly seventy minutes or more that is intended for commercial release.

feed spool   Holds the unexposed film in the film chamber.

field mixer   Used for mixing microphones on location.

fill light   Fills in the harsh shadows created by the key.

film chamber   The space in the camera where the unexposed and exposed film is stored.

film plane   The place where the film is exposed.

filters   *(audio)* Options on an audio recorder that affect a wide range of frequencies above or below a certain point. *(visual)* Glass or gel material that alters the color, quantity, or character of light.

filter slots and holders   Small slots found either in the film chamber or on the exterior of the camera where a filter in a holder can be inserted.

fine cut   In editing, the fine-tuning of the rough cut.

first assembly   Putting the desired takes in the order laid out in the script. Also called *stringing out*.

fish eye   A lens that sees almost a full 180 degrees in front of the camera.

flange   The lip on the back of the lens that is inserted into the camera.

flares   Small points of light on the lens that can create undesired effects on the film.

flash frames   The overexposed frames at the beginning and ending of every shot.

flashing   Running unprocessed film past a small light to create effect.

flatbed   Tabletop editing machine in common use.

fluid camera technique   An approach to efficient shooting that smoothes out or eliminates entirely any bumpy camerawork.

fluid heads   Common professional tripod head used to produce smooth movements.

focal length   The length of a lens, calibrated in millimeters or, less common, inches.

focus ring   Ring on the lens where focus is set for every shot.

Foley   Method of creating sound effects in a specially equipped studio.

footage counter   Indicator that keeps track of how much film has been shot.

foot-candle   Unit of measure of light based on volume of light 1 foot from a candle.

force processing   Overdeveloping film, generally used to compensate for underexposure. Also called *pushing*.

format   The size of the film stock and the image size. There are three standard formats that are in general use: 35mm, 16mm, and Super 8.

frame counter   Gauge on the camera that counts individual frames, helpful in such applications as animation.

frame rulers   Linear, rulerlike representations of film used in editing to count frames.

frames per second (fps)   The number of individual frames photographed per second; the professional frame rate is 24 fps. Slower speeds create fast motion, and higher speeds yield slow motion.

freeze frame   A printing technique that repeats individual frames to freeze the action.

French flag   A small flag on an articulated arm that mounts on the camera, used to cut lens flares.

frequency range   The spectrum of audible and inaudible sound, represented in hertz.

frequency response   Refers to how evenly and completely a specific recorder or playback format reproduces the audible range.

front-surfaced mirror   A mirror that is coated on a surface (of a shutter, for example) for optimal optical performance.

***f*-stop**   A diaphragm in the lens that is used to regulate the amount of light reaching the film plane.

full-body shot   Shot that includes a person from head to toe.

gaffer   Key crew member who heads the lighting crew and is responsible for the technical implementation of the DP's lighting plan.

gaffer's tape   A 2-inch-wide tape used for a multitude of purposes on a set.

gain controls   A name for the amplitude controls found on audio-recording equipment.

gang synchronizer   Consists of interlocked rolling drums (gangs) with sprocket teeth; sound and picture are locked into gangs and fed through the synchronizer in sync.

gear heads   Movement of tripod head is controlled by separate gears that are in turn controlled by hand cranks.

gel   A colored cellophanelike material used on a light to change its color.

generation   The family tree of an image or piece of sound; successive copies will eventually degrade from the original.

grain   Similar to pixels on a computer, it is a general term for the silver halide crystals that are the building blocks of the photographic image.

gray scale   Represents a series of distinct shades of gray, from black to white.

grip   The jack-of-all-trades on the set.

grip equipment   Specialized clamps and tools used to mount instruments.

half-moon shutter   A half-disc–shaped shutter that rotates in front of the gate.

handheld camera   An approach that can give a sense of urgency or chaos to action, often making the viewer feel like a participant in the action.

Hazeltine   Equipment used to analyze each individual shot prior to printing.

head   Mechanism with pan and tilt controls on which the camera is mounted. Also refers to the beginning of a shot or roll.

headroom   *(audio)* Room above 0 VU where the recorder still reproduces an undistorted signal. *(visual)* Compositional space above a subject's head.

hertz (Hz)   Measurement of the pitch of a sound.

high-angle   Shooting from above that tends to diminish a subject.

high-frequency attenuators (HFAs)   Audio filters that cut frequencies above a preset level.

high hat   A tripod head mount that stands about 6 inches tall, used for mounting camera on tabletops and other surfaces.

high-key   Even, fairly flat lighting; one could call it nonjudgmental lighting.

high-pass filters   Audio filters that allow high frequencies to pass through while filtering out low frequencies.

HMI lighting   A relatively new line of daylight color temperature instruments.

hyperfocal distance   The closest focus point that includes infinity in the depth of field.

inches per second (ips)   The standard measurement of the rate of travel of audiotape.

inching knob   Used to manually move the camera's action backward or forward.

incident light meter   A light meter that measures how much light is falling on a subject.

intermittent movement   The alternately moving and stationary movement of the film as it is being exposed.

invisible editing   Conventional approach to cutting in which the editing is designed to go largely unnoticed by the viewer.

jump cut   A cut in which there is a jump in time between the shots.

keepers   Keep the film tight against the sprocketed rollers in the camera.

Kelvin (K)   Measurement of color temperature.

key grip   The head of the grip crew.

key light   Usually the major source of illumination, generally a beam of light that casts harsh shadows.

kicker light   A light that comes in and brushes or rims the cheek when the fill is not covering the area adequately.

lab   The motion picture processing laboratory.

Latham's loops   A bend in the film where the continuous motion of the sprocketed rollers and the intermittent movement of the pull-down claw are reconciled.

latitude   The range of lighting values within which a film stock will produce a usable exposure.

lavalier mics   Small clip-on mics that are frequently used for interviews, although they have a wide variety of applications in film. Also called *lavs*.

lens mount   The method with which the lens is attached to the camera.

lens perspective   Refers to the way lenses represent space.

lens speed   Refers to the maximum aperture, as wide as a lens's diaphragm will go.

lens support system   Rods that extend from the body of the camera to support the weight of the lens, avoiding undue stress on the camera's lens mount.

lens turret   A moveable plate in front of the film gate with which you can rotate different lenses in front of the film, allowing you to switch lenses between shots.

light leaks   Any unwanted light striking the film, caused by irregularities in the camera's tight-fitting junctions.

light struck   Footage that is exposed to light in the loading process. All efforts are made to minimize the amount of film subject to this effect.

light valves   Shutterlike devices in a printer that can be opened and closed to control the volume of a color in the print. The three colors of light are controlled individually.

lighting continuity   Creating photographic consistency between the shots.

lighting ratio   Representation of the relationship between the key and the fill. Also called *contrast ratio*.

lighttrap   Chamber where the film passes out of the magazine, designed to ensure that light will not seep in.

limiter   Audio recorder feature that adjusts peak signals that are liable to be distorted.

line inputs and outputs   Plugs used to transfer audio from one machine to another.

line signal   Specific type of audio signal that is used to transfer from machine to machine.

lined script   A version of the script created by the script supervisor while filming, it uses vertical lines to detail what action is being covered from each setup.

location scouting   The process of finding locations suitable for individual scenes.

long shot (LS)   A shot that includes the full human body or more.

look   The visual character of an individual film stock, mostly has to do with issues of grain, color separation, and how stocks respond to under- and overexposure.

loop setters   Small guards above and below the gate on automatic-threading cameras that create loops of the appropriate size and shape.

lost frames   Concerns how the requirements of the negative cutter affect a film's cutting, specifically how you need to account for the frames that are ruined in cement splicing.

low-angle   A shot in which the camera is below the subject, tending to make characters or environments look threatening, powerful, or intimidating.

low-frequency attenuators (LFAs)   Audio filters that cut low-frequency signals.

low-key   Contrast lighting that is atmospheric and might be considered judgmental.

low-pass filters   Audio filters that allow low frequencies to pass through while cutting high frequencies.

mag stock   Audio stock that is the same size and dimension as the film itself; the medium for audio cutting in conventional film editing. Also called *fullcoat.*

magazine (mag)   A separate film chamber that is mounted on the camera.

married print   Where the two entities—picture and sound—are finally joined together.

master mix   The product of the mixdown of the mixtracks, it is the final sound for a film.

master scene technique   Common approach to shooting scenes, in which the sequence of LS-MS-CU is used to move from general to very specific information.

master shot   A shot that establishes the setting: where the characters are, any important objects that may be present, and so on. Also called *establishing shot.*

match cut   A cut in which the action matches from one camera angle to the next.

maximum aperture   The widest f-stop opening on an individual lens.

mechanical and friction heads   A simple tripod head in which the movements of the pan and the tilt are simply metal on metal. They are more useful for still photography.

medium shot (MS)   A shot of a person from roughly the waist up.

memory   Phenomenon in which a battery memorizes the small amount of charge it needs to be topped off if it has not been totally discharged often enough.

mic signal   A specific audio signal that is created by a microphone.

mini plug   A smaller version of the quarter-inch plug, generally used as a microphone input on consumer cassette recorders and video cameras.

minimum aperture   The smallest f-stop opening on an individual lens.

mirrored butterfly shutter   Shutter shaped like a butterfly that, as it rotates, alternately sends light to the film plane and to the viewing system.

mixtracks   The sound rolls created in the editing process.

MOS   Shots executed without sound being recorded.

Nagra   A popular audio recorder for sync-sound filming.

negative cutter   Person who matches the original to the edited workprint. Also called *conformist.*

negative cutting   The process of conforming the camera original to the edited workprint.

negative film   Stock that has all the lights and darks reversed from how they are normally perceived.

nicad   Rechargeable nickel-cadmium battery used for many cameras with electric motors.

nonsync sound   Sound recorded separately from the picture.

normal exposure   The exposure that produces a clear and true-to-life picture.

normal lens   A lens that essentially gives a normal representation of space.

oblique angle   Shot where the camera is tilted laterally, often used to suggest imbalance. Also called *Dutch angle.*

ohms   A unit of measurement of the resistance to a signal passing through a line.

optical effects Effects done during final printing, such as dissolves, fades, wipes, supers, and so on.

optical master The photographic printing element for a film's sound track, it is a blank piece of film except for a narrow strip of diamond-shaped patterns opposite the side with the sprocket holes.

optical printer Used to rephotograph existing footage, it is essentially a camera shooting into an apparatus that projects the film.

opticals Graphic effects that are created at the lab prior to final printing, including split screens, keyholes, freeze frames, spins, wipes, and a host of other effects.

optical track The photographic sound track that is printed on the edge of the final film.

orange mask Leader which is the shade that creates black in the resulting color prints from color negative.

original The film that actually ran through the camera when shooting.

outtakes Unused shots, usually stored together on rolls for easy review.

overexposure Film that received too much light, resulting in overly bright images.

overhead Drawn view of a scene from above, helpful for planning blocking and camera positions.

overlapping dialogue cut A cut in which the transition from one shot to the next occurs during a line of dialogue.

over-the-shoulder (OTS) A shot done over a character's shoulder.

pan A shot in which the camera is simply pivoted horizontally on the tripod.

parallax A problem on rangefinder cameras where the viewfinder is not seeing precisely the same frame as the film is seeing.

parallax adjustment An adjustment to correct parallax problems.

peak program meter (PPM) An improvement on the VU meter that reads the peak of every signal from the microphone or line. Also called *modulometer*.

perforations Sprocket holes on the film which facilitate transportation and exposure.

phantom mics Mics powered by the recorder's battery rather than an internal battery.

phasing A complex phenomenon in which specific frequencies are canceled out and thus not recorded.

photographic consistency The challenge of creating shots that will match photographically when cut together.

photographic darkroom bag A double-zippered bag used to load and download raw stock in total darkness. Also called *changing bag*.

pickup pattern Refers to how a mic picks up sound that is coming from different directions. Also called *polar pattern*.

picture lock The point when the editor determines that picture editing is completed, usually followed by extensive sound effects and music editing.

pitch Distance between sprocket holes on the film stock.

plant mics Mics planted on a set to pick up sound in areas that are difficult to boom.

plastic memory Tendency of the film stock to stiffen in the shape in which it was left.

point-of-view Shot that represents the vision or the viewpoint of a specific character.

postproduction The editing stages of a film, including scoring, titling, and all finishing processes.

potentiometers (pots) A name for the amplitude controls on audio-recording equipment.

preproduction The process of putting the film in position to shoot.

presence The innate audio ambience of a given space. Also called *room tone*.

pressure plate Holds the film flat against the gate area in the camera.

prime lens Any fixed focal length, that is, nonzoom, lens.

principal shooting Denotes the concentrated shooting schedule of a film's scenes.

printer A contact printer where film is duplicated.

printer lights The individual controls on the three primary colors of light—red, green, and blue—in a printer.

printer points Increments in the intensity of a printer light.

printing cues The instructions to the printer lights and fader unit needed for every shot.

printing down Using the intensity of printer lights to deal with overexposure.

printing program A computer-generated edit decision list which will run the printer lights and fader unit.

printing up Using the intensity of the printer light to deal with underexposure.

production Includes all the actual shooting.

production board A large board that cross-references the scenes with the resources needed to execute them. This is now largely computerized.

production designer   The person responsible for the design of all the film's settings.

production manager (PM)   The person responsible for the day-to-day running of a film's production.

production office   Central command center for a film shoot.

production sound   The sound recorded while filming. It is generally, though not exclusively, dialogue.

production values   An umbrella term that refers to the amount of resources devoted to the image.

proxemics   From the word *proximity,* refers to the distance between subject and camera.

pull-down claw   The mechanism that advances each individual frame for exposure.

quarter-inch plug   An audio plug used extensively as a mic or line connection. Also called *phone plug.*

quick-release plate   A detachable plate that is used to secure the camera to the tripod head easily.

rack focus   Physically shifting the focus ring as the shot is being executed.

rangefinder viewing   A viewing system in which the operator looks through a facsimile lens that is mounted on the side of the camera.

raw footage   The rolls of uncut footage.

raw stock   The unexposed film purchased from the manufacturer.

RCA plug   Probably the most common audio line connection, found on a wide range of equipment from consumer stereos to VCRs.

reaction shots   Wordless shots of characters reacting to action.

recanning   Putting a short end back in its packaging when rolls are downloaded at the end of a day or for any other reason.

reflective light meter   A light meter that measures how much light is reflecting off a subject.

reflex viewing   The industry standard viewing system in which the operator is actually looking through the camera's lens while filming. Also called *through-the-lens viewing.*

registration pin   A small pin that holds the image steady as it is being exposed.

release print   Designed for exhibition, all subsequent prints that use an acceptable answer print as the guide.

rerecording mixer   An employee of the mixing facility who orchestrates the mix at your instruction.

resistance   The force in a tripod head against the operator's movement.

reversal film   Has all colors and shades rendered normally on the original.

rewinds   Mechanism on a viewer or an editing bench for hand-winding the film.

RGB   Acronym for the three primary colors of light: red, green, and blue.

riding gain   The process of watching the display on an audio recorder, manipulating amplitude control to ensure that the sound is being optimally recorded at all times.

rough cut   The first complete cut of a film.

rule of thirds   Draws lines that divide the frame into thirds horizontally and vertically, used as guides for creating a balanced composition.

run-through   Rehearsing a scene at normal speed, generally used to watch for technical problems.

sandbags   Used to secure light stands and other equipment against tipping over.

scene   The basic unit of a script, with action occurring in a single setting and in real time.

scratch track   A conventional sync track that serves as a guide in editing.

script supervisor   The crew member responsible for keeping track of continuity as well as other general script considerations.

selects   The shots that have been selected for use in the first assembly.

series 9 filters   The most common size of filters and ring adapters for 16mm.

set lights   Instruments used to create effects in parts of the set.

setup   The basic component of a film's production, it refers to each individual camera position, placement, or angle.

shallow focus   An approach in which several different planes of sharp and soft focus are incorporated within a single image.

sheet negatives   Used to photograph title cards. Also called *Kodaliths.*

shock mount   A suspension system that absorbs any moderate shocks to the microphone or boom.

shooting for the edit   Denotes the importance of considering while shooting a scene how it is going to be edited.

shooting script   A detailed, annotated version of the script usually put together by the director.

short ends   The remaining unexposed portion of a roll at either the end of a day's shooting or when a fresh roll needs to be loaded.

shot   Commonly defined as the footage created from the moment the camera is turned on until it is turned off.

shot list   A less formal alternative to the storyboard, it is a list of brief written descriptions of the intended shots.

shot/reverse shot   Involves shooting all of one person's dialogue and then picking up the camera and moving it to the reverse shot to shoot all of another person's dialogue.

shoulder   The precipitous drop-off at the overexposure end of a film stock's latitude.

shutter   Constantly rotating in front of the gate, it blocks the light while the film is being pulled down and then allows the light to reach the film when the frame is stationary for exposure.

shutter speed   The amount of time each frame is exposed. In motion pictures, it is usually a constant that is dependent on fps (frames per second).

signal path   The route that an audio or video signal takes.

silver halide crystals   Crystals suspended in the film's emulsion that change their properties when struck by light and subjected to chemical developers.

single perf   Film stock with sprocket holes on only one side. Also called *one row.*

slate   The clapboard that is used to start sync scenes.

slug   Leader or junk picture that is used to fill in the empty spots on the sound rolls. Also called *sound fill.*

slug rolls   Rolls of junk picture or leader into which nonsync sound is cut.

SMPTE Universal leader   Standard countdown leader from the Society of Motion Picture and Television Engineers. Also called *Academy leader.*

sound effects (SFX)   Incidental sound cut to action, not music or the spoken word.

sound mixer   The person who operates the tape recorder and is head of the sound crew.

sound log   Similar to a camera report, the log of the daily activity of the sound crew.

sound perspective   Refers to the way we expect to experience sound at specific proxemic positions.

spill   Excess light from an instrument.

split reel   Reel with a threaded center so the two flanges can be detached.

spreader   An apparatus with three arms that extend that is put on the floor to hold the tripod legs in position. Also called *spider* or *tri-downs.*

spring-wound motor   A camera motor driven by a spring similar to that found in a mechanical clock.

sprocketed rollers   Feed the film into and out of the area where each image is exposed.

spuds   The mounting piece on most small light stands.

squawk box   An amplifier/speaker used on an editing bench.

standard legs   Tripod that extends from roughly four to around seven feet, used for shots that are done at a standard height.

Steadicam™   A device that mounts on the camera operator's chest, giving fluid movement to what are essentially handheld shots.

storyboard   Has each shot drawn on one side of the page with the script material it covers—dialogue, action, and so on—on the other side. Also called *board.*

straight cut   A cut from the end of one line of dialogue to the beginning of the next.

stress   Aesthetic result of an unbalanced image. Also called *tension.*

sunshade   Mounted on the front of a lens, it shades the lens from direct light.

Super 8   The smallest format in common use and the amateur standard for years.

Super 16   An adaptation of the 16mm format that uses the area of the film that would be taken up by the second row of sprockets for additional image area.

superimposition   Two shots laid on top of each other; can either be achieved in the camera while shooting or in the editorial and final printing processes. Also called *supers.*

sync   The synchronization between sound and image.

sync beep   A single frame of mag stock that creates a beep that is cut across from the Academy 2. Also called *sync pop.*

sync rolls   The mag stock transfers of the production sound.

synchronous motor   A speed-controlled motor that produces a virtually perfect 24 fps. Also called a *crystal* or a *D.C. Servo-controlled motor.*

syncing up   Using the slate to match the production sound with the image.

tail   The end of a shot or roll.

tail slate   A slate done at the end of a shot as opposed to at the head.

takes   The number of attempts at a shot needed to produce at least several usable versions.

take-up spool   Takes up the film after it has been exposed.

tape-direct switch   Gives the choice of monitoring the playback or record heads.

target   The series of markings on the viewing screen.

telephoto lens   A long lens that magnifies the subject in a manner similar to binoculars.

tilt   A shot with the camera moved vertically on a tripod head.

timer   A lab employee who goes through the entire film and analyzes each individual shot for color and exposure. Also called the *grader.*

timing   The process of evaluating each shot before printing.

toe   The precipitous drop-off to underexposure at the edge of a film's latitude.

tracking shot   A shot that follows alongside, in front of, or behind a moving subject.

trim bin   Bin for hanging film during editing.

trimming   Changing the shape, quality, or intensity of the light an instrument produces.

trims   In editing, frames trimmed from the shots you are using.

tripod   Three-legged camera support; what is referred to as a tripod is actually two separate pieces—the legs and the head.

tripod threading holes   One or more holes in the bottom of the camera body that are used to attach the camera to the head.

t-stops   Take into account the light that is lost passing through a lens.

tungsten (T)   Lamps rated for motion picture photography that are 3,200° K. They produce the same color a black-bodied surface does when it is heated to 3,200°.

TV safe frame   A frame on the viewing screen that defines the boundaries of the image once transferred to video.

tweaking   Fine-tuning what each instrument is accomplishing in a lighting setup.

two-shot   So named because it shows two people from roughly the waist up.

underexposure   Film that received too little light, resulting in dark areas of the frame.

unintentional splice   Splice where an attempted cut was put back together again.

upright editing machine   An older design than the flatbed, which still sees limited use.

variable shutters   A control on the camera that allows the operator to change the shape of the shutter.

video assist   A tiny video pickup device that is mounted in the viewing system of the film camera, giving a video representation of the shot.

viewer   A standing viewing machine on which you can analyze the film a single frame at a time or at any other speed you desire.

visual shorthand   Accomplishing an action visually in as economical a way as possible.

visual subtext   Information that is not present in the content and structure of the narrative but implicit in the visual presentation.

VU (volume unit) meter   Meter that gives a visual representation of the level of the audio signal being fed to the record head.

walk-through   An initial rehearsal in which the technical personnel and the actors walk slowly through a shot to identify potential problems.

wide-angle lens   A lens that gives a wide view of a scene. Also called *short lens.*

wild camera   A camera that cannot do synchronous-sound filming.

wind noise   Unwanted sound created by wind hitting the microphone.

wind zeppelin   Has a baffle design that cuts much of the interference from wind. Also called *wind shield.*

wireless mic   A mic, generally a lavalier, that is plugged into a radio transmitter; the signal is then sent to a receiver on a recorder. Also called *radio mic.*

workprints   Duplicate prints made for editing that are frame-for-frame replications of the original and are made by a motion picture processing laboratory.

XLR   The standard mic connection on most professional audio and video equipment. Also called *Canon.*

Zero VU (0 VU)   Often presented as the point that the audio signal should not exceed because it will distort, although there is some room above it for viable recording.

zoom lens   A lens with a variable focal length.

Index